DATE DUE

AUG 1 1 2005		
GAYLORD		PRINTED IN U.S.A.

INTERNATIONAL POLITICS
POLICYMAKERS AND POLICYMAKING

INTERNATIONAL POLITICS

POLICYMAKERS AND POLICYMAKING

ROBERT L. WENDZEL
University of Maine

JOHN WILEY & SONS
New York • Chichester • Brisbane • Toronto

Library of Congress Cataloging in Publication Data:

Wendzel, Robert L   1938–
    International politics.

    Bibliography: p.
    Includes index.
    1. International relations.   I. Title.

JX1391.W46   327   80-36681
ISBN 0-471-05046-6

Printed in the United States of America

10 9 8 7 6 5 4 3 2 1

TO KAREN

PREFACE

This book is a text in international politics, written mainly for students who are taking their first course in the discipline. It emphasizes the importance of concerning oneself with real world situations, and it stresses the necessity of dealing with such situations on a pragmatic, specific basis.

The approach is primarily analytical, and its central organizing feature is the "policymaker focus." One can study international politics in a variety of ways, focusing attention on any or several of a wide range of phenomena. And one may choose from different levels of analysis, ranging from the global "system" to the nation-state to various substate entities. Human knowledge is far from adequate, and many of today's differing approaches are helpful in aiding our understanding. But at some point, no matter what the approach, it is necessary to come to grips with the fact that it is real flesh-and-blood human beings in authoritative positions that formulate and implement the policies of the various actors that make up the system; in other words, regardless of what analytic method one adopts it is essential at some point to deal with the fact that in the real world *policymakers* inevitably will and do play a central role. For this reason we focus our attention on policymakers right from the beginning, and stay with this concentration throughout the analysis.

My analytical approach, with its central organizing feature of the "policymaker focus," is a five-part composite.

1. It involves a concern for the policymaker's actual perceptions and actions. A considered effort is made to view things through the policymaker's eyes.
2. It includes an examination of the many factors that significantly affect the policymaker, whether he or she is aware of them (and correctly perceives them) or not. Thus it is broader than just the policymaker's perceptions.
3. My approach includes a continuing effort to induce the student to "put himself or herself in the policymaker's shoes." Not only does this stimulate interest but also it is the only way that students can appreciate the complexities and problems with which policymakers must deal.
4. The book contains a normative element. Frequently, there is an attempt to provide some guidelines as to how policymakers pre-

sumably "should" try to proceed in certain cases, what they probably "should" at least attempt to do, and so on.

5. It provides a dose of realism for the reader by drawing attention to,
and concentrating on, what policymakers in the real world think is
important, and by emphasizing what they actually do or do not do.
Regardless of the opinions and preferences of observers, it is real
world policymakers who make the critical choices of international
politics.

Although the book is analytical, it will have eminent practical value. By
focusing on the policymaker, it gives the student an understanding of the basic
options that policymakers realistically might have available in concrete situations and the vast array of difficulties that they may encounter. Its pragmatic
specificity also provides the student with a useful analytical foundation for his
own examination of concrete situations. Furthermore, although historical and
descriptive material is employed first for the purpose of illustrating analytical
concepts, it has been carefully selected to also provide a basic understanding of
most of the substantive issues of major contemporary significance as well.

My organizational approach is, first, to analyze the fundamental context
for the policymaker's activities—the basic features of the international political environment within which he or she works. The types of international parties and their attributes and importance, how international governmental functions are performed, the degree of cooperation, competition, and conflict that
exist, and the role of ethics, law, ideology, and power are examined in Part I.
In Part II, Chapters 3–6, we discuss the steps in policy formulation, analyzing
the importance of the question of who is involved in particular situations, the
determination of objectives, ascertaining capability, determining orientation,
and external means of increasing capability. Part III, Chapters 7–8, provides
an analysis of the foundation of capability, the tangible and intangible building blocks underlying international influence. In Part IV, Chapters 9–12, I
examine the instruments of policy implementation, analyzing the use of economic, military, communication, and negotiating techniques in carrying out
policies that were previously decided. And Part V, Chapters 13–15, closes the
analysis by investigating the problems, constraints, and limitations that real
world policymakers encounter when trying to formulate and implement the
optimum policy. I particularly emphasize frequently made intellectual mistakes, seemingly "inherent" practical problems, and domestic constraints.

The organization of the topics and subject matter is quite deliberate.
First, it has a certain intrinsic logic. Nevertheless, since there are many teaching approaches in the discipline and no arrangement is equally well suited to
all, I have arranged and packaged the subject matter in a manner that allows

considerable instructor flexibility, because the various parts can be productively interchanged according to the particular professor's classroom requirements. For example, whereas in my courses the parts are studied in sequence (because I prefer to provide the student with the framework for and tools of analysis before discussing complicating obstacles and limitations), others might be interested in discussing domestic constraints and common policy-making problems earlier and wish to use Part V immediately after Part I. Given the multitude of teaching approaches in use today, this flexibility is a considerable asset.

A strenuous effort has been made to make this book both easily readable and interesting (without sacrificing either precision or the depth of analysis). After all, a book is of little value to students unless they *can* and *will* study it. Therefore, academic jargon is avoided unless it is clearly necessary. Traditional concepts are used when their meaning is clear, but an effort is made to avoid ambiguous carryovers from the past, no matter how venerable they may be. To add clarity and precision to the analysis, I have introduced, at some points, new commonsense terminology that specifically and accurately identifies the concepts being used.

This book is not a panacea. It does not provide, as no book can, an encyclopedic description of all international politics, nor does it provide a remedy for all the world's ills. Furthermore, it is written with full knowledge that a myriad of texts already exist, many of which are highly useful; it would be both presumptuous and inane to suggest that this book is "better" than all of them regardless of one's interest and purpose. There is, however, a considerable and quite significant gap in today's literature. There is no comprehensive text that focuses throughout on the individuals who make and carry out policy, no comprehensive text that focuses on *policymakers*. This book hopefully fills that gap.

Several people made valuable contributions to the book. The complete list is too long to include here, however, and a partial accounting must suffice. I begin by acknowledging all those who provided constructive inputs to the different editions of my core text, *International Relations: A Policymaker Focus*, a work that provided the genesis for this book. Their assistance is gratefully acknowledged there and has continued to be of benefit. Three individuals deserve special mention for their contributions to this book. Robert Hoover of Utah State University read the entire manuscript and made several extremely valuable comments *re* organizational matters. Robert Bledsoe of the University of Central Florida painstakingly checked an enormous number of factual points and his efforts contributed directly to the book's accuracy. And Frederick H. Hartmann of the U. S. Naval War College provided truly immense assistance across a broad spectrum of conceptual, factual, and editorial considerations. All of these men receive my sincere thanks. I also wish to acknowledge my editor at Wiley, Wayne Anderson, who was patient, encouraging, and helpful throughout. Finally, I cannot overemphasize the persistent and consistent help and support I received from my wife, Karen; it was invaluable. Indeed, without her this book would not have been written. Obviously, if errors exist they are mine alone.

Robert L. Wendzel

CONTENTS

PART 3   THE FOUNDATION
OF CAPABILITY   **159**

7   Capability Components: Tangible   **161**

8   Capability Components: Intangible   **212**

PART 4 POLICY IMPLEMENTATION INSTRUMENTS

GRAPHICS

Part 1
THE INTERNATIONAL ENVIRONMENT

On January 14, 1975 a spokesman for the U. S. Department of State said that the United States was legally free to breach the Vietnam cease-fire agreements because of various violations previously committed by Hanoi. At first glance one might assume that this statement meant that Washington was deeply concerned with these alleged violations of the law and that various legal considerations were important in determining the nature of the response. Some observers did make this assumption but others disagreed. Some felt that the reference to the law was just a "cover." According to this line of reasoning, policymakers were much more worried about what they perceived to be Hanoi's increasing power than about any legal niceties, and this statement was a warning not to go too far. In addition, some analysts speculated about the presumed unethical nature of such violations and wondered whether American policymakers were really responding for moral reasons, and still others believed that the statement was just a tactical move in what was perceived to be an ideological struggle against communism.

How important are such factors? Do policymakers generally pay any attention to law or ethics? Is power all that counts? What kind of world do we live in? What is international politics all about, anyway?

The answers to these questions are extremely important. Unfortunately, they are also terribly complicated and one usually cannot reach definitive conclusions. Some general understandings are possible, however, and are very necessary. If the policymaker does not understand the general nature of the international environment, he or she may formulate and seek to implement policies that are contrary to the usual "facts of life." To the extent that the policymaker does so, his or her policies will fail.

Part 1 provides a basic analysis of this international environment within which the policymaker must work. We will proceed by seeking to answer the following seven questions:

1. Who are the primary parties (actors, units, components) whose actions and interactions comprise the essence of international politics and what are their characteristics?

2. How are governmental functions performed in the international political system?

3. What impact do ethical and moral considerations have on policymakers as they formulate and implement policy?

4. What is the role of international law? Are policymakers significantly influenced and regulated by it in their activities?

5. Does ideology play a significant role in determining various aspects of policy? If so, what is it?

6. How important are power factors, how prevalent are considerations of capability? Is international politics really just a constant power struggle, with everything else of only minute importance?

7. Should the policymaker assume that most relations are conflictual in nature, or are other types of relationships also important?

1
The Parties And How
They Are Governed

In order to understand international politics one must know something of the basic nature of the units that are involved in it, and have a reasonable comprehension of to what extent and how the interrelations of those units are governed by phenomena external to themselves. Who are the primary parties (actors, units, components) whose actions and interactions comprise the essence of international relations, and what are their characteristics? How are governmental functions performed in the international political system?

THE PARTIES

There are two major types of parties in international politics: state and nonstate. Traditionally the former have received the lion's share of the attention, and justly so. As the analysis will show, however, nonstate actors are becoming increasingly important.

States

The primary parties (units, actors, entities) of international politics are the 150 or so states (also variously called nation-states, nations, or countries). They have been the primary unit of international action for over 300 years and are still so today despite the occasional importance of other entities.[1] It is states which cause most of the major problems of international politics, and if those problems are solved (or not solved) it will in most instances be the result of state action or inaction; it is states that will determine whether nuclear war occurs, meaningful arms control agreement is achieved, productive steps are taken to alleviate world hunger, natural resources are constructively utilized, etc. It will be state policymakers who will formulate and implement the policies that will largely determine the world's future.

Attributes of Statehood. States vary enormously in terms of geography, population, ideology, ethical systems, political structure, capability, history, and so forth, but despite their differences they exhibit certain common attributes, and it is these that give them their "statehood." From the policymaker's perspective there are three such attributes that have major operational significance: *territoriality, the right of external autonomy and equality, and the right of internal control.*[2]

The first and most prominent state attribute is *territoriality.*[3] The entire earth's surface is subject to the authority of political units with a territorial basis. A state exists within a more or less defined geographic area with vaguely or specifically delineated boundaries; without territory there is no state.

This requisite of territoriality obviously has implications for the policymaker. Considerations of territorial defense or acquisition are pertinent in a wide range of situations and, in some cases, possess overriding importance. As we point out in depth in Chapter 3, the defense of one's home territory is a fundamental policy objective, one for which in all but the most unusual circumstances states would be willing to make a maximum expenditure of resources (including going to war). Governments exercise direct authority over population, resources and many other components of capability within a specific territorial area. Because these factors are of considerable significance as the foundation of international influence, the location and configuration of boundaries is critical.

Usually, international boundaries are clearly delineated on maps (and on the ground as well) by various indicators, and they are accepted as legitimate.

---

[1]The modern nation-state system developed in Europe with the breakdown of feudalism. In the fifteenth and sixteenth centuries feudal princes began to consolidate and enlarge their domains through conquest and marriage. Eventually this process culminated in the establishment of unified, centralized states organized on a national basis and ruled by absolute kings. These were the precursors of the states of today.

[2]Two other requisites for statehood are a permanent population and an economic system. Obviously a state cannot exist without inhabitants, and there must be some set of arrangements by which capital and labor are combined to produce and distribute goods and services.

[3]See John Herz, *International Politics in the Atomic Age*, Columbia University Press, New York, 1959, Parts I and II, for a different view.

This is not always true, however. In portions of the Arabian Peninsula, for example, there are no clearly defined frontiers. The lack of precise boundaries and the resulting uncertainty can easily lead to (and be used to justify) conflict. The lack of a definitive border delineation was a significant factor leading to the 1962 Sino-Indian War.[4] And particular boundaries are not always accepted as legitimate. Often there is a clearly drawn line but one party simply does not accept its validity and considers land on the other side of the demarcation to be its "home" territory (or simply desires to acquire territory to satisfy various other objectives).

Occasionally, nonpolicymakers have speculated that the attribute of territoriality is diminishing in significance due to the global interdependence that exists in a number of functional areas. But the evidence of state action does not bear this out. In other words, to *policymakers* territoriality is still of enormous importance, and in their actual formulation and implementation of policy territorial concerns continue to loom very large. In 1977–1978, for example, Somalia and Ethiopia fought an undeclared war over control of the territory of Ogaden Province in southeastern Ethiopia. Surely it would be a matter of importance to American policymakers if a foreign power sought to detach a part of the territory of the United States.

Or turn to the Middle East. In June 1967 a war none of the parties had really sought occurred, and Israel for the third time decisively defeated her Arab enemies.[5] Consequently, the mountainous Golan Heights were taken from Syria, Israeli forces occupied Egypt's Sinai Peninsula, the Gaza Strip was conquered, and Jordan lost the West Bank and the old city of Jerusalem. These territorial shifts had an enormous impact and inevitably became major sources of tension in the Arab-Israeli conflict. Very simply, the Arabs wanted "their land" back, and the Israelis, who had won, would not return it unless they could be shown how such action would benefit their security. In 1973 Egypt and Syria even launched a limited war in an effort to bring progress toward "eliminating the consequences of aggression."[6] In 1974 and 1975 some tradeoffs were made and limited Egyptian-Israeli and Syrian-Israeli disengagement agreements were achieved, but the territorial issues remained unresolved.[7] In March 1979 the Egyptian-Israeli Peace Treaty was signed. For Egypt the primary objective achieved by the treaty was the regaining of control over the remainder of the territory lost in 1967, while the major reason most other Arab actors opposed the treaty was their belief that its signature greatly decreased the chances that they could achieve their territorial aims. To the pol-

---

[4] Also see p. 275.
[5] For an examination of the developments leading to this war see Chapter 14, pp. 380–385.
[6] Also see Chapter 10, pp. 277–278.
[7] Re the disengagement agreements see Chapter 6, pp. 137–138.

icymakers of these Middle Eastern states the attribute of territoriality is of such a vital character that war has been (and may again be) necessary.

A second attribute is *external autonomy and equality*, that is, the right to international legal equality and the freedom to pursue whatever foreign policy one desires (although presumably this is to be done within the confines of international law). Every state is supposed to possess certain rights including those of self-defense, territorial integrity, and political independence. It can sign treaties, enter alliances, or exchange diplomats. It is presumed to be free from external interference in the choice of foreign policy objectives, orientations, and instruments. It has the right to maintain armed forces and the ultimate authority to determine whether or not to wage war. In fact, a state is assumed to be free from any restraint on its external conduct except that which is self-imposed, mutually agreed to, results from prudent calculation, or is generally accepted international law (and even this can be debated).

Essentially what this means is that each state is presumed to have the right to play by the same rules as all the others in its external relations. For example, it was as legitimate for the Soviet Union to extend foreign aid (via the provision of military assistance) to Ethiopia in 1977 as it had been for the United States to provide aid to that state in the 1954–1977 period. Similarly, because all states have the right to sign or not sign treaties, and because each state will make that decision for itself, it is as legitimate for Israel *not* to become a party to the Nonproliferation Treaty as it is for her to become one; obviously, some states have, some have not. In these instances, as in all others, state policymakers will decide what to do (or not do) based on their calculation of how particular actions (or inaction) will affect the achievement or protection of their particular objectives. The point here is not the wisdom or ethics of a particular choice, but rather the fact that because of the right of external autonomy and equality policymakers have the right to make the choice and carry out the policy on the same basis as everyone else.

It is apparent that the right of external autonomy and equality is sometimes violated. States, in fact, are not always treated equally, efforts to play by the same rules as others are often frustrated and condemned, and sometimes other actors massively interfere with efforts to exercise this right. It is a fact of international political life that what is good for the goose is not always believed to be good for the gander, that frequently states interpret certain kinds of actions to be acceptable if they do them but not if someone else does. Nevertheless, the vast majority of the time the attribute *is* assumed by policymakers to be operative and it *is* honored much more than it is violated. As such it has considerable operational validity.

A third attribute of statehood is the *right of internal control* and the means to achieving it. A state, because it is a "sovereign" (translate: "independent'') political unit, is largely free to govern as it wishes within its own territory; there is no superior agency to which it owes allegiance.[8] Its governmental and economic systems may be organized in any manner it desires. Its government is the supreme lawmaker within its borders, and foreign political units cannot make and enforce rules or settle disputes on its territory without its consent. The state has the final authority over the people within its boundaries, literally holding the power of life and death.

Policymakers are highly resistant to any action they perceive to be an infringement on this right. Soviet reactions to President Carter's human rights campaign are instructive in this regard.[9] Following the signature of the Final Act of the Conference on Security and Cooperation in Europe (CSCE) in Helsinki, Finland, in August 1975, within the Soviet Union a Moscow group known as the "public Group for the Assistance of the Fulfillment of the Helsinki Agreements in the USSR" was established by Russian dissidents to monitor Soviet implementation of the Agreement's human rights provisions. By early 1977 this group had published 19 reports, many of which were highly critical of the Kremlin's compliance record.

At the end of January, not long after Jimmy Carter assumed office, the U. S. State Department criticized Moscow for what it said were efforts to intimidate dissident Soviet physicist Andrei Sakharov, a move Mr. Carter subsequently endorsed. Four days later the Russians arrested Aleksandr Ginsberg, a member of the Moscow group who also was administering a fund left by the exiled author Aleksandr Solzhenitsyn to help political prisoners and their families; a week later the group's leader, Yuri F. Orlov, was arrested also. Sakharov then wrote President Carter a letter, requesting the President's support for human rights advocates in the U. S. S. R. and Eastern Europe. Mr. Carter wrote back, assuring Sakharov that the United States would continue its "firm support to promote respect for human rights not only in our own country but

---

[8]The concept of sovereignty was originally developed by the French philosopher Jean Bodin. Writing amidst the near anarchy in sixteenth-century France following the Wars of Religion, he sought to strengthen internal control and promote national unity. His ideas of absolute power over citizens and subjects exerted vast influence on his contemporaries and have been influential to this day.

[9]One might have thought Mr. Carter would have learned something from the Trade Reform Act episode. As part of their attempts to develop closer relationships in the early 1970s, the United States and the Soviet Union sought to increase trade. The 1972 Summit Agreements gave impetus to this desire. When the U. S. Congress passed the Trade Reform Act in December 1974 and made the granting of nondiscriminatory trade status to the Soviets contingent upon a Russian agreement to liberalize their Jewish emigration policy, the Soviets responded by nullifying their Summit trade pledge. They stated that such a provision was an unacceptable interference in their internal affairs; Jewish emigration from Russia was Moscow's business and no one else's.

also abroad."[10] Shortly thereafter, ex-dissident Vladimir Bukovski was received by the President at the White House.

The Soviets were furious. Behind the scenes Ambassador Anatoly Dobrynin protested vigorously, and publicly the Communist Party newspaper *Pravda* ran a number of stories charging the United States with attempting to interfere in the internal affairs of the Soviet Union under the guise of so-called concern for human rights. In mid-March another prominent member of the Moscow group, the Jewish activist Anatoly Shcharansky, was arrested and charged with treason.

President Carter, however, failed to heed the Soviets' warning. Speaking at the United Nations on March 17 he said that no U. N. member could claim that mistreatment of its citizens was solely its own business. In a major response on March 21, Communist Party General Secretary Leonid Brezhnev, stated:

> Our opponents would like to find forces of some sort opposed to socialism inside our countries. Since there are no such forces, because in socialist society there are no oppressed or exploited classes or oppressed or exploited nationalities, some sort of substitute has been invented and an ostensible "internal opposition" in socialist countries is being fabricated by means of false publicity. That is the reason for the organized clamour about the so-called "dissidents" and why a world-wide hullabaloo is being raised about "violations of human rights" in socialist countries. . . .
>
> Washington's pretensions to teach others how to live are, I am sure, unacceptable to any sovereign state, not to mention the fact that neither the situation in the United States itself, nor U. S. actions and policies in the world at large justify such pretensions.
>
> I repeat: we will not tolerate interference in our internal affairs by anyone, no matter what the pretext. Any normal development of relations on such a basis is of course, unthinkable.[11]

A few days after Mr. Brezhnev's speech Secretary of State Cyrus Vance arrived in Moscow with the Carter administration's proposals for a SALT II treaty. To Washington's dismay the proposals were summarily rejected. Although there were disagreements over certain substantive provisions, it was evident from the contemptuous nature of the rejection that Moscow's action was largely a response to Carter's "interference" in Soviet "internal affairs."

[10]Quoted in U. S. Department of State, *Special Report: Second Semiannual Report to the Commission on Security and Cooperation in Europe, December 1, 1976–June 1, 1977,* June 1977, p. 6.

[11]Novosti Press Agency Publishing House, *L. I. Brezhnev: Speech at the 16th Congress of the Trade Unions of the USSR, March 21, 1977,* Moscow, 1977, pp. 27–28, 30–31.

In light of the fact that the human rights campaign not only was not helping Soviet dissidents but also was producing negative results on other fronts, Washington began to reduce its pressure, and through the summer and early fall of 1977 much less was heard about human rights. Apparently the lesson had not really sunk in, however, because at the Belgrade follow-up meetings to review the implementation of the CSCE Final Act the United States again strongly condemned the Soviets and various Eastern European states for alleged violations. While the Russians angrily said that discussion of the supposed implementation deficiencies of another state was barred by the principle of nonintervention in internal affairs (and was designed to divert the meeting from its main purpose of strengthening security and expanding cooperation in Europe) the American delegation not only discussed the well-known cases previously mentioned but also brought up problems it said were faced by religious and ethnic minorities in the U. S. S. R. Given these major differences, the Belgrade meetings ended in March 1978 without even a substantive concluding document.

Washington still was not finished, but as its public criticism continued so did Soviet repression. In May the Kremlin convicted Yuri Orlov of "anti-Soviet agitation," sentencing him to seven years imprisonment (after which he would be liable to an additional term of five years in internal exile). In early June Mr. Carter, in a commencement address at the U. S. Naval Academy, said of the Russians "The abuse of basic human rights in their own country, in violation of the agreement which was reached at Helsinki, has earned them the condemnation of people everywhere who love freedom."[12] In July, two days before Secretary Vance arrived in Geneva for more arms limitation talks with Soviet Foreign Minister Andrei Gromyko, the Soviets began the show trials of Shcharansky and Ginsberg. Both men were quickly convicted, Shcharansky being sentenced to 3 years in prison and 10 in a "labor camp," Ginsberg to 8 years in a hard-labor camp.

Although the Carter administration apparently was unable to accept it, as this example poignantly shows state policymakers react vigorously to what they feel are external efforts to interfere with the right of internal control. This is not a matter of the substantive merits of the particular case but a question of the "rules of the game," of the international political facts of life.

Despite everything said above concerning resistance to perceived interference with the right of internal control, it is evident that policymakers of external units, wittingly and/or unwittingly, sometimes do violate this attribute. As we discuss later, many states are highly susceptible to external interference (some request it), and certain orientation options and policy implementation instruments are appropriately suited for such action.[13] Nevertheless, if one evaluated most states in terms of the degree of internal control or external interference, he or she would find most were near the internal control end of the spectrum. Generally speaking, policymakers at least begin with this assumption and make adjustments from there.

One final comment is required. The preceding discussion, after analyzing the nature of the attribute of the right of internal control, has pointed out the degree to which it is honored and the inevitable hostility produced when it is violated. But one should not deduce from this that it would not ever be rational to violate this right. Depending on who is involved in the situation, the nature and importance of the various parties' objectives, capability relationships, resources needed for other objectives, and so forth, in a particular case it might be worth the risk. But when trying to determine whether or not to undertake violative action one should fully take into account the tenacity and intensity with which policymakers defend this right and the consequent enmity that will be produced when attempts at violation occur. If one is going to interfere with this attribute, he or she must be cognizant of the hostility the action will engender and calculate that the objective the violation is intended to achieve (and it "better" be achieved) is of such importance that the hostility can be accepted. What one must not do is assume that such hostility will not be produced.

Implications of So Many States. Earlier we noted that there are 150 or so states in today's world. That there are so many states is an important fact. For the policymaker there are seven implications of this point that have major operational significance. As will become clear (as the student reads the remainder of the book), because there are so many states:

1. And because there are enormous differences among them—each state having its own history, geographical setting, ideology, political system, culture, capability foundation, ethical code, etc.—state particularization and uniqueness is a fact of life. While there are certain attributes common to all states, the specific characteristics vary immensely and often are the most critical factors. Consequently, the various states cannot productively be dealt with as if they were interchangeable units.

2. Policymakers will find it extremely difficult to establish priorities, formulate an effective yet coordinated policy, and accurately monitor implementation.

3. There will be immense needs for specialized knowledge and current information.

---

[13]Especially see Chapter 5, p. 117, and Chapter 10, p. 281.

4. And because each state not only deals with several others but has a number of relationships with them, numbers 2 and 3 above are even more troublesome than they would first appear.
5. Most situations will be extremely complicated. Many parties will be involved (all pursuing their own objectives), an inordinately complex web of interactions will occur, and specific developments will have both multiple causes and differential effects.
6. Outcomes often will not be predictable, and the influence of any single state frequently will be minimal.
7. In light of the preceding six points, it is inevitable that there will be a considerable number of differences, disagreements, and conflicts.

Given the operational attributes of states and the implications of the fact that there are so many, it is apparent that the policymaker faces a difficult task in formulating and implementing an effective policy. As we will see, there are a number of factors which make this job much more difficult than even this would imply, however. One of these is the fact that there are actors other than states in international politics.

Nonstate Parties

Although it is a fact that the primary parties in international relations are states, and one should always assume that states are involved unless otherwise specified, there are certain nonstate actors that occasionally play significant roles. These vary widely in terms of permanence, scope, and purpose.

United Nations. Perhaps foremost among the nonstate parties is the *United Nations*, a universal membership, permanent, general purpose organization. Theoretically competent to deal with any international issue anywhere in the world, its permanent institutionalization has forever changed the international scene. Procedures are different than before its existence, problems that might previously have been ignored now receive the glare of publicity, and new mechanisms are available to handle disputes. Small states are able to receive unprecedented status and have their grievances heard, sometimes wielding influence disproportionate to their economic and military strength. A wide range of functional activities are carried out under its auspices. The style and tone of international relations, as well as the content, have been permanently altered. Because of these facts policymakers need to consider the role of the United Nations in a wide variety of situations.

The American public has seldom viewed the United Nations with much objectivity. Rather than accepting the organization's existence as an established fact and seeking to understand its role in international politics, people have tended to choose up sides and be "for" or "against" the United Nations, depending on whether the organization seemed likely to further United States policy interests or not. As a result, public opinion has fluctuated enormously. In the early post-World War II years people had wildly unrealistic hopes and expectations for the new organization and gave it strong support; in contrast, in recent times many have come to believe it is at best futile, and it may even be harmful; therefore, they are "against" it.

Although state policymakers have held varying views of the United Nations' utility, their approach has usually been a good deal more pragmatic than that of the public. As a general rule they have viewed the United Nations simply as one of the nonstate actors in the international environment, an entity which is an established part of the scene. Policies with respect to the United Nations have not been pro or con the organization. Instead, they have been formulated and implemented in accordance with policymakers' perceptions of whether the United Nations would be helpful or detrimental to their party in the specific case. In other words, policymakers tend to be "for" on *some* issues, "against" on *some*, and perhaps indifferent on *some*, but the particular attitude is directly related to the specific case and the manner and degree to which the policymaker expects the United Nations to affect his or her state's interests.[14]

International organizations do not just spring up overnight, nor are they creations that mysteriously emerge from the realms of grand philosophy. International organizations are initiated and grow (or do not) as a product of the ideas, actions, and interactions of specific human beings acting in the name of the entities they represent (i.e., as a result of actions of state policymakers). So it was with the United Nations. The United Nations came into existence in 1945 following a number of multilateral wartime conferences.[15] The United Nations was preceded by the League of Nations, which had been created after World War I, and the League was the outgrowth of historical trends, some of which were nearly a century old.[16] It should be evident then, that numerous policymakers from various states over extended periods of time believed it to be in their interest to have some form of international organization. Apparently this is still the case; if states did not believe it was to their advantage to belong to the United Nations, they would not do so.

---

[14]A useful article on the "for" and "against" issue is Inis L. Claude, Jr., "The Symbolic Significance of the United Nations," *The Virginia Quarterly Review*, Autumn 1971, pp. 481–504.

[15]See Jack C. Plano and Robert E. Riggs, *Forging World Order: The Politics of International Organization*, Macmillan, New York, 1967, Chapter 3.

[16]The best analysis of this phenomenon is Inis L. Claude, Jr., *Swords Into Plowshares: The Problems and Progress of International Organization*, Fourth Edition, Random House, New York, 1971, Chapter 2.

The Security Council. The major political organs of the United Nations—those most important in terms of peace and security—are the Security Council and the General Assembly.[17] The *Security Council* is the smaller of the two, today having 5 permanent and 10 nonpermanent members, and it was expected by the framers to be the more important.[18] Indeed, according to the U. N. Charter the members conferred ". . . on the Security Council primary responsibility for the maintenance of international peace and security. . . ."[19] In order that no one fail to get the message, in Article 12 it was stated that while the Security Council was exercising its functions the General Assembly ". . . shall not make any recommendation with regard to that dispute or situation unless the Security Council so requests."[20]

Some people have assumed that through the Security Council the United Nations was expected to maintain international peace and security; and indeed, according to Article 1 of the Charter this *is* one of its purposes.[21] Therefore, in these people's eyes, since the United Nations obviously has not done this, it has failed. But was this really the expectation of its founders? If not, then it is hardly reasonable to criticize the United Nations for not doing what it was never intended to do in the first place.

The answer to the question lies in understanding the oft-maligned veto rule. According to Article 27, decisions on all nonprocedural matters "shall be made by an affirmative vote of seven members including the concurring votes of the permanent members."[22] Since the permanent members were the United States, the Soviet Union, France, Great Britain, and China, this meant that all parties who were expected to be major powers in the postwar world had to concur for a decision to be reached on substantive issues.[23] Conversely, a negative vote, or veto, by any one of these states could prevent action. If a permanent member was not involved in a situation, it could block decisions involving a determination that an aggression had occurred, prevent the determination of who was at fault if it had, and prevent any sanctions from being imposed or enforced. If it was a party to a dispute a permanent member could not prevent

---

[17]The other organs are the Secretariat, Trusteeship Council, Economic and Social Council, and the International Court of Justice.

[18]Originally it had five permanent and six nonpermanent members, but a Charter amendment in 1965 enlarged it by adding four nonpermanent members.

[19]Article 24, paragraph 1 of the U.N. Charter. Plano and Riggs, p. 560.

[20]Ibid., p. 558.

[21]Ibid., p. 555.

[22]Ibid., p. 561. The "seven" was changed to "nine" with the expansion of membership in 1965.

[23]This provision has subsequently been interpreted to the effect that if a resolution has obtained the requisite number of affirmative votes and no permanent member casts a negative vote the resolution passes.

consideration of the issue, but it *could* prevent enforcement actions against itself.

The implications of these procedural facts are enormous. Each of the Security Council's permanent members has the power to totally hamstring the operations of the enforcement system of the United Nations against itself, and the capacity to preclude any serious action against any of its allies (or anyone else, for that matter). It is apparent from the records of the various negotiating conferences preceding the United Nations' creation that these states knew this only too well; the veto provision was included deliberately. *Obviously, then, the major powers did not expect the United Nations to maintain peace between, or control the use of force by, themselves.* In terms of later developments, therefore, the United Nations could not possibly have been a major "container" of communism, or of anything else resulting from the actions of the permanent members and those they supported. Its own Charter precluded such a role.

Given the foregoing, what *was* contemplated in the peace and security realm for the United Nations? If the United Nations could not act when conflicts occurred between the major powers, or where one of their allies or clients was involved, what could it do? The answer is that even in the ideal, even if the permanent members of the Security Council cooperated and agreed that a situation had arisen that required collective action against a particular state, the United Nations enforcement procedures *were expected to be employed only against minor powers.*[24] *Therefore, the types of crises of potentially the greatest international significance were excluded from the U. N. system since they inevitably would involve the activities of the major powers and/or their allies or clients.*[25]

It must again be stressed that this limitation of the capacity of the United Nations to act in peace and security matters was deliberate. The United Nations was an organization created by states, and the major powers had no intention of surrendering to it any of their decision-making capacity *re* vital interests and fundamental objectives; even less were they interested in forming an international body that might undertake action against themselves. Additionally, state policymakers recognized the fact that it would be futile, and probably destructive to the United Nations, if the organization were set up with the purported capacity to handle peace and security matters in situations where one of the major powers would oppose it. Finally, neither the United States nor the U. S. S. R. would have joined the United Nations if the veto had

[24]Originally most American policymakers believed that the Security Council's permanent members *would* be able to cooperate and agree, and that these states thus would be able to act in concert to preserve the peace.

[25]The most relevant Charter provision here is Article 51, which recognizes the "inherent right of individual or collective self-defense."

not been included; it would either be a United Nations with limited capacity, or no United Nations.

The General Assembly. With the development of the Cold War in the years after World War II, it quickly became apparent that the U. N. security system would not even be able to operate in the limited fashion envisaged in the Charter. In the Security Council the Soviets used the veto extensively, preventing cooperative behavior of any sort. All attempts to negotiate agreements for the forces presumably to be available for use by the Security Council (as required by Article 43), were casualties of United States-Russian hostility. With the Security Council's impotence so apparent, pressure began to build in the West for a strengthening of the role of the second of the United Nations' major political organs, the General Assembly; it was not clear how this ought to be done, however, given what seemed to be the clear provisions of the Charter.

This was the situation in June 1950 when North Korean military forces invaded South Korea.[26] Initially, the Security Council responded by adopting American resolutions opposing the invasion. It was able to so act because the Russians were boycotting the United Nations, having walked out in January to protest the refusal of the Security Council to remove the representative of Nationalist China from his seat in favor of a representative from the People's Republic. But in August the Soviet delegate returned and the Council was deadlocked. Shortly thereafter in the General Assembly the United States proposed what was called the "Uniting for Peace Resolution," and this was soon adopted by a vote of 52 for, 5 against, and two states abstaining.[27] The Uniting for Peace Resolution provided that when the Security Council was unable to act because of the veto, the General Assembly could consider the conflict immediately with a view to making appropriate recommendations.[28] The Assembly thus adopted the position that the United Nations would not be prevented from acting because of the lack of great power unanimity; it too could act in peace and security matters. Since the adoption of the resolution both organs have considered such issues. But even if the General Assembly acts it cannot *require* its members to do anything; in these cases, as in all others, it can only *recommend* certain courses of action.[29] Whether such recommendations will be followed will depend on the judgment of the policymakers of the members

---

[26]For more on this see Chapter 14, pp. 401–402.

[27]Decisions on important questions in the General Assembly require a two-thirds majority vote of members present and voting.

[28]The Resolution also recommended that each member state maintain within its armed forces units earmarked for U. N. service. Although there were a number of vague declarations of support, this soon became a dead letter.

[29]Because of the failure (discussed above) to provide armed forces for the Security Council, the Council too can only recommend coercive action.

concerning whether their state's interests would be helped more (or harmed less) by going along with the recommendations than by not doing so.

Much of the General Assembly's time is devoted to efforts to adopt, or prevent the adoption of, resolutions. Prior to the mid-1950s Assembly proceedings were often dominated by debates on Cold War issues and related resolutions. During this period the United States and its allies and clients almost always were in the majority. This is no longer true. Beginning with the admission of 16 members in 1955, membership has rapidly increased, and today the organization is approximately three times its original size. Since so many of the new members were states that only recently had become independent, issues related to imperialism subsequently came to occupy center stage, and to some extent they still do. The General Assembly today is controlled by the newer states. Frequently headed by the Afro-Asian bloc, often supported by most of the Communist states, it is the new states that are usually "victorious," and the United States frequently finds itself outvoted.

There are five important points to remember with respect to General Assembly resolutions.

1.   No one has to comply with them; the organization cannot compel compliance.[30] In the organization's first decade the Soviets often refused to comply, and today the targets of "anti-imperialist" resolutions frequently do likewise.
2.   Often resolutions are proposed and passed in the full knowledge they will be vigorously opposed by the target. In such a case the purpose is to increase pressure in the hope of bringing about capitulation, or, in cases where it is apparent that capitulation will not occur, to reap propaganda benefits.
3.   Because every Assembly member has one vote, many resolutions are passed by a collection of states whose capability is minute in comparison with the capability of the states that are the resolutions' targets.
4.   Many of the resolutions concern issues that are not perceived by policymakers of the major powers to be of great import (at least to them).
5.   Many significant issues are never seriously considered for the simple reason that the majority does not wish them to be.[31]

Other U. N. Capabilities. In spite of the numerous difficulties discussed above, the United Nations does have certain capabilities in peace and security

---

[30]There may be efforts to compel adherence, but if so they will come from states (although policymakers may use the United Nations as a forum for their operations).

[31]The Nigerian Civil War of the late 1960s and the 1975–1976 Lebanon War being good examples.

matters, and its members have several times put them to use. First, the United Nations can be employed as a *fact finder*. Acting as a party external to a given situation, U. N. representatives can "impartially" investigate the issues and report their findings. In the 1958 Lebanon crisis, for example, the Security Council dispatched a United Nations Observer Group to Lebanon (UNOGIL) to investigate and report on allegations to the effect that agents of the United Arab Republic were infiltrating and smuggling weapons into Lebanon.[32]

The United Nations is employed as a fact finder in three different kinds of situations. First, there is the case where there is real doubt about what happened. Sometimes conflicts arise from ignorance and/or misperception, and a party may wish to preclude hostilities by discovering what the facts actually were. Second, a party may want a fact finder when it is convinced it knows what the situation really is, but believes that others do not. In this case the party believes its position will be validated, and his or her state's claims upheld and legitimized, once all the facts are known. When used in this fashion, of course, the fact finding could as easily increase tension as decrease it, depending on what the facts actually are and how states react to the report. And third, sometimes a party may agree to fact finding even if it anticipates the result might be harmful; the reason is that investigation takes time. Perhaps while it is occurring other maneuvers can be undertaken that will more than offset the harm flowing from whatever the fact finders will produce.

Another capability of the United Nations is *mediation*.[33] Parties to a dispute may decide it would be useful to have the United Nations or its representative, which (or who) presumably would be impartial, offer its (his or her) suggestions for a reasonable settlement. For example, a U. N. Commission for Indonesia, acting as a representative of the Security Council, was quite effective as a mediator in the conflict between the Netherlands and Indonesian nationalists over the struggle for Indonesian independence; the four armistice agreements ending the 1948–1949 hostilities in Palestine were achieved with the considerable help of U. N. mediator Dr. Ralph Bunche; in late 1958 and early 1959 a special representative of the secretary-general was able to help restore calm between Cambodia and Thailand following a period of high tension, broken diplomatic relations, and border incidents; and in 1962 another special representative of the secretary-general succeeded in bringing Indonesia and the Netherlands to an agreement over the status of West New Guinea.

Of course, there also have been a number of failures. One of the most notable recent ones involved the inability of Gunnar Jarring to in any way facili-

[32]For additional information on the Lebanon crisis see below, Chapter 13, pp. 369–371, and Chapter 14, p. 392. For an excellent examination of the UNOGIL operation, including its problems, see Rosalyn Higgins, *United Nations Peacekeeping, 1948–1967: Comments and Commentary, Volume I: The Middle East*, London, Oxford University Press, 1968, pp. 530–603.

[33]For more comments on the functions of a mediator see Chapter 5, pp. 112–115.

tate a settlement of the Arab-Israeli dispute after his appointment as special representative in late 1967; despite concerted efforts to be neutral, his performance was perceived by the Israelis to be exceedingly biased.[34] Another failure occurred during the first Palestine War when the U. N. mediator, Count Folke Bernadotte, was assassinated by Israeli terrorists who believed his proposals were consistently pro-Arab.

The fact that the United Nations exists and can offer its services as a mediator is important; policymakers know that a competent third party is available, that individuals with skill and experience can readily be obtained for mediatory activities if such are desired. It is important to remember though, that whether or not mediation will be undertaken will be determined by the parties to the dispute, not the United Nations.[35]

Another U. N. capability is *interposition*.[36] This involves the physical interposing of some type of U. N. presence between disputants.[37] Often this occurs after the cessation of hostilities, the major functions of the U. N. unit being to observe, supervise, and report on compliance with or violations of the ceasefire. Following the 1948–1949 Palestine War, for example, the United Nations Truce Supervision Organization was dispatched to observe and report on the implementation of the Armistice Agreements. Sometimes the mandate is broader. In 1956, following the Israeli-British-French invasion of Egypt in the Suez crisis, the United Nations Emergency Force was created to direct and administer the cessation of hostilities, bring about and supervise the withdrawal of forces, and then seek observance of, and report on, the cease-fire.[38]

The interposition of a U. N. presence often contributes to a decrease in tension by the simple fact that it geographically separates former belligerents. It also may act as a shield and deterrent to further action. Three of its characteristics are very important. First, it is primarily a nonfighting force; although often composed, at least partially, of military personnel, it is pacific in nature. Second, it will only be employed if the parties to the dispute so desire; furthermore, since interposition units must be dispatched to some particular piece of

[34]Also see Chapter 5, p. 115.

[35]And whether it will be successful will be determined by the degree to which it achieves the requisites essential to a problem-solving agreement. See Chapter 12, p. 332.

[36]On one occasion the United Nations exercised another related capability. In 1960, when the former Belgian Congo became an independent state, chaos and violence erupted. A U. N. Congo Force was subsequently established and sent, its mission to save lives, restore order, help speed the evacuation of foreign troops, and prevent foreign interference. Before it was finished however, it became an active combatant, supported a particular faction, and put down an attempt at secession. The action led to an enormous financial crisis and almost tore the organization apart. It is unlikely to be repeated.

[37]Sometimes the particular U. N. unit will also perform mediating and/or fact-finding functions.

[38]For more on the Suez crisis see Chapter 13, pp. 364–367.

territory, and since states vigorously maintain their right of internal control, the units can be located only where and under such restrictions as the state controlling that territory allows.[39] Finally, the units usually come from states with no major interest in the dispute in an effort to ensure impartiality.

The final capability the United Nations provides is as a *permanent forum for negotiations.* In a sense, the United Nations is a permanent, institutionalized, multilateral diplomatic conference. During its regular sessions and its frequent special meetings, representatives of the world's states are more or less continuously in contact as they work through the United Nations to achieve their various policy objectives. This constant contact and interaction provides innumerable opportunities for bargaining. Of course, there are certain issues policymakers feel should not be ventilated at this forum, but the point is that the opportunities for negotiation—whether via open debate or private bilateral or multilateral meetings in the corridors—are ever present. This can be especially useful in exploratory talks of a private nature. Information can be gathered, general positions stated, procedural issues explored, and an assessment of the prospects for substantive talks made away from the limelight and before one's prestige is committed to a formal negotiating session. Whether policymakers choose to use the United Nations as a forum for negotiation, of course, is a matter for their determination.

To sum up, the United Nations has played, and continues to play, a rather limited role in international peace and security matters. It was expected to operate only with respect to minor powers, and often it has not even done that. On the other side of the coin, it has provided a number of useful capabilities and state policymakers have sometimes put them to good use. Regardless of how valuable one thinks it has or has not been, *the key point is that the United Nations was, and is, what the states have made it. The United Nations is essentially state controlled, and as such is more a reflector than a determiner of policies; it will or will not be useful to the extent and in the manner that the states so desire.* Because the United Nations is without the independent capacity to make or enforce binding rules or to settle disputes between its constituent units, policymakers usually do not consider it to be an effective international party separate from its members.

Regional Organization. A second type of nonstate entity that occasionally acts as an international party is the regional organization (the Organization of American States, the Organization of African Unity, the Arab League, etc.). It is *unusual* for state policymakers to consider such entities as distinct parties separate from their membership, however, for two reasons. First, regional or-

---

[39]In 1967 the UNEF had to be withdrawn from Egypt when in mid-May Cairo asked it to leave; it could not stay without the host state's consent.

ganizations seldom have "supranational" authority, power over and above their constituent parts. Second, seldom are they to any degree "integrated," unified in terms of institutions, practices, and attitudes to the extent that it is reasonable to expect that change within the territorial boundaries covered by the organization will be solely peaceful. There is one regional organization in today's world, however, in which a meaningful if restricted supranationalism and integration *do* exist, namely, the European Community. It deserves a closer look.

As Europe lay prostrate after World War II various policymakers began to seriously consider the pros and cons, and the practicality, of European unification. There were differing hopes and desires, of course. Some saw a potential united Europe as a security community, a collectivity able to withstand foreign attack but internally peaceful; some thought in terms of economic gain, visualizing a huge common market within which economic policies would be coordinated, protected by a wall of tariffs; some put the two concepts together and envisioned a powerful military-political-economic force. At the same time that such ideas were being discussed, perceived concrete security and economic needs led to increasing interstate interaction, and a number of traditional military alliances, economic cooperation agreements, and consultative arrangements were achieved.[40] These concrete agreements combined with the integration ideas that were being considered provided the basis for specific integrative action.

In 1950 French Foreign Minister Robert Schuman proposed pooling French and German coal and steel production within a common market under a supranational organization, and suggested that other European states be invited to be members also. By April 1951 France, Germany, Italy, and the Benelux countries ("the Six") had signed a treaty that created the European Coal and Steel Community (ECSC), and in July 1952 the organization officially came into being.[41] French policymakers had had three basic reasons for proposing ECSC. One, obviously, was economic gain. Second, given Germany's enormous economic potential, Paris was concerned about being economically dominated; French policymakers hoped that tying the two economies together in these critical areas would prevent this from occurring. Finally, and crucially, it was hoped that the industrial intertwining would make war between the two states not just unthinkable, but actually impossible.[42] Policymakers from the other states sought economic gains, some hoping that this would be the be-

---

[40]See Chapter 6, pp. 141, 146.

[41]Useful on the origins and early development of the ECSC are William Diebold, Jr., *The Schuman Plan*, Praeger, New York, 1959, and Ernst B. Haas, *The Uniting of Europe*, Stanford University Press, Stanford, Cal., 1958.

[42]At this point, France was as worried over the possibility of a resurgent militarist Germany as she was over the Russians.

ginning of a movement toward eventual economic union.[43] A few hoped for even more, that the ECSC would be the first step toward political unification.

Although efforts toward political and military unification were unsuccessful, in the economic sphere progress continued. In 1957 the Six signed the Treaty of Rome, which provided for the creation of the European Economic Community (EEC). The EEC's goal was to eventually establish a common market within which there would be the free movement of goods and services, capital, and individuals. In 1967 ECSC, EEC, and the European Atomic Energy Community (which had been formed in 1958) were combined into the European Community (EC).

The institutions of the EC today do possess a degree of supranational authority within the economic sphere. Each of the members (now nine with the entry of Britain, Denmark, and Ireland in 1973) has accepted the fact that the EC Council of Ministers can make certain types of decisions that are binding on the constituent units, including those who disagree. Two points are important in this connection. First, because to this time the participants have recognized the value of the EC and usually have believed that what benefits EC (in the long run at least) also benefits the individual states, they generally have entered the consultation process with a cooperative supportive attitude, have attempted to fashion a consensus that would be mutually beneficial, and generally have worked diligently to avoid confrontation.[44] Second, although the formal procedures are somewhat variable and occasionally complicated, it has been an unwritten but generally accepted rule that unanimity should be achieved on major issues.[45] These two points in combination mean that seldom has the question of whether a party is bound even arisen.

The EC has made considerable progress toward the creation of an economic common market (although its capital and labor markets, currencies, and national economies are far from unified). Furthermore, it does possess a degree of supranational authority within its rather limited subject matter area. Also, and of major importance, European integration appears to have advanced to the state that war among the nine is highly improbable, a rather startling change as compared to just a generation ago. Though these are important facts, they do not make the EC a recognizable international party distinct from its members except in a very limited sense. *It's very important to remember that essentially the EC, as the EC, is operative only in the economic sphere. In all other areas—political, legal, ethical, organizational, military, whatever—*

[43]The Germans, in addition, were interested in being accepted as postwar equals, and in taking steps that would eventually lead to the removal of foreign control and occupation.

[44]This has not always been true, of course, as the "vetoes" by French President Charles De-Gaulle of Britain's attempts to join in 1963 and 1967 attest.

[45]For more on the "Community method" see Leon N. Lindberg and Stuart A. Scheingold, *Europe's Would-Be Polity*, Prentice-Hall, Englewood Cliffs, N. J., 1970, pp. 96–97.

except as such areas are perceived (by the states) to be related to economic matters, the nine operate individually as traditional independent states. This is not to say that their cooperation on economic issues may not have some spillover effect; in some cases no doubt it does. Nevertheless, it is of cardinal significance to recognize that, as a rule, on noneconomic matters the members of the EC act individually in accordance with their perception of their individual state interests, and they seek to achieve their own particular state objectives. And even in the economic arena nationalism has been prevalent. Members have frequently had national economic gain as their immediate objective and have sought to achieve EC consensus appropriate to that end; and, as mentioned earlier, capital and labor markets are still not common, there is no uniform currency, and the different states often have had (and continue to have) national economic policies that were (and are) antagonistic. And there is another issue. In the past it has usually been in the interest of the states to go along with the EC. What if, in the future, such ceases to be the case? What would happen, for example, if there were a major European energy shortage and the EC adopted a certain policy but a particular member desired an alternative that would be much more (individually) advantageous? Would it subordinate its own interests to the EC policy? Might not we find that operationally the supranational "authority" would not exist? One should not underestimate the EC's importance, as the EC, but it is essential to view the organization within the framework of its real, many, and varied limitations. Real world policymakers (usually) do just that.

Multinational Corporations. Another nonstate party is the multinational corporation (MNC). MNCs are business firms with production and marketing activities beyond the borders of any one state; their primary objective is to make a profit. Generally, MNCs send abroad "a package of capital, technology, managerial talent and marketing skills to carry out production in foreign countries," sell their products in several states, and have a number of foreign subsidiaries.[46] Economic operations usually are tightly integrated, both in terms of production and marketing. Decision making tends to be highly centralized, with control being exercised by the parent company.[47] Naturally, policies are adopted that are perceived to enhance the firm's economic position.

Since World War II the growth of MNCs, especially of United States MNCs, has been striking. From 1950 to 1966 the number of affiliates of Amer-

---

[46]The quote is from Joan Edelman Spero, *The Politics of International Economic Relations*, St. Martin's Press, New York, 1977, p. 89. I have drawn heavily from Ms. Spero's work, Chapters 4 and 8, in the descriptive material that follows.

[47]This is not always the case, of course. For a useful discussion of variations among MNCs see David H. Blake and Robert S. Walters, *The Politics of Global Economic Relations*, Prentice-Hall, Englewood Cliffs, N. J., 1976, pp. 80–88.

ican MNCs more than tripled. In the 1960 to 1971 period the value of stock of U. S.-owned direct foreign investment rose from $32.8 to $86 billion, and during the same period West German, Japanese, and British foreign investments also increased dramatically.[48] The economic magnitude of the MNCs is enormous. In the early 1970s the yearly value added by each of the top 10 MNCs exceeded the gross national product of over 80 states.[49] Using another standard, the combined assets of all MNCs were estimated at more than $200 billion.[50] It is not exaggeration to say that a significant part of international economic activity today is accounted for by MNCs.

The economic strength, primary objective, and organizational characteristics of these business entities are such as to bring them into potential conflict with states. Let's briefly analyze this issue in terms of the MNC's effect on economic development, dominance of the host's economy, economic control by the host state, and influence in the political process.

MNCs and Economic Development. When discussing the role of MNCs in economic development one must be chary of making many generalizations. For one thing, the number and importance of MNCs varies enormously from state to state. Generalizations, therefore, can only be useful as possible guides for further analysis of the specific case. Secondly, unfortunately, there frequently is relatively little hard evidence on which to base a conclusion; most of what has been said or written has been a combination of hypothesis and political opinion based on limited and possibly distorted information.

Though any judgment therefore must be tentative, what evidence there is appears to indicate that generally the (strictly) economic impact of MNCs on developed states has been more positive than negative.[51] Investment has been considerable, leading to greater production and employment, highly sophisticated technology has been introduced, and idle host country resources have been put to work. In the less developed countries (LDCs) though, the record is more mixed. While there has been a high level of capital investment, in some instances much of the financing has come from local sources (which has the additional detrimental effect of harming the local competitors); while it is true that there often has been a transfer of high-level technology, in certain cases subsidiaries have paid unreasonably high fees for its use (thus raising the cost) and sometimes the technology has not been high grade; when the technology

---

[48]Spero, p. 91.

[49]Joseph S. Nye, Jr., "Multinational Corporations in World Politics," *Foreign Affairs*, October 1974, p. 153.

[50]David W. Ziegler, *War, Peace, and International Poliics*, Little, Brown, Boston, 1977, p. 402.

[51]Abdul A. Said and Luiz R. Simmons, "The Politics of Transition" in Abdul A. Said and Luiz R. Simmons, eds., *The New Sovereigns: Multinational Corporations as World Powers*, Prentice-Hall, Englewood Cliffs, N. J., 1975, p. 8.

has been top level, local firms often have been unable to meet the competition; finally, while money has been pumped into local economies and employment has increased, many times the best jobs have gone to foreigners and most of the profits have returned to the MNC's home base.[52]

Dominance and control. Policymakers in many host states fear that MNCs will dominate their economies. In certain situations they have grounds for their fears. In many of the developed economies, for example, foreign-based MNCs dominate high-technology industries. To take one instance, by the early 1970s United States MNCs controlled 80 percent of Europe's computer business, 50 percent of its transistor industry, 65 percent of its telecommunications, and 90 percent of its microcircuit industry.[53] In many LDCs, MNCs have long controlled the raw materials and extractive industries, which are the primary economic asset of many of these states. More recently, MNCs have taken the lead in the development of manufacturing capabilities. In these cases there is a real possibility that the host may become an economic dependency.[54] State policymakers are only too aware that the particular industries in question often are critical in terms of economic development, and sometimes are significantly related to national security.

In some of the LDCs it is not just the dominance of key industries that is a concern, of course. In certain of these states MNCs have such enormous overall economic strength in comparison to the host that their policies can easily distort, and even defeat, the state's economic plans. A major withdrawal or addition of funds can defeat host state monetary policy, for example, or the opening and closing of facilities can increase employment or unemployment, or balance of payments and resource allocation efforts can be largely nullified, etc.[55]

But there is another side to the dominance problem. In the first place, in quantitative terms very few host state economies are actually dominated. In other words, in terms of numbers most state economies are *not* dominated by MNCs. This is true even in the LDCs since most of the MNCs' operations occur in just a few countries. Second, in those developed countries where high-technology industries are under significant foreign control, most other sectors of the economy are not (even allowing for the multiplier and ripple effects). And third, in most states most of the time relations between the MNC and the host *are highly cooperative*, each hoping to benefit from the MNC's activities;

[52]Blake and Walters, p. 92, indicate that the negative aspects are more appropriate to MNCs operating in extractive industries than to those involved in manufacturing.

[53]John Spanier, *Games Nations Play*, Third Edition, Praeger/Holt, Rinehart and Winston, New York, 1978, p. 354.

[54]For more on economic dependencies see Chapter 6, pp. 152–153.

[55]For a useful discussion of the dominance and control issue see Spero, Chapter 8.

they *both* have an interest in economic gain, and believe that if the MNC benefits the host state will also.

But the foregoing does not negate the fact that there is a real issue, a real actual and/or potential source of conflict. Partly this is due to the existence of specific, documented instances of dominance. In part, perhaps for the most part, it is a result of host state policymakers' apprehensions about what *could* happen, about what MNCs *might* do. Foreign-based MNCs, viewing particular states as just a portion of a larger production and marketing area, economically huge, organizationally centralized and integrated, not dependent on local financing, can make decisions and carry out policies in the interest of the firm; the impact of a particular action on the host's economy does not have to be a major consideration. It's not that the host state may not be considered, but only that if it is such will occur only in the context of what is best for the firm. The real issue then is the degree to which the host can effectively exercise one of the basic attributes of states, the right of internal control.

Theoretically, of course, there is no problem. Host states could simply refuse to allow new MNCs to establish themselves, and they could nationalize those already there. And sometimes such courses are pursued. Most times they are not, however, for the simple reason that, as noted above host state policymakers believe that MNCs, despite all the actual and potential problems they (may) cause, (on balance) have beneficial effects and should not be eliminated.[56] What state policymakers have been doing in certain instances, in their effort to control MNCs but not destroy the "goose that lays the golden egg," is to increase the regulation of such entities in an effort to establish more mutually beneficial relationships that contribute significantly to host economy control and development.

Political influence. When discussing the political influence of MNCs the first point to note is that many of the major issues of international politics are outside of, or only peripherally related to, the MNCs' usual concerns. Most issues directly related to peace and security matters, for example, matters of vital interest to state policymakers, are simply not dealt with by MNCs. Similarly, issues concerning ideology, state prestige, international ethics, and many other subjects are usually not within MNCs' spheres of interest. Starting from this premise, that most international political issues are not of major concern to MNCs, one moves on to note that even in the sphere of general economics MNCs generally are not very concerned. The most accurate way of explaining what MNCs *are* interested in is that they are concerned with the few *specific* issues that they believe will affect their profits.

---

[56]In fact, many states today compete in an effort to attract MNCs. For an examination of the reasons why MNCs are wanted, see Jack H. Behrman, *National Interests and the Multinational Enterprise*, Prentice-Hall, Englewood Cliffs, N. J., 1970, Chapter 2.

What can we say about MNC influence within this limited sphere of interest? Generally it appears that in the developed countries MNCs seldom have had much direct impact on the political process. Although occasionally they have made campaign contributions (both legal and illegal) and undertaken public relations campaigns to oppose or support certain factions or positions, these have been the exceptions rather than the rule, and even when such activities have been undertaken they usually have not been very effective. In another sphere, MNCs may occasionally have had a degree of indirect impact on the politics of certain developed countries via some influence on local culture and social structure, although no definitive conclusions are yet possible. Generally speaking, the primary importance of MNCs in developed countries has been that by their particular characteristics certain issues have become salient that otherwise might not have been, and both the perceptions of, and options available to, state policymakers have been somewhat changed.

In the LDCs the *general* answer still is that usually MNCs do not have a direct impact on the domestic political process, but in this case the generalization hides almost as much as it reveals. In a number of instances MNCs *have* intervened extensively in host state politics, and sometimes they have done so very effectively. As noted earlier, MNCs are concentrated in a relatively few LDCs, so "by definition" they are not influential in most LDCs. In those states where they are concentrated, however, because of their enormous economic strength their mere presence affects the agenda of government, the salience of issues, and the options available. Often, they have been an active participant in these arenas. Public relations campaigns, campaign contributions, economic pressures, even bribery on occasion, have been employed to further various firms' economic interests. And once in a while MNCs have interfered in host state politics to the extent of illegally seeking to prevent candidates from being elected and/or seeking to bring about a regime change.[57] Thus, while the general rule is that MNCs do not interfere in a major way in host state politics in the LDCs, there have been enough exceptions to make it apparent that each situation must be examined individually.

There is considerable controversy over the degree to which MNCs act specifically as political agents of their home state. There *have* been instances in which MNCs have acted as an arm of the home government, doing things such as serving as a cover for intelligence work or a conduit for foreign aid.[58] On the other hand, because the firm's interests are paramount in its policymakers' eyes, MNCs occasionally have followed policies directly contrary to the desires

---

[57] A flagrant example of this occurred in the early 1970s Chilean campaign of the International Telephone and Telegraph Company in which ITT sought to prevent the election of Salvadore Allende as president and then, once he was in office, sought his overthrow.

[58] Spero, p. 200.

of the home state. In the October 1973 Arab-Israeli War for example, American-based oil companies refused to sell oil to the U. S. armed forces for fear of harming MNC relations with the host Arab states.[59] American MNCs also have sought to sell products to particular foreign states that the Defense Department had restricted because of the goods' strategic value. The usual situation is not either of these however; most of the time MNCs are not an extension of home state policy but neither do they act contrary to the parent state's interests. *Instead, the MNCs seek to balance home and host state concerns in a way that will create the context most conducive to the firm's economic gain.*

As our analysis has shown, MNCs are a major economic force in today's world, though precisely what their impact is remains controversial. While they have been very important in a few situations dealing with certain limited kinds of issues, most issues and relationships do not involve MNCs. Furthermore, even in those that do, ultimately state policymakers, with the right of internal control and their capacity to use military force, will usually be the ones to make the critical decisions. Thus, while MNCs sometimes are a party of significance and each situation must be studied with that possibility in mind, one should begin with the assumption that states will be the major actors, because usually they are.

National Liberation Organization. The final nonstate actor is what might be called the national liberation organization (NLO).[60] In the Vietnam War, of course, the Viet Cong was an NLO. Today there are many such entities, the Irish Republican Army, the South-West African People's Organization, and the Eritrean Liberation Front being three more that quickly come to mind. NLOs vary enormously in size, organizational structure, internal unity, economic and military strength, popular support, ethics, and ideology. But they do have certain features in common. First, NLOs do not possess legal authority over a specific territory; they are seeking to "liberate" that territory from the current regime and obtain that authority. Second, nationalism is the driving force behind most NLOs, nationalism based on shared perceptions (within the NLO) of the past and common (again, within the NLO) hopes for an independent state for their people in the future. And third, usually NLOs employ the military policy instrument across a wide spectrum of uses short of all-out warfare, and also make extensive use of communications.[61]

---

[59]Richard Barnet and Ronald E. Muller, *Global Reach: The Power of the Multinational Corporations*, Simon & Schuster, New York, 1974, p. 77.

[60]Such entities receive a number of labels, such as freedom fighters, patriots, guerillas, insurgents, terrorists, etc. Frequently the label chosen is a reflection of the labeler's view of the entity.

[61]See Chapter 10 for more on the military instrument, and Chapter 11 for more on communications.

NLOs are very important in some regions today. To take one example, since 1967 various Middle East NLOs, such as the Palestine Liberation Organization, the Popular Front for the Liberation of Palestine, the Democratic Popular Front for the Liberation of Palestine, and others, have become significant regional actors.[62] Though the Palestine Arabs are frequently divided by personal rivalries and ideological and tactical differences, are sometimes manipulated by the Arab states' policymakers, and often become enmeshed in intramovement leadership and organizational conflicts, all Palestinian NLOs agree that Palestine is "their land" and it must be liberated from the Israelis (Zionists). Through the military and/or communication activities they have undertaken since the 1967 war the various units have been able to focus attention on their case and thus have "made" the Palestinian issue a key element in the Arab-Israeli conflict.[63] Many policymakers today, in fact, consider the Palestine problem the heart of the matter. All leading Arab state policymakers endorse the Palestinian cause, and their policies must be formulated and implemented accordingly. Although the Palestinian NLOs are, naturally enough, an anathema to the Israelis, because they are a major party to the dispute Israeli policymakers, too, must take them into account. Whether these Palestinian NLOs will be successful or not is debatable, but clearly their importance is not.

In certain situations, then, NLOs can be significant international actors. Unfortunately, beyond stating this fact there are few generalizations of much value. The degree to which a particular NLO will be influential will be a function of a number of factors we discuss elsewhere, such as capabilities and capability relationships, characteristics and skills of the particular parties, relative state permeability, alliance and aid relationships, the effectiveness of the military and communication policy instruments, etc. The key point to note at this juncture is that there are a number of situations in which NLOs do play a major role, and one must always be alert to that fact.

This analysis of the actors in international politics began with the statement that the 150 or so states are the primary units of action. Despite the evidence indicating the existence of various other entities, the essential validity of this statement remains unimpaired. But as the analysis shows there are other possibilities and to neglect them would be a distortion. The policymaker must begin with the various states involved but be alert to the fact that nonstate parties could play a significant role in any given situation.

---

[62]Following the Arabs' defeat in the first Arab-Israeli War (1948–1949), the Palestinians placed their hopes in the policies of the Arab states. As a result of the decisive Israeli victory in the June 1967 war, the Palestinians decided that they would have to take the lead in liberating their homeland because the Arab states could not.

[63]The word "made" is used advisedly. In the 1948–1967 period many non-Palestinian policymakers did not perceive this issue to be of major importance, but a number now do. Whether in fact it *was* of such importance but just not recognized as such is another question.

GOVERNMENTAL FUNCTIONS

What are the major characteristics of the international political world within which the policymaker works? One has already been noted, namely, that its primary components are states. The second major feature is that *there is no central institution or set of institutions to perform governmental functions.* Compare this to domestic political systems. Although they differ in terms of the particular form the institutions may take, all domestic systems have some centralized arrangements for making rules, interpreting and applying them, settling internal disputes, and enforcing decisions.

With respect to rulemaking, in democratic political systems there is a legislative process by which laws are passed; in authoritarian governments there are the commands of the leadership. The Communist Party of the Soviet Union determines the regulations under which Russians will live, while in Great Britain it is parliamentary rule. No matter what the state or governmental system, there is some central apparatus for making the rules that authoritatively allocate the values for that society.[64] There is no central institution to perform this function in international politics.

The situation is similar with respect to executive functions. On the domestic political scene there is a central government that holds a preponderance of coercive power. It is charged with the responsibility of enforcement of the laws and decisions concerning their interpretation, and is responsible for enforcing the decisions made to settle internal conflicts. Because of its monopoly (or near monopoly) of the instruments of violence, it is able to carry out its enforcement duties. There is no comparable international agency, no "executive" with international military forces at its disposal.

Finally, in every political system disputes must be settled. Every domestic political system has some agency that is designed to perform this function. In the United States it is primarily the judicial branch of government. It is, in most cases, the ultimate arbiter of conflict. As was true with respect to rulemaking, application, and enforcement, the international political arena provides no central institution for discharging the function of conflict resolution.

The lack of central institutions, of "government" if you will, is only part of the problem. Another very important characteristic of international relations is what might be called *the absence of a sense of community.* Within most states there is usually some degree of consensus on political values. The general nature of the objectives to be sought and the types of means appropriate for their achievement are widely, if imperfectly, accepted. Over time, policymaking procedures become somewhat regularized and understood (at least by those in authority) and the norms of behavior and "rules of the game" are

---

[64]This phrase is borrowed from David Easton, *The Political System: An Inquiry Into The State of Political Science*, Knopf, New York, 1953.

considered axiomatic. Transgressions of these factors tend to be viewed with disfavor and the assumption is that an effort will be made to apprehend and penalize the transgressor.

Within this framework of shared values and expectations, the rules made and applied by the central institutions tend to be followed as a matter of course. Usually obedience is not even an issue. The government, after all, has a "right" to perform these functions so long as it does so within the limits of the consensus, so the rules are expected to be followed. Even if obedience becomes an issue, the citizen will usually obey the law because he or she accepts the government's "legitimacy," its authoritative right to carry out governmental functions. If the citizen breaks the law and is caught and convicted, he or she expects to pay a price.

Because of this sense of community, most laws within domestic societies are obeyed voluntarily. It is considered both right and beneficial to behave in this fashion. Unfortunately there is no such sense of community in international politics. There is no shared network of values, no consensus on either means or ends. Whether to follow certain rules is an issue, indeed, so is the very content and determination of the rules. Similarly, value conflicts are often at the root of disputes. Because of these facts even if there were central institutions the problem would only be half solved. Without a sense of community even the appropriate apparatus would not be permanently successful.

Because there are no central institutions to make, apply, and enforce the rules, since there is no agency to resolve conflicts, and because there is no international sense of community, the policymaker acts within an environment that might be called *decentralized anarchy.*[65] Each party acts as its own legislator, executive, and judge. No state possesses the authority to make decisions for any party other than itself. This being so each tends to look out for "number one" and seeks to influence others for its own benefit.

Because of this anarchical decentralization, and because policy differences will inevitably arise, conflicts must be settled by the states themselves. Because of the lack of centralized institutions and a sense of community there is little to indicate that a dispute will be settled to any party's satisfaction. Thus there is an ongoing process of attempting to demonstrate the benefits of acceding to "our" point of view.

Ultimately the only way one party may compel another to act in the desired fashion is through the threat or use of force. Otherwise it may just refuse and there is no institution capable of "persuading" it to change its mind. Similarly, only the possession of sufficient military strength and the will to use it can hope to guarantee survival (if even that can). Since there is no central au-

---

[65]The term is adapted from John Spanier, *Games Nations Play: Analyzing International Politics*, Praeger, New York, 1972, pp. 51–56.

thority with this capacity, the use of military might by the individual parties becomes the ultimate arbiter.

This brief analysis has shown that because there is no central institution or set of institutions to perform governmental functions in the international political world and because there is no sense of community the policymaker operates within a decentralized anarchical system in which force is the ultimate test. This does not necessarily mean, however, that policymakers always think force is all that really counts and that other factors are unimportant in influencing the formulation and implementation of policy; far from it. Although policymakers of state and nonstate parties alike must always be cognizant of the importance of capability and power factors, there are other features of the international environment that also have an impact, such as ethics, law, and ideology. Chapter 2 discusses the general role of both power and nonpower factors for international political policymakers.

2
Ethics, Law, Ideology, Power

Within the decentralized anarchical international environment described in Chapter 1, policymakers formulate and implement policies designed to achieve their particular party's objectives. In this chapter we analyze the general influence of ethics, law, ideology, and power on policymakers as they carry out this task.[1] Although few definitive conclusions can be presented because of the complexity, uncertainty, variability, and differences pervading the system, some general understandings are both possible and necessary. If the policymaker does not understand the basic "facts of life" in international politics he or she may formulate and implement policies that are far from productive. The following five questions are specifically addressed:

1. What impact do ethical and moral considerations have on policymakers as they formulate and implement policy?
2. What is the role of international law? Are policymakers significantly influenced and regulated by it in their activities?
3. Does ideology play a significant role in determining various aspects of policy? If so, what is it?

---

[1]The word "general" is used advisedly. As always, one should take the general interpretations as guides only, and pragmatically apply and modify them according to the characteristics of the specific case.

4. How important are power factors, how prevalent are considerations of capability? Is international politics really just a constant power struggle, with everything else of only minute importance?

5. Should the policymaker assume that most relations are conflictual in nature, or are other types of relationships also important?

THE ROLE OF ETHICS

What role do ethical considerations play in the calculations of policymakers? To what extent do considerations of right and wrong, good and evil, influence their decisions? Are moral issues and value questions just raised for propaganda reasons, or do they really have an impact on the people who make policy?

Very often these questions are discussed in order to promote a particular point of view, and as such are couched in terms of a purported incompatibility between ethical considerations and what is called power politics.[2] It is sometimes assumed or postulated that ethical concerns and capability analysis based on self-interest are irreconcilable. It is suggested that policymakers perceive (or at least should perceive) a clear distinction between these contradictory factors. Furthermore, it is implied that policymakers have a clear choice in this matter; they can choose one or the other and which one is up to them.

Such a characterization is both oversimplified and inaccurate (as should become obvious by the end of this book). The analysis below demonstrates several instances in which ethics did play a role in policy calculations, thus underlining the point that ethics do count. But as will be shown later other considerations, including capability analysis, have sometimes been of similar or greater importance. In many cases it will be apparent that the process was very complex and several factors were involved, that there was no clear choice, and that different factors sometimes led to the same conclusion.

Types of Influence

Ethics are often important in the *formulation of long-range goals,* particularly those dealing with the kind of international system one hopes will develop. Ethical factors also may influence the selection of specific policies considered

[2]This purported incompatibility has led to much scholarly and public debate over what was called "Realism" and "Idealism." See in particular Edward H. Carr, *The Twenty Years' Crisis, 1919–1939*, Macmillan, London, 1939; Thomas I. Cook and Malcom Moos, *Power Through Purpose: The Realism of Idealism as a Basis for Foreign Policy*, Johns Hopkins Press, Baltimore, 1954; Hans J. Morgenthau, *In Defense of the National Interest*, Knopf, New York, 1951; and Hans J. Morgenthau, *Politics Among Nations*, Fifth Edition, Knopf, New York, 1973.

ιο be appropriate to achieving such objectives. Various policymakers have advocated, and sought to achieve:

> a system of equal, free, and self-determining nationalities, each organized into its own state and living peacefully side by side.[3]

Former President Woodrow Wilson emphasized the necessity of self-determination and believed strongly that permanent peace could not be achieved without it; it was both the goal and the means. The principle of equality has sometimes possessed a similar status. The idea is that if all states have equal rights and obligations the major source of conflict (inequality) will be eliminated. According to this conception, security rests on cooperation and "real" cooperation is possible only among states who are equal politically and juridically.[4] Ethical considerations such as these may influence long-range desires and be in the back of policymakers' minds in their daily routines. As such they will be a persistent component in the policymaking process, although their impact will vary with time and circumstance.

Ethical concerns also *affect the self-image one possesses.* Many American policymakers apparently have come to assume that the United States is the repository of moral virtue and other states are just waiting in line to be enlightened. Somehow the conception arises that "our way" is ethically superior and other states will surely see this and request us to share our bounty. In such a situation the policymaker's approach to all situations will be conditioned by his or her ethical self-image.

Lest one misunderstand, however, it should be recognized that this phenomenon is not the province of any one state but instead it is rather common. Each party tends to see itself as the most virtuous, both in general terms and in the context of each particular situation. From the viewpoint of a Vietnamese Communist, for example, the Viet Cong were morally superior to Washington. As he saw things the United States had sabotaged the Geneva Agreements, prevented free elections, and thus prevented the unification of his country under popular leadership; he saw American assistance to Saigon as a process of penetration designed to turn Vietnam into an American colony. Aiding a repressive regime, Washington turned the Southern zone into a military base and eventually perpetrated outright aggression against the Vietnamese people by the most technologically destructive means. If one believed this way then he was ethically correct in opposing the United States and its "puppet." One rea-

---

[3]John H. Herz, *Political Realism and Political Idealism,* University of Chicago Press, Chicago, 1951, p. 67.

[4]See Frank Tannenbaum, *The American Tradition in Foreign Policy,* University of Oklahoma Press, Norman, 1955, pp. 158–159.

son the Viet Cong were so effective was that they believed they were in the right; ethical concerns did matter and influenced specific actions.

This is not a new phenomenon, of course. As John Stoessinger pointed out in his study of the developments leading to World War I, the major policy-makers of *all* the belligerents in that conflict tended to see themselves as "honorable, virtuous, and pure."[5] To take just one example, the leaders of Austria-Hungary believed that they were fighting to protect what in their eyes was the bastion of European civilization.[6] Thus they did not even consider the possibility that their attack against Serbia could be an act of "aggression"; Austria-Hungary, as they saw it, was preserving what was good and virtuous, and they were only doing what was necessary to achieve their objectives; because they were the most ethical party, they had an obligation to act, and to act successfully.

Ethical considerations may also *provide the catalyst for action or make the action undertaken much more intense.* This could be either because of the substance of what was done or because of the manner in which the actions were carried out. Both of these factors had an impact on American policy-makers and their decision to enter World War I. When President Wilson said that the United States entered the war to "make the world safe for democracy," ethical concerns were critical in his mind. German violations of neutral rights, for example, were considered ungentlemanly. The sinking of merchant ships, particularly the *Lusitania*, and the eventual unrestricted submarine warfare, infuriated Americans; these things were just not done. Real resentment was aroused by:

> Germany's violations of American rights and the gentlemanly code of international ethics and decency. . . In their view German policy was deliberately, unalterably, and by the very nature of Germany's rulers inhumane, autocratic, militaristic, expansionist, and utterly barbaric in its standards of international conduct. On the other hand, they were convinced that the preservation of American ideals, American interests, and civilization itself depended on a British victory.[7]

Finally, and rather critically, ethical concerns *often act as a constraint;* certain objectives or means are modified or rejected for ethical reasons. In the Cuban Missile Crisis one of the alternatives considered for removing the Soviet missiles was what was called a surgical air strike (that is, a surprise bombing

---

[5]John G. Stoessinger, *Why Nations Go To War*, Second Edition, St. Martin's, New York, 1978, p. 27.

[6]They were concerned with a number of nonethical factors also, of course, but that does not negate the fact that ethical concerns were of some importance.

[7]Robert Osgood, *Ideals and Self-Interest in America's Foreign Relations*, University of Chicago Press, Chicago, 1953, p. 236.

raid). President Kennedy and his brother Robert (the Attorney-General) both rejected this option, partly on ethical grounds. It reminded them of an American-perpetrated Pearl Harbor. As the Attorney-General put it:

> I could not accept the idea that the United States would rain bombs on Cuba, killing thousands and thousands of civilians in a surprise attack. Maybe the alternatives were not very palatable, but I simply did not see how we could accept that course of action for our country.[8]

Certainly one method of weakening the adversary is to simply kill many of its leaders. In 1939, thousands of Polish officers were captured by the Russians and placed in prisoner-of-war camps. In early 1940 some 15,000 of them were murdered in the Katyn Forest massacre.[9] Thus, when Stalin suggested to Churchill in early 1944 that the way to resolve the German problem was to liquidate 50,000 German officers, he was taken very seriously. Churchill, however, found the suggestion reprehensible and made it plain he never would consider such action. Ethically he simply could not tolerate it.

The Rest of the Picture

The fact that policymakers often take ethical factors into account when formulating and implementing policy seems established beyond doubt. But this simple statement, while very important, does not give the whole picture. For one thing, there are cases where this does not occur, such as in the Katyn Forest massacre or the Nazi slaughter of six million Jews. One must also be aware of the fact that ethical statements are often deliberately used to rationalize and/or hide unethical behavior. It is also apparent that people seek to interpret their behavior in a way that seems just and correct, and are often able to manipulate facts and situations to this end. Sometimes, if considering the ethical issue would be inconvenient or embarrassing, policymakers may just ignore or refuse to deal with it.

Another difficulty is the natural tendency toward "psychologic," the tendency to interpret the same behavior as ethical if "we" do it but unethical if "they" do.[10] When the Japanese bombed Chinese cities in the 1930s killing many noncombatants, they were condemned for immoral behavior. Ger-

---

[8]Robert F. Kennedy, *Thirteen Days: A Memoir of the Cuban Missile Crisis*, Norton, New York, 1971, p. 15. Certainly tactical and strategic considerations also entered the picture however.

[9]The evidence is overwhelming on this point although the Russians have always denied it and charged Germany with perpetrating the act. The fact that Moscow even bothers to deny the charge shows that there is some concern over its implications.

[10]Charles E. Osgood, *An Alternative to War or Surrender*, University of Illinois Press, Urbana, 1962, pp. 26–30.

many's massive atacks on Coventry, London, and Rotterdam received similar disapproval. By the end of World War Two such raids were standard practice for all parties, however. The Allies presumed their activity was justifiable because the objective was presumed to be more ethical. In Vietnam, the Communist interpreted his presence to be ethical and the presence of American forces to be aggressive, and vice versa. Though India had long condemned Western colonialism for its denial of self-determination, in 1961 New Delhi had no compunction about taking the enclave of Goa from Portugal and subjecting the native Goans to Indian rule. Since (as noted above) there is no sense of community and no central set of governing institutions, each party is the definer and interpreter of the ethical factor in any situation. Given the differences in perspectives, objectives, and means it is obvious why so many differences arise.

Another problem for the policymaker is that *it is often terribly difficult to determine what is or is not ethical in a specific case.* In September 1938 British Prime Minister Chamberlain agreed to the surrender of certain German-inhabited strategic portions of Czechoslovakia to Germany at the Munich Conference. A man of impeccable principles, he believed he was acting ethically because he thought this agreement would ensure peace. World War II began a year later. His action was unwise, but was it unethical? Or take the Korean War, which began in June 1950. By mid-1951 the fighting had stabilized and armistice negotiations began. Most issues were resolved quickly but the question of returning war prisoners stalemated the talks. The United Nations Command insisted that no one should be forced to return to his country against his will, surely an ethical consideration, and the Chinese resisted.[11] Peking's position, traditional in international relations, was that everyone is returned regardless of individual wishes. While talks were floundering because of the United Nations' ethical considerations, the killing, wounding, and maiming went on. Was the United Nations' position more ethical than if it had returned the prisoners and stopped the carnage?

In the minds of some, the difficulty of determining what is or is not ethical is directly relevant to aspects of the problem of nuclear deterrence and/or combat.[12] In the realm of strategic nuclear deterrence, for example, the idea that party A will be deterred from attacking party B because A knows B can retaliate by killing untold millions of A's citizens means that millions of innocent people are the hostages and potential targets of nuclear war. Is this unethical, since noncombatants are consciously and deliberately included in the equation? Is it ethical to threaten nuclear attack on (their) innocent people in order to prevent a nuclear attack on (your) innocent people? Does the answer to this

---

[11]The U. N. Command also had other motivations, such as publicly humiliating the Chinese.
[12]For an in-depth discussion of deterrence, see Chapter 10, pp. 282–290.

question depend on whether the deterrence works? In other words, is strategic nuclear deterrence ethical if it prevents war but not if it doesn't? Or, reducing the geographical scope of our analysis, what would or would not be ethical with respect to nuclear combat and/or deterrence in the European region? Would it be ethical for NATO to launch a nuclear attack on Eastern Europe and the Soviet Union, inevitably killing millions of innocent people, if Warsaw Pact conventional forces were overrunning NATO's armies? Is it ethical to even threaten such for deterrent purposes? Again, is the answer dependent on the pragmatic test of success? In these cases, as in most, determining what is or is not ethical is very difficult.

Another facet of this problem arises because of the fact that *there is no universal standard of ethics*. Different states have different cultures and social structures, and different cultures and structures spawn different ethical systems. Thus what is considered "good" or "bad" varies from one state to another. Policymakers' conceptions of what is "just"are at least partly shaped by their culture and social structure. Because of these facts policymakers from different states will almost inevitably have different conceptions of what is or is not ethical. It is hard enough to find agreement on what is ethical between people from the same state. When cultural and structural variations are added the problem is compounded.[13]

An eternal ethical question is *to what extent does the end justify the means*? Is it ethical for one to help a dictatorship survive if it will help him in turn? Was Churchill's willingness to work with Stalin in order to defeat Hitler justifiably ethical? To what extent are high-level bombing raids that kill innocent civilians justifiable if one believes he is fighting a "just" war? The dropping of the atomic bomb on Hiroshima resulted in over 70,000 Japanese deaths. Although more than 100,000 lives were lost as a result of both bombs (the second landed on Nagasaki on August 9, 1945), it is generally estimated that nearly one million were saved, the anticipated cost of an invasion of the Japanese homeland. Was the decision to drop the bombs ethical or not? And don't all parties believe their cause is "just"? An important point to note here is that there are many situations in which the individuals involved do not even raise this question because the answer seems (to them) self-evident. For example, America's World War II policymakers did not discuss *whether* the atomic bomb should be used, only *where, when,* and *how.* As they saw it, given the objective it was "obvious" that it should be dropped, that the end justified the means.

What about the simple act of lying? Many policymakers accept lying as a necessary part of international politics. A few, like Adolf Hitler, lied with im-

---

[13]A useful article in this regard is Henry A. Kissinger, "Domestic Sources of Foreign Policy," *Daedalus,* Spring 1966, pp. 503–525.

punity. Most do so less often, but many engage in the practice when it would prove useful. In the 1977–1978 war between Ethiopia and Somalia over control of Ethiopia's Ogaden province, for example, each side felt it advisable to prevaricate. Somalia insisted none of her regular troops were involved, that the combatants were ethnic Somalis in Ethiopia rising against their tyrannical rulers. This just was not so; at least 10,000 Somali troops were directly engaged in combat. On the Ethiopian side for months policymakers insisted that Soviet and Cuban advisers were present in very small numbers and even then only in nonmilitary roles. This, too, was simply untrue; more than 10,000 Cuban troops and 1000 Soviet military personnel were involved in the Ethiopians' successful expulsion of the Somali forces.

The question of the extent to which the end justifies the means is raised with particular poignancy by the use of terrorist tactics by national liberation organizations.[14] NLOs are seeking to create and/or obtain control of a state. In their quest to attain this objective frequently NLO policymakers have determined that tactics of spectacular violence will prove useful to that end. In their eyes they are "freedom fighters" or "patriots" involved in a war for independence; innocents, of course, will get hurt, but this is war and the cause is "just." Thus, if the Irish Republican Army plants a bomb in London and shoppers are killed, or if one of the Palestinian organizations hijacks an Israeli airliner or blows up a bus in Jerusalem, it is simply a necessary part of the struggle (obviously the targets of such actions view things differently). Is it ethical to seek to harass one's opposition, to increase social and political disunity, to wear down the adversary, to focus world attention on one's plight, by methods that are deliberately calculated to kill and wound civilians? Does the end justify the means?

How does one compare one act with another? Which was more ethical or unethical, the starving to death of over a million Russians by Germany during the World War II siege of Leningrad, or the British-American air raid on the German city of Dresden in 1945, which killed about 135,000 Germans? Is high-altitude bombing more ethical than the face to face gunning down of over 100 Vietnamese peasants by American soldiers at Songmy or the mass executions of South Vietnamese by the Vietcong around Hué in the 1968 Tet offensive? Was it more ethical for the United States to decide to honor past commitments and for the first time agree to sell sophisticated fighter aircraft to Saudi Arabia, as it did in early 1978, or would it have been more ethical for Washington to have decided to renege on past commitments and not agree to sell such aircraft to the end of moderating the arms race (even though it knew the Saudis

---

[14]We are not using the term "terrorist" in a judgmental fashion here, but only for identification reasons, that is, so that the reader will immediately identify the type of activity under consideration.

had an offer from France to sell them equivalent planes if Washington backed out, and that the Saudis would, in fact, buy them)? Which would have been the more ethical decision?

Policymakers find themselves in confused and troubled waters where ethical factors are concerned. It is clear enough that questions of right and wrong enter into a wide range of calculations but it is also obvious that sometimes they don't and sometimes ethics are deliberately used to rationalize or hide what is really happening. Additionally, it is unfortunate but true that each party tends to think it is the most ethical. Finally, very often it just is not clear what is or is not the most ethical thing to do. This being so, all a policymaker can do is analyze the specific situation with these considerations in mind and attempt to ascertain what elements characterize the particular case.

THE ROLE OF LAW

What is the role of law for the policymaker? Often the subject of international law is "studied" in order to demonstrate either its great (or potentially great) impact or to show that it has little value. Neither approach is very helpful to the policymaker. He or she needs to determine the actual role that law plays, and understand the role it can play, without regard to proving its worth or limitation.

When speaking of international law one is referring to the rules and norms of conduct that parties recognize as binding in their relations with other parties. Such rules may prescribe certain actions, prohibit certain modes of behavior, or perhaps specify and define the conditions that lead to the operationalizing of various rights and/or obligations.

Modern international law developed with the transformation from feudalism to the modern state system in Europe. With the creation of the territorial state with its attributes of complete internal control and freedom from external authority, it became necessary to develop some rules for international intercourse. It was perceived to be necessary to provide for immunity for diplomatic agents, to define the nature and limits of national territorial jurisdiction, to create an acceptable body of regulations to handle the expansion of international economic relations, and to provide common rules for international maritime activities. Policymakers generally recognized their mutual self-interest in these and similar areas. Thus it was necessity and self-benefit that led to the creation of international law.

Sources of Law

What are the sources from which international law springs? The first is *custom*. Customary law comprises rules that states have come to consider as binding on themselves because of generally accepted usage over long periods of time. For reasons of self-benefit, habit or fear states will follow a certain course of action. As this becomes "the way things are done" it acquires some validity, until a time is reached when it is considered obligatory.[15] Most of the rules governing the freedom of the high seas would fall into this category. Policymakers are forced to be aware of international custom in their daily activities.

A second major source, considered by many today to be the most important, is the international treaty.[16] Treaties may be bilateral, such as the Treaty Between the United States of America and the Union of Soviet Socialist Republics on the Limitation of Anti-Ballistic Missile Systems (the ABM Treaty), or multilateral like the Treaty Banning Nuclear Weapon Tests in the Atmosphere, in Outer Space and Under Water (the Limited Test Ban Treaty), or the Non-Proliferation Treaty (NPT).[17] Treaties may codify or clarify existing custom, rules, and relationships, create new rules or relationships, or specify the conditions under which particular rules and relationships are or are not operational.

From the policymaker's perspective there are two key points to remember about treaties. First, once a treaty is signed and ratified there is a recognized rights and obligations relationship. One is bound to do or not do certain things, thus limiting his or her party's autonomy accordingly. Therefore, treaties must be entered into cautiously with careful attention given to their specific provisions.

Second, and equally important, no state is bound by a treaty it has not legally accepted. Thus the policymaker does not need to worry about being legally obligated by agreements between other states. This point is so obvious yet it is sometimes neglected. For example, the United States was not a party to the 1954 Geneva Agreements ending the first Indochina war. Thus all the later talk about American violations was misinformed because Washington could not violate an agreement to which it was not a party.[18]

The fact that a state is not bound by a treaty to which it is not a party is relevant, of course, in all kinds of issue areas. In the area of arms control, for

[15]Technically, this should not be confused with mere frequency of conduct without obligation, which is known as comity. In practice, however, the distinction is difficult to make.

[16]For our purposes "treaty" means any international agreement signed, ratified, deposited, and accepted as binding, regardless of whether the parties label it a treaty, agreement, convention, protocol, or whatever.

[17]For more on these treaties see Chapter 10, pp. 293–295.

[18]However, Washington unilaterally pledged that it would not use force to disrupt the settlement, and said it generally favored free elections for divided countries. Whether in fact it followed its own stated policy is obviously a matter of controversy. See U. S., Department of State, *Bulletin*, August 2, 1954, pp. 162–163.

example, since neither France nor the People's Republic of China are parties to any arms control agreement, they are in no way limited in their construction and deployment of weapons systems no matter how much others may be. Also, since neither is a party to the Limited Test Ban Treaty each is free to conduct whatever nuclear tests it feels advisable, whether they be in the atmosphere, under water, or wherever. Though much attention today is focused on U. S.-Soviet bilateral arms control negotiations, and rightly so, it must be remembered that if Moscow and Washington achieve an agreement it will be binding only on those states, and will not control the arms activities of nonparties like China and France. Looking at some other issue areas, suppose one is analyzing the question of the feasibility of halting the sale of conventional weapons to all parties in particular regions, or the problem of preventing nuclear proliferation. Immediately, it will be necessary to recognize that unless *all* potential supplying states become parties to the appropriate treaties, because nonparties will not be legally bound there will be no legal constraints on their actions.[19]

Because no two states are parties to all the same agreements and to no others, and because states are bound only by those to which they are parties, the rules binding on each state are different from those binding on any other. Because of this there is no universal or quasi-universal standard in many areas. Instead there may be a multitude of conflicting, confusing, and overlapping rules, or sometimes there may as yet not be any system of rules for a given type of activity. Obviously these situations allow the policymaker considerable flexibility of action, the freedom to interpret things to his or her own benefit without being charged with departing from the common standard.

In addition to custom and treaties, there are several somewhat less significant sources of international law, namely, *judicial decisions*, so-called *general principles*, and the *writings of scholars*. Occasionally states are parties to a controversy before an international court, in which case the policymaker would obviously be concerned with the judicial decision. This, however, is not the usual situation. The reason is that the primary source of international judicial jurisdiction is the willingness of the states to submit their dispute for judicial determination, and states are simply unwilling to submit matters of major significance.[20] After all, in a judicial proceeding there is always a loser and

---

[19]This does not mean to say that the only means of achieving the objective would be having all states be parties to an appropriate agreement, of course. Nevertheless, the fact that one is not bound is a matter of considerable import.

[20]There is a provision (Article 36) in the Statute of the International Court of Justice (the United Nations Court) providing for compulsory jurisdiction. Only about 30 percent of U. N. members have availed themselves of this optional clause, however, and even they have so weakened it with restrictions and reservations that there is very little about it that remains "compulsory."

no state wants an outsider (the court) to have the power to make it be that loser. The inevitable result is that policymakers usually consider judicial decisions to be a source of only secondary importance.

The same conclusion is true of general principles and the writings of scholars. The very generality of the principles means they are susceptible to widely varying interpretations, and policymakers will take advantage of this. Scholarly writing abounds with conflicting views and controversy thus providing a basis for determining what someone considers the law to be (or have been), but it also allows one considerable latitude in interpretation. Both of these sources may be consulted but neither will be considered binding.

It is essential to remember that the policymaker is seeking to ascertain "what the law is" within the international environment described in Chapter 1. To reiterate, this means there is no central legislative organ to pass the laws, no executive to enforce them, and no judicial agency competent to settle disputes. Instead it is the individual states that perform these functions. Coupled with the lack of a sense of international community, this leads to a decentralized anarchic situation where force is the ultimate arbiter.

Why Law is Obeyed

Since only the states can punish a lawbreaker, why is the law obeyed? *A point of immense significance is that it usually is obeyed.* The rules, guides, and norms of behavior accepted as binding by states in their mutual relations are in most instances scrupulously observed. In most of their activities policymakers are very concerned with acting in accordance with recognized legal procedures.

Why is this so?[21] We indicated above that international law originated because of perceived needs, the knowledge that it would be advantageous to all if there were certain accepted modes of operation in selected areas. This is still the most common reason for not violating the law; it is *simply to one's benefit to obey.*

In addition to the specific advantages that may flow from observing certain rules, there are two related considerations. First, there is the *expectation of reciprocity*, that is, the idea that other states will reciprocate by also undertaking certain obligations. It is hoped that this will lead to a situation of mutual self-advantage with each party having more to gain than lose by observing the law. The second related aspect is that *stability and predictability* are enhanced when actions are undertaken according to prescribed procedures. Without some regularization the ordinary relations among nations would be chaotic and it would be impossible to develop even a semirational policy. This, too, adds pressure to be law abiding.

    [21]The author is particularly indebted to K. J. Holsti, *International Politics: A Framework for Analysis*, Second Edition, Prentice-Hall, Englewood Cliffs, N. J., 1973, pp. 417–420.

Another reason law is obeyed is, simply, *habit*. Certain transactions are carried on routinely and little consideration is given to change. There is no reason not to follow the traditional pattern as long as things are going well. Furthermore, various parties develop a vested interest in the continuance of existing procedures, making change even less likely. Usually a crisis or an outside stimulus must intervene before the policymaker will react. Until that time, he or she will not question the existing order.

International law is also observed in order to enhance one's *prestige*. A state that develops a reputation for following the rules stands to receive certain benefits. Because there is no central agency for enforcing the laws it is up to the states to do it. Seldom will they enter agreements they assume will be broken and thus require enforcement.[22] A state that constantly defaults on its obligations will simply not be trusted nor dealt with as openly as one that is law abiding.

The final reason for not violating the law, of course, is *fear of punishment*. It is in this area that international law is "weak" in comparison to domestic law. The lack of a central enforcement agency means that the only coercive sanctions available are those possessed by the states themselves. If none of the previously discussed reasons for observing the rules are appropriate, and no state is able and willing to enforce compliance, then the law can be broken without punishment being suffered.

When Law is Usually Violated

We have seen that policymakers may and often do consult a wide range of sources to find out what the law is, and they usually attempt to formulate their policies in accordance with the generally accepted rules. The vast majority of international conduct occurs within regularized patterns of activity, and policymakers recognize that it usually is to their benefit to observe the law. Despite these facts, the law obviously *is* broken in certain cases, and often there is not much a state can do about it unless it is willing and able to compel compliance.

In what kind of situations do these violations readily occur? The answer is really quite clear: *in any case where one of the parties perceives a significant threat to its fundamental objectives it will quickly dispense with legal considerations that might inhibit their achievement.* What this means is that the policymaker does not consider legal factors to be of primary importance in a crisis, when there is a conflict that one thinks might endanger his or her state's sur-

---

[22]Our discussion here is limited to agreements the policymaker hopes will solve a problem. For a discussion of nonsolution agreements see Chapter 12, pp. 327–332.

vival, territorial integrity, belief system, or governmental-economic organization. These types of situations, while in the minority quantitatively, are clearly the most significant in terms of peace and security. And because there are no central mechanisms to force policymakers to consider international law in crisis situations, legal factors remain of secondary significance in determining policy and the outcome where peace and security are heavily involved.

Because policymakers usually prefer not to violate treaty provisions openly, but will not let legal considerations inhibit their efforts to achieve fundamental objectives, frequently "escape clauses" are written into agreements. In the Non-Proliferation Treaty, for example, each party has the right to withdraw if *it* decides that "extraordinary events" related to the Treaty's subject matter have jeopardized its "supreme interests." A similar clause is embodied in the 1972 Soviet-American ABM treaty.[23]

Although they have little impact as a constraint or determinant of crisis policy, legal considerations often do play some role, however. First, even in a crisis policymakers seek to characterize their activities as being in accordance with international law. Sometimes this is not a deliberate manipulation of facts and principles but rather the employment of one of several possible legitimate interpretations. As was noted earlier, there is no universal standard in many areas so different interpretations often occur. Quite naturally policymakers will tend to interpret things to their benefit, and often they do so sincerely believing that they are not distorting things at all.

Second, if policymakers cannot make at least a semiplausible argument to the effect that their policy is in accord with some legitimate interpretation, they may invoke *rebus sic stantibus*, a doctrine meaning that the treaty is void or voidable because fundamental circumstances have altered since its inception. *Rebus sic stantibus* is a well-established principle in international law though there is, as one might expect, considerable disagreement over its appropriate usage.[24]

Third, policymakers may seek to use the law tactically to justify and support positions already taken. A decision may be made on the basis of capability considerations, for example, and then the policymaker will put together a legal argument to justify that decision. Cases in point would be the 1948–1949 Berlin Blockade and the Cuban Missile Crisis of 1962. Although elaborate legal justifications were developed in support of American policies there is little

[23]For the texts of these agreements see U. S. Arms Control and Disarmament Agency, *1977 Edition: Arms Control and Disarmament Agreements: Texts and History of Negotiations*, June 1977, pp. 84–88, 132–135.

[24]Useful is Gerhard Von Glahn, *Law Among Nations: An Introduction to Public International Law*, Third Edition, Macmillan, New York, 1976, pp. 448ff.

evidence to indicate that legal considerations significantly influenced the policymakers' decisions.[25]

It is important to remember that international law is but one of several factors impinging on policymakers as they formulate and implement policy, and they will evaluate it in that context. Given the international political environment of decentralized anarchy, and this is a very salient point, *it is the parties* who will determine law's role, and they will do so in terms of their perception of its relative importance and utility *to them*, both generally and in the specific case.[26] In most instances they will act in ways they sincerely perceive to be legal because it is in their interest to do so, but if it comes to a choice between obeying the law and attaining one's fundamental objectives, the law certainly will lose.

THE ROLE OF IDEOLOGY

Another element that may influence the policymaker's calculations is ideology. Ideology has been defined as:

> The more or less coherent and consistent sum total of ideas and views on life and the world (belief system, doctrine, *Weltanschauung*) that guides the attitudes of actual or would-be power holders.[27]

This concept, the complex of ideas that supposedly explains past and present plus providing guidelines for the future, has also received other names such as belief system, social myth, or doctrine. Regardless of the label given to it, it roughly translates as one's world view.

Although one can argue terminology and definition, policymakers are not concerned with such activities.[28] Their interest is in the operational effects of

[25]Lawrence Scheinman and David Wilkinson, eds., *International Law and Political Crisis: An Analytic Casebook*, Little, Brown, Boston, 1968. This was certainly not the first work to reach this and most of the other conclusions contained therein. However, it had special merit in that it examined a series of cases empirically and the findings substantiated much of what had been observed much less systematically before. It also is written and organized concisely so that the ordinary student can use it with relative facility, a rare quality.

[26]It might be noted that because law tends to undergird and formalize the status quo its importance and utility will often be dependent on one's relative contentment or dissatisfaction with that status quo. A satisfied party tends to be very law abiding, while a discontented one may be faced with the choice of not achieving its objectives or violating the law.

[27]John H. Herz, "Ideological Aspects—International Relations," *International Encyclopedia of Social Sciences*, Cromwell-Collier-Macmillan, New York, 1968, p. 69. The term "Weltanschauung" roughly translates as "world view."

[28]Academics are, however, and the definitions are many. Those interested in pursuing this further should consult the standard work in the area, Karl Mannheim, *Ideology and Utopia: An Introduction to the Sociology of Knowledge*, Harcourt Brace, New York, 1936. For a useful con-

the phenomenon. To what extent do these ideas and views on life and world influence the actual formulation and implementation of policy? Are they primarily general idea systems that affect only long-range goals or do they directly
impinge upon specific detail? Are they more important than other considerations such as law, ethics and capability, or less so? These and similar questions
may be critical as the policymaker tries to understand and anticipate the actions of his opposite numbers.[29] Unfortunately, there seldom are clear-cut
answers.

Let's examine two ideologies and their impact to see if we can get a better
understanding of the phenomenon's operation. First we will briefly analyze
the "liberal" American belief system, and then we will take a more detailed
look at the role of communism in the conduct of Soviet foreign policy.[30]

The American Liberal Ideology

Ideology has played a significant role in American foreign relations.[31] Until
the post-World War II era most twentieth-century policymakers uncritically
accepted certain beliefs as the "fundamental truths" of international relations. With the development of the Cold War a few began to question these basic "truths," but many held to the original assumptions in the belief (or hope)
that the conflict was an aberration and a new age of cooperation would develop once the Communists were overcome. Although the Vietnam war destroyed
these hopes or beliefs for some, many Americans believe that Vietnam was just
one more aberration; in their eyes, the original "truths" are still valid today.

The American liberal ideology begins with the assumption that *people are
basically good*. Most of the time people will do what is right if just given the
chance. There are no major, inherent national differences in this regard; although they may be in different stages of development and thus act somewhat
differently at particular times, underneath, whether people are Ethiopians,
Chinese, Americans, or Russians, they are all essentially good. This assump-

---

cise discussion see Richard W. Sterling, *Macropolitics: International Relations in a Global
Society*, Knopf, New York, 1974, Chapter 6.

[29]For a textbook that emphasizes the importance of seeing things from within different world
views, see Steven J. Rosen and Walter S. Jones, *The Logic of International Relations*, Third Edition, Winthrop, Cambridge, Mass., 1980.

[30]This analysis must, of necessity, encompass a variety of generalizations. Naturally, not all
American policymakers subscribed completely to the beliefs listed below. Similarly, communism
does not perform precisely identical functions for all Soviet leaders.

[31]For a discussion of the basic beliefs, see Moos and Cook, Morgenthau (both works), Robert
Osgood, and Tannenbaum, cited above. Also very useful are Frederick H. Hartmann, *The New
Age of American Foreign Policy*, Macmillan, New York, 1970; George Kennan, *American Diplo-
macy, 1900–1950*, University of Chicago Press, Chicago, 1951; and Ernest W. Lefever, *Ethics and
United States Foreign Policy*, Meridian, New York, 1957.

tion has two very significant operational consequences. First, since most people are good it follows that if a certain individual, group, or government is bad, he (it) is an aberration; presumably, therefore, his (its) removal will restore "goodness" to its rightful position. World War I and World War II were fought to eliminate a certain few aberrants from the scene, the assumption being that their removal would lead to more normal (good) situations and peace would ensue.[32] These wars thus were fought to end war, to eliminate the "bad guys" and get back to normal.[33]

The second consequence of the assumption that people are basically good is a belief that ethical concerns can provide a realistic basis for policy. Since most people are essentially good, ethical factors, presumably, will often be decisive in determining policymakers' choices, in all countries (unless the policymakers are aberrations, like those mentioned above). Even when confronted with difficult decisions, most policymakers thus will act ethically (as defined by Americans, of course). Therefore, deception, lying, breaking agreements, the deliberate use of force, etc., just are not the norm; one can reasonably expect that most foreign policymakers will conduct their affairs in an above-board and honest manner, seeking international relationships based on trust and mutual benefit, and can act accordingly. Leaders who do not play by these rules will "stand out like a sore thumb." Those aberrants who act unethically, who play "power politics" and use force to achieve their objectives, will be evident to all; since most people are ethical, such leaders inevitably will arouse great opposition.

Another component of the American liberal ideology, one closely related to the belief in people's goodness, is the idea that *people are essentially alike*, all having the same basic interests, desires, and fears (all people are created equal). Since states are governed by people, they too, at least generally, must have a *similarity of interests*. Because, as noted above, most people are good and act ethically, these similar state interests must also be good and ethical. Since peace is more ethical than war, most states must be seeking peace most of the time.[34] Presumably, therefore, most states would feel it in their interests to band together to deter aggression, or to join collectively in a war to halt it.

In addition to these characteristics, people are also assumed to be fundamentally *rational*. With the proper guidance and education they can know

---

[32]It also was believed that there was a clear distinction here, that war and peace were mutually exclusive and there were no mixed or gray areas in between. Once war ended, *its opposite*, peace, would ensue.

[33]Given the nature of the objective, no quarter could be given. Thus, war was total and had to be pursued until total victory and unconditional surrender were achieved.

[34]The fact that the United States grew to "maturity" in the nineteenth century, which from the termination of the Napoleonic Wars to the early twentieth century was the most peaceful period in the history of the nation-state system, was highly significant in this regard; since America "grew up" in a time of peace its policymakers assumed that peace was the norm.

what ought to be done, both generally and in specific cases. Since they are good, want peace, and generally act in a rational fashion, they will seek and learn how to manage international relations in a relatively peaceful manner.[35] Therefore, if "they" are opposed to "us," it must be because they are misinformed or don't understand (or are held in the grip of an unscrupulous few). Once we "educate" them, once they understand the fact that we are "good" and they are "good," there should be no grounds for conflict. Being rational they will eventually comprehend this fact. Much of the basis for President Roosevelt's World War II policy toward the Soviet Union was his belief that if the Kremlin really "understood" Americans it would see there was no real reason for conflict. Consequently, the President "bent over backward" to convince Stalin of Washington's good faith.[36]

None of this would mean much, however, if people were the prisoners of events. Americans have rejected this assumption, believing that *people are basically able to shape and control their destinies*. Events do not control people, people make events. After all, hadn't the United States seized its opportunities; hadn't it totally transformed the land and established continental, indeed, hemispheric political supremacy? And hadn't the United States achieved enormous economic progress? Not realizing how much they had been aided by unique circumstances and the policies of other states, most Americans believed that they had gotten where they were solely by their own efforts. Therefore (they believed), since Americans had determined their destiny, others could determine theirs.

Furthermore, at least according to the American liberal ideology, if states are willing to act decisively *problems can be solved*. As noted above, Americans looked back on their own history with a sense of pride; many problems *had* been solved. The idea of "we shall overcome" was deeply rooted. Little children were told, only half in jest, that there is no such word as "can't." If there are problems, with good, rational individuals with similar interests working together they *can* be solved, so let's get at it. There is no reason things can't be better if we just act decisively.[37]

Finally, it has long been believed that *people in all states should have the right to choose their own form of government, and that if they have this right they surely will choose a Western-style democracy*. Such a governmental system (it is believed) allows the individual to achieve his or her fullest potential and provides the greatest degree of freedom consistent with public order, so

---

[35]How many times has it been said that such and such a war would not occur because it would make no sense, because it would not be rational.

[36]For a solid analysis uncluttered by the usual morass of praise or condemnation, see Jules Davids, *America and the World of Our Time: U.S. Diplomacy in the Twentieth Century*, Third Edition, Random House, New York, 1970, Chapters 9–13.

[37]America's continual involvement in efforts to resolve foreign conflicts provides ample evidence of this.

obviously that is what people will choose. Furthermore, it is "clear" that most democratic governments will be controlled by good, reasonable people intent on, and capable of, solving problems. Given these facts, it is apparent that the more democratic a state's government the more peaceful will be its policies.

The concepts of the American liberal ideology lead to a very optimistic view of international relations. Because most people are basically alike and fundamentally good, they must want what "we" want, that is, a peaceful world of democratic governments. Because people are reasonable, able to control things, and solve whatever problems arise, what is there to prevent progress? Peace is the normal state of affairs, and cooperation is to be expected on most issues. Conflict is unusual and the result of some particular aberration; eliminate the "bad apples" and conflict will disappear. Power and capability concerns are not usually very critical since most people are good and rational and war is bad and irrational. When such matters are important it's because the few aberrants are active; once they are gone, harmony will return. Whatever the trouble let's take care of it and move on to a better world.

The optimism of those believing in the American liberal ideology has led to unrealistically high expectations, and the impact of specific events has sometimes brought frustration and disillusionment. The confrontation with unyielding reality has led many to reassess these beliefs. In consequence, many policymakers today are more cognizant of the role that power plays than was the case previously. These individuals also tend to be less optimistic than before; it no longer is "self-evident" to them that peace is the normal state of affairs, nor is it plain that all problems are soluble. Not all Americans have undertaken such a reassessment however; some, policymakers and observers alike, continue to embrace most aspects of the liberal ideology, with all the consequences that entails.

Soviet Communism: Functions

What about the impact of ideology on Soviet foreign policy? What functions does communism perform for Moscow's policymakers as they act on the international stage?[38] First, Communist ideology provides *a vision of things to come* (a function fulfilled by ethics for many non-Communists). It is believed that, through the inexorable working of fundamental laws of history, class will struggle against class until capitalism perishes and the whole world comes to communism. Capitalism, as all systems containing separate classes, contains

---

[38]A subject as complex as this is highly controversial and defies neat, categorical answers. Because of the complexity of Communist ideology we will not analyze its major components as such; such an effort is beyond the scope of this work. Instead, we will focus on certain *conclusions* about its general impact on policymaking for foreign affairs, touching only incidentally on the substance.

the seeds of its own destruction. The exploiters, the owners of the means of production (capitalists), will eventually be overthrown by the exploited, the workers (proletariat). Since the mode of production determines every aspect of societal life, the elimination of conflict over its control by means of the successful class struggle will eliminate conflict itself. The state will no longer be necessary and will just wither away, and each person will contribute according to his ability and receive according to his needs. This is the long-range goal, the future state of affairs that Communists seek to create.

Second, Communists believe that *conflict is unavoidable until their final triumph*. As indicated above, class struggle over control of the means of production is inevitable until only the workers are left. Through the dialectic process, history is the clash of economic contradictions, and change is continual.[39] The exhaustion of domestic profit possibilities will lead capitalist economies to seek foreign markets. This quest will inevitably lead to intercapitalist war. Furthermore, socialism (communism) and imperialism (capitalism) cannot exist side by side for an extended period of time, and any "coexistence" can only be temporary. Conflict (although not necessarily war) is inevitable here too, but communism will eventually triumph.[40] Thus, a Communist sees no harmony of interests among states and no possibility of long-run peace or stability until his or her system emerges victorious. Until that day conflict and change are just in the nature of things.

Third, Communist ideology provides the *general framework within which all international activity is analyzed. It is the fundamental philosophy that provides standards for evaluating various policies*. Whether something is "good" or "bad" will be determined by its place in the historical process and the degree to which it helps or hinders the inevitable ultimate result. Information will be interpreted through the lens of Communist thought and placed in various ideological categories. As Soviet Communist Party General Secretary Leonid Brezhnev said in his address to the CPSU Central Committee at the 25th Party Congress in early 1976:

> In their struggle, Communists act on the general laws, norms and patterns governing the development of the revolution and the building of socialism and com-

---

[39]The dialectic process means that the outcome is determined by a clash of opposites. A given situation gives rise to tendencies for its destruction, and the result is a synthesis, a merging of the two to form a new situation. The process then begins anew and continues over and over until the final synthesis is achieved.

[40]Disagreement over this point was an important factor in the development of the Sino-Soviet dispute. Whereas Lenin had spoken in terms of a series of terrible collisions inevitably occurring, in 1956 Khrushchev said that there was no fatal inevitability of war. He did not, however, say that conflict could be avoided, just that it might not be military; he also did not say that war was unlikely. Another point to note is that the Soviet leader did not alter the traditional communist view of the inevitability of *intercapitalist* war.

munism . . . Deep understanding of these general laws and norms, and reliance on them in combination with a creative approach and with due consideration for the concrete conditions in each separate country, were and remain the inalienable and distinctive feature of the Marxist-Leninist.[41]

Communist ideology thus is the model through which reality is perceived and by which it is interpreted. For example, the landing of Allied troops in Russia near the end of World War I would be seen as a futile attempt by international capitalism to prevent its own inevitable destruction by destroying the Bolshevik regime, rather than as an effort by former allies to bring Russia back into the war against Germany. And World War II came about, according to Stalin:

> . . . as an inevitable result of the development of international economic and political forces on the basis of modern monopoly capitalism. Marxists have repeatedly explained that the capitalist system of world economy contains the elements of a general crisis and armed conflicts, that consequently the development of international capitalism in our time takes place not peacefully and evenly but through crises and war catastrophes.[42]

Ideology also provides a *basis and method for analyzing specific problems*. For example, one might decide whether or not to provide assistance to a particular revolutionary group by determining the general stage of history in which he finds himself, ascertaining the ownership of the means of production, discovering the particular phase of the dialectic process characterizing this situation, calculating the relative strength of the pertinent class forces, and finally determining whether or not these specific tactics will advance or hinder the revolutionary process. Similar methodology could be applied to issues like whether to engage in warfare, negotiating temporary agreements with capitalists, etc.

Finally, communism provides the *vocabulary* within which Soviet strategy and tactics are hammered out. Decisions over relations with the United States are debated in terms of the inevitability of war, the class struggle, the relative strength of socialism (communism) and capitalism, and so on. This linguistic factor is not trivial although it may seem so at first glance. The mere fact that Soviet and Chinese policymakers argue out their dispute in ideological terms indicates, unless one assumes them to be totally phony, that they consider ideological factors to have considerable importance. Furthermore, the con-

---

[41]Compass Publications, Reprints from the Soviet Press, *L. I. Brezhnev: Report of the CPSU Central Committee and the Party's Immediate Objectives in Domestic and Foreign Policy, XXVth Congress of the CPSU, 24 February 1976*, White Plains, New York, 1976, p. 43. Hereinafter this will be cited as Brezhnev, *25th Congress Report*.

[42]Quoted by Paul E. Zinner, "The Ideological Bases of Soviet Foreign Policy," *World Politics*, July 1952, p. 497.

stant use of concepts and terms tends to reinforce the speaker's beliefs and they may become internalized as unquestioned bases for action.

It is evident that Communist ideology provides Soviet policymakers with a vision of the state of affairs they believe will eventually develop, a belief in the inevitability of conflict and change until that time arrives, a framework within which to analyze all international activity, and the vocabulary within which to determine and execute policy. In terms of everyday policymaking it serves still another function by creating a certain sense of security. Soviet policymakers can act with considerable *confidence* because they know that in the long run communism will triumph. The fundamental laws of history are inexorable. In Soviet eyes recent developments give ample evidences of the workings of these laws. As Mr. Brezhnev has stated:

> This is an epoch of radical social change. The positions of socialism are expanding and growing stronger . . . The class struggle of the working people . . . against the exploiting order is gaining in intensity. The scale of the revolutionary-democratic, anti-imperialist movement is steadily growing.

> The governments of capitalist countries are making repeated attempts to moderate the contradictions and come to terms on joint anti-crisis measures. But the nature of imperialism is such that each endeavors to gain at the expense of others, to impose its will. The differences surface in new forms, and contradictions erupt with new force.

> . . . the developments of recent years forcefully confirm that capitalism is a society without a future.[43]

Because of their views of the certainty of the eventual outcome, Soviet policymakers can afford to be *patient*. There is no need to hurry, no particular date by which their objectives must be accomplished. This being so they can be *flexible*, adjusting their tactics and strategy to the changing situation. If the situation is not ripe for revolution, then wait. If there seems to be a setback, it is only temporary. There is a certain ebb and flow to the historical process, and wise policymakers will adjust their actions to it. Therefore, one need not be anxious or frustrated over specific incidents, because the ultimate outcome is clear.

Soviet Communism: Questions

Although communism does influence Soviet policymakers in the significant ways discussed, there are still some key questions to be answered. To what extent is ideology used as a tool to justify action taken on other grounds? To what extent is reality twisted to fit preconceived molds? Even when the general

---

[43]Brezhnev, *25th Congress Report*, pp. 38, 39, 40.

tenets are accepted by policymakers, to what extent are specific decisions determined?

These first two questions can be handled as a unit. The flexibility and inconsistencies in Communist ideology allow Soviet policymakers much leeway in "reinterpreting" and "updating" their ideas when necessity so requires. For example, when it became obvious shortly after World War I that the expected worldwide revolution was not going to occur in the foreseeable future, the party leaders were able to speak in terms of socialism in one country (U. S. S. R.) with that becoming the base for the eventual revolution. Thus, policies aimed at consolidating the regime's internal power were followed instead of those actively fomenting revolution abroad, and were justified as necessary to solidify the "dictatorship of the proletariat." The imperialists would eventually be destroyed from this base. Lenin's original concepts provided no hint that only a portion of the world would be Communist, but when this occurred it proved necessary and possible in practice to rationalize the fact.

Another example involved Soviet relations with capitalist states. A strict interpretation of most Communist thought allows for little in the way of friendly relations with capitalists. In practice, however, Communist Russia has had to choose the lesser capitalist evil on many occasions just to protect itself (the revolutionary base). After the First World War she preferred Germany to the West; from 1933–1939 she continually warned against the Nazis; from 1939–1941 she was Germany's partner, yet from 1941–1945 she was the ally of Britain, France, and the United States against Germany. Today she is more friendly to the leading capitalist country, the United States, than to Communist China. None of this is to gainsay the specific decisions, each of which was designed to protect the Soviet Union. And each was explained ideologically as being part of the dialectic process, the struggle to resist fascism, protection of the revolutionary base, and so on. But clearly it is important to note that Communist thought could be and was used very "flexibly" in order to justify actions whose objective often was simple survival and whose major decision component was consideration of capability.

The fact that Communist ideology was so flexible brings up another point. Very often ideological factors reinforce other considerations such as power. The fact that one may be stressed does not automatically mean another is neglected, or indeed not benefited by the action undertaken. It has been reasonably argued that to even consider power and ideological factors separately involves a distortion because they are related, the latter providing the framework within which the former is considered. Much of Soviet history shows a process of mutual reinforcement, ideology and power considerations leading to the same result.[44]

[44]Frederick H. Hartmann, *The Relations of Nations*, Fifth Edition, Macmillan, New York, 1978, Chapter 24.

Another key issue is the degree to which, even when general concepts are accepted as valid, a particular course of action is mandatory. Let's again take the example of world revolution.[45] Soviet policymakers have never denied that this is still one of their fundamental objectives, and indeed shall be achieved at some point in time as part of the inevitable historical process. But what does this mean in terms of particular cases? Are Soviet policymakers going to be actively fomenting revolution in all situations? Do all revolutionary groups deserve support or just those that are Communist or Communist controlled? Should Communists not seek immediate revolution but collaborate with nationalists whose policies help to achieve Soviet national objectives? Should resources be expended to support revolution abroad that could be used to shore up military defense at home? Should one seek to overthrow all capitalist regimes as soon as possible, even those that might provide assistance against common third party enemies? Should revolution be sought with the same tactics and at the same pace in all situations, or should they be adjusted to practical circumstances?

Each of these questions, and many others of a similar nature, have considerable practical importance and have received different answers at different times. In each case the broad assertion gives no clue as to what to do in the particular contingency. This lack of precision is a necessary concomitant of flexibility and allows for the use of ideology as a tool, but this means that it seldom can provide a blueprint for specific action. And this one case is representative of most of the general facets of Communist ideology. Merely knowing that someone is a "true believer" is often not particularly helpful in predicting his actions in a given situation.

It has been shown that Soviet policymakers have often used ideology as a tool and have acted on nonideological bases. Ideology has been twisted and manipulated to support traditional capability-based decisions. It was also noted that general concepts often give us little clue as to what specific policies may be undertaken. But these facts should not lead one to underrate the significance of the earlier analysis of the functions Communist ideology performs. The clear vision of the future and the certainty of final victory provide for great strength, tenacity,and patience. The fact that all acts are evaluated, all information is interpreted and particular problems are analyzed within a given framework gives the Russians a distinctive perspective, and an outsider must try to place himself within that context if he or she is to understand Soviet policy at all. The fact that a distinctive vocabulary is used and the same words have different implications for different people makes it necessary for those dealing with the Soviets to be sure that there are mutually accepted interpretations of all agreements. Finally, the fact that conflict and change are considered inherent in the nature of the historical process allows outsiders to know

[45]Ibid., raises many of these points.

that the Soviets never expect a stable, nonconflictual situation to develop until they emerge triumphant.

Soviet Communism and Détente

Our analysis of orthodox communism to this point has made it clear that unless major ideological changes have occurred Communist policymakers do not foresee a world in which cooperative relationships are dominant (at least until communism's victory). But perhaps such changes *have* occurred. In the past two decades or so a new word has frequently been used to describe American-Soviet relations: "détente." The "Cold War" is over, some say, and there now is a "détente." Specific definitions of détente vary considerably, of course. Almost all include certain elements, however; a general relaxation of tensions, increased recognition of common Soviet-American interests, a reasonable degree of cooperation and consultation, and cautious policies designed to avoid confrontation. Some define détente more optimistically, speaking of conducting interstate relations in a peaceful and relatively harmonious manner, extensive cooperation, the avoidance of policies that would cause or exacerbate confusion, a refusal to seek unilateral advantage, and so forth. This latter conception usually flows from beliefs that the U. S. S. R. has become a status quo power and Soviet policymakers want and intend to conduct their relations with non-Communists on a permanently cooperative, nonconflictual basis.

Traditional Communist ideology, of course, would preclude the optimistic view of détente. As explained above, according to Communist doctrine history is determined by certain immutable, objective laws, and conflict is inevitable until Communism's eventual triumph. It is important to understand that this is *not* a matter of personal qualities or perceptions, and thus it *cannot* be altered by changing leaders, removing misperceptions, or negotiating new agreements. It is, according to Communist ideology, *inherent* in the nature of things. *Thus a permanent, stable, cooperative international order simply would not be possible.* There may be periods in which the correlation or balance of historical forces is such as to yield a temporary equilibrium, *but it is temporary.* This does not mean that cooperative arrangements might not be possible (or even beneficial) in specific situations. Indeed, there are circumstances in which it might be advantageous for Communists to make deals with non-Communists, the SALT I Agreements and various economic arrangements being cases in point. But such specific arrangements would exist within the context of the overall conflictual dialectic of history; they would not be a substitute for, or change in, this dialectic; they would simply be a particular part of the continuing process.

Today Soviet leaders say they believe in détente. Has their ideology changed? Do the historical laws no longer operate? Is conflict no longer inevitable, given the Soviet-American détente?

A recent Soviet publication put it this way:

> The ideological struggle is not an invention of the Communists. It is a permanent condition of human society, an objective reality, an integral feature of the life of mankind. To abolish it, to eliminate it is not within the power of any government.[46]

Thus détente, the Communists believe, does *not* alter the ideological basics. Let's look at some specifics. How does it affect the class struggle? Does détente advance the cause of Communism? During his 1976 address to the 25th CPSU Congress Mr. Brezhnev stated:

> Now that détente has become a reality, the question of how it influences the class struggle arises often both in the international working-class movement and among its opponents.
>
> Some bourgeois leaders affect surprise and raise a great to-do over the solidarity of Soviet Communists, the Soviet people, with the struggle of other peoples for freedom and progress. This is either outright naiveté or more likely a deliberate befuddling of minds. What could be clearer, after all, than that détente and peaceful coexistence refer to interstate relations. This mainly means that disputes and conflicts between countries are not to be settled by war . . . *Détente does not in the slightest cancel out, nor can it cancel out or alter, the laws of the class struggle . . .*
>
> *We make no secret of the fact that we see détente as the way to create more favorable conditions for peaceful socialist and communist construction.*[47] (my emphasis)

The same official adherence to Communist ideology is evident with respect to other specific features, détente or no détente. The resulting conclusion is inescapable. If Soviet policymakers believe what they say they believe, if they truly subscribe to their professed ideology and are not simply mouthing orthodox phrases and dogmas unrelated to operational policymaking, the cooperative sort of détente envisioned by many outside the Communist world is not at all what the Soviets foresee.

The brief examination of the American liberal ideology and the more detailed look at the role of communism in the conduct of Soviet policy have dem-

---

[46]Mikhail Golubnichy, *Detente, The Soviet Viewpoint: The Only Way*, Novosti Press Agency Publishing House, Moscow, 1978, p. 59.

[47]Brezhnev, *25th Congress Report*, pp. 45–46.

onstrated that ideology is often a significant factor in policymakers' calculations. But just as was true with respect to ethical and legal considerations, there are many times when it is not decisive. There is another key input for policymakers, the consideration of capability or power factors, and it is to this that we now direct our attention.

THE ROLE OF POWER

It is obvious to even the most casual observer that power (capability) plays some role in international politics.[48] Wars do occur, various degrees of force and/or coercion are used, and conflicts of all sorts are recurring elements in the news. But simply reporting this fact does not help us, or the policymaker, determine how important this factor really is. Are such developments typical or unusual? Do policymakers expect such things or are they surprised when they occur?

Many analysts and practitioners consider power to be the most crucial feature of international politics. The noted authority Hans Morgenthau writes:

> International Politics, like all politics, is a struggle for power. Whatever the ultimate aims of international politics, power is always the immediate aim.[49]

According to Morgenthau, history and logic combine to support this conclusion. Policymakers are well aware of the importance of power, and they think and act in power terms. Many other analysts agree. Thus, it is said that an observer can understand international politics from the policymaker's perspective, in a sense be looking over his or her shoulder as he or she works, if that observer too thinks in those terms.[50]

Why do policymakers so frequently think and act in terms of power? Why are thinking about power, attaining maximum power, and using one's power such pervasive features of international politics? There are basically two schools of thought in this regard: (1) it is a result of certain qualities in human nature, or (2) it is a logical result of certain features of the international environment. The first, exemplified by Morgenthau but quantitatively in the minority, emphasizes what are said to be certain inherent features of human existence. It is argued that society is governed by objective immutable laws that have their roots in human nature, and human nature is fixed and unchange-

---

[48]No definition of power or capability will be attempted at this point, leaving the student to his or her common-sense interpretation of what it really means. In Chapter 4 the policymaker's conception of this factor will be discussed.

[49]Morgenthau, *Politics Among Nations*, Fifth Edition, p. 27.

[50]Ibid., p. 5.

able.[51] One of the facts of life is that people are not basically good, as many American policymakers have assumed. On the contrary, all peoples possess an insatiable desire for power. Furthermore, they are not rational either: "Reason, far from following its own inherent impulses, is driven toward its goals by the irrational forces which it serves."[52] Peoples' constant desire for power will bring about conflict, and they are not sufficiently rational to prevent it. Because of this the best a policymaker can do is expect and accept this fact and accommodate and adjust his or her own actions to these unalterable realities.[53]

The much more prevalent basis for the conclusion that policymakers are primarily influenced by, and concerned with, capability considerations results from some of the characteristics of the international environment discussed earlier. Because there is no set of central governing institutions to make rules, apply them, enforce decisions, and settle disputes, the states have to perform these functions themselves. Each state possesses the ability to make its own decisions, including the decision to use force. Each state can only rely on itself for survival. Because all states possess military strength and because there is no one else to rely on, self-help through the threat or use of force becomes the ultimate arbiter in all situations. For these reasons each state will automatically fear and distrust the others, and always be somewhat insecure. The more one state becomes secure by increasing its capability, the more others become insecure. It is a vicious circle as each state seeks to accumulate more and more. This is what leads to "power politics." As John Spanier puts it:

> The state system thus condemns each state to a continuing struggle for power because each faces a security dilemma. Nations seek power not because the maximization of power is their goal; they seek it because they wish to guard the security of their "core values," their territorial integrity and political independence. And they act aggressively because the system gives rise to mutual fear and suspicion; each state regards its brother state, so to speak, as a potential Cain.[54]

[51]Ibid., p. 4.

[52]Hans J. Morgenthau, *Scientific Man vs. Power Politics*, University of Chicago Press, Chicago, 1946, p. 154.

[53]My analysis of Morgenthau is drawn from a combination of his *Politics Among Nations, In Defense of the National Interest*, and *Scientific Man vs. Power Politics*, all cited above. Two points are important in this regard. First, because he has written so prolifically and covered so much ground, there are many different ways of interpreting and summarizing his work; this is mine alone. Second, one must remember that Mr. Morgenthau hit the scene like a cannon shell shortly after the Second World War and his work was revolutionary. He wrote to challenge the previously prevalent academic emphasis on ethics and law, and did so very successfully. A great academic debate followed. The student should consult the works listed in footnotes 2 to 4 and 31 above. Also useful in this regard are Hans J. Morgenthau, "Another 'Great Debate': The National Interest of the United States," *The American Political Science Review*, December, 1952, pp. 961–998, and Robert W. Tucker, "Professor Morgenthau's Theory of Political Realism," *The American Political Science Review*, March, 1952, pp. 214–224.

[54]Spanier, *Games Nations Play*, Third Edition, p. 56.

If power was as important and sought as constantly as these analyses seem to indicate, regardless of whether it was because of human nature or the characteristics of the system, then what a jungle the policymaker would live in.[55] One would have to assume that everyone was constantly struggling, fearful and suspicious of all. No one could be trusted. Conflict would be the usual order of things, and cooperation would be only a means of increasing one's capability. No one would be above suspicion and one would always have to expect the worst. The only thing the policymaker would need to consider is power, because nothing else would really matter.

But is this really descriptive of the totality of international behavior? The answer is emphatically "NO!"[56] Were it true, policymakers would have a much simpler (if somewhat more frightening) task than they actually do in terms of the types and categories of data involved. But as was demonstrated in previous sections, law, ethics, and ideology do play some role in international politics. Policymakers in fact are often influenced by such factors and many times do take them into account when making decisions. This is a fact and it alone demonstrates that power is not all that matters.[57] Thus, even if the concept of human nature has some validity, and modern research at least raises some doubt, even if it is fixed and unchangeable, an even more dubious assumption in light of much evidence pointing to the influence of one's environment, and even if it includes an insatiable desire for power, a debatable and unverifiable assumption, it is obvious that many other factors are involved and power is far from the only force determining the thoughts and actions of policymakers.

Similarly, it is also evident that regardless of system characteristics states are not always seeking to maximize power. Despite the arguments about the nature of the system condemning each state to a "continuing struggle for power," the evidence shows that in fact states don't always pursue such a policy. As we see in Chapter 3, states choose from a wide range of objectives and

---

[55]We say "as these analyses seem to indicate" advisedly here. As indicated in footnote 53 Professor Morgenthau's work is very complex and allows much variation in analysis. Furthermore, although it is not always possible to tell precisely when he is describing "reality" and when he is proposing a theory that experience can never totally achieve, it is clear that *sometimes* he is describing only what he thinks the essence of politics *ought* to be, not what he thinks it is. See particularly his *Politics Among Nations*, Fifth Edition, pp. 4–10. Spanier too, as he explains on pages 70–71 of his Third Edition, is presenting a model from which particular observations are deduced. Naturally, in the real world there will be degrees of variation from the model. In any event the issue here is not the precise views of Morgenthau or Spanier, but the role of power.

[56]Both Morgenthau and Spanier would accept this but would still stress the overarching importance of power and suggest that all else is relatively insignificant.

[57]State practice is the most powerful evidence one could develop. For various academic arguments see the works cited in footnote 53 above.

these vary in their relationship to power, particularly in the sense of "struggling" for its "maximization."

In analyzing the actual behavior of various states one quickly sees that in some cases it would not only be incorrect but would also be a great distortion to say that power maximization was their goal or that they were constantly struggling for its attainment. Who would characterize modern American-British or American-Israeli relations in such a fashion? Would the creation of the World Bank be meaningfully described as part of a power struggle? How about ordinary international trade agreements or Canadian-American negotiations over navigation procedures on the Great Lakes? For some states almost no aspect of their activity seems usefully characterized in this way. Swedish neutrality would be an example. And, as George Quester has said:

> Surely Iceland and Switzerland are nations, but they devote almost no effort to influencing the outside world politically, and thus are barely interested in power, much less deterministically dominated by it.[58]

If power is not all pervasive then how should one describe its role? Certainly it does have some degree of significance. The key point is that its significance can only be determined in light of the particular situation. Because of the system's characteristics it is true that there is always the possibility that power will be very important and may be decisive. Perhaps force will even be used. Since there is always this potential the policymaker must continually consider capability factors. For the same reason it is necessary to be very careful to recognize that one must act to protect his or her country and that conflicts can occur. On the other hand, the policymaker must also remember that other factors may enter into policy calculations and cooperation also might be possible; conflict is not the only type of relationship that can occur. Thus, although the policymaker must always take power factors into account other factors cannot be ignored. There are no *a priori* conclusions one can reach about the relative importance of the different phenomena in particular circumstances. It is essential to analyze the specific situation and the particular policymakers involved to see which factors are most pertinent in each case.

In this regard, as in so many, the factor of perception is terribly important. The policymaker must, of course, be aware of the role that ethics, law, ideology, and power usually play and then attempt to deduce the specific application from the generality. But it is essential to go beyond a superficial analysis and take into account the fact that different individuals "see" things differently. Different people operate from different perspectives and seldom

---

[58]George H. Quester, *The Continuing Problem of International Politics*, Dryden Press, Hinsdale, Ill., 1974, p. 13.

observe the situation in an objective manner. Although the world policymakers perceive may be quite different from that which an objective outsider might see, *they will in fact act on the basis of their perception.* Thus the policymaker must try to determine the particular perception of every other participant policymaker and, recognizing that each will act on the basis of his or her own subjective interpretation, act accordingly.

CONFLICT, COMPETITION, COOPERATION

The foregoing analysis has shown that law, ethics, ideology, and power are important in international politics, the role that each plays depending on many different factors. It is clear that although there are times that the policymaker must accord the highest priority to questions of capability there are times this is not so. Given these facts alone one would expect that there would be a wide variety of relations ensuing among states. In addition, one needs to recall that there are 150 or so states (plus nonstate actors) participating in international politics, each with its own history, geographic setting, political and economic system, and so forth. Each has its own policymakers and their differing perceptions of and susceptibility to the general factors that have been analyzed, each seeking some of a wide range of possible objectives via a vast array of policy techniques (see Part 4), all of this occurring within a decentralized anarchical system allowing each considerable latitude of choice. The end result is an amazingly complex system.

What does this mean in terms of conflict, competition, or cooperation? Do most of the relations in this complex world involve conflict? Is cooperation the norm? What should policymakers assume as they attempt to formulate and implement policy? The answer is that they should *assume* nothing. Because of the bewildering variety and immense quantity of international interactions, the policymaker deals with an unbelievably complex world. As the previous discussion has shown, even understanding the most basic concepts is an extraordinarily difficult task. It is clear enough, of course, that conflicts occur and do so for many reasons. Maybe states are simply seeking incompatible objectives such as each wanting to exercise control over the same territory, or perhaps one desires the stabilization and the other the overthrow of a particular government. In a situation where objectives are fundamentally opposed, if they cannot be adjusted and states seek them with an intensity precluding meaningful compromise, conflict will be the result. There also are less concrete reasons for disputes. Prestige may become involved and make compromise impossible; the snowballing phenomenon may set in until a conflict develops that no one anticipated; perhaps incorrect or inadequate information or certain preconceptions bring about unnecessary conflict; sometimes policy is conducted so ineptly that it leads to trouble, or perhaps there just was not adequate time to think things out. Maybe ethnic, racial, or religious differences cannot be reconciled. And the list could be extended. Not to belabor the point further, it is obvious that there are a wide variety of conflictual relations.

But there are a number of relationships that are not conflictual. Sometimes relationships are produced that are basically *competitive*. For example, states may compete for the support, gratitude, neutrality, or cooperation of a particular third party via a program of foreign aid. American economic and Soviet military aid to India would be a case in point.[59] Or states may compete in terms of economic growth, the "space race," or propaganda activities, as Moscow and Washington have so often done. Perhaps parties to a particular treaty will compete to see who can obtain the most advantages under the agreement without technically violating its provisions. In these and relations of a similar nature, competition, not conflict, is the rule (although it could lead to conflict).

Finally, there are *cooperative* relations. As was true with respect to conflictual relationships, there are many varieties of cooperative relationships also, ranging from those that are very limited and informal to arrangements approaching both complete agreement on objectives and on the coordination of means.[60] Although one might assume that cooperation automatically implies a commonality of objectives, this is not necessarily the case. For example, in the early 1950s both the United States and Pakistan wanted an alliance. Washington's main goal was to contain Communist China, Pakistan's to receive American weapons for possible use against India. Although a relationship of limited cooperation ensued, the parties were cooperating to achieve different ends. Sometimes states cooperate in the negotiation of a particular agreement but have very different reasons for their cooperation. The 1939 Soviet-German Nonaggression Pact is a case in point.[61]

Of course, there are those situations in which cooperative relations exist between states that do have common objectives. The United States and the Western European countries cooperated by forming NATO to attain the common objective of deterring a Soviet military attack.[62] As noted earlier, in 1957 France, West Germany, Italy, and the Benelux countries created the European Common Market in a common attempt to break down nationalistic barriers to economic growth.[63] In 1973 Egypt and Syria cooperated in the planning and undertaking of a limited military assault against Isiael. Even in a conflict situ-

---

[59]For a thorough examination of foreign aid see Chapter 9, pp. 250–263.

[60]For discussion of the advantages and disadvantages of different levels of cooperation see Chapter 5, pp. 119–126.

[61]For more on the Nonaggression Pact see Chapter 6, p. 145 and Chapter 12, pp. 327–328.

[62]There also were other reasons. See Chapter 6, footnote 19.

[63]See Chapter 1, p. 21.

ation there may be common objectives, and cooperation may occur. Frequently, for example, belligerents cooperate by tacitly consenting to a limitation of their war's territorial scope.

Not only are international politics in general thus a mixture of conflictual, competitive, and cooperative relations of varying configurations and intensities, this is also true with respect to the relations of any two parties. American-Soviet conflicts since World War II have made headlines and rightly so, given the capability of these states, their potential for destruction, and the depth and intensity of their disputes. But there have been other relationships as well. We already have mentioned certain elements of competition, to wit: foreign aid, economic growth, the "space race," etc. Perhaps more interesting is the fact that there have also been a number of areas of U. S.-Soviet cooperation. The tacit consent to limit their competition to nonviolent means is one example. Another was the signing of the Limited Nuclear Test Ban and Non-Proliferation Treaties as the superpowers sought to limit the dangers of nuclear weaponry. In the 1970s economic, medical, scientific, and cultural cooperation increased, as did political-military concern and consultation over the growing capability of the People's Republic of China. And, of course, the Strategic Arms Limitation Agreements of May 1972 provide another example. Thus one sees a real mixture of conflict, competition and cooperation even between Washington and Moscow.

As a policymaker one must avoid prejudging this issue. Things are just too complicated and unpredictable to make an *a priori* judgment. The interactions of the policies of international parties do not produce any "characteristic" relationship. There may be conflict, competition, or cooperation, or a mixture of the three, but a policymaker simply cannot know in advance. As is true in so much of international politics, one just has to be situation-specific.

In Part 1 we have provided a useful understanding of the essence of the international environment within which policymakers work. We now go to Part 2, the formulation of policy within that environment.

Part 2
POLICY FORMULATION

Within the context of the major features of the international political environment described in Part 1, there are a series of steps that the policymaker *should attempt* to follow in formulating an optimum policy. These steps provide the subject matter of Part 2. It is important to note that this discussion is, in some part, normative. While policymakers in fact frequently do try to employ the procedures and analytical techniques that are examined in Chapters 3–6, at times they do not. Also, as our analysis in Part 5 will make clear, the policymaker's task is more complicated than Chapters 3–6 would suggest because there are a number of constraints and limitations under which one must labor. Finally, for the sake of clarity the material in Part 2 occasionally tends to oversimplify matters because it involves a somewhat artificial separation into steps of activities that in practice are very much interrelated and that sometimes are undertaken almost simultaneously. These facts do not, however, detract from the utility of presenting an analysis that (1) is a great aid in helping the observer to understand how policymakers in fact do proceed much of the time, and (2) establishes certain guidelines that policymakers should try to observe to the greatest extent possible. To present such an analysis is the purpose of Part 2.

3

The Parties and Their Objectives

It might logically be assumed that one would begin the process of policy formulation by determining what his or her party's objectives should be. And indeed, in practice this sometimes (though not always) is exactly what is done. But such is not the optimum starting point. The policymaker who so acts is making two mistakes. First, this policymaker is bypassing a very critical and deceptively difficult task, namely, precisely ascertaining who really is involved in, and who holds the key to the outcome of, the specific situation. Second, such action, focusing as it does solely on the objectives of one's own party, fails to give sufficient attention to what the other involved parties are seeking, what their objectives are. Taking the appropriately defined steps in the correct sequence is of considerable importance.[1]

WHO IS INVOLVED?

The policymaker's first step is to ascertain who is involved in the particular situation being considered. How many parties are there, what are their relationships, and who will be critical in determining the outcome? It seems like this would be easy, but it is not, and very often differences in this analysis underlie severe disagreements over the policy to be adopted.

[1] Useful and somewhat similar is Hartmann, *The New Age of American Foreign Policy*, Chapter 1.

There are any number of situation configurations with which a policy-maker must deal but it is useful to think of them in terms of seven basic categories: (1) two primary parties; (2) a primary party and a coalition of equals; (3) a primary party and a coalition headed by a dominant party; (4) two or more coalitions of equals; (5) several primary parties; (6) two or more coalitions with each headed by a dominant party; and (7) any of the preceding with the addition of parties adopting any of the orientations described below that do not involve concern with the substance of the problem (such as neutral problem solver or balancer). The policymaker must attempt to determine which configuration characterizes the situation in question and what this means in terms of the appropriate target for his or her policy. In each instance he or she is searching for the key party or parties, the one(s) who can wield decisive influence.

This task is always important but it can be critical in a crisis. In this situation the key question often is who is the "enemy?" Even this limited aspect of the problem can be exceedingly complex. Perhaps an example would be helpful: let's analyze the Vietnam conflict in the early and mid-1960s as it was (and might have been) perceived from Washington.

Who really was involved? Who was the "enemy"? Was this war fundamentally a domestic power struggle between two South Vietnamese factions, the Saigon government and the Vietcong (VC), later supplemented and expanded by outside forces? Was the VC the primary enemy of the Saigon government and was it essentially an organization of South Vietnamese dissidents? Or was the VC a front organization for the Democratic Republic of Vietnam (DRV), operating in accordance with instructions from the North? Or did the VC and DRV constitute a coalition of equals, neither dominating the other? Or were both the VC and DRV engaged in a war of national liberation largely controlled and directed by the People's Republic of China (PRC)? Or was this a three-way coalition? Or were these three, separate parties? Or were all three a part of a centrally directed Communist monolith seeking to communize the entire globe, with this being but one theater of that struggle? These were not mere hypothetical problems. On the contrary, they constantly confronted policymakers and received different answers at different times (although the policymakers were not always aware of their own confusion and the significance of the issue).

American conceptions shifted erratically among three possibilities. The enemy was: (1) a primary party, monolithic communism; (2) a primary party, Hanoi, and the VC was its creature; and (3) a primary party, China. Configuration number one was dominant (two primary parties) although the identity of the parties was a matter of dispute. On "our" side, at some point Washington took over the primary role from Saigon; as to "their" side, American policymakers never did reach a permanent conclusion concerning who the enemy really was (the complexity of the overall issue is demonstrated by the fact that even within a given configuration there can be wide differences of opinion).

Secretary of State Dean Rusk illustrated American confusion rather clearly in his testimony before the Senate Foreign Relations Committee on February 18, 1966.[2] At one point he said:

> We must view the problem in perspective. We must recognize that what we are seeking to achieve in South Vietnam is part of a process that has continued for a long time, a process of preventing the expansion and extension of Communist domination by the use of force against the weaker nations on the perimeter of Communist power... The Communist world has returned to its demand for what it calls a world revolution... So what we face in Vietnam is what we have faced on many occasions before. The need to check the extension of Communist power in order to maintain a reasonable stability in a precarious world.

This would seem to be clear enough. The enemy is Communist power and this is part of a gigantic effort to revolutionize the world. Yet later in the very same speech Secretary Rusk evidenced his lack of clarity when he referred to the act of aggression by *Hanoi*:

> But the evidence is overwhelming that it is in fact something quite different. A systematic aggression by Hanoi against the people of South Vietnam.

Elsewhere he said:

> These facts demonstrate beyond question that the war in Vietnam is as much an act of outside aggression as though the Hanoi regime had sent an army across the 17th parallel.[3]

When this conception was dominant, the Administration directed its activities toward Hanoi:

> For months now we have done everything possible to make clear to the regime in Hanoi that a political solution is the proper course. This is the simple message that we have tried to convey to Hanoi through many channels. The regime in Hanoi has been unwilling to accept any of the possibilities open to it for discussion.

---

[2]For the text of his testimony, see U. S. Department of State, *Bulletin*, March 7, 1966, pp. 1–17.

[3]This seems to have been the more generally accepted American interpretation. See U. S. Department of State, *A Threat to Peace: North Viet-Nam's Effort to Conquer South Viet-Nam*, Publication 7308, 1961, and U. S. Department of State, *Aggression from the North: The Record of North Viet-Nam's Campaign to Conquer South Viet-Nam*, Publication 7839, 1965.

Clearly, if the enemy was the monolithic Communist bloc of Cold War fame the key would lie not in Hanoi but presumably in Moscow.[4]

Yet perhaps this was neither expansion by a Communist monolith nor an act of aggression by Hanoi. Rusk himself so indicated on October 12, 1967 when he opined that Communist China was the real instigator, or at least the underlying menace involved in the Vietnam war. At a press conference he said that it was really China that was testing Washington here, that "Peking has nominated itself by proclaiming a militant doctrine of the world revolution and doing something about it."

This was not an abstract discussion divorced from policy implications. If China was the main enemy then all American policy had to be calculated on the basis of an expansionist China instigating a war of national liberation.

President Johnson seemed equally unclear. In his famous "Patterns for Peace" speech at Johns Hopkins University on April 7, 1965, he stated:

> The first reality is that North Viet-Nam has attacked the independent nation of South Viet-Nam.

Yet later he said:

> Over this war—and all Asia—is another reality: the deepening shadow of *Communist China*. The rulers in Hanoi are urged on by Peiping. . . *The contest in Viet-Nam is part of a wider pattern of aggressive purposes.*[5] (emphasis mine)

Other officials also demonstrated similar confusion but there is no need to further belabor the point. Much of Washington's difficulty in determining what should be done in Vietnam stemmed directly from this failure to determine with whom one should be (or was) dealing.

It should also be pointed out that the problem was even more complex than these "official" interpretations might indicate. Many nonpolicymakers held still another view. They also believed in the two primary parties configuration but felt that these primary parties were simply different South Vietnamese factions, the VC being essentially composed of southern insurgents. Two noted experts on Southeast Asia, George Kahin and John Lewis, put it this way:

> In sum, the insurrection is Southern rooted; it arose at Southern initiative in response to Southern demands . . . It gained drive under the stimulus of Southern

[4]If the real enemy was non-Vietnamese there would be no serious study of the history, culture, and politics of Vietnam because such subjects would be deemed essentially irrelevant to the outcome of the struggle. If the "locals" were mere pawns in the larger struggle one might feel that it made no difference that there had been a victorious anticolonial revolution led by Ho Chi Minh and that he was the most popular figure in the country.

[5]See U. S. Department of State, *Bulletin*, April 26, 1965, pp. 606–610.

Vietminh veterans who felt betrayed by the Geneva Conference and abandoned by Hanoi . . . They lost patience with the communist North and finally took matters into their own hands. Hanoi, despite its reluctance, was then obliged to sanction the Southerners' actions or risk forfeiting all chance of influence over the course of events in South Vietnam. Contrary to U. S. policy assumptions, all available evidence shows that the revival of the civil war in the South in 1958 was undertaken by Southerners at their own—not Hanoi's—initiative.[6]

This issue is not restricted to U. S. policy in Vietnam, of course, but has relevance to many other situations. For example, what configuration exists, who is involved in, and who holds the key to the outcome of, the Arab-Israeli dispute? Is the primary configuration one of an Arab coalition of equals versus Israel? If so, is Egypt, now that it has signed a peace treaty with Israel, still a coalition member? Perhaps an Arab coalition is involved but it is a coalition headed by a dominant party not a coalition of equals. If so, who is that dominant party? Or, maybe the configuration is one of two coalitions of equals, the United States and Israel on one side and Syria, Jordan, and the PLO on the other. Perhaps it is not any of these. Perhaps there are two coalitions of equals, as hypothesized above, plus a party intent on exacerbating matters to prevent a settlement, such as the U. S. S. R. Or is the situation different still, the configuration being one of several primary parties and no cohesive alliances? If that is so, which of these primary parties will prove decisive? Will it be the Palestinians? If one answers this question affirmatively, just which Palestinians is he or she talking about? And might it not be the Arab oil states, not the Palestinians, who will prove decisive?

Or switch to the problems of a divided Europe. Are there really just two primary parties, the Americans and Russians, with everyone else of minor importance? Or is the situation one involving two alliances headed by dominant partners in confrontation? Are opposing coalitions disintegrating and cross-alliance policies becoming more important? Is it really a case of several relatively independent parties all seeking their own objectives? What is the role of the Germans, West and East? Do they really hold the key?

Even if at some point a policymaker was able to determine who was involved in situations such as those described above, even if at some juncture he or she could ascertain what configurations existed and who held the key to the outcome, his or her task would not be finished *because the identity of the participants and who holds the key can change.* The 1970 Jordan civil war is a case in point. First, some background comments are necessary to place the situational developments in perspective. By 1970 various Palestinian NLOs—The Palestine Liberation Organization, The Popular Front for the Liberation of Palestine, etc.,—had concluded that the Arab states were largely ineffectual in

[6]See George McTurnan Kahin and John W. Lewis, *The United States in Vietnam: An Analysis in Depth of America's Involvement in Vietnam*, A Delta Book, New York, 1967, p. 119.

the quest to "liberate" Palestine; the states' decisive defeat by Israel in the 1967 war despite the massive arms and training assistance they had been receiving seemed to make this all too clear.[7] In light of this conclusion the NLOs had themselves become active, undertaking a wide range of limited military actions against the Israelis. Frequently, these operations were launched from bases in Jordan.

The Palestinian NLOs' activities constituted a major problem for Jordan's King Hussein. First, quite predictably the Israelis often retaliated. Hussein was continually faced with the dilemma of either engaging the Israelis and risking all-out war (and almost certain defeat), or allowing them to conduct military operations in Jordanian territory at will, damaging his prestige and credibility both among his own people and throughout the Arab world. Second, the guerillas, in point of fact, were almost a "state within a state"; they disregarded Jordanian laws, established their own government structures and systems of taxation, and in general acted like an army of occupation. Yet, although they clearly challenged Hussein's right of internal control, because nearly two-thirds of his subjects were Palestinians and because of the fact that the Palestinian cause had enormous appeal throughout the Arab world, the king tended to act with caution.[8]

Now to the events leading to the civil war. A number of incidents, including small armed clashes involving the king's forces and various guerilla units, had occurred intermittently for some time. In most cases, Hussein had acted moderately, and in June 1970 he even agreed to certain "progressive" cabinet changes so as to avoid a direct confrontation; the NLOs, too, usually had sought to avoid all-out combat. But when in August Hussein accepted the so-called Rogers cease-fire plan (an American proposal to restore the Arab-Israeli cease-fire that had been accepted after the 1967 war but had since deteriorated) the guerillas were furious; they were totally opposed to any proposal that might lead to a partial settlement with Israel because such would not provide for the liberation of Palestine. Consequently, they launched another round of raids, increasing the tension level enormously. Then came what for Hussein was the last straw; early in September members of the Popular Front for the Liberation of Palestine hijacked four Western-owned airplanes, forcing them to land in what was called "liberated territory" in Jordan. Hussein was being made to look foolish.

> On the ground . . . only twenty miles from his palace in Amman, a detachment of Jordanian troops stood in a wide circle, impotently facing an inner circle of PFLP

[7] An excellent and fairly brief account of the growth of the guerilla movement is William B. Quandt, Fuad Jabber, and Ann Mosely Lesch, *The Politics of Palestinian Nationalism*, University of California Press, Berkeley, 1972.

[8] The Palestinians had been displaced from (what they believed to be) their lands in the 1948–1949 and 1967 wars.

commandos who guarded the planes and threatened to destroy them and their occupants at the first hostile move from the army.[9]

Hussein had had enough. On September 17 Jordanian troops unleashed a massive armed attack against the guerillas.

At this point no one doubted who was involved. It was the forces of the king against a loose coalition of Palestinian NLOs. In the first few days of the war things went badly for the Palestinians; although they fought fiercely they were no match for Hussein's troops. Suddenly, a new element entered the picture. As the Jordanians drove northward the *Syrian* government declared that it was supporting the Palestinians; soon tanks and troops of the Syrian trained and commanded Palestine Liberation Army moved south to engage the Jordanians. Clearly, the situation had changed. The Syrians had become a key participant. There was even more to it than this would indicate, though. The United States, which had long supported the independence of Hussein (indeed, which considered his survival a matter of vital interest), believed there was a strong probability that the *Soviet Union* was behind the Syrians' move.[10] Was it? If it was, then perhaps Moscow held the key via Damascus. Though it was not at all evident what the situation actually was, it was clear that it had been changed from what it was before.

But the policymakers' task was still more complicated than even this would imply. Not only did policymakers have to alter their analysis because of observed and possible changes with respect to who had already become involved, they also had to think (as one always should) in terms of who might logically be expected to become involved in various alternative future circumstances.[11] It was evident that *Israeli* policymakers would not accept the establishment of a guerilla, or guerilla-controlled, government in Jordan, for example. In order to be ready to prevent such an occurrence Israeli Defense Forces had taken up positions for possible military intervention. Thus, though Israel was not involved at this point, under certain circumstances she might be.[12]

---

[9]Malcolm H. Kerr, *The Arab Cold War: Gamal 'Abd al-Nasir and His Rivals, 1958–1970*, Third Edition, Oxford University Press, New York, 1971, p. 147.

[10]Very useful on the American view and the resulting policy responses are William B. Quandt, *Decade of Decisions: American Policy Toward the Arab-Israeli Conflict, 1967–1976*, University of California Press, Berkeley, 1977, Chapter 4 and Henry Kissinger, *The White House Years*, Little, Brown, Boston, 1979, Chapter 15.

[11]Similar thinking influenced U. S. policy in the Korean war. Concern over possible Soviet involvement was important in the American decision not to take military action against the Chinese mainland.

[12]Such intervention proved unnecessary when Hussein's forces—with a gratuitous assist from Syrian Defense Minister Hafez Assad who purposely failed to provide air cover for the "PLA" armor in order to advance his internal political fortunes—crushed the guerillas, ending the war. It was in "honor" of this, incidentally, that the guerilla unit known as Black September was formed.

How would the Syrians react to that? And, if the Syrians then directly intervened, what would Washington and/or Moscow do?[13]

The Jordan civil war and the other examples make it very evident that determining who is involved and who holds the key to a particular situation is not
an easy assignment. Yet it is absolutely essential that this be done, and done
well. If it is not, the policymaker will not even know whom to make the primary target of his or her policies. If that is so, unless one is very lucky the best
that can be hoped for is policy ineffectiveness, and quite possibly one will
move toward a situation that will be highly detrimental.

DETERMINATION OF OBJECTIVES

Once one has determined who is involved one must attempt to discover what
each wants; what are their objectives?[14] At the same time one must be provisionally formulating one's own, determining what outcome(s) or state(s) of affairs one would like to see produced.[15]

All international actors have a wide range of objectives that they potentially may seek to achieve or protect. These may vary in terms of importance,
breadth, the intensity with which they are sought, the time frame within which
one hopes to achieve them, and the resources one is willing to allocate to their
attainment. They may also differ in the extent to which a party really expects
them to be attained, as well as the sources from which they come.

When one speaks of "objectives" one is talking about the "ends" of policy. However, it should not be assumed that it is possible to neatly distinguish
between "means" and "ends," and that the "ends" are definite and final.
Few objectives are ends in themselves. Instead they are usually means to the
achievement of further ends (which in turn are often means to further ends,

[13]Both President Nixon and Dr. Kissinger believed confrontation with the Soviets was a definite possibility. See Secretary Kissinger's comments, U. S. Department of State, *Bulletin*, July 23,
1973, p. 149, and Richard M. Nixon, *"U. S. Foreign Policy for the 1970s: Building for Peace," A
Report to the Congress by Richard Nixon, President of the United States*, February 25, 1971, pp.
127–128.

[14]At this point in the process the policymaker generally begins with the assumption that the
policymakers of all states act in a unified, rational fashion, although one recognizes that this is an
oversimplification and sometimes just plain wrong. However, one must begin here and make adjustments and allowances later. See Part 5 for various qualifications.

[15]It is important to note that the formulation at this juncture is, or at least should be, only
provisional. One ought not to attempt a definitive determination with so many steps still to be undertaken, with the costs and benefits of so many factors still to be assessed.

and so forth). What the situation really involves is a means-end chain of varying degrees of complexity.[16]

Fundamental Objectives

All states seek certain fundamental objectives, certain objectives so important and lasting that in all but the most unusual situations policymakers will undertake a maximum expenditure of effort and resources to achieve or protect them, including going to war. The first of these, and the most fundamental, is pure *survival*. At rock bottom all of the policymaker's decisions must be based on their anticipated effect on the continued existence of his country. One must always ask, "is this helpful or harmful to security?" Survival is composed, at a minimum, of two parts: first, protecting the lives of a majority of the population, and second, defending the country's sovereignty or political independence (i. e., its capacity to make independent decisions concerning its internal affairs and external policies).

Because all states operate within an environment of decentralized anarchy where military strength is the final arbiter, because all have the ability to use force, because ultimately each can rely only on itself for survival, and because the number of actual and potential conflicts in international politics is enormous, it is understandable why survival considerations inevitably condition a large number of policy decisions. Whether they like it or not, policymakers, of necessity, *have* to be concerned with survival threats and with choosing the most appropriate means of eliminating, countering, or altering them. In this regard, because of the uncertainties inherent in the international system and the stakes involved, when it looks as if survival may be at issue policymakers generally believe it is only prudent to assume the worst re the objectives of a potentially threatening party. If one is going to err, it is felt, one should err on the "safe" side; the policymaker cannot take the risk of underestimating the survival threat, given what the possible consequences could be.

A second fundamental objective, and one that is often considered to be a matter of survival, is *territorial integrity*. In most cases the defense of one's home territory is critical. A state that loses its *entire* territory, of course, ceases to even be a state, as happened to Poland in the eighteenth century.[17] From 1795 until the end of World War I "Poland" did not exist. As this illustrates, there have been cases in which one's territory has just been relinquished, but

---

[16]See Keith R. Legg and James F. Morrison, *Politics and the International System: An Introduction*, Harper, New York, 1971, pp. 140–142.

[17]In a series of three partitions, in 1772, 1793, and 1795, Poland was divided among Prussia, Russia, and Austria (Austria was involved only in the first and third partitions).

this is highly unusual. Occasionally policymakers have "accepted" the loss of just a portion of their territory in the hope of preserving the remainder. Perhaps the most famous example of this was the "acceptance" by the Czechoslovakian government of the loss of certain German inhabited strategic territories to the Nazis following the Munich Agreement in 1938.[18] In that case territorial integrity was violated but a certain territorial base was retained. But these two cases were extraordinary, very much the exception to the rule. The policymaker must assume that parties will consider preservation of their home territory to be a fundamental objective and will fight to protect it.

This does, however, raise another issue: what *is* one's home territory? It is not always clear where one state ends and another begins. It must be remembered that each state has its own conception of what is "home," and sometimes these conceptions are different. The People's Republic of China claims that 500,000 square miles of Soviet Asia actually "belongs" to China. These territories, "taken" from China by Tsarist Russia in the "unequal" treaties of 1858, 1860, and 1864, include segments of the Soviet Republics of Kazakhstan, Kirghizia, and Tajikistan, as well as the Amur River Basin and the Maritime Territory.[19] The Soviets, of course, dispute the Chinese contention. Whose "home territory" is it? After World War II Germany was split into East and West, and the ancient citadels of Prussian (German) power were incorporated into Russia and Poland. What is, or is not, "Germany?" What about other divided nations, such as Korea? Who "owns" land taken by conquest? And what about areas concerning which there has never been agreement as to whose home territory it is, such as the West Bank of the Jordan or the city of Jerusalem? These are pertinent, highly troublesome questions.

Because the preservation of territorial integrity, of one's "home territory," is almost always a policy objective of primary importance, if a party has had its territorial integrity massively violated its policymakers likely will feel strongly about reacquiring those lost lands and make a major effort to devise policies appropriate to that end.[20] There can be instances in which this does not occur, such as in situations where the former governing unit(s) is (are) so altered in nature and/or reduced in capability that recovering the lost terri-

---

[18]Of course the remainder was not preserved in this case. The best general account of the Munich Crisis is Sir John W. Wheeler-Bennet, *Munich—Prologue to Tragedy*, Second Edition, Macmillan, New York, 1963. A very useful and brief introduction replete with valuable documents, is Frances L. Lorwenheim, ed., *Peace or Appeasement? Hitler, Chamberlain and the Munich Crisis*, Houghton Mifflin, Boston, 1964. The best introduction to the Munich era is still Winston S. Churchill, *The Second World War, Vol. I: The Gathering Storm*, Houghton Mifflin, Boston, 1948.

[19]See footnote 36 following.

[20]This may involve the use of force, of course, but it also may not. For an example of the latter see the discussion of West German Chancellor Konrad Adenauer's approach in Chapter 13.

tories would be impossible, but these are the exception not the rule. In most cases a party that has had land taken from it will make a major effort to get it back, Germany's attempts to avenge her enormous World War I losses being a case in point. Sometimes, of course, conditions are such that immediate action is precluded, but that does not mean the underlying objective has been abandoned. Syria's desire to regain land taken from her by Israel in 1967 has not diminished even though the conditions for achieving the objective have not been propitious. While the restoration of territorial integrity is not in each and every case a fundamental policy objective, and though the intensity with which it is sought will vary with situational conditions, policymakers of parties other than the ones whose territory was despoiled generally find it only prudent to assume the aggrieved entity will make a major, sustained effort to get "its land" back.

A third objective that has often been considered fundamental is the *preservation of a state's belief system from externally imposed change.*[21] States often consider the basic principles, beliefs, values, customs, and traditions by which they live to be of such importance that they would be willing to fight to maintain them. Certainly the United States would consider the protection of some democratic principles worth fighting for. Attempts by a foreign country to prevent the free exercise of religion or to prohibit freedom of association in the United States, for example, would not be tolerated. South Africa would not freely accept foreign-induced changes in its Apartheid programs. And, as we saw in Chapter 1, the Soviets bitterly resisted President Carter's human rights campaign, perceiving it to be an effort to alter their belief system.[22]

There are times when events occur in other states that may not have as their immediate objective the alteration of one's belief system, but a judgment is made to the effect that they could well produce this result. If such a situation seems to be developing there will be a strong temptation for policymakers of the "threatened" state to see if there is some way to take preventive action.[23] In late 1967 in Czechoslovakia—a Soviet satellite that had been relatively quiescent under Soviet control for nearly two decades—intellectuals began to openly protest the government's manifold restrictions on the freedoms of press and speech.[24] Soon a reform movement was in full flower, and Alexander Dubček, a liberal reformer, was appointed First Secretary of the Czech Communist Party. In the spring of 1968 censorship of the press was eliminated, and

---

[21]Both this and the following fundamental objective are directly related to the third attribute of statehood, the right of internal control. See Chapter 1, pp. 6–10.

[22]See Chapter 1, pp. 7–9.

[23]There will not always be, of course.

[24]Philip Windsor and Adam Roberts, *Czechoslovakia: Reform, Repression and Resistance*, Columbia University Press, New York, 1969.

other civil rights seemed achievable. The Soviet Union was vitally concerned. Moscow perceived these activities to pose a potentially severe threat to its own belief system. Consequently, it undertook a wide range of nonviolent military maneuvers designed to "persuade" the Czechs to mend their ways.[25] When those proved unproductive Soviet military forces, along with troops from several other Warsaw Pact states, invaded Czechoslovakia and imposed the Kremlin's will. The "Prague Spring" was over.

A fourth fundamental objective often is the *protection of the existing political or economic system from externally imposed change*. Obviously the Soviets would fight to preserve their existing governmental structure against the imposition of more democratic institutions, as would North Korea, Vietnam, China, and others. The leaders of Israel would not accept a change in the governmental structure that would allow true binational Arab-Israeli control. Washington would consider preservation of its mixed-capitalist economic system critical, and conversely the Soviets would certainly act to prevent the imposition of any system based on private ownership of property and the means of production. Historically, the rulers of East Germany have paid little heed to the various Western plans for German reunification that have embodied the requirement of free, all-German elections. Lebanon's Christian leaders long opposed external (and internal) plans to alter the "favorable" Christian-Moslem relationship in the governmental structure, plans designed to take into account the "pro-Moslem" demographic and confessional changes that occurred after the National Covenant was agreed to in 1943. As these examples show, policymakers strenuously oppose external efforts to alter their state's political or economic system. Most of the time, in fact, if necessary they will go to war rather than acquiesce in such a development.

Middle-Range Objectives

Fundamental objectives are essentially conservative, something to be defended or protected.[26] There are many other objectives states may seek which vary in significance depending on the situation. They may become exceptionally important and require the expenditure of considerable resources, or may receive lower priority. Generally their achievement is sought within a foreseeable period of time, although not immediately. Such *middle-range objectives* some-

---

[25]Also see Chapter 10, p. 271.

[26]They are also more separable on paper than in practice. In most cases they are interrelated and often they compete with one another for limited resources. The policymaker is usually confronted with an uncertain choice among related alternatives none of which is totally acceptable or unacceptable. Although it is useful to analyze them separately, one must remember that in reality things are much more complicated.

times resemble fundamental objectives, but there are salient differences in terms of their permanence, the perceived level of importance, and the intensity with which they are sought.

Middle-range objectives span the gamut of desires and a wide range of classification schemes are possible. For the policymaker, however, it is useful to divide them into political, material, ideological, and prestige objectives, even though he recognizes that there is considerable imprecision and overlapping here.

Political objectives deal primarily with capability and security relationships. An example would be the acquisition of additional territory, or the retention of that previously conquered but not essential for survival. Another might be the creation of political dependencies as the Soviets did in Eastern Europe after World War II. Perhaps the objective is to negotiate a limitation of strategic weapons as the United States and Russia did in interim fashion in May 1972. A state might seek to increase its diplomatic bargaining power by increasing its military strength. Policymakers may determine that it would be useful to add the capabilities of other states to their own and form alliances, as the United States did with great frequency in the late 1940s and 1950s. Maybe a state will embark on a policy designed to deny strategic assets to its adversary while acquiring new assets for itself.[27]

Material objectives include anything affecting economic growth and development. Policymakers naturally are concerned with such matters. As we discussed earlier, in the late 1950s France, West Germany, Italy, Belgium, the Netherlands, and Luxembourg created the European Economic Community in an effort to break down nationalistic barriers to Europe's integrated economic growth.[28] In an attempt to alleviate the impact of poor harvests the Soviet Union has frequently purchased wheat from the United States. To keep its economy fueled Washington buys oil from Nigeria, Canada, Venezuela, and various Persian Gulf states. For Japanese policymakers since World War II economic development and the expansion of economic influence have been *the* major subjects of attention. Much (perhaps most) of Canada's foreign policy is designed to promote economic growth. In many of the world's less developed countries (LDCs) the achievement of material objectives is a pressing, everyday concern.[29] For states that depend on external sources for capital, technology, and expertise, the attainment of productive trade and foreign aid

---

[27]It has been hypothesized that this is what the Soviets are trying to do in Africa, the Middle East, and South Asia. See the provocative testimony of Avigdor Haselkorn in U. S. Senate, Subcommittee on Near Eastern and South Asian Affairs, Committee on Foreign Relations, *Hearings: Middle East Problems*, 95th Congress, 1st Session, May 18, 1977, pp. 6–18ff.

[28]See Chapter 1, pp. 20–21.

[29]Also see Chapter 7, pp. 197–198.

relationships is a high-priority matter. In an effort to provide a framework within which trade would flourish, and provide a procedural base and some accepted principles for trade negotiations, in 1947 the Western powers created the General Agreement on Tariffs and Trade (GATT).

Ideological objectives may include the spreading of a particular system of beliefs. Attempts by Communist leaders to "convince" their neighbors of the validity of Marxism-Leninism would be an example. When President Wilson took the United States into the First World War to "make the world safe for democracy," he was in part seeking an ideological victory.

Another ideological objective would be persuading another party which professes the same ideology as you to accept the "correct" (your) interpretation. Disagreement over the "correct" interpretation of communism has been one of the major issues in the Sino-Soviet dispute.[30] In 1956 Nikita Khrushchev broke with orthodox Leninist and Stalinist doctrine by stating that there was no "fatal inevitability" of war between socialists and capitalists. Because of the overwhelming strength of the camp of socialism, capitalist leaders might be deterred from going to war. The Chinese strongly disagreed. Orthodox communism allowed no room for this capacity to avoid war; a series of terrible collisions was inevitable. If, in contrast to orthodox doctrine, some capitalists in some situations could choose to refrain from actions previously considered inevitable, such as those leading to the terrible collisions foreseen by Lenin, if in some cases they could avoid the inexorable laws of history, then why couldn't they in others?[31] Where would it stop? Persuading the other party of the correct interpretation clearly was a matter of some import.

The protection or enhancement of *prestige* is extremely important to policymakers. Even though the January 1974 Israeli-Egyptian agreement to disengage forces along the Suez Canal fit in with Russian political objectives, the Kremlin let Washington know it was displeased because Dr. Kissinger had not consulted with the Soviets enough in the negotiation process; the Soviets wanted equal status with America. During these same negotiations Egyptian President Anwar Sadat said he was not able to accept a particular "Israeli" proposal, even though the substance of the proposal was to his liking. That being so, at Kissinger's suggestion an "American" proposal was formulated embodying most of the same provisions. Because he did not think his prestige would be harmed by working with Washington, Sadat found this acceptable. Certainly one of the prime objectives of France in building its own independent nuclear force was the enhancement of prestige that automatically accrues from being a nuclear power. Once the United States decided to withdraw from Vietnam, minimizing the damage to its prestige became a major goal; concern

---

[30]See Chapter 6, pp. 147–149, for more on the Sino-Soviet dispute. Re relations between Communists and capitalists, see Chapter 2, pp. 50–54.

[31]Excellent is Hartmann, *The Relations of Nations*, Fifth Edition, pp. 478–483.

over the perceived loss of prestige had much to do with the level and intensity of Washington's subsequent actions in the Mayaguez incident.

A prudent policymaker will recognize the importance of this factor and not place his or her counterpart's prestige in jeopardy any more than unavoidable. President Kennedy heeded this maxim in the Cuban Missile Crisis by allowing Khrushchev a means of withdrawing the Soviet missiles that did not humiliate the Communist leader; the president did not want to provoke a spasm reaction. Failure to give sufficient weight to this element can be harmful to the pursuit of other goals. Hanoi's objective of eliminating American military forces from South Vietnam proved much more costly as a result of its massive conventional assault across the demilitarized zone in March of 1972. President Nixon responded by mining key North Vietnamese ports and initiating heavy bombing of the North. The president obviously felt that there was no need to kick Uncle Sam in the backside as he was leaving. Another example occurred in mid-1956 when Secretary of State Dulles withdrew America's offer to finance the construction of Egypt's High Aswan Dam in a highly offensive manner; a week later an angry Gamal Nasser responded by nationalizing the Universal Suez Maritime Canal Company, and the Suez crisis began.[32]

Specific Immediate Objectives

Finally, the policymaker needs to formulate the specific immediate objectives. After assessing the relationship of the particular situation to fundamental objectives and then considering what middle-range goals should be sought, it is necessary to ask "what is the immediate objective that fits in best with the overall plan?"

Suppose, for example, one has determined that the fundamental objective of survival is endangered because one is not sufficiently achieving the middle-range objective of economic growth. Perhaps what is needed is a critical natural resource such as petroleum, and one has none in one's possession. The specific immediate objective then might be to obtain the needed petroleum in the most feasible manner. After an assessment of the situation one would know whether to attempt to negotiate a trade agreement, seek to purchase oil, agree to adopt certain positions in the United Nations on certain issues, provide military assistance, use force, or whatever.[33]

It is important for policymakers to keep clearly in mind the identity of, and the relationship between, the immediate, middle-range, and fundamental

[32]For more on the Suez crisis see Chapter 13, pp. 364–367.

[33]Although the classification scheme is different, an excellent example of this kind of analytical approach may be found in William D. Coplin, Patrick J. McGowan, and Michael K. O'Leary, *American Foreign Policy: An Introduction to Analysis and Evaluation*, Duxbury, North Scituate, Mass., Table 4.2, 1974, pp. 86–90.

objectives that are being protected or sought in the particular situation. If this is not done, distortions and mistakes may occur that result in severely detrimental policies. Immediate objectives of relatively minor intrinsic importance may take on "great value" just because a state is seeking them, and their achievement may be sought with an intensity and at a cost that are totally disproportionate to their intrinsic worth. Furthermore, because their relationship to fundamental objectives has become blurred it could be that their pursuit will counterproductively endanger fundamental objectives. Although it is not an easy task, it is essential that a policymaker not let the achievement of a specific immediate objective become an end in itself; he or she must keep its intrinsic value and the linkage to middle-range and fundamental objectives in mind.

Sources of Objectives

To this point the picture that has been presented has been oversimplified because it concentrated only on "our" objectives. In actuality what the policymaker must do is make a *simultaneous comparative analysis* to determine the objectives of all the parties. In each case one must ascertain the fundamental, middle-range and immediate goals, determine their relationships, and evaluate the significance of his or her conclusions. In order to undertake this task with any degree of confidence it is very helpful to examine another issue: What are the sources of the objectives for the parties in question? From where do their objectives come?

Once again the task is complicated. Some objectives seem to spring from several sources while others seem to just develop. Furthermore, all attempts at classification distort reality somewhat. A policymaker, however, needs to know where objectives come from if he or she is to understand them and perhaps influence future goal formation, and must attempt the task no matter how difficult.

There are several rather general sources of objectives. As noted in Chapter 2, *ideological and ethical factors* often influence goal formation. Communism provides the lens through which Soviet leaders see the world and the rationale for much of their action. A policymaker looking at ideological factors would, among other things, expect the Soviets to only sign agreements they believe would hasten the inexorable dynamic of history; one would not expect them to try to obtain agreements to permanently eliminate conflict. The policymaker would expect Communist leaders, because of their belief that capitalists are compelled to seek overseas expansion, to have as a major political objective the containment or countering of that expansion. American values similarly condition the nature of United States objectives.[34] A policymaker

---

[34]"So much so that many analysts have extensively criticized American policy on precisely this point. Also see Chapter 2, pp. 47–50 and footnote 31.

looking at the American liberal ideology would expect Americans to try to achieve highly "ethical" solutions to problems and be very concerned with the ethical or moral aspects of any situation. He or she would expect Americans to optimistically try to solve problems and not just let them take their course, and to seek to promote peace by achieving greater "understanding" between parties.

A second general source is *historical tradition and precedent*. The American objective of preventing significant European encroachment in the Western Hemisphere was enunciated in the Monroe Doctrine in 1823 and continues to this day.[35] For hundreds of years Britain sought specifically to prevent the domination of the Low Countries (Belgium, the Netherlands) by a dominant Continental Power to protect against a cross-Channel invasion, and generally to maintain a relatively equal Continental distribution of power. For much of its history (both before and since the advent of communism) Russia has sought to acquire additional territory, to create a buffer zone around its geographic heartland for defense in depth, and to break out of its landlocked position by acquiring ice-free ports (particularly through the Dardanelles Strait to the Mediterranean). These and similar factors are often taken by policymakers as "givens," automatic and continual sources of objectives.

When analyzing historical factors, however, one should keep two points in mind. First, it is not just narrow precedent that is important, but more generally a state's total historical experience. The Chinese belief that territory over which they lost their dominion during periods of imperial weakness should rightfully be under their control (territory that includes what today are Vietnam, North and South Korea, Laos, Kampuchea, Burma, and parts of Malaysia, Indonesia, and Russia) will inevitably lead them to be concerned with regaining that dominion, even if they have not "traditionally" sought to do so.[36] A newly independent state with little tradition of any kind may well pursue objectives that are decidedly anticolonial because of its experience.

A second point is that although historical factors are important they are not necessarily controlling. For centuries England supported the survival of the Ottoman Turk Empire for the purpose of protecting the British imperial lifeline through the Mediterranean to the East (and India, Singapore, Hong Kong, Australia, etc.). This often meant opposition to traditional Russian efforts indicated above. The altered circumstances of World War I, however, brought about an agreement with the Russians against the Turks. The point is

---

[35]This concept had originally been proposed by the British as an Anglo-American venture. Washington was unwilling to cooperate, however, and proceeded on its own. In actuality the Doctrine's success in the nineteenth century was more a result of British naval strength and European concern elsewhere than it was due to American power.

[36]The Chinese list 19 specific territorial losses. A useful map reprinted from a 1954 Chinese textbook may be found in Hartmann, *The New Age of American Foreign Policy*, pp. 340–341.

this: although a policymaker must look at a state's historical patterns and experience for clues to objectives, and recognize that it is an important source, he must avoid being mesmerized by the past and assume that nothing will change.

In addition to such general sources, *specific internal needs* may generate objectives. Population pressure on the food supply may bring about the goal of territorial expansion, and/or increased production, and/or population control. Economic needs may prescribe certain goals. LDC policymakers often feel compelled to seek external capital and technological aid because of the deficiency of their domestic economies in these spheres. The United States is dependent on foreign sources for more than 90 percent of its industrial diamonds, bauxite, and manganese, more than half its chromium and zinc, and approximately half its oil; clearly, Washington will have the objective of somehow obtaining these important resources. Sometimes a particular regime is incapable of enforcing the right of internal control. This frequently will lead to a request for external aid, as it did in 1958 when Lebanon's Camille Chamoun called on Washington for assistance and American marines were dispatched to the Middle East.[37] The list of possibilities is almost endless. The policymaker must examine the subject country's domestic conditions to ascertain what needs may spawn what objectives.

A wide range of external factors may also come into play. Policymakers *perceive threats to national security* and respond accordingly. The American objective of containment of communism arose in this fashion. Alliances are often formed for security reasons, as was true with NATO. Obviously, a major impetus to the quest for stronger armed forces is the perception that security is threatened. The Kremlin's concern with what it perceives to be a growing Chinese threat is one of the major factors behind the search for détente with the West. Jerusalem's perception that an independent Palestinian state on the West Bank would soon constitute a Palestinian-Soviet threat to Israel's survival dictates the objective of preventing the establishment of such an entity.

Perception of a security threat is not the only external source of objectives, however, although official statements may sometimes try to make it look that way. There are also *opportunities to take advantage of situations created by foreign events and conditions.* Domestic unrest provides great possibilities for penetration and intervention. The need for foreign assistance yields the opportunities for influence that go with giving such assistance. The disintegration of an alliance, such as the Sino-Soviet combine, may provide the opportunity to increase one's influence with both countries. A revolution that deposes an adversarial regime may put a more amenable one in its place.

Another external source is the *need to handle a common problem.* Of course, this could involve the two (external) sources discussed above, but it is much broader than that. The mutual Soviet-American recognition of a need to

---

[37]For more on the Lebanese crisis see Chapter 13, pp. 369–371, and Chapter 14, pp. 396–397.

limit strategic weapons led to the SALT Agreements of May 26, 1972. Multilateral acceptance by six European countries of the need to break down nationalistic barriers to economic growth led to the creation of the Common Market in 1957. Concern over economic and environmental issues today is leading to international attempts to solve these difficulties.

Another example of responding to the need to solve a common problem occurred in 1960. For decades prior to that time world oil prices and production levels had been determined by seven huge multinational oil companies, the so-called "seven sisters." Policymakers in the states in which the oil was located and from which it was shipped believed that they had too little influence and that their states were not receiving their fair share of the economic benefits. To remedy their common problem, in 1960 Saudi Arabia, Iran, Kuwait, Venezuela, and Iraq formed the Organization of Petroleum Exporting Countries (OPEC).[38]

Another source is the *needs of the leadership*. Any regime requires some degree of internal support if it is to stay in power. Given this fact, there is always the temptation to create incidents or proclaim possible threats to security in order to maintain this support. Throughout much of the 1950s and 1960s Red Chinese leaders were able to use the spectre of an American invasion to rally popular sentiment behind them. Today, charges of similar Soviet intentions serve the same purpose. Many leaders of newly independent, less developed countries are particularly prone to this activity. Prior to independence they often assumed that all of their troubles were caused by the colonialists. With the imperialists' departure, however, it has been discovered that significant problems (such as low economic growth) remain and that they are extremely difficult to solve. In order to divert attention from failures at home a dynamic, sometimes frenetic foreign policy may be undertaken.

To this point the sources examined have been limited in one critical respect: they are outside of the policymaking process itself. Each of these factors will compete for the policymaker's attention but they will "get through" in varying degrees with differing amounts of effectiveness. One also needs to examine a more proximate source of objectives, namely, *the actual process by which the decisions concerning objectives will be made*. One must seek to determine the locus of decision and ascertain the identity of the key policy influencers. Are there key elites whose will shall prevail? Are there interest factions who control certain issues? Do some decisions really seem to be the product of bureaucratic conflicts? What effect do institutional and structural factors have? These and similar questions must be asked.[39]

---

[38]Since OPEC's creation its membership has expanded considerably. The other members are Libya, United Arab Emirates, Algeria, Qatar, Nigeria, Abu Dhabi, Indonesia, Ecuador, and Gabon (associate member).

[39]Many of these questions are analyzed in depth in Chapter 15.

This brings us to the final consideration, one that policymakers often respect more than observers: *it is human beings who make decisions*. In Chapter 8 the significant impact that individuals have on capability is analyzed; personal factors are equally important here. Whatever the objectives that are decided on, they are chosen by particular people with all their virtues and frailties.

In an excellent little book, *Why Nations Go To War*, John Stoessinger notes that many of the abstract forces often cited as causes of war (nationalism, militarism, alliance systems, economic factors, etc.), had less impact on the cases he studied than did individuals. His analysis indicated that "the personalities of leaders . . . have often been decisive."[40]

Whether a particular individual will be decisive in a given case cannot be prejudged, of course, but it is clear that some individuals will make the final determination of objectives. This being so, the final task with respect to sources is to determine who are the key individuals in any situation and analyze their characteristics.

Complicating Factors

In seeking to identify and categorize objectives and establish the linkages among them, there are a number of factors (in addition to those already discussed) that complicate the task considerably. *First, all parties are involved in a number of situations simultaneously, not just in this one, and the importance they attribute to a given situation, and the objectives they are seeking to protect or achieve therein, are in part a function of their perceptions of the importance and requisites of these other situations.* Although in 1948 the members of the Arab League decided to attack the fledgling state of Israel at the termination of Britain's Palestine mandate, none of them were willing to commit all of their forces. While they all shared the immediate objective of preventing the creation of the Jewish state, each had inter-Arab, nationalist-colonialist, and domestic situational concerns that were perceived to be of such significance that only portions of their armies could be spared for use against the Zionists. The policymaker trying to ascertain the various parties' objectives in a given situation thus must determine where this particular situation fits in terms of each of the party's overall policy priorities.

There is a closely related point that complicates matters further—a policymaker sometimes will do something in a particular situation primarily to achieve extrasituational objectives. In contrast to the example of the Arab

---

[40]John G. Stoessinger, *Why Nations Go to War*, Second Edition, St. Martins, New York, 1978, p. 226. Obviously the jury is still out on the issue of the causes of war. For an excellent summary of many of the current theories see Rosen and Jones, Third Edition, Chapter 10.

League forces noted above, this is not a case where one can only do so much in situation W because he or she has to commit resources to X, Y, and Z; in this case one's situational actions are (in part, at least) designed so that they will have a certain impact on extrasituational targets. When this occurs it is difficult to discover what the parties' situational objectives are since they are conceived as a result of projections as to how they will affect extrasituational matters. For example, American policy in Vietnam in the Nixon-Kissinger years was, to a considerable extent, a reflection of the administration's views as to how various actions or outcomes would affect U. S.-Soviet relations. Dr. Kissinger was seeking to achieve a relaxation of tensions with the Russians along a broad front, hoping such a relaxation would result in the creation of a stable international equilibrium. It was his view that every situation, including Vietnam, was linked to every other in this effort. He further believed that "since a stable equilibrium with Russia would depend on America's steadfast honoring of her commitments, an abrupt or precipitous withdrawal was no longer possible."[41] Therefore, objectives and policies in the Vietnam situation were determined in considerable part by their anticipated effect on the web of extrasituational relationships that existed between Washington and Moscow.

Another complicating factor is that in a given situation parties frequently are attempting to achieve or protect a number of objectives. Because of this, one's task is not a matter of simply ascertaining state X's specific immediate objective and determining the linkage between it and X's middle-range and fundamental goals, because state X may well have more than one objective. When the People's Republic of China invited President Nixon to come to China in the early 1970s, one of its immediate objectives was to decrease the tension between Washington and Peking.[42] But it also thought the trip could assist in the achievement of a multiplicity of other objectives, including a worsening of American-Soviet relations, increasing China's prestige, perhaps signaling and/or bringing about the weakening of Washington's commitment to preserve the independence of the nationalist Chinese government on Taiwan, tying the United States closer to Peking and thus deterring any potential aggressive moves by the Soviets, and possibly providing the PRC with an opportunity to show Washington it was not an aggressive state to the end that the United States might increase the rate of its troop withdrawals from the Far East.[43]

[41]John G. Stoessinger, *Henry Kissinger: The Anguish of Power*, W. W. Norton, New York, 1976, p. 50.

[42]Also see Chapter 14, pp. 389–391.

[43]In the "Nixon Doctrine," first announced by the President in mid-1969, the United States had decided that, while it would keep all its treaty commitments, if new hostilities developed it would look to the nations directly threatened to assume primary responsibility for their own defense. As a result, American troop levels in Asia (not only in Vietnam, but elsewhere also) were beginning to decline.

Yet another complicating factor is the fact that a policymaker may change objectives. This might be due to an alteration in situational conditions. In the Korean war, at first the United States' objectives were to prevent the conquest of South Korea by the invading Communists and bring about a return to the status quo *ante*. Once U. N. forces had recaptured the south and driven the invading forces back to the original boundary (38th parallel), however, Washington changed its objective to the "liberation" of North Korea and sent its troops across the boundary accordingly. Objectives also may be changed because the previously formulated objectives had proved to be unattainable. Syria's original objective with respect to the 1975–1976 "civil war" in Lebanon was to help bring about a peaceful resolution of the conflict, one that substantively would favor the Moslem-Palestinian coalition. When this proved impossible and Syrian prestige seemed endangered, the objectives became salvaging Syrian prestige and compelling a cease-fire without regard to the precise impact on the different Lebanese factions.[44] International relationships are fluid, and policymakers attuned to the dynamics of particular situations may well think it advisable to alter their objectives as situational and extrasituational conditions change. One who is attempting to discover what other parties' objectives are thus cannot stop with ascertaining what they are originally. The investigation must be continual so as to handle the possibility of change.

A related type of difficulty is that a policymaker's evaluation of the importance of achieving a particular goal may change, and the relationship between that objective and those of more fundamental importance may change correspondingly. For example, fostering cooperative relations with certain oil producing states, such as Saudi Arabia, has long been an objective of American foreign policy. Until the early 1970s, however, it received relatively low priority because policymakers saw little linkage between it and achieving or protecting fundamental objectives. By middecade, however, given the enormous U. S. dependency on foreign petroleum sources and the necessity of obtaining huge quantities of oil to keep the economy running, officials in Washington perceived a much more direct linkage and fostering cooperative relations with such states became a matter of considerable importance. When this type of change takes place the intensity and persistence with which a goal will be sought, the resources and prestige a party is willing to commit, and the risks one is willing to take, will change considerably. In terms of our categories, the objective has been moved from the specific immediate category to that of the middle range, and new maneuvers will become the (immediate) means to this end.

Finally, the task of determining what other parties want is made difficult by the facts that either these parties may not be sure themselves, or they are ex-

---

[44]Also see Chapter 5, p. 116, and Chapter 9, p. 257.

tremely inconsistent, seeking first one goal then another. It may be that a state has been drawn into a situation unexpectedly and is simply "playing it by ear" while assessing the facts and alternative policy courses. In May 1967 Egypt and Israel found themselves in a situation in which unanticipated events kept altering the situation and developments seemed to "snowball" out of control.[45] In the early stages of the crisis neither party was certain of what was happening and neither was sure as to what its situational objectives ought to be. A problem also can occur when a party's policy formulation process itself has been faulty and has produced a blurry and/or incompatible set of objectives. Or, perhaps a policymaker is more concerned with other problems and thus has not sufficiently thought out his or her policy with respect to this one. Whatever the causative factors, it is evident that it is extremely difficult to discover what a particular party's objectives are if that party itself doesn't know.

As our entire discussion of the determination of objectives has illustrated, ascertaining what the various parties are seeking is a task of enormous difficulty. By using the identifying categories, establishing linkages, examining sources, and taking into account the complicating factors, one can systematically attack the problem and significantly improve the odds. Given the importance of the job, this is a not unimportant point. But no matter how the policymaker approaches the problem or how well one employs the concepts, he or she can never be completely sure of success. Determining others' objectives will always be an imprecise activity, and uncertainty will be ever present.

Objectives: Closing Comments

As we have mentioned before, at the same time that the policymaker is trying to discover what the other parties' objectives are he or she also is determining his or her own. Some closing comments are in order. One point is immediately apparent: *one's perception of other state's objectives will significantly influence the determination of one's own.*[46] For example, whether a party should try to form a defensive alliance will in part be determined by whether the policymaker perceives a security threat and believes such an alliance will help counter it. Whether X builds a particular weapons system may in part be a reflection of military developments in Y.[47] Thus, it is in the nature of things that many times objectives will be primarily responsive. This is true for all actors; there is a constant interaction of events and perceptions in international poli-

---

[45]See Chapter 14, pp. 380–385.

[46]Which really makes it another "source."

[47]For a stimulating yet succinct discussion of this phenomenon as applied to arms races, see David W. Ziegler, *War, Peace, and International Politics*, Little, Brown, Boston, 1977, pp. 222–225.

tics, and all actors find some of their policies largely reactive. Sometimes, in fact, one may not even have been concerned with a given problem until conditions changed and others were perceived to be seeking certain things. For example, the United States paid little attention to the Mediterranean area until the post World War II era. It was only after Britain announced it was pulling out and Washington saw a Soviet threat that it responded with the Greek-Turkish Aid Program and the Truman Doctrine.[48]

To ascribe determinative significance to the impact of other states' objectives, however, would be an error. As we saw earlier in the chapter, objectives spring from a number of sources; this is true for all parties. While perceptions of what other parties are seeking will certainly be an element in one's calculations, ideological factors, regime needs, security concerns, opportunities for advantage, the need to handle a common problem, internal needs, historical factors, etc., also will be weighed. Though other states' objectives are important, they are not the only consideration.

Ideally, what the policymaker does is identify and categorize what needs to be protected or achieved in the particular situation, establish priorities among the various possible objectives and the linkages between them, examine them to make them as compatible and consistent one with another as possible, and devise the most appropriate means for producing the desired outcome(s). This is an extremely difficult task, as the student by now should plainly see. Operating in the ever-dynamic, decentralized anarchical world of international politics with its multitude of different political actors acting and interacting in so many different ways, each uniquely influenced by a number of environmental features and seeking its own objectives, the policymaker is confronted with an awesome job.

In addition to all the difficulties discussed to this point, there are yet three more factors that the policymaker must keep in mind. First, if one hopes to have a reasonable chance of obtaining one's objective, or at least of doing so at a cost that's not wholly disproportionate to the objective's value, it is essential to formulate objectives within the framework of a realistic assessment of capability relationships.[49] Although it may not be accurate to assert that "means determine the ends that may be sought," it is certain that goals *should* be determined in the light of capabilities.[50] Second, every objective, every action, has differential effects.[51] This means, first, that no matter what the ob-

---

[48]See Dean Acheson, *Present at the Creation: My Years in the State Department*, Norton, New York, 1970, Chapters 22, 24, 25. For further discussion see Chapter 9, p. 259.

[49]For more on ascertaining capabilities see Chapters 4, 7–8.

[50]The quote is from Howard H. Lentner, *Foreign Policy Analysis: A Comparative and Conceptual Approach*, Charles E. Merrill, Columbus, Ohio, 1974, p. 199.

[51]See Chapter 14, pp. 396–400, for an in-depth discussion.

jective one decides on, its successful achievement or protection will still yield both costs and benefits, and second, there will be an impact on more than one party and the impact will be different on each. Therefore, no choice will be perfect. The policymaker will be trying to decide on the objectives that (apparently) will yield the most favorable benefit-cost ratio in terms of the anticipated net impact on all parties. Third, and very importantly, no one state controls everything that happens. Therefore, whatever the policymaker's choice, it may be (or become) inappropriate because of occurrences beyond his or her control.

Despite all the foregoing, the policymaker must proceed; the policymaker cannot, as observers can, avoid determining his or her party's objectives just because doing so is difficult. And the importance of this task must be underlined. The objectives are the states of affairs and situational outcomes toward which the entire rest of one's policy is directed. If these original choices are wrong, the question becomes simply one of how efficiently and rapidly a party is moving in the wrong direction, how well one is doing in protecting or achieving the wrong goals.

4

Ascertaining Capability

Once a policymaker has discovered who is involved in a particular situation, and discovered the other parties' objectives and provisionally determined his or her own, it is time for the third step in policy formulation: ascertaining capability. Terms like capability, power, and influence have given rise to interminable and sometimes meaningless quibbling over definitions. Unfortunately, because policymakers so often deal in the currency of power and influence one cannot simply dismiss the issue as irrelevant. Rather than discussing the issue in abstract terms, however, our approach will be to view it from the policymaker's perspective. To the policymaker no single definition is sufficient because the concept is composed of several parts.

BUILDING BLOCKS

What then does the policymaker mean when he or she speaks of capability? *First, he or she is concerned with the identification and measurement of key tangible and intangible elements that can provide the building blocks for the exercise of international influence.* Examples would be military capacity, economic strength, geographic factors, population characteristics, natural resources, and so forth. In this sense power is the sum of a set of components, a specific quantity of factors whose aggregate is directly related to the achievement of a state's objectives.

Usually this facet of the concept is closely connected with concern about the importance of force and war-making capacity. Because of that, analyses of the "elements of power" or "components of capability" frequently are directed toward an understanding of how, and to what extent, the various building blocks contribute to military strength.[1] For example, economic factors such as the level of industrialization or energy production are examined in terms of their actual or potential contribution to military capability, or particular geographic assets are discussed with respect to their strategic value. In a similar fashion, demographic factors such as age distribution and spatial density, the degree of societal cohesiveness or the lack thereof, natural resource sufficiency or deficiencies, governmental efficiency, etc., these and other components are evaluated primarily in terms of the degree to which they contribute to a party's capacity to use military force.

It is essential that one go through this step and thoroughly analyze these raw materials of capability since they often do affect the success or failure of a state's policies. In fact policymakers usually do so and are influenced by their conclusions. For this reason all of Part 3 is devoted to an examination of such components. However, any analysis that stops here is both oversimplified and inaccurate because capability is much more (or less) than such a sum of certain ingredients (a fact that has led some observers to go too far the other way and almost dismiss the components as irrelevant) and it is exercised via many instruments in addition to the military.

RELATIONAL QUALITY

A second part of the policymaker's conception of capability is its relational quality. Capability involves a relationship between parties; policy actions and interactions occur as states affect other states. It makes no sense to speak of capability only in absolute terms because a useful analysis must include the relative and comparative aspects. Party W is concerned with capability in the particular case only because it has determined that its situational objective(s) cannot be achieved or protected unless party Y does or does not do something. Therefore, it needs to know how "strong" party Y is.

Because capability is not meaningful unless discussed in relation to other parties, abstract comments like China has such and such military capability or Egypt possesses X degree of economic strength have little utility in and of themselves. The question to ask is "compared to whom"? For example, al-

---

[1]Although much of the literature today is placing less stress on this view, occasionally a newer work gives it a reemphasis. See Rosen and Jones, Third Edition, Chapter 7.

though China's military strength might be immense compared to Nepal it certainly would not be relative to that of the Soviet Union.

Taking the relational factor into account, one can say that, operationally, capability is exercised in the following situations:

1. A party is able to overcome its adversary.
2. A party is able to influence the behavior of another party at least partially in the way that it wants to and in a direction that the target otherwise would not have gone. This may involve a modification of the target's activity by getting it to do something or stop doing something, or within each of these major categories to increase or decrease the scope and intensity of its actions.
3. Capability also is exercised if the target is persuaded to continue an existing policy that it otherwise would have changed or to refrain from undertaking new actions it otherwise would have initiated. Thus, influence may continue after a target modifies behavior in the sense of reinforcing the new policy.

Three additional points are important here. First, *it is usually the case that, to some extent at least, influence is mutual.* In other words, seldom is capability exercised in one direction only; in most situations the target state will have some influence on the supposed influencer. Because situations often involve many parties the pattern of influence relationships may be very complicated. Each state is a target of signals and actions from many sources as well as being a sender. One should not make the mistake of assuming that influence will be equal in all directions, however. Quite the contrary; generally relationships are asymmetrical and certain states considerably more powerful than others. One must also remember that usually it is necessary to speak in terms of degrees of influence and not total dominance, although occasionally this may not be the case.

Second, *in any relationship there is the element of feedback.* After the policymaker undertakes some action and responses occur, the situation is different from the original. Information concerning the differences soon begins to "feedback" to the initiator. As a result of the receipt of data on situation changes, the initiator may have to modify policy to meet the new requirements. Perhaps capability has been exercised effectively and the target's behavior has been so altered that pressure can be decreased, or maybe the data indicates that the previous actions were counterproductive and the target is actually escalating unwanted activity. In any event, feedback is a dynamic, complicating, uncertainty-increasing element in all capability relationships.

Third, *a policymaker may avoid, modify, initiate, or halt certain actions because of his or her perception of another party's policy, even though that other party has made no explicit attempt to exercise capability.*[2] The policy-maker in such a case is anticipating what would or would not occur in various contingencies, and makes the decision before, and in the absence of, acts by the other party. One may decide, for example, not to order an invasion of a given state because his or her projection of the likely reactions and consequences indicates that such would be counterproductive. In this kind of situation the other party may not deliberately exercise capability, but a capability relationship nevertheless occurs; as a result of the policymaker's projections of the consequences of possible alternative policy courses, behavior is being influenced.

SPECIFIC POLICY CONTEXT

The third facet of the policymaker's capability concept is that it is meaningful only within a specific policy context. Capability is really a means to an end, and can be most usefully operationalized in terms of a cost-benefit analysis concerning a state's achievement of its objectives. Capability is exercised via influencing other states in such a way as to increase the degree to which one achieves his or her objectives without a corresponding increase in cost, maintains his capacity to achieve his objectives while decreasing the cost of so doing, or increases the degree of achievement and decreases the cost thereof.

As indicated earlier, one must define the problem at hand by identifying and examining the number and importance of the parties involved, and then proceed to an analysis of their objectives and the provisional formulation of his own. Capability becomes relevant only in relation to these parties and objectives.

It is this facet more than any other that shows that the building blocks approach to capability has its limitations. Certain combinations of ingredients cannot be directly applied to some situations. For example, the nuclear arsenal of the United States had very little direct impact on French policy toward Washington in the mid-1960s. A major objective of American policy was to maintain NATO diplomatic unity. When the French decided to pursue their own policies in certain areas the disparity of American and French nuclear striking power was irrelevant. Obviously Washington was not going to use nuclear force against its ally.

Similarly, one sees that American nuclear power has very little value in persuading nonaligned states to modify their behavior or objectives. In fact, its use is inappropriate to many military conflict situations such as guerilla

---

[2]Useful is David A. Baldwin, "Inter-Nation Influence Revisited," *Journal of Conflict Resolution*, December 1971, pp. 478–479.

warfare, various revolutionary activities, limited conventional wars, or even defense. It is pertinent primarily with respect to the objective of deterrence, and basically to situations involving possible Soviet attacks.[3]

Another kind of situation that's relevant in this regard is one in which capability can be exercised, but the costs and risks involved in the particular policy action are perceived to be disproportionate to the value of the objective the policy is designed to achieve. In this policy context the question is not whether it is *possible* to achieve or protect one's objectives, but whether or not the *cost* of doing so is too high. There is no doubt, for example, that had the United States chosen to use all of its military strength in the Vietnam war it could have defeated and conquered North Vietnam. The costs and risks that the course of action would have entailed, however, were far in excess of the value of such a victory, so such a policy was not adopted. In analyzing capability relationships the policymaker needs to visualize and seek to produce outcomes not just in terms of whether the capability component relationship will allow them to be achieved in the particular situational context. He or she also must ask the question: At what cost?[4]

SUSCEPTIBILITY

Another facet of capability analysis is the examination of each party to determine its overall and specific susceptibility.

Vulnerability

The degree to which a party is susceptible to the exercise of capability is partly a function of its vulnerability.[5] To what extent is it vulnerable in this particular situation to the specific type, quantity, and quality of capability the other parties wish to use? A landlocked state such as Czechoslovakia, for example, is not vulnerable to an amphibious military assault. Perhaps a party is seeking to bring about a policy modification via the exercise of foreign trade pressures. One must then discover if the target is dependent to any appreciable degree on trade, and whether the initiating party is in a position to materially affect price and supply matters. Perhaps one is investigating the question of resource sufficiency or deficiency, with special reference to petroleum. Obviously a state like the Soviet Union, which is a net oil exporter, is less vulnerable to an oil em-

---

[3]See Chapter 10, p. 282–290.

[4]The word "must" is used advisedly. Obviously, policymakers don't always do this. For example, it is quite apparent that cost-benefit thinking of this nature did *not* occur *before* America's massive involvement in the Vietnamese conflict.

[5]Also see Chapter 9, p. 246–247.

bargo than the United States, which now imports nearly one-half the oil it uses.[6]

An important point here is that all parties are different; each actor has its own particular combination of strengths and weaknesses. Therefore, the vulnerability mix of each of the parties also is unique. A policymaker seeking to discover the situation-specific vulnerabilities of other parties, then, cannot fruitfully begin with preconceived, general notions. The approach, to be productive, needs to be specific, differentiated, and particular.

Responsiveness

A second major determinant of susceptibility is responsiveness, the degree to which a party "allows" itself to be influenced.[7] There are certain situations in which many of the factors seem to indicate that capability ought to be able to be effectively exercised, but in practice it cannot. Frequently the reason is that, in effect, the target simply and effectually says "no!" In the Vietnam war in the mid-1960s the United States sought to coerce DRV leaders to come to the bargaining table on Washington's terms via a policy of controlled escalation.[8] Particularly important in this regard was a program of systematically escalated bombing. In their efforts to achieve that objective American policymakers very carefully assessed each projected escalation in terms of what the "rational" response to it "should" be, and then undertook specific actions accordingly. Surely, it was thought, North Vietnamese policymakers would reconsider their views and modify their policy appropriately as the frequency, intensity, area subjected, and importance of the targets selected were gradually upgraded; surely, before being confronted with the possibility of their country's total destruction, they would give in; but, of course, as we all know, they did not. Hanoi was terribly "unresponsive," "unwilling" to be influenced. For them, fundamental objectives were at stake and a maximum sacrifice would be made if necessary. The American failure to comprehend this—plus, perhaps, an overestimation of the capabilities of "rational" analysis—led to some highly counterproductive policies.

Responsiveness is a factor of enormous importance, one that needs to be assessed with great care. Certain generalizations are of some help in this regard. It is evident, for example, that responsiveness varies from party to party, and fluctuates with time and circumstance as well. It also is clear that the *same* party will demonstrate different degrees of responsiveness as conditions

---

[6]For more on U. S. resource vulnerability see Chapter 7, p. 180, and Diagram 2.

[7]See Karl W. Deutsch et al., *Political Community and the North Atlantic Area*, Princeton University Press, Princeton, 1957.

[8]Useful and succinct is Kahin and Lewis, Chapter 8.

change. It also is apparent that the (category of) objective(s) being sought will have a bearing on responsiveness, as will a number of intangible components of capability such as societal characteristics, governmental efficiency, and policymaker quality.[9] In some instances, framework features like ethics or ideology may be salient.

Beyond the elementary guidance provided by general statements of this nature, however, the policymaker is on his own. Just because party W suffers more in a war, for example, does not mean it will be more responsive, or that it will lose.[10] As the Vietnam war showed, the supposedly less powerful country with very low responsiveness may be the one that is most successful in achieving its objectives, the one, therefore, that actually exercises capability. Unfortunately, determining responsiveness is far from easy. As is so often true, the policymaker has to proceed, with caution, on a case by case basis, examining the practical specifics of the particular situation. Though the general guidelines are helpful, they only point the direction. To be operationally useful, hard-headed pragmatic analysis must follow.

INTENTIONS/WILLINGNESS

When attempting to determine the significance of comparative capabilities in a given situation *the policymaker must take into account the intentions of each party and their willingness to use whatever power they may have.* Sometimes there is a tendency to become too concerned with attempts to measure potential capability and one does not pay sufficient attention to the party's intentions. For example, whereas the United States possesses military strength far superior to that of Canada, it has no intention of using it against its northern neighbor. The mere existence of exercisable power, while creating the possibility of conflict and thus being a necessary part of any situation calculation, does not automatically lead to the conclusion that a conflict situation exists (if international relations were nothing but an unceasing power struggle, however, such might be the conclusion). Even states with objectives directly contradictory to one's own may have no intention of using capability at a given time. The fact that a policymaker's adversary possesses a given weapons system is obviously more dangerous to one's security than if that system was possessed by his ally, but whether this adversary intends to use it or not is a critical factor.

The necessity of assessing intentions is clear. This does not mean it is not important to determine strategic situational implications irrespective of inten-

---

[9]See Chapter 8, pp. 212–231.

[10]See Steven Rosen, "War Power and the Willingness to Suffer" in Bruce Russet, ed., *Peace, War and Numbers*, SAGE, Beverly Hills, 1972, pp. 176–178.

tions, though; far from it. Indeed, much of our analysis of the tangible components of capability (Chapter 7) is directly relevant to such matters. And it is obvious that the building blocks, relational, specific policy context, and susceptibility features already discussed are enormously important, and their situational contextual implications are of considerable significance. Regardless of what their intentions might be, for example, if the Soviets were in a position to control all of Europe, by that fact alone they would pose a potential survival threat to the United States for geopolitical-strategic reasons, no matter what they "intended" to do.[11] Or, if the Soviets themselves should face a hostile China to the south, a powerful Germany to the west, a resurgent Japan to the east, and a strategically potent United States at various points around Russia's periphery, they would have to draw certain policy implications regardless of those parties' intentions. Nevertheless, while one obviously cannot ignore situational implications, it is not enough to just analyze them and end the analysis there. The policymaker must take the next step and assess his or her counterpart's intentions. In each of the above described situations it would be of enormous importance for one to determine whether the other party(ies) intended to attempt to exercise its (their) capabilities and actualize the potential threat(s) or whether those threats will remain latent (as in the American-Canadian case).

But ascertaining the intentions of the relevant parties is still not enough, because policymakers—like everyone else—do not always actually try to do that which they had fully intended. In terms of capability analysis, this means that when the time comes to actually try and operationally exercise their power policymakers sometimes may not be willing to do so. The United States has strategic and tactical nuclear weapons systems available for the defense of Western Europe. Washington's official policy position is that if the appropriate contingencies develop it will employ these weapons systems. But, as the French have repeatedly asked, would it really be willing to do so, at least in the absence of a direct threat to its own territory? If, for example, Warsaw Pact forces were overrunning Western Europe but there was no indication the United States itself would soon be attacked, would Washington really be willing to respond with tactical "nukes" and risk the devastation that possible Soviet nuclear counterretaliation could wreak on the United States?

Discovering if, to what extent, and how a given party will actually be willing to seek to exercise capability in a particular situation is an enormously complicated job. One must attempt to determine the mix of, and linkages between, the objectives that the party is trying to achieve or protect, and analyze

---

[11]An interesting, rather provocative geopolitical analysis encompassing and enlarging on this point is Colin S. Gray, *The Geopolitics of the Nuclear Era: Heartlands, Rimlands, and the Technological Revolution*, Crane, Russak & Co., New York, 1977.

the pertinent capability components, relational factors, and susceptibilities in the specific policy context. *But this is only part of the task, because the willingness to use capability is not solely a function of capability factors.* As we saw in earlier chapters, policymakers are influenced in varying degrees by party attributes, ethics, law, and ideology. Furthermore, the entire remainder of the book is devoted to an analysis of many other features that may have an impact, such as the spectrum of orientation options potentially available, the implications of the use or nonuse of various external means of increasing capability, the availability and prospective utility of different combinations of policy implementation instruments, and the constraints and limitations on policymaking in the international political world and/or on the domestic scene. It, therefore, is imperative that neither policymaker nor observer make the mistake of assuming that a given party will or will not seek to exercise capability solely on the basis of a particular perception of capability relationships. While capability will no doubt be considered, it will only be one of the influencing elements.

Because a policymaker's willingness to use capability is variable and is the result of the interaction of a wide range of factors, counterpart policymakers frequently see opportunities to undertake actions to influence one's decision. They may seek to directly deter via a military buildup of their own. Or, they may proceed more indirectly. Sometimes they seek to bring about an alteration in the nature and prominence of certain of the environmental framework features such as ethics or ideology, or at least in one's perceptions thereof. On other occasions they may try to divert attention and/or increase the counterbalancing pressures by manipulating alliance factors, altering the situation by obtaining new allies, encouraging the fragmentation of one's coalition (if he or she has one), or preventing one from obtaining new allies.[12] Maybe it is possible to increase the adverse pressures by encouraging parties who have objectives in conflict with those of the target. And there are other options. The possibilities are legion. *The key point to remember is that the willingness to exercise capability is a variable, not a given, and a wise counterpart policymaker will seek to influence it.*[13]

SYSTEMIC DETERMINATION

As we have seen, in seeking to ascertain capability relationships in specific situations it is essential that one determine the various parties' responsiveness to

[12]For more on counterbalancing interests, see Hartmann, *The Relations of Nations*, Fifth Edition, pp. 18–19, 266–267.

[13]And thus exercise one's *own* capability.

the exercise of power by others, and their willingness to exercise whatever power they have. To this point we have assumed that these are variables and that policymakers' choices are not inexorably determined by certain features of the international political world, by "the system" as it were. Are there cases when this is not so? Are there situations in which certain actions are automatic, regardless of policymaker desires? Are the willingness to exercise or not exercise one's power, and/or the responsiveness and/or lack thereof to power's use, somehow inexorably controlled in certain contingencies by factors external to the policymakers of international political actors? There are two theories (models) that have enjoyed considerable prominence in international politics, theories that do indicate a certain automaticity in this regard: the balance of power and the domino theory.

The Balance of Power

The term "balance of power" is one of the most venerable and oft used in the literature of international relations. Inevitably perhaps, through this long and frequent usage it has acquired a number of overlapping and sometimes confusing meanings, and it has been used for a variety of purposes. Other studies have usefully explored the ambiguities and confusion in detail, a task beyond the scope of our concern.[14] We are interested in the balance of power concept when it is used to describe a *system* of international politics, and only with a particular aspect of that—the degree to which there is an "automaticity" of policy responses, the extent to which policymaker choice is controlled by systemic factors. Relating this to ascertaining capability, the question is: To what extent are involvement, responsiveness, and the willingness to use power, in specific policy contexts, automatically (or nearly so) determined when the balance of power system exists?

First, just what is a balance-of-power system? Although there are disagreements as to its precise components, there is sufficient consensus for us to be able to present the following list as at least representative:

1. There are several independent parties.
2. Power must be distributed in such a fashion that no one party can be stronger than all the remaining combined.
3. The parties are constantly struggling to maximize their power.
4. Each party is suspicious of every other.

---

[14]See especially Inis L. Claude, Jr., *Power and International Relations*, Random House, New York, 1962.

5. The only antidote for power is countervailing power.

6. Parties have no long-term ties or alliances.[15]

In a general sense the balance of power system is purported to operate as follows: when any party threatens to become dominant, the other parties will seek to prevent this from occurring and will form alliances designed either to restrain or defeat the threatener. With respect to specific actors, this means first, that the potentially threatened party(ies) is willing to use its power and resist. It also will seek external allies and will try to convince these allies to exercise their capability in this situation. Second, and critically, parties other than the (potential) aggressee will become its allies and be willing to use their power. How automatic are such developments? Morgenthau writes: "The aspiration for power on the part of several nations, each trying to maintain or overthrow the status quo, *leads of necessity* to a configuration that is called the balance of power and to policies that aim at preserving it" (emphasis mine).[16]

Though appealing, as a view of how international politics actually works (even in multilateral situations with power distributed as per the model's stipulations) this is both an oversimplification and a distortion, and as applied to many situations it is just plain wrong. Even allowing for the fact that there are many kinds of situations to which it does not apply—cooperative relationships, conflicts initiated by weaker states, etc.—even when it purportedly is applicable there are major difficulties.[17] The following is an illustrative if not exhaustive list:

1. Not all parties (if any) are continually struggling to maximize power. As we have already demonstrated in depth, parties have a wide range of relationships, are influenced by a number of factors, and seek a variety of objectives. Capability changes brought about by the threatening party, therefore, will be only one of many factors in policymaking calculations.

2. The potentially threatened party may choose not to resist, or may respond unilaterally.

3. Parties other than the aggressee may avoid involvement, as historically they so frequently have (the failure to ally with Czecho-

---

[15]There are other "rules" or "conditions" that may be operative with respect to aspects of the system other than its automaticity. In addition to Claude, *Power and International Relations*, see Edward Vose Gulick, *Europe's Classical Balance of Power*, Cornell University Press, Ithaca, 1955. For a more theoretical view see Morton Kaplan, *System and Process in International Politics*, Wiley, New York, 1957.

[16]Morgenthau, *Politics Among Nations*, Fifth Edition, p. 167. Later, on the same page, he uses the word "inevitable."

[17]Some of these, of course, are more relevant at one time than another, and pertain to some situations and parties more than to others.

slovakia at Munich, for example). In other words, they are *not* always willing to exercise their power in this manner.

4. Because parties other than the aggressor have an enormously varied set of orientation options from which to choose, they may become involved in any one of several ways other than cooperating via an alliance.[18] The model grossly underestimates the latitude of policymaker choice.

5. Parties sometimes do have long-term commitments, so they may not have the flexibility essential for quickly allying with the threatened party.

6. Parties other than the aggressee may, instead of allying with the aggressee, cooperate with the aggress*or* in the hope of obtaining a share of the spoils.

The conclusion, therefore, is clear: on the basis of both logic and historical evidence there is no automatic response, no mechanistic determination of choice as postulated in the balance of power system.[19] In some cases parties become involved and are willing to exercise their capability in such a fashion, and in some cases they are not. *The key point is that in each situation the policymakers decide! It is not automatic!* Involvement, relationships, susceptibilities, and the willingness to try and exercise capability in specific policy contexts will be the product of situation-specific policymaker choices, not balance of power systemic determination.

The Domino Theory

The domino theory posits a scenario very different from that envisioned in the balance of power system. If an aggression occurs, goes the argument, parties must be willing to use their power to halt it immediately, because if they don't act quickly and decisively the parties adjacent to the aggressed-upon actor will become more and more demoralized; if aggression is not stopped at once, instead of forming alliances and vigorously resisting the aggressor (as the balance of power system postulated) other parties will progressively lose the will to resist. The result, of course, is that eventually, they too will succumb. Their willingness to exercise power will disappear, and they will be highly responsive to the exercise of power by the aggressors on them. The particulars of the situation are not important in this regard; no matter who is involved, the nature of the objectives they are seeking, the historical background, where and under

[18]See Chapter 5 for discussion of orientation options.
[19]To make our point we have chosen to discuss the balance of power system in its most deterministic form. Some theorists adopt a less mechanistic view, and our assessment of their views, of course, would have to be modified accordingly.

what circumstances the action takes place, and so on, if the aggressing party is not stopped at once, the other parties will soon capitulate.[20] Party differences also are unimportant in the domino theory. The parties are viewed as interchangeable units that exhibit uniform behavioral responses to the appropriate stimulus. Whether the actors are similar or very different, have similar or divergent outlooks, are large or small, etc., is all essentially irrelevant. In certain circumstances certain things are automatic no matter what the specifics.

For much of the post-World War II era, American policymakers formulated policy at least partially on the basis of these beliefs.[21] In early 1954, for example, when considering the possible implications in Asia of the impending "fall" of Indochina, President Eisenhower compared the situation to a row of falling dominoes; knock over the first one and the rest will certainly fall too. Policymakers in the Truman administration applied essentially the same principle to postwar problems in the Mediterranean, though their phraseology was somewhat different. They compared that situation to the effect of one rotten apple in a barrel; if the rotten one is not eliminated, all the others will inevitably become damaged, too. Perceiving a Communist threat to Greece, American policymakers therefore concluded that if the "Greek apple" were allowed to become rotten (if Greece fell to the Communists) Iran and other parties to the east would become infected, infection would be spread into Africa through Asia Minor, and to Europe through Italy and France.

It is undeniable that successful aggression has an impact, and that the results produced by such an occurrence may be adverse to various parties in innumerable ways. But to leap from that undeniable fact to the conclusion that after one such development the adjacent parties will simply give up, will inexorably lose the will to resist, is wholly unwarranted. All policy actions have differential effects, and the specific results vary enormously with the parties, time, and specific situational conditions.[22] Parties are not interchangeable units; different actors have their own unique mix of features, and they do not respond in identical fashion to similar stimuli.[23] And, as we have consistently pointed out, policymakers are subject to a number of influences in the formulation process, and have a number of responses from which to choose. Furthermore, (usually) to policymakers it *does* make a difference who is involved, what objectives are being sought, etc. And the proposition that one will automatically decide not to try to achieve or protect fundamental objectives like

[20]Though not necessarily a part of the domino theory, there usually is an accompanying belief to the effect that the aggressor, encouraged by the success, will perpetrate more aggressions.

[21]They believed that the West's capitulation to Hitler at Munich proved their point. This was rather strange logic since, at least eventually, the Nazis *were* confronted, and they lost.

[22]For more on the concept of differential effects see Chapter 14, pp. 396–400.

[23]For more on party uniqueness see Chapter 8, pp. 231–235.

territorial integrity, or even survival, just because some *other* party is conquered, approaches absurdity. Would India and Pakistan, for example, automatically decide not to defend themselves if China invaded and conquered Burma? It is patently obvious that, historically, other states have not just given up after a successful agression. Did the Axis win World War II?

The domino theory shares a fatal defect with the concept of a balance of power system: it postulates a degree of automaticity in the willingness or nonwillingness to use one's power that simply does not exist. Although they are influenced by strategic circumstances, policymakers in the decentralized anarchy of the international political world are not *controlled* by inherent-systemic forces, and they can *choose* from a whole spectrum of options in response to particular actions by others. *When trying to ascertain capability it is essential to realize that there are no automatic relationships, no inherent responses as to when, how, and how much power will be used in specific situations.*

Having discovered who is involved in the particular situation, discovered the other parties' objectives and provisionally determined one's own, and ascertained the capability relationship of the parties, the next step is to determine the appropriate nature and level of involvement. What are one's options in this regard, what are the major types of orientation one might choose? This is the subject matter for Chapter 5.

5

Determining Orientation

Having discovered who is involved and what situational configuration exists, determined the other parties' objectives and provisionally determined one's own, and ascertained the capability relationships and linkages pertinent to the specific context, the policymaker next needs to take the fourth step in policy formulation, *determining orientation*. When we say a policymaker is "determining orientation" we mean one is deciding on the degree and nature of his or her party's involvement in a particular situation.[1] Orientation will vary with time and circumstance, and because each state deals with many problems at once it may have several different orientations simultaneously. With respect to a given situation, however, usually only one orientation is possible (although there may be some that overlap, a factor that shall be considered in due course).

---

[1]The concept of a means-end chain (discussed in Chapter 3) is relevant here. Once the policymaker has determined the degree and nature of involvement (the orientation) that would be most efficient in achieving or protecting the previously decided-on objectives, achieving that degree and type of involvement itself becomes the specific immediate objective (and the means to the achievement or protection of other objectives). The concept applies in similar fashion to external means of increasing capability, discussed in Chapter 6.

There are ten orientation options from which to choose, each with its own characteristics.[2] These can be usefully divided into three categories: (1) nonconcern options, those in which the policymaker is not really concerned with the outcome of the specific situation, (2) concerned nonissue options, those in which the party is concerned with the outcome but not because of his views on the substantive issues involved, and (3) issue options, those in which one is concerned with the outcome primarily in terms of substantive situational issues.

NONCONCERN ORIENTATION OPTIONS

If a policymaker is not concerned with the outcome of a particular situation there are three orientations from which to choose: (1) avoidance, (2) minimal nonalignment, or (3) participatory nonalignment.

Avoidance

The first of the nonconcern orientation options is simply *avoidance*; just do not become involved. As part of its general European policy from 1815 to 1917, for example, the United States studiously avoided involvement in European conflicts.[3] For centuries prior to the mid-1800s Japan refused to become involved in conflicts beyond her immediate geographical area, a course of action similar to that followed by China.

A rational choice of avoidance rests on the premise that noninvolvement will not be harmful to one's security (or at least less harmful than the projected consequences of involvement). There are several situations in which this might be the case. First, the situational issues may be irrelevant. For example, the resolution or nonresolution of the Arab-Israeli conflict is essentially irrelevant

---

[2]The purpose of this chapter is to get one to carefully think about the various choices a policymaker might have with respect to the degree and nature of his party's involvement in any situation. Thus it is a logical exercise designed to demonstrate the advantages and disadvantages of various possible choices rather than an attempt to describe what a policymaker necessarily does in a given case. On the other hand, one should not assume that this type of thinking does not occur. Although the procedures may not be identical and real life situations are more complex, policymakers inevitably concern themselves with their options for involvement and must engage in thinking similar to that described below.

[3]The term "isolation" has been used to describe a general foreign policy approach of noninvolvement. Because we are focusing on a given situation and recognize that a state may avoid one situation but be deeply involved in another the more limited terminology has been adopted. However, many of the same factors enter into considerations of the specific situation and the general approach. Holsti, Chapter 4, is particularly useful in this regard.

to Peruvian policymakers, so they have no reason to become involved. Second, the issues may be relevant but be of so little significance in comparison to other concerns that they are not worth the allocation of one's time and resources. Third, in some situations it may be that a party's noninvolvement would require or allow the involved parties to act in a way that inevitably is beneficial. If the United States employed an exclusively offshore deployment in Asia, one could argue that China's neighbors (including Russia) would be forced to take on whatever burden of containment was necessary.[4] After all, it certainly would not be in the interests of the Asian states to come under Peking's control, nor would it please the Kremlin. Presumably, therefore, they would resist such a development. Fourth, policymakers may perceive the situation to be devoid of possible benefit, to be a case of "heads you win, tails I lose." For example, policymakers of the People's Republic of China have consistently declined to participate in nuclear arms control negotiations, seeing no way that any agreements could be achieved that would benefit Peking. They contend that the Non-Proliferation Treaty, Limited Test Ban Treaty, and other arms control measures only favor the United States and the Soviet Union; it is essential, in the PRC's view, that other states acquire nuclear striking capability and the American-Russian "duopoly" be broken. Therefore, to participate in negotiations with the superpowers on these topics would be at best futile and could be counterproductive.[5] Last, but certainly not least, it may be that the situation is one in which the policymaker sees the possibility of constructive results but recognizes that his or her party is in no position to help produce them. This is similar to the "heads you win, tails I lose" scenario except that the difficulty here is not inherent but instead is a result of a lack of operational capability. In recognition of this problem a policymaker may rationally opt to avoid involvement.

Of course, avoidance is not always wise. There are many situations in which issues are both relevant and significant, parties acting to achieve or protect their objectives will hinder the protection or achievement of one's own unless prevented from doing so, there are possibilities for gain, and one does have a degree of operational capability. When these conditions obtain the policymaker needs to choose an orientation option that entails some type of involvement. Each situation must be separately evaluated to see if avoidance would be effective or not.

---

[4]See Hartmann, *The New Age of American Foreign Policy*. This is not to imply that China is expansionist, but only to state that if it is her neighbors would, just to protect their own interests, shoulder the burden of containment.

[5]Of course, Peking does not object to a massive disarmament of the superpowers and would be happy to participate in negotiations leading to that end.

In addition to considering the *wisdom* of this orientation one also must deal with the question of whether other parties will permit it. Geographical barriers such as high mountains and wide seas were major factors in allowing the United States, Japan, and China to be uninvolved for long periods of time, but modern technology has significantly reduced their impact. Furthermore, the parties of the modern world have become increasingly interdependent economically. In addition, a wide variety of policy instruments are available, and used, for purposes of penetration and subversion, and these may require a response. Finally, a state may be drawn into a dispute by obligation (perhaps through an alliance), threat, or attack. Thus even though a policymaker may determine that avoidance would be the orientation most appropriate to the achievement or protection of his or her party's objectives in a given situation, external factors may preclude its choice.

Minimal Nonalignment

A second orientation option is *minimal nonalignment*. In this instance one does not avoid involvement but the participation is low level and one does not take sides on whatever the issues may be. The policymaker determines that it is necessary to be minimally involved either in order to protect his or her party's interests or because some participation is forced on him or her. However, the policymaker also feels that a neutral stance on the issues is beneficial because the specific situational issues are not pertinent to the achievement of his or her objectives, and/or one cannot significantly influence the outcome anyway, and/or an attempt to resolve the problem might require more resources than he or she is willing to commit, and/or any deviation from neutrality entails considerable risk.

Countries like Sweden and Switzerland have productively employed this orientation with great frequency, and done so across a wide spectrum of issues. Minimal nonalignment also has been effectively utilized by states such as Romania and Norway in intra alliance and/or intrabloc dispute situations. Canada has avoided substantial involvement in the Arab-Israeli conflict, but has minimally participated in certain situations by contributing contingents to various United Nations' peacekeeping forces. And throughout most of the 1960s and 1970s Japan adopted this orientation toward the Sino-Soviet dispute.

Minimal nonalignment allows considerable independence and flexibility of action as well as minimization of any risk of antagonizing any of the parties by taking a conflicting position (although they might be unhappy because one did not support their view). It allows a concentration of attention, effort, and resources on other issues in accordance with one's priorities. However, it suffers from many of the same potential drawbacks as avoidance including lack of direct influence on the parties and the issues (and thus the possible occurrence of actions detrimental to one's interest) as well as the possible difficulty of remaining unaligned and only lightly involved. Because there is a low level of participation the parties may well feel inclined to make one a target of their actions in order to alter the involvement level and issue stance.

Participatory Nonalignment

A third orientation possibility is *participatory nonalignment.* In this case the policymaker decides to be actively involved with the parties in this situation but involved in the pursuit of his or her party's objectives without respect to the situational issues. The parties will be dealt with not in terms of their positions on the problems at hand but instead on the basis of whether and how they affect the policymaker's nonsituation concerns; it is the policy not its source that is important. The policymaker may thus consider the employment of a wide range of policy instruments with respect to the situational parties but one does so without primary concern for their impact on the issues involved; this just is not his or her party's problem.

Participatory nonalignment sometimes has been utilized with considerable effectiveness. For example, following the rift with the Soviet Union in the late 1940s Yugoslavia frequently employed it to good effect as a means of retaining its independence of action between the Soviets and the West. India, too, generally rejected association with one Cold War bloc or the other, flexibly maneuvering and manipulating to her benefit between rivals each bidding for her favor. But perhaps the foremost practitioner of this approach was Egypt's Gamal Abdel Nasser. Nasser chose this orientation (which he called ''positive neutrality'') for essentially pragmatic reasons; in his view, it was the most effective means of obtaining the objective of the removal of foreign influence from the Arab world. To Nasser the Cold War was not the most pressing problem, foreign influence was. Therefore, he did not take sides on Cold War issues. But because that conflict situation existed he was able to participate in ways beneficial to Egypt, playing the hopes and fears of one side against the other. By shrewdly taking advantage of Washington's and Moscow's Cold War concerns, Nasser was able to extract military, political, and economic benefits for Cairo in ways that allowed a gradual dimunition of the situational capability of non-Middle Eastern parties, as well as an enhancement of his own. Today, many of the LDCs of Africa and Asia find this orientation works equally well for them.

Although participatory nonalignment often has yielded positive results for its employer, there also have been times when it has not. Upon reflection, the reasons for this are apparent. The policymakers of the parties who are the targets or objects of this orientation naturally are displeased by the disregard of what to them are important situational issues. Additionally, and in some cases more importantly, they may well resent the methodology of what they perceive as a cold-blooded effort to manipulate them as if they were puppets on a string. As we examine in detail later, Nasser produced just such a reaction from Washington in the mid-1950s.[6] Thus while it is a fact that participatory nonalignment has been, and still can be, used to good effect in certain situations, it is equally true that it contains a number of potential disadvantages and that, historically, these have sometimes become operational and more than offset the benefits obtained.

Both minimal and participatory nonalignment are likely to become more feasible options in the 1980s. As fluidity increases and alliances become less cohesive, as economic and environmental interdependence increases, and as more power centers develop in the continued shift away from bipolarity, orientation options that maximize flexibility and conflict avoidance will likely have more appeal.

CONCERNED NONISSUE ORIENTATION OPTIONS

In addition to nonconcern orientation options the policymaker also has certain options from which to choose that demonstrate a concern for the situation's outcome, but it is a concern unrelated to the merits of the specific situational issues; in these instances one is concerned with the situation and its probable outcome, but not because of the substance of the situational issues. There are three concerned nonissue orientations: the balancer, the neutral problem solver, and the exacerbater.

Balancer

The first of the concerned nonissue orientations is the *balancer*. When exercising this option one agrees to commit strength to the "weaker" side(s) in order to bring about a "balance," a relatively equal capability distribution. The catalyst for action is the previous inequality in capabilities and one's assessment of the consequences likely to flow therefrom.

It should be noted that this option is not chosen because of the nature of the issues, objectives, or parties involved, but because of an evaluation of the consequences presumed to result from perceived capability differentials. This being so, the balancer is not necessarily concerned with the resolution of issues per se, but with preserving situational stability and either deterring the outbreak of conflict or preventing the stronger side from winning. Such an option

---

[6]See Chapter 13, pp. 364–365.

also precludes close association with one party or antagonism to another, because the needed flexibility could not be preserved in such a case.

The balancer option can be critically important because the balancer may hold the key to whether a situation is stabilized or deteriorating. To successfully employ it, one must have sufficient capability to be able to influence the outcome, be sufficiently flexible on issues and parties to be able to make the requisite adjustments, and be willing to actually commit enough resources to do the job. This is a combination that very few parties actually possess in today's world.

The balancer orientation has been utilized on a number of occasions historically as parties have sought to rectify capability distribution inequalities and the consequences they have believed to flow therefrom. Frequently, however, what has been perceived to be a balancer orientation has actually been something else. Many times parties have ended up achieving a "balance" in capability distribution not because that was their objective, but because that was the extent of their capability; they would have preferred an unequal capability distribution in favor of their side (a "favorable balance") but just were not able to obtain it. There also have been situations in which a "balance" was achieved primarily as a consequence of different parties' pursuance of specific objectives via other orientations, their actions being undertaken for reasons other than concern for capability distribution and the "balance" simply being a product of the particular policy choices. In these situations balanced or unbalanced capability distributions unrelated to situational issues were neither the catalyzing agent nor the objective. It has often been said that Great Britain employed the balancer option for lengthy periods prior to the twentieth century. Though it is true that Britain often (but not always) acted to support the weaker side in Europe and changed positions rapidly, one can argue with some force that specific objectives such as preventing control of the Low Countries by a dominant Continental Power, etc., were the underlying reasons for her action, not any abstract concern with capability distribution or balance.

Neutral Problem Solver

The second concerned nonissue option is *neutral problem solver*. Here the policymaker is concerned with resolving the issues at hand, going beyond mere stabilization, restoration, or deterrence as in the balancer choice, actively seeking to settle whatever differences exist. One may or may not be particularly concerned about the precise substance of the resolution. Perhaps this option will be chosen only if it seems that a certain type of settlement is possible or maybe just solving the problem is enough.

There are two facets to the neutral problem-solver orientation: *mediator* and *compeller*. The former has been the most publicized. When employing the mediator facet one (who is not primarily involved in situational issues) seeks to aid situational parties settle a dispute via peaceful negotiations. Mediation has been employed to good effect any number of times. President Theodore Roosevelt successfully mediated the end of the Russo-Japanese War of 1904; the Soviet Union helped mediate the end of Indo-Pakistani hostilities in the mid-1960s; in 1969 Egypt's Gamal Nasser mediated between Lebanese security forces and Palestinian guerillas, allowing the achievement of what became known as the Cairo Agreements; in mid-1978 President Carter's successful mediation between Egypt and Israel enabled these ancient enemies to agree on two "frameworks" for peace, and later his efforts were significant in bringing about the peace treaty of March 1979.

Former American Secretary of State Henry Kissinger was one of the most effective mediators of modern times, being the catalyst behind the achievement of the Israeli-Syrian and (two) Israeli-Egyptian disengagement agreements in 1974 and 1975. A look at his activities prior to the January 1974 Egyptian-Israeli agreement would be instructive. The October 1973 Arab-Israeli War had ended with neither side being a decisive winner, although the Israelis clearly had gained the upper hand by the time hostilities terminated.[7] The fact that there was neither victor nor vanquished seemed to Kissinger to create a situation conducive to problem-resolving negotiations. Other factors aided in creating a promising context. First, neither side, at this point, saw any rational purpose in renewing hostilities; there was no objective toward the achievement of which (at this juncture) the use of force was deemed appropriate. Second, the cease-fire was tenuous and the situation on the ground created an atmosphere of urgency. The Egyptian Third Army was encircled by Israeli forces on the east bank of the Suez Canal, and on the west bank the Israelis had cut the Suez-Cairo road, endangering Suez city and perhaps even Cairo. Egypt, and the Russians, could not tolerate this situation indefinitely. Third, the war had produced a psychological paradox. Although eventually the Arabs had begun to lose, because they had fought so much more effectively than they had in any of the previous wars they perceived themselves as "winners." In their eyes the "myth" of Israeli invincibility had been shattered, and Arab credibility, and pride, had been enhanced. In consequence, for the first time the Egyptians believed negotiations might be made to yield some really positive results.[8] On the other side of the ledger, the Israelis, who had begun to "win," acted as if they had lost. Perhaps, they thought, it was time to be more flexible.

The context thus was propitious. But direct talks between these bitter adversaries were unlikely; an outside third party was necessary to provide the cat-

---

[7]For more on events preceding the October War, see Chapter 12, p. 349.

[8]Creating such a possibility had been Sadat's objective in launching the war. See Chapter 10, pp. 277–278.

alyst, to help overcome the legacy of so many years of enmity. The United States was acceptable to both Cairo and Jerusalem as a (passably if not completely) neutral nonbelligerent. Hopeful of preventing a new round of hostilities and achieving a degree of stability, Washington leaped at its opportunity. Dr. Kissinger immediately undertook what became known as "shuttle diplomacy," physically shuttling (traveling) back and forth between Egypt and Israel. In this situation, as is always the case, it was necessary to overcome *both* substantive and prestige difficulties. The Secretary recognized this full well and sought to ameliorate problems of both types. His tactics were flexible and varied. Sometimes he merely provided "good offices," just acting as a message carrier; often he went further, seeking to precisely clarify positions and explain specific viewpoints; frequently he attempted to create a degree of empathy and understanding; on occasion, he offered *his* ideas for settlement; though usually calm and precise, once in a while he would emotionally threaten and/or cajole and/or implore the leaders to be more flexible. As a result of his skillful efforts, the parties' desire for an agreement, and a growing recognition that substantive differences might be reconcilable, by January 1974 all parties agreed on the principles of partial but not total Israeli withdrawal and the creation of off-limits zones. Following this achievement Dr. Kissinger undertook an incredible blitz of activity, journeying back and forth in an almost nonstop effort to narrow the differences on concrete issues such as the exact deployment of forces, the width and control of buffer zones, and precise demilitarization arrangements, and on prestige factors such as the document form and the degree of private versus public commitment. Finally, and to a considerable extent as a direct product of the Secretary's efforts, on January 18, 1974 the Egyptian-Israeli disengagement agreement was signed.

Dr. Kissinger, as was true of the mediators in the other examples mentioned above, diligently worked to resolve the issues in dispute; his concern was less with the specific substantive content of a settlement than with the fact that a settlement be achieved. In terms of technique, as all good mediators he provided his good offices and clearly communicated between the parties, constituted a third party from whom suggestions could be taken without loss of prestige, made substantive suggestions as to reasonable compromises, attempted to clarify issues and positions, tried to get each party to see things from the other fellow's perspective, and attempted to demonstrate the advantages that would accrue from a settlement.

There are some dangers in this mediation facet of problem solver, however. A policymaker choosing this option risks meddling in affairs that the parties to the situation may prefer to keep private. Often states can exercise capability more effectively without the interference of a third party, and feel that an outsider will be a hindrance to settlement. Furthermore, an outsider sometimes allows the parties to avoid coming to grips with the real issues in the hope than an "easier out" may be found. A key point may be whether one is asked to participate or offers services on his own initiative. In the latter case the policymaker must be especially careful to anticipate the likely reaction of the parties. Even if assistance is requested one must consider the probabilities of success and the possible consequences of failure.

An obvious danger is that of antagonizing one of the parties by what it perceives to be an inept handling of the job. Following the 1967 Arab-Israeli War, the United Nations Security Council appointed Gunnar Jarring as Special Representative to try to bring about a permanent peace based on Resolution 242 of November 22, 1967. His handling of his assignment so infuriated the Israelis, however, that by mid-1971 he had lost all credibility as a mediator. Israel felt that Dr. Jarring consistently violated any reasonable concept of neutrality. The crowning blow was the so-called "Jarring initiative" of February 8, 1971, an identical letter sent to both Israel and Egypt in which Jarring requested, as an "inevitable prerequisite" of peace, that Israel "give commitment to withdraw its forces from occupied UAR territory to the former international boundary between Egypt and the British Mandate of Palestine" (in exchange for certain Egyptian concessions).[9] Of course, the determination of secure and recognized boundaries was a critical issue; to request this commitment in advance seemed clearly out of line for a neutral mediator.

One final point needs to be made. No matter how adept or inept a mediator is, his or her efforts constitute only one part of the situation. As we have seen, a mediator can be of help to situational parties in overcoming prestige difficulties, misunderstandings, and misperceptions, help them empathize with and understand their counterparts, aid in devising language acceptable to all, point out areas of possible substantive compromise, etc. But it is imperative to remember that a mediator has no binding authority; a mediator cannot compel anyone to do anything, and his or her activities can be dispensed with at any time. Furthermore, a mediator cannot alone create in the parties or the situation the conditions requisite for a problem-solving agreement, to wit: a real desire to settle, reconcilable substantive objectives, and an outcome that does not unduly harm the participants' prestige.[10] And ultimately, it is the *parties* who must agree. While one should not underestimate that which a good mediator can accomplish, it is important not to overestimate it either.

The second type of neutral problem solver is that of a *compeller*. Once again the policymaker is concerned with the outcome of the situation but not

---

[9] For text see *New Middle East*, April 1971, p. 44.

[10] For more on the conditions essential for a problem-solving agreement, see Chapter 12, p. 332.

because of the substantive issues involved; he or she just wants things settled. Here, however, mediation has been judged to be ineffective and more coercive measures are required.

Why might a policymaker seek to compel an agreement if not greatly concerned with the substance? There are three basic reasons. First, one may perceive that other problems are more fundamental and this one is diverting attention, effort, and resources into low-priority channels. Thus it is necessary to get things concluded one way or another and move on to more important matters.

Second, and more frequently, there is often a fear that unless a problem is solved now it will become more serious. More parties may be drawn into it meaning more points of view will need to be reconciled, positions may harden as public statements are made and interests become vested in certain policies (eg. the United States in Vietnam under Lyndon Johnson), the level and intensity of disagreement may increase, prestige may become involved and make compromise more difficult, and eventually events may just seem to snowball out of control.[11] Thus the policymaker may decide that the problem should be solved now or else it may become insoluble.

Third, occasionally a party may previously have employed other orientations unsuccessfully, each failure incrementally damaging prestige; in such situations policymakers sometimes conclude that they have little choice but to try and compel a settlement. In the 1975–1976 Lebanese civil war Syria first sought to mediate between Christians and the anti-Christian Moslem-Palestinian coalition, but she was unsuccessful. Then Damascus tried to bring the hostilities to a "favorable" conclusion via an orientation of limited support, introducing certain Syrian-controlled Palestinian guerilla units to aid the anti-Christian coalition; this too was unproductive. Finally, his prestige and credibility deteriorating, President Hafez Assad acted as a compeller, sending in regular troops and armor. Subsequently a cease-fire was obtained, policed by forces of the Arab League (nearly all of whom were Syrian).

The compeller orientation has certain limitations. First, in many situations it simply cannot be effectively employed because one does not have the capability to compel a settlement; compeller is an option available only to those who have a certain degree of situational capability. Second, for the parties who do use it, there are severe risks. Obviously the tension level will increase, at least until the situation becomes stabilized; those being compelled will not be pleased. Also, because the situation will be considerably altered and the party doing the compelling will have its capability enhanced, and because all actions affect more than one party and affect each one differently, actors other than the compeller and compellee may reevaluate and alter their previous

---

[11]See Chapter 14, pp. 380–385, for an example of snowballing.

course of action. In consequence, objectives may be changed; or, the intensity with which particular objectives are sought and resources allocated to their achievement or protection may be altered; or, nonconcern orientations may be replaced by concerned nonissue or even issue orientations; and so on. In the complex, dynamic, decentralized anarchy of international politics the threat or actual employment of openly coercive orientations inevitably produces searching reappraisals by a host of actually and potentially affected parties. The ramifications of those reappraisals are scarcely predictable.

The prudent policymaker, after having determined who is involved and what their objectives are, and after investigating the situation and concluding that a settlement is essential, must ascertain capability relationships in order to see if the compeller orientation is even feasible. If one concludes that it is, he or she must then assess the import of the costs and risks attendant to this option, and carefully weigh them against the projected benefits of its successful employment. Only after such a judicious analysis should a policymaker decide to become a compeller.

Exacerbater

Another major orientation option is *exacerbater*, involvement in the situation in such a way as to prevent a settlement. Although one sometimes makes the hopeful assumption that parties always want problems solved, history shows that many times this simply is not so. Often policymakers seek to make trouble, to prevent any solution from being found, and to exacerbate existing difficulties. Chaos, confusion, and/or the persistence of difficult problems provide fertile ground for various kinds of penetrating or subversive activities, for example. Social disunity of various kinds may be desirable if one wishes to undertake guerilla warfare. The continuation or aggravation of a territorial dispute may be desirable because it allows an outsider to have its assistance sought; perhaps if the problem were solved it would no longer be needed. If party X has unwisely become involved in a conflict situation of minimum intrinsic importance but seems (for whatever reason) unable or unwilling to extricate itself, if party Y is adversarial Y may attempt to prevent any settlement and thereby continue the drain on X's capability and morale.

A recurrent hypothesis has been that the Soviet Union frequently utilizes the exacerbater orientation in the Middle East, trying to keep things stirred up so that some of the parties will turn to Moscow for assistance. It is primarily the need for anti-Israeli weaponry and economic assistance, the argument goes, that prompts many Arabs to seek Russian aid. To what extent would the Soviets be needed if the Arabs and Israel were living together peacefully?

Several of the Arab parties opposed to the implementation of the 1978 Camp David peace "Frameworks" employed this option, feeling that if those agreements were fully implemented the Arab front against Israel would be badly split and Arab capability severely reduced; Israel, they felt, then would simply hold on to all the nonEgyptian Arab territory it acquired in the June 1967 war, and the possibility of an independent Palestinian Arab state would be even more remote.[12] Thus, Syrian "peacekeeping" forces in Lebanon engaged in skirmishes with Christian troops in Beirut, increasing the risk of Israeli intervention, and escalating inter-Arab pressures on Egypt; Palestinian leaders called for Egypt's isolation in the Arab world, and the possible imposition of economic and/or political sanctions, hoping to dissuade Sadat from his path toward Egyptian-Israeli peace; in Baghdad a conference of Arab leaders convened and voted monies to increase the military strength of Syria and Jordan, and to supply more aid to Palestinian guerillas in the occupied territories. Through these and a variety of other actions Arabs opposed to the Camp David accords sought to exacerbate Egyptian-Israeli and Egyptian-Arab difficulties to such an extent that Sadat would not sign a peace treaty with Israel. Of course, they were not successful, the treaty being signed in March 1979.

The obvious drawback to the exacerbater orientation is that the situational parties that are seeking to achieve or protect objectives that involve issue resolution inevitably will be displeased if they realize that instead of trying to aid them a party is seeking to prolong or aggravate situational difficulties. As a result there may be a strong negative reaction. In mid-June 1972 Egypt expelled several thousand Russian advisers after the Kremlin refused to provide military aircraft equivalent to the F-4 Phantoms Washington was supplying to Israel. Sadat said Moscow was following a no-war, no-peace policy by declining to aid Egypt in developing the offensive capability necessary to "liberate" the occupied lands; while that might serve Russia's interests, it did not serve Egypt's.

ISSUE ORIENTATION OPTIONS

To this point our analysis has dealt with orientation options that varied in the degree of involvement and concern with the disposition of issues at hand, but none of them were primarily related to the substance of the problem and the various situational alignments. Now it is necessary to turn to substantive orientations. Although there are infinite variations and gradations of friendship and hostility and support or opposition, and any categorization is both some-

---

[12]On September 17, 1978 "A Framework for Peace in the Middle East Agreed at Camp David" and "Framework for the Conclusion of a Peace Treaty between Egypt and Israel" were signed by Egypt's Anwar Sadat and Israel's Menachem Begin. For texts see U. S., Department of State, *The Camp David Summit*, Publication 8954, September 1978.

what arbitrary and a matter of degree, the policymaker still can usefully approach this matter in terms of four fundamental categories: (1) limited support or cooperation, (2) complete support or cooperation, (3) indirect opposition, and (4) confrontation.

It is necessary to point out that there can be some overlap in these categories. Limited support of party A may involve indirect opposition to party B and vice versa, and complete support of X may bring about confrontation with W and vice versa. However, it is also possible that indirect opposition can occur without supporting anyone, that complete support may not yield confrontation, and that confrontation can occur bilaterally. Although one may sometimes be looking at two sides of a coin, sometimes one is not.

Limited Support or Cooperation

If a party is involved in a multilateral situation and policymakers calculate that certain parties and/or positions should be supported, they may choose to keep this support relatively *limited* and any relationship with like-minded parties loose and *informal*. There might be several reasons for this. First, this approach allows for considerable flexibility. Because there is no deep commitment it is possible to vary tactics and the degrees and types of support. Sometimes, of course, a low level of assistance is all that is required. In early 1977 for example, France airlifted Moroccan troops to Zaire where, along with government forces, they were able to repel an invasion by rebels based in Angola.[13] But if a low level is insufficient one always has the option of escalating. When in late 1975 the outcome of the war in Angola was still in doubt the Soviets decisively escalated their military aid to the forces of the Popular Movement for the Liberation of Angola (MPLA) and Cuban combatants were introduced; in consequence the tide of battle was turned. The Russians and Cubans followed similar tactics with a major increase in the level of military assistance to Ethiopia early in 1978 in the war with Somalia. The results were similar, too, the Soviet-Cuban aided party emerging victorious. One also can decrease support with relative ease if the level is already low; there has not yet been a major commitment, little prestige has been involved, and the supported party has not become significantly reliant. It is much easier to retrench gracefully prior to a major involvement than after one.

A second potential advantage is that the flexibility inherent in this option creates some degree of uncertainty, and this may be beneficial. For example, if a state is not sure whether or not another party will defend country X, it may hesitate to take the risk of attacking. If a potential adversary always knows

---

[13]A little more than a year later French Legionnaires were flown to the same country to turn back a similar invasion.

what one will do it can plan its moves accordingly; sometimes it may help to keep one's counterparts guessing.

Sometimes a policymaker will choose this option simply because it is abundantly clear that certain common objectives exist and no stronger stand is necessary. For example, the United States does not need to make an explicit formal commitment to Israel in every phase of the Arab-Israeli conflict because it is obvious that Washington will not allow Tel Aviv's destruction.

A policymaker analyzing various options also would note that limited support is a comparatively low-cost, low-risk orientation, certainly less risky than complete support. There is a relatively minimal resource allocation, and one's prestige is not on the line to the extent it would be if a deep commitment existed. Furthermore, since this choice assumes that one's security is not directly involved (or else there would be a greater commitment), there tends to be less danger of being the primary target of hostile activity (although obviously there would be exceptions to this because one cannot always choose whether or not he is a target), and less possibility of creating concern about what one's future objectives might be.

Within a few months of the end of the Vietnam war, relations between Vietnam and its erstwhile Communist allies in Kampuchea (Cambodia) began to deteriorate.[14] A number of border clashes occurred, each party undertaking a variety of limited military operations against the other. The People's Republic of China opted to become involved in this conflict; Peking was not overly concerned with the intrinsic merits of the parties' claims and counterclaims, but it still opted to give the Kampuchean government of Pol Pot limited support. The reason: a perception that the recently unified Socialist Republic of Vietnam was an ally of the Soviet Union, and together they intended to try to dominate Southeast Asia.[15] While one might argue intentions and ultimate objectives, there was no disputing the fact that Hanoi and Moscow had greatly increased cooperative relations. As a result of its perception, throughout much of 1977 and 1978 China supplied Kampuchea with large quantities of foreign aid, and publicly endorsed its charges against Hanoi. Chinese policymakers did not at this juncture opt for complete support, however, because of possible third party reactions. They recognized that complete support might produce "Middle Kingdom fears" elsewhere in the region, and could elicit Soviet moves of a nature Peking was not prepared to counter.[16] But these risks could

---

[14]Cambodia was renamed Democratic Kampuchea in 1976.

[15]Reunification was officially proclaimed on July 2, 1976. The student should note that "the situation" and "who is involved" are different for different parties; China and Kampuchea had different definitions and concerns.

[16]"Middle Kingdom fears" refers to beliefs that China would try to reassert domination over lands it had dominated at the height of Chinese imperial glory. See Chapter 3, p. 83.

be minimized with the orientation of limited support, and it was regularly employed during these years to the end of denying (via Kampuchea) the establishment of Soviet-Vietnamese hegemony.[17]

Lastly, a state may decide to give informal limited support because it feels compelled to do so. Perhaps it really would prefer to avoid this issue but because a strong ally, regional leader, or client is deeply involved the policymakers feel that they have no choice. Maybe this is an issue on which previous statements have been made that indicate a certain viewpoint, or a treaty relationship makes at least nominal support necessary. In other words, there are times when the policymaker really would prefer not to give any support at all but the benefits of that course of action are more than offset by the costs.

The limited support orientation also has a number of possible disadvantages. First, the very flexibility involved can turn out to be detrimental. Since states seek to anticipate the actions of others, certainty is often a desired quality. The parties one is supporting want to be able to "count on" his actions and may well be resentful of what they feel is perfidy. Also, the lack of certainty may increase the likelihood of adversarial activity rather than decrease it. For example, if the Germans had been sure that the British would enter World War I (which they were not) they might have acted differently. American policymakers in much of the post-World War II era assumed that uncertainty was an invitation to aggression and thus sought to construct a ring of alliances to deter potential Communist attack.

One's friends may also resent the fact that the support is so limited. In both the Korean and Vietnam conflicts the United States felt that its allies were not carrying their fair share of the load. Nominal or limited support may be considered to be phony, or an unwillingness to expend one's own resources when someone else will do it. This kind of feeling can easily spiral into mutual charges of bad faith and eventually have severe intracoalition repercussions.

Finally, although the costs and risks are less than they would be with complete support, the opportunities for gain are also. In 1975 the United States was providing limited support (foreign aid) for the alliance of the National Front for the Liberation of Angola (FNLA) and the National Union for the Total Independence of Angola (UNITA) in their struggle against the Soviet-backed Popular Movement for the Liberation of Angola (MPLA). By late in the year, as Soviet assistance to the MPLA increased and Cuban combatants were introduced, it became increasingly apparent that the FNLA/UNITA alliance was losing. Washington was not willing to match the Soviet escalation, however, opting to keep its support very limited; shortly thereafter, when the

---

[17]Though the U. S. S. R. and the SRV did not come to dominate Southeast Asia, China's limited support of Kampuchea was ineffectual in preventing the SRV's "blitzkrieg" invasion and the overthrow of the Pol Pot regime.

MPLA emerged victorious, American influence in Angola virtually disappeared. If a policymaker employs the orientation of limited support he or she needs to recognize the fact that self-imposed limitations may correspondingly limit achievements.

The second half of this "friendly" orientation is *limited cooperation on substantive situational issues*.[18] Obviously, there are a number of situations in which the objectives the parties are seeking in their mutual relations are such that working together would be beneficial. Nevertheless, the cooperation that ensues may be limited. Why might one opt to cooperate in no more than a limited fashion? There are several reasons. First, it may be that in a given situation greater cooperation is simply not possible; in the 1972 American-Russian strategic arms limitation talks policymakers realized that broad agreements were out of the realm of possibility and limited their actions accordingly. While recognizing the political and economic advantages that would flow from integrating their coal and steel industries, in the early 1950s France and West Germany had too many divergent interests, differing perceptions, and antagonistic historical-emotional legacies to cooperate in any more than a limited manner. At this time the formation of the European Coal and Steel Community was the furthest they could possibly go.[19]

Second, frequently there is a belief that it is useful to begin small. If cooperation cannot be achieved on the little things it cannot be achieved at all; if it can, perhaps a degree of positive momentum can be created and efforts can be productively stepped up. A third advantage is the flexibility such a low level of cooperation allows; not having invested great resources or prestige in a given situation, one can alter (or even reverse) course without incurring significant loss. Finally, and often most importantly, policymakers may choose to keep cooperation limited because of third party concerns. Policymakers recognize full well that no situation is just bilateral; though the cooperation itself may be, it is conducted within a complex world of interacting relationships, is itself the product of a multitude of influences, and affects a number of different parties in varying ways.[20] Therefore, the policymaker cannot "go overboard" in one situation because such action would cause major problems with third parties (and/or fourth, fifth, etc.). In an effort to preclude such developments, and since policymaking is an uncertain art at best, policymakers often feel it is wise to proceed in a very cautious, limited fashion.

---

[18]We are distinguishing "cooperation" from "support" analytically, although in practice, of course, there is a certain amount of overlap. As used here, "cooperation" is used in connection with the friendly mutual relations of the parties (it is "internally" focused), whereas "support" concerns helping another party achieve goals external to their mutual relationship.

[19]Italy and the Benelux states also were parties. For more on the background see Chapter 1, pp. 20–21, and corresponding footnotes.

[20]See Chapter 14, especially pp. 391–400.

An instructive recent example of limited cooperation was manifested in late October 1978 when Japan and the People's Republic of China signed a treaty of "peace and friendship." Limited cooperation was all that was possible for the parties in this situation. Memories of historic conflicts, ideological differences, rival claims to sovereignty over the Senkaku Islands, conflicting views on the problem of Korean reunification, divergent (although not totally opposed) perceptions of the Soviet threat, these and other considerations precluded more. But, although complete cooperation was not possible, even cooperation of a limited nature could yield some real benefits. First, it would, it was hoped, open a new era in Sino-Japanese economic relations, a possibility with potentially enormous implications. Second, each party also had political objectives, Peking trying to move the Japanese toward an anti-Soviet stance, the Japanese attempting to increase stability and enhance the likelihood of a neutralized Asian mainland. And although they differed in their perception of the degree and intensity of the Soviet threat, each also hoped that the degree of cooperation was sufficiently minimal to avoid provoking counterproductive Russian responses.[21]

Complete Support or Cooperation

In some situations of mutual interest, the limited support or cooperation option is insufficient to achieve one's objectives. If the issues in question are perceived to be of considerable importance, such as those affecting one's ability to achieve fundamental objectives, the policymaker might feel it necessary to undertake a major expenditure of resources and be desirous of working closely with another party or parties toward the goal of a favorable substantive outcome. If so, he or she likely would choose the orientation of *complete support or cooperation*.

Complete support inevitably produces certain results. Situational certainty is increased, a fact that can be either good or bad. Predictability will be appreciated by one's friends, as will the degree of support. No suspicions of failing to do one's share or sham participation will be in evidence. Similarly, adversaries will be aware of what is going on and be required to calculate accordingly. Presumably losses will not occur because of confusion or misperception about what a party will do. In fact, the mere existence of such support may directly affect a situation's outcome; the fact that the United States would fight to prevent a Soviet military takeover of West Germany obviously has an impact on that situation's result. Finally, because of the deep involvement com-

[21]Much to Japan's chagrin, on November 3, 1978 Russia and Vietnam signed a clearly "unneutral" friendship pact. Though China already was nearly at sword's point with Hanoi and Moscow, Japan had been trying to cultivate cooperative relations with both.

plete support entails the policymaker is in a position that permits bringing to bear all one's options for increasing external capability and making maximum use of the vast array of foreign policy tools available.

For several years following the "creation" of the Federal Republic of Germany in 1949, its leaders utilized the orientation of complete support toward the United States.[22] As a result of World War II Germany had been economically devastated, her territorial integrity had been shattered, and Western leaders were fearful of a Soviet takeover; the United States at this time was in the forefront of the struggle against Communism, advocating the doctrine of containment and employing a wide range of military, economic, and communication policy instruments in pursuance of that objective.[23] In light of West Germany's objectives of territorial reunification and economic-political reconstruction and growth, her weakness and America's strength, the commonality of mutual interests, and the degree to which Washington could supply the FRG's immediate needs, West German policymakers deduced that complete support of the United States was clearly the orientation to choose.

While complete support yields opportunities for considerable gain, it also has certain potential drawbacks. For one thing, the very certainty eliminates much of one's flexibility and its accompanying advantages (noted previously). Second, it is more costly in terms of resource expenditure. Because all states are limited in resources and because resources allocated to one situation are not available for others, the policymaker must husband his or her party's resources and distribute them on the basis of carefully determined priorities. One must be certain that this situation warrants a major commitment.

Another difficulty is that such a level of support automatically carries with it a substantial investment of prestige, making compromise more difficult. Particular groups and/or individuals have a vested interest in having the policy work. This being so there is a danger of being locked in, unable to adjust to changing circumstances. Furthermore, there may be a tendency to assume that just a little stronger and/or longer commitment will "solve" the problem. Because the commitment is so serious the policymaker may feel that failure (or anything that could be interpreted as failure) is simply not acceptable, and make his decisions accordingly. Certainly Lyndon Johnson's Vietnam policy is a case in point.[24] Yet because no one can guarantee success, a high level of support may simply lead to a demonstration of ineptness rather

[22]For more on the "German problem" see Chapter 13, pp. 362–364.

[23]For more on containment see Chapter 13, pp. 358–362.

[24]So much is written that one hardly knows what to recommend. Perhaps the most useful works to begin with are David Halberstam, *The Best and the Brightest*, Random House, New York, 1969, and New York Times, *The Pentagon Papers*, Bantam, New York, 1971.

than capacity. It is also possible that the certainty engendered will not yield the desired results; perhaps a party's adversaries had already anticipated the position taken and had decided that confrontation was their best route. Finally, it is possible the adversary will interpret strong support of one party to mean that another will not receive support. In 1950 when American Secretary of State Dean Acheson defined the United States defense perimeter in a way that did not include South Korea, some Communist leaders interpreted this to mean that support for South Korea was excluded and that country would not be defended by American forces.[25]

The second facet of this orientation is *complete cooperation*.[26] There are some circumstances in which the parties have common or complementary objectives in their mutual relations, the issues are of considerable importance, and the maximization of cooperative relationships is necessary for their resolution. Syria, a state composed of a melange of disparate, highly partisan ethnic, religious, and social groups, a party that has simultaneously embraced the potentially conflicting ideologies of pan-Arabism and Syrian nationalism, an entity in the 1950s caught up in Cold War, inter-Arab, and Arab-Israeli problems, was by late 1957 on the verge of disintegration. Most of the traditional political factions had, for one reason or another, been discredited. The three that retained any credibility were the Baath (Arab Socialist Resurrection) Party, the Communists, and the military.

The Baathists, whose fundamental objective was independent pan-Arab unity, believed Egypt's Gamal Nasser was the man who could bring this about. This, along with what they felt was the possibility of a Communist takeover unless action was taken to prevent it, led them to advocate a merger of their country with Egypt. The military, split into a number of competing factions, each suspicious of the other, also worried about a Communist takeover, concerned about Baathist influence, saw in Nasser an answer to their problems. They, too, advocated union. Even some of the Communists, believing Nasser to be tied to Moscow and feeling he could be manipulated, sought union. Thus, when in response to their entreaties Nasser laid down a number of highly

---

[25]However, one should not jump to the conclusion that this exclusion was the sole basis of what has been called the "invitation" to attack. See John W. Spanier, *The Truman-MacArthur Controversy and the Korean War*, Norton, New York, 1965, Ch. 2. For the view that Acheson's omission *was* critical, see Robert T. Oliver, *Why War Came to Korea*, Fordham University Press, New York, 1950. Also see Chapter 14, pp. 401–402.

[26]To reiterate what was said earlier, we are speaking in terms of *gradations*, using the term "complete" only to make the point. Cooperation can never be absolutely "complete" in the sense that there would not be the slightest differences or disagreements. Complete cooperation in the security realm would involve what has been called pure collective security. See Hartmann, *The Relations of Nations*, Fifth Edition, Chapter 20.

restrictive conditions for the merger, most Syrian leaders promised complete cooperation. Only in this manner, they felt, could their problem be solved. In February 1958 Egypt and Syria merged to become the United Arab Republic.[27]

Seldom, of course, does cooperation occur this completely. Nevertheless, under certain conditions it appears with a degree of regularity: when parties have similar (or at least compatible) government structures, ideologies, and ethical systems; have common perceptions of the definition, causes, and possible solutions to the problems at hand; and neither party is perceived as a threat to the other's fundamental interests. The United States and Great Britain generally fit these criteria and employ this orientation in their mutual relations a great deal. It is evident though, that there are few situations in which all these conditions are present; therefore, complete cooperation is infrequent. Because of the decentralized, anarchical, complex nature of the international political world, policymakers seldom feel it prudent to cooperate too extensively with anyone, whether said party is purportedly friendly, neutral, or hostile; ultimately one must base all decisions on the projected effect of any action on survival, and in that regard one's only sure ally is oneself.

A final comment with respect to the orientation of complete support or cooperation: the greater the level of support or cooperation one undertakes, the greater the adverse consequences of failure. When a major effort is made, if it is unsuccessful prestige may decline noticeably, influence significantly decrease, etc. Given this rather obvious but enormously important fact, the wise policymaker will employ this orientation judiciously, doing so only when firmly convinced that the objective is worth the risk.

Indirect Opposition

Moving from the "friendly" to the "hostile" side of the spectrum, the policymaker may decide to employ the issue orientation of *indirect opposition* (which may involve limited support for certain parties in some cases). The policymaker's analysis of the situation may indicate that if certain parties achieve their objectives his or her party's interests will be harmed, but it appears that an orientation of direct confrontation would be unwise. There are several reasons why indirect opposition may be preferred. First, it may be that a party wishes to have its opposition secret (or at least disguised). Perhaps nonsituation parties would act adversely, either *re* the situation or with respect to nonsituational issues, if the opposition were open; also, maybe negative domestic pressures would increase greatly.

In 1964 the United States had not, as yet, dispatched American combat units to Vietnam. Officially it was not engaging in military operations against

---

[27]In 1961 Syria seceded from the union.

the North, but secretly throughout the year Washington was progressively escalating pressure on Hanoi via a wide range of clandestine military activities. Under what was known as Operation Plan 34A, there were overflights for intelligence purposes, kidnappings, the parachuting of sabotage and commando teams in to blow up bridges and railroad depots, the bombardment of coastal installations by PT boats, and so forth. As a rule most of the "dirty work" in the various operations was done by South Vietnamese troops, with the Americans only acting as "advisers." The attacks were the result of a monthly schedule of raids drawn up in the field by the American military, and cleared for action by Washington. U.S. policymakers did not want nonsituation parties, or the American people, to be aware of what was happening; the indirect opposition orientation seemed to meet its requirements well.

A second advantage of this orientation is that generally the costs and risks are lower than they would be in a direct confrontation. As a rule a relatively small amount of prestige is involved, and if the operation is unsuccessful relatively little loss will be suffered.[28] Furthermore, because the opposition is indirect one is less likely to be the target of direct retaliation than in a confrontation situation. This is true even if the "indirect" aspect is clearly a fiction and all the parties know it. In mid 1977 Somalia attacked Ethiopia under the guise of supporting a bid for "freedom" by the ethnic Somalians (living in Ethiopia) of the Western Somali Liberation Front; in the Korean War it was only Chinese "volunteers" who fought against the United Nations Forces, not the army of the People's Republic of China. The fact that in both these cases an effort was made to avoid a total confrontation, meaning the resultant challenge was less direct, made it easier for the perpetrators' opponents to avoid undertaking direct retaliation.[29]

Another advantage of indirect opposition is that the policymaker can alter orientation, change the level and nature of his or her party's involvement, with relative ease.[30] During World War II the Soviet Union and Britain occupied Iran, later being joined by forces from the United States. The allies' objectives were to protect Iran as a valuable corridor for shipping war supplies to Russia, and prevent its oil from falling into German hands. A treaty was soon signed with the Iranian government to the effect that within six months of the end of the war all foreign troops would be withdrawn. As the war drew to a close it became apparent that Moscow had no intention of honoring its pledge. Furthermore, in the northern border province of Azerbaijan a revolt by Commu-

---

[28]However, if one's participation is so thinly disguised that everyone knows who really is involved, and if it is a major unsuccessful operation, this may not be so.

[29]This, in itself, was not the only reason in either case, although it was an important influencing element.

[30]And certainly more easily than if one is at a confrontation level.

nist-dominated elements was instigated, and with the assistance of Soviet troops, who prevented the Iranian government from quelling the uprising, in December 1945 the Autonomous Republic of Azerbaijan was proclaimed. Also, since the latter part of 1944 the Russians had been (unsuccessfully) seeking major oil concessions from Iran, and pressure was continuing in that regard. When the date set for the withdrawal of foreign troops came—March 2, 1946—Soviet forces were still there and gave no indication they were planning to move; there was no sign that the other pressures were abating, either.

The Kremlin's opposition to Iran, to this point, had been strong but indirect; policymakers were in a position from which they could escalate or deescalate with equal facility. Iran appealed to the U. N. Security Council, charging Russia was attempting to coerce her into granting oil concessions and was planning to detach the Azerbaijan area. A number of countries, led by the United States, vigorously supported Teheran and indicated serious consequences would be forthcoming if the Soviets did not disengage. In light of this strong reaction, and given the possibility Washington might perceive some linkage between this situation and Soviet maneuvers in the more important (to Russia) region of Central and Eastern Europe and undertake countering actions there, Moscow relented and announced it would soon withdraw its troops (which it did). Shortly thereafter, an agreement was reached with Iranian authorities settling the Azerbaijan and oil concession issues.

Confrontation

In some conflictual situations indirect opposition is not deemed sufficient, however. In these cases one may have to employ the final orientation option, *confrontation*. In the decentralized anarchy of international politics there are some situations that the policymaker perceives to involve certain parties with considerable capability seeking objectives clearly contrary to his or her own, and he or she has no means to resolve the problem except to confront these adversaries and "draw the line." (For many reasons, including the immense dangers of modern warfare and presumably a preference for the peaceful settlement of disputes, scholars sometimes fail to give sufficient emphasis to this option despite the obvious fact that it is often chosen).

Confrontation is similar in some ways to complete support: it involves a judgment that the issues are important, requires a willingness to take high risks, requires the recognition that considerable resources may have to be expended, will inevitably place one's prestige on the line, obviously will result in antagonism from the adversary, and (if one is rational) will only be employed in a situation in which success or failure matters immensely.

But confrontation differs importantly from complete support in two respects. First, it is an orientation the policymaker adopts as a result of a calculation of the probable impact on the state's fundamental objectives of certain anticipated actions by other party(ies), regardless of whether one's allies agree or not. The policymaker has determined that it is imperative that the source of the perceived threat to the state's objectives be "confronted" come what may, and whether friends perceive the situation similarly and act in concert accordingly is of secondary importance. Confrontation is an orientation independent of other parties except the one(s) that is(are) the source of the threat, it is based on a judgment that one's security is significantly endangered, and it will be carried out with or without external assistance. The United States' decision to confront Russia in the 1962 Cuban missile crisis, for example, was not a matter of supporting someone else but was based on calculations about the impact of Soviet actions on American security.

A second difference, sometimes of great importance, is that since confrontation is unilateral in conception and implementation it is directly, specifically, and only concerned with one's own security, whereas complete support focuses initially, and perhaps primarily, on the security of the supported party, affecting the security of the policymaker's state only derivatively. To illustrate, if the United States employed the orientation of complete support with respect to helping Israel deter a military attack by an Arab state, the original focus would be on the survival of Israel; only derivatively would there be concern for American security. By way of contrast, if Washington again chose to directly confront the Soviet Union over what were judged to be unacceptable Soviet activities in Cuba it would be because of direct concern with the impact of those activities on American security.

Obviously there are circumstances in which complete support of one's ally is undertaken and one would have opted for confrontation had not the ally itself chosen to confront the adversary; when such a scenario exists the orientation calculations are reinforcing, the independent determination of the policymaker's own requirements blending with the desire to support allies or friends. Nevertheless, knowing which orientation is the "real" source of a policy action is important; the intensity of activity, one's "staying power," and the willingness to expend resources are more likely to be at a maximum if the policymaker has acted from a confrontation orientation. The reason for this, quite simply, is that usually a confrontation orientation is not chosen unless the policymaker perceives that there is a major threat to fundamental objectives and believes that ultimately there may be no one to count on but oneself. If such conditions obtain and the policymaker goes ahead anyway, it is likely that he or she will do everything in his or her power to succeed; therefore, if opposed the probability of conflict is high.

The fourth step in the policy formulation process, determining orientation, is of critical importance. In the first three steps the policymaker's activities are primarily investigatory and deductibe in nature; finding out who is

involved, what the varous objectives are, ascertaining pertinent capability relationships, these are essentially intellectual tasks. But when one determines
orientation, although the activity contains a strong investigatory-analytical
component it goes beyond that; it also includes elements of policy content and
action. The particular orientation option one chooses, beginning as it does the
bridging between policy formulation and implementation, sets the framework
for all later developments; the determining of orientation gives an initial direction and emphasis that partially precludes (and/or makes more costly) other
alternatives, enhances the likelihood of achieving some objectives while decreasing the probability of obtaining certain others, and totally forecloses the
possibility of some outcomes. It is a choice of enormous importance.

6
External Means of
Increasing Capability

To this point our analysis has focused on the four basic steps of policy formulation, steps that all policymakers should take to whatever extent they can. Many times, however, because of the pervasive importance of capability considerations, a fifth step is required, an analysis of various external means of increasing relative strength (internal capability components are discussed in Chapters 7 and 8).[1]

TERRITORIAL CHANGES

The first category of such external techniques is territorial change. There are three basic changes a policymaker might seek: (1) territorial acquisition, (2) detaching territory from one's adversary without acquiring it, and (3) creating functional and/or spatial off limits zones.

---

[1]Aspects of this "step" are directly related to and/or are extensions of certain subjects discussed earlier, especially orientation options. Activities designed to increase capability via external means are of such operational significance and pervasiveness, however, that they deserve an explicit, in-depth analysis in their own right.

Territorial Acquisition

The *acquisition of territory* has a major effect on capability through its impact on the internal components of power. As a general rule adding land means adding strength (although, as is pointed out in Chapter 7, additional size does not always mean additional capability).[2] By definition more land means the country is bigger. This simple geographical fact allows more room for the deployment and dispersal of critical facilities, forces and populace, provides room for additional growth, and makes a state more difficult to successfully attack, conquer, and occupy. Economically, too, it may be beneficial. Perhaps additional arable land will be obtained so agricultural output can be increased, or industrial complexes will be captured so manufacturing can increase, or a critical natural resource can be acquired to fuel the economy. Sometimes a particular strategic geographic advantage may be developed if a certain area is acquired. For example, when Israel captured Sharm al-Sheikh in the 1967 June War she gained the capacity to command the entrance to the Gulf of Aqaba.[3] New territory usually means additional population, which also may contribute to strength (although it could also be a drain if it is uncontrollable, there is not enough food, shelter, etc.). As discussed in the analysis of territorial integrity, sometimes territory is considered "ours" and its acquisition may greatly increase domestic political support. And one could give many more examples.

Although there are many possible advantages one could gain from territorial acquisition, the policymaker needs to carefully weigh the anticipated net benefits against the projected costs of acquisition. Except in highly unusual circumstances the days of relatively easy expansion are over. For example, although historically it was possible for Russia and the United States to expand continentally with little resistance, equivalent opportunities no longer exist (for them or anyone else). A similar feature of bygone days was imperialistic expansion, the acquisition and subjugation of nonadjacent areas populated by different and less technologically advanced peoples.[4]

Today, the policymaker seldom has the option of acquiring territory with little resistance. As explained earlier, territoriality is an attribute of statehood with major operational significance, and in the actual formulation of policy territorial concerns usually loom very large.[5] Maintaining territorial integrity,

---

[2]See p. 165.

[3]Possession of Sharm al-Sheikh allows one to effectively control the narrow Straits of Tiran at the entrance to the Gulf. For further discussion of the events leading to the 1967 war, see Chapter 14.

[4]This fascinating topic has been the subject of innumerable studies. The beginning student might start with John A. Hobson, *Imperialism, A Study*, University of Michigan Press, Ann Arbor, 1965, and E. M. Winslow, *The Pattern of Imperialism*, Columbia University Press, New York, 1948.

[5]Also see Chapter 1, pp. 4–6.

defending one's home territory against external attack, is a fundamental objective, a goal for the achievement of which a party almost always will make a maximum effort (including going to war).[6] This means that a policymaker considering attempting to acquire territory must assume that the target of the projected action in all probability will resist with all means at its disposal; except in highly unusual circumstances the target will utilize an orientation of confrontation and will seek its objectives with great vigor. Even if the scenario involves an LDC as the target and the potential attacker is a nonadjacent major power resistance likely will be severe, because in most instances there will be other nonadjacent major powers who will come to the LDC's aid to prevent massive territorial acquisitions by their rival. Outright imperialism is no longer in fashion, and there are no more unclaimed lands. Because of these facts, the acquisition of a particular territory must be of singular importance in order for such action to be attempted.

Another point to remember is that it makes a difference from whom territory is sought. Obviously one reason for this is the level of resistance one will encounter; China would notice the difference between Russia and Nepal. It is also important because of the fact that the loser is weakened and in terms of one's basic security it is more significant if some states are weakened than others. For example, it clearly would make a difference to the United States whether the loser were China or Bhutan, even if the land acquired had the identical qualities. When Germany obtained the immensely valuable Skoda munitions works from Czechoslovakia as a result of the 1938 Munich capitulations the West also lost them. If they had been taken from a neutral country the West's absolute strength would not have decreased and the relative increase in German capability would have been considerably less.

A final consideration is this: the successful acquisition of a particular territory may produce an outcome much less favorable than that which had been anticipated. For one thing, because of the acquisition parties other than those directly involved will inevitably reconsider their policies. The changed territorial configuration will alter capability relationships, and the fact that a party acquired additional territory may lead to a different perception of what that party's objectives may be in other situations. This could lead to an increase in the tension level and more potential and/or actual conflictual relationships. Second, the party(ies) from whom the territory is acquired obviously will be less than pleased and in many instances will not accept the loss as permanent. If this condition obtains, a major (perhaps fundamental) policy objective will be the land's recapture, the restoration of territorial integrity.[7] Finally, it may turn out that the acquisition increases internal difficulties. The possible rea-

---

[6]Also see Chapter 3, pp. 75–77.
[7]Also see Chapter 3, pp. 76–77.

sons are legion. Perhaps the land is economically unproductive, constituting a net resource drain; maybe elements of the populace conduct and/or provide a haven for guerilla operations by national liberation organizations against their new governors; possibly the new people are culturally, racially, or ethnically very different and the country's societal cohesiveness decreases. And there are many other potential difficulties. When a policymaker is considering the possibility of attempting to acquire additional territory then, it is not enough to calculate the costs and risks of acquisition and recognize the importance of the identity of the projected target. One also needs to very carefully evaluate the plusses and minuses in the state of affairs that will exist if "success" is achieved.

Detachment Without Acquisition

A second type of territorial change involves *detaching territory from one's opponent although not acquiring it yourself*. One reason leaders of most Arab governments favor the creation of an independent Arab Palestine is because this would require the detachment of certain territory from Israel and weaken her accordingly. The Soviet Union has encouraged a separatist movement among the six million people of the Chinese province of Sinkiang as a means of weakening Peking's position in their border dispute. In the two World Wars Germany encouraged the Ukrainians to break away from Russia and set up their own state.

A recent successful use of this technique occurred in the India-Pakistan war of 1971 and the creation of Bangladesh.[8] Separated by more than 1000 miles of Indian territory, East and West Pakistan were very different culturally, economically, and ethnically. The Bengali peoples of the East were understandably bitter over their subordination to the Western Punjabs; ethnic rancor and discrimination were apparent. A symbolic indication of this occurred in late 1970 when, after a devastating cyclone struck the Bengali coast, President Yahya Khan waited almost two weeks to visit the scene of the disaster. Politically, economically, and socially the Westerners ruled.

At the same time the intense antagonism between India and Pakistan resulting from the religious and territorial disputes that developed out of the partition of British India in 1947 continued unabated. The deep animosities that had led to the original fighting festered and it was clear that the 1965 war had settled nothing.[9]

---

[8]For an excellent concise introduction to this topic, see Rounaq Jahan, "India, Pakistan, and Bangladesh" in Gregory Henderson, Richard Ned Lebow, and John G. Stoessinger, eds., *Divided Nations in a Divided World*, David McKay, New York, 1974, pp. 299–336.

[9]The territory of Kashmir was divided between the two countries after the original partition. In 1965 warfare broke out over it anew, with neither side emerging victorious. See Russel Brines, *The Indo-Pakistan Conflict*, Pall Mall, London, 1969.

In December 1970 elections were held. To the surprise and dismay of President Khan and the People's Party (Western) the Awami League of Sheikh Mujibur Rahman won an overwhelming victory in the East. The Awami League had advocated complete regional autonomy for East Pakistan, and there was little doubt (in light of its electoral victory) that once the new National Assembly convened Mujibur Rahman would be elected Prime Minister and the Assembly would vote the League's program. To preclude this, President Khan refused to call the Assembly into session, arrested Mujibur, and banned the League. The Bengalis responded with widespread civil disobedience, and this was followed by a full-scale rebellion and a proclamation of the independence of the new state of Bangladesh. President Khan responded by sending in the (Western) army to crush the rebels. Extreme brutality was employed by (West) Pakistani authorities, the number of people massacred perhaps reaching a million.

Indian policymakers at first reacted cautiously, adopting an orientation of limited support and restricting their involvement to caring for the (literally) millions of refugees fleeing into their country.[10] By midyear, however, Pakistani troops were chasing Bengalis across the border, and several armed clashes occurred. Considering the economic pressures the refugees were creating and the possibilities for weakening their adversary, the Indians chose to escalate. Covert aid was extended to the rebels (known as the Mukti Bahini), and Mrs. Gandhi's government made preparations for direct involvement. In August India signed a treaty of friendship with the Soviet Union, a clear signal to China (which was friendly to Pakistan) not to intervene. In October and November aid to the Mukti Bahini was increased. Then, on December 1 Indian troops "defensively" advanced five miles into Pakistan and the government demanded a total Pakistani withdrawal.[11] Khan's response was a surprise (and futile) air attack on India; this in turn provided just the right pretext for a major Indian invasion of the East. With surprising ease the Pakistanis were defeated, and on December 16 they surrendered. The independence of Bangladesh thus was confirmed.

India had not initiated this problem although her long-standing dispute with Pakistan had helped to create a volatile situation. By carefully taking advantage of developing events, however, she was able to intervene effectively with the result that territory was detached and her primary antagonist weakened accordingly.

---

[10]They fled to the Indian state of West Bengal, whose people were ethnically and culturally similar and who received the refugees with a degree of sympathy.

[11]By this time winter snows had closed the Himalayan passes, "reinforcing" the Indian-Soviet treaty's impact on deterring possible Chinese intervention.

Off-Limits Zones

The final territorial change a policymaker may seek is to make certain zones "off limits" either territorially or functionally. This may occur through mutual agreement, consent, or simply as a result of the policies of contending parties in competition but unwilling to push things to the point of conflict.[12] Usually such territories are considered too important to allow the other side to possess or utilize but not worth the costs and risks that would be entailed in attempted acquisition. In such a case it is in the interest of all to remove them from the "game."

This has occurred many times. Afghanistan occupied such a position for centuries, separating the British in India from the Russian bear. In 1907 this status was confirmed by the Anglo-Russian agreement on the Middle East. Switzerland was permanently neutralized at the Congress of Vienna in 1815 and has had her neutrality respected. In more recent times, Austria was neutralized as a result of the 1955 peace treaty that "officially" ended World War II and brought about the withdrawal of Soviet troops.[13]

Sometimes areas become off limits without any official agreement. Policymakers may realize that all parties would benefit from eliminating these areas from competition but realize that it would not be feasible or necessary to seek a formalized arrangement. The result then may be a tacit consent to the situation. Siam (Thailand) and Abyssinia (Ethiopia) were "declared" off limits in this fashion for lengthy periods, as was Korea.

The number of areas permanently out of bounds is very small, however, for the obvious reason that such a status is dependent on outside parties for its continuance. Because of this fact policymakers do not often try to create such an arrangement. Even when it is sought, the rate of success is poor. Thailand, Ethiopia, and Korea, indicated above, are no longer "safe," nor is Tibet. Belgium was declared "perpetually neutral" in 1839 but, being the main highway from Germany into France, was trampled in World War I. Washington and Moscow sought to remove Laos as a bone of contention in 1962 but the agreements soon became relatively ineffectual.

Sometimes specific areas are declared off limits in a functional sense through some kind of limitation on militarization. There are many examples of demilitarization. According to the terms of the Versailles Treaty ending World War I, that part of Germany between the Rhine River and the border with France (Rhineland) was demilitarized; the 1954 Geneva Agreements ending the Indochina war established a demilitarized zone on either side of the

---

[12]The term "neutralization" is sometimes used to describe declaring a territory off limits by mutual agreement, although it also has a wide range of other meanings.

[13]See William B. Bader, *Austria Between East and West, 1945-1955*, Stanford University Press, Stanford, Cal., 1966.

provisional military demarcation line established in the area near the 17th parallel; as part of the Israeli-Syrian General Armistice Agreement that halted the fighting after the 1948–1949 Palestine War, demilitarized zones were established in those areas that were to go to Israel under the United Nations Partition Plan but that were occupied by the Syrians. A number of agreements have been signed by various parties in an effort to keep certain specific geographic areas out of the strategic arms race, including treaties that prohibit the establishment of military bases or fortifications or the testing of weapons in Antarctica, forbid the placing in orbit of objects carrying nuclear weapons or the installation of nuclear weapons or military facilities on celestial bodies, and prohibit the stationing of weapons of mass destruction on the ocean floor.[14]

In each of these cases the parties recognized that making certain areas free of military activity would enhance their security. This is usually the purpose of such arrangements. This was particularly apparent in yet another instance of demilitarization, the El Auja case. When the Palestine war ended Israeli forces were occupying the little town of El Auja, a small desert village on a strategic road junction near the Egyptian border.[15] Cairo said it was the gateway to the Egyptian Sinai and could not remain in hostile hands; Israel said it was the logical invasion route into the Negev (Israel's southern desert) and a hostile force could launch an attack from there and cut her in half. When U. N. Mediator Ralph Bunche suggested demilitarization, both sides accepted, recognizing each other's security would be protected.

The May 1974 Israeli-Syrian disengagement agreements provide a good example of limited (de)militarization. In addition to the establishment of a U. N.-controlled area of separation, three zones of force restrictions were set up on each side of the no-man's-land. Within the first 10 kilometers each way only 6000 men, light artillery, and 75 tanks were allowed; in the next 10 kilometers no heavy artillery and a maximum of 500 tanks; and in the last 5 kilometers heavy artillery and missiles were prohibited.[16] Similar kinds of arrangements were stipulated in the September 1975 Egyptian-Israeli Sinai II Accords.[17] A U. N.-controlled buffer zone was set up between Egyptian and Israeli forces within which certain manned surveillance and watch stations and

---

[14]The treaties are (1) The Antarctic Treaty, (2) the Treaty on Principles Governing the Activities of States in the Exploration and Use of Outer Space, Including the Moon and Other Celestial Bodies, and (3) the Treaty on the Prohibition of the Emplacement of Nuclear Weapons and Other Weapons of Mass Destruction on the Seabed and the Ocean Floor and in the Subsoil Thereof. For more on these treaties see Chapter 10, pp. 292–293.

[15]This is concisely and perceptively discussed by Earl Berger, *The Covenant and the Sword: Arab-Israeli Relations 1948–1956*, University of Toronto Press, Toronto, 1965, Ch. 3.

[16]*Jerusalem Post*, June 4, 1974, p. 4.

[17]For text, see United Nations, Security Council, Report of the Secretary General, Addendum S/11818/Add. 1*, September 2, 1975.

unmanned electronic sensor fields would be located to provide tactical early warning capability. On either side of this buffer designated Limited Forces and Armaments areas were established. Forces were limited to 8 standard infantry battalions, 75 tanks, 72 artillery pieces, and 8000 personnel. The parties also were prohibited from locating in these areas weapons that could reach the lines of the other side, and from emplacing antiaircraft missiles within 10 kilometers of their respective rear zonal lines.

Attempts to totally and partially demilitarize various areas have had mixed success. On the negative side, Hitler reoccupied the Rhineland in 1936, the Vietnam DMZ was violated with alacrity, the Syrian-Israeli DMZs became foci of violence and antagonism, and Israel reoccupied El Auja prior to its Sinai assault in 1956. On the other hand, the provisions of the Antarctic, Outer Space, and Seabed Treaties, and the requirements of the limited forces zones in the Middle East disengagement agreements, have been (and were) well observed. Just as is true with respect to all other agreements, parties will adhere to demilitarization arrangements only so long and insofar as those arrangements are perceived to aid in the achievement or protection of one's objectives; if that ceases to be the case, policy will be altered.

It would be useful to conclude this topic by providing a representative list of the objectives a policymaker might be seeking if he or she tried to use external means of increasing capability in this fashion:

1. Prevent one's adversary from increasing capability by denial of territory, particularly territory of special strategic significance.
2. Reduce general tension level between the parties by removing (or at least dampening) one source of conflict.
3. Reduce general tension level between the parties by demonstrating that agreements can be reached on at least some issues.
4. By eliminating one issue, be able to allocate more resources to other objectives.
5. Lower tensions and reduce probability and intensity of border incidents, aggravations, or accidents by reducing geographical proximity; especially important in terms of militarization limitations.

ALLIANCE ADJUSTMENTS

A second major category of maneuvers for increasing relative capability is alliance adjustment. There are three basic types: alliance formation, alliance prevention, and seeking to bring about the fragmentation of an opposition coalition.

Alliance Formation

The underlying rationale for *alliance formation* is simple. A policymaker perceives that his or her party's objectives cannot be achieved, or achieved as efficiently without outside help. Therefore an attempt is made to add the capabilities of one or more other parties to his or her own in the pursuit of said objectives. The assumption is that collective, cooperative behavior backed by increased strength will maximize the attainment of specific goals at the minimum possible cost.

Sometimes it simply may not be possible to achieve one's goals without outside help. There was just no way that Britain could be victorious in World War II without the assistance of Washington and Moscow, for example. European economic cooperation could not be achieved unilaterally, so the Common Market was created in 1957. For years the major oil producing states of the Third World could not, individually, break the grip of the huge MNCs that controlled world oil price and production levels (let alone use petroleum as a lever of influence); to remedy their common problem in 1960 they formed the Organization of Petroleum Exporting Countries (OPEC).

There also may be situations in which one believes that an objective may be obtainable but the costs of unilateral activity would be excessive. In the early 1950s when NATO adopted its Forward Strategy (defending Western Europe against the Soviets at the Iron Curtain), it was evident to American policymakers that West Germany should help with its own defense. This led to Bonn's limited rearmament and inclusion in NATO in 1955.[18] A more controversial example occurred in World War II. By early 1945 it was apparent that the United States would be able to win the war against Japan, but it looked as if the cost would be enormous; no one yet knew if the atomic bomb would work, and it was estimated that an invasion of the Japanese homeland would entail a million casualties. In light of these considerations, at the Yalta Conference President Roosevelt agreed that he would accept Russia regaining (fundamentally) the territorial position she had held prior to the 1904 Russo-Japanese War in exchange for her entering the war against Japan within three months after Germany surrendered. To the president, the costs of unilateral activity were excessive.

Whether a policymaker decides that an alliance should be formed or not is (usually) a decision of policy, not principle, and this means that there are many different types of alliances formed for many different purposes. There are relatively loose diplomatic coalitions, economic trading blocs, and bilateral or multilateral military arrangements. Alliances differ in terms of subject matter,

---

[18]The French were greatly disturbed at the prospect of Germans with weapons, which, given the history of German-French relations in the preceding 100 years, was understandable.

parties, geographical scope, the nature of the commitments undertaken, duration, degree of integration, and commonality of interests.

Despite this range of possibilities policymakers are usually pretty clear about the reasons for a particular alliance. Often a perception of threat and the resulting insecurity is the prime driving force. It is clear, for example, that one of the major factors leading to the formation of NATO was the Western fear of a Soviet military assault on Western Europe.[19] Similarly, the December 2, 1954 Mutual Security Pact between the United States and the Republic of China (Taiwan) was the result of their mutually perceived threat to Taiwan from Red China. The consummation of such threat-perception alliances sometimes allows alliance members a freedom to pursue interests they could not have sought without some measure of security. The Western European states would not have followed the policies that led to their rapid economic growth in the 1950s without the protective shield of NATO.

Although it is sometimes assumed that military alliances are always defensive and deterrent in nature this is not necessarily so. The Tripartite Pact concluded by Germany, Italy, and Japan on September 27, 1940 prepared the way for their war against the United States, for example. Obviously, joint planning and execution is advantageous for offensive as well as for defensive actions.

There are times when alliances are concluded for less obvious reasons. Perhaps a particular regime decides that greater domestic support is needed for certain programs. The specter of an invasion is often created in order to rally the people behind their government, and concluding an alliance could be the consummation of this illusion.

Another reason would simply be to receive the tangible benefits of military and economic aid that often come with alliance agreements. This could be used to keep the local populace under control and prevent rebellion. Such aid also might be used for foreign policy objectives other than those anticipated by the supplying state. American weapons flowing to Pakistan were "supposed" to be used to restrain Red China, but the Pakistanis used them against India in 1965. It is obvious enough that Pakistan's reasons for receiving American assistance were different from Washington's reasons for giving it.

Finally, a policymaker may seek an alliance for nonalliance effects. Perhaps the situation is such that more important objectives may be sought in the

---

[19]Seldom if ever is a policy undertaken solely because of a single factor. In most situations there are interrelated causes and each decision has a differential impact (as is pointed out in detail in Chapter 14). NATO, for example, was consummated only after it became obvious that World War II unity had disintegrated, several specific disputes had arisen, attempts to negotiate agreements had failed, and it seemed to many European and American policymakers that a unified strengthened Western bloc was a necessity. Despite the multitude of causal factors, however, the presumed major purpose of the alliance, to deter a Soviet military attack, was relatively specific.

future and it is hoped that an alliance will create a beneficial relationship that will be helpful in their achievement. Or it may be that not only more important objectives are sought but also a wider range of cooperative action, and this is to be just the start. Or lastly, perhaps an alliance may be concluded because of the anticipated impact on third parties (not third party "targets"). As an example, take the Brussels Alliance of March 17, 1948, signed between Belgium, the Netherlands, Luxembourg, Great Britain, and France. Although complete in itself as a defensive military pact, a major purpose for its conclusion was to show Washington that these European countries would do what they could to prevent or combat a Russian attack; shortly thereafter NATO was formed.

It is generally assumed that alliances make new commitments and/or add emphasis to existing ones. Another presumed effect of alliances is to add precision or clarity to the situation. While these characteristics are often present, such is not always the case and the point should not be overstressed. For example, in the Dual Alliance of Germany and Austria-Hungary signed in October 1879 each party agreed to support the other if Russia attacked. This was certainly precise and added a commitment to the previous situation. However, the Manila Pact of 1954 (that signified the creation of SEATO) required only that each party would act to meet the common danger in accordance with its constitutional processes.[20] The confusion over what this really meant was demonstrated by the fact that Washington said it was required to defend South Vietnam by the SEATO Treaty and Protocol whereas the other signatories said there was no such obligation (in that situation). A policymaker thus may add new commitments or emphasize old ones, and he or she may add certainty, stability, and precision to the situation, but the degree of change is dependent on the particular case.

When calculating whether to seek an alliance or not one must also recognize the possible disadvantages that might accrue. It must be remembered that states have a wide range of objectives only some of which are common. Others may be complementary, some are divergent, and some hostile. When joining an alliance either common or complementary objectives are sought and the alliance is presumed to help in their achievement. Noncommon objectives may be temporarily submerged or placed lower in priority, but they may reassert themselves later as conditions change. It is possible that a fall out among allies as noncommon objectives come to the fore may be more serious than if the alliance had never existed (witness the Sino-Soviet dispute).

Another problem is that alliances sometimes foster unrealistic hopes of the degree of cooperation that will ensue. The United States was chagrined at its

---

[20]For text, see U. S., Department of State, *Southeast Asia Treaty Organization*, Publication 6305, 1956.

NATO allies relatively unsympathetic view toward Israel in the October 1973 Arab-Israeli war, for example, but since each party views things in terms of its own objectives this was easy to understand. Whereas Washington was concerned with supporting Israel within the framework of a Soviet-American detente, its allies were worried about their oil supplies being shut off by the Arabs (plus being unhappy over America's lack of consultation with them concerning U. S. policy). Because of the differences in perspective, states also contribute different amounts to an alliance based on their assessment of its worth and the willingness of others to contribute, and this too can fuel differences among friends. A major issue today concerns the relative military and financial contribution of various members of NATO.

Another potential disadvantage is the lessening of autonomy that automatically ensues following alliance formation. The policymaker must remember that once a party joins an alliance its options are more limited; new obligations have been undertaken, resources expended, prestige invested, etc. As noted above, even in nonobligatory situations there may be pressure from alliance members to act in certain ways in the interest of alliance solidarity; nevertheless, though sometimes difficult, usually these problems can be handled without producing major negative consequences. Much more freedom limiting are situations in which events make alliance obligations operational. In some contingencies, of course, all members will agree on the degree of obligation and the nature and timing of the various actions required so the limitation on choice is not a problem. But there are other contingencies in which a party's alliance obligations may (unless one reneges on one's obligations) constrain choice severely, possibly even drawing one into an unwanted conflict. The system of rigid, competitive alliances that existed in Europe in the years immediately prior to World War I had such an option-limiting effect, and helped produce a situation in which a number of parties perceived themselves as having no choice but to fight.

Finally, alliances targeted on specific parties quite naturally worsen relations with those parties, and the net impact of this worsening may be more negative than positive. The tension level between the parties certainly will be raised, and the possibility of hostilities may also be increased. Because one is trying to increase relative capability, although the actions do not inevitably produce counteractions they certainly provide an incentive for the target to attempt to accomplish the same thing, either internally or via the formation of a counteralliance. The incorporation of West Germany in NATO in May 1955, for example, was followed within a week by the formation of the Warsaw Pact. And if a policymaker is himself or herself reacting to an alliance his or her action may reinforce the target's belief in its necessity for that alliance, and encourage efforts to strengthen and broaden it.

Alliance Prevention

The second major category of alliance adjustments is *alliance prevention.* Just as it is valuable for party X to enhance its relative capability by forming alliances, it is similarly valuable for its adversaries to do so. Clearly it is in X's interest to prevent this from occurring, to prevent X's opponent from obtaining allies.

How does one go about this? It will be remembered that all international politics is a dynamic mixture of cooperative, competitive, and conflictual relations of various configurations, involvements, and intensities. Similarly, the relations of any two parties also are a mixture. Each international party in fact deals with several others at any given time, having a number of relationships with each. The result is an extremely complex web of interactions. In an environment as fluid and uncertain as this, all choices affect a number of parties and have both costs and benefits. This includes choices for or against alliance formation. When a party enters an alliance it has (sometimes intuitively) determined that its net cost-benefit calculus will be improved by that action. Inevitably, certain objectives not served by the alliance have been subordinated to those the alliance is designed to achieve or protect, and policy options designed to achieve those nonalliance objectives have been foregone. *The way a policymaker operates to prevent an alliance from being formed is to alter the cost-benefit calculus of the leaders of the sought-after party in such a fashion as to make it more advantageous for them not to become the ally of one's opponent than to do so.*[21] The policymaker seeks to increase the conflictual proportion of the relationship mix between his or her opponent and the sought-after party, simultaneously enhancing the cooperative (or decreasing the conflictual or competitive) proportion of his or her own unit's relations with that actor. In more concrete terms, one tries to persuade the target that its nonalliance objectives should take priority, that they cannot be reasonably achieved if the alliance is formed, that if no alliance is formed the policymaker can help the target achieve them, and (thus) that the decision should be made against alliance formation.

Adolf Hitler's policy toward the Soviet Union in 1939, taking advantage of conditions and persuading Stalin not to ally with the British and French, provides a useful example. At first glance conditions could hardly have been less propitious. From the time of Hitler's coming to power in 1933 the Soviets had viewed him as a threat. Internally he had battled the Communists ferociously, and once gaining power persecuted them ruthlessly. In foreign policy

---

[21]Hartmann's discussion of the "cardinal principle" of "counterbalancing interests" is pertinent here. Hartmann, *The Relations of Nations*, Fifth Edition, especially pp. 18, 266.

one of Hitler's first acts as chancellor was to abrogate what had been a very fruitful German-Soviet mutual rearmament agreement. More than this, the Nazi leader stridently denounced both the Bolsheviks and the Russian people generally, labeling both as subhumans only one step above the Jews. Soviet leader Josef Stalin was firmly convinced that it was only a matter of time before the Nazis attacked. As a result of this conviction, from Hitler's accession onward Stalin had made a concerted effort to be more cooperative with the West (even if only temporarily), and in 1935 the U. S. S. R. had signed a five-year military defense pact with France. The same year a Soviet-Czech treaty also was signed.

The other major European actors in this situation were France and Britain. From the end of World War I on the French had had one fundamental end Paris had constructed a broadranging alliance system throughout Eastern Europe. One of the key links was a 1924 treaty with Czechoslovakia. By 1935 this system, if implemented, could have restrained Germany. Britain, however, saw things differently. London believed it was essential to make sufficient concessions to Berlin to satisfy what were perceived to be the Germans' legitimate and limited territorial objectives. Once that was done, it was thought, the British could maximize their own gains via the appropriate use of various nonconcern and concerned nonissue orientations. London's approach to the Nazis, therefore, was quite different from that of Paris, as witnessed by a naval agreement she signed with Germany in June 1935.

Although it hardly seemed likely at the time, events in the 1935–1939 period would prove to be such as to give Hitler his opportunity with Stalin. Let's briefly trace these developments. First, in 1935 Germany openly repudiated the disarmament clauses of the Versailles Treaty. Shortly thereafter came a crisis over an Italian attack on Ethiopia. Neither Britain nor France desired to use their forces against Italy in Africa, so they followed an ambiguous and somewhat vacillating course, one that encouraged Hitler and concerned Stalin.[22] While the League of Nations was busy with the Ethiopian crisis, Hitler reoccupied the Rhineland, again openly violating the Versailles Treaty. France, seemingly paralyzed, did nothing, while Britain did not consider the move too serious since, after all, it was German territory. In March 1938 the Germans "peacefully" annexed Austria; Britain and France just watched. Then, in September, the infamous Munich Agreement was signed, dismembering Czechoslovakia, ceding the Sudetenland to Germany, giving the German army the important Skoda munitions works and some valuable mountain fortifications.

---

[22]It was not yet clear which way Italy would go. Only recently she had taken a strong stand against Nazi action in Austria, and Britain and France did not want to permanently alienate her.

British Prime Minister Neville Chamberlain believed "peace in our time" had been achieved.

The Russians, who had not even been invited to Munich, worriedly saw the Germans moving East. Although they had an alliance with France, Paris, by refusing to honor the Franco-Czech Treaty, destroyed its alliance credibility; to Stalin, the Franco-Soviet Pact had become worthless. France and Britain now declared they would guarantee Czechoslovakia's new frontiers. But when in March 1939 Hitler annexed the remainder of that country Britain again failed to act, and the French, unwilling to confront Hitler alone, did likewise. Stalin strongly suspected that the British and French were seeking to embroil Germany and Russia in a mutually devastating war, the objective being the destruction of two menaces at once. Though he did negotiate with them re a possible alliance against Hitler, the talks were fruitless. The West Europeans, torn between the Nazis and the Communists, were either unable or unwilling to make the kinds of commitments Stalin desired.

Hitler was fully cognizant of Stalin's belief that London and Paris hoped to have the Germans and Russians destroy each other, and he began to skillfully fan these fears; Stalin's suspicions, already considerable, now reached even greater heights. The Nazi leader also played another card. A very important but sometimes underemphasized result of World War I was the fact that Russia, as Germany, had suffered enormous territorial losses; Communist or not, states that lose territory usually very much want to get it back, and the Soviet Union was no exception. This objective would be much more likely to be achieved if there were not an alliance with Britain and France than if there were one, and Hitler intimated that in the absence of such an alliance he would be most willing to cooperate. German-Soviet negotiations now were hurriedly undertaken, and Hitler specifically agreed that the Soviets ought to have a sphere of interest in Eastern Europe, regain a portion of Poland (lost in World War I), and recover Bessarabia from Rumania (similarly lost). These agreements soon were embodied in a secret protocol attached to the 1939 German-Russian Nonaggression Pact.[23] The possibility of a Soviet-British-French alliance was (at least at this time) dead.

Even though the situation in the 1930s had hardly been propitious for Hitler's efforts at alliance prevention, the Nazi leader—aided and abetted by British and French ineptitude, Stalin's fears, and certain other Soviet concerns—had been able to take advantage of the flow of events and exploit the Soviets' nonalliance interests shrewdly thereby preventing an alliance with Britain and a renewal or new pact with France. The strength of his opposition (Britain and

---

[23]Stalin also had a number of other reasons for making this agreement. See Chapter 12, pp. 327–328.

France) had been rendered relatively less than it would have been had the alliance(s) been formed, and the number of immediate antagonists had been reduced by one.

Alliance Fragmentation

The third basic type of alliance adjustment is *acting to bring about or encourage the fragmentation and possible dissolution of the opposition's alliance.* Let's briefly examine the problem of NATO fragmentation and then look in more depth at an example with great relevance for today, the Sino-Soviet rift.

When the North Atlantic Treaty Organization was established in 1949 the world power distribution was bipolar; the Soviet Union and the United States were so far superior in capability to everyone else (that it appeared?) that only the superpowers mattered. World War II unity had been replaced by the tensions of the Cold War, and there was a shared, intensely perceived threat of a Russian military attack in both Western Europe and Washington. Other issues were felt to be of considerably less significance; it was believed that the Soviet threat had to be countered by a defensive military alliance.

But over time many conditions changed.[24] Behind the NATO shield, and with Marshall Plan aid, Western Europe prospered. As states regained strength and became less dependent on Washington (even competing now in many areas) they began to assert their own independent conceptions of policy. A second alteration was in the area of threat perception. No longer did a Soviet attack appear imminent as a nuclear stalemate developed between the superpowers. Thus the major reason for NATO's existence seemed to be losing its significance. Third, this stalemate seemed to tie the hands of the superpowers and make it unlikely that one would undertake military action against the other. This allowed the smaller alliance partners more flexibility of action. Fourth, as discussed earlier, France began to question the credibility of America's promise to automatically aid Europe against a Soviet attack now that Washington was also vulnerable. Fifth, a growing fragmentation in Eastern Europe encouraged cross-alliance relations with less fear of retaliation. Sixth, the general movement of the United States and Russia after 1962 toward some kind of detente encouraged similar actions by the secondary allies. And seventh, intraalliance disagreements themselves, over both substance and coalition decision-making procedures, exacerbated the difficulties. These factors combined to produce a much less cohesive alliance.

[24]Useful in this regard are Francis A. Beer, *Integration and Disintegration in NATO*, Ohio State University Press, Columbus, 1969; Edwin H. Fedder, *NATO:The Dynamics of Alliance in the Postwar World*, Dodd Mead, New York, 1973; and Wolfram Hanrieder, *The United States and Western Europe*, Winthrop, Cambridge, 1974.

Now let's examine the Sino-Soviet dispute. The Soviet Union and People's Republic of China signed a treaty of alliance and friendship on February 14, 1950, officially creating the Sino-Soviet axis. In the West this was presumed to be a mere formalization of the status quo within the Soviet bloc. Over most of the next decade, amid innumerable statements of the permanent fraternal friendship of all Communists, billions worth of economic aid and technical assistance flowed from Moscow to Peking as did considerable military assistance. In return, the Chinese followed the Soviet ideological and political line, and occasionally helped to bridge the differences between Moscow and her European satellites.[25]

Yet a conflict began to develop in the late 1950s and by the early 1960s a full-fledged rift had occurred. What had happened?[26] There seem to have been many contributing factors. First, there were several framework features. Number one, the mere increase in Chinese capability over the decade naturally led her to assert her own views. Second, the vast territorial claims that China makes against Moscow began to throb like an open wound.[27] This was more troublesome because of a third factor, namely, the Chinese view of their own history. Considering themselves to be the "Middle Kingdom" receiving tribute from inferiors around them, they traditionally considered non-Chinese to be barbarians. Russians were felt to be particularly uncivilized. In turn, the Russians harbored a deeply felt (racial?) animosity toward the Chinese, seeing them as the latest in a long line of Asian threats stretching back to the Middle Ages. Fourth, there were personal antagonisms. Contrary to the belief of many Westerners, the Soviets had not always been particularly helpful to the Chinese Communists. In the 1920s they had forced the Chinese leadership to work with Chiang Kai-shek, for example, and after World War II Stalin had advised Mao (that "radish Communist") against fighting Chiang.[28] This resentment lingered on. Another personal element was Mao's belief (after Stalin's death in 1953) that he was the most authentic "revolutionary" left

[25]The Soviets assumed that a certain degree of "gratitude" would develop as a result of their aid; very little did, as is usually the case. See Chapter 9, pp. 256–258.

[26]There are a wealth of studies on this subject. Rather than footnote each point I will simply state that, in addition to standard texts on Soviet and Chinese Foreign Policy, the following works have been especially helpful and I am indebted to all of them: Edward Crankshaw, *The New Cold War: Moscow v. Peking,* Penguin, Baltimore, 1963; William E. Griffith, *Sino-Soviet Relations, 1964–65,* M.I.T. Press, Cambridge, 1967; William E. Griffith, *The Sino-Soviet Rift,* M.I.T. Press, Cambridge, 1964; G. F. Hudson, Richard Lowenthal and Roderick MacFarquhar, *The Sino-Soviet Dispute,* Praeger, New York, 1961; Klaus Mehnert, *Peking and Moscow,* G. P. Putnam, New York, 1963; and Donald S. Zagoria, *The Sino-Soviet Conflict, 1956–1961,* Princeton University Press, Princeton, 1962.

[27]See Chapter 3, p. 76.

[28]For further discussion of the Chinese Communist Revolution see Chapter 10, pp. 279–280.

alive and the major strategic thinker within the Communist camp. Finally, the problems confronting the Chinese—obtaining territorial "unification," trying to counter perceived security threats of overwhelming magnitude without either adequate military or geopolitical defenses, achieving a degree of economic development above even the most minimum level, creating domestic stability and order—were both enormous and in many ways dissimilar in degree and/or kind from those confronting the Soviets. Inevitably this led to differences in perspective and policy choice.

All of these framework features provided an explosive setting. As the years went by Chinese leaders began to assert their own policy interests and their desire to have an equal share in decision making within the Communist camp. Perhaps these problems in themselves would have been sufficient to bring about the rift, but this will never be known since several specific policy issues also arose.[29]

In the mid 1950s a major dispute arose over the "correct" interpretation of Marxist-Leninist thought (and over who was the correct interpreter thereof). At the 20th Congress of the Soviet Communist Party in 1956 Nikita Khrushchev stated that there was no "fatal inevitability" of war between the Socialists (Communists) and capitalism because of the strength of the Socialist camp. This seemingly contradicted the orthodox Leninist position that communists and capitalists could not exist side by side for any length of time, and that a series of terrible collisions would inevitably occur. The Chinese stoutly defended Lenin's precepts and felt that Moscow was demonstrably incorrect as well as overly cautious.[30] Furthermore, as we noted earlier, Peking was alarmed by the logical problem Khrushchev had created; if capitalists in some situations had the ability to avoid what previously were considered to be the inexorable laws of history, why couldn't they in others? Who could know what this might lead to?

A second problem area concerned trade and aid. Despite the considerable assistance received Chinese policymakers felt that Moscow's efforts were insufficient. First, most of the economic assistance had to be paid for out of exports, instead of being free. Second, on a per capita basis it was less than other states such as Outer Mongolia received. It also seemed as if neutrals like Egypt were treated better. Finally, and of particular significance, the Soviets refused

---

[29]It is extremely difficult to ascertain cause and effect here, both with regard to the relationship between the framework features and the specific policy issues, and within each grouping. We truly have a case of interrelated events (see Chapter 14 for more examples) and make no attempt to single out or define specific relationships.

[30]Although many interpreted Khrushchev's speech to indicate that a more accomodating policy toward the West would be forthcoming, his "adventurous" actions in the Second Berlin Crisis and Cuban Missile Crisis showed otherwise. See pp. 348 and 402–405.

to help the Chinese develop their own nuclear capability despite a 1957 promise to give Peking a sample bomb and data on its manufacture.

There were several other specific disagreements: (1) the Chinese bitterly resented Russia's refusal to help in the liberation of Formosa (Taiwan), a fundamental objective of Peking's policy. They also were irritated by Moscow's lukewarm support in the 1955 and 1958 crises over the offshore islands;[31] (2) there was disagreement over how to deal with nonaligned countries. The Chinese believed in continuously working for revolution by aiding local Communist parties, whereas the Russians were willing to aid non-Communist nationalists who might weaken Western influence (such as Egypt's President Nasser); (3) in 1958 the Chinese sought to revitalize their economy in what was known as the Great Leap Forward. Moscow said it would not work, refused aid, and said "I told you so" when it was a failure; (4) by 1960 there was serious fragmentation within the Communist bloc. The open Chinese courtship of Albania and others obviously aggravated relations with Russia; (5) in October 1962, after several years of intermittent tension and disagreement over precise boundary locations, Chinese troops attacked certain Indian provinces. The Soviets not only failed to support Peking, they actually provided armaments to New Delhi (pursuant to previous agreements);[32] (6) when Khrushchev agreed to remove Soviet missiles from Cuba in 1962, China called it appeasement of the capitalists; and (7) the Soviet signature of the Limited Nuclear Test Ban Treaty in 1963 was directly in opposition to Chinese desires for a nuclear capability.

In both of the cases, NATO and Sino-Soviet, potentially incompatible objectives were originally subordinated in view of the bipolar distribution of capabilities and the common perceptions of threat. As time passed and the nonsuperpowers gained strength, however, they began to assert themselves. Perceptions of threat became less certain and specific intraalliance policy differences arose. Particular incidents occurred that added to the fragmenting momentum, and a flexibility of approach became more evident. In the Sino-Soviet case open antagonism developed as specific incidents combined with certain fundamental features and changed conditions to produce a full-fledged dispute (that has erupted into border violence several times).

---

[31]Following their defeat by Communist forces in 1949 the Chinese Nationalists retreated to the island of Taiwan (Formosa). All Chinese consider Taiwan to be an integral part of China, and ever since their victory Communist leaders have announced their intention to liberate it. Nationalist forces, even after their loss, held onto some tiny islands between Taiwan and the mainland. In 1955, and again in 1958, the Communists shelled these islands heavily. In each instance American policymakers made it clear that they would participate in the islands' defense. The Russians, although condemning the American stance verbally, gave no indication they would do more than talk.

[32]See Chapter 10, p. 275 for further discussion.

A policymaker external to these or other alliances may be in a position to encourage fragmenting pressures. In a vein similar to alliance prevention, one's objective is to alter the cost-benefit calculus of certain parties, here to the end of making it more advantageous for them to leave the alliance than to stay in it. Recognizing that all policy choices have both advantages and disadvantages, that certain objectives are served by any alliance but others are not, and that certain nonalliance objectives and the policy options designed to achieve them have been foregone by alliance parties in the interest of alliance formation and cohesion, the external policymaker may be in a position to alter the target's policy by demonstrating the superior cost-benefit advantages of nonalliance objectives and the means of achieving or protecting them. If one is able to accomplish this, a degree of fragmentation will result. But there is a very important point to note here, that is, *in neither of our examples did external parties create the alliance schism; in both cases it resulted from intraalliance developments.* In other words, alliance fragmentation began in spite of, not because of, the policies of outsiders. Although external parties acted to take advantage of and encourage dissolution, they did not productively do so until after intraalliance fissures had developed.

This is not to say that a policymaker should never seek to bring about fragmentation. All situations are different; alliances vary in numerous ways as do the circumstances, the participants, etc.; if the opportunity presents itself, certainly one should carefully investigate whether, without entailing excessive risks, there might be a means of altering a particular party's cost-benefit calculus in a manner that would encourage dissolution. But it must be remembered that the alliance in question was formed for some reason; indeed, if it is your adversary's alliance, perhaps it was formed with you as the target. In many cases, perceived attempts at divide and rule may produce the opposite effect— driving the very alliance partners one is hoping to split together against what is perceived to be a common threat. In most situations it is dangerous for an external policymaker to unilaterally seek to create the conditions for, or actually bring about, alliance fragmentation. It is much more feasible to study the particulars and capitalize on trends already in existence.[33]

The evidence of state practice makes it clear that even in this age of nuclear weaponry policymakers continue to consider alliance adjustments to be of considerable importance. In the early and mid 1950s the Soviets (unsuccessfully) went to great lengths to prevent the Federal Republic of Germany from joining NATO, on numerous occasions they have undertaken very strong ac-

---

[33]Even the detachment of Italy from the Triple Alliance in World War I was possible only because of the existence of objectives that could only be accomplished at the expense of her alliance partner, Austria-Hungary, and objectives with which her alliance objectives directly conflicted.

tion to maintain (and enhance) the strength of the Warsaw Pact, and since the early 1960s they have expended much effort to develop an extensive if relatively informal alliance system via the use of so-called "Friendship treaties" in areas around their periphery and at strategic locations in the Third World. The United States has been greatly concerned over NATO's lack of cohesion, has sought to solidify its bilateral alliance ties, and has, by reorienting its Asian policy, acted to encourage exacerbating factors in the Sino-Soviet dispute (and has thereby increased Russia's security problems). Of course, nonnuclear parties also have continued to manifest concern with alliance adjustments, ranging from the forming of temporary alliances to overcome a common foe (such as the Patriotic Front formed in the 1970s by antagonistic feuding black nationalist factions in Rhodesia, their only unifying bond being the desire to eliminate the existing government) to actions designed to fragment the opposition's alliance (e.g., Israel's 1978 efforts that ultimately led to the signing of a separate peace treaty with Egypt without a stipulated binding linkage to a comprehensive Middle East settlement). Alliances or the lack thereof continue to affect capability relations, perceptions of threats to fundamental objectives, tension levels, the probability that force will or will not be employed, etc.; nuclear age or not, nuclear party or not, policymakers need to, and usually do, pay close attention to alliance formation, prevention, or fragmentation.

AUTONOMY LIMITATIONS

The final category of external techniques to increase relative capability is autonomy limitations. There are two basic types: (1) the creation of dependencies, and (2) manipulation of one's adversary's internal capability components. In each case the objective is to increase relative capability by decreasing the adversary's strength.

Creation of Dependencies

There are several possible types of dependencies but it is useful for the policymaker to think simply in terms of either economic or military dependence.[34]

---

[34]Historically another major type of dependency creation was the establishment of satellite states, the most prominent example being the post-World War II establishment by the Soviet Union of complete political, military, economic, and ideological control over the nominally independent states of Eastern Europe. Relying on the presence of the Red Army, cooperation between secret police organizations, and a ruthless use of economic, military, and communication techniques, almost complete subordination was achieved. Though important historically, only rarely is the creation of such dependencies a feasible option for policymakers today. One cannot, however, say that it is wholly passe; circumstances can be visualized in which it still would be feasible.

Economic dependency can be established in a wide range of circumstances.[35] There are many states that have much of their economic health based on the production and sale of one particular product.[36] Not only is it the source of revenue for internal purposes, it is also the primary means of obtaining foreign exchange to purchase foreign goods. Since many of the LDCs are essentially one product economies, and since export earnings often account for 75 to 80 percent of LDC foreign exchange resources, many times such parties are extremely vulnerable to external pressures. If one is in the position of being the primary market for their primary product considerable leverage may be possible and his or her decisions may have great impact. Of course, the availability of alternative markets, substitute products and so forth will affect this.

A similar possibility of foreign trade manipulation occurs if one's state is the primary supplier of necessary goods and services unobtainable domestically. If one needs certain machine parts in order to develop its aircraft industry and must rely on foreign sources for them, his or her economic position is clearly weak. Also, a state may be the primary supplier of critical resources, either natural or in the form of capital or technology. Perhaps the United States cannot run its industrial machine effectively without South African diamonds or OPEC petroleum, or Israel's economy cannot develop without American economic assistance to cover its balance of payments deficits. In each case some degree of economic dependence is established.

Each of these variations has one facet in common, namely, an outside party plays a primary role because it is the major purchaser or supplier of an economic necessity. The degree of dependence will depend on many things including target vulnerability, alternative sources or markets, substitutability, bargaining skill, willpower, priority of objectives, relation to other issues, and the use of other instruments of policy.

But there is another kind of economic dependency one might seek to create, this one more insidious and deep seated. A very effective means of control occurs when one is able to manage or control the major economic enterprises within a given country. Control may be established by capital investment from governmental and/or private sources. Perhaps a given sector of the economy simply cannot develop and considerable outside financing is necessary. In this

---

[35]This analysis assumes that the policymaker is able to control and direct the personnel and institutions of his or her own state. This is obviously not always the case as the discussion in Chapter 15 demonstrates. Despite the fact that this assumption departs to some extent from reality, it is highly useful for the purpose here of showing various aspects of the creation of dependency. The student will simply have to recognize that in some "real world" situations policymakers have less autonomy and authority than these comments would indicate, and would have to adjust accordingly.

[36]Pertinent to the entire discussion of the creation of dependency is the analysis of the economic policy instrument in Chapter 9.

case particular outside sources may, via the quantity and terms of financing, take over effective control. The banking and financing institutions of all market economies play a key role in growth and development through their impact on credit and the money supply, and penetration of these institutions may give one a lock grip on local economic performance.

Many times outside parties establish new firms or take over the ownership of existing ones. In these cases much production and employment comes under the control of foreign entrepreneurs. This is particularly critical when such enterprises operate in key sectors of the economy. Sometimes top and middle management is either foreign or foreign selected, and its decisions are at least partially designed to achieve foreign rather than local objectives. Today, as discussed in some depth in Chapter 1, multinational corporations participate in certain aspects of international politics with an impact that sometimes is equal to or greater than that of many states.[37] Although domination occurs less frequently than is sometimes imagined and alleged, there have been a number of instances in which foreign-based MNCs in fact have come to dominate host state economies, creating what amount to economic dependencies. It should be again pointed out though, as it was in Chapter 1, that (although there are exceptions) MNCs usually act in their own interest and not as agents of their home state. Thus, in most of these cases the party whose capability is being relatively enhanced is a nonstate actor, the MNC.

A second type of dependency to be established is *military*. In the discussion of alliance formation it was stated that often a major motivating force is the desire to increase relative capability by combining strength. While this is sometimes true it often is not the whole story. Sometimes a powerful state will seek an alliance with a less powerful one in order to establish its dominance over the latter. Anytime a lesser power joins an alliance it runs this danger. There are those in the United States and Western Europe, policymakers and analysts alike, who believe that the creation of military dependencies was a major (though not the only) Soviet objective in the plethora of friendship treaties it concluded in the 1960s and 1970s with states around its periphery and in strategically significant areas of Africa, South Asia, and the Middle East.

Military dependency may be established in specific ways. Perhaps an agreement has been reached to establish a military base. The presence of foreign troops on one's soil provides many opportunities for leverage. Maybe the dominating state is involved in training and directing local forces, or perhaps in supplying their needs in terms of weapons systems and replacement parts. Obviously the recipient in this case is under some pressure to adhere to the wishes of the supplier. Many times various kinds of assistance programs have certain restrictions concomitant with them. Another point, sometimes over-

---

[37]See Chapter 1, pp. 22–27.

looked, is that the constant contact provides innumerable opportunities for subtle influences, influences often unseen by outside observers.

But military dependence does not necessarily mean equivalent political influence. Dependency can arouse resentment and a policymaker in today's world must recognize that there are alternative sources for his recipient. While the dependent state has certain needs it also is trying to achieve its *own* objectives. Depending on its own analysis of the relationship between the assistance and its needs, in the context of supplier alternatives and its vulnerability it may suddenly seek to become less dependent. As indicated above, in the summer of 1972 when Egyptian President Sadat concluded that Soviet aid was prolonging rather than altering the territorial situation with Israel, Soviet advisers were peremptorily expelled.

A policymaker thus finds that the creation of economic or military dependencies does not automatically bring about a significant increase in relative capability. Because it sometimes does, however, it certainly is an option to consider. Furthermore, it has a number of characteristics that give it considerable appeal. First, generally the process begins on a voluntary, cooperative basis so one is not open to charges of imperialism (although this is still a question of degree). Indeed, in many instances the parties that later become dependent are the ones that originally most energetically seek, and for a while work hardest to sustain, the very programs that eventually result in their dependency; frequently they vigorously request the sale of new arms, the formation of alliances, foreign loans, technology transfers, the investment of foreign capital, etc. Second, it is very difficult to determine just when a dependency does or does not exist; a policy designed to achieve this objective thus is difficult both to detect and to counter, by either the target or interested extrasituational parties. Third, there are a whole host of tactics one can employ, meaning tactical flexibility is considerable. Finally, relatively minimal resource and prestige commitments are required; the costs and risks are comparatively small.

Capability Component Manipulation

The second major type of autonomy limitation is the manipulation of the adversary's internal capability components.[38] The policymaker may be trying to limit his target's capacity to control his internal power factors and thereby decrease his relative strength, or perhaps to actually decrease the quality or quantity of the resources. Possibly one is even seeking to influence the composition or structure of the target government itself. Through a wide variety of possible actions one seeks to intervene in the affairs of another, interfering with (or

---

[38]The discussion here is restricted to means short of guerilla warfare. That topic will be considered in Chapter 10.

penetrating) the internal processes of that country to its detriment and his party's resultant benefit.[39]

Attempts to manipulate internal capability components (variously called covert, subversive, or clandestine actions) are widespread in international politics, being the province neither of particular parties nor of particular time periods. In the 1930s, for example, the Nazis provoked numerous incidents, infiltrated key organizations, indulged in kidnappings and various types of terrorism, staged demonstrations, and promoted racial enmity, etc., in both Austria and Czechoslovakia. Since gaining power in 1917 Soviet Communists have been extensively involved in manipulative activities, the coup in Czechoslovakia in 1948 being perhaps their most successful effort. The United States has had an extensive covert action program since the late 1940s, engaging in acts that have ranged from financially supporting (to the tune of three million dollars) the election of Christian Democrat Eduardo Frei in the 1964 Chilean election to the organizing and abetting of the overthrow of the Arbenz regime in Guatemala in 1954. Despite frequent pretensions to the effect that they are always innocent victims, many of the smaller states also heavily engage in efforts to manipulate internal capability components. Clearly, for example, in the 1970s a number of African states were involved in efforts to undermine the regime of Ian Smith in Rhodesia, and in the late 1950s and 1960s agents of Egypt's Gamal Nasser ranged throughout the Arab world promoting the Egyptian leader and his brand of pan-Arabism. And national liberation organizations, of course, almost "by definition" undertake such activities.

Policymakers desirous of taking this step have an enormous variety of potential methods at their disposal. The following is no more than a sampling. A major component of capability involves the degree of support that a government receives from its populace, and a major objective may be to lessen that support. Perhaps there are ethnic, racial, or religious rivalries that can be exploited, or class differences containing the seeds of conflict that can be worsened. Maybe one can infiltrate the leading labor organizations, arouse or exacerbate their bitterness toward management and bring about disastrous strikes. Sometimes it is possible to infiltrate the media of communications and turn key spokesmen against the government. Perhaps there is a situation that may be used to create a scandal and bring down a certain official or administration, or maybe there is general unrest and one can help sponsor civil disturbances. Possibly, through covert propaganda facilities, the policymaker can deluge a receptive population with "news" about its government's failures and duplicity. Maybe false rumors can be started or stories "planted" in the press to

---

[39]While much ink has been used attempting to distinguish between intervention and interference, developing a precise definitional distinction is of little concern to policymakers. Here the terms are used interchangeably.

create further disaffection. All of these and many other procedures affect the support a government receives.

Of course more tangible power components may be affected also. Governmental factors influence capability and perhaps it is possible to seriously impede the policymaking machinery or deliberately distort the information process on which it is based. Perhaps one can harm military capability by ferreting out defense secrets or by influencing training procedures or strategic conceptions so as to leave the adversary unprepared for the most likely contingencies. Perhaps equipment and facilities can be sabotaged. Possibly economic capacity can be harmed by infiltrating key organizations and then manipulating them in ways contrary to the state's objectives, or maybe one can contribute to an inflation psychology by various covert methods. Perhaps the policymaker can influence the outcome of internal power contests, including elections, and bring about a regime change. And so the list could be extended but to no good purpose at this time; the point is clear enough.

Increasing relative capability by manipulating the adversary's internal capability components is becoming more important, both quantitatively and qualitatively. The reasons seem clear enough. First, the use of techniques for this purpose is difficult to detect and prove. Second, the cost, in terms of personnel, equipment, finances, and prestige, is relatively small. This means that nearly all states can afford to use such techniques. Third, there is less risk of opposition retaliation or public condemnation if discovered than if more traditional means were used. Fourth, most states are vulnerable to some kind of manipulation, including the superpowers. Because of the dangers of modern general warfare, and the nuclear stalemate as well, even the superpowers are unlikely to use all out force unless grossly provoked. One may certainly expect to see a continuation of this trend throughout the decade.

COMMENTS

Having decided what external means of increasing relative capability may be productively utilized in the specific situation the policymaker has nearly completed the policy formulation process, previously having discovered who is involved and what situational configurations exist, determined the other parties' objectives and provisionally determined his or her own, ascertained the capability relationships and the linkages pertinent to the particular policy context, and determined which orientation options could be most fruitfully employed. The reader may have noticed that we said "nearly completed." The reason the word "nearly" was used is that the task of policy formulation is never "finished." *Policy formulation is a dynamic, ongoing process in which new judgments and appraisals, reappraisals, alterations, and modifications are continuous, inevitable, and pervasive.* This, for example, is why we continually spoke of the "provisional" determination of one's objectives; except for achieving or protecting those outcomes of fundamental importance (such as survival) one's objectives are always provisional and subject to alteration. The student must remember that the real-life policy formulation process is vital and dynamic, constituting an everchanging challenge to policymakers.[40]

There is one key aspect of the policy formulation process which, for reasons of textual space and symmetry, has not yet received the in-depth treatment it deserves, namely, the analysis of internal capability components. This is the task to which we turn in Part 3.

Part 3
THE FOUNDATION
OF CAPABILITY

In Chapter 4 it was pointed out that capability analysis
is a critically important part of the policy formulation
process. As discussed therein, the policymaker must recognize the relational nature of power and the fact that
capability analysis is relevant primarily when utilized in
terms of specific policy situations. These facts are per-
fectly accurate and provide necessary warnings against
simply compiling a list of a state's internal capability
components and assuming that their sum equals
"power." But one must not go too far in this regard.
Although the mere possession of a given mix of components does not automatically guarantee influence, without strength in certain areas a state can not be influential. A state's capability is ultimately based on certain
internal factors and in the long run they will in large
part determine its influence-potential. To put it another
way, the internal capability components are the essential
building blocks that comprise the foundation for international influence.

   When thinking about the components of capability
the first things that come to mind are the tangible factors: geographical influences, population characteris-

tics, natural resources, economic strength, and military power. It is apparent that such factors are highly significant and that they must constitute a major part of any capability calculus. These tangible elements will be analyzed in depth in Chapter 7. But the story does (or should) not end at this point because there are a number of intangible features that also need to be taken into account, features that significantly affect the degree to which, and how, the tangible components will be utilized. These intangible elements—governmental functions, characteristics of society, individual policymaker quality, and party uniqueness—provide the subject matter for Chapter 8.

7

Capability Components: Tangible

There are certain factors that directly impact on a party's international capability, tangible features that constitute building blocks for the operational exercise of influence. The major tangible components are geography, population, natural resources, economic strength, and military strength.

GEOGRAPHY

One of the most important and enduring components of capability is geography.[1] Its major constituent parts are location, size, climate, topography, and shape.[2]

Location

The location of a state in relation to other states is a geographical fact of immense importance. Who is or is not one's neighbor has significant strategic implications and can have considerable impact on one's national security.

---

[1]Usefully related topics are the discussion of the state attribute of internal control in Chapter 1, the examination of fundamental objectives in Chapter 3, and the analysis of increasing capability externally via territorial changes in Chapter 6.

[2]Another geographical factor is natural resources. Because of its scope and significance, however, we shall give it separate treatment.

Let's look at a specific example. Assume that one's state has several thousand miles of common border with a state that has great potential strength, and that the latter claims that over 500,000 square miles of its territory are being illegally occupied. Assume further that there is competition for the leadership of an ideological movement, disagreement over the correct ideological interpretation of certain elements within that movement, there are military forces of considerable strength arrayed against each other along the border, and that serious incidents occur. Furthermore, suppose that over the last 15 to 20 years there have been a series of disagreements over practical policy questions such as military assistance and economic programs, and that today there is a great power that is wooing both states and at the same time is a potential adversary. If one is a policymaker in this position the fact of geographical proximity combined with the factors previously mentioned obviously presents a policy situation very different from any faced by the United States. This, of course, represents a simplified and generalized thumbnail sketch of the Sino-Soviet border situation as seen from Moscow.[3] Quite clearly if Canada were hostile and powerful American-Canadian relations would be vastly different.

It is essential in discussing location and proximity, of course, to look at more than just one neighbor. The Soviets not only share Siberia's lengthy southern frontier with China, they also have a resurgent powerful offshore neighbor to the east (Japan), several unreliable and potentially hostile eastern and central European satellites to the west, and beyond them as a "near-neighbor" the already powerful and potentially yet more powerful Federal Republic of Germany, a state whose territorial situation remains highly troublesome.[4] This locational configuration, plus the mixed but potentially adversarial relationship with the United States, inevitably creates a multithreat perspective, a perspective in which geographical factors figure enormously. A related point of note is that such geographical features strongly impact other components. To take but one example, within the multithreat perspective just described, and irrespective of whatever "offensive" objectives the Kremlin conceivably might have, Russia's geostrategic circumstances (including her huge size, covered in the next section) dictate that its military needs to have a very large standing army with great reserves, huge quantities of tactical air defense weapons systems, an immense logistical infrastructure, considerable intermediate- and medium-range air striking power, and naval strength to shortstop whatever adversarial resupply may come to its opponents via the sea lanes.[5]

---

[3] Also see Chapter 6, pp. 147–149.

[4] See Chapter 3, p. 76, Chapter 13, pp. 362–364, and Chapter 14, pp. 394–395.

[5] Of course the Soviet armed forces also have many other characteristics. Here we are only speaking of those attributes that are more or less inevitable in light of the geostrategic circumstances.

The geographical position of the United States is not at all similar to that of the U. S. S. R. (and her policymakers' perceptions consequently are often equally asymmetrical). The continental United States is separated from the Eurasian continent by bodies of water approximately 3000 miles wide to the east and 6000 miles wide to the west. For the eighteenth, nineteenth, and early twentieth centuries this sea distance was an immense defensive asset as the oceans constituted significant barriers to invasion.[6] Because of changes in technology, of course, they are no longer as formidable as they once were since the high seas can act as highways as well as barriers and intercontinental missiles can cross them without difficulty. Nevertheless, the lack of proximity to one's potential adversaries is still a matter of some import because it is much more difficult to successfully attack and/or occupy across thousands of miles of ocean than across adjacent frontiers. Furthermore, because of the lack of proximity border incidents and disputes are much less likely to occur.

Consider this fact: only the United States, among the medium or great powers of the world, "grew up" in a location where it had no great power neighbors, and continues to exist in such a favorable position.[7] This lack of great power neighbors allowed a much wider range of policy orientation options than otherwise would have been possible, permitting, for example, Washington to choose an orientation of avoidance for most of the nineteenth century. Had it been located adjacent to a potential adversary this would not have been feasible.

Two other locational factors need mentioning. First, sometimes a state is strategically significant primarily because of its location, much more important than it would be if it were situated somewhere else. Korea, because of its proximity to China, Russia, and Japan, is a good example. Mozambique is another, located in southeastern Africa and sharing common borders with six other countries: South Africa, Zimbabwe (Rhodesia), Zambia, Swaziland, Malawi, and Tanzania. Proximity to major and/or large numbers of states automatically confers a degree of value. Many times policymakers are concerned with what to the general public seem to be relatively insignificant countries for reasons that are not apparent; often strategic location is the answer. In such instances certain countries become important as a result of their proximity to states of greater intrinsic strategic value, not because of any inherent worth of their own.

---

[6]Of course wide oceans do not, by themselves, provide an insuperable obstacle to attack and many lands were successfully invaded across wide oceans prior to, during, and after this period. Nevertheless, the seas *did* provide an immense defensive advantage in comparison to countries who were faced with the situation of a common land boundary with a potentially hostile, strong state.

[7]See Hartmann, *The New Age of American Foreign Policy*, Chapter 2.

The second point is that because of their location certain states possess or are in a position to largely control certain specific geographic assets. Such assets may be enormously important. The Cape of Good Hope at the southern tip of Africa is a case in point. Around it pass most of the West's internationally exchanged oil and an immense quantity of strategic supplies. Because of this it is obvious that South Africa's control and direction would be very important even if for no reason other than her location.[8] Since the outer limits of location are the state's boundaries and since boundaries sometimes change, the frontiers of one's location also are sometimes altered. Such a change may affect the control of strategic geographic assets.[9] As a result of World War II Russia reacquired Southern Sakhalin and obtained the Kurile Islands (which lie to the north of the Japanese island of Hokkaido). The main base for the Soviet Pacific Fleet is Vladivostok, seaborne access to which is via the Sea of Japan. Transit by the southern straits could easily be blocked by forces based in the Japanese islands, but because of Moscow's possession of the Kuriles Russian ships can move into the Sea of Okhotsk and reach Vladivostok from the north. As Colin Gray points out:

> The physical geography of its Siberian littoral, with its offshore island chains, explains very clearly why the Soviet Union will never cede the Kurile Islands back to Japan. If the Kuriles were returned to Japan, the Japanese (or a hostile power using Japanese-provided facilities) could render the Sea of Okhotsk a "closed sea" to the Soviet Union.[10]

Size

The second major geographical factor is size.[11] The Soviet Union is more than two and one-half times as large as the United States, stretching 7000 miles east to west and 3000 north to south and comprising nearly one-seventh of the land area of the earth. This territorial vastness has significantly contributed to the failure of all modern attempts to conquer her (as Napoleon, Hitler, and others found out when, in a sense, the country began to conquer them).

---

[8]Of course there are other reasons, natural resources and ethical concerns being two of the most important.

[9]See Chapter 6, p. 132, for another example.

[10]Gray, p. 43.

[11]For analytical reasons our discussion considers each geographical factor separately. In reality they are related and the policymaker must analyze the impact of the particular "mix" on capability. For example, massive size plus proximity can easily be viewed by one's neighbors as "automatically" posing a security threat. See Alain-Gerard Marsot, "The Chinese Perspective," in Sudershan Chawla, Melvin Gurtov, and Alain-Gerard Marsot, eds., *Southeast Asia Under the New Balance of Power*, Praeger, New York, 1974, Ch. 4.

Large size automatically yields certain benefits. It gives a nation's army room to retreat without surrender, room to hide to fight another day. It also allows the location and dispersal of critical population, economic, military, and governmental facilities and centers far from the borders, thus increasing their chances of survival in case of invasion or nuclear attack. Although this may be thought to have less significance today because of the advent of nuclear weapons, since most countries and most conflicts are nonnuclear and since even the nuclear powers may participate in nonnuclear warfare, it is still of considerable importance. A final military advantage of great size, if combined with a large population, is that a defeated large country would be very difficult to occupy and control. As A. F. K. Organski has stated, "The occupation of China would be formidable: it would require more soldiers and administrators than the United States possesses."[12]

A very small country possesses none of these advantages and is much more vulnerable to invasion, conquest, and occupation.[13] However, Japan's decisive defeat of China and Russia in 1894 and 1904, and Israel's four consecutive military victories over its Arab adversaries underline the fact that size alone is not determinative.

But it is not an unmixed blessing to be big. For example, a large area is sometimes considered to confer the nonmilitary advantage of providing room for a substantial population, itself a major component of power. This is true, but in and of itself means little; mere space can just as easily be a source of weakness and a temptation to invasion as a source of strength. An area must be able to support a large population for it to be a positive element, and this capacity depends on factors other than size. For example, the Rub al Khali (the "Empty Quarter") in Saudi Arabia is useful only as a barrier to invasion because it is incapable of supporting human life on any scale.

Great size can have other disadvantages. There is a point beyond which efficiency decreases. As has been true in Russia, for example, there can be difficulties in developing the efficient transportation and communication systems necessary to tie the country together. Sheer size can easily multiply the number and the complexity of the problems with which the government must deal, and this in turn may well lead to a burgeoning, overbearing governmental bureaucracy. If additional size means that various nationality groups will be incorporated within the borders, this too could lead to internal discontent.

Though great size does have its drawbacks policymakers seldom feel that the disadvantages equal the advantages. Therefore, other things being equal, if

---

[12]A. F. K. Organski, *World Politics*, Second Edition, Knopf, New York, 1968, p. 129.

[13]This factor may contribute to an exceptional security consciousness and a marked tendency to act quickly and decisively when threats are perceived. This certainly has been one of the prime factors shaping Israel's political-military policy.

one has the choice between decreasing, maintaining, or increasing territory the latter almost always will be chosen. It is important to remember the obvious yet sometimes underemphasized point that boundaries are created by people. This being so, people can change them. To illustrate, witness the changes in Israel's geographic configuration following the June War of 1967, changes that allowed her to occupy territory about seven times larger (in terms of square miles) than her pre-1967 area (see Map I). Many Israelis feel that, given the size, firepower, and initiative of Egypt's and Syria's forces, if Israel had not had the strategic depth provided by the Sinai desert and the Golan Heights the nature and perhaps the outcome of the October 1973 hostilities would have been quite different.

Control of one's neighbors may have an effect similar to extension of size because it moves the area of potential border conflict closer to the enemy and further from the homeland. Certainly the activities of the Soviet Union after World War II in Central and Eastern Europe extended Soviet "boundaries" far into Europe. In case there would be an attack again from or by Germany, the attack would begin far from the heart of the fatherland.[14]

Climate

The third geographical feature affecting capability is climate. Certain points are evident in this regard. There needs to be sufficient heat, a long enough growing season, sufficient rainfall (or irrigation possibilities), and soil of minimum quality in order for a country to produce crops. Otherwise it will be dependent on foreign sources to keep from starving.[15] Obviously there are areas of the world where these climatic conditions are not present: great portions of Canada, Alaska, Greenland, Soviet Union, western China, and Antarctica are too cold and their growing season is too short; desert areas in the Middle East, North Africa, and the interior of Australia are too arid for cultivation, and there are many areas of the world where the soil is too low in nutrients or is so rocky it is nigh unto impossible to grow crops even with artificial fertilizers and modern technology.

Another climatic consideration is whether there are areas of the world that are so hot or so cold that human beings cannot function optimally with the result that these areas can never produce states with significant capability.

[14]For a concise examination of this point as it figured in Soviet policymaking in the immediate post-war era, see Adam B. Ulam, *Expansion and Coexistence: The History of Soviet Foreign Policy, 1917-67*, Praeger, New York, 1968, Chapter 8.

[15]See pp. 188-190 for further discussion of agricultural capacity. Although "soil" might be discussed with reference to natural resources, because of its obvious relationship to the other conditions discussed it was felt that it made more sense to include it under this heading.

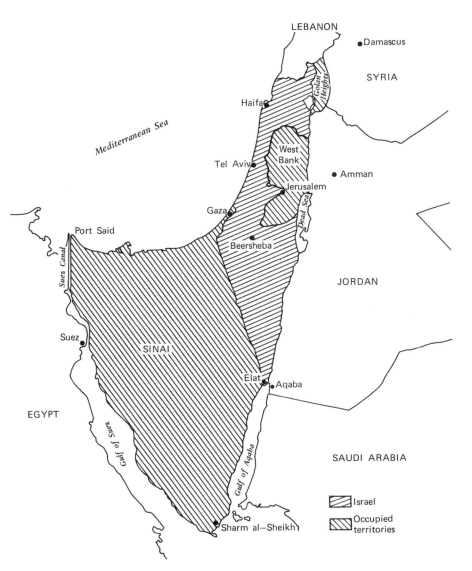

Map I. "Israel" before and after 1967 war.

It has been suggested that a great power cannot exist outside of the temperate zones, that the human organism cannot function efficiently outside the middle latitudes and therefore parties external to such regions are doomed to insignificance. A cursory glance at history reveals clearly that many of the greatest powers and empires indeed have been located in the temperate zones. But was this a cause-and-effect relationship or not? After all, many great civilizations of the past such as the Mayans and the great African empires flourished in relatively tropical and semitropical climates. Some observers seem to assume that the nontemperate areas of the world will never produce a great power because they have not done so in industrial times. Are climatic conditions between 20 degrees north and 20 degrees south of the equator so enervating that significant consistent human achievement is precluded?

No one really knows the answer to this question. Because of this it really is not very productive to make sweeping statements concerning the effect of climate on capability. There is no gainsaying the fact that human vitality and energy levels are to some degree effected by climate, but no one knows precisely how and how much. Three additional points are worth considering in this regard. First, what is "comfortable" to one people may be very uncomfortable to another, and vice-versa. Since there have been great powers in almost all non-arctic areas of the world at one time or another, obviously many have come from areas certain other parties would view as highly unpleasant. It is simply a fact that enormous climatic variations exist and at one time or another most all populated regions have produced actors with significant capability. To a West European the long, dry Mediterranean summer may hardly be conducive to vigorous activity but the past has been filled with the exploits of Assyria, Babylonia, Persia, Rome, Greece, the Arabs, and so on. A second point is that, as history shows, people are highly adaptable: although there are (still undefined) limits, within certain bounds people have made numerous adjustments in the quest to "get along" with their climate. And as modern knowledge grows changes in diet, activity, personal hygiene, and medicine may enable further productive responses to occur. Finally, it is at least plausible to suggest that with advancing technology it may become possible to modify the environment within which people work sufficiently to largely mitigate the various energy-inhibiting effects of climate. This would not be total, of course, and it would be expensive and time consuming, but it is a process that conceivably is within humanity's grasp. One cannot be sure it will happen on any grand scale, but even microchanges might significantly enhance the ability of peoples long accustomed to oppressive conditions to increase their performance levels.

Topography

A fourth major geographical facet is topography. Topography, of course, has an impact on climate. Wind, temperature, rainfall, and soil conditions are influenced by the lay of the land, by the relative position of waterways within the country, by the height and location of mountains and valleys, and so forth. Topography also has important internal effects on the country. The location of plains, mountains, rivers, lakes, and valleys will have a considerable impact on both transportation and communication. These factors also have an extremely important effect on the location, density and unity of the population, the ease of moving military forces from one point to another, and on patterns of economic distribution and development.

Topographical factors also have an important strategic value vis-à-vis other nations and have sometimes set limits on expansion. Great mountain ranges like the Himalayas, the Alps, and the Pyrenees have served this function. A lack of natural barriers also is important. Consider the situation with respect to peninsular Europe from the perspective of a Soviet policymaker. There are no natural barriers separating the U. S. S. R. from its western neighbors. Historically many times the north European plain from Germany's Rhine River eastward has provided a convenient avenue for invasion. Indeed, there is a 700-mile-wide gateway into (and out of) the Soviet Union between the Black and Baltic Seas. And once attacking forces are into European Russia there are no major impediments until one reaches the Ural Mountains, no land over 1400 feet high. These topographical facts inevitably condition the intensity and nature of the response by the Soviet Union and the states of Western Europe to each other. This has considerable significance with the division of Germany and the impact (or potential impact) that a reduction of forces in Central and Eastern Europe on the part of the United States and the Soviet Union might have.

Though topographical features have considerable strategic significance and definitely shape and condition parties' policies in many ways, they are not wholly determinative (any more than any other single factor ever is). For example, even major barriers to attack can, under the right conditions, either be overcome or circumvented; they make the task more difficult but not impossible. On the Syrian side of the 40-mile-long armistice demarcation line with Israel that was established after the 1948-1949 Palestine War sit the mountainous Golan Heights (see Map I). Along the northern half of the line the mountains rise very steeply at or near the frontier, while along the southern part they slope more gradually for a few miles before accelerating their rate of rise. Naturally difficult to climb, either immediately or shortly after crossing the boundary, in the 1949-1967 period they were heavily fortified by Damascus and came to constitute a formidable defensive position. Despite all this, Israeli Defense Forces successfully captured the Heights in less than three days in the June 1967 war.

Because of topography the Golan Heights have enormous strategic salience in the Arab-Israeli conflict. Prior to 1967 the Syrians were able to lob mortar shells down on the Israeli settlements below with relatively little opposition. Obviously the Israelis do not desire to restore that situation. The Heights also are important for other reasons. They contain one of the sources of the Jordan River and overlook Lake Tiberias (Kinneret, the Sea of Galilee), thus potentially imperiling Israel's vital water supply; the Transarabian pipeline crosses them on its way to terminals in Lebanon; finally, the great city of Damascus is directly accessible across flat land to the east. Given the Heights' strategic importance it is extremely unlikely that any Israeli policymaker would negotiate an agreement that provided for full withdrawal and a restoration of Syrian sovereignty. Because of their geographical features the Golan Heights have too much strategic value to be an object of this kind of bargaining.

Shape

The final geographical feature affecting capability is shape. In some cases a state's configuration can be of enormous significance, especially if other geographical features such as size also are disadvantageous. As noted earlier, pre-1967 Israel was very small. More than this she possessed relatively long frontiers and very little depth, and thus was constantly faced with the possibility of a knifelike attack cutting her in two. This was particularly true with respect to the area usually referred to as the West Bank, land that had been controlled by Jordan since the 1948-1949 Palestine War. The armistice lines had been drawn in a manner such that at some points Jordanian forces in the West Bank could advance to points less than 10 miles from the Mediterranean Sea, and no part of central Israel (which contained three-fourths of her population and industrial infrastructure) was more than 15 miles from the water. These factors, plus the topographical fact that the central plains flat lands contain no topographical barriers (in direct contrast to the Judean and Samarian mountains and hills in the West Bank) created what the Israelis perceived as a strategic Achilles heel and a constant temptation to attack by a hostile party.[16] Israel's victory in 1967 gave her much more defensible boundaries by resting her eastern boundary on the Jordan River, greatly lessening the danger of divide and conquer tactics (see Map I). The greater security afforded by the changed geographical configuration will certainly make Israeli policymakers hesitant to relinquish military control over the West Bank. Never again do they wish to be put into a position where a blitzkrieg might effectively partition the country.

Sometimes the implications of shape are altered by a change in neighbors. The country of Czechoslovakia was created from portions of the defeated Austro-Hungarian Empire after World War I. A long narrow state, she was bordered on the west by an unhappy Germany and shared more than one-half of her northern frontier with that same country. Germany had been stripped

---

[16]This has direct relevance to Israel's adamant opposition to the creation of an independent Palestinian state in this area. Valuable in understanding the Israelis' strategic perceptions is Yigal Allon, "Israel: The Case for Defensible Borders," *Foreign Affairs*, October 1976, pp. 38-53.

of many territories by the Allies after the war and her people were bitterly resentful.[17] It was very clear that most Germans wanted those territories back, and would be willing to make sacrifices to get them. In addition, there were significant German minorities in many non-German states, including nearly three million in the Sudetenland region of Czechoslovakia, and the Nazis wanted them in an enlarged "Germany" also. In addition to having this potential enemy to the west and north, a considerable portion of Czechoslovakia's southern boundary was shared with the Germanic state of Austria, itself an object of Nazi expansion. Thus, when Hitler annexed Austria in March 1938 he flanked the Czechs on three sides and their defense problems became much more extreme (a not unimportant consideration at Munich in the fall).

POPULATION

A second major component of capability is population. To properly determine its role one must analyze questions of size, ratios of productive to nonproductive elements, educational levels, density, and spatial distribution and trends.

Size

The first aspect to be investigated is sheer size. How many people are there in this particular country? It is sometimes said that the relationship of population size to capability is such that it is probably impossible to be a medium or great power without a relatively large population.[18] Why is this so? The reason usually given first is that a large population is necessary to have an effective military force.

It is true that there has been no modern military power with more than local influence that did not have a large population, and it is also true that despite advanced technology large masses of human beings still fight many wars. Furthermore, large modern armed forces require vast quantities of men to manufacture, supply, operate, and repair their highly sophisticated weapons and support systems. Finally, in a war of any length, a large population is necessary to keep the domestic economy in operation so it can contribute to the war effort.

Although these statements are accurate, if one stopped analyzing at this point one would get a very distorted picture. This argument deals primarily

[17]Germany lost Upper Silesia, the Polish Corridor, Danzig, Eupen-Malmedy, part of Schleswig-Holstein, and Alsace-Lorraine.

[18]Morgenthau, *Politics Among Nations*, Fifth Edition, p. 125. He states: "no country can remain or become a first-rate power which does not belong to the more populous nations of the earth."

with one kind of military conflict, a conventional war over a considerable length of time between relatively equal modern adversaries. Although this is important, there are several types of conflict to which this concept is inappropriate. The development of a nuclear striking force does not necessarily require a large population, nor does the ability to launch a decisive first-strike attack with highly sophisticated forces against technologically inferior and less trained opponents. Perhaps even more critically, in today's world a wide range of guerilla and insurgent military activities may be successfully undertaken by states without large populations.[19] None of this is to gainsay the potential military advantage that a large population can yield, but only to point out that one must evaluate it in terms of the nature of the conflict and the parties involved.

A second reason that possessing a large population is usually important is its relation to economic strength. A large population is essential for the development of an economic system sufficiently advanced to provide the array of economic tools necessary to influence other parties over an extended period of time. And unless a state has a large number of people it is extremely difficult to develop both the quantity and the quality of skills and capabilities that are required by the highly interdependent, specialized, and technologically advanced systems of the industrialized world.

A large population contributes to economic strength not only in terms of productive capability but also on the consumption side of the equation, that is, as a (actual and/or a potential) market for the goods and services of others. The lure of the potentially enormous market provided by China's masses has been a significant international factor for centuries, and other populous states such as the United States and the U. S. S. R. possess a similar significance. A state with a large population thus has a tool that may be of considerable importance in terms of trade manipulation possibilities, policymakers being able either to offer material rewards and promises to those with whom they are dealing or to apply pressure by denying or threatening to deny access to their state's market. Clearly a large population is significant because of its actual and potential impact on economic strength. And although it is a truism, it also is a fact that a state without economic strength cannot exercise decisive political influence for very long.

Another advantage of possessing a large population relates to a state's ability to avoid subjugation after suffering military reverses. A heavily populated state would be harder to occupy and control than one with few people, all else being equal, and once an enemy was in occupation the possibilities for ef-

---

[19]However, support or acquiescence of the population of the target country is helpful as was aptly demonstrated by the Vietcong in the Vietnam War. For further discussion of guerilla warfare, see Chapter 10, pp. 278–282.

fective protracted resistance would be greater. This would be especially true if the victorious party itself were relatively small; the enormous population disparity between Israel and her Arab neighbors has impacted Israeli policymakers on this exact point. And imagine anyone trying to occupy and effectively control the more than 850 million Chinese.

Despite these many advantages it nevertheless is clear that merely possessing a large population does not automatically bring about significant power.[20] It is also obvious that one cannot say that the larger the population the greater the capability or else China would be the most powerful nation in the world with India second and so on (see Table 1). Indeed, not only is it self-evident that many factors other than population influence capability, one cannot even say that size is necessarily the most important aspect of the population component. What other facets must be investigated?

Table 1   Population of Selected States, 1970–1976 (Millions)

State	*1970*	*1976*	*Annual Rate of Increase 1970–76 (%)*
China	771.8	852.1	1.7
India	539.1	610.1	2.1
U. S. S. R.	242.8	256.7	0.9
United States	204.9	215.1	0.8
Indonesia	119.5	139.6	2.6
Japan	104.3	112.8	1.3
Brazil	92.5	109.1	2.8
Bangladesh	68.1	80.6	2.8
Nigeria	55.1	64.7	2.7
W. Germany	60.7	61.5	0.2
United Kingdom	55.4	55.9	0.2
Egypt	33.3	38.1	2.2
Poland	32.5	34.3	0.9
South Africa	22.5	26.1	2.6
Zaire	21.7	25.6	2.8
Colombia	20.5	24.3	2.9
E. Germany	17.1	16.8	−0.3
Cuba	8.6	9.5	1.7
Saudi Arabia	7.7	9.2	3.0
Israel	2.9	3.5	3.0
Lebanon	2.5	3.0	3.1

Source: UN Statistical Yearbook 1977, New York, 1978, p. 68–74.

[20]In some circumstances states can even have "too many" people. See as follows, pp. 175–177.

Productive Population Elements

Another task one must undertake is to determine the proportion of the population that is available for productive efforts. What percentage of the people are within the productive age brackets, in terms of both economic and military activity? Children and the elderly are basically non-productive in these terms, constituting a net drain on a state's resources. Although the exact boundaries of the "productive years" vary with time, circumstance, and culture and so cannot be definitively determined, a good rule of thumb is to use 15 to 60 as the economically productive years and 18 to 35 for military service.[21]

Other questions are related to this facet of the productive population elements. In most countries men are the prime contributors to economic and military development, and therefore male-female ratios are important. Even though this is slowly changing in many states, it still should be investigated (but evaluated in light of altering conditions). Often particular racial, religious, or ethnic groups are not permitted to contribute fully, thus depriving the society of their resources. The extent and nature of this denial must be ascertained and its implications examined.

These issues are important because they give us an indication of the proportions of the state's population that add to or detract from its capability. A nation with a large percentage of its people in the productive categories is doubly fortunate: it has more people who are productive as well as fewer who require their support. It is important in this regard to project several years into the future, to try to anticipate the ratio of productive to nonproductive elements at various future times. Obviously things change, and the ratios will change also.[22] A state that currently has a large percentage of its population under 15, for example, as the children grow older (other things being equal) will have a much better productive to nonproductive ratio.

Educational Level

The general educational level is very important. Education clearly affects the populations' skills' levels, both in terms of quantity and quality. Without a reasonably literate population an industrial economy cannot begin to function. In fact, the differentiation, specialization, and interdependence of all modern governmental, social, and economic systems probably could not occur

---

[21]The life expectancy of the population is an important part of this question. In many of the less-developed countries people simply do not survive long enough to be within the productive years for very long.

[22]As explained in Chapter 4, capability is meaningfully operational only when discussed relationally. Since the ratio in each state will change over time, the states' relational ratio also will change.

(at least not efficiently) without mass education. And certainly there cannot be significant technological development without advanced education.

Lack of educational quantity and quality also affects military capability. For example, armed forces with low skills levels simply cannot compete with highly sophisticated military machines if there is a direct, unrestricted confrontation.[23] A prime example of this was provided by the contrast in 1956 and 1967 between the highly mobile and exceptionally sophisticated Israeli armed forces and their numerically superior but less educated Arab neighbors. The Egyptians had excellent equipment but simply did not have the "know-how" to use it effectively. This was particularly significant in 1967 inasmuch as they had received intensive Soviet training and the result was still an Egyptian debacle.

This type of contrast is one that is difficult to significantly alter in a short time because one cannot change the educational level of a country overnight. The increased efficiency of the Egyptian armed forces in the October 1973 war with Israel does not disprove but rather confirms this argument. The intensive efforts to improve Egyptian quality after 1967 only partially succeeded. There was just too large a gap. Even the advantage of a surprise attack with sophisticated weaponry was not enough to overcome the deficiency. The lack of high-grade educational performance has handicapped certain states with large populations that otherwise might be much more influential, such as India, Indonesia, and Brazil.

Density and Spatial Distribution

Population density and spatial distribution also need to be examined. Is the country densely populated, thus making it highly susceptible to nuclear devastation? Are there "too many" people on "too little" land, making it impossible to raise enough food to support them? Is population growing rapidly, thus making things worse? Will these factors lead to demands on the government for territorial expansion? Even if the overall people per square mile figures are low, is the population concentrated in a few high density areas and thus susceptible to quick elimination? Are the major population centers near the frontiers? These and related questions need to be asked.

A major phenomenon in much of today's world, one related both to population density and to the overall question of population size and economic productivity, is *overpopulation*; there are "too many" people. In capability terms this means that for a number of states they would be "stronger" if they had less people and those that they did have were spread out over more land.

[23]One must always remember that the United States imposed limitations on its activity in Vietnam in terms of the types of weapons used and the deployment of forces.

Table 2   Population of Major Regions, 1965–1976 (Millions)

Regions	1965	1970	1976	Annual Rate of Increase 1965–1976 (%)	Annual Rate of Increase 1970–1976 (%)
World	3288	3610	4044	1.9	1.9
Africa	309	352	412	2.7	2.7
Northern America	214	226	239	1.0	0.9
Latin America	247	283	333	2.7	2.8
Asia	1824	2027	2304	2.1	2.2
Europe	445	459	476	0.6	0.6
Oceania	17.5	19.3	21.7	2.0	2.0

Source: UN Statistical Yearbook 1977, New York, 1978, p. 8.

The stark reality for many policymakers is that they must devote much of their attention to simply trying to keep their people fed. The population explosion is very real. Between 1750 and 1900 world population doubled, and it doubled again by 1950. Starting from a different point but illustrating the same problem, whereas in 1965 there were nearly 3.3 billion people in the world, it has been projected that there will be almost twice that many by the year 2000.

The problem is severely compounded by the fact that the vast majority of the growth is occurring in the already "overpopulated" and relatively less developed countries in Asia, Africa, and Latin America (see Tables 1 and 2). In general, birthrates are considerably higher in these LDCs than they are in the developed states, and better health care, sanitary conditions, and food production and preservation have led to a drastic decline in the death rate (and thus a decrease in infant mortality and an increase in the life span).[24] In consequence, the LDC population is expected to grow more rapidly in the next several decades than that of the developed states. Although projections of growth are risky and imprecise, there is little doubt that the LDCs will possess at least 75 percent of the world's population by the turn of the century (see Table 3 and Diagram 1). Unfortunately, "by definition" the LDCs have enormous economic difficulties (in part *because* of their population problems) and have neither the economic infrastructure, the skills, nor the capital to make much progress toward remedying their deficiencies in the foreseeable future (as shall be examined in detail following).

"Excess" population is a condition that often breeds chaos and bitterness, providing a fertile ground for parties implementing the orientation of indirect opposition via guerilla war and propaganda techniques. Economic strength is harmed, popular support for the government jeopardized, and soci-

[24]See Werner J. Feld, *International Relations: A Transnational Approach*, Alfred, Sherman Oaks, Cal. 1979, p. 44.

Table 3   Population Growth Rates and Shares, Major Regions and Selected States, History and Projections

	Annual Av. Growth Rate (%)			Share of Population (%)		
	1950–55[a]	1970–75[a]	1995–2000[b]	1950[a]	1970[a]	2000[b]
World total	1.7	1.9	1.6	100.0	100.0	100.0
Developed regions	1.3	0.9	0.6	34.3	30.0	21.7
Developing regions	1.9	2.3	1.9	65.7	70.0	78.3
Northern America	1.8	0.9	0.7	6.6	6.3	4.7
Europe	0.8	0.6	0.5	15.7	12.7	8.6
U. S. S. R.	1.7	1.0	0.7	7.2	6.7	5.0
Africa	2.1	2.6	2.8	8.7	9.7	13.0
Latin America	2.7	2.7	2.4	6.6	7.8	9.9
China	1.6	1.7	1.0	22.3	21.4	18.4
India	1.7	2.4	1.8	14.1	15.0	16.9
Other Asia	1.9	2.4	2.0	18.3	19.8	22.9
Oceania	2.25	2.0	1.45	0.5	0.5	0.5

Source: U. S. Department of State, *World Population: The Silent Explosion*, 1978, p. 4.

[a]Estimated.

[b]Projected.

etal cohesiveness decreased. There simply are too many people for the state's economic, political, and social capacity. Unless population growth is significantly slowed in these areas, and there is precious little to indicate that it will be, things are likely to get worse. Overpopulation will continue to be a drain on resources, preventing a state from achieving even moderate foreign policy objectives without excessive costs.[25]

Trends

Finally, one must be certain to analyze trends. Demographic factors, like all the components of capability, are everchanging, and it is essential to assess them in terms of their past, present, and probable future(s). The world is dynamic, not static, and a useful analysis must take this into account. To take only one example, suppose one is concerned with issues of comparative population size. It would be essential in such a situation to ascertain whether populations were increasing or decreasing, and how fast, in both absolute and com-

[25]Despite the fact that this problem may exist, population size still may have the positive attribute of making this country harder to conquer. Also, the mere existence of an overwhelming population disparity will yield the larger nation some influence because it could simply innundate the smaller with human waves if necessary.

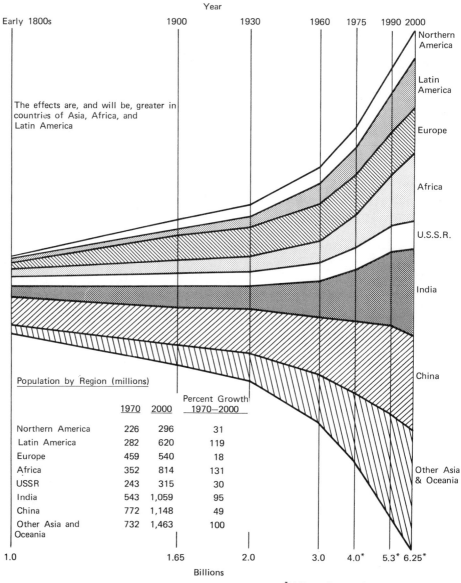

The Population Explosion
Where the People Are Likely to be in the Year 2000

Population by Region (millions)

	1970	2000	Percent Growth 1970–2000
Northern America	226	296	31
Latin America	282	620	119
Europe	459	540	18
Africa	352	814	131
USSR	243	315	30
India	543	1,059	95
China	772	1,148	49
Other Asia and Oceania	732	1,463	100

*U.N. medium projection variant

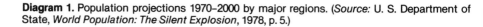

Diagram 1. Population projections 1970–2000 by major regions. (*Source:* U. S. Department of State, *World Population: The Silent Explosion*, 1978, p. 5.)

parative terms. From the Franco-Prussian war of 1871 until the beginning of World War II French population barely increased while Germany's grew rapidly. This signified a relative increase in German strength unless France could offset it in other areas (which she could not). The Germans, in turn, were worried about the growth of the Soviet Union. Today Russia and much of the rest of the world cast anxious eyes on the more than 850 million Chinese. All the aspects of the population component—size, productive elements, educational level, and density and spatial distribution—need to be examined not only in terms of their current status but also via a projection of past and present into the future; although such an exercise is hazardous and imprecise, it also is imperative.

NATURAL RESOURCES

Natural resources are another component of capability. While no one would suggest that a nation that is richly endowed with natural resources will automatically become a great power, it is clear that the possession of large quantities of high quality resources provides a base on which capability can be built. A modern industrialized economy cannot function without critical resources including coal, iron, and petroleum as well as a wide variety of other minerals. Similarly, a modern military machine is dependent on certain strategic resources.

Six Basic Points

When analyzing the role of natural resources in capability determination the policymaker must keep six basic points in mind. *First, it is necessary to distinguish between the mere possession of natural resources and their use. Resources contribute to economic and military strength primarily as they are developed.* Minerals, for example, must be drawn from the earth and processed before they enter into the production process. If a state does not have this extracting, processing, and producing capacity its mineral resources contribute little to its usable strength.[26] One way around this problem is to grant development concessions to foreign countries or companies. In such a situation the country possessing the resource gains something in terms of political power and economic benefits, but also loses some resource benefits to the concessionaire. On the other hand, this is still a net gain because, by definition, without the concessionaire the resources would not be developed. A conflict situation

---

[26]However, knowledge of their mere existence can sometimes provide bargaining leverage.

can develop, however, as the possessing state learns to develop its own capacity or wishes to increase its share of the benefits.[27]

A second point is that a country must also have political control over its own territory if it is to receive the optimum benefits from its resources. If it is a dependency of a foreign state, such as many Eastern European countries have been in relation to the Soviet Union in most of the post-World War II era, it obviously does not have full control over the use of its resources and therefore cannot reap all their benefits. Policymakers of many of the Third World states that have gained independence since World War II fear a "neoimperialism" by ex-colonial powers or MNCs that (they believe) is designed to produce just such a result.

Third, all states' resource endowments are unique; no two states have the same quantity, quality, and mix of resources. This fundamental asymmetry that exists between various parties' resource situations makes comparisons difficult. The problem is compounded by the fact that it is hard to assess the relative advantage accruing from the possession of one particular resource against the merits of possessing another. Resources, after all, vary in utility according to circumstance, situation, and need; iron is not equivalent to oil, uranium to alumina, or copper to manganese. And whatever the situation is now it surely will change over time.

Fourth, resources reflect not only potentials but also limitations. The lack of resources will set (or at least should set) limits on the objectives one would formulate, and in point of fact *will* eventually set limitations on their achievement. Because of this, obtaining sufficient resources and reducing vulnerability to resource deficiency manipulation often are significant policy goals.

Fifth, no major state is wholly self-sufficient. To take only one example, the United States imports more than 90 percent of its industrial diamonds, manganese, cobalt, natural rubber, and bauxite, almost 90 percent of its chromium and tin, more than half the zinc and nickel it uses, nearly half its petroleum, and more than a quarter of its iron ore (see Diagram 2). In addition to its obvious needs for imports in energy production and related areas, the United States also has a number of other industries that are heavily import dependent (see Table 4).

Sixth, natural resources sometimes provide a nation or a group of nations with political power that they would not otherwise possess. An example today certainly is the possession of great petroleum resources by several Arab nations of the Middle East. However, possession of natural resources can also make a nation the object of political activities, which it would otherwise escape. One

---

[27]Much of the discussion of multinational corporations in Chapter 1 is relevant here. Also see Chapter 3, p. 85.

U.S. IMPORT DEPENDENCE AND IMPORT SOURCES
(1977 estimates except where noted.)

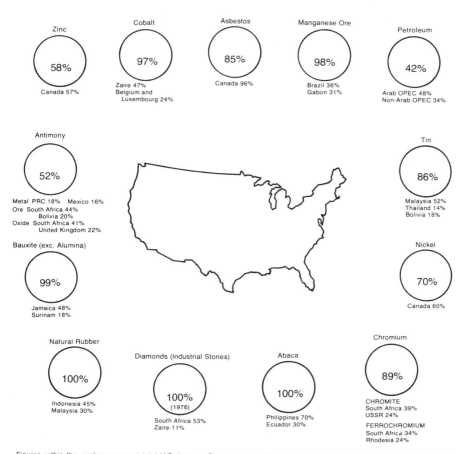

Zinc

58%

Canada 57%

Cobalt

97%

Zaire 47%
Belgium and
Luxembourg 24%

Asbestos

85%

Canada 96%

Manganese Ore

98%

Brazil 36%
Gabon 31%

Petroleum

42%

Arab OPEC 48%
Non-Arab OPEC 34%

Antimony

52%

Metal PRC 18%   Mexico 16%
Ore South Africa 44%
Bolivia 20%
Oxide South Africa 41%
United Kingdom 22%

Tin

86%

Malaysia 52%
Thailand 14%
Bolivia 18%

Bauxite (exc. Alumina)

99%

Jamaica 48%
Surinam 18%

Nickel

70%

Canada 60%

Natural Rubber

100%

Indonesia 45%
Malaysia 30%

Diamonds (Industrial Stones)

100%
(1976)

South Africa 53%
Zaire 11%

Abaca

100%

Philippines 70%
Ecuador 30%

Chromium

89%

CHROMITE
South Africa 39%
USSR 24%

FERROCHROMIUM
South Africa 34%
Rhodesia 24%

Figures within the circles represent total U.S. imports. Figures outside the circles indicate principal foreign suppliers and the percentage they comprise. For example, the U.S. imports 85% of its asbestos; 96% of that comes from Canada and 4% comes from other foreign sources.

Diagram 2. U. S. import dependence and import sources (1977 estimates except where noted). Figures within the circles represent total U. S. imports. Figures outside the circles indicate principal foreign suppliers and the percentage they comprise. For example, the U. S. imports 85 percent of its asbestos; 96 percent of that comes from Canada and 4 percent comes from other foreign sources. (*Source:* U. S. Department of State, *The Trade Debate*, May 1979 (revised), inside front cover.)

Table 4   U. S. Import-Dependent Nonenergy Industries

Industries	Imports
Tires (radials, aircraft tires)	Natural rubber
Paper, paper goods, printing, and publishing	Paper base stocks (pulp and newsprint)
Steel	Chrome, manganese and nickel
Electronics and electrical machinery	Nickel, cobalt, tungsten and assembled electrical components
Aluminum	Bauxite
Plastics	Petroleum for feedstocks
Insulation	Asbestos
Canning	Tin
Metal working and machinery	Tungsten, nickel, cobalt and manganese
Fertilizer	Potash

Source: U. S. Department of State, *The Trade Debate*, Washington, D. C., 1978, p. 20.

of the major concerns of the contending powers in the Congo crisis in the early 1960s was the fact that the Congo contained vast quantities of copper, uranium, and cobalt.[28] And the fact that Angola possesses considerable oil reserves, iron ore deposits, and diamonds, and may contain significant amounts of manganese, uranium, titanium, phosphate, and gold, greatly enhanced her worth to external actors in the mid-1970s "civil" war.[29]

Obtaining Resources

Because resources are so vital and no country is self-sufficient, the attainment of requisite resources often becomes a foreign policy objective. Historically, the necessity for resources was often a prime motivating force for territorial acquisition or colonialism. Today this direct method is much less fashionable and alternative techniques are usually used.

The most often used method is simply to negotiate a trade agreement. Most states must rely on trade to obtain resources since they need them, do not

---

[28]In mid-1960 Belgium began to withdraw from its African colony, the Belgian Congo. Immediately, civil war developed. Belgian paratroopers returned to restore order, and this led the Congolese "government" to request U. N. assistance. A U. N. Congo force was created to replace the Belgians but it was soon caught up in a civil conflict as several Congolese factions sought power. The situation was made worse as the Soviets and Americans turned it into a Cold War as well as a nationalist-colonialist issue. For a perceptive analysis see Ernest W. Lefever, *Uncertain Mandate: Politics of the UN Congo Operation*, Johns Hopkins, Baltimore, 1967.

[29]For additional comments on this conflict see Chapter 5, pp. 119 and 121–122.

have them, and cannot get them any other way. Because there presumably are mutual benefits involved in any trade agreement each party has a stake in maintaining cooperative relations. However, the degrees of dependence and vulnerability will affect the nature of this stake.[30] Sometimes, since the transportation facilities needed to bring the resources from a foreign country to one's own are so important, control of these facilities becomes critical.[31] British and French dependency on the Suez Canal as a trade route was certainly a major factor in their 1956 decision to attack Egypt.[32]

Policymakers may strive to reduce interdependence and vulnerability via domestic programs. First, they may engage in extensive exploration of their own country hoping to discover heretofore untapped resources. Second, sometimes natural or synthetic substitutes can be devised. Third, various new processes are sought, perhaps increasing the yield of existing resources, using lower quality resources, or providing for a combination of resources into new materials. In an effort to lessen the United States' energy deficiencies, for example, under the Carter administration initiatives were undertaken to investigate more intensively the potential of solar energy, devise more economical processes for obtaining petroleum from oil shale, and to develop synthetic fuels.

States will vary widely in their ability to adjust to the rising demands for materials. They differ in the degree to which they possess the basic essentials, and in their capacity to develop and use them. They differ in their capacity to supplement whatever deficiencies they may have from foreign sources, and in their domestic ability to find alternatives. Finally, they differ in the degree to which they can make the resources which they do have, whether through possession or access, invulnerable to action by their adversaries. The policymaker must carefully analyze each of these factors.

The Big Three

Although it is not possible to discuss in detail the significance of all natural resources, it would be highly useful to briefly analyze the fundamental resources without which a country simply cannot become a strong economic power: coal, iron and petroleum.[33] For over 100 years *coal* has been the world's most important source of energy. Without abundant coal the Soviet Union's industrialization would have been much more difficult, and coal formed the bed-

---

[30]Trade can also be used as a weapon. See the discussion in Chapter 9, pp. 240–250.

[31]Also see above, p. 164.

[32]This was not the only reason, however. The British perceived Egypt's President Nasser to be a threat to British influence throughout the entire Middle East (which he was) and Prime Minister Eden called him another Hitler. The French saw Nasser as a threat to their interests not only in the Middle East but in North Africa as well.

[33]This discussion is heavily influenced by Sprout and Sprout, pp. 286–290.

rock of the industrial structure of modern Germany. Britain's industrial dominance in the 19th century rested upon a long lead in the utilization of good quality and relatively accessible coal, and the pace of American industrialization has been achievable partly because of its immense coal reserves.

Coal is important first because of the fact that it is the primary fuel for the production of various ores. Second, coal-fired boilers generate a large part of the world's electricity. Third, in many areas of the world its steam is still used to propel ships and railway locomotives. And fourth, in some areas it has become a primary raw material in a wide range of chemical industries. Because of the political problems involved in obtaining petroleum today it is quite possible that coal will become even more essential in the future.[34]

A second critical resource is *iron*. There is no way to develop a modern industrial society without great quantities of iron because without it one cannot develop a strong steel industry, and steel production is one of the major indicators of the overall strength of an economy. In addition to pure steel production, a wide variety of alloys (in which iron is combined with other metals) are critically important today, alloys designed to increase the toughness, resiliency, and durability of the metals.

As we mentioned earlier, resources contribute to economic and political strength primarily as they are developed, as they are extracted, processed, and enter into the production process. Usually the highest quality and most accessible materials are obtained first, and over time extraction becomes more difficult and costly, and quality declines. This has been the pattern of iron ore mining in the U. S. S. R., and ore extraction is becoming increasingly difficult and costly. Moreover, a steady decline in the quality of the ore has compelled the steel industry to allocate a growing share of its investment capital to new ore mining capacity, facilities to upgrade the ore, and facilities to improve the quality of the iron charge for blast furnaces.[35] Clearly, it is necessary that resource quality and accessibility be assessed as well as quantity when evaluating the contribution a particular component can make to operational capability.

A third major natural resource is *petroleum*. A modern economy just cannot run without oil nor can a modern war machine with its concomitant mechanized weaponry and vehicles. The Middle East is the world's largest oil producing area and contains approximately 60 percent of the world's published proven oil reserves. The dependence of the non-Communist industrialized world on Middle East petroleum is staggering. Japan, for example, obtains over 90 percent of its oil from that region, Western Europe more than 60 per-

---

[34]Although petroleum limitations may hinder the use of coal since much of the machinery used in obtaining coal requires petroleum to function.

[35]U. S. Congress, Joint Economic Committee, *Soviet Economic Problems and Prospects: A Study prepared for the use of the Subcommittee on Priorities and Economy in Government of the Joint Economic Committee*, 95th Cong., 1st Sess., August 8, 1977, p. 6.

cent. The United States, too, is a major importer of Middle Eastern petroleum, currently acquiring nearly one-fourth of the oil it consumes from that area.

Although American dependence on foreign oil is well known it is a phenomenon of fairly recent origin. Indeed, prior to the 1970s there was no oil security threat. But with high quality domestic reserves less ample and accessible and a fall in the use of coal and the production of natural gas, by the time of the OPEC embargo of 1973 the United States was importing more than 25 percent of the oil it consumed.[36] And since that time, stimulated by the embargo, American dependence on petroleum imports has increased enormously (see Tables 5 and 6). The result, of course, is a considerable decrease in one of the subcomponents of capability, one that directly and indirectly affects several others.

It is essential that one always evaluate resource issues with a sense of time perspective and project past and present trends into the future. The Soviet Union for years has been one of the world's largest oil producers (in some years *the* largest), and a net exporter of considerable magnitude. But under all but the most optimistic of scenarios the likelihood is that by the mid to late 1980s this will change.[37] The Soviets are emphasizing current production rather than exploration and development, domestic demands continue to rise, they are not discovering new reserves as rapidly as they have been depleting existing ones, and whatever new reserves they do find will probably be located in the climatically inhospitable and less-accessible areas offshore or further east into Siberia. If U. S. intelligence projections are anywhere near accurate the Soviets will be pressed to even meet their domestic concerns, let alone continue their exports to the Eastern European states (and to certain non-Communist states that purchase oil with the hard currency the Soviets use to buy technology from the West).

It is evident that natural resources constitute a key element of capability, a component with a multiplicity of interrelated effects. Let us conclude our examination by suggesting that one investigating any particular situation place his or her analysis within the framework described above, specifically answering the following questions with respect to each situational party:

1. What resources does it need?
2. What does it possess, in terms of quantity, quality, variety, and accessibility?

---

[36]For more on the embargo see Chapter 9, pp. 243–244 and 249. Although one generally speaks of the "OPEC" embargo, not all of the 13 members of the cartel participated.

[37]Of particular value is the testimony of CIA Director Admiral Stansfield Turner to the Subcommittee on Priorities and Economy in Government of the Joint Economic Committee of the U. S. Congress, June 23, 1977. See the *Hearings, Allocation of Resources in the Soviet Union and China —1977*, 95th Cong., 1st Sess., Part 3, pp. 5-16, 33-36.

Table 5 U. S. Petroleum Imports by Source, 1973–1978

Imports from OPEC Sources (thousands of barrels per day, average)

	Algeria	Indonesia	Iran	Libya	Nigeria	Saudi Arabia	United Arab Emirates	Venezuela	Other OPEC	Total OPEC	Arab Members of OPEC
1973	136.0	213.3	222.8	164.4	458.8	485.7	70.6	1134.9	106.4	2992.9	914.7
1974	190.1	300.4	468.8	4.4	713.4	461.3	73.9	979.1	88.4	3279.8	752.5
1975	282.4	389.6	280.4	231.8	761.8	714.6	116.7	702.5	121.4	3601.3	1382.6
1976	432.2	538.8	298.5	453.3	1024.7	1229.8	254.4	700.1	134.0	5065.8	2424.1
1977	558.6	541.0	535.0	722.6	1143.0	1380.4	335.3	690.4	286.7	6193.1	3182.2
1978	628.0	530.4	544.7	642.7	902.9	1137.4	378.4	633.0	221.5	5619.0	2915.5

Imports from Non-OPEC Sources (thousands of barrels per day, average)

	Bahamas	Canada	Mexico	Netherlands Antilles	Puerto Rico	Trinidad and Tobago	Virgin Islands	Other	Total
1973	170.8	1312.9	15.2	573.6	99.3	250.6	329.2	523.5	3274.2
1974	159.3	1067.6	8.4	509.6	90.4	241.2	391.7	384.2	2852.4
1975	152.0	845.2	71.4	323.6	89.7	240.9	406.5	306.1	2435.4
1976	116.5	599.3	87.1	274.6	88.1	272.6	422.3	373.5	2234.0
1977	170.5	516.9	179.4	210.9	105.1	289.3	466.2	675.8	2614.1
1978	157.4	461.6	316.9	229.5	89.4	251.0	426.8	647.9	2580.5

Source: U. S. Department of Energy, *Monthly Energy Review*, May 1979, pp. 34–35.

Table 6 U. S. Dependence on Petroleum Imports, 1973–1978 (in millions of barrels per day)

	Arab/OPEC	All OPEC	All Countries	Domestic Demand
1973 average	0.91	2.99	6.26	17.31
1974 average	0.75	3.28	6.11	16.65
1975 average	1.38	3.60	6.06	16.32
1976 average	2.42	5.07	7.31	17.46
1977 average	3.18	6.19	8.81	18.43
1978 average	2.92	5.64	8.23	18.82

Source: U. S. Department of Energy, *Monthly Energy Review*, July 1979, p. 16.

3. Can it develop what it has?
4. Does it have control over its resources?
5. How vulnerable and dependent is it on foreign sources?
6. Can it find alternatives, internationally or domestically?
7. What changes are likely in the foreseeable future, and what will their impact be?
8. To what extent, and how, will resource deficiencies limit its immediate, middle-range, and long-run capability, particularly in the area of economic productivity?

ECONOMIC STRENGTH

A prime element of capability is economic strength. Traditionally, its importance has been explained by its close association with and influence on military capacity. In this respect the degree of industrialization is critical. The well-known authority, Hans Morgenthau, states:

> The technology of modern warfare and communications has made the overall development of heavy industries an indispensable element of national power. . . . Thus it is inevitable that the leading industrial nations should be identical with the great powers, and a change in industrial rank, for better or for worse, should be accompanied or followed by a corresponding change in the hierarchy of power.[38]

This is an oversimplification, however. The military instrument of policy has a wide range of potential uses, only one of which is fighting a conventional war of considerable duration, the type of "modern" warfare scenario that Morgenthau envisages. Granted, in this respect the argument is valid and is thus pertinent to many situations.

[38]Morgenthau, *Politics Among Nations*, Fifth Edition, pp. 119-120.

But there are others to which it is inappropriate. For the development of nuclear strength one could argue that the relative degree of industrialization is important but not determinative because a moderately developed economy with technological expertise and a solid financial base might be sufficient. Even more significant is the fact that many of the uses of the military instrument involve various types of limited or sublimited war.[39] These activities often do not require a high level of economic development. Thus although the concept of economic war potential is relevant to some cases, it must be analyzed in light of the specific situation and evaluated accordingly.[40] None of this denies the relationship of economic and military power, but only points out the complexity of the relationship.

Economic strength today is critically significant in its own right. First, the mere existence of a powerful economy exercises an influence because of its potential impact.[41] The U. S. economy's potential as a market, for example, will inevitably influence the policies of some states. Similarly, its immense productive capacity automatically makes it a potential threat to competitors or a possible source of goods, services, and capital.

Beyond mere existence, however, lies the realm of economic policy techniques (discussed more fully in Chapter 9). States often use economic tools to seek to achieve their objectives, and the stronger the economy the more varied and credible the options. One cannot effectively promise a program of technical or financial assistance if it cannot be given, nor can he threaten deprivation without the strength to deprive.

Agricultural Capacity

A major component of economic strength and one that sometimes receives insufficient attention is agricultural capacity. One can view the process of economic development as the shift from an agricultural to an industrial economy. This shift cannot be accomplished, however, unless and until each agricultural worker produces enough food to allow others to be set free to participate in the modernization process (unless one is dependent on foreign sources, a very risky situation). If a state is not self-sufficient or nearly so in food production, it is at a great disadvantage relative to those that are.

When a policymaker seeks to analyze agricultural capacity where does he or she begin? The first question to ask is: Can the state produce enough food

---

[39]See Chapter 10, pp. 272–282.

[40]See Klaus Knorr, *Military Power and Potential*, D. C. Heath, Lexington, Mass., 1970, pp. 19-20.

[41]The performance of American industry in World War II and its potential for the postwar period had a significant impact on Stalin's policies. See Adam B. Ulam, *The Rivals: America and Russia Since World War II*, Viking, New York, 1971, Ch. 1.

to feed itself? Great Britain has been in serious jeopardy in wartime because she produces less than one-half of the food she needs. Historically this required that she have a great navy to protect the sea lanes over which her vital food supplies were shipped. Given Britain's post-World War II imperial retrenchment and relative power decline, should hostilities of more than a limited local nature occur she might well become dependent on American naval forces to perform this function (especially if her foe possessed considerable sea denial capability).

A serious deficiency in gross agricultural capacity confronts a policymaker with a number of problems. Internally it requires one to develop policies and make resource and labor force allocations that disproportionately emphasize one sector of the economy at the expense of others; nevertheless, because of the depth of the problem policymakers often have little choice.[42] In some states things are so bad that people live at subsistence levels and famines are common. Some potentially great powers, such as India, almost constantly face this threat. Externally, policymakers of such states are compelled to negotiate with commodity supplying parties (whether ideally this is what they would prefer or not), and to do so from a position of relative weakness. Operational capability is certainly minimal in such circumstances. And, of course, as mentioned earlier, in wartime a severely production-deficient party is highly vulnerable to adversarial pressures.

The second major facet of agricultural capacity is productivity, the efficiency and level of output per acre, worker, capita, etc. Many states are able to produce enough food to feed their population but only through the overemployment of resources in agricultural activities. This is a major problem today in many of the "have not" nations of the world. Many times great powers are also confronted with this misutilization of resources. For example, approximately 30 percent of the Soviet Union's labor force is involved in agricultural production as compared to less than 5 percent for the United States. If the Soviets were able to transfer this 25 percent differential to industrial, consumer, and service pursuits they would be able to vastly increase economic productivity.

In analyzing the questions of insufficient absolute production and low productivity one must also look at the probabilities of changes. To what extent is the soil of this particular country capable of producing much greater quantities and higher qualities of food? Is the climate such that this could occur? Through the use of various fertilizers, irrigation schemes, better qualities of

---

[42]There may be a number of domestic political concerns involved here also. If little progress is made it may well be that societal cohesiveness and popular support will decrease, political opponents will call for and/or act to bring about regime change, external parties will intervene via indirect opposition and/or limited support, etc.

seed and plant, better management, more efficient organization, and the application of higher levels of skill, knowledge, and technology, is it possible for these states with agricultural difficulties to overcome to some extent their agricultural problems?[43]

Economic Development

The real key to economic strength is encompassed by what is usually called economic "modernization" or economic "development."[44] Highly modernized or developed economies are characterized by a high degree of economic differentiation, a complex division of labor, highly organized and standardized production systems, machinery being the major element of work energy, high levels of productivity, and high levels of total output.

How does a policymaker determine the degree to which a particular economy is developed? Unfortunately there are several indicators and there are serious difficulties associated with each. In addition, one runs into data problems. Many governments do not keep accurate national accounts and some hide or distort information that could be unfavorably construed. Despite these obstacles there is enough information to get a general idea of strength, and if one uses a combination of various economic indicators he can get a reasonably accurate picture.

The first standard is *gross national product* (GNP). GNP is an indicator of the total output of a given economy at market price, thus being a measure of production, not potential. As such it reflects total output in all areas, and all changes in consumption, investment, and military or other governmental expenditures would be reflected. Relative GNPs provide a useful place to start any comparison because they indicate comparative magnitudes of strength and the limitations on a particular country's capability to support internal and external commitments.[45]

There are, however, several difficulties with using GNP data. In the first place, unpaid labor such as occurs in households, and the value of goods ex-

---

[43]One should note the fact that due to rapidly increasing population it is quite possible that even if food production and productivity are increased, in many of the most populated parts of the world this may be insufficient to sustain what is already a very substandard level of existence.

[44]The processes of development and modernization are complex and composed of many interrelated factors only one of which is the economic. The most useful introduction to the general subject is Cyril E. Black, *The Dynamics of Modernization*, Harper, New York, 1966.

[45]As always, identifying the parties in a situation is important. With respect to relative GNPs the question becomes "relative to whom?" Although Japan's GNP is of moderate size relative to that of the United States it is overwhelmingly larger than its regional competitors in East Asia. On the possible implications of this point see Donald C. Hellman, *Japan and East Asia: The New International Order*, Praeger, New York, 1972.

changed via barter (which occurs to a great extent in less developed and some socialist economies) are not included. Second, because GNP figures are based on monetary value they may not reflect the true contribution of any particular segment of the economy to that country's political commitments. For example, what is the true value of the motion picture industry to the capability of the United States? A third problem is that when one is comparing economies it is difficult to translate prices from one economic system to another because of the nature of the different systems and currencies. Prices may be artificially set and the official ratio between currencies may not reflect their actual value relationship. Fourth, states have different economic data systems, and converting individual state data (even if its available) to common categories and concepts is a difficult task. Thus methodological errors may occur and the resultant product may be somewhat inaccurate. Finally, because currency values fluctuate, inflationary and/or deflationary factors may skew the result. Nevertheless, although there are clearly a number of difficulties it still is possible to develop common data and bases and make comparisons that are meaningful at least in terms of comparative magnitudes.

An examination of current GNP data shows that the United States is by far the world's strongest economic power (see Table 7). It alone accounts for nearly one-fourth of world GNP.[46] If the United States' production is combined with that of its NATO allies the sum is a figure approaching 50 percent, and if Japan is added the proportion exceeds one-half. Looking at Western Europe as a whole, the countries comprising the European Communities produce nearly 20 percent of the world GNP. The Communist states constitute another major economic force, accounting for about 22 percent. It is evident that the relatively few states included in the above categories produce an overwhelming percentage of the earth's goods and services: the converse is also true, that the vast majority of the countries produce only a miniscule proportion.

The policymaker must analyze not only current GNP but also trends and changes. Four features of today's world economy are especially interesting in this regard. First, her growth rate having declined significantly the Soviet Union no longer is gaining on the United States as she was in the 1950s and 1960s, the GNP ratio having remained about 2 : 1 in Washington's favor since 1970. Second, the major oil-exporting states of OPEC (the Organization of Petroleum Exporting Countries) achieved almost unbelievable growth in the 1973-1976 period. Though in some cases this has slowed somewhat, their growth rates in most instances still are among the world's highest. Third, Japan's GNP continues to advance more rapidly than that of any other indus-

---

[46]Data for this and the succeeding paragraph are derived from U. S. Department of State, *Special Report: The Planetary Product "Back to Normalcy" in 1976-77,* June 1978.

Table 7   GNP, Selected States, 1976

State	GNP (in U. S. $ billions)
United States	1,706.50
U. S. S. R.	857.00
Japan	538.65
W. Germany	422.03
France	335.63
China (PRC)	249.10
United Kingdom	215.13
Canada	159.18
Brazil	111.00
India	101.40
Poland	92.24
Australia	79.70
Iran	68.70
E. Germany	66.16
Sweden	64.98
Czechoslovakia	57.95
Saudi Arabia	48.90
Switzerland	46.32
Argentina	40.73
Indonesia	34.00
Denmark	32.82
Venezuela	32.20
South Africa	31.89
Nigeria	30.40
Norway	25.99
Libya	14.00
Egypt	13.00
Israel	12.20
Chile	10.40
Bangladesh	9.9
Cuba	8.9
Ghana	4.60
Zambia	3.00
Syria	2.60
Somalia	0.2

Source: U. S. Department of State, *The Planetary Product "Back to Normalcy" in 1976–1977*, June 1978, pp. 30–36.

trialized state. And fourth, many of the poorer states are now growing more rapidly than some of the industrialized countries. There is an important caveat to be remembered here, however. Because the statistical base on which poor states build is very small, in many cases even though their rate of growth exceeds that of some of the developed countries their absolute deficit in GNP continues to increase.

A second major indicator of the degree of development is *gross national product per capita*. There are tremendous differences in this regard as Table 8 indicates. Two points are especially pertinent here. First, the immense gap between the rich and poor states is actually *increasing* despite the fact that the less developed countries (LDCs) are growing. Most of the LDCs are the same states that are suffering the pangs of overpopulation discussed earlier in the chapter, and the prospects for narrowing the gulf in the near future are not bright.[47] A second point is that even within the general category of the developed states there are significant disparities in GNP per capita; American GNP per capita is over twice that of the Soviet Union, for example.

Certain cautions are necessary when evaluating GNP per capita figures. First, because the concept involves GNP all the difficulties connected with that concept apply. Second, because the term uses the mean average, in some cases it may provide a distorted picture in that it may hide gross inequalities in income distribution. In a number of LDCs, for example, wealth and property are concentrated in the hands of a small elite while the masses subsist in squalor; whether you and I split $100 evenly or I take $99 and you get $1, the result is still $50 per capita. Third, production per capita figures do not automatically reflect economic strength for foreign policy objectives because different economies allocate economic resources differently and for a tightly controlled economy the precise per capita figures may not be that important. The Soviet Union, for example, was able to compete with the United States in a strategic arms race in the late 1950s despite the fact that its per capita production was considerably less than that of the United States.

A third major standard of economic development is *energy production and consumption* (see Table 9). This indicator includes all energy sources: coal, oil, nuclear power, solar energy, hydroelectric power, and natural gas. No nation can develop and operate a modern industrialized economy without a great supply of energy. It is useful in this regard again to consider gross as well as per capita figures. This is particularly true with regard to the People's Republic of China where per capita consumption is low but over the last few years total production has increased rapidly. Another important consideration in today's energy hungry world is the degree to which a party produces enough (or almost enough) energy to meet its domestic needs. If it does not and is heavily dependent on energy imports, such as Japan is, it is extremely vulnerable; if, on the other hand, a party produces far more than it consumes, such as Saudi Arabia, it may be in a position to utilize the economic policy instrument with some efficacy. When evaluating the issue of energy sufficiency one must not stop with gross statistics of the sort presented in Table 9, however,

---

[47]Some argue that this widening gap portends disasters that threaten to engulf not only the less developed states but the rich countries as well. See Charlotte Waterlow, *Superpowers and Victims: The Outlook for World Community*, Prentice-Hall, Englewood Cliffs, N. J., 1974.

Table 8   GNP Per Capita, Selected States, 1976, and Average Annual Real Growth Rates 1960–1976 and 1970–1976

		Growth Rates (%)	
State	P.C. GNP (in $)	1960–1976	1970–1976
Kuwait	13,960	− 3.2	− 2.2
Switzerland	9,160	2.3	0.5
Sweden	9,030	3.0	2.1
Canada	7,930	3.7	3.5
United States	7,880	2.4	1.7
Norway	7,800	3.9	4.5
Denmark	7,690	3.3	1.5
W. Germany	7,510	3.3	2.0
Belgium	7,020	4.1	3.2
Australia	6,990	3.1	1.9
France	6,730	4.3	3.3
Libya	5,970	7.3	− 6.6
Japan	5,090	8.0	3.9
E. Germany	4,520	3.2	3.8
Saudi Arabia	4,420	6.5	9.5
United Kingdom	4,180	2.7	1.7
Poland	2,880	4.0	5.3
Israel	2,810	5.1	3.3
U. S. S. R.	2,800	3.8	3.1
Venezuela	2,540	2.6	3.1
Iran	2,060	8.0	8.2
Argentina	1,580	2.9	1.8
Brazil	1,300	4.8	7.4
South Africa	1,290	2.2	1.4
Chile	1,050	1.1	− 2.3
Cuba	840	1.1	0.5
Syria	830	2.2	2.2
South Korea	700	7.3	8.7
North Korea	670	5.2	6.8
Rhodesia	530	2.2	1.5
Nigeria	400	3.5	5.4
China (PRC)	370	5.2	4.3
Egypt	280	1.9	3.1
Indonesia	280	3.1	5.3
Tanzania	180	2.6	1.7
Mozambique	150	1.4	− 4.3
India	140	1.2	0.5
Zaire	130	1.4	0.4
Bangladesh	90	− 0.4	− 0.8

Source: World Bank, *1978 World Bank Atlas: Population, Per Capita Product, and Growth Rates,* Washington, D. C., 1978, p. 6.

Table 9   Energy Production and Consumption, Selected States

State	Production Total 1973	1976	Consumption Total 1973	1976	Consumption Per Capita 1973	1976
World	8,448	8,952	7,767	8,318	2,041	2,069
United States	2,145	2,050	2,470	2,485	11,738	11,554
U. S. S. R.	1,402	1,674	1,169	1,350	4,684	5,259
Saudi Arabia	567	644	11	18	1,272	1,901
China	513	615	504	590	633	706
Iran	461	467	36	50	1,154	1,490
Canada	287	259	213	230	9,632	9,950
Poland	176	200	152	181	4,553	5,253
United Kingdom	175	198	314	295	5,599	5,268
W. Germany	170	166	365	364	5,885	5,922
Libya	161	146	2	4	889	1,589
Nigeria	151	154	5	6	81	94
India	94	121	112	133	196	218
Indonesia	100	114	18	30	136	218
Mexico	61	91	65	76	1,160	1,227
E. Germany	78	79	106	114	6,273	6,789
Japan	37	38	426	415	3,918	3,679
Egypt	13	27	10	18	294	473
Brazil	22	26	62	80	615	731
Zaire	0.58	2.37	2	2	76	62
Bangladesh	0.96	1.14	2	3	32	32

Source: UN Statistical Yearbook 1977, New York, 1978, pp. 384–387.

Quantities in million metric tons of coal equivalent and in kilograms per capita.

even though they are useful in certain cases. In most instances it is necessary to investigate the pertinent subcategories. To take one illustration, while in gross terms the United States' energy production-consumption deficiency does not appear overly serious, as our earlier analysis (and Diagram 2 and Table 6) demonstrated there is a critical problem with respect to one major source: oil.

Another significant measure of economic development is *steel production* (see Table 10). Steel is a basic ingredient in nearly all heavy industrial and military goods. To some extent steel production is a measure of flexibility because often it can be shifted relatively easily from civilian to military uses and vice versa. One must also remember that although steel in its simplest form is an alloy of iron and carbon, in the last 50 to 100 years scores of alloys have been developed in which steel is combined with other elements to produce materials that have a much greater strength, resistance to corrosion, hardness, or other desired properties. As Table 10 clearly demonstrates, there is a tremendous disparity between a very few states and the rest of the world in this area also.

Table 10   Crude Steel Production, Selected States

State	1968	1972	1976
World	528,700	626,400	675,000
U. S. S. R.	106,537	125,592	144,805
United States	119,262	120,875	116,121
Japan	66,893	96,901	107,399
W. Germany	41,159	43,706	42,415
China	15,000	23,000	27,000
Italy	16,963	19,815	23,446
France	20,410	24,054	23,221
United Kingdom	26,277	25,293	22,274
Poland	11,008	13,131	15,231
Czechoslovakia	10,555	12,727	14,693
Canada	10,161	11,859	13,137
Spain	4,971	9,564	11,085
Romania	4,751	7,401	10,733

No other state produces 10,000 per year, entire remainder of world less than 100,000 total.

Source: UN Statistical Yearbook 1977, New York, 1978, p. 330.

Production figures in thousand metric tons.

A final indicator of the level of economic development is the *percentage of the state's labor force engaged in nonagricultural work*. If the majority of the labor force is involved in simply producing enough food to keep the nation fed there will not be sufficient resources available for industrialization. Such is the case in most of the LDCs today. In India, for example, nearly 80 percent of the people depend on the land in one fashion or another for their livelihood, and many other states have comparable situations. For most such parties significantly improving agricultural capacity in a short time is just not possible, and one may reasonably expect the percentage of the labor force engaged in nonagricultural pursuits to remain low.

Priorities, Emphases, and Allocations

Another issue of primary importance in analyzing economic capability is who gets what part of the pie? What sectors of the economy are emphasized, what are the state's priorities, and how are economic resources in the form of land, labor, and capital allocated? Policymakers in all countries are confronted with insistent demands from a wide variety of sources and have insufficient resources to meet them. Therefore decisions must be made concerning which demands are to be met and which are not, and the degree to which those demands that are to be met shall be satisfied. Although there are a wide variety of possible categories of allocation, for our purposes the most useful are personal consumption, capital formation, and government expenditures (subdivided into military and nonmilitary).

In all nations there is *a conflict between demands for a rapid improvement in the standard of living, that is, immediate personal consumption, and the necessity for new capital formation* (investment in productive capacity to bring about future economic development). States whose economies are primarily consumer oriented leave a smaller proportion of their resources available for economic growth and development. The significance of this fact depends, of course, partly on the degree of consumer orientation.

It also depends on the absolute level of development a state has already obtained. Although one cannot stipulate the relationship with mathematical certainty, it is essentially true that the higher the rate of investment in fixed capital the higher the rate of increase in gross national product. New capital can be obtained from domestic or external sources but most of it must come from savings in the domestic economy. In a highly developed economy the rate of capital investment need not be particularly high because there is already a high level of capital development. In other words, the rate of investment may be small but the absolute level of investment could still be considerable.

In a less developed country, however, a very high rate of capital investment as well as large absolute quantities will be required.[48] The problem is that there simply are not sufficient domestic savings available to provide the necessary capital for rapid economic growth. How can the less developed countries save 10 to 15 percent of their national income per year when annual per capita income may be no more than a couple of hundred dollars (or even less)?

The problems of economic growth for less developed countries are magnified by the facts that these are usually the regions in which population pressure is the highest, where economic infrastructures are seldom adequate (marketing, distribution, transportation, and communications systems, etc.), technological levels are low, skills and technical talents are largely nonexistent, and the vast majority of the labor force is employed in subsistence agriculture. Often difficulties are compounded by the fact that such states are also dependent on foreign sources for their cash income, being primarily one-product economies.

In many of these countries the inhabitants have become aware of the advancements of technologically developed economies, have recently become independent, believe that they were unjustly held back by colonial powers, and

---

[48]For an excellent introduction to this problem of economic development in the less developed countries, see Lester B. Pearson, *Partners in Development*, Praeger, New York, 1969. A highly useful anthology that focuses on the interrelated factors in development and the difficulty of ascertaining the most effective approach is Frank Tachau, ed., *The Developing Nations: What Path to Modernization*, Dodd Mead, New York, 1974.

demand the economic benefits that exist elsewhere. This is part of what is called the "revolution of rising expectations." Yet given the lack of domestic capital and these other economic handicaps, even with considerable external economic assistance it is highly doubtful that in the foreseeable future rapid economic progress can be made.

But the policymaker usually seeks external assistance because there is little alternative. The other presumed options are to increase production and/or reduce consumption. The reduction of consumption is hardly feasible since "by definition" one is talking about countries with extremely low per capita consumption. And one cannot simply wave a magic wand and increase production because that is the very problem, the problem that production cannot be increased. The problem is right at the beginning; capital begets capital but how does one get it in the first place?

As the analysis of indicators of economic development and Tables 7 to 10 demonstrated, the disparities in the level of economic strength from state to state frequently are enormous. In addition to all the difficulties in LDC development just discussed, LDC policymakers in many instances find that their party is economically dependent in terms of trade and/or capital investment and/or foreign aid on one or more of the developed market economies of North America, Western Europe, or Japan. Although the developed economies many times do depend on the LDCs for natural resources and raw materials (see Diagram 2), the LDCs reciprocally depend on the developed states for markets. The relative weakness of the LDCs and the asymmetrical nature of the dependence relationships have given rise to efforts by LDC leaders to improve their relative position, to a "North-South" dialogue with the South seeking what has been called a new international economic order. Preferential trade agreements, transfer of technology on preferential terms, linkage of prices received for exports to prices paid for imports, a favorable reorientation of the international monetary system, increased capital for development and more favorable terms, measures for debt relief and/or mitigation, stabilization of commodity markets and prices, these are but some of the specific immediate objectives being sought. The extent to which LDC policymakers will be able to operationally exercise capability and persuade policymakers of the developed states to make major policy modifications is problematical, however, (at least in the near future) given the relative cost-benefit alterations such modifications inevitably would produce, the immense disparities that exist in the parties' overall capabilities, and the many divergences in approach and conflicts among the LDCs themselves.

Another allocation question concerns *government expenditures.* In analyzing this factor one is concerned with the relationship of government expenditure to national economic output, the role of the government in terms of controlling and directing production, the wisdom with which it participates in and/or manages the economy, the extent of participation and management, and the degree to which government expenditures are allocated to military purposes.

In all societies today governments play a major economic role. Policymakers are confronted with increasing demands for more and better social programs and services, and for protection of the environment as well as for a higher standard of living. One must balance these against demands for capital formation and for resources for external commitments, including those of military defense and military related activities.

The proportion of gross national product allocated to military purposes varies considerably from country to country and over time.[49] In terms of absolute dollar equivalents, in 1977 Saudi Arabia had the highest per capita expenditure for military purposes, nearly twice as much as the second-ranked state. With respect to the percentage of gross national product devoted to military expenditures, Israel led the way with nearly 30 percent followed by Syria at around 16.4 and Jordan at 15.5. Concerning expenditures by the superpowers the Soviet Union annually spends about 11 to 13 percent of its GNP on defense whereas the United States spends approximately 6 percent of American GNP. Turning to the European theater, most of the NATO countries spend in the 3 to 5 percent range as do their counterparts in the Warsaw Pact (excluding the Soviets). It should also be pointed out that there is a distinct upward trend in military expenditures in many of the LDCs of the "South," which results in the uneconomic utilization of what already are meager economic resources. This diminishes current consumption and imposes further hardships in areas where the standard of living already is low, and it prevents the use of such resources for future economic development.[50]

The statistics of military allocation provide some indication of the general scale of a country's military efforts. The rapidly increasing costs of not only direct participation in warfare but also the maintenance of large standing military forces, of research and development, of producing and testing highly sophisticated weapons, and perhaps of maintaining a military presence and supporting military forces overseas, may become so prohibitive that they will become increasingly unsupportable for many countries.

The discussion of economic strength can be closed with the reiteration of a couple of points made previously. First, while it is true that no single component of capability is the only determinant of national power, economic

[49]The data below is drawn from the International Institute for Strategic Studies, *The Military Balance, 1978-1979*, London, 1978, pp. 88-89.

[50]This is not to make an *a priori* judgment as to the wisdom of such activities. In the decentralized anarchy of international politics the military policy instrument has a number of valuable usages, as we point out in Chapter 10.

strength is obviously a critical element. Second, one must remember that economic capability is significant not only because of its impact on the state's potential for military activity, but also in its own right.

MILITARY STRENGTH

The last of the tangible power elements the policymaker must investigate is military strength, today perhaps the most controversial of all capability components. Nowhere is it more true that one must analyze capability with respect to the specific policy context in which one is operating, and assess capability in relation to the particular objectives and conditions thereof. There are many situations in which the utility of military power is much less than one would expect from mere assessment of its components.[51] Despite this fact and while not underestimating its importance, the policymaker must recognize that the es- sence of the existence of independent states is their capacity to make their own decisions, and these decisions often involve judgements about the potential or actual use of military force. In the decentralized anarchy of international politics military force has been and remains the ultimate arbiter of conflict. More than this, policymakers know that the military policy instrument can be usefully employed in a number of ways other than total combat, and they would like to have the capacity to optimize these other usages as well.[52] Whether observers like it or not, it is a fact that wars of various kinds *do* occur, statesmen frequently *do* employ military strength, and policymakers *do* sometimes choose to risk or engage in hostilities. Military strength *is* and *will continue to be* a vitally important building block for the operational exercise of capability.

Quantitative and Distributive Aspects

Part of the policymaker's assessment of military strength involves a consideration of quantitative and distributive factors. In this regard he is concerned with such questions as the size of forces in being, the number of bases, the types and numbers of weapons, and so forth. A simple determination of the military manpower possessed by the Soviet Union, the United States, or the People's Republic of China gives some indication of military strength. In 1978, for example, the PRC had 4,325,000 in the armed forces, the U. S. S. R. 3,638,000, and the United States 2,068,800.[53] A comparison of such quantitative factors is often useful. Even if the Burmese army of 153,000 was well trained and

---

[51]Much of Chapter 4 is directly relevant here.

[52]See Chapter 10 for a discussion of these other usages.

[53]International Institute for Strategic Studies, *The Military Balance, 1978-1979*, London, 1978, pp. 90-91.

equipped with extremely sophisticated weaponry, its relative size deficiency of nearly 3½ million compared to the army of the People's Republic of China would be impossible to overcome in combat. This points out the fact that the policymaker is not concerned with absolute figures in the abstract but rather with comparing the strength of his or her country's forces (and those of its allies) with those of its potential adversary(ies). Usually in making such comparisons policymakers also take care to be theater specific and to include only the data that is relevant to the particular situation. To illustrate, when comparing NATO and Warsaw Pact manpower, since not all the states in each alliance are likely to be involved in the same theater of battle, policymakers usually break the figures down into two regions: Northern and Central Europe (taken together) and Southern Europe. To show the difference this makes, in terms of manpower in combat units in the Northern and Central Europe sector the Pact forces hold a 943,000 : 626,000 edge, whereas in Southern Europe NATO forces outnumber Pact personnel 550,000 : 388,000.[54]

But such gross figures are far from the whole story. When analyzing quantitative factors one must develop meaningful categories. As one gathers data on air forces, for example, it is not just how many bombers, but how many of what kind? Which fighters are designed primarily for offensive operations, and how many are interceptors? Not only how many missiles, but how many of what range, what payload, located where, how reliable, how vulnerable, and so on. To develop meaningful categories it is necessary, in other words, to specify both performance characteristics and the mission to be performed; otherwise one may be comparing apples and oranges.

When examining forces in being one must also be concerned with the distribution among the various branches. How large, for example, is the army as compared to the navy or air force? The relevance of this distinction is illustrated by the case of China. Even a cursory examination shows that Peking's naval and air forces are clearly insufficient to allow it to be a conquest threat (at this point in time) to anyone other than its land neighbors.[55] A significant concentration of personnel in any branch has direct and obvious implications for capability and strategy.

When analyzing various states' armed forces the policymaker faces serious problems of comparability. Not only are there differences in the distribution of personnel and weapons among branches, the mix within each branch is considerably different. How does one compare bombers and missiles, or armored and infantry divisions? Even when trying to compare like categories one finds equivalence hard to determine. For example, if one is comparing armored divisions, how does he or she take into account the fact that divisions

[54]Ibid., p. 109.
[55]Ibid., pp. 55-57.

are structured differently in different countries? A Soviet armored division contains 11,000 men and 325 tanks, a U. S. division 16,850 men and 324 tanks, and a Chinese division 10,000 men and 270 tanks.[56] Mechanized and airborne divisions are structured differently from armored divisions, and these structures also differ from country to country. Obviously, simple comparisons by the number of divisions would be extremely misleading. It is essential that one know the way the parties structure their various divisions if comparisons are to be meaningful.

Because all parties face somewhat different problems, operate from different perspectives, and proceed on the basis of different assumptions, the problem of developing useful categories for comparison is complicated even further. Frequently policymakers deal with this issue by orienting their thinking on the basis of mission and including within their categories a variety of considerations. To take but one example, in the U. S. Defense Department's *Annual Report for Fiscal 1980* Secretary Harold Brown made the following comments:

> I am, of course, aware that we estimate the Soviets as having more than 45,000 tanks, while the United States has only 10,000. But while we recognize the Soviet armor threat, that raw comparison does not convince me of Soviet military superiority in Central Europe, or make it advisable for the United States to buy another 35,000 tanks. Our allies happen to have tanks as well; and anti-tank launchers—of which we and our allies have already acquired more than 17,000 (and more than 40,000 anti-tank missiles)—are also relevant to stopping tanks. It is most unlikely, in any event, that the Soviets could bring all those tanks to bear against the United States and its allies. Simply counting up tanks, or ships, or aircraft, or missiles is not a sufficient basis for determining the relative effectiveness of two opposing forces.[57]

Forces in Being, or Potential? Some observers have suggested that when assessing the quantitative and distributive aspects of military strength only forces in being need to be considered, that estimates of potential are not necessary. Such a view seems to imply that any war would be over quickly, and thus the quantities of personnel and equipment only potentially available are largely irrelevant. Just as the assumption that most wars will be of considerable duration is an oversimplification, the assumption of decisively fought short wars, perhaps with nuclear weapons, also is too all-encompassing. It is undeniable that never before have so many parties had such quantities (and varieties) of weapons

---

[56] Ibid., p. vii. These are average figures and can only be treated as approximate since military organization is flexible and formations may be reduced or reinforced.

[57] U. S. Department of Defense, *Department of Defense Annual Report Fiscal Year 1980*, p. 11.

with great lethality. Moreover, it is evident that a rapid shift from peace to war production and a rapid increase in the production of weapons systems and supplies is more difficult in some states now than previously because of the increasing complexity and sophistication of these parties' military equipment. These factors (along with many others) make it perhaps more probable that short decisive wars will occur than was the case any time previously, but they certainly do not guarantee it. There are many other possibilities. Often, for example, wars occur between parties that simply don't have highly advanced weapons systems. Frequently these take on many of the aspects of a war of attrition, similar in some aspects to a conventional conflict like World War II. Also, it is possible for wars to occur between great powers and lesser powers in which the great power, for whatever reason, decides not to fully use its capability and becomes involved in a long-standing conflict (Korea, Vietnam). Furthermore, it has been speculated that even confrontations among the great powers might be somewhat conventional. This was one basis for NATO's adoption of the doctrine of flexible response, attempting to provide some conventional options and not require an automatic response with nuclear weapons.[58] Finally, there are many conflict situations involving guerilla activities that involve the use of forces and resources for a considerable length of time; in these cases forces in being are not decisive at all. Whether forces in being would be decisive in any particular hostilities would depend on a host of factors, including the size and efficiency of the attack; the degree of warning and the response thereto; the size, manning, and readiness of defensive forces; appropriateness of tactics and strategy; effectiveness of alliances (if there are any); effectiveness of decision making; luck; and the impact of the qualitative features discussed as follows (personnel, technological sophistication, and leadership). In contingencies in which forces in being are not decisive another factor becomes important—reinforcement capacity. Reinforcement capacity is a major concern for NATO policymakers. As they see it, if war should occur in Europe there is little doubt the Soviets would mass their forces and concentrate fire-power in an effort to shock and then breakthrough NATO defenses; both Soviet military doctrine and their force posture and deployment indicate such a scenario. If NATO forces are able to slowdown this blitzkrieg (and not cross the nuclear threshold) reinforcement will be necessary on both sides. Unfortunately for the West, the Pact is capable of a much faster buildup in the first few weeks of fighting (and the disparity would be increased if local surprise had been achieved). Given the importance of the United States and the Soviet Union in the respective alliances their role will be crucial, and America's reinforcement task—intercontinental reinforcement by sea and air—clearly is much more difficult than that of the U. S. S. R.

---

[58]For further discussion of "flexible response" see Chapter 14, p. 398.

If hostilities are not terminated quickly another factor must enter the equation, namely, mobilization potential.[59] In analyzing this factor the policymaker must take into account several factors mentioned earlier: the military age structure of the population, its size, male-female ratios, and educational and skills levels. One must also examine the state's capacity to organize and allocate its resources effectively, and its morale and leadership qualities. Critically important in this regard is the economic base.[60] The question is: "Does this party have the overall capability to support a sustained war?" The lack of such capacity has done much to influence Israel's military strategy. Tel Aviv's emphasis on firepower and mobility coupled with an offensive strategy is dictated by her presumed inability to sustain a war of attrition.

It is evident from the foregoing that the prudent policymaker will not limit the analysis to forces in being. While the hostilities which may occur may be short and decisive they also may not be, and in some situations other factors such as reinforcement capacity and mobilization potential will be highly important.

Qualitative Factors: Personnel

It should be obvious that the policymaker must not halt his or her analysis after examining quantitative factors; quite clearly, qualitative considerations must be studied also. Before commencing the discussion of such qualitative factors two important caveats need to be introduced. First, the distinctions among the factors to be discussed imply a degree of separateness that is somewhat beyond that which actually exists; the factors are interrelated. Second, and in a similar vein, the distinction between quantitative and qualitative features also is somewhat artificial. As our previous analysis has shown, one cannot discuss quantitative features wholly separately from qualitative considerations; the reverse is equally true. Thus while it is highly useful for the purposes of clear thinking to analyze the categories separately, it is essential to remember that in the real world they are always at least somewhat interrelated.

For purposes of analysis, qualitative considerations can be usefully subdivided into the categories of personnel, the level of technological development, and leadership. The quality of the troops involved in a particular conflict may be decisive. In both 1967 and 1973 the superb quality and morale of the Israeli forces, fighting what they perceived to be wars for survival, more than offset the firepower of their Arab opponents. Perhaps even more to the point is the

---

[59]For an excellent introduction to the entire subject of military potential see Knorr, Chapter 2.

[60]In the discussion of economic capability it was stated that the relevance of economic strength to military capacity varies with the kind of conflict, and that in some situations the relationship may not be significant. It is equally true, however, that in other cases it is.

example of the success which the Vietcong had against the immensely superior firepower of the United States in the Vietnam war. The Vietcong's skill, their propensity to harmonize with the native population, their ability to make use of the geographical factors, their high morale and dedication, and their ability to gain critical information allowed them to neutralize Washington's vast technological advantages.[61]

When investigating military alliances a major issue frequently is the degree of commitment and reliability of the forces of the various alliance members. To illustrate, given the polycentrism of, and the unrest of the populace in, Central and Eastern Europe, the Soviets clearly have to be concerned over the reliability or the lack thereof of various Warsaw Pact contingents. If a European war broke out, would the Czechs support the Russians? How about the Hungarians? Is 1956 an old and faded memory? Certainly the East Germans hold no love for Soviets. At the time of the uprisings in East Berlin in 1953 (uprisings crushed by Soviet force) "the People's Police units called in generally refused to attack the insurgents and were soon kept away from the scene for fear they would join the rebels."[62] Who would East Germans fight, West Germans or Russians, if hostilities occurred? And what would the Rumanians and Poles do? These and related questions cannot be definitively answered at this point, but they are questions of vital significance to policymakers in both the Warsaw Pact and NATO. Without doubt one's answers will severely impact the assessment of the importance of some of the NATO-Pact quantitative disparities discussed earlier.

Qualitative Factors: Technological

Another major component of military strength is the level of technological development and sophistication. Although other factors also are important and in some kinds of conflicts can partially offset technological superiority, it is equally true that wars have often been decided by the technological factor and policymakers clearly would like to have technological supremacy. Enormous sums are spent today for research and development, testing, production, and deployment of highly advanced weapons, support, and control systems.

All policymakers would like to have the technological advantage. When Israel purchased American F-4 Phantom jets and used them to counter Egyptian artillery in the war of attrition in 1969 and 1970, they achieved a technological advantage. This led to an Egyptian request for Soviet surface-to-air

---

[61]One must always remember, however, that the United States acted within certain self-imposed limitations, such as the nonuse of nuclear weapons.

[62]Peter H. Merkl, *German Foreign Policies, West & East: On the Threshold of a New European Era*, ABC CLIO, Santa Barbara, Cal. 1974, p. 197.

missiles and a later generation of MIG fighter interceptors to counter the Israeli edge. A major concern of American policymakers in recent years has
been the growing vulnerability of the United States' land based inter-continen-
tal ballistic missile (ICBM) forces. In the late 1970s the U. S. S. R. was deploying new highly accurate ICBMs at a rate of about 125 a year, missiles with considerable hard-target (silo destroying) kill capability.[63] Most of these missiles
were MIRVed, adding to the threat.[64] Furthermore, the U. S. S. R. also was
rapidly enhancing the capability of its submarine launched ballistic missile
(SLBM) force. Projecting these trends into the near future Secretary of Defense Brown stated it was conceivable that at some point in the early to mid-
1980s the Soviets "could eliminate the bulk of our ICBM silos and still retain a
large number of warheads in reserve."[65] To counter the growing ICBM vulnerability the United States was engaging in a number of measures to upgrade its
deterrent forces including research and development for the MX mobile land-
based ICBM (which also would be more accurate and carry more warheads
than existing missiles), the deployment of new longer range Trident I missiles
in its Poseidon submarines, the development and 1981 deployment of the new
Trident submarine (which would be quieter, faster, have longer range, and
carry more missiles than its predecessors), and further development toward the
1982 deployment of air launched cruise missiles (ALCMs) on existing B-52
bombers.[66]

Today the development of modern weaponry as a result of scientific and
technological advances is enough to stagger the mind. The explosion of one
nuclear warhead in the one-megaton range would make a hole almost 300 feet
deep and a half mile across.[67] Everything in the immediate area would be destroyed and a huge fireball would develop. Within four or five miles all com-

---

[63]The statistics are provided in U. S. Department of Defense, *Annual Report Fiscal 1980*, p.
72.

[64]MIRV is an acronym for Multiple Independently Targeted Reentry Vehicle. It refers to a
cluster of several warheads on one launcher, each warhead capable of being independently directed to a separate target. A MIRVed missile employs some type of warhead dispensing postboost
vehicle that maneuvers to achieve successive requisite positions and velocities to dispense each warhead on its trajectory toward the desired target. In the future it is possible that the warhead reentry
vehicles will themselves maneuver after they reenter the atmosphere.

[65]U. S. Department of Defense, *Annual Report Fiscal Year 1980*, p. 15. The Secretary was
careful to point out that he strongly doubted such an attack would be forthcoming however, and
that the U. S. retaliatory capacity would remain large even without its ICBMs.

[66]A cruise missile is a pilotless guided missile which utilizes aerodynamic lift to offset gravita-
tional pull and propulsion to counteract drag. ALCMs are relatively slow airbreathing missiles
whose flight path remains in the earth's atmosphere.

[67]A megaton is equivalent to one million tons of TNT. This is the size of the warhead carried
by the American Minuteman II. As of mid-1979 the Soviets had deployed about 200 SS-18s, which
in their single warhead mode carry an 18-25 MT warhead.

bustibles would ignite and any humans that survived would be hideously burned. All structures in this area would be destroyed and various materials would cut through the air like bullets. Windstorms of hurricane velocity would develop as would devastating soundwaves. Radiation would be horrendous and be spread over the miles by the wind. No one knows precisely what the genetic effects would be on the survivors nor what areas would remain uninhabitable due to radioactivity.[68]

This description is briefly illustrative of what might occur with only a single megaton blast. Suppose a larger attack occurred. An American submarine armed with Poseidon missiles today conveys more firepower (in terms of TNT equivalents) than was dropped by all of the Allied air forces on Germany in World War II. The noted defense analyst, Herman Kahn, speculates about deaths of 2 to 160 million, the continuing genetic impact of nuclear war, and then states that military planners should understand the importance of being able to accept retaliatory blows in the sense of being able to distinguish among 2 million, 5 million, 20 million, 50 million, and 100 million American or Soviet deaths.[69]

Today both the Soviet Union and the United States possess nuclear striking forces of frightening potential.[70] Diagrams 3 and 4 give a simple quantitative comparison of the number of missiles deployed by each at various stages since the early 1960s, while Table 11 provides a summary breakdown of the situation in mid-1979 including data on warheads and strategic bombers.

When analyzing the strategic nuclear relationship in an effort to determine whether essential equivalence exists things are even more complicated than this might imply. Several other factors also have to be considered. One is target vulnerability, one aspect of which was discussed above. Another concerns "payload" or "throw weight," the weapons and penetration aids carried by the delivery vehicle. Soviet missiles generally utilize larger warheads with higher explosive yields than those used by the United States.[71] There are certain offsets here, however. First, because explosive force is exerted in all direc-

[68]For useful discussions of the possible consequences of a nuclear exchange see National Academy of Sciences, *Proceedings of the Symposium on Postattack Recovery from Nuclear War*, Washington, D. C., 1967, and U. S. Congress, Office of Technology Assessment, *The Effects of Nuclear War*, May 1979.

[69]Herman Kahn, *On Thermonuclear War*, The Free Press, New York, 1969, pp. 20 and 472. A key question in all this is, how much is too much? What is the unacceptable level of damage necessary to deter? See Chapter 10, for further discussion.

[70]Britain, France, and China have small nuclear forces and other states possess the potential for such. See Chapter 10, p. 267, and corresponding footnote.

[71]According to the Chairman of the Joint Chiefs of Staff, in 1979 the Soviets enjoyed a 11.3/7.2 million pounds throw-weight edge. U. S. Department of State, *SALT II: Senate Testimony, July 9-11, 1979*, "Chairman of the Joint Chiefs of Staff, General David C. Jones," Current Policy No. 72A, p. 34.

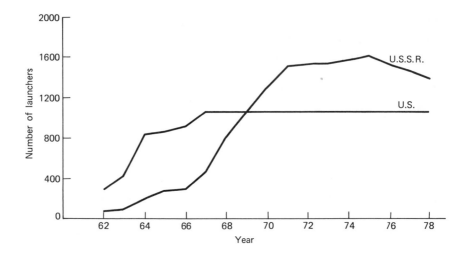

Diagram 3. U. S. and U. S. S. R. ICBM launchers, 1962–1978. (*Source:* The International Institute for Strategic Studies, *The Military Balance, 1975–1976*, London, 1975, p. 73; *The Military Balance, 1976–1977*, London, 1976, p. 75; *The Military Balance, 1978–1979*, London, 1978, pp. 82–83.)

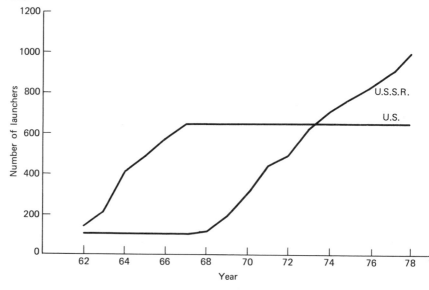

Diagram 4. U. S. and U. S. S. R. SLBM launchers, 1962–1978. (*Source:* The International Institute for Strategic Studies, *The Military Balance, 1975–1976*, London, 1975, p. 73; *The Military Balance, 1976–1977*, London, 1976, p. 75; *The Military Balance, 1978–1979*, London, 1978, pp. 82–83.)

Table 11   U. S.–U. S. S. R. Strategic Force Levels, 1979

	U. S.	*U. S. S. R.*
ICBM launchers	1054	1398
ICBM launchers equipped with MIRVs	550	608
SLBM launchers	656	950
SLBM launchers equipped with MIRVs	496	144
Heavy Bombers[a]	573	156
Total force loadings	9200	5000

Source: The data for all but the last category are from the official statements of the United States and the Soviet Union on June 18, 1979 at the signing of the SALT II Treaty. See U. S. Department of State, *SALT II Agreement*, Selected Documents No. 12A, 1979, p. 49. The data on force loadings is from U. S. Department of Defense, *Annual Report for Fiscal Year 1980*, p. 71.

[a]This includes, for the United States, B-52s used for miscellaneous purposes and those in reserve, mothballs, and storage; it does not include 68 FB-111s. Soviet figures do not include Backfire.

tions a warhead with twice the yield will not destroy twice the area. The term "equivalent megatonnage," usually defined as two-thirds the power of explosive yield, takes this into account. Still, even by this measure the Soviets are well "ahead" in this category. But there is yet another major characteristic: accuracy.[72] It is a generally accepted fact that in terms of the capacity to destroy hardened targets (such as missile silos) accuracy is critical, the rule of thumb being that an improvement in accuracy by 50 percent is equivalent to an 800 percent increase in yield. In this category the United States currently is leading but the Soviets appear to be rapidly catching up. Other elements such as command and control systems, reliability, retargetability, etc., also have to be taken into account. When analyzing "capability" in the sphere of strategic nuclear forces the policymaker is dealing with an issue that almost defies comprehension.

Qualitative Factors: Leadership

The final qualitative aspect of military capability is leadership. This encompasses many factors. It involves the degree to which leaders are able to bridge the gap between officers and regular soldiers and between various branches of the armed services as a whole. It concerns the quality and the appropriateness of the military training program. It includes the efficiency and capacity of the staff and the command, control, and communications structure(s). It involves the degree of receptivity to innovation and change, flexibility or lack thereof in

---

[72]Accuracy is usually expressed in terms of Circular Error Probable (CEP), the estimated radius of a circle within which 50 percent of the warheads are expected to fall.

terms of strategy and tactics, the capacity to analyze and correctly assess the impact of military information, and the extent to which leaders are able to produce vigorous sustained action by both front line and supporting elements. Finally, and crucially, good leadership involves correctly anticipating and visualizing the scenarios most likely to occur, the types of hostilities in which a party is most likely to be engaged, the subsequent preparing of one's forces adequately and appropriately for *those* kinds of contingencies, and then following through with appropriate execution.[73]

There have been many failures in leadership strategy. Two quick examples will underline this point. First, the classic case of the Maginot line psychology of the French between World War I and World War II. The revolutionary effect of mobility on the tactics of war demonstrated at the end of World War I was not appreciated sufficiently by French policymakers. They therefore built a wall of steel and concrete between themselves and the Germans and neglected to develop their own mobile armored forces. The German General Staff, on the other hand, fully alive to the potentialities of armor, mobility, and heavy firepower, planned and later executed what became known as the lightning war (blitzkrieg). The onslaught of Hitler's Panzers and divebombers against the French in World War II led to a devastating French defeat.

Another example occurred in the 1967 Arab-Israeli War. The Egyptian air force had a numerical superiority over Israel's. Unfortunately (for Cairo) its defensive strategy envisaged an Israeli attack from the East directly across the Sinai Peninsula and Egyptian radar was deployed accordingly. The Israelis circumvented this defense line with a series of strikes from the West, coming around behind the Egyptians and destroying nearly three-fourths of the Egyptian air force on the ground in the first two hours of the war. This defect in the Egyptian leadership cost them any possibility of winning. Of course, the reverse of the poor strategy is the good strategy. For examples one can simply point to the above cases, citing the brilliance of the German General Staff in the development of the blitzkrieg and the shrewdness of the Israeli air command in deciding on the routes of its attack on June 5, 1967.

The problem of the correct strategy is becoming more and more difficult to solve given the myriad of types of conflict that are possible and the fact that no country has unlimited resources. It is virtually impossible for a policymaker to be prepared to meet all contingencies and develop appropriate strategies to meet all possible types and levels of conflict. One can never wholly foresee the future, what kind of hostilities will occur where and under what circumstances, and once the shooting starts it's very difficult to predict what will hap-

---

[73]One major difficulty of the American effort in Vietnam was that Washington trained the ARVN (South Vietnamese) forces to fight a conventional war and thus they were ill equipped to handle the guerilla tactics of the Viet Cong.

pen anyway. More than this, no party has sufficient resources to fully prepare for all eventualities. The best the policymaker can do is carefully analyze the likely contingencies, rank them in terms of importance and probability, and then, on this basis, allocate resources and devise what seem to be appropriate strategies. Hopefully one will anticipate correctly or nearly so in most instances. Nevertheless, inaccuracies are to some degree inevitable; no one is infallible. Therefore, it is essential that the policymaker's plans provide a level of flexibility sufficient to at least partially counter unanticipated contingencies. Where this is not done the outcome may well be counterproductive.

To this point our analysis has focused on the tangible components of capability. One should not end his or her examination here, however, because there also are a number of intangible features that need to be taken into account. To these we now turn.

8

Capability Components: Intangible

The internal components of capability discussed in Chapter 7 were, for the most part, tangible. Because of this (many of) their various aspects could be quite easily measured. Much more elusive but no less important are the intangible components of capability: governmental functions, characteristics of society, individual policymaker quality, and party uniqueness.

GOVERNMENTAL FUNCTIONS

The first of the intangible capability components is *governmental functions*, the forms, structures, and processes of government in the particular state. *The central concern in this regard is the degree to which the government can bring the country's potential capabilities to bear on the specific problem at hand, and the efficiency and dispatch with which this can be done.* If policymakers cannot actualize potential capability then such potential might as well not exist. If they can bring it to bear but only in a very inefficient manner, then they either will be less likely to achieve their objective, or do so only at a disproportionate cost. This is important at anytime but may be particularly crucial in short run crisis situations.[1]

---

[1]Obviously the total of a state's resources is important as well as is their quality, as has been discussed in our analysis of the first five components of capability. But in the short run the governmental factor could be critical. It has been stated that, "in the short run, then, power differentials among states in the international system stem much more from differential abilities to allocate resources to foreign policy pursuits than from differential endowments in basic resources." See Puchala, p. 181.

Because no state possesses unlimited resources, allocation choices must be made. Decisions concerning the comparative merits of domestic and foreign policies are required, resulting in some resources being used for each type. Additionally, choices must be made among various external programs, which means that no single problem or project can be allocated more than a portion of the resources theoretically available for foreign affairs. How and to what extent does the organization and operation of the governmental system facilitate or hinder this decision-making?[2]

In examining these issues one must avoid oversimplified answers. It has sometimes been assumed that policymakers in authoritarian governments automatically possess major advantages compared to those in more democratic systems. It is postulated that they are not subject to public opinion constraints, are able to act with secrecy, speed, and decisiveness, are able to "shift gears" whenever appropriate, and are able to use whatever means they consider appropriate. Conversely, it is suggested that democracies fall short in these areas.

This argument has some degree of validity but entails major difficulties because it does not accurately describe the realities of the authoritarian policy-making process. It categorically assumes that the "advantages" noted above exist at all times but that is not so; sometimes they just are not there. Most of the time the differences between authoritarian and democratic systems in these areas are differences of *degree, not kind*.

All governments, for example, require some degree of acceptance by their populace to exist, and so policymakers are concerned with what people think. This may be less true in authoritarian systems than in democracies but it still is a factor of some importance. If an authoritarian government requires support from its people, then the "people's opinion" makes some difference. Sometimes an authoritarian rules by the sword, of course, but this is not common. And when he or she does it is only a mixed blessing because the more costs incurred in domestic political control the fewer resources available for foreign policy. It is true that sometimes resources *can* be allocated by fiat but if this is necessary it often leads to, or is a symptom of, considerable internal unrest.

Another point is that authoritarian governments as well as democracies are composed of congeries of people and interests that both compete and cooperate in the policymaking process, and this can lead to inefficiency, confusion, misdirected policies, and delays in both systems. Following the shooting down of an American U-2 spy plane in the Ural Mountains by a Soviet rocket on May 1, 1960, for example, there was great uncertainty and factional disagreement in Moscow as to the appropriate response.[3] Four days of embar-

---

[2]Much of the analysis here is directly related to the problem of domestic constraints. For a more detailed analysis see Chapter 15.

[3]See Michael Tatu, *Power in the Kremlin: From Khrushchev to Kosygin*, Viking, New York, 1968, Chapter 2.

rassed public silence went by. Then, after considerable discussion within the Central Committee of the Communist Party, Premier Khrushchev reported the incident in a speech to the Supreme Soviet. But the Soviet leader deliberately adopted a relatively moderate tone, trying to walk a tightrope between those who wanted a vigorous condemnation of capitalist espionage and those who didn't want to jeopardize the upcoming Paris summit. On the same day as Khrushchev's speech Washington issued a "cover" story, claiming the plane had only been engaged in meteorological work and had crossed the border accidentally. In the Kremlin debate continued, and on May 7 Khrushchev denounced Washington's cover story as well as American espionage activities generally. But the Soviet leader was still very careful to leave the United States a way out with its prestige only slightly harmed, stating he was willing to believe that President Eisenhower did not know a plane had been sent over the Soviet Union and had failed to return. American policymakers failed to grasp this opportunity, however. The same evening as Khrushchev's May 7 speech the State Department announced the flight was "probably" undertaken by an unarmed U-2 plane, and two days later Secretary of State Christian Herter acknowledged extensive American aerial surveillance for intelligence gathering purposes, said that such had been occurring for some years, and intimated it likely would continue. Shortly thereafter, President Eisenhower publicly assumed full personal responsibility for the flight. It was not until all this occurred that the various Soviet domestic interests coalesced, but at this juncture they did and Mr. Khrushchev responded with great intensity; given the prestige challenge which Washington's actions and statements posed, he really had little choice. For our purposes the salient factor is not the incident's outcome, but rather the simple fact that there existed a lack of consensus and direction in the Kremlin prior to a certain point. As this example shows, even in highly authoritarian systems there sometimes is considerable factional disagreement, uncertainty, and confusion.

Outsiders, dealing with a core of individuals who are operating within and trying to dominate an intensively and extensively controlled political system, sometimes fail to perceive the internal factionalism that exists. On some occasions the facade of unity hides a bitter (domestic) power struggle. For example, most Americans were unaware of the shakiness of Khrushchev's rule in the early 1960s and were caught by surprise when in late 1964 he was ousted by comrades Brezhnev and Kosygin. Perhaps even more to the point, the mere existence of China's Great Proletarian Cultural Revolution of the mid and late 1960s was not apparent in the West until well after it had begun, and throughout its duration it remained a considerable puzzle.[4] In both of these instances

---

[4]In the mid-1960s a serious struggle for power developed in the Chinese Communist Party. Under Mao Tse-tung's leadership a great purge of Party and bureaucratic "reactionaries" was instituted. Thousands of youthful Red Guards spread Mao's slogans throughout the country, casti-

foreign policy activities were hindered by, and in part were products of, domestic political developments, just as they sometimes are in democratic systems.

Despite all the foregoing, however, it is still true that democratic policymakers are *relatively* less free to formulate and implement policy as they desire than are their authoritarian counterparts, and they often find it more difficult to act as rapidly. These difficulties have sometimes led to vast governmental efforts to deceive and mislead the populace, the obvious recent example being the contrast between the announced and actual American policies in Vietnam in most of the 1960s.[5] But this "difficulty" can also be an advantage if one assumes that a policy more responsive to the public will receive more support. Furthermore, more open systems tend to allow a greater interchange of concepts and data, presumably leading to more informed decisions. In addition, democratic structures supposedly tend to place more emphasis on individual initiative and creativity, which in turn should lead to more imaginative and innovative policies (although obviously it does not always work this way).

What conclusions can one draw so far? Perhaps only the negative one that no particular type of system is automatically more effective than any other. What this means for the policymaker is that he must get down to specific considerations and avoid *a priori* judgments resulting from mere system classification.

What are some of the key questions that need to be asked? First, *what is the form and structure of the target government?* It is obvious that the form of government alone does not dictate the nature of the political process, but it is also true that the particular structure does have an impact. Witness, for example, the United States system of checks and balances with an intermingling of functions. This means that no policymaker can ignore certain institutional features. The fact that foreign policy programs must be funded by Congressional appropriations means that an American policymaker must frame his or her policies with a wary eye on Capitol Hill. In 1973, after the signature of the Peace Agreements on Vietnam, the Congress voted to cut off funds for bombing in Cambodia. The president vetoed one bill, but under severe pressure for a further tightening of the purse strings he agreed to end the bombing by August

---

gating the "imperialists" who were impeding the revolution. Unexpectedly strong resistance was encountered, however, and the entire party, military, and governmental structures were in turmoil. Serious fighting occurred in some areas and eventually the Red Guards themselves had to be curbed. Out of the chaos Mao emerged supreme but the Party was weakened and military interests became more important.

[5]We would again suggest starting with Halberstam and the Pentagon Papers. Also useful in this regard and generally with respect to the issue of American governmental deception, is Lincoln Bloomfield, *In Search of American Foreign Policy: The Humane Use of Power*, Oxford University Press, New York, 1974, pp. 99-112.

15, 1973. In 1975-1976 Congress voted to cut off all military and financial assistance to the FNLA/UNITA coalition in the Angola war. Another structural feature of some import in the American system is the fact that all treaties must be ratified by the U. S. Senate. Thus the president, if wise, will consult with the Senate and attempt to judiciously accomodate his policies to its views, as President Carter did with respect to the Panama Canal Treaties. President Wilson's failure to do this led to the rejection of the Treaty of Versailles and the League of Nations at the end of World War I.[6]

The second question is, *what is the current political situation and what are the actual political processes in the particular state?* It is essential that one go beyond an examination of the formal institutions of government and seek to determine who actually holds power, how decisions actually are made, what in practice is (are) the process(es) by which rules are promulgated, interpreted, applied, and enforced, and how disputes are really settled. There frequently is a great discrepancy between the "official" and the "real." In early 1958, for example, despite their official positions the president and prime minister of Syria actually were almost devoid of policy influence. Real power was shared by leaders of the Baath Party, the military, and the Communists, and it was they (especially the Baathists) who engineered Syria's merger with Egypt. In the Soviet Union, despite what the U. S. S. R. constitution provides, all important decisions are actually made by Communist Party leaders. Despite what the constitution stipulated, when in Lesotho in 1970 the government lost the election it suspended the constitution, declared a state of emergency, and simply refused to relinquish its power. In Japan most foreign policy decisions are actually the result of intra-political party factional bargaining by the Liberal-Democrats. In these and innumerable other instances the "paper" form of government has (had) little to do with the actual political process.

Another question the policymaker must ask is *to what extent is this particular party flexible, able to adjust to changing conditions?* Are there historical precedents that will eliminate or dictate certain options and objectives? Is there a prevailing ideology that is similarly rigidifying? Do the policymakers have their judgments largely determined by role perceptions that do not allow them freedom of activity, or by superior-subordinate relationships that prevent consideration of new ideas? Are the organizational processes such that particular groups have an inordinate influence over the policymaker to the extent that certain options will never be realistically considered? Do bureaucratic factions have vested interests in existing policies to such a degree that suggested alterations will be thwarted by bureaucratic infighting? Do the standard operating procedures of the foreign policy apparatus stifle creativity and innovation?

---

[6]Today, presidents often resort to an "Executive Agreement" instead of a treaty since it has the same impact as a treaty but does not require senatorial consent.

Are international problems viewed as abstract generalized issues of "Good" and "Evil" thus obliterating meaningful concrete distinctions and precluding policy modifications?

Another set of questions concerns the information gathering system. Is it such that adequate quantities of information can be obtained? Are the sources reliable? Are, for example, so-called "national technical means" (reconnaissance satellites and various forms of electronic espionage) sufficient to verify compliance with strategic arms control agreements? Another question is, is the data obtained accurate and undistorted by misperception and incorrect interpretation? Israel was well aware of Egyptian and Syrian military redeployments prior to the October 1973 war but most of its policymakers did not think an attack was probable.[7] Can the information be communicated to the right people at the right time? Will it be used in an efficient manner so that a rational decision is likely to be made? Do bias and prejudice exist within the system that would prevent certain options from being realistically considered, and in some cases almost ensure that certain other factors will be taken as givens? Do policymakers have certain preconceptions that preclude careful consideration of information from certain sources, or automatically eliminate particular policy choices?

Finally, one must seek to determine if the government is organized in such a way that policymakers are able to provide the specific means of policy implementation that are appropriate for given objectives. In other words, to what extent are they able to translate potential into real power or prevented from doing so by the mere nonexistence of correct instrumentalities? For example, suppose a particular country has a highly diversified and highly differentiated modern economy with a strong industrial base. This mere existence gives this country a certain potential for action. If the economic strength cannot be utilized via its contribution to military and economic instruments of statecraft, however, instead being devoted to higher levels of domestic consumption, its contribution to that state's capability is limited.

There is no automatic answer to the question of governmental strength. Only by analyzing the specific governmental components of the countries under consideration can one determine the degree to which policymakers may be organizationally able to translate capability potential into realizable power.

CHARACTERISTICS OF SOCIETY

Another component of capability is what one can call the characteristics of the domestic society: the degree of societal cohesiveness, and the degree of support that the government receives from its populace.

---

[7] Also see Chapter 15, p. 433.

Degree of Cohesiveness

The degree of cohesiveness can have a significant impact on capability. Generally speaking, the more a society is fragmented the more attention, effort, and resources required to deal with this problem and the less available for foreign policy pursuits. Even when minorities are mercilessly crushed as in the case of the Nazi slaughter of six million Jews, the state is still diverting its attention and resources from foreign policy objectives.[8] Furthermore, the potential contribution of these groups is, of course, never actualized.

The causes and types of fragmentation are many and only a few can be discussed here. One is the existence of major *ethnic, tribal, or racial differences*; these often lead to conflict. Whereas the United States became a "melting pot" and a variety of ethnic groups eventually melded into society (except for blacks and Indians), in the 1970s alone bloody civil wars based on ethnic disunity occurred in Pakistan, Chad, the Sudan, Ethiopia, and (originally) Cyprus. In the late 1960s a tribally based civil war occurred in Nigeria that caused nearly two million deaths. In the late 1970s in South Africa the minority white government continued to impose its rule on the black majority, while in Rhodesia a partially racially based guerilla-civil war took place. In Iran there have been periodic hostilities between the majority Persians and the Kurds as the latter have sought independence. In World War II many Ukrainians joined forces with the Nazis to fight their Russian masters. And today—in cases ranging from the Karens of Burma to certain of the 60 or so ethnic groups in the Ivory Coast—ethnic and/or racial and/or tribal differences threaten to fragment society in a great number of states. Obviously such divisions are detrimental to capability.

Religious differences too can cause disunity. The tragic dispute between Protestants and Catholics over the future of Northern Ireland continues to this day. The division of the Indian subcontinent into the separate states of India and Pakistan following Britain's departure in 1947 was largely the outgrowth of Islamic-Hindu hostility. During the Vietnam war the Saigon government (South) was often hampered by Catholic-Bhuddist enmity. And the little country of Lebanon, its population approximately half Moslem and half Christian with each faith itself splintered into numerous sects, suffered a major crisis in 1958 and in 1975-1976 was almost torn apart by a civil war that produced upwards of 20,000 deaths; in both instances, though there also were other factors involved, religious antagonism was a major causal element.

---

[8]The Nazis argued that the result of the extermination of the Jews would be a strengthening of Germany, because the "backstabbers" would be removed. Although untrue in this instance, the principle could hold true in other cases.

In addition to these and other subnational factors, in some cases elements of the population feel an allegiance that crosses state boundaries. Such *transnational* attraction can be terribly disruptive. Most of the subnational factors discussed above also have transnational implications. A number of ethnic groups, tribes, races, and religious groups have been split by various territorial boundaries, and many consider such arrangements to be both artificial and temporary. Indeed, in many cases transnational ethnic, tribal, racial, or religious affinities are major contributing causes of conflict. It is essential that one not assume that if a group is split transnational loyalties are secondary. The post-World War II division of Germany and the development of Cold War blocs does not mean that all Germans have given up their desire for a unified country. Indeed, former West German Chancellor Brandt's phrase, "two German states within one German nation," shows the feeling of being one German people despite the political realities of the day. The division of Korea similarly does not eliminate a feeling of oneness and certain transnational attractions. Sometimes an ideological flavor is added, exacerbating matters. Pan-Arabism, the idea that the Arabs are really all one people and present state frontiers have no legitimate basis, was the philosophical core of Egyptian President Gamal Nasser's policy in the 1950s and 1960s (and performs the same function for the activities of the Baath parties of Syria and Iraq today). And, of course, there also are comprehensive ideologies with transnational appeal, such as international communism.

It is apparent that there have been a great number of instances in which subnational and/or transnational factors have produced societal cleavages that have severely diminished capability, and doubtless there will be many more. But the operational policymaker must be careful not to assume too much in this area. For example, though societal fragmentation certainly is not helpful, the fact that a society is fragmented does not inexorably mean that the fragmented party cannot have an effective foreign policy. Almost 50 percent of the Soviet Union's population is composed of ethnic minorities, and many of them bitterly dislike the majority Russians. Nevertheless, obviously the Soviet Union is a very powerful country. Similarly, one cannot automatically assume that the existence of such cleavages will bring about the downfall of the government in times of crisis. In 1970 and 1971 there was violent civil conflict in Jordan between King Hussein's forces and various guerilla organizations. The population of Jordan was about two-thirds "ex-Palestinian" and many observers had assumed that if a crisis occurred the Palestinians would revolt against the King. In actuality when the conflict occurred the majority of the population simply ignored it.[9]

[9] Also see Chapter 3, pp. 71–74.

The key questions the policymaker must ask in this regard are:

1. How much and what kind of disunity is there?
2. To what extent will its existence divert interest, attention, effort, and resources from foreign policy objectives?
3. How much would the country add to its capability if the problems were solved, and how much is it losing now?
4. Is the fragmentation likely to lead to policy alteration, regime change, or even civil war?
5. Is the country likely to "solve" the problem?
6. How vulnerable is the country to foreign penetration and influence because of this?
7. What should be the appropriate policy response?

Popular Support

The degree of societal cohesiveness is related to a larger issue—the extent to which the populace supports the current regime and/or its policies. In analyzing this subject (in terms of both its regime and policy-support aspects) one first needs to answer a number of basic questions:

1. First, and rather obviously, to what degree is the general public supportive, indifferent, or apathetic, both re this situation and in general? Although the influence of public opinion varies from country to country and with time and circumstance, in all states it plays some role and must therefore be investigated.[10]
2. What are the attitudes, political strengths, and levels of involvement of the interest factions, groups(ings), and opinion-influencing elites who are in a position to have an impact on policymakers?
3. How intensely, broadly, and deeply are the various positions, attitudes, beliefs, and opinions of the particular segments held, and how likely (and susceptible) are they to change? If significant change(s) is (are) likely, what will its (their) net impact(s) be?
4. If there is compliance with or support for the particular regime and/or its policies, is it largely voluntary or is it the product of fear and sanctions? In other words, is the "support" that exists genuine or imposed?
5. If the prime causes of "support" are sanctions and fear, to what extent are such really effective, how much of a diversion of effort and resources from foreign policy pursuits do they require, and to

---

[10]Also see Chapter 15, pp. 407–412.

what degree does their utilization cause counterproductive effects in relations with situationally pertinent international parties?

6. If sanctions and fear are freely employed, what is the probability that their targets will be driven into more vigorous opposition, and what would the consequences of that be?

After answering these basic questions the policymaker must then address the issues of *time* and *relevance*. Is the degree of support temporary or permanent? To illustrate, is the American public's disenchantment with foreign military involvements, a disenchantment flowing largely from the Vietnam war, likely to continue into the foreseeable future, or will it erode with the passage of time? Second, is this attitude one that applies to a broad range of issues, or is it highly specific? Again using the impact of the Vietnam war as an example, is the American public inclined to support a "less involved" policy as a general principle, or is its view targeted specifically on Vietnam (or Asia, or...?)? Finally, one must decide whether the level of support is a relevant consideration with respect to the specific situation being analyzed.

The importance that popular support for governmental policies has sometimes had, and the difficulties when it has been lacking, can be amply documented. Certainly the disintegration of the support of the American people for continued involvement in Vietnam led to a weakening of the government's capability to achieve its stated objectives. The collapse of support by the Chinese people for Chiang Kai-shek's government was a significant contributor to Mao Tse-tung's rise to power.[11] The inability of the Saigon government to obtain more than a modicum of public support was directly related to its inability to defeat its opponents despite massive American aid. Contrast these situations with the magnificent popular support that the English people gave their government in World War II, and the intense support of the Israeli populace against the Arabs in their various conflicts, and one can easily see how important it can be.

These, however, are dramatic and extreme cases. What about the more ordinary situation? Are there any guidelines one can follow that will help to answer the questions raised above? Perhaps there are. Although they are neither foolproof nor easily operationalized, the following still are useful to the policymaker as kinds of rules of thumb:

1. Every government, to some extent, responds to domestic demands placed upon it by its populace. The more responsive it is, the more likely it is to be supported. In LDCs, for example, frequently there

---

[11]This is vividly described in U. S. Department of State, *United States Relations with China with Special Reference to the Period 1944-1949*, Washington, D. C., 1949. Also see Chapter 10, pp. 279–280.

are major demands by the general public for noticeable and continuous improvement in the standard of living, and for an equalizing
redistribution of wealth. The more LDC policymakers can effectively respond to these demands, the more likely they will be supported.
2. Every government has certain priorities among its objectives. The
more important the objective, the more intensive will be the government's efforts to obtain popular support, and the more critical for
that government that it be obtained.
3. The more the government's objectives and policies are consonant
with the country's traditions, norms, belief system, and historical
experience, the more likely they will receive support.
4. The smaller the discrepancy between the people's expectations of
government and governmental achievement, the greater the support.
Conversely, the greater the discrepancy, the less the support. If the
people in a particular LDC have been promised an improved standard of living and an equalization of wealth and do not get it, they
may well turn against the regime.

THE INDIVIDUAL POLICYMAKER

Another component of capability one must analyze is the impact of specific individual policymakers. It was said in Chapter 1 that the primary actor in international politics today is the nation-state. This is true. One must always remember, however, that when someone says that "Soviet Russia" is following
such and such a policy, or "Egypt" reacted violently to this or that, he or she
is speaking in metaphorical terms. In reality only human beings make decisions. The state does not take action; human beings act and make decisions in
the name of the state. If one speaks then of the containment policy of the
United States one is actually talking about a policy formulated by some specific individuals responsible for American foreign policy. What this means to the
policymaker is that the analysis must include identification of the key personnel and an analysis of their specific characteristics.

Particular Characteristics

Ascertaining the particular characteristics of the individual decisionmaker is
an important task because different individuals have different impacts upon a
state's foreign policy. Obviously international politics is not just the interaction of so-called great people. It is also evident, however, that history shows
that it *does* make a difference who occupies a position of influence at a particular time. It clearly made a difference when Hitler came to power in Germany,
and no one doubts that Winston Churchill left a personal imprint on British

foreign policy in World War II. Clearly Henry Kissinger's particular qualities significantly influenced the course of American policy. It is doubtful that the Chinese Communist Revolution would have proceeded as it did if someone other than Mao Tse-tung had been its leader. Anwar Sadat made major changes in Egypt's policy toward Israel after taking over from Nasser, Willy Brandt had a special impact on West Germany's policy toward the Soviets, and Charles DeGaulle greatly altered French policy. Specific individuals some-times do make a considerable difference.

One begins the process of identifying key policymakers by *ascertaining the locus of decision*. Is there a key decisional unit, or is effective authority scattered among several agencies and groups? What are the influence relation-ships and linkages that exist and how do they impact the present situation? Then, within the context of the answers to these questions, one must find out who are those particular human beings who are most influential in this area and whose authoritative acts are, for all intents and purposes, the acts of the state?[12] Obviously, one must obtain and accurately evaluate a great deal of in-formation about the particular state under consideration in order to perform this task effectively.

The second step involves an assessment of the policymaker's basic person-ality structure. What particular traits characterize this policymaker's behavior, and how relevant are they to his or her policymaking activities? Is the policy-maker basically trusting or distrustful? Unquestionably, President Nixon's tendency to distrust friend and foe alike significantly influenced his *modus operandi*. Is this individual essentially rational and will particular situations be analyzed in an essentially rational manner? Whereas President Kennedy handled the Cuban Missile Crisis in a highly rational fashion, on the eve of World War I Kaiser Wilhelm's actions were almost devoid of rational basis. How does this individual react to various kinds of stimuli? Are there certain patterns of behavior that occur with regularity in certain kinds of situations? In his World War II negotiations with the Western Allies, Josef Stalin fre-quently responded to questions in a quiet, sensible, unassuming fashion, covering "with honey" what was a superb tactical thought process.[13] Is the particular person's personality such that everything must be interpreted in all-or-nothing terms in order for him or her to feel confident? Are one's beliefs absolute and unshakable? To John Foster Dulles the United States was in-volved in an all-out struggle to preserve the "Free World" from conquest by an inherently aggressive international Communist bloc, and nothing could

---

[12]One of the more useful innovations in the study of political science is decision-making anal-ysis. A particularly valuable introduction to this topic is, Richard C. Snyder, H. W. Bruck and Burton Sapin, eds., *Foreign Policy Decision Making*, Free Press of Glencoe, New York, 1963.

[13]See George F. Kennan, *Memoirs: 1925-1950*, Little, Brown, Boston, 1967, pp. 279-280.

convince him otherwise. Is this policymaker basically an insecure, outer-directed person? Was a sense of personal insecurity partially responsible for President Truman's determination to be "tough," to "stand up to the Russians?"[14] Is the particular individual impatient with those who disagree and will this lead him or her to ignore or even oppose policymakers whose help is needed? Is this, in part at least, the explanation of what led to the precipitous downfall of Ghana's Kwame Nkrumah, after nearly a decade of leadership (during which his country had become a focal point of African independence)?[15] These and questions of a similar nature are highly pertinent. In the "real world," policymakers always have certain perceptions of the personalities of their counterparts, whether formed deliberately or not, and these perceptions influence both policy formulation and policy implementation.[16]

Previous Experience

Another cluster of factors one must analyze can be combined under the label of previous experience. This could involve anything from childhood and teenage experiences to social background and level of education, up through and including previous policymaking activity. Studies of Woodrow Wilson's childhood have argued, for example, that his later lack of perceptivity, his inability and/or unwillingness to compromise, and his messianic zeal were primarily the result of childhood influences, especially his relationship with his father.[17] Perhaps Anwar Sadat's determination to recover every inch of territory taken from Egypt by Israel in the 1967 war was, at least in part, an outgrowth of the attachment to the land he had formed during the years of his rural-village upbringing. *It is important that one seeking to understand a policymaker's current and future behavior have some knowledge of that person's early experiences.*

A person's educational experience also may be pertinent. Much of Henry Kissinger's diplomacy, for example, flowed from the ideas and theories he de-

---

[14]See Walter LaFeber, *America, Russia, and the Cold War 1945-1975*, Third Edition, Wiley, New York, 1976, p. 17.

[15]See Christian P. Potholm, *The Theory and Practice of African Politics*, Prentice-Hall, Englewood Cliffs, N. J., 1979, pp. 50-52.

[16]One of the major factors determining Khrushchev's behavior in the early stages of the Cuban Missile Crisis was his perception of Kennedy as "weak." See John G. Stoessinger, *Nations in Darkness: China, Russia and America*, Third Edition, Random House, New York, 1978, Chapter 12.

[17]See Sigmund Freud and William C. Bullitt, *Thomas Woodrow Wilson: A Psychological Study*, Houghton Mifflin, Boston, 1967, and Alexander George and Juliette George, *Woodrow Wilson and Colonel House*, Day, New York, 1956. Most observers do not consider these studies to have *proven* such relationships, however, but only to have developed sufficient data to advance them as reasonable hypotheses.

veloped first as a student and then as a professor, especially those related to Metternich and the Congress of Vienna.[18] Dr. Kissinger's study of history and politics convinced him that before one could achieve peace it was necessary to first achieve stability, that to achieve stability it was necessary to employ policy backed by force, that in the course of diplomacy no party's survival could be endangered or stability would be unattainable, that all major issues are closely interrelated, and that true stability (and therefore peace) requires a balancing of interests and power such that no party is dominant and no party is totally satisfied or dissatisfied.[19] Let's look at a couple of examples of how these fundamental ideas influenced later policies. Because without stability peace would be impossible and because today stability cannot be achieved without Soviet acquiescence, a détente was essential; because all issues were seen as interlinked, the course and pace of the Vietnam negotiations were influenced by external events and conducted with an eye on external parties; because no party's survival should be endangered and no one could be fully satisfied or dominant if peace were to ensue, it was necessary to establish balanced Arab-Israeli equilibrium during and after the October 1973 Middle East war (and to work with Moscow); and many more illustrations could be provided. Policymakers find it useful to analyze their counterparts' educational experiences when trying to understand current and future policies.

The simple fact of being alive in a certain time period and drawing certain "lessons" from the events of the day also can be important. Because the majority of American policymakers after World War II had lived through and "experienced" the results of the appeasement at Munich, there developed what has sometimes been thought of as the Munich complex, the idea that one cannot negotiate with an aggressor and a tough uncompromising approach must be taken against all who are perceived to threaten world peace. When President Truman was informed of the North Korean assault against South Korea in June of 1950, he specifically thought of the 1930s and the danger of history repeating itself.[20] And President Johnson, when speaking of why the United States was in Vietnam, said it was the "central lesson of our time that the appetite of aggression is never satisfied."[21] Post-World War II Soviet leaders, having lived through the "Great Patriotic War" and having seen what a nationalistic Germany that had lost a preceding war (and been disarmed) had been able to do, were not much comforted by Western assurances that the West Germans posed no conceivable threat to Russia. In the 1930s British

---

[18]Very useful is Stoessinger, *Henry Kissinger: The Anguish of Power*, Chapters 1-4.

[19]Compare this with our discussion of the "balance of power." See Chapter 4, pp. 101–103.

[20]See Harry S. Truman, *Memoirs, Vol. II: Years of Trial and Hope*, Doubleday, New York, 1956, pp. 332-340.

[21]This is part of the President's famous Johns Hopkins speech of April 7, 1965, reprinted in Kahin and Lewis, p. 424. Also see the discussion of the "domino theory," Chapter 4, pp. 103-105.

leaders, having witnessed the terrible slaughter of World War I, were determined to do everything possible to avoid another war; undoubtedly the terrible memories of the earlier hostilities had much to do with Chamberlain's policy at Munich.

Finally, personal involvement in specific historical situations may do much to shape one's later outlook. As an Egyptian soldier in the 1948-1949 Arab-Israeli War, Gamal Nasser felt humiliated by the inadequacy, inefficiency, and corruption that characterized the Egyptian army's performance. He resolved that if he ever had the chance he would remedy these deficiencies. After he took over the government in the early 1950s he sought to build up Egyptian military strength and prevent any slights to Arab dignity. Thus when Israeli forces launched a successful attack into the Egyptian-administered Gaza Strip in early 1955, he was humiliated and intensified his existing quest for military assistance. When he was unable to obtain arms "without strings" from the West he was further humiliated, and reacted with a wounded sense of dignity by obtaining arms from those who attached no conditions, the Communists.[22]

Ho Chi Minh's attitude re the utility of negotiating an agreement with the United States to end the Vietnam war certainly was influenced by his earlier personal experiences. As we recount in more detail in Chapter 12, on March 6, 1946 Ho's Democratic Republic of Vietnam signed an agreement with France.[23] Although a portion of that agreement provided that there should be a referendum in Cochinchina concerning that territory's future, the French quickly violated this provision and set up a puppet government. Then, in 1954 Ho was a party to the Geneva Accords that "ended" the Indochina war. On the basis of these accords it was expected that free elections would be held throughout Vietnam within two years. Ho, undoubtedly the most popular man in the country at the time, expected to win these elections, but he was foiled because they were never held; the Saigon government (with varying degrees of American support) refused to participate. In light of such experiences it is understandable that the Vietnamese leader exhibited considerable suspicion, skepticism, and great care during negotiations, and would have even if there had not been ideological, racial, security-threat, or war-produced differences.

Concept of Role

Another component of the policymaker's makeup is his or her concept of role. What does this individual believe are the responsibilities and powers of whoever occupies this particular position; what role is he or she supposed to play?

---

[22]See Chapter 13, p. 364, for further discussion.
[23]See Chapter 12, pp. 329-330.

What are the factors one must investigate in this regard? First, it is important to look at history. In most cases, previous position occupants will have established certain norms and precedents and the reactions to various activities will be on the record. Although the record of the past will not necessarily be controlling, what has happened previously will place certain pressures on the policymaker. Second, it is necessary to determine who the "relevant others" are and what they think because the policymaker's role concept is partly determined by what such relevant others do or do not expect. For example, even if thinking it desirable no member of the Politburo of the People's Republic of China would find it advisable to advocate freedom of political party organization, given the role expectations of other Politburo members. Similarly, since an American secretary of state is directly responsible to the president others expect that policies and views supportive of the Chief Executive will be advocated, not the contrary.

An important point to note here is that role expectations tend to become more set as a person occupies a particular position for a considerable length of time. Precedents become established, procedures become routinized, and there seems to be less room for individual initiative. As these expectations become more deeply entrenched and widely shared particular individuals and groups develop an interest in maintaining the status quo and it is difficult for change to be effected. The individual policymaker's freedom (and influence) in such a situation may be very limited.[24]

Sometimes one may be forced to make some decisions that he would prefer not to make. This is a typical problem for the vice-president in the United States. Hubert Humphrey was expected to support President Johnson's Vietnam policy, even though he did not always agree. Very often a man of differing experience and outlook than the president, the vice-president is still a member of the team and because of his position is expected to support that team without reservation. Diplomatic representatives and military officials also are frequently confronted with this requirement.

It clearly is necessary for one to investigate and determine the extent to which, and in what ways, particular policymakers will feel constrained to do or not do certain things simply because of the concept of role they hold re the positions they occupy. But it is important not to go overboard in this regard, to keep this issue in perspective. In the first place, as we have repeatedly emphasized, policymakers are subject to a whole range of influencing forces. Role concept, while important, is only one of these. Second, even in terms of role concept there are several qualifying features. For one thing, every individual brings to the position a unique blend of characteristics, views, and experiences. Consequently, each person will perceive and evaluate the various factors dif-

[24]Much of the discussion of bureaucratic politics in Chapter 15 is relevant here.

ferently, have a somewhat different role concept, and react to the constraints in his or her own unique fashion. Also, although precedents and others' expectations do become established sometimes they change. Indeed, one may act on the basis of what appear to be established precedents and still find difficulties, as President Nixon discovered in the reaction to his deployment of military forces into Cambodia in the latter stages of the Vietnam War. Furthermore, in fluid and/or new situations there may not yet be set role expectations; no precedents or guidelines may yet have been established. Finally (although it is a matter of degree), in certain highly authoritarian systems key individuals may operate in a policymaking context that is relatively devoid of established procedures and/or constraint-imposing policy influencers. In Uganda in the late 1970s Idi Amin had few role constraints limiting his freedom of choice.

Physical and Mental Health

The next factors to be investigated are physical and mental health. Sometimes one forgets that it is people that are being dealt with, and people have stresses and strains, get tired, have "bad days," or get sick. The strain of responsible policymaking positions is immense, and the deterioration of public leaders has often been significant. In the twentieth century both Presidents Wilson and (Franklin) Roosevelt died while in office, and President Eisenhower suffered severe physical ailments. Stalin died while in power, as did Mao Tse-tung, Ho Chi Minh, Gamal Nasser, Jomo Kenyatta, and others.

Any number of times a deteriorating physical condition or mental state has had an impact on policymaking. For example, President Roosevelt was seriously ill at the 1945 Yalta Conference. Although the precise degree to which this sapped his energy and hindered clear thinking in his negotiations with Stalin is not determinable, there is little doubt that it had some influence. British Prime Minister Anthony Eden was in ill health during the Suez crisis. During the early stages of the crisis this was of little moment, but once things began going badly and the United States, Russia, members of the Commonwealth, much of the Third World, and even most of his own countrymen, joined in opposition his deterioration accelerated and was a significant contributor to his decision to halt the attack. On the eve of World War I Franz Joseph, the emperor of Austria-Hungary, was an exhausted, nearly senile old man.[25] Between the time of the assassination of Crown Prince Franz Ferdinand at Sarajevo and the commencement of hostilities, he was incapable of really understanding what was happening and what the consequences of various alternative policies likely would be. On June 22, 1941 the Nazis launched Operation Barbarossa and attacked the Soviet Union. Stalin, who had stubbornly refused to believe

---

[25]Useful is Stoessinger, *Why Nations Go To War*, Chapter 1.

such an attack was imminent, collapsed in shock; for nearly two weeks he locked himself in his study and took no part in policymaking; the strain was just too much.

What all this means is that when one is analyzing the capability component of the individual policymaker it is essential to investigate the specific person's physical and mental health. To what extent is the particular individual unable physically and/or mentally to handle the complexity, the stresses, and the energy demands? To what degree is this person prevented from doing the clear thinking the job requires? In what ways, and how much, will his or her physical and/or mental difficulties accentuate particular personality traits that hinder rational policymaking? It is evident that to the extent that a policymaker is physically or mentally incapacitated that individual is less able to effectively do the job than if he or she were well (and the more susceptible that person is to being influenced by his or her opposite numbers).

Knowledge and Skill

An individual policymaker's particular characteristics, previous experience, concept of role, and physical and mental health all are important, and one seeking to ascertain that person's impact on capability must investigate them thoroughly. But they are not the whole story. To complete the analysis one must study the factors of *knowledge* and *skill*.[26]

"Knowledge," as used here, refers to the breadth and depth of one's understanding of the principles of international politics. Does the particular policymaker know the characteristics and roles of the various units involved in international relations, and does this individual understand the extent to which these units' interrelations are and are not governed by phenomena external to themselves? Is he or she aware of the implications of the fact that there are so many international parties? Does this individual understand the role that ethics, law, ideology, and power usually play, or does he or she give one of these more or less emphasis than it warrants? Is this person cognizant of the fact that international politics in general, and the relations of any two parties in particular, are a variable mixture of conflict, competition, and cooperation? Is the policymaker aware of the essentiality in the policy formulation process of first determining who is involved and who holds the key to a particular situation? Does this person understand the importance of keeping clearly in mind the identity of, and the relationships between, the immediate, middle range, and fundamental objectives that are being protected or sought in the specific

---

[26]There is some overlap of categories here because the factors previously discussed may affect knowledge and skill. Nevertheless, there are general differences both in substance and breadth as will become apparent.

instance (and their relationship to, and the degree to which they are influenced by, extrasituational matters)? Does this individual understand the range of factors, such as situational alterations and the multiplicity of objectives, that make the determination of other parties' objectives so difficult? Is he or she aware of the importance of willingness and susceptibility in ascertaining capability? What about orientation options? Does this policymaker understand the full range of alternatives and the advantages and disadvantages of each? Does this person realize that not all negotiations are designed to achieve agreements and that not all agreements are designed to permanently solve problems? The list could go on and on.

"Skill" in policymaking also is very important. What we are analyzing here is the policymaker's ability to formulate and implement policy optimally; to what extent can this person maximize the net achievement or protection of the appropriately prioritized objectives at the minimum net cost, given the context and circumstances in which he or she is operating? This involves a number of considerations, only a few of which need be mentioned at this point.[27] Does this party usually choose the orientation that is most appropriate to the specific situation? When using external means of increasing capability and seeking to induce opposition alliance dissolution, does this individual skillfully alter the target's cost-benefit calculus in such a way as to encourage fragmentation, or are the alliance partners driven together by the crudeness of his or her efforts? Do this individual's words and actions continually signal something different from that which is intended? Is communication not undertaken with great care, words and phrases being employed without regard to their special precise meanings? Is prestige given insufficient consideration? Does the particular policymaker too often employ abstractions and generalizations as the basis for policy, and is there a failure to empathize? Is this person unable to discern nuances, unable to distinguish between the meaningful and the trivial? In particular cases does this party fail to give sufficient weight to specific tangible factors like geography or economic strength? Does he or she not take into account differential effects, the interrelatedness of events, or the impact of the past? Does this party not understand the limitations of foreign aid and thus use that policy instrument incorrectly? Does this person lose sight of the requirement of political rationality in wartime, and/or does he or she not employ the military policy option most appropriate to the situation? As with respect to knowledge, here too the list could go on and on.

The knowledge and skill of the individual policymaker are very important. There is much in international politics, of course, that is beyond any individual policymaker's ability to control or significantly influence. Furthermore, he or she perforce represents a particular party with certain characteristics

---

[27]All of them are analyzed in more detail in other parts of the book.

amid a number of choice-limiting constraints, and does so in a situation that always is somewhat uncertain, complex, and unmanageable. But the individual policymaker still has considerable leeway, and the choices that are made frequently can have an enormous impact on the situation's outcome. The broader, deeper, more precise, and more sophisticated one's knowledge, and the greater the skill with which one operates in formulating and implementing policy, the higher the probability that his or her party will be able to achieve or protect its objectives and do so at the lowest possible cost.

PARTY UNIQUENESS

The final capability component the policymaker must analyze is *party uniqueness*. Every international party is a unique blend of features, a composite of attributes that is different from each and every other. International parties are not interchangeable, homogenous entities that can be easily categorized, and they cannot be usefully analyzed in simple, mechanistic ways. The policymaker who fails to recognize party uniqueness, the particular characteristics and perceptions of the specific parties and policymakers in the situation, will at best have moderate success, and more likely will be ineffective.

Parties differ enormously in their particular features, in geography, natural resources, population, economic strength, military capability, societal characteristics, ideology, governmental systems, and so on. Because of this, different leaders will not perceive issues related to these features in the same way. Israel's pre-1967 lack of geographical depth and size, for example, inevitably conditioned her policymakers' perception of the degree to which territory is important for national security. Policymakers of a state without such shape and size weaknesses quite possibly would not have the same perception, and if they did not empathize they would fail to understand Israeli policies. Israel's policymakers' concerns over particular geographical features must be of major importance when one is trying to ascertain Israeli capability. To use another example of geographical uniqueness, no other state has the same attributes as the Soviet Union: one-seventh the earth's land surface but landlocked much of the year, vulnerable western approaches, several thousand miles of common border with a bitter adversary (China), a major power offshore neighbor located to the east (Japan), a major possibly revanchist "near neighbor" to the west (West Germany), and a number of possibly antagonistic lesser states to the immediate west. In a geographical setting such as this Soviet policymakers understandably must be extremely sensitive to alterations in capability and policy in, or that affect, the various parties around the U. S. S. R.'s periphery. Non-Soviet policymakers should be alert to the Russians' unique situation and seek to determine how it will affect Soviet perceptions and policies in any particular case. To illustrate, when analyzing arms control matters and seeking to determine what constitutes military "equivalence" it is essential that the United States—whose geographical situation is so different from the Soviets, having no major power neighbors—recognize that Russian policymakers inevitably will operate within a multithreat perspective *even if Washington is excluded*. The Kremlin's view of what is necessary for "equivalence" will in part be conditioned by the number of actual or potential threats she sees around her, and that is very different from what may be "seen" by the United States.

There are many other examples of the differences in particular features. Some states, like Somalia, have elements of "their" population outside current national frontiers, others do not. States vary enormously in natural resource endowments, needs, and vulnerabilities. Some parties have major strategic and general purpose military capability, some only limited war strengths, some are weak in nearly all military spheres. Obviously, there are immense variations in the level and rate of economic development. The differences in these and other features contribute to the development of particularized objectives, different party priorities and perceptions of what is important and what is not, divergent perceptions of what is or is not ethical, varying assessments of what others' objectives are or are not, and so forth.

Historical Experience and Perceptions Thereof

Perhaps the most salient of all the aspects of party uniqueness, however, are *historical experience and the policymakers' perceptions thereof. Every party's historical experience is different from the historical experience of every other*. The Soviet Union was invaded by Germany in World War II, the United States was not. France has been defeated by Germany three times in little more than a century, Britain has not. Israel has had four wars for survival since World War II, Japan is the only country to have suffered a nuclear attack, and so on. Sometimes, of course, even though there are a number of unique specific experiences there are similarities in terms of categories of particular actions. Several states may have thrown off the shackles of colonialism and become independent, a number of parties may have launched guerilla war operations, etc. This leads to a tendency to stereotype and categorize. But two points are important here. First, though actions may fit into like categories they still will have specific dissimilar, unique properties. Second, and of crucial importance, no party will have the same historical *composite* as any other; *it is the totality of the party's historical experience that must be evaluated*. While specific developments have more or less importance within a party's total historical experience, they are but a part of the mosaic and must be viewed as such.

But there is more to it than just the party's actual experience, important as that may be. *Of critical significance is how its policymakers perceive that expe-*

rience. What policymakers "see" in the present and visualize or anticipate for the future is, to a considerable extent, a reflection of what they perceive to have been the past. In this sense, what *actually* happened is less important than what they *think* did. Perceptions of their party's specific and total historical experience will affect policymakers' views of the operational principles of the international environment within which they work, influence the determination of the content of, priority among, and linkages between objectives, affect the ascertainment of capability (especially one's assessment of willingness to use power and party responsiveness), impact on one's views of the utility and specific use of various policy implementation instruments such as foreign aid, negotiations, and the military, affect policymakers' perceptions of the degree of (and what should be the response to) threats and deterrents in particular situations, and so on. Indeed, almost everything policymakers do, in some way, will be affected by their perceptions of their party's unique history.

Another point, and one that cannot be overstressed, is that because of different histories and perceptions thereof, the same issue will not be perceived in the same way by policymakers of different parties. In other words, *policymakers will not "see" the same "reality."* Let's take as an example the contrasting views of the Arabs and the Israelis concerning who has the more legitimate claim to Palestine. *First, let's look at the issue from the Arab's perspective.* Prior to World War I, the area known as Palestine was part of the Ottoman Turk Empire.[28] During World War I Great Britain made a series of promises to the Arab leader Sharif Husein to the effect that if the Arabs would ally with Britain and revolt against the Turks (Britain's adversary), once victory was achieved the Arabs could become independent. Although Palestine was not specifically mentioned as being in the territory included in this pledge, it was not excluded and the Arabs made it quite clear that they considered it to be part of what was promised. On the basis of these promises the Arabs, who constituted more than 90 percent of Palestine's population, joined the alliance and launched the revolt. But when the war ended independence was not achieved. Instead, Palestine was governed by Britain as a League of Nations mandate. The Arabs cried "foul" and refused to cooperate or to accept the mandate's legitimacy. Over the next two decades strife was nearly constant. Another element was added that exacerbated the difficulties and frustrated the Arabs even more. With Britain's permission, Jewish Zionists were entering Palestine, settling, buying land, changing the population ratio, preparing (in the Arabs' view) to make Palestine into a Jewish state. Although Britain proposed a number of compromises Palestine's Arabs rejected them all; they would accept nothing less than independence; after all, it was "their" land. Of

---

[28]Palestine was not a separate entity, however. At this time the term was used to describe an area everyone agreed existed, but it did not have clearly defined boundaries.

course, the advent of the Nazis in Germany and the horrors of World War II just increased the Zionist pressures.

When World War II ended, in Palestine the Arabs, Zionists, and British continued their three-way struggle for control.[29] Finally, Britain, unable to resolve the problem, dumped it into the lap of the United Nations. On November 29, 1947 the U. N. General Assembly voted to partition Palestine into separate Jewish and Arab states, with an internationalized Jerusalem. All the Arab states voted against this plan, saying it was illegal (who gave the United Nations that power?) and unethical. The Arabs refused to accept this division of "their" land, and after the British withdrew they went to war against the Zionists.[30] The Arabs argued that they, having been a majority of the population of Palestine for over a thousand years and having been promised the land in World War I, had a better historical claim to the land than the Jews. Furthermore, *they* had not been the ones who had persecuted the Jews, and *they* should not be the ones forced to suffer for European savagery. The only "just" solution for Palestine was for it to become an independent Arab state in which the Jews could live as a minority.

Now let's examine the issue from the Israeli perspective. The Israeli view is so different that one would hardly know the parties were addressing the same issue. Zionism, the movement for a return to the Promised Land and the creation therein of an independent Jewish state, has ancient roots. In the Holy Scripture it is said that Abraham was commanded by God to leave his home and lead his people to a land God would show him, and that there God would make of him a great nation. Abraham obeyed his God, ultimately settling in Canaan where the Lord appeared and said "To your descendants I will give this land."[31] After living in bondage in Egypt and escaping in the exodus, the Hebrews (eventually) returned and conquered Canaan. With the death of King David their country split into two Kingdoms. In 721 B.C. the northern kingdom of Israel was overcome by Assyria, its people disappearing forever from the pages of history. In 586 B.C. the southern kingdom of Judah was overcome by Babylonia, and its people deported. After the Persians replaced the Babylonians many Jews (men of Judah) returned. Later, during parts of the first and second centuries B.C. they even had limited independence. But in 63 B.C. Judea was overwhelmed by the Roman colossus, and in 135 A.D., following an unsuccessful revolt, the Jews were "permanently" expelled; the "Diaspora" had be-

---

[29]The student should constantly remember that we are giving the Arab view.

[30]This is somewhat of an oversimplification, on two counts, but neither detracts from the essential point being made. The qualifications are, first, that intermittent (usually) small-scale hostilities had been underway for some time. Second, the Arabs were far from united operationally. With respect to their perceptions of the relative merits of the conflicting claims to Palestine, however, there was total unanimity.

[31]*The Holy Bible*, Genesis 12:7 (RSV).

gun. From 135 A.D. to the twentieth century there was no independent Jewish entity. For 2000 years Jews were forced to try to assimilate in foreign lands. Frequently they suffered intensive and extensive persecution, sometimes even death. Throughout their trials the Jews never forgot their Promised Land; one day there would be a Return.

Modern Zionism began in the late nineteenth century as it became evident to many Jews that only an independent Jewish state would solve their problems. In World War I the British, anxious to influence the Russians and Americans, and to assert their own interests vis-a-vis the French in the Middle East, issued the Balfour Declaration. This document provided that the British would view with favor "the establishment of a national home for the Jewish people" in Palestine. When the war ended and the Palestine mandate was established Jews were allowed to immigrate, and by 1939 they constituted about 30 percent of the Palestinian population. When after World War II the United Nations voted partition the Zionists accepted; they had come home, to the Promised Land. Never again would they be homeless or subjected to foreign rule.

The differences in historical experience and perceptions thereof on the part of Palestine's Arabs and the Israelis are so enormous that it is understandable that what is perceived as reality differs totally. What *is* "reality" in this instance? Policymakers on both sides here sincerely believe they understand reality yet what they perceive and believe is monumentally different.

The examination of party uniqueness concludes our discussion of intangible capability components, and the analysis of intangible internal capability components completes the discussion of policy formulation. In Parts 1 to 3 we have examined the fundamental characteristics of the international environment within which the policymaker operates (Chapters 1 and 2), analyzed the steps that should be undertaken to formulate an effective policy in a particular situation (Chapters 3-6), and discussed the basic internal components of capability that provide the foundation for achieving international influence (Chapters 7-8). We now go to Part 4, a study of the instruments of policy implementation.

Part 4
POLICY IMPLEMENTATION INSTRUMENTS

Once the policymaker has decided what his or her policy should be he or she must determine the most appropriate means of implementation. Since there are a wide variety of possible implementation instruments, it is not possible to discuss each one individually. Policymakers often break them down into two categories, however, those that are relatively tangible (such as economic and military activities) and those of a more intangible nature (such as communication and negotiation). We shall follow the same pattern, the economic and military instruments providing the subject matter for Chapters 9 and 10, communication and negotiation for Chapters 11 and 12.

9

Tangible Implementation Instrument: Economic

The first tangible implementation instrument to be discussed is the economic.[1] Because of the essentiality of economic strength to capability and the complexity and interdependence of modern economic life, policymakers in all states must be alert to the potential influence of the economic tool and consider their options very carefully.

The number and variety of economic options might seem to be immense, since almost every facet of economic activity could conceivably be utilized in some fashion. In the real world, however, the policymaker's range of choice may well be much more limited, for two simple reasons: (1) the domestic economy is so weak that many of the (theoretically) possible options in fact do not exist; and (2) domestic political pressures impose constraints that preclude (or at least inhibit) the use of the economic instrument in certain ways.

Thus the policymaker's options may be greatly circumscribed by the conditions in his or her own state. Since this is so one must recognize that the following discussion will carry within it the critical assumptions of capability and freedom from constraints. To the extent that the components of capability an-

---

[1]The concept of a means-end chain is relevant here and to the discussion of all the other policy implementation instruments as well. Though instruments essentially are means designed to achieve or protect previously decided on objectives, once a policymaker has determined which is (are) the appropriate instrument(s) to use successfully utilizing it (them) becomes the immediate objective. For more on the means-end chain see Chapter 3, pp. 74–75.

alyzed in Chapters 7 and 8 are insufficient or the domestic pressures examined in Chapter 15 prevent options from being utilized, the policy instrument is functionally nonexistent.

Two additional background comments are necessary at this juncture. First, it is essential to recognize that the economic instrument may be used to achieve or protect nonmaterial objectives as well as those that are primarily economic in nature. Indeed, while the anticipated material impact of the technique's utilization presumably will be an element in all policymaker calculations, very frequently political and/or prestige and/or ideological objectives hold higher priority. In other words, the economic tool is not used solely for the pursuit of economic goals. Second, political concerns always condition economic policy. Sometimes this is the result of a conscious policy choice and policymakers deliberately employ the economic instrument in a manner other than that which they assume would be the most economically productive. But even when this is not true, even when economic activities are not deliberately "politicized," in a broad sense they automatically are because they are the result of the actions and inactions of the policymakers of international political parties; even a decision to not let "politics" interfere is a decision made *by* policymakers of international political units, and it will impact *on* such parties. Therefore, there is no such thing as a "nonpolitical" "economic" international economic policy.

TRADE POLICY

International trade is a factor of major importance in policymakers' calculations. The volume of goods, services, resources, and capital exchanged internationally continues to grow and it becomes more and more apparent that various economic problems have worldwide implications (see Table 12). Because a host of economic interdependencies and vulnerabilities exist there are a great many situations in which there may be opportunities to exert influence.

Trade Manipulation: Techniques

When attempting to achieve or protect a particular party's objectives via the use of international trade there are a number of different manipulative techniques one might be able to use.

Tariffs. The first of the trade manipulation techniques is the selective employment of *tariffs* (taxes imposed on foreign-made goods coming into the country). Sometimes tariffs are imposed for primarily domestic reasons. In some cases one is seeking to protect certain types of domestic production from foreign competition. The European Economic Community through its Common Agricultural Policy protects and stimulates agricultural production within the

Table 12　World Trade: Exports and Imports, 1965, 1970, 1975, 1978 (billions of U. S. Dollars)

Area and State	1965	1970	1975	1978[a]
	Exports, f.a.s.[b]			
Non-Communist				
Developed countries	129.7	225.9	583.3	853.4
United States	27.5	43.2	107.6	140.2
Canada	8.5	16.7	34.1	47.5
Japan	8.5	19.3	55.8	99.9
European Community	64.8	113.0	298.4	444.0
Other developed	20.4	33.6	87.4	121.8
Developing countries	35.2	54.3	203.7	296.1
OPEC	10.7	17.6	111.5	145.0
Other	24.5	36.7	92.2	151.1
Communist	23.2	34.7	90.4	133.3
Total	188.1	314.9	877.4	1,282.8
	Imports, c.i.f.[c]			
Non-Communist				
Developed countries	136.7	235.3	610.9	889.2
United States	23.2	42.4	103.4	184.0
Canada	8.7	14.3	36.2	45.8
Japan	8.2	18.9	57.9	80.2
European Community	69.3	116.9	301.9	440.9
Other developed	27.3	43.0	111.5	138.2
Developing countries	37.0	56.6	189.5	291.3
OPEC	6.5	10.0	52.7	104.1
Other	30.5	46.6	136.8	187.2
Communist	22.6	34.2	100.8	133.5
Total	196.3	326.1	901.1	1,314.0

Source: Economic Report of the President, January 1979, p. 302.

[a]Preliminary estimates.
[b]Free-alongside-ship value.
[c]Cost, insurance, and freight value.

Common Market via the placing of variable duties on all agricultural imports. In other situations policymakers may utilize tariffs in an effort to discourage consumption of a particular product, or maybe tariffs are imposed because certain parties feel it is a simple and relatively convenient way of raising revenue.

But often a policymaker is seeking to apply economic pressure to a particular foreign state and is using tariff manipulation as the instrument. Even if this is not the policymaker's sole objective, a tariff automatically has an international impact. Usually, the higher the tariff, the higher the price. This means, assuming other things remain constant, the foreign goods will be less competitive and (unless demand is highly inelastic) fewer will be sold. If this occurs the foreign producer might be persuaded to modify its policy in the manner desired by the tariff imposer; in some instances it may be that the explicit or tacit threat of such tariff imposition may produce the desired policy change.

Many times such efforts are not effective, however. In August of 1971 President Nixon imposed a "surcharge" of 10 percent on all imports into the United States that were not already subject to quota (quantity) restrictions. One objective of this tax was the provision of relief to American import-competing industries, another an improvement in Washington's balance of payments position.[2] The primary objective though was to bring about major policy modifications by the targets of that policy, America's trading partners in Europe and Japan, but this did not happen. Instead, the tariff simply created considerable ill will.

A policymaker may also manipulate his or her party's tariff structure in such a way as to reward the target of his or her actions. For years the United States has accorded Yugoslavia preferential treatment in order to help her maintain her economic independence of the Soviet Union. And as was indicated in Chapter 1, as part of its détente policy Washington recently sought to extend tariff benefits to the Soviets themselves (in early 1975 Moscow rejected that offer, however, because it contained a Congressionally-imposed provision requiring freer Jewish emigration).[3]

There are some situations in which, because of previous agreements, policymakers are not always free to employ tariffs as selectively as they might wish, however, having given up that capacity in exchange for other benefits. In 1947 the major western powers formed the General Agreement on Tariffs and Trade (GATT) to the end of promoting free trade on a nondiscriminatory basis and reducing trade barriers. At the same time procedures for multilateral tariff-reduction negotiations were agreed upon. Since GATT's establishment seven sets of multilateral trade negotiations have been conducted. During this period the members' trade with each other has increased enormously, and tariffs on dutiable manufactured and semimanufactured goods have been significantly reduced. In this case various parties mutually agreed to relinquish to a certain degree their capacity to selectively employ tariffs in the hope that freer trade would promote joint and singular economic gain.[4]

Quotas. *Quotas*, quantitative restrictions, provide a second category of trade manipulation possibilities. The importing party may simply place a numerical

---

[2]It was hoped that less money would go out as imports became more expensive. The United States continued to experience a balance of payments deficit, however.

[3]See Chapter 1, footnote 9.

[4]There are a number of important spheres in which GATT principles have not been adhered to, however. A useful summary may be found in Spero, p. 72ff.

limit on the number of certain kinds of goods that can be imported. In this situation the foreign producer can sell its goods under its own price arrangements but the quantity is limited. As measured by value, 6.4 percent of the manufactured products imported into the United States in 1977 were quota items.[5] Specifically (in the area of manufactured products), Washington maintained quota restrictions on imports of textiles, color television receivers from Japan, stainless and alloy tool steel, and nonrubber footwear from South Korea and the Republic of China. On occasion the United States has accomplished the same result that quotas would achieve by prevailing on other states to adopt "voluntary" export limitations, by persuading certain parties that it is in their interest to place quantitative ceilings on the amount of a particular good that they will export to the United States.

Embargoes or Boycotts. The third category of trade manipulations involves the use of *embargoes* or *boycotts*. A boycott is a refusal to import. It may be selective, involving specified commodities, or be general, a refusal to purchase any commodities produced by a particular country. An embargo is a refusal by one country to sell its goods to another. This also may be specific or general. Embargoes and boycotts have been utilized on a number of occasions. As the Cold War developed, for example, the United States and its NATO allies instituted an embargo on the sale of military equipment and "strategic" nonmilitary goods to the U. S. S. R. and other Communist states. The objective in these instances was to weaken the perceived enemies (and/or to prevent them from increasing their military capability via the route of purchasing critical items from their presumed targets). Similarly, following Fidel Castro's ascension to power in 1959 and his increasingly close relations with the U. S. S. R. the United States used a wide range of restrictive economic instruments in an effort to weaken the Cuban economy, decrease societal cohesiveness and popular support, and compel a policy modification (and bring about a regime change?). Washington began the process with selective boycotts and quota reductions and escalated the pressure until eventually a complete economic and travel boycott was in effect.

More recently, shortly after the October 1973 Middle East war commenced the Arab members of OPEC began to apply severe economic pressure on those industrialized countries they perceived to be supporting Israel, especially targeting the United States. On October 16 six Persian Gulf States announced a 70 percent increase in the posted price of oil, and the next day a declaration was issued to the effect that exports would be cumulatively reduced by 5 percent a month until three conditions were met: (1) the Israelis withdrew from all "occupied" territories, (2) the "legitimate rights" of the Palestinians

[5]U. S. Department of State, Office of Special Trade Activities, August 1, 1978 (personal communication).

were restored, and (3) all appropriate U. N. resolutions were implemented. Two days later Libya proclaimed a total embargo on oil exports to the United States, and by October 21 all the Arab oil producers had followed suit.

Subtle NTBs. There is yet another category of manipulative devices, a category which encompasses a variety of mechanisms with but three common character-istics: (1) they can be manipulative, (2) they do not involve tariffs, and (3) they do not seem, at first glance, to be highly trade restrictive. These can be called, appropriately enough, *subtle nontariff barriers (NTBs).*[6] Subtle NTBs fre-quently are employed to effectuate orientations such as exacerbater or indirect opposition or in order to increase relative capability via the manipulation of the target's internal capability components. They lend themselves to such usage because they seem so "reasonable," because often they do not appear to be directed *against* foreign trade at all. Since there are a number of subtle NTBs we must content ourselves with only a few representative illustrations. It may be that in a particular case state X has sanitary, safety, and environmental regulations that make it difficult for party Y to sell its goods in X. States that export food products, for example, are directly and significantly affected by such health and sanitary regulations. Perhaps government procurement prac-tices are such that foreign producers are placed at a disadvantage. Some states provide export subsidies in certain areas to give particular exporters an advan-tage, and sometimes tax relief is granted to make one's exports more competi-tive; obviously such advantages are at the same time detriments to exporters from other states. And there are many more examples one could give. Because of their subtlety and a certain opprobrium that many parties attach to openly coercive trade manipulation devices, it appears that policymakers seeking to manipulate trade are more and more turning to subtle NTBs.

Blatant NTBs. Two other trade-effect options that are occasionally utilized might be labelled *blatant NTBs.*[7] These nontariff barriers are so openly coer-cive in purpose that a policymaker (presumably) would not seriously consider their utilization unless the situation was highly conflictual and the objectives of considerable value. One blatant NTB is *preemptive buying.* This involves the purchase of particular goods or commodities so that the target of the ac-tivity will not have them available. During World War II the Allies often sought to outbid the Axis for materials that neutrals were willing to export to either side. *Dumping* is a second kind of blatant NTB maneuver. This involves the sale of goods at an artificially depressed price to drive the price of this par-ticular good down on the world market so as to make it less profitable for

---

[6]Because of their subtlety, the effects of such NTBs are difficult to precisely assess. It is quite clear that they restrict trade in many areas, however.

[7]Embargoes and boycotts also could fall into this category, although for analytical purposes it is useful to keep the categories separate.

other countries having to sell it. This obviously would have an inihibiting effect on the trade of the country or countries in question.

Exchange Rate Manipulation. The final technique invoives the *manipulation of currency exchange rates*. This can best be explained by example. Assume a purely bilateral relationship between countries X and Y, and that each country's currency can be freely converted into (exchanged for) that of the other. In order for country X to purchase goods from country Y, it needs to have its currency converted into that of country Y, because Y wishes to be paid in its own money. Some ratio of currency exchange, therefore, inevitably will be established. For any number of reasons (such as inflation) it may be that country X's currency is "overvalued," that is, the price of X's currency to Y is higher than it should be in terms of what goods it will buy. In such a situation X's exports to Y tend to be held back because of their cost, whereas imports from Y are encouraged since X's "overvalued" currency will purchase more of Y's currency than it would at a realistic rate of exchange and this extra currency can buy more of Y's goods. An option X's policymakers might have at this point would be devaluation, making X's currency worth less in its foreign exchange purchasing power. Since devaluation means it now would take more of X's currency to purchase Y's currency, and a given amount of Y's will purchase more of X's than it would before, other things being equal imports from Y to X will become more expensive and X's exports to Y will become cheaper.[8]

Policymakers also may *revalue* their currencies upward. The impact on import and export prices here would be the reverse of that engendered by devaluation. With revaluation, imports will be encouraged because more foreign currency will be purchased with a given amount of one's own money, and exports will be discouraged because it will take more foreign currency to purchase a given amount of one's own. Note that such an action, to the extent that it is effective, tends to be deflationary in the importing country due to the increase in the quantity of the relatively cheaper imported goods.

Trade Manipulation: Effectiveness

To what extent is the policymaker's use of trade manipulation techniques effective?[9] As we discussed in Chapter 4, capability can be operationally exer-

---

[8]In 1971 and again in 1973 the United States devalued the dollar in an effort to counter growing balance of payments deficits. This objective was not accomplished, however, the causes of this deficit being far too deep seated to be remedied by exchange rate manipulation.

[9]The strictly economic impact of the various techniques is, of course, beyond the scope of this book. Obviously, the international political policymaker ought to consult professional economists and take their views into account before making a final judgment on trade manipulation. Our analysis proceeds on the basis of an assumption (which would have to be verified in each case) to the effect that the particular manipulation technique would, all other things being equal, have the expected economic impact.

cised when one is able to influence the policy choices and behavior of another party in the way that one wants to, thereby causing results other than those that would have occurred in the absence of his or her activities.[10] This may involve a modification of the target's behavior by getting it to do or not do something, or bring about an alteration in the intensity and/or scope of the target's activities within one of these categories. Capability also can be exercised by persuading the target to continue an existing policy it otherwise would have discontinued, or by persuading it to refrain from undertaking new actions it otherwise would have initiated.

When a policymaker is analyzing a particular situation with respect to the degree to which trade manipulation techniques might allow the effective exercise of capability, certain questions receive top priority. If a policymaker is looking at an exporting nation one of the first things to ask is, to what extent is the target's economy dependent on exports? There are two subcomponents to this question. First, (see Table 13) what percentage of GNP do exports comprise? Second, to what extent are exports important in particular economic spheres, especially those crucial to this particular state's development? Another major question is: To what extent does the target rely on the sale of just one or two products for its foreign exchange earnings? (See Diagram 5.) Are "we" in a position to materially affect the sale of that (those) product(s)? Finally, the policymaker needs to investigate the degree to which the target's exports go to a single market. To what extent is it dependent on one particular actor in the marketing of its product(s)?

Each of these questions helps the policymaker ascertain the *vulnerability* of the exporting country to trade manipulation. If a state depends heavily on foreign trade for its economic development it needs to export goods in order to obtain the foreign exchange required to purchase the necessary imports.[11] If it

Table 13   Exports and Imports as a Percent of GNP for Selected Developed States, 1976 (billions of U. S. dollars)

	Exports	*Imports*
Netherlands	53	50
West Germany	29	27
United Kingdom	28	30
Canada	24	24
Italy (1975)	24	25
France (1975)	20	19
Japan	14	14
United States	7	7

Source: U. S. Department of State, *The Trade Debate*, Revised, May 1979, p. 11.

[10]See Chapter 4, especially p. 94.

[11]Of course one may be able to supplement his or her capacity by other means for a while, but basically this statement is correct.

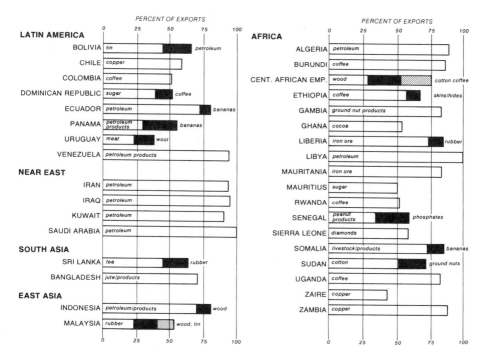

Diagram 5. Developing-country dependence on primary products for foreign exchange earnings. (*Source:* U. S. Department of State, *The Trade Debate*, May 1979 (revised), inside back cover.)

cannot export enough or the prices it receives are too low, (such as has been the case with many developing nations that must rely primarily on the export of primary products) it must receive immense economic assistance or its economy will not progress. Similarly, to the extent that states rely primarily on the sale of one product, such as many Latin American and African states have had to do, any fluctuation in the quantity and price of the sales of that product can have a terrific impact. And if the situation is such that this one product is exported primarily to one country, also a typical situation, the policymakers of that importing state may be in a position to exercise overwhelming influence.

Similar questions would be appropriate with respect to the question of the vulnerability of importing nations.[12] What proportion of its economy is dependent on imports? To what extent is a particular product an essential component of its economic system? And finally, to what extent is it dependent on one particular source for this particular import?

What does history tell us with respect to the effectiveness of trade manipulation techniques in producing the desired policy modifications? Despite cer-

[12]For more on U. S. dependence, also see Chapter 7, pp. 180–182, and Diagram 2, p. 181.

tain popular misconceptions to the contrary, the record shows that such policies have usually *not* yielded the benefits originally envisaged. Why might this be so? There are several possible explanations. First, threats of economic deprivation, and policies that attempt to bring this about, inevitably create immense feelings of hostility. Although hardship may occur, people learn to tolerate it, and the very resentment engendered by the hardship makes them more willing to stand the deprivation. Sometimes tolerating hardship becomes a goal in itself. People come to believe that it is their patriotic duty to show their willingness and capacity to suffer rather than give in to pressure.

Another point is that sometimes people simply learn to adapt. A restructuring of their domestic economic situation may occur as improvisation and innovation develop, and perhaps there will even be an underlying change in values. Third, some states possess relatively diversified economies and are just not very vulnerable. The more diversified a particular party's imports and exports and the greater the range of suppliers and markets, the less susceptible it is to trade manipulation. For actors with these characteristics the interruption of economic relations would not be critical (although it might cause some inconvenience).

Another point of some moment is that even if a product is of exceptional importance the policymaker usually will bend every effort to find an alternative rather than submit to the crude use of economic coercion. If one is the policymaker for an exporting country one will seek to find alternative markets. If one is the policymaker of an importing country one will seek to find alternative sources. Since in most situations the pressures applied are not universal but emanate from a particular source (or combination of sources) alternatives usually exist. Also, there usually are breaks in any system of sanctions. And if one is the policymaker for a country being embargoed he or she will seek to find or develop a substitute product to replace the one being denied. The only kinds of items that may not be readily substituted for are those that require a certain technological capability one simply cannot either achieve, acquire, or make use of, or those that depend on the utilization of certain natural resources that one cannot obtain elsewhere (and even this difficulty can be overcome in some instances). Finally, of course, in some situations the target may be able to neutralize one's efforts by taking effective countermeasures. For example, if state R devalues its currency state B may reciprocate by devaluing its currency thus eliminating any advantage that might have been gained by R.

What, in fact, were the results of the embargoes discussed above? The strategic embargoes targeting the Soviet Union and the People's Republic of China had little positive impact. In fact, if anything the embargoes were counterproductive because of the encouragement they gave to (already existing) desires for self-sufficiency, the targets' drive to produce the necessary commodities themselves, and their efforts to develop alternative sources and substitutes.

And the American embargo and boycott of Cuba, while isolating Cuba from her traditional trading partner, similarly forced Castro to find alternative markets and sources.[13] In none of these cases was the target's policy modified in a way beneficial to the parties imposing the embargo, nor were the targets prevented from obtaining or marketing the restricted goods. Indeed, as pointed out above, if anything, because of the actions that the embargoes (in part) stimulated the targets ultimately were stronger than if the embargoes had never been imposed.

On the other hand, the Arab oil offensive of late 1973 was partially successful. On November 6, 1973 the European Economic Community issued a declaration that recognized the "rights" (not just the "aspirations") of the Palestinian people. And shortly thereafter Japan adopted a very pro-Arab stance with respect to the solution of the Arab-Israeli conflict. The United States, too, demonstrated an effort to adopt a more evenhanded approach to the problem, as witnessed by the American-instigated disengagement agreements of 1974 and 1975.[14]

Despite these "positive" accomplishments, the oil embargo was not as effective as some Arab policymakers had hoped. Although Washington did act during the October war to prevent a total Israeli victory, and followed up with efforts designed to bring about at least a partial troop withdrawal, key American policymakers such as President Nixon and Dr. Kissinger made no attempt to compel the Israelis to pull back to the pre-1967 lines or to meet the OPEC members' stated demands. Furthermore, while quite clearly the embargo was one of the important elements influencing United States policy formulation and implementation, it is not evident exactly how large a role it played or how different American policy would have been had it not existed. Indeed, given Dr. Kissinger's conception of the importance of balance and equilibrium in the negotiating process it can not unreasonably be hypothesized that Washington's policy would have been essentially the same whether there was an embargo or not.[15]

What ought one to conclude about the use of trade manipulation techniques? *Basically, that only in rare cases do they produce the desired policy modifications, and in some instances they even can be counterproductive.* This

---

[13]This is not to say that American measures did not have some economic effect, for they did. But in no way did they bring about a policy modification on the part of the Cuban government. On the contrary, their imposition simply reinforced Castro's existing predilection to the effect that he needed to ally himself tightly to the Communist block and develop Cuba's internal capability components as rapidly as possible.

[14]And, quite clearly, the specter of another Arab oil embargo provided impetus for further American mediation efforts in the area, including those that led to the 1979 Egyptian-Israeli Peace Treaty.

[15]For more on Kissinger's views, see Chapter 8, pp. 224–225.

is not to say that trade manipulation never is effective nor that it never should be considered. It is an option that occasionally is useful and might, in the right situation, if rationally employed vis-à-vis the right target, be of some value. In certain instances moderate changes in the tariff and quota structure could bring about the sought-after policy adjustments. This would most likely be true in a situation where the product is of critical importance and where one is the primary supplier or market. In each case the degree of vulnerability, which is a reflection of the degree of need for trade in general, concentration with a single partner, and the significance of the particular product in question, must be weighed against the possibility of the development of substitutes and alternatives, the willingness to adapt, patriotic belt-tightening, and reciprocal action. Generally, the number of situations in which a careful cost-benefit assessment would indicate that trade manipulation would yield a positive operational result is small. In consequence, trade manipulation should only be used sparingly and with considerable circumspection.

FOREIGN AID

The second major economic implementation instrument is foreign aid, the transfer of cash, credit, goods, or technical assistance from one party to another. Used primarily (although not exclusively) in connection with orientations reflecting various degrees of support and cooperation in the pursuit of common or complementary objectives, foreign aid has long been a commonly accepted policy technique. In the eighteenth and nineteenth centuries, for example, European states often provided loans to "backward peoples" as a means of gaining a colonial foothold. Subsidies of equipment and money were regularly a part of military alliances. After World War I the United States made large loans to some twenty countries.

It was not until after World War II, however, that foreign aid was used extensively and systematically. The United States led the way. Responding to the perceived threat of a Soviet takeover of Europe, American policymakers responded with a variety of assistance programs (see below). This was the beginning of a global effort that to this point has cost more than $235 billion.

Although Washington has provided far more foreign aid than any other party, many others have significant programs.[16] After Stalin's death the new Soviet leadership embarked on a large (although selective) assistance program that has continued to this day, and foreign aid has been and remains a substantial component of the foreign policies of a number of other states including

---

[16]It should be pointed out that a state can have a relatively small program but that program can be highly significant if it is concentrated in a few selected areas. For example, although the overall magnitude of the Japanese effort is small compared to that of the United States, it is very important in the politics of East Asia. As early as 1967 Japan extended a greater absolute amount of assistance to the region (excluding Vietnam) than did the United States. See Hellman, p. 109.

Japan, West Germany, Australia, France, Italy, Sweden, Canada, Great Britain, Saudi Arabia, and China. Obviously, not all states have the economic strength to employ this instrument on an extended scale. Therefore, in terms of a program of great overall magnitude foreign aid is basically an instrument utilized by the policymakers of the major powers. Nevertheless, even states with little economic strength occasionally may be able to (and do) productively use foreign aid in a limited number of carefully selected situations.

Categories of Aid

What are the major categories (types, kinds) of foreign aid programs? The first is *development assistance*: foreign aid is provided on the grounds that it will contribute in a meaningful way to the recipient's economic development. This has been the rationale for much of America's economic assistance.[17] These programs may involve cash grants, the presumed purpose of which would be to enable countries to obtain capital necessary for rapid development, or favorable credit arrangements such as long term low interest loans, the procedure favored by the Soviet Union during most of the 1950s and 1960s.[18]

A second major category is *military assistance*, the supplying of money and materials for military uses (including aid for defense support programs). The U. S. military assistance program was developed after World War II in connection with the policy of containment. At first the program consisted primarily of nonrepayable grants to alliance partners. Until the early 1960s these efforts constituted the largest part of Washington's effort but then the economic sector became preeminent. In the early and mid-1970s another shift occurred (the emerging alteration being particularly accelerated by the 1973 Arab-Israeli War and the Arab oil embargo) and once again military aid became dominant. There were two important differences between this and the program of the 1940s and 1950s, however. First, reflecting the increased capabilities of the Western European states, the decline of SEATO, and Washington's concerns with both the Arab-Israeli issue and the oil-rich states of the

---

[17]Helpful in understanding this rationale, even though its statistics are now somewhat dated, is Joan M. Nelson, *Aid, Influence and Foreign Policy*, Macmillan, New York, 1968.

[18]In the 1950s and 1960s there was much controversy concerning whether the American approach (emphasizing grants) was inferior to the Soviet approach, which emphasized credits and loans. American policymakers assumed that grants, because they were outright gifts, would bring about greater gratitude than a loan which had to be repaid, and in some cases this seemed to be true. On the other hand, in certain situations grants apparently had a tendency to make the recipient feel as if he were accepting charity and made him resentful of that fact. Thus in some cases the more "expensive method," and that is the loan, was politically more palatable to the recipient nation than the cheaper gift. A useful discussion of the advantages and disadvantages of each may be found in Joseph S. Berliner, *Soviet Economic Aid*, Praeger, New York, 1958.

Persian Gulf, the major recipients were different: now the weapons went primarily to Saudi Arabia, Iran, and other Middle Eastern parties instead of to America's Cold War alliance partners. Second, instead of being in the form of nonrepayable grants, the "assistance" was purchased; foreign military sales became the primary component of the program.[19]

Many parties other than the United States, of course, are actively involved in arms transfers, some on a substantial scale (see Diagram 6). In 1977, for example, the Soviet Union concluded agreements for weapons transfers to less developed countries that were valued at nearly $4 billion, and actually made arms deliveries worth $3.265 billion to these same parties.[20] In fact, from July 1977–June 1978 there were more than 130 identified arms agreements, agreements involving an enormous number of states. In addition to the United States and the U. S. S. R., Switzerland, Japan, Brazil, Portugal, and China were suppliers, and the number of recipients was considerably larger.[21] And even this understates the total arms traffic because various clandestine unidentified arrangements are not included, nor are transactions involving supply by nongovernmental independent arms merchants.

The third main type of foreign aid is *technical assistance*, the transfer of knowledge and skills from one party to another. Relatively inexpensive, technical assistance allows personnel from the assisting party (whether it be a state or a nonstate actor such as an MNC) to advise and cooperate with the recipient in a coordinated attack on such practical problems as fishery development, improvement of crop yields, control of disease, the construction of roads, educational advancement, hydroelectric power generation, and so forth, and to do so on a more personal level than is usually true in general economic development programs. Technical assistance efforts have constituted a very small proportion of total foreign aid activities since World War II. For certain actors, however, they at times have been a highly important segment, the People's Republic of China's rather extensive involvement in sub-Saharan Africa in the late 1970s being a case in point.[22] Because of the relatively low degree of productive results engendered by other types of aid programs and the comparatively low (economic) cost of technical assistance, it seems likely that technical assistance efforts will grow in significance in the future and come to comprise a larger share of total foreign aid activities.

[19]Continuing U. S. balance of payments problems also were a component of the policymakers' calculations in this regard.

[20]U. S. Central Intelligence Agency, National Foreign Assessment Center, "Communist Aid to Less Developed Countries of the Free World, 1977," November 1978, p. 1. Hereinafter this will be cited as U. S. CIA, "Communist Aid to LDCs, 1977."

[21]See IISS, *The Military Balance, 1978-1979*, pp. 104-107.

[22]See U. S. CIA, "Communist Aid to LDCs, 1977," p. 10.

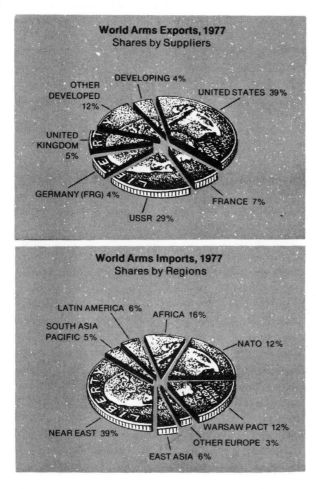

World Arms Exports, 1977
Shares by Suppliers

DEVELOPING 4%
OTHER DEVELOPED 12%
UNITED STATES 39%
UNITED KINGDOM 5%
GERMANY (FRG) 4%
FRANCE 7%
USSR 29%

World Arms Imports, 1977
Shares by Regions

LATIN AMERICA 6%
AFRICA 16%
SOUTH ASIA PACIFIC 5%
NATO 12%
NEAR EAST 39%
WARSAW PACT 12%
OTHER EUROPE 3%
EAST ASIA 6%

Diagram 6. World arms transfers 1977. (*Source:* U. S. Arms Control and Disarmament Agency, *Arms Control, 1978*, 1979, p. 41.)

Foreign Aid Objectives

What have policymakers providing foreign aid sought to achieve via this assistance? What have been the various programs' objectives? One must be careful to analyze this question with great care. Frequently there is a considerable disparity between the stated objectives and the real ones, between rhetoric and reality (although obviously this is not always the case).[23]

[23]Useful is Hans J. Morgenthau, "A Political Theory of Foreign Aid," *American Political Science Review*. June 1962, pp. 301-309.

Economic Development. Economic development has been a major objective of many foreign aid programs. While it is undoubtedly true that policymakers of assisting parties have sometimes sought other goals under the guise of, or in conjunction with, economic development, it is equally undeniable that in many instances development has been a basic objective.[24] For many Americans the objective of economic growth has a certain ethical content. It is believed that all human beings deserve a certain minimum standard of living and those who are more fortunate have an obligation to help bring this about. There also are individuals in aid-providing states who believe that the states of the developed world "owe" the formerly colonized areas and peoples of Asia, Africa, and Latin America (the LDCs of the so-called Third and Fourth Worlds) something, and this "something" includes foreign aid.[25]

American policymakers, however, while not ignoring ethical considerations, usually have sought to assist in economic development because of what its achievement was presumed to lead to in turn, namely, democratic government, the development of a capitalist economic system, and a more open society on the part of the recipients.[26] These in turn, some have assumed, lead to peaceful foreign policies. Some policymakers also assume that with more economic development states become more stable and this will reduce the probability of internal unrest. This in turn reduces the possibility of external exploitation. It is also argued that development will enable the recipients to remain independent and avoid becoming dependent on outsiders for their security and survival. Thus, some policymakers have believed that economic development and technical assistance have great potential for bringing about peace and stability in a system of states based on the principles of western democracy and economic capitalism.

What does the record show in this regard? Obviously, as the cases of Germany and Japan in the 1930s and the Soviet Union today demonstrate, there is no automatic relationship between economic development and democracy.[27] If one looks at the recipient states since the Second World War one finds that many are not concerned with democracy at all, and those that are concerned

[24]Naturally this has often been a major objective of the *recipients*.

[25]It is important to note in this regard that few *policymakers* in the developed world subscribe to this view, at least to the extent that it significantly influences their aid policy calculations.

[26]The primary middle range objectives have been essentially political, as described here, and there has been a certain presumed linkage to goals of a more fundamental nature. It is true, however, that many policymakers have hoped that certain material benefits also would ensue, such as the development of better export markets, increased opportunities for private foreign investment, etc.

[27]On the other hand, it may be that a certain *minimum* level of economic development is a prerequisite to the establishment of a successful democracy. There is much to indicate that where abject poverty exists and there is no hope for the future, freedom with responsibility also will be absent.

define it only in terms that are consonant with their traditions and objectives. Those who had or sought a governmental system Americans might consider democratic prior to receiving aid, mostly the Western Europeans, have continued to do so. Those who previously had not, mostly leaders of non-Western less developed countries, did not start. Thus there is little historical evidence to indicate that economic development necessarily leads to Western-style democracy.

Even less promising conclusions appear with regard to the relationship between economic development and capitalism. In many less developed countries capitalism has been equated with the exploitation of the masses by the private privileged classes, both colonialist and native. Capitalism is an anathema, and economic development is hardly likely to increase the use of capitalistic devices within the system. Actually the evidence indicates that there is more of a tendency to move in the direction of less private enterprise and ownership of the means of production, and a greater degree of state control, than vice-versa.

Similarly, one cannot predict with confidence that development will be stabilizing; it depends on the characteristics of the recipient and the relationship of the level and type of performance to the demands and expectations of key groups. The process of economic development is uncertain and complex and there are times when it may be disruptive rather than stabilizing. In many of the less developed countries order has been maintained for generations only through the ruthless use of force by the ruling classes. If economic development occurs and if new groups arise to challenge the control of the privileged, a potentially revolutionary system develops. Generally it is the groups that have already begun to rise who are the most revolutionary in their expectations. Economic development, instead of increasing stability, may increase instability and create precisely the opposite of the stable situation that the policymakers had hoped to create.

The idea that development will increase the likelihood of a peaceful foreign policy also is unsubstantiated. Both rich countries and poor countries have attacked and been attacked, and there is little hard evidence to indicate that simply because a country is economically developed (or developing) it will pursue a peaceful foreign policy.

In addition to recognizing the lack of necessary correlation of these elements, the policymaker must also ascertain whether or not economic development is really possible in a given case. The extreme difficulties facing the less developed countries as they seek to modernize and grow were discussed earlier.[28] Development is a task of immense proportions, one that economic assistance in and of itself often cannot influence significantly. Many times the amount of capital required is so large, the development of the economic infra-

[28]See Chapter 7, pp. 197–198.

structure so complicated and time-consuming, the upgrading of educational and skills levels such a gargantuan undertaking, and the changing of human and cultural traits such a laborious and uncertain process that the odds against any significant growth are overwhelming.

What this means for the potential provider as well as the recipient is that expectations must be kept at a relatively low level or else considerable disenchantment may set in with each side blaming the other. The parties, assuming they both sincerely desire economic development, must face this situation realistically so as not to be overly disappointed if rapid progress does not occur. If it is decided that the odds are favorable, they each must be prepared for a long term program of a fairly significant size.

The policymaker of a potential providing state also needs to ask whether or not economic development is a "good" objective in a particular case. Since development presumably means the recipient will be "stronger," one must ask whether or not that would be in his or her state's interest. This is not the kind of judgment one can make *a priori*. If the recipient is more friendly toward one's adversaries than toward oneself then presumably it would be better if that state were weaker rather than stronger.

Sufficient Gratitude. A second major objective of many policymakers of providing states is what might be termed the achievement of *sufficient gratitude*. The providing policymaker expects the recipient, in return for the economic assistance, to have enough gratitude to at least be sympathetic toward the assisting state's foreign policies and perhaps sustain or modify his own behavior according to the assisting state's desires. It is the idea that I help you, and out of gratitude for that help I expect you to be sympathetic to me or to continue or change what you are doing in the way I want you to. This has been, and continues to be, a major objective of aid programs.

Much to their chagrin, both the Soviet Union and the United States have discovered that the objective of sufficient gratitude is seldom achieved. When President Kennedy took office in 1961 he determined to set the United States on a new course with respect to Egypt. As a part of his program nearly a billion dollars worth of food was given to Cairo over the next three years. In return Washington wanted President Nasser to cease his anti-American outbursts, become more moderate with respect to the Arab-Israeli issue, cease supporting the Algerian rebels, and perhaps accept a position of favorable neutrality with regard to American policy in the Congo. None of these changes occurred.

As part of its price for extensive economic aid to the People's Republic of China the Soviet Union expected Mao Tse-tung to follow Soviet dictates on several issues in the late 1950s, but instead the Sino-Soviet conflict developed.[29] If the Soviets had received "sufficient gratitude" from Peking the Chinese would have been somewhat more willing to do as they were bidden. Soviet threats to reduce this assistance, and then its actual reduction, instead of compelling a modification of Chinese policies simply increased Peking's hostility.

For two decades prior to the 1975-1976 civil war in Lebanon the Soviet Union had been Syria's primary arms supplier. When Syria's President Assad was considering becoming involved in the Lebanese conflict the Soviets, recognizing the dispute's unpredictability and worried that action by Damascus might damage radical Arab unity and/or provoke Israeli counteraction, counseled against such a maneuver. To back up their "advice," the Russians threatened to slow down the weapons supply if their counsel was ignored. Assad's "gratitude" was not sufficient to enable Moscow to persuade him, however, and (as we discussed in Chapter 5) Syria did intervene, beginning with mediation and eventually escalating to the point of dispatching thousands of troops to compel a cease-fire. The Soviets responded as they had said they would and sharply reduced the flow of arms, but Assad did not alter course.

Gratitude means very little in international politics. Recipient policymakers know that assistance is provided on the basis of self-interest, and they take it in the same way. Their reasons may be very different from the provider's, and they may put the aid to unexpected uses. They may seek aid only for prestige or simply for purposes of maintaining themselves in power, for example, or even use it against one of their provider's other friends. Seldom do they feel they "owe" anyone any gratitude for aid. And for the same reasons discussed in connection with the effectiveness of trade manipulation, recipients are seldom amenable to foreign aid pressures.[30] They adapt themselves to get along without, they resent efforts at coercion and fight it, there are alternative sources and they know it, and so forth.

None of this is to say that there never are cases in which a small amount of gratitude develops, nor that one can say with certainty that actual or threatened aid manipulation never can be effective in producing policy modifications. Regarding the first point, no doubt at times aid can be one means of helping to achieve and maintain a certain level of cooperation between likeminded parties, parties with similar or at least compatible objectives. And the possibility of not obtaining assistance, or of a reduction in current programs, certainly will enter into a recipient policymaker's calculations; occasionally it

[29]See Chapter 6, pp. 147-149.

[30]Useful is Klaus Knorr, *The Power of Nations: The Political Economy of International Relations*, Basic Books, New York, 1976, Chapter 7. After having studied 25 post-World War II cases of attempts to coerce aid-receiving states into policy modifications, Dr. Knorr found that success was achieved in only 2.

may be that, in the context of one's overall policy patterns and objectives and a recognition that cooperative relationships with a given party are imperative, such activities will produce the desired outcome. The mid-summer 1972 Soviet threat to reduce arms deliveries to Hanoi unless progress were made in negotiations with the United States was just such an instance.[31] But these comments do not negate the essential points. Even if a little "gratitude" develops very seldom will it have an appreciable impact on recipients in terms of placing the providing state in a position to exercise operational policy modifying capability, that is, in terms of increasing the recipient's "responsiveness." And in those relatively few cases where capability can be exercised it usually is because of the importance of certain other factors, not because of any feeling of gratitude on the part of the recipient.

In recent years the United States, the Soviets, and other aid suppliers, becoming more cognizant of the limitations of foreign aid in producing policy modifications, have become somewhat more selective in their programs. Gone are the days when (some) policymakers assumed that major policy alteration benefits could be obtained across a broad spectrum of situations with a variety of aid recipients. Consequently, today foreign aid efforts tend to be specific and concentrated. In (fiscal) 1977, for example, two countries (Saudi Arabia and Iran) accounted for about two-thirds of America's foreign military sales; and in (calendar) 1977 five states (Syria, Algeria, Ethiopia, India, and Libya) accounted for almost 90 percent of Soviet arms sales.[32]

Most contemporary policymakers are aware that although policy changes have often occurred in close temporal proximity to assistance maneuverings, in most instances the modifications have preceded rather than followed the manipulations. In other words, foreign aid has followed recipient policy change rather than causing it. The U. S. agreement to help Egypt reopen the Suez Canal in early 1974 came only *after* Egypt had adopted a somewhat neutral position between Washington and Moscow. The Soviet offer to finance the Egyptian High Dam came after the Egyptians had been rebuffed by the United States. Soviet aid to Iraq was begun only after the July 1958 coup; it did not lead to it. Generally speaking foreign aid does not itself cause a major modification of policy. Instead, the opportunities for developing and cementing new relationships occur first and then foreign aid may be an effective instrument to achieve that limited objective.

Support. A third major objective of foreign aid is providing support for the recipient. In these situations the policymaker does not attempt to persuade the recipient to modify its policy. It may be that one is not concerned with the

---

[31]See Stoessinger, *Henry Kissinger: The Anguish of Power*, p. 64.
[32]U. S. CIA, "Communist Aid to LDCs, 1977," p. 1.

issues per se and is seeking either to exacerbate situational difficulties or to bring about their resolution via a balancer orientation; maybe relations with the recipient already are cooperative and one is seeking common or complementary objectives via a support or cooperation orientation. In any event, the recipient's policies already are satisfactory to the provider; even if they are not exactly what the assisting party desires, they are at least generally acceptable. The problem in this situation is that the recipient does not have capability sufficient to achieve or protect certain objectives to the extent that *the provider* desires.[33] The purpose of assistance in these situations is to support the recipient and remedy the capability deficiency.

Some support assistance has been of an emergency short-term nature. In the immediate post World War II era the Communists put severe pressure on Turkey and Greece. From Turkey Moscow demanded territorial concessions, a favorable revision of the Montreaux Convention governing the Dardanelles Straits, the conclusion of a defense treaty similar to those which the Russians had concluded with their Balkan satellites, and leases for military bases. In Greece, Communist-led rebels had been fighting government forces since the latter stages of World War II, and had intensified their activities following the British evacuation.

Faced with this situation American policymakers felt compelled to act. One of the major moves was the passage of the Greek-Turkish Aid Program. This measure was signed into law on May 22, 1947 and provided some $400 million worth of economic and military assistance.[34] The quick dispensation of emergency funds was a major force in thwarting Communist efforts.[35]

Sometimes support may be provided in an emergency situation but on a longer-term (though not indefinite) basis. During the same period that the Greek-Turkish Aid Program was developed it became painfully obvious to American policymakers that Western Europe, devastated by World War II, was in a state of economic disintegration. Perceiving a major Soviet threat and afraid that such chaos was an open invitation to mischief, and recognizing that the Western European states could not help themselves, the Truman administration decided to act. If the Western Europeans would take some initiative and provide the United States with a comprehensive plan for European eco-

---

[33]The reader should note the italicizing here and recognize that the provider's and recipient's objectives may or may not be the same.

[34]For a fascinating brief discussion of the background and objectives of this program, see Acheson, pp. 262-271, 290-301. Also note that Truman's speech requesting congressional action led to a relatively open-ended commitment of American strength. See Hartmann, *The New Age of American Foreign Policy*, pp. 126-128.

[35]Washington also used the military instrument in a limited, nonviolent way via a series of demonstrations of force, and coupled this with some diplomatic (and not so "diplomatic") threats. It was this *combination* of instruments that turned the tide.

nomic reconstruction, Washington would help in developing the final details and provide the necessary financial help. The Europeans did provide such a blueprint and this led to the European Recovery Program (Marshall Plan). Over the next four years Washington gave more than $13 billion in economic assistance. The aid was enormously successful and the result was a startling economic recovery. By the end of the program production had either reached or exceeded prewar levels in nearly all areas.

In neither the Greek-Turkish Program nor the Marshall Plan did American policymakers seek to bring about major policy modifications because the recipients already had objectives that were compatible with American desires. The problem was that they did not have the capability to achieve those objectives. The assistance programs provided this capability.[36]

A third type of supportive assistance is a little different. *Sometimes there is a more or less continuing program that purposely is not of a quantity or quality sufficient to enable the recipient to totally achieve that which it may desire.* For example, although for years the Soviet Union has supplied Syria with economic and military assistance, Soviet policymakers have made sure that the quantity and quality of this aid has not been sufficient to enable Damascus to enhance its capability to the point of constituting a major threat to Israeli security. The reason: if Syria were in such a position and hostilities commenced, the possibility of escalation and a resultant U. S.–U. S. S. R. confrontation would be considerable. Therefore, from Moscow's perspective it has been only prudent to keep its aid below any level that could lead to such a development.

This type of assistance can give the policymaker many problems, however. Generally the provider in such cases is attempting to do two things. First, he wants to provide enough support to allow the recipient some hope of achieving his objectives but not enough to really help him do it. And second, he seeks to develop sufficient gratitude in the recipient so that the latter's policies will reflect the provider's interests. But this is a very risky operation and the recipient can easily become very disenchanted with the provider if he refuses to give the quantity and quality of aid desired (as was indicated earlier with respect to the expulsion of Soviet "advisors" from Egypt in July 1972).

Finally, sometimes the provider may have a program of continuous, nearly unlimited, support. It is probably incorrect to say that any providing state will just give whatever is sought, but it is certainly clear that there are cases in which the recipient is assured of having its legitimate needs met on a continuing basis. Although Israel does not automatically receive everything it asks

---

[36] In both of these cases the recipients had the will and capacity to carry through to success. No amount of external assistance will be sufficient if these ingredients are missing. The United States provision of $2 billion worth of futile aid to the Nationalists in the Chinese civil war is eloquent testimony to that fact.

Washington to provide, American policymakers make absolutely sure that she receives everything necessary to maintain a first-class military machine, and make sure that the rest of the world understands that this is a permanent, firm commitment (as permanent and firm as anything can be).

In this kind of relationship the recipient is as influential as the provider. Although Israel is dependent on the United States for assistance, because of its commitment Washington is not in a position to apply as much pressure as it might appear.[37] It is true that, given her policies and the potential strength of the Arab forces surrounding her, Israel might have trouble finding alternative arms sources (although this might not be true) and thus the United States would presumably have some leverage. But if Washington decreases its aid all that happens is that Israel is weaker, and this is not Washington's objective. If American policymakers desire a militarily secure Israel they must provide aid. If they must, and Israel knows they must, then in a sense the Israelis are "in the driver's seat."

Foreign Aid: No Choice?

Policymakers considering the use of foreign aid not infrequently feel as if they are confronted with an impossible dilemma. On one hand, they are aware of the numerous difficulties with aid programs. They know only too well that aid often does not contribute significantly to economic development, and that even when it does it frequently leads to counterproductive differential effects. They know that seldom do aid recipients develop a degree of gratitude that is sufficient to allow the provider to effectually exercise policy-modifying capability. They further realize that historically aid often has gone down the drain as a result of some policy debacle by the recipient (Egypt's loss in the 1967 war despite the massive Soviet aid program) or because of regime change or reorientation (the overthrow of the Shah of Iran in early 1979 despite billions in U. S. arms aid, Somalia's anti-Soviet reorientation following Moscow's aid to Ethiopia in 1977). Furthermore, they are fully cognizant of the fact that their efforts may be offset by those of their competitors. Policymakers also know that many recipients employ the orientation of participatory nonalignment to the hilt, playing one potential source against another in an effort to extract maximum gain from, and minimal allegiance to, all. Another problem that develops if one is in a situation where aid has already been provided is even though giving assistance may not yield highly positive results any movement toward significantly reducing or eliminating it likely will produce strongly negative consequences. Finally, sometimes an aid provider may unwittingly allow itself

---

[37]Of course, if maintaining Israel's strength was not deemed so critical, the situation would be different and the United States would be in a position to use its leverage.

to be gradually drawn into situations the contours and potential consequences of which have not been thoroughly analyzed—and they thus may well be negative—such as the United States did in Vietnam.

But despite all these actual and/or potential difficulties, operational policymakers often feel that they have no choice but to provide aid. They reason this way: although aid is not always successful in increasing the providing party's influence, sometimes it is, and at least somewhat cooperative relations are established during the process. Furthermore, recipients and potential recipients want aid, and will react adversely to negative decisions. And in nearly all situations there are other sources to which these parties can and will turn, parties that will be more than happy to become an aid provider. For example, just because the United States does not provide arms to a particular state does not mean arms will not be provided; there are many sources for arms. Because of this sort of reasoning, in some instances at least the result is that aid is provided simply because of the feeling that there really isn't any choice.

While there are a limited number of contingencies in which the policymaker's choices are so circumscribed, usually this is not the case and if aid is given on this basis it is the result of a far too narrow and oversimplified view of the international political world. Two brief comments should make this quite clear. First, as Chapters 10-12 will show, policymakers may seek to achieve or protect their objectives via the utilization of the military and/or the communication and/or the negotiation policy implementation instruments, as well as through the use of foreign aid (which is only one-half the economic instrument). Just because one does not utilize foreign aid does not mean his or her party's policies cannot be implemented. Second, foreign aid is most often useful in connection with orientations involving varying degrees of support and/or cooperation. Not only are their other means of implementing those orientations, there are many other orientations and perhaps a different one would be more beneficial. To give one example, suppose party X adopts an orientation of avoidance with respect to party B, providing no aid, and suppose C then jumps right in and provides aid to B. As we have seen above, aid often is not productive. Therefore, why should X assume that, if aid would not be effective if employed by X it will be if used by C? Why would B not be significantly influenced by X if X provided aid but be significantly influenced by C when C provides it? Indeed, might not avoidance actually save X the possible negative consequences that sometimes develop in aid relationships? This of course is just illustrative, and there are many other comments one could make to substantiate the point.

None of the foregoing is to suggest that aid should not (or should) be provided in any particular case. Nor is it to suggest that there are no occasions in which the "boxed-in" scenario is unrealistic. In certain specific situations it could be that cooperative relations are deemed essential, the recipient is a party of major importance, the issues at stake are vital, there is an adversary just waiting to provide aid if you don't and the recipient will obtain it from that source if necessary, there are no feasible implementation instrument alternatives, and time is of the essence. In such a contingency it might be that aid is the only realistic option. *But a cardinal point here is that such situations are rare; seldom do all these conditions obtain.* Most of the time policymakers have considerably more flexibility than such a scenario allows.[38] So, although it is not always true, most of the time if one decides to provide aid only because there seems to be no other reasonable choice it is a reflection either of a lack of appreciation of the depth and variety of policy formulation and implementation options that are available or a lack of their efficient utilization.

CONCLUDING REMARKS

Before leaving this chapter a few concluding remarks are in order. First, (most) policymakers have learned that the economic instrument is considerably less effective than many assumed in the 1950s and 1960s. Seldom can it be used in such a way that the recipient will modify its policy under the threat or actual use of economic deprivation. Second, seldom does much gratitude develop in return for assistance. Third, seldom is the economic tool particularly effective by itself. Instead, it is useful primarily as a part of a coordinated package of policy instruments. Fourth, often it has been successfully used to help sustain or support recipients whose interests and policies are already favorable. And fifth, in some cases its use has actually been counterproductive, creating conditions that were harmful to the provider.

---

[38] This analysis excludes, of course, the constraints and choice-inhibiting factors discussed in Part 5.

10
Tangible Implementation Instrument: Military

The second major tangible instrument of policy implementation is the military. Because all international parties operate within an environment of decentralized anarchy, because all have the capacity to use force, because ultimately one's only sure ally is oneself, because the number of actual (let alone potential) conflicts is enormous, and because conflicts may endanger fundamental objectives, it is evident that in the very nature of things policymakers will make a large number of conflict-oriented decisions related to the protection or achievement of fundamental objectives.[1] And because in the international political world military strength is the ultimate arbiter of conflict, it also is obvious that policymakers must continually make judgments concerning the potential or actual use of military force. This requirement is nothing new. As Lerche and Said have pointed out: "Reconciling policy considerations to the threat, initiation, conduct or avoidance of war has long been one of the major concerns of the statesman."[2]

But there have been some dramatic changes in the nineteenth and twentieth centuries that make the current policymaker's task much more difficult. Due to many factors including an intensification of nationalism, the indus-

[1]See Chapter 3, pp. 75–78, for more on fundamental objectives.
[2]Charles O. Lerche, Jr., and Abdul A. Said, *Concepts of International Politics*, Second Edition, Prentice-Hall, Englewood Cliffs, N. J., 1970, p. 92.

trial, scientific, and technological revolutions, and changes in international morality, wars today have a tendency to become total. Entire populations sometimes become involved, both as participants and targets. Objectives tend to be universalized and conflicts become struggles between "Good" and "Evil." It is no exaggeration to say that we are living in an age of unmatched carnage.[3]

The problem has been compounded by the nuclear revolution. The immense destructive potential of today's weapons systems almost defies comprehension.[4] The wrong move might literally be a matter of life and death for millions. And with ballistic missiles, supersonic aircraft, and who knows what other scientific marvels, such horrible destruction can be efficiently and accurately delivered in a very few minutes. When one analyzes these facts (in the context of the tendency toward total war) he sees why it is imperative that the policymaker be ever so careful when contemplating actions involving the threat or actual use of the military tool.[5]

In most instances policymakers do act with such care, but not always. It is not easy to stay calm and cool when formulating and implementing policies in conflict situations that may endanger one's fundamental objectives, especially when those policies may involve the killing, wounding, and maiming of real flesh-and-blood human beings. But the fact that war and/or the possibility thereof raises intense emotions does not negate the need to act rationally. Indeed, perhaps it just reinforces it. Although policymakers sometimes do adopt a very short-sighted view and fight a war only to achieve total and complete military victory without regard to political consequences, frequently they more productively recognize that military policy needs to be coordinated with other policy instruments in a manner that will achieve positive political results after the war is over. In other words, they recognize that the world will go on after the termination of hostilities, and they seek to project the consequences of particular alternatives into the future and choose the one that best achieves their objectives with the most favorable overall cost-benefit ratio, whether that be one that involves a total military victory or not.

The requirement of political rationality applies across the entire spectrum of uses of the military, and indeed there are many. Although there are various classification possibilities, a useful approach, and one that policymakers often employ, is to analyze one's options in terms of the level of activity and amount

[3]The introductory student could usefully consult Morgenthau, *Politics Among Nations*, Fifth Edition, Chapters 20 and 22, and Hartmann, *The Relations of Nations*, Fifth Edition, Chapter 8. Also very helpful is Raymond Aron, *The Century of Total War*, Beacon, Boston, 1954.

[4]Also see Chapter 7, pp. 206–209.

[5]This very problem is one of the reasons that some policymakers increasingly resort to the careful *nonuse* of the military instrument in their policies.

of violence anticipated, threatened, controlled, or undertaken.[6] This shall be our approach also.[7]

Before considering these different categories specifically, three additional points need to be made. First, the degree to which a policymaker can effectively use the military instrument is greatly affected by his or her own state's military capability. Obviously a policymaker cannot employ a tool if one has no tool to employ. Thus the particular purposes for which the military instrument may be used by the policymaker in question must be determined in light of the quantitative, distributive, and qualitative components of military capability discussed earlier.[8] Second, the reader should not assume that in real life the options are as neatly packaged and clearly differentiated as our analysis might seem to imply. For analytical reasons the distinctions are highly useful, and they are reflective of the type of thinking that policymakers very frequently do engage in. But reality is always more complex than one's conception thereof, and the categories in practice sometimes tend to blur and shade over one into another.

Third, because of party uniqueness the various options are viewed, used, and reacted to differently by different parties. This point cannot be over-stressed. As always, it is essential to become situation specific, to analyze specifically who is involved, what their objectives are, etc., etc.

NONACTIVITY—PRESTIGE

The first way in which the military instrument is "utilized" is via the enhancement of prestige through the mere existence of a degree of capability. In this sense there need not be purposive military activity as such; in these situations nonactivity will serve the purpose.

Because of the importance of military capability historically, the possession of a strong military force has often been a mark of international status. This fact has long been accepted by policymakers and is a point not lost on the leaders of the less developed countries. One of the first goals of Egypt's President Nasser on gaining power in the early 1950s, for example, was the development of a strong military. Today policymakers of LDCs often seek to obtain

---

[6]Different national perceptions are important in this regard. Our analysis focuses on the activity and violence levels as seen by the policymaker of the country considering the use of the military. What are low levels for one country may be very high for another.

[7]This analysis does not specifically deal with a situation of total combat, either offensively or defensively. The military aspects of such activity are beyond the scope of this work, and the pertinent political points have already been covered, namely, total victory must not be the ultimate aim and political rationality must govern the conduct of the conflict.

[8]See Chapter 7, pp. 200–211.

weapons systems for which they have little operational need (systems which in some cases their personnel are even incapable of satisfactorily operating). In such instances one's objective usually is the bolstering of the particular leader's or regime's prestige (internally as well as externally), the weaponry adding little or nothing to effectual military strength.

The acquisition of nuclear striking capacity is a particularly significant means of increasing prestige because of the vast qualitative difference between nuclear and nonnuclear weapons.[9] Given the immense destructive potential of even a few nuclear warheads, possession of even minimal nuclear striking ability is a matter of considerable political prestige, a fact recognized by policymakers in all countries.

Today five states have operationally deliverable nuclear capability: the United States, the Soviet Union, Great Britain, France, and the People's Republic of China. In addition, India has exploded an atomic device and could easily obtain striking capability, and many other states have the potential for such acquisition.[10] The spread of nuclear knowledge, reactors, and materials has made the problem of nuclear development much less formidable than it was just a few years ago. There is no doubt that at least an additional 20 states today could develop nuclear strength if they desired, including West Germany, East Germany, Japan, Egypt, and Israel. For better or worse, the decision whether or not to acquire nuclear weapons now lies largely beyond the control of the superpowers. Up to this point it is evident that the disadvantages of acquiring nuclear weapons have outweighed the projected advantages for most of the "threshold" states, since most of those that could have developed nuclear weapons have not actually done so. This does not alter the fact, however, that essentially the choice is theirs to make and they can become nuclear powers if they so desire.

Possessing a strong military force also enhances one's prestige in the sense of providing a strong negotiating base, of providing a "position of strength" from which to bargain. Recall from the discussion in Chapter 7 that from the end of World War II until the mid-1960s the Soviet Union was clearly inferior to the United States in strategic nuclear capability. During this era no agreements were achieved between these states limiting the construction of strategic weapons systems. It was only as the Soviets began to attain strategic nuclear parity, and thus were able to negotiate from a position sufficiently strong to allow a compromise that would permit what were perceived to be comparable risks to the parties' fundamental objectives, that meaningful ne-

---

[9]Obviously, enhancing prestige is not the only reason one might want to obtain nuclear weapons.

[10]Fear of the possible consequences of such a proliferation led to the negotiation of the Non-Proliferation Treaty. See pp. 293–294.

gotiations were undertaken and an agreement (SALT I) finally achieved.[11] Somewhat paradoxically it thus appears that, in some cases at least, it is necessary to produce more or "better" arms before one is in a position to agree to arms control.

A somewhat analogous situation has existed with respect to aspects of Egyptian-Israeli relations. Prior to Egypt's effective limited war in October 1973 there had been three other sets of hostilities in the post-World War II era, the Israelis being decisively victorious in each. In none of these instances had productive negotiations occurred following the termination of hostilities.[12] But the Egyptians (along with the Syrians) established in the October War, for the first time, that they had a credible military force, that the Israelis (even though they eventually emerged "victorious") were not invincible. As a result Israeli policymakers (and the Americans) reappraised the strategic situation and evidenced much more willingness to be flexible. Negotiations soon commenced and (aided by U. S. mediation efforts) in 1974 and 1975 disengagement agreements were signed. Following further talks and American assistance the parties achieved the Camp David Framework Agreements in September 1978, and on March 26, 1979 Egypt and Israel signed a peace treaty.[13] Quite clearly the evidence of military strength provided by the events of October 1973 allowed Egypt to achieve a certain amount of prestige, and this in turn permitted the effective "utilization" of the military policy instrument via a nonactivity option.[14]

In the situations discussed above, policymakers have gained (or sought) increased prestige through the mere possession of a strong military force. They have not actually employed the instrument in any active way, but sometimes even nonactivity can be beneficial.

NONVIOLENT ACTIVITY

Military forces are sometimes effectively used in a nonviolent manner.[15] Usually this occurs within some kind of negotiating context with each move

---

[11]This is not to say that the change in weapons ratios was the sole cause, of course; many other factors also were involved. For more on SALT I see pp. 295–296.

[12]Armistice Agreements were signed in 1949 after the first war, but they did little to advance the cause of peace.

[13]Also see Chapter 12, p. 337.

[14]Once again it is necessary to remind the student that unicausal explanations seldom provide a complete picture. While the establishment of military prestige was both essential and important in this instance, other factors such as the personality and perceptions of President Sadat, America's skillful employment of the mediator orientation, etc., also were salient.

[15]One of the most effective instances of this occurred in the Cuban Missile Crisis. See Chapter 14, pp. 402–403.

designed to communicate a particular capability and possible intent to a specific party.

In most instances nonviolent activity is used coercively in what are essentially conflict or quasi-conflict situations. Let's look at some brief examples. In the analysis of territorial changes in Chapter Six the May 1974 Israeli-Syrian Disengagement Agreement was briefly discussed.[16] This agreement was to run for six months and expire November 30, 1974. Syrian policymakers, in order to maximize uncertainty in the hope that this would persuade their Israeli counterparts to make substantial concessions, refused to publicly indicate whether or not they would agree to an extension of the United Nations Disengagement of Forces (UNDOF) mandate.

Throughout much of 1974 the Israelis had been building extensive fortifications on the occupied Golan Heights.[17] As the time drew near for a decision on extension, construction was speeded up. When this did not bring about any assurance from the Syrians, the Israelis decided to begin large-scale military maneuvers on their side of the neutral zone. These maneuvers simulated various types of combat using both reservist and regular army troops. Particular emphasis was placed on those types of warfare most likely to occur between the Syrians and the Israelis, and the Israeli armed forces publicly emphasized maneuvers of an offensive character. Israeli policymakers did not engage in violence. Their use of the military, however, was very effective and played some role in the resultant Syrian decision to extend the UNDOF mandate.

Another example of the effective use of the deployment of military force occurred in mid-1934. In July the Nazis staged a coup in Vienna, Austria, and murdered Chancellor Dollfuss. In response, Italy, under the leadership of Mussolini, concentrated heavy troop formations on the border (at this time Mussolini had not yet decided to join with Hitler). Upon seeing this troop deployment Germany disavowed the coup; the Italian nonviolent activity had been successful.

Another example occurred in early 1957. Following the Suez crisis of 1956 (in which Britain, France, and Israel had "unsuccessfully" attacked Egypt), the popularity of Egypt's President Nasser rose dramatically and seemed to pose a threat to many Western-oriented Arab policymakers.[18] One such leader, Jordan's King Hussein, was under immense internal pressure to reorient both his domestic and foreign policies to bring them into line with Nasser's. Strikes and riots occurred as he resisted, and a series of incidents developed that seemed to be leading to a full scale civil war. The United States, interested in support-

---

[16]See Chapter 6, p. 137.

[17]*Jerusalem Post*, October 22, 1974, p. 1. In 1974 there was more construction than during the entire period between the June 1967 War and the Yom Kippur War of October 1973.

[18]Also see Chapter 13, pp. 374–376.

ing Hussein as a Middle Eastern counterweight to Nasser, announced that it considered the independence and integrity of Jordan to be vital to American interests, and dispatched the Sixth Fleet to the Eastern Mediterranean.[19] Such gunboat diplomacy proved to be very effective, and the crisis soon abated. Privately administration officials left no doubt that this was a calculated show of force.[20]

Sometimes a coercive nonviolent show of force does not bring the desired result, however. Such activity is designed to threaten the target, to warn that unless the desired modification of behavior occurs actions detrimental to the target may be forthcoming. The specific immediate objective is to produce a certain policy modification without resorting to violence. But the policymakers of the target party have certain objectives they are trying to achieve or protect, and the degree of importance of these objectives will be important in determining their response. They will evaluate the threatening action through their own unique perceptual lenses and according to their calculation of the costs and benefits of various alternative responses. Presumably they anticipated certain risks and costs prior to undertaking their present policy, maybe even anticipating this particular threat. Perhaps they have already gone so far that they feel that they have no choice but to continue, or maybe they feel the costs of enduring the executed threat are less than those that would be incurred by giving in. It also may be that they feel the threatener does not have the capability or the will to carry out its threat.

In August 1957 the Syrian Government uncovered an alleged American plot to overthrow the existing regime. Because of Syria's increasingly close relations with Russia, her "leftist" domestic structure, her rabidly anti-Israeli attitude, and her antagonism to Western-supported Arab leaders like Jordan's King Hussein, it was clear that Washington would oppose her on many issues.

Whether there was a CIA-engineered plot is not clear from the evidence but the Syrian policymakers certainly thought there was.[21] They expelled three American diplomats and Washington retaliated by declaring the Syrian Ambassador unwelcome. Remembering the success of its military demonstrations in the Jordanian crisis a few months earlier, Washington had the Sixth Fleet ostentatiously engage in maneuvers in the Eastern Mediterranean.

This time, however, it backfired. Instead of being cowed, Syrian policymakers stepped up their anti-American campaign and stated that such gunboat

---

[19]This occurred so suddenly that 150 sailors were left in port. *New York Times*, April 25, 1957, p. 1.

[20]Ibid., p. 2.

[21]This point is very interesting although irrelevant to our concern. For an interesting discussion see Patrick Seale, *The Struggle for Syria: A Study of Post-War Arab Politics 1945-1958*, Oxford University Press, London and New York, 1965, Chapter 21.

diplomacy substantiated their charge that the United States was the real imperialist in the region, a major enemy of all Arabs.[22]

In the Syrian case the military maneuvers were mere bluff; the United States hoped its actions would produce the desired outcome, but if that did not occur Washington was not prepared to use force. This was quite in contrast to Soviet policies in Czechoslovakia in 1968. For many months the Czechoslovakian Government had been steadily moving toward a more democratic government, and this was perceived by Moscow as a threat to its system. In the spring of the year the Warsaw Pact states held scheduled military maneuvers inside Czechoslovakia, but when it came time to withdraw they were especially slow. This implied threat brought no appreciable alteration in Czech policies. Then the Soviets staged some war games near the frontier. Once again Czech policymakers refused to bend. As is discussed below, in August the Russians (with the "assistance" of other Warsaw Pact states) invaded; they were not fooling. Here the Czechs guessed wrong, but the point for our discussion is that the nonviolent use of the military was again ineffective.

Except in those situations in which the party engaging in nonviolent military activity is overwhelmingly superior in capability to the target and/or the target has no likely allies, such activity contains a considerable element of risk. When confronted with such maneuvers target policymakers inevitably feel pressure to respond vigorously in some manner; that response could be a countering use of nonviolent activity, or even a resort to force. Clearly the target policymakers' prestige and credibility—both internally and externally—will be harmed if they don't do something, and (for obvious reasons) they may well perceive a real threat to their party's fundamental security objectives. When Austria-Hungary declared war on Serbia in July 1914 it also mobilized forces beyond those needed to defeat that country, the purpose being to deter a possible Russian intervention. But the Russians perceived this additional mobilization as directed against them and countered with a partial mobilization of their own. Soon all of the (soon to be) belligerents were mobilizing and engaging in military maneuvers, and the hostilities of World War I were not long in coming.[23] As the earlier examples showed, the nonviolent use of the military to produce policy alterations does not always lead to counteraction of this nature. It is, however, a distinct possibility and the policymaker must continually recognize this fact.

---

[22]Their case was not harmed when Secretary Dulles said he hoped that "the people of Syria would act to allay the anxiety caused by recent events." That looked like an invitation for a coup. The quote is from U. S. Department of State, *American Foreign Policy: Current Documents, 1957,* p. 1038.

[23]It is an altogether too simple explanation to attribute the outbreak of World War I solely to such developments. Nevertheless, they were a major contributing factor. Also see Chapter 13, pp. 376–378.

Nonviolent military activity occurs most frequently in conflict or near conflict situations. As we have mentioned several times, military force is the ultimate arbiter in the decentralized anarchy of international politics; thus even a nonviolent use of the military instrument may carry considerable policy-modifying potency vis-a-vis recalcitrant actual or potential adversaries. On occasion, however, nonviolent activity may occur in a cooperative setting; although there are a number of means of enhancing cooperative behavior that often are more appropriate, in some instances the military can be fruitfully utilized. For example, in recent years the Soviets have been prone to send elements of their (expanding) navy to ports of friendly African and Asian states as a means (and symbol) of improving bilateral relations. And after the signature of the American-mediated Israeli-Egyptian disengagement agreement in January 1974 the United States dispatched ships to Egypt to help Cairo clear the Suez Canal of mines. Activities such as these can't help but enhance cooperation.[24]

LIMITED ISOLATED VIOLENCE

Moving up the scale, the policymaker may conclude that some degree of force or violence would be useful but warfare should be avoided. Thus the operation should remain limited in terms of objectives, targets, and duration, and probably would involve a particular incident (or series of incidents) or a one-shot military operation.

The Israeli Government has long made use of limited military violence. As discussed above, in late 1974 the Syrian Government had not given any public indication concerning whether or not it would approve an extension of the UNDOF mandate. About the same time the Palestinian question put Israel on the diplomatic defensive. At the Rabat Conference in October Arab leaders called for the creation of an independent Palestinian Arab state, agreed that the Palestine Liberation Organization (an organization Israeli policymakers characterized as being composed of gangsters and murderers) was the "sole legitimate representative" of the Palestinian Arabs, and stated that any portions of the old Palestine Mandate recovered from Israel would be the responsibility of the PLO. In late November the United Nations General Assembly voted to affirm the Palestinians' "right to national independence and sovereignty" after listening to PLO leader, Yasir Arafat, state his case.

---

[24]It should be pointed out that policymakers in cases such as these may also have an eye on nonsituational parties. As mentioned in Chapter 3, sometimes one's policy in a given situation is designed primarily for its extrasituational impact. Even if not so designed, because all actions have differential effects (see Chapter 14) nonsituational parties will be impacted in some manner.

In order to emphasize its own military strength and the fact that it would not be pressured into negotiating with the PLO, Israeli military units undertook a wide variety of attacks against PLO supported facilities in Lebanon. These attacks included several small infantry forays that destroyed installations and equipment as well as inflicting minor casualties, and air sorties as far into Lebanon as Beirut. In each case the operation was specific, its military objective was clear, and its political objective was to demonstrate that Israel had the military strength and political willpower to make its own decisions concerning with whom it would negotiate over land it controlled.

Another example of limited military operations occurred on the night of August 20, 1968 as troops from the Soviet Union, East Germany, Poland, Hungary, and Bulgaria crossed the Czechoslovakian border and proceeded to occupy their "ally." In this case the objective was primarily to eliminate a regime that was becoming too "liberal" (read: "capitalist" and "democratic") for Soviet policymakers' tastes. The Soviets did not expect much military resistance, and they did not get it. As a result their limited violence proved successful.

In the aftermath of the final collapse of South Vietnam's armed forces and the American evacuation in the spring of 1975 United States prestige and credibility in Asia (and elsewhere?) was, in the eyes of both many American and many non-American policymakers, at a low ebb; the provisions of the painfully negotiated 1973 Paris Peace Agreement were in shambles, and it was evident that the DRV would soon "unify" Vietnam under its aegis. Fortuitously for Washington, at this juncture an opportunity to regain at least some of its lost prestige presented itself when on May 12 Cambodia seized the American cargo ship *Mayaguez*. Availing itself of this opportunity the United States responded swiftly and directly, dispatching marine units to recover the vessel and its crew. Whether the operation was conducted as efficiently as it ought to have been, whether the level of violence was appropriate to the level of provocation, whether the crisis diplomacy of the Ford Administration was sufficiently prudent and careful, even whether the objectives were correct, are all matters of dispute, but none of these concerns are relevant to our discussion. The point here is that in this situation policymakers in fact utilized limited isolated violence as the means to achieve their objectives.

Although there are many other examples, it would be superfluous to give them. It is clear that policymakers often decide to engage in the limited use of violence, and sometimes it works. But many times it does not. And there is an additional difficulty. Unless one is in a situation in which the target is overwhelmingly inferior in capability, has no possibility of obtaining external assistance, or has no intention of resisting anyway (a highly unlikely contingency in the absence of the two foregoing conditions), there is an enormous risk that what begins as an exercise in limited isolated violence will escalate into some type of warfare. It is essential to recognize that the extent to which the violence remains limited and isolated depends not just on the initiating party but also in considerable part on the reaction of the target. Thus, while it is certainly essential that one plan operations very carefully so as to minimize the probability of violent counteraction, *there is no way to ensure that even with the best of planning there in fact will not be significant retaliation, nor that if this occurs spiralling reciprocal escalation will not also soon follow.* It is all well and good to speak of managing and controlling crises and the role of violence therein, but the policymakers of the parties being attacked (again, unless said parties are hopelessly outclassed in terms of capability and have no possibility of obtaining assistance) may prove to be highly "unmanageable." If the policymaker planning to use limited isolated violence is prepared to escalate should events show that to be necessary, then perhaps such a possible reaction may not be of great moment. But if not, if a violent counteraction would require a response that would entail costs beyond the benefits one could possibly attain, then the policymaker should engage in limited violence only with a great deal of caution because in most instances significant counteraction is a real possibility.

LIMITED WAR

Sometimes it appears that one can achieve his objectives only with the sustained but limited application of force. Limited wars are not new, of course, but with the tendencies toward total war and the appalling destructiveness of modern weaponry the necessity of keeping conflicts limited has gained a new urgency.

In some senses, of course, nearly all wars are limited. Although there are exceptions, it is highly unusual for a party to seek the annihilation of its adversary with every means available. Even in World War II some types of weapons were not used and some methods were not employed. Despite this fact, there is still an important distinction to be made here. *The concept of limited war implies a conscious effort to use the military instrument for rationally defined political purposes, and to keep the conflict under control by definitely limiting or excluding certain factors.* A point of some significance in this regard is that because different parties have different perceptions, orientations, and objectives the same conflict can be quite limited for one participant but relatively unlimited for another. For example, although Washington saw the Vietnam war as a limited conflict, for Vietcong policymakers it was a struggle for survival.

What are the major limitations one may seek to impose? The first lies in the area of *objectives.* In a limited war situation the policymaker is only seeking certain carefully defined and restricted political goals. Limited wars are not fought to achieve total victory, nor are they designed to subjugate an adversary or make massive territorial acquisitions. The nineteenth-century Prussian, Prince Otto Von Bismarck, was a practitioner of limited war *par excellence*. After decisively defeating Austria in the Seven Weeks' War (June to August 1866), for example, he refused to annex many of the territories that he had captured. His purpose had been to demonstrate Prussian superiority in North Germany and make some limited territorial gains. This he had accomplished. By going no further he avoided incurring permanent Austrian hostility.[25]

Another example was provided by the Sino-Indian conflict. In conjunction with a festering boundary dispute and the political contest for Asian supremacy, Communist Chinese forces attacked India's Himalayan provinces in late 1962. The Chinese easily overran their opposition and demonstrated that they had the capacity to conquer the entire subcontinent if they should desire, but they did not.[26] This attack accomplished two carefully limited objectives. First, it clearly established Peking's military superiority. Second, it reaffirmed China's position on borders, namely, that the existing frontiers were artificially imposed and had no legitimacy; the true borders of China were those of the Middle Kingdom.[27]

Frequently the element of prestige is of importance in the decision to engage in limited warfare. Certainly prestige preservation was one of the major reasons President Truman opted to militarily oppose the North Korean attack on South Korea in June 1950, for example, and prestige enhancement had much to do with China's effort to "punish" Vietnam with a limited invasion in February 1979. Domestic regime prestige needs also may lead to limited war operations; perhaps the chief policymaker's internal support is eroding and a foreign policy success will restore his or her personal popularity. But prestige-induced limited warfare frequently produces a highly volatile situation. Unless the attacker is successful prestige will be harmed rather than helped, and inevitably this will produce pressure to broaden one's objectives and delimit operations. Policymakers undertaking limited war for prestige reasons need to be inordinately careful to avoid placing themselves in a situation in which they must escalate or be humiliated.

A very important factor in achieving limited objectives via the limited application of force is clear communication. The policymaker must make sure that other parties *know* his or her objectives are limited or else he or she is inviting counter action. In their 1979 attack on Vietnam the Chinese time and again made it evident that they did not intend either conquest or territorial ac-

---

[25]Useful is Hartmann, *The Relations of Nations*, Fifth Edition, pp. 336-337.

[26]Because the Cuban Missile Crisis was occurring simultaneously it is unlikely that any outside power capable of preventing this would have done so. They had their own troubles.

[27]See Chapter 3, pp. 76, 83.

quisition, that their goal was simply to "punish" Vietnam; once that had been done they would withdraw. In the examples discussed above Bismarck and Mao also were able to communicate clearly. They were able to succeed for the reason that outsiders who might have become involved did not do so because they were aware that the militarily superior parties in each situation sought only some rather carefully limited goals, goals that did not significantly endanger these outsiders' efforts to achieve or protect fundamental objectives.

But such clear communication is not always possible, and even when the message seems clear the recipient may either misperceive or simply not believe it.[28] As we discovered in our earlier analysis of the determination of objectives (Chapter 3), ascertaining objectives is a critical but terribly complicated and uncertain task. What *are* a particular party's objectives, and *are* they limited? Chamberlain thought Hitler's objectives were limited, but he was wrong. Doubly frustrating is the fact that sometimes the policymakers themselves are not sure what they are after, or they may start out with one goal but change as the situation changes. The original American objective in Korea was simply to prevent a North Korean conquest but Washington opted for territorial unification when battlefield conditions improved (and later changed again in the light of battlefield reverses).

Policymakers also may seek to *limit the means employed* and deliberately exclude the use of certain weapons systems.[29] As has been mentioned previously, the United States deliberately excluded the use of nuclear weapons in the Vietnamese conflict. Although there have been minor exceptions, generally speaking chemical and biological weapons have not been extensively used in warfare. The assumption behind weapons exclusion is that the situation can be more easily controlled and escalation can be prevented if one avoids using certain parts of his arsenal. Presumably his adversary will recognize that mere destruction is not desired and that survival is not the issue.

One may also seek to *limit the participants*. Indeed, a major reason for limiting objectives and/or excluding the use of certain means is to avoid provoking others into participation. Sometimes one has his or her eye on a specific nonparticipant. American policymakers in the Vietnam conflict were constantly looking toward Peking and stating that various military raids were in no way a threat to Chinese security.

The concern also may be more general. Although one cannot say there is a precise relationship between the intensity of warfare and the number of com-

---

[28]For more on problems of communication see Chapter 11.

[29]The reference here is to the nonuse of weapon systems that a state possesses. Obviously a state cannot employ weapons it does not have but that type of "limitation" is not meaningful for our purposes.

batants, it is usually true that, other things being equal, the fewer the number of participants the more controllable the situation becomes. For example, suppose in the next Middle East war (assuming there is a next Middle East war) all of the Arab states become heavily involved against Israel (one must remember that this never has occurred in previous conflicts). If such were to happen it is quite possible that, for those participants, the war would become unlimited and someone's survival would be at stake. Should that occur the conflict would be very difficult to control.

Another way a policymaker may seek to control a conflict is by *limiting the targets* of his or her activity. The less vital a particular target is to a state's survival the more the policymaker for that state can tolerate its being attacked, and vice versa. This type of limitation may refer simply to declaring (tacitly or explicitly) certain geographical areas off limits. In the Korean War, for example, the Chinese enjoyed what became known as a "privileged sanctuary" in that the United States did not (except for minor incidents) attack the territory of the Chinese state itself. Similarly, the United States was allowed its "privileged sanctuary" in the sense that many of its troops and supplies came from Japan and Peking made no effort to attack her.

Sometimes the participants seek to make use of targeting in order to apply pressure to another belligerent. In the Vietnam conflict it was not until early 1965 that the United States began to bomb Hanoi's "privileged sanctuary" in the north, and then it began in terms of areas near the demilitarized zone. When Washington was not able to bring Hanoi to the bargaining table on the terms it desired it increasingly chose targets that were more vital to the North Vietnamese war effort such as port facilities in Haiphong, steel complexes, electrical facilities, and so forth. As we know, however, the gradual escalation did not prove successful.

A very successful recent use of limited warfare occurred in October 1973. After his ascension to power in 1970 Egyptian President Sadat sought to bring about some progress toward the "removal of the consequences of Israeli aggression," that is, some Israeli movement away from the Suez Canal and the return of some of the territories taken by her in the 1967 war. By late 1973, despite all his efforts, no progress had been made. Because of this on October 6, 1973 Egypt launched a military assault across the Suez Canal, and began the Yom Kippur (Ramadan) War.

The Egyptian attack clearly was only a limited warfare maneuver. The Egyptians did not have the military capability to defeat Israel, and knew it. Instead they hoped to make a good military showing, which in fact they did, and thus improve their bargaining position. This would compel Israel to think very seriously about negotiating some type of compromise agreement, forcing her to recognize that merely digging in on the banks of the Canal was not a sufficient policy.[30] Sadat made it clear that he would not accept this indefinitely and that such a policy would prevent any possibility of a peace settlement.

Sadat also was seeking to demonstrate to the remainder of the world that the Arabs were developing a military capability of some note and other states (particularly the United States) should recognize that no longer was Israel guaranteed of a sure military victory. He hoped that once outsiders recognized this fact, they would make more of an effort to help bring about a settlement. As mentioned earlier, in early 1974 and 1975 the United States did act as a problem solver and helped bring about the Israeli-Syrian and (two) Israeli-Egyptian disengagement agreements.

A policymaker choosing to engage in limited warfare is embarking on a highly risky venture, one with scarcely predictable results. When United States forces crossed the 38th parallel in the Korean war and began the quest for (Korean) territorial unification its action heightened Peking's fears of an American invasion; although Washington did not seek or expect an expanded war, as we all know it got one. In late 1978 Idi Amin's Ugandan army initiated limited warfare operations across the border into Tanzania. Spurning all offers of mediation, the Tanzanians counterattacked and drove the invaders out. Not satisfied with restoring the status quo *ante bellum*, they then invaded Uganda and in the spring of 1979 forced the Ugandan dictator to flee the country. It is fine in the abstract to talk about "limiting" warfare and "managing" crises, but in the real world the task is extremely difficult. Of course, as we saw earlier in some instances it has been done. But given the risks, prudent policymakers will deliberately choose to undertake limited warfare only with great circumspection, and they will do so only after a careful analysis demonstrates that the objectives are worth taking high risks to achieve and no other means yields as favorable a cost-benefit calculus with respect to attaining the desired outcome.

GUERILLA WARFARE

There is one type of limited war that deserves separate treatment because of its importance today, and that is guerilla war.[31] Utilized primarily in furtherance of the orientations of indirect opposition and/or limited support (and sometimes in execution of the exacerbater option), guerilla wars are undertaken by a wide variety of states and national liberation organizations and most generally occur in the less developed countries of Asia, Africa, and Latin America. *The term "guerilla warfare" covers a broad range of conflicts and situations,*

---

[30]This statement is not meant to imply that the Israelis actually *were* following such a policy. These comments refer only to *Egyptian perceptions* and objectives.

[31]Also variously called sublimited war, war of national liberation, people's war, ambiguous conflict, or unconventional war.

but two elements are always present: there is some degree of revolutionary ac-
tivity against the existing government, and (at least initially) the tactics are un-
conventional with an emphasis on mobility, harassment, and infiltration.

The "book" on guerilla war was "written" by Mao Tse-tung in the Chinese Communist revolution.[32] The Chinese Communist Party was established in 1921 at the instigation of the Communist International in Moscow, and took its place among the series of revolutionary factions competing for power in the wake of the collapse of the Manchu Empire.[33] Under Soviet direction the Chinese were compelled to collaborate with the Kuomintang (the Chinese Nationalist Party). This uneasy partnership was dissolved in 1926 and 1927 as the Nationalists, under the leadership of the Moscow trained General Chiang Kai-shek, launched a military campaign aimed at gaining control over all of China. Although that objective was never totally achieved, Chiang did inflict a series of military defeats upon his rivals and emerged as the most powerful force in the country. When a series of Communist insurrections failed in the late 1920s the Party was driven from the cities into the northwest provinces.

Until this time Mao had been only one among several leading Communists. After it became clear that the Russian-dominated policy had failed and the existing leadership was inept, however, Mao and his associates were able to take over. Taking advantage of Kuomintang incompetence and the beginning of the Japanese onslaught he began a guerilla campaign.

Mao recognized that traditional Marxist doctrine predicting the revolution of the industrial proletariat was inappropriate to the Chinese situation because no industrial proletariat existed. Showing the flexibility of good leadership, he placed *his* emphasis on the peasants and capitalized on their disaffection with the Kuomintang. Alternately fighting and collaborating with the Nationalists (as they continued their efforts against the Japanese) he built both a highly disciplined political party and a very effective military machine. Tactically he used the difficult terrain for evasive tactics, avoiding direct combat situations that might drain his military strength. Mobility and surprise were his assets and when it looked like he might lose a battle he quickly retreated.

When World War II ended China was still in turmoil. There was no effective military or political control, transport and communication facilities were

---

[32]Mao actually did much writing, but the comments here are referring to his example and the fact that many later revolutionaries adopted his methods. For an understanding of his basic ideas in this sphere see Mao Tse-tung, *On Guerilla Warfare,* Praeger, New York, 1961.

[33]The Manchus lost power in 1911. The succeeding years were characterized by governmental impotence and warlord rule. The country was divided into a series of military fiefdoms, each controlled by a regional warlord or military leader, and the central government became little more than a puppet of whichever warlord happened to be in control of the region at the time. Soon two "central governments" competed for control, one in the imperial capital of Peking, the other at Canton.

disrupted, inflation was rampant, and corruption continued unabated. Full-scale civil war developed. Mao continued to avoid massive confrontations and harassed and frustrated his opposition. He made use of captured or abandoned equipment plus some weapons turned over by the Russians in Manchuria. Mao was not concerned with defending or obtaining particular pieces of territory or lines. In reality there are no front lines in this kind of activity; the front is everywhere. His forces concentrated on small-scale operations against communication lines and supply depots, ambushed convoys, and generally used hit-and-run tactics.

In an effort to cut their losses the Nationalist forces retreated to the cities (a traditional Chinese defense technique) thus leaving the countryside to the Communists (which was precisely what the latter desired as they continued to build their strength on the peasantry). Eventually the cities became isolated and supplies were cut off. Counterthrusts became nearly impossible and the civilian population (at least most of it) just stood back and watched, ready to join whichever side seemed to be winning.[34] It was not so much that the government was despised by the people as it was that the public was indifferent. Early in 1948 the Communists took the offensive as morale among even the best Nationalist formations began to crack. Chiang's demoralized troops simply lost the will to fight. With Nationalist strength dissipating the Communists were now able to engage in direct confrontation and usually emerged victorious. In early 1949 Peking fell to Mao's forces. Before the year was out Chiang retreated from the mainland to Formosa and Mao was in control. In October he proclaimed the People's Republic of China with its capital in the old imperial city of Peking.

Since the time of Mao's successful guerilla war numerous others have sought similar goals in more or less the same fashion. Frequently external parties (for their own reasons) provide a particular belligerent NLO with assistance. The People's Republic of China and (North) Vietnam for example, have played major roles in supporting wars of national liberation in Asia, and scores of other "people's" forces have been aided by foreign actors in their quest for power.[35] Economic and military assistance, inflammatory propaganda activities, aid in disrupting the government's decision-making system, help in exacerbating ethnic, racial, or religious cleavages and conflicts, efforts to enhance the appeal of disruptive transnational factors, highlighting and emphasizing discrepancies between the people's expectations and the level of the regime's performance, in these and many other ways external parties can be of considerable help to the guerillas.

[34]This often is the situation in successful revolutions. Seldom do the masses rise up and overthrow their government. Instead, they simply fail to give it support. This is not always the case, however, as the overthrow of the Shah of Iran in early 1979 demonstrated.

[35]Also see Chapter 5, pp. 119, 121–122.

But despite the many techniques available, external parties usually cannot initiate and successfully carry out guerilla warfare on their own; revolution is seldom exportable. The basic role of outsiders is one of assisting, of facilitating the insurgents' activities and exacerbating the problems of the existing government. The reason for this limitation is that guerilla activity cannot be effective without some degree of popular support, and this will be forthcoming only if the populace is somewhat alienated from the government to begin with.[36] Although policymakers of external parties may be able to magnify internal discontent and provide the discontented with certain capabilities, seldom can they create the conditions for successful insurgency in the first place.

Successful guerilla warfare is more than a military operation. While flexible unconventional military tactics are an essential component of the guerrilla's strategy, advocacy of politically and socially popular causes, exploitation of societal cleavages, alienation of the populace from the government, the selective use of terror, in short a broad spectrum of political/psychological techniques are utilized to obtain a degree of popular cooperation or acquiescence and destroy the enemy's will to continue. If the insurgency is in some measure succeeding, then, in fact, to some extent these objectives are being achieved. Consequently, a well-organized guerilla campaign cannot be effectively countered or controlled solely by military methods. This does not mean military countermeasures are not important. They are. The government must be able to inflict military defeats on its opponents, be able to demonstrate its military competence. But to succeed it must do more than this. If it ultimately is going to halt the insurgency, in addition to achieving some military successes government policymakers will have to become responsive to the demands of the populace and do something to alter the conditions that alienated people (and thus allowed the guerillas to get started) in the first place. Whether or not policymakers will find such alternatives palatable in terms of their own personal, regime, and perceived national interests, or whether in fact such demands are actually possible to meet given the objective conditions of the particular situation are both questions which can only be answered on a case by case basis.

It is highly probable that policymakers of external parties will aid national liberation organizations in their guerilla activities with considerable frequency in the 1980s. There are several reasons why this is so, why such activity is frequently perceived to be a quite useful tactic:

1.   It is often possible to keep one's participation relatively disguised (or maybe even secret), thus minimizing the risk of a direct confrontation and any possible impairment of fundamental objectives.

[36]See Chalmers A. Johnson, "Civilian Loyalties and Guerilla Conflict," *World Politics*, July 1962, pp. 646-661.

2.   The consequences of failure tend to be relatively small due to the relatively small commitment.
3.   Such operations are relatively inexpensive. The weapons and supplies required are comparatively meager and thus are within the capability of nearly all states.[37]
4.   Only a small number of participants are required to start and never does the personnel requirement become excessively large.
5.   Because of the dangers of nuclear warfare policymakers are actively seeking alternative uses of force.
6.   States are much more permeable than in the past and it is difficult to prevent penetration.
7.   Conditions in many countries are ripe for revolutionary activities, and many of the problems seem unlikely to be remedied in the foreseeable future.

DETERRENCE

The policymaker also may employ the military instrument for purposes of deterrence.[38] Basically, deterrence means that policymaker A seeks to prevent policymaker B from doing something by threatening B with unacceptable costs if he does. By posing this threat A is seeking to preclude certain types of activity (usually activities involving military attack). Deterrence involves a critical psychological relationship between the "deterrer" and "deterree," and when successful is characterized by the effective nonuse of military force.

Our approach to this topic will be threefold. First, in brief and simplified terms we will specify and define the components most generally accepted by deterrence theorists and practitioners as constituting sound deterrence. Second, we will analyze the evolution of American strategic doctrine and policy and examine the role of some of the components of sound deterrence therein.[39] Third, we will provide what is sometimes neglected in the analysis of deterrence—a placing of the discussion within the broad perspective of the political policymaker.

[37]This, of course, can change. If the guerilla forces alter their tactics to engage in confrontations, their needs will drastically increase. At this time external aid may be decisive.

[38]The subject of deterrence is so complicated and amorphous that one hardly knows where to begin. Volumes have been written and an entirely new area of specialization, deterrent theory, has emerged. Unfortunately there is little agreement among scholars or policymakers. As John Raser has said, "what looked like a forest to early deterrent scholars is now seen to be a tractless jungle and its explorers are unable to set up any guideposts reading 'this way to safety'." John R. Raser, "International Deterrence," in Michael Haas, ed., *International Systems: A Behavioral Approach*, Chandler, New York, 1974, p. 320.

[39]Because of its seminal importance, our discussion focuses primarily on strategic nuclear deterrence.

Components of Deterrence

What are the requirements for effective deterrence? *First, the policymakers must act as rationally as possible.*[40] There must be accurate evaluations of the capabilities and intentions of the relevant parties, different national perceptions must be taken into account, careful precautions must be taken so as to prevent organizational inefficiency from disrupting planned policy, and the costs and benefits from each potential decision must be accurately calculated and balanced. If rationality is not present no system of deterrence can be guaranteed to be effective. If states are headed by people who are "trigger happy," careless, power hungry, unstable, or whatever, or if there is not careful control over subordinates and they undertake senseless activities, deterrence may be unworkable.

There are a number of other difficulties with respect to this requirement of policymaker rationality. First, quite clearly there is no universal agreement as to what is or is not "rational" in a particular situation, and what "rationally" would deter one individual might not deter another. Different national perceptions, of course, also would loom large in this regard. Second, in time of crisis, when the need for rationality is most evident, its existence may be least likely. As policymakers find themselves confronted with conditions that conceivably could endanger fundamental objectives they may become less rational than they would be in less stressful situations. Third, it is arguable that in certain situations, such as one involving the opportunity to cripple most of a potential adversary's strategic forces in a surprise attack with some of one's missiles while holding others in reserve to deter retaliation, it might actually be rational to initiate hostilities. Finally, no matter how rational policymakers are, the possibility of war by accident, miscalculation, or unauthorized use still remains and it is unaffected by deterrence considerations. What is the point of this discussion? Simply this. While it is certainly true that rationality is an essential component of sound deterrence, the "common sense" view that because nuclear war would be horribly destructive no *rational* person would launch it glosses over a number of complex, very real problems.

The second component of deterrence is *credibility*. This involves several elements. First, in order for credibility to be established one must have the military capability to inflict what is considered by the deterree to be an unacceptable level of damage. Second, credibility requires the capacity to communicate the extent of one's capability to the deterree. Obviously a state will not be deterred on the basis of the second state's military strength if it is not aware that

---

[40]Total rationality is impossible, of course, since one can never know all the information relevant to a particular subject, be aware of all the possible alternatives and their consequences, and so on. Here we simply mean that the policymakers do everything within their power to think and act on the basis of evidence and logic.

the second state has this strength. Usually such communication is relatively easy.

A third component of credibility is the willingness to use power. One's threat to carry out an activity that will bring about unacceptable damage must be believed by the target of that threat; otherwise, there will not be a deterrent effect. The target must think that the threatener is willing to do what it said it would. Simply because a party has a certain level of military strength does not necessarily mean that it is willing to use it. Once again communication, in this case communication of willingness, is terribly important.

A critically important fact to note is that *credibility depends on the beliefs and perceptions of the target of the deterrent policy, that is, the deterree.* It is not what the deterr*er* thinks is important that will be decisive, but the thoughts and ideas of the deterr*ee.* When analyzing the question of what is an unacceptable level of damage to Russia, it is not important what would be unacceptable to *American* policymakers but rather what level of damage is unacceptable to *Soviet* leaders.

The final component of effective deterrence is *stability*. What makes for a stable deterrent relationship? Not overwhelming superiority. While party A, which has no desire to attack party R but has enormously superior nuclear striking capacity in comparison to R's, may consider such a situation to be highly safe and stable, from R's perspective the situation may be highly dangerous and because R may see things in this manner the result is instability. Even if, in objective terms, the parties' nuclear forces are comparable, if one party's *perception* is such that the other would strike first if it could successfully do so the situation again could be unstable. Perhaps that party indeed would attack at an appropriate moment, or maybe the policymaker who felt his or her state was the likely target would launch a preemptive strike to avoid the perceived adversary's possible first strike. After all, when such terrible weapons are available the one that strikes first just might be able to destroy the other side's forces and avoid retaliation. What appears to be necessary to remedy this instability is to have a situation of *mutual retaliatory invulnerability*, a situation in which both parties know that their retaliatory forces could withstand a first strike and respond by delivering an unacceptable level of damage on the attacker. When both parties have this capability, and each knows it, the situation seems to be relatively stable.

U. S. Strategic Deterrent Policy

Following World War II American policymakers assumed that if there was to be another war it would be general, the result of a Soviet attack on Europe.[41]

---

[41]See Chapter 13 for further comments on American postwar perceptions.

The resulting American posture was a basic reliance on the *threat of atomic retaliation*. Since the United States was the only state to possess nuclear weapons at this time this was a first strike/counter city strategy.[42] If the Soviets launched an attack the United States would retaliate with a nuclear response on the major cities of the Soviet Union. From the Soviet point of view, in light of the American atomic monopoly, this kind of policy was credible but it also was threatening and destabilizing.[43]

The testing of a Soviet atomic bomb in August 1949 and the victory of the Chinese Communists (who were presumed to be controlled by the Soviets) initiated some changes. The National Security Council undertook a strategic review and in April 1950 issued a posture study (NSC 68) which placed somewhat more emphasis on the dangers of less than total war and called for a substantial increase in defense spending. The onset of the Korean War two months later gave additional impetus to these changes.

When the Eisenhower Administration took office in 1953 it decided to take a new look at military strategy. The main policy architect was Secretary of State John Foster Dulles, and the new policy was called *massive retaliation*. The Administration was worried about the spiraling costs of defense. It felt that reliance on a more unified strategy emphasizing the role of one of the services (Air Force) would be both less expensive and more effective. The strategic policy was enunciated by the secretary in early January 1954 when he said that henceforth the United States would consider responding to provocations with massive retaliatory power by means and at places of its own choosing.[44]

Massive retaliation was not really very different from the first-strike/counter city policy of the Truman administration. It could not help but be destabilizing and threatening to Soviet policymakers. The Russians were busily engaged in building their own nuclear force, testing thermo-nuclear devices, and developing delivery systems that could threaten the United States. Because of this the policy of massive retaliation came to resemble a mutual suicide pact. Since there was no defense against nuclear attack it was as if Mr. Dulles was saying, "if you destroy us I will make sure we take you with us when we go."

Many came to believe that this policy had severe deficiencies. It implied in all cases the threat of (and perhaps preparation for) total war, regardless of the

---

[42]First strike in the sense that the United States would be the first to launch a nuclear attack. The trigger for such a strike was presumed to be a prior Soviet assault.

[43]Although there was no Soviet attack on Western Europe at this time, and thus one can argue that deterrence was effective, one could argue that this deterrent policy was designed to prevent a war that the Soviets themselves never contemplated. If that is so the Soviets could only see it as a potentially aggressive accumulation of power.

[44]John Foster Dulles, "The Evolution of Foreign Policy," U. S. Department of State, *Bulletin*, January 25, 1954, pp. 107-110.

extent and type of provocation.[45] Although the secretary was vague in terms of precisely what would happen if the Soviets provoked Uncle Sam, the possibility of massive response was there. Apparently he assumed this would be sufficient to deter both general and limited wars.

Both logic and a spate of local conflicts convinced many, observers and policymakers alike, that massive retaliation *by itself* was insufficient as a strategic doctrine. It allowed policymakers no flexibility of response. This did not seem rational, because there were many situations in which such a massive response would not be appropriate. Because of this there were doubts Washington would actually be willing to retaliate, and this damaged its deterrent's credibility.

Another policy problem was developing about this time because of changing capability relationships. American strategic forces were highly vulnerable to a Soviet attack, and as the Soviets enhanced their striking power the survivability of Washington's retaliatory capability seemed increasingly endangered. Because of the possibility of a successful Russian first strike Washington's response would have to be automatic and immediate. Quite naturally this led to greater emphasis on the development of invulnerable retaliatory forces (second-strike capability). If a state is committed to not launching a first strike, and if its adversary can launch a surprise attack and wipe out one's nuclear forces, then the situation is very unstable. Stability requires that states possess weapons that can survive a surprise attack and be capable of delivering a retaliatory blow of unacceptable proportions.

When the Kennedy administration took over the beginnings of change that occurred in the latter Eisenhower years received further impetus. Greater emphasis was placed on the development of mobile Polaris missile submarines in order to decrease vulnerability. There was an effort to develop a greater mix of retaliatory forces (a combination of strategic air command forces and land and sea based missiles, the so-called strategic "Triad") so that there would always be at least one retaliatory force available. And as land-based missiles began to be deployed in underground concrete silos there were efforts to "harden" these shelters to provide the greatest possible resistance to an attack.

In 1962 a shift in strategic doctrine occurred. In a major speech in Ann Arbor, Michigan, Secretary of Defense McNamara announced what became known as the *doctrine of counterforce*.[46] The basic idea of counterforce is de-

---

[45]Extensive reliance on massive retaliation seemed to mean that, when faced with low level or limited provocation, one's options were limited to massive response or acquiescence. This dilemma had much to do with the development of limited war capacity, discussed above, and the doctrine of flexible response, discussed in Chapter 14. For the view that nuclear weapons make huge conventional forces obsolete see Bernard Brodie, *War and Politics*, Macmillan, New York, 1973, Ch. 9.

[46]See U. S., Department of State, *Bulletin*, July 9, 1962, pp. 64-69.

terrence by threatening to destroy military targets (instead of population centers). Under this operation cities would be spared and every effort made to minimize casualties among civilians.

Counterforce was also an intrawar deterrent doctrine. The idea here was that should war-preventing deterrence fail, a counterforce strategy would be the least immoral method of fighting a war because it would involve the least number of noncombatant casualties. In this sense it was hoped that deterrence would operate within the framework of a nuclear war, and that a nuclear war could be a limited war.

It was also assumed that counterforce targeting would give one's opponents an incentive to avoid striking cities. As Professor Rosi put it, "by retaliating in a controlled manner against military targets in the U. S. S. R., while avoiding Russian cities, the United States would seek to negotiate a truce before an all-out, city-destroying attack was launched by either side.[47]

The difficulty with a counterforce strategy is that it inevitably has first strike implications. Obviously attacks against an adversary's forces are more effective if launched before the latter's weapons have been fired. Although one might say that his posture was second strike counterforce, and mean it, opposition policymakers would be compelled to consider the contrary. This is precisely what the Russians did, and the result was the addition of considerable impetus to the arms race.[48] The more one sought to make counterforce credible, to increase his capability to destroy his opponent's forces, the more destabilizing it became. And neither side really believed the other would avoid its cities anyway.

McNamara never made it quite clear if Washington was shifting completely to counterforce or not, and by the mid-1960s some changes were apparent. The new policy was the *doctrine of assured destruction*. This was a second-strike/counter value strategy. Although the precise terms varied from time to time, the doctrine's essential postulate was that the United States should, after absorbing a Soviet attack, have the retaliatory capacity to destroy an unacceptably large portion of Russia's population and industrial capacity (usually the proportions stipulated were one-third and two-thirds respectively).[49] Developing a force of this capacity required both an increase in offensive strength and a decrease in vulnerability. Washington increased its

[47]Eugene J. Rosi, ed., *American Defense and Détente: Readings in National Security Policy*, Dodd Mead, New York, 1973, p. 98.

[48]Useful in this regard is Edgar M. Bottome, *The Balance of Terror: A Guide to the Arms Race*, Beacon, Boston, 1971, Part IV. Another very important stimulant was the adverse (as the Soviets saw it) outcome of the Cuban Missile Crisis, the Kremlin believing it was forced to accept a humiliating defeat because of its strategic inferiority. See Chapter 7, Diagrams 3 and 4.

[49]According to Morton Halperin, however, the original figures were 25 percent in both cases. See Morton H. Halperin, *Defense Strategies for the Seventies*, Little, Brown, Boston, 1971, p. 73.

emphasis on hardening of missile silos, and began testing the MIRV. The Soviets, too, stepped up their efforts. The problem, of course, was that as each party sought to enhance its offensive capability and decrease its vulnerability so as to be able to withstand a first strike and still be able to effectively retaliate, it was also increasing its offensive options. Quite naturally defense planners of the potential target perceived such activities as potentially threatening, and thus what were designed to be stabilizing moves also had certain destabilizing tendencies.

When Richard Nixon became president American superiority in missile launchers was decreasing.[50] In light of this fact, the immense costs of the arms race, domestic political factors inhibiting new missile programs, and the recognition that the most stable deterrent situation seems to involve mutually invulnerable retaliatory forces, the President adopted the *strategy of sufficiency*. While maintaining the assured destruction capacity discussed above, he sought to stabilize the situation and prevent the Russians from gaining superiority. These efforts led to the Strategic Arms Limitation Agreements of 1972 in which overall quantitative limits were placed on the strategic missiles each side could possess. With the development of essentially equivalent nuclear capability policymakers now spoke in terms of *mutual assured destruction* (MAD). Deterrence now seemed stabilized because it was mutual.

But the SALT Agreements and perceptions of parity did not prevent the arms race from continuing, nor did they stop the growth of strategic doctrine. On February 5, 1974 Defense Secretary Schlesinger proposed a refinement of the sufficiency-assured destruction posture.[51] Within this framework Mr. Schlesinger advocated "*selective targeting options.*" In language that seemed to combine counterforce and flexible response concepts, he indicated that Washington intended to "shore up deterrence across the entire spectrum of risk," providing selective options for "measured responses" against a wide range of military targets. This facet of the approach clearly was concerned with intra-war deterrence. The old question, of course, arises: Is the increased capability required to accomplish this objective a stabilizing or destabilizing factor?

With these developments American strategic doctrine seemed to stabilize. When the Carter administration assumed office it quickly adopted the posture

[50]See Chapter 7, Diagrams 3 and 4 for an examination of the trends.

[51]See the secretary's testimony before the Senate Armed Services Committee. U. S. Congress, Senate, Committee on Armed Services, *Fiscal Year 1975 Authorization for Military Procurement, Research and Development, and Active Duty, Selected Reserve and Civilian Personnel Strengths*, Hearings, 93rd Congress, Second Session, February 5, 1974, pp. 1-163. With respect to the current status of American assured destruction capability the secretary testified that the United States could retaliate, even after an attack "more brilliantly executed and devastating" than he thought the Soviets could deliver, and destroy more than 30 percent of Soviet population and 75 percent of Russian industry (and still have something left for the Chinese).

of its predecessor. Policymakers stated that a rough strategic equivalence existed between Washington and Moscow and that American retaliatory forces could withstand a major Soviet attack in sufficient numbers to strike back with devastating power against the appropriate target system; to the extent that control, selectivity, and deliberation were useful, they too could be provided.[52] For better or worse, there seemed to be considerable agreement in the United States on both what America's strategic doctrine was, and on what it should be.

Perspectives

Strategic deterrent policy is designed to enhance the protection or achievement of one's fundamental objectives by the effective nonuse of military force. Party X's potential adversary is prevented from endangering X's capacity to survive, its sovereignty and political independence, territorial integrity, belief system, and essential political and economic systems, through the knowledge that if it attempts to do so X will retaliate with a military response of unacceptable proportions. To this point our analysis has focused on the elements of deterrent doctrine, practice, and theory that are traditionally discussed in this regard, examining what is usually conceived of as an essentially bilateral relationship and focusing on weapons system changes and relationships and various perceptions thereof.

While such an analysis is important and certainly is a necessary part of any productive study of deterrence, by itself it is incomplete. To stop the analysis here, or to flesh it out by simply adding further detail and depth to the discussion of the existing categories, still leaves the analysis too narrow to be operationally meaningful. Deterrent policy is an important part, but only a part, of the overall foreign policy of a given party, and it needs to be examined in that overall context if it is to be kept in perspective. A number of specific points are especially pertinent to remember in this regard.[53]

First, no situation is truly self-contained, and no relationship is completely bilateral. Situational policymakers often are greatly influenced in their situational actions by nonsituational actors and conditions. With respect to deterrence what this means, on one hand, is that whether or not a party is deterred (or decides to attack) may well be significantly influenced by factors external to the bilateral strategic relationship. For example, whether the Soviets are deterred from (or encouraged to) attack the United States may be as much a re-

[52]See the testimony of various officials before the House Defense Appropriations Subcommittee early in 1977. U. S. Congress, House of Representatives, Subcommittee of the Committee on Appropriations, *Department of Defense Appropriations for 1978*, Hearings, 95th Congress, First Session, 1977, Part 2.

[53]Several of the following points were significantly influenced by an unpublished manuscript of Frederick H. Hartmann's tentatively titled *The Game of Strategy*.

flection of Soviet-Chinese relations and interactions as it is of U. S.-Soviet nuclear capability factors. This point has a second implication: situational actions always affect nonsituational actors, and may in fact be designed with that in mind. The Soviets certainly do things re the United States, for example, the major objective of which is to influence policymakers in Peking.

Another point of importance here is that all parties are different. Assumptions of, and discussions concerning, the probable impact of particular weapons system and/or doctrinal changes sometimes occur in a kind of antiseptic vacuum that ignores the very considerable differences between international parties. The result often is a highly distorted picture. It *does* make a difference who is involved. Each party is unique, and the uniformity of behavior in response to certain stimuli that is posited in such discussions simply does not exist. No two parties face the same strategic situations, and no two view situations in the same manner. And as we have seen in our earlier discussions, policymakers have an enormous range of options from which to choose when responding to particular stimuli. The conclusion, therefore, is that the reactions to particular stimuli definitely are party specific and variable, and they can differ immensely with the party and the situation.

Third, parties act for many reasons, not just as a result of policymakers' perceptions of capability relationships. Narrowly conceived deterrence theory sometimes postulates that once party X has a certain force superiority and the other side's retaliatory forces are at least potentially vulnerable, war is much more likely. This may be so, but as a generalization it is far too broad. Did the United States attack the U. S. S. R. in the early 1950s? Obviously many other factors enter into such decisions. Certainly a party's overall strategic circumstances are important, as is the entire matter of whether policymakers believe that their objectives can be served by nuclear war. The degree of support or isolation from allied assistance also can be critical. Other factors such as the general state of bilateral relations, the bilateral and overall international tension level, the possible influence of (and impact on) third parties, other objectives and priorities, internal regime needs, ideological considerations, the sheer matter of willpower—on and on goes the list of factors that could be influential in determining whether or not a war will be launched in any particular case. Also to the point in this regard is that sometimes, at least historically, parties have undertaken major military efforts *knowing* they were not necessarily superior (Pearl Harbor). While capability relationships are important and significantly enter into deterrent and hostility-initiation calculations, they still are but one factor among many.

ARMS CONTROL

Finally, policymakers may seek to engage in arms control. Operating in the decentralized anarchy of the international political world where force is the ultimate arbiter of conflict and a party's only sure ally is itself, men and women in responsible policymaking positions have generally given short shrift to suggestions and plans for broad and general disarmament. They know that, in fact, with the world being what it actually is, all international parties will feel the need to maintain a certain level of military capability and all parties *will* utilize the military policy instrument in a number of ways. At the same time policymakers also are cognizant of the enormous dangers posed by nuclear weaponry, and some have felt that perhaps certain advantages could be obtained and/or costs reduced and/or baneful effects minimized if in certain situations arms could in some way be controlled or limited. But because of the ever-present decentralized anarchy and the importance of military strength in achieving and protecting fundamental and middle-range political objectives, policymakers quite naturally have gone very slowly and with great caution in voluntarily limiting their capability. Consequently, they have been able to negotiate agreements with their potential adversaries in only a small number of cases.[54] Yet because they have been able to do so at least on occasion arms control has sometimes been perceived to be a productive means of policy implementation in certain contingencies.

Because of the importance of military strength, agreements directly limiting or controlling the numbers, types, and attributes of major weapons systems, especially those of a strategic nature, have been the most difficult kind to achieve. They are, however, the most significant and we will discuss them in more depth later. Other, more narrowly focused, arms control agreements have proved somewhat easier to obtain, agreements concerning discrete issues perceived by policymakers to be somewhat less central to the protection or achievement of fundamental objectives.

Discrete, Less Central Agreements

Agreements have been concluded with respect to four major kinds of discrete, less central issues.[55] *One such issue has been concern over the possibility that a nuclear war might occur as the result of inadequate communication, accident, or unauthorized attack.* When the Cuban Missile Crisis erupted in 1962 American and Soviet policymakers encountered severe difficulties in communicating rapidly and accurately with each other. Because of this, what to that time had been a relatively abstract concern suddenly became concrete. As a result, in the aftermath of the crisis American policymakers proposed the establishment of direct communication links between Washington and Moscow. Negotiations

---

[54]Technically "arms control" could also be applied to a party's unilateral activities, but we will use it only in the more generally accepted sense of international agreements and understandings.

[55]Useful and succinct is Barton and Weiler, Chapters 6, 14.

commenced toward this end, and on June 20, 1963 the United States and the Soviet Union signed the so-called "Hot Line" agreement, the objective being to provide the basis for a direct communication system that would allow the rapid clarification of intentions and the prevention of accidental or unauthorized war. Telegraph-teleprinter equipment subsequently was established at terminals in Washington and Moscow, providing facilities for the direct transmission of encoded printed messages from one head of government to the other. Later, at the same time the Soviets and Americans were negotiating with respect to certain measures limiting strategic weapons (see more below) they also undertook to improve their direct communication system. As a result, on September 30, 1971 an agreement became operational whereby satellite communication circuits would be added to the full-time duplex wire telegraph circuit (and backup radio telegraph circuit) already in existence. Multiple-terminal satellite communications were subsequently established in January 1978, re-placing the original Hot Line circuits.

At the same time the agreement to improve the direct communication system was concluded another agreement, the "Agreement on Measures to Reduce the Risk of Outbreak of Nuclear War Between the United States of America and the Union of Soviet Socialist Republics," entered into force. In this pact the parties agreed to notify each other in case of an accidental or unauthorized missile launch or if unidentified objects were detected by missile warning systems. Each party also pledged to notify the other in advance of any planned launches beyond its own territory in the direction of that other, and to maintain and improve its organizational and technical arrangements to guard against the accidental or unauthorized use of weapons under its control.

Agreements of this nature are not foolproof, of course. And, obviously, they do not provide any protection against deliberate warfare, do not reduce or limit weaponry, and may even yield certain opportunities for deception. But, on balance, American and Soviet policymakers deemed them to be useful in that they helped enhance the odds of achieving the common objective of avoiding accidental or unauthorized war.

A second type of agreement has been one designed to declare certain geographical areas off limits with respect to nuclear weapons.[56] In these agreements policymakers have sought to take preventive action before problems developed in certain areas by banning in those zones certain types of military activity. In 1959 12 countries signed the Antarctic Treaty, and the agreement entered into force June 23, 1961.[57] The treaty opens the continent for scientific

---

[56]For more on off-limits zones see Chapter 6, pp. 136–138.

[57]The parties were Argentina, Australia, Belgium, Chile, France, Japan, New Zealand, Norway, South Africa, the Soviet Union, the United Kingdom, and the United States.

observation, stipulates that it is to be used exclusively for peaceful purposes, prohibits all measures of a military nature including the establishment of bases and fortifications, and prohibits any nuclear explosions or the using of the continent for the disposal of radioactive waste. In 1967 the Treaty on Principles Governing the Activities of States in the Exploration and Use of Outer Space, Including the Moon and Other Celestial Bodies was signed. This treaty provided that the parties thereto would not place in orbit around the earth any objects carrying nuclear weapons, install nuclear weapons on celestial bodies, or station nuclear weapons in outer space in any manner. Also, the establishment of military installations and bases and the conduct of military maneuvers on celestial bodies was forbidden. Then, in 1971 an agreement was reached prohibiting the emplacement of nuclear weapons and other weapons of mass destruction on the seabed and the ocean floor beyond the parties' 12-mile coastal "seabed zone."

The third kind of discrete, less central agreements have been those involving some limitation on the testing of nuclear weapons. In an effort to reduce radioactive fallout, take advantage of the nuclear-war consciousness prevalent in the aftermath of the Cuban Missile Crisis, and limit the proliferation of nuclear weapons, in 1963 the governments of the United States, the United Kingdom, and the Soviet Union signed the Treaty Banning Nuclear Weapons Tests in the Atmosphere, in Outer Space and Under Water. Over 100 nations have since signed and ratified this accord. Two of the nuclear nations, France and China have not, however, and have been free to continue their atmospheric testing programs.

Underground nuclear tests were not covered by the Limited Test Ban Treaty, however, and the LTB nuclear signatories altered their efforts accordingly. In 1974 this "gap" was at least partially filled when the Soviets and Americans signed the Threshold Test Ban Treaty (TTBT). Designed to become operational in 1976, this treaty prohibited underground nuclear tests above the "threshold" level of 150 kilotons.[58] Such "gap filling" would be more apparent than real, however, because by this juncture both parties had fully tested their large-yield warheads and were most interested in testing new lower-yield warheads to be utilized as MIRVs, warheads that could still be tested underground and not violate the terms of the TTBT.

The last of the discrete less than central agreements was the Non-Proliferation Treaty (NPT), which was signed in July 1968 and entered into force

---

[58]The TTBT was submitted to the U. S. Senate for ratification in 1976 but no action had been taken when Mr. Carter assumed the Presidency. The new president declared the treaty wholly inadequate and pursued negotiations for a comprehensive test ban. Though the TTBT thus never entered into force, the Soviets and Americans in practice have generally complied with its basic obligations.

March 5, 1970. The specter of a world filled with states with nuclear military strength has long been a concern to many, policymakers and observers alike. In the decentralized anarchy of international politics such a situation would seem to be courting disaster. In line with this kind of thinking the Soviets and Americans in 1966 and 1967 hammered out the provisions for a nonproliferation agreement. The heart of the treaty, in the eyes of these parties, lay in Articles I and II. According to these provisions each nuclear weapon party agrees not to transfer nuclear weapons or devices, or control over such, to any non-nuclear party, nor to in any way assist or encourage a nonnuclear weapon party to manufacture or acquire such weapons. Conversely, nonnuclear weapon parties agree not to manufacture, control, or acquire nuclear weapons or devices. Another major treaty provision, one of great significance to the nonnuclear weapon parties, is that the nuclear states pledge to facilitate the fullest possible exchange of equipment, materials, and information for the peaceful uses of nuclear energy. In an energy-hungry world this is an obligation of no little importance.

As we noted briefly earlier, today there are five major operationally nuclear capable states: the United States, the Soviet Union, Britain, France, and China. In 1974 India exploded a nuclear device, and at least 20 other parties today have the capability to fabricate a device in no more than a few weeks or months (or may already have clandestinely done so). The situation is more precarious than this might indicate though, for two reasons. First, neither France nor China are parties to the NPT. Second, and perhaps even more importantly, all nuclear reactors, including those designed exclusively for peaceful uses, produce plutonium as a by-product and plutonium can be used instead of uranium to fabricate nuclear weapons. Therefore, although potential weapons manufacturers may not be able to obtain or produce enough enriched weapons-grade uranium to manufacture nuclear explosives, if a party has a chemical reprocessing plant its plutonium can be separated from other elements in the spent nuclear fuel produced by the reactor and be used for the manufacture of weapons. Although such a procedure is not simple, requires certain kinds of complex facilities and skills, and is expensive, and although nonnuclear parties to the NPT have pledged not to develop nuclear weapons, the facts that several of the near-nuclear nations are not NPT parties and that more than 40 countries have some kind of peaceful nuclear energy program leads one to conclude that even today the problem of nuclear proliferation is one of considerable magnitude.

Limiting Strategic Weapons

To date in the post-World War II era only one major set of agreements limiting strategic weapons has entered into force, the United States-Soviet Union

SALT I agreements of 1972.[59] As mentioned earlier, when operating in the decentralized anarchy of the international political environment parties are loath to voluntarily agree to limit their military capability in the slightest. Consequently, agreements of that nature have been few and far between. Nevertheless, some have been concluded. Why? What are the policymakers' objectives in such agreements, what are they trying to accomplish?

SALT I. Before answering this question, let's examine the key provisions of the agreements signed to date. SALT I negotiations began in 1969, and in May 1972 they produced an ABM Treaty and the Interim Agreement on Certain Measures with Respect to the Limitation of Strategic Offensive Arms. Under the ABM Treaty each side was limited to two antiballistic missile sites, one around its national capital and one around an ICBM complex.[60] The treaty further limited the parties to no more than 100 ABMs at each site. Since that time the issue of ABMs has been dormant and real arms "control" has been achieved.

The Interim Agreement on Strategic Offensive Arms signed at the same time froze the number of ICBM and SLBM launchers at the level of those operational as of July 1, 1972 or those under construction at that time, freezing them for a period of five years. The United States did not have additional missiles under construction at this juncture so the agreement "froze" the American forces at the already existing levels of 1054 ICBMs and 656 SLBMs. The Soviets *were* involved in a major construction program, however, so the establishment of upper limits was significant.[61] The levels agreed on for the Russians were 1618 ICBMs and 740 SLBMs. Each party had the right to expand the number of SLBMs, the United States to 710 and the Russians to 950, but they could do so only if they dismantled an equal number of older ICBMs or launchers of SLBMs on older submarines.

Four points of considerable import should be noted in regard to the interim agreement:

1. A number of strategic systems capable of striking the other parties' homeland with nuclear weapons, such as strategic bombers, were not covered.
2. Only quantitative limits on missile launchers were established. No qualitative features, such as accuracy or the number of RVs per missile, were in any way limited.

---

[59]"SALT" stands for Strategic Arms Limitation Talks. In June 1979 the SALT II agreements were signed, but as of this writing SALT II had not yet been acted on by the United States Senate.

[60]In July 1974 the parties signed a protocol reducing the number of sites to one for each party.

[61]See Chapter 7, Diagrams 3 and 4.

3. Although it was not apparent on its face, the agreement was designed to support strategic parity, what has been called essential equivalence. Although the Soviets were permitted a numerical advantage in launchers, this was the only area in which they were ahead at the time, and it was this area alone that was controlled. The United States was well ahead in strategic bombers, missile accuracy and reliability, and MIRVs, and its lead in these spheres compensated for the disparity in numbers (and these areas were not controlled).

4. Most of the parties' major ongoing strategic programs were *not* covered.

Objectives. As one examines the terms of the agreements achieved to date (and the provisions of the pending SALT II agreements as well) certain facts are readily apparent. In all cases the parties were very careful not to do anything they believed would harm their deterrent capability. Each side clearly operated on the assumption that mutual deterrence was essential and an ongoing part of the international scene, and the agreements allowed for the continuation of a number of existing and planned strategic programs. In consequence, little attention was paid to what many nonpolicymakers see as major goals of arms negotiations, a halt to the arms race and/or large-scale reductions (disarmament). Other factors frequently cited by nonpolicymakers as reasons for arms control, such as economic costs, seem to have been similarly uninfluential.

What then, have been the objectives policymakers have sought in these agreements? There seem to have been a cluster of goals, all of which can in one way or another be subsumed under the rubric of *enhancing strategic stability*. Breaking this concept down into its subcomponents, the agreements limiting strategic weapons appear to have been designed to do the following:

1. Help stabilize the strategic balance and mutual deterrence, building on the principles of parity and the essential equivalence of existing and future forces.

2. By stabilizing the strategic deterrent balance, striving to minimize tensions between the parties, at least to the extent that those tensions are caused by alterations and/or perceived threatening imbalances in strategic weapons systems.

3. By building on the principles of parity and essential equivalence, eliminate whatever destabilizing first strike or preemptive strike tendencies there might be as a result of perceived strategic imbalances.

4. By stabilizing the strategic balance and mutual deterrence, adding a degree of predictability and reliability to each state's security prob-

lem, thus optimizing the potential for rationality in policymaking procedures.

5. For all of the foregoing reasons, creating a situation in which the parties perceive similar risks to the achievement and protection of their fundamental objectives.

6. Finally, creating an atmosphere and symbol of greater confidence which, in combination with the more stable deterrent-strategic balance situation, allows for the development of significantly broader and deeper levels of bilateral cooperation in a number of other areas of mutual interest.

Conditions Essential for Agreement. Before concluding this analysis, a couple more comments need to be made. First, as we have said time and again but cannot say too often, policymakers act for many reasons, objectives spring from many sources, many issues are dealt with simultaneously, extrasituational concerns and influences are very important, etc. What we have described above are the objectives that are primarily related to certain types of arms control agreements. As always, a full-fledged analysis would have to be broadened to take all these other kinds of considerations into account.

Second, it is important to ask: What conditions are essential in order for meaningful weapons limiting arms control agreements to be achieved?[62] While no one can answer this query with certainty, the following list includes elements that appear to be necessary even if they are not always sufficient.

1. There must be at least a rough equivalence in strategic capability, and the parties must know it.

2. The agreement's provisions must not be harmful to any party's deterrent capability.

3. There must be policymakers who are committed to arms control as a means of decreasing bilateral tension and enhancing mutual cooperation.

4. The potential costs and the risks to fundamental objectives must be perceived as approximately equal.

5. The parties must truly desire a stable bilateral strategic relationship.

6. The parties' extrasituational objectives and concerns must not be harmed.[63]

---

[62]We are concerned here with specific conditions that are directly pertinent to weapons limiting arms control agreements. All agreements, at least to the extent they are designed to "solve" problems, must meet the four conditions spelled out in Chapter 12, p. 332.

[63]At times extrasituational influences may even be helpful. For example, certainly the Soviets became more amenable to U. S. efforts after the beginning of Washington's withdrawal from Vietnam and the Nixon initiatives toward China.

There is one other condition that must obtain, one that needs separate treatment: *the agreement must be verifiable*. Each party to an arms control agreement must have the capability to monitor every other party's activities to the extent and in such a manner as to be able to verify that these other parties are complying with the terms of the agreement. In other words, one must be able to determine whether or not the other signatories are cheating. If policymakers do not believe their party has this capability they simply will not conclude an agreement. Pacts with one's adversaries, dealing with such critical subject matter, are not entered into solely on the basis of trust.[64]

Massive on-site inspection would be valuable in verification, but for obvious reasons such has never been agreed to. The SALT I agreements, and several others as well, are monitored by "national technical means" of verification, that is, various technical intelligence gathering and ordering techniques that operate outside the territory of the observed state. National technical means include high-resolution photography from reconnaissance satellites, line-of-sight, over-the-horizon, terminal and shipboard radars, various ground-, air-, and sea-based electronic devices, and a variety of other sensors. Because of their concern on this point the parties also have included provisions in their agreements by the terms of which deliberate concealment measures that impede verification are prohibited, as is deliberate interference with verification activities.

Arms control, like all the other uses, and "nonuses" of the military instrument of policy, is utilized only when and to the extent policymakers deem it appropriate to the achievement or protection of certain objectives. Arms control, in other words, is only one among a wide range of implementation techniques. Even with respect to the achievement of stability it is but one of many alternatives a policymaker may choose. To be properly evaluated, therefore, arms control must be placed in the perspective of the overall policy patterns of the parties, weighed against the parties' objectives, compared to the cost-benefit ratios of other alternatives, etc.

In Chapters 9 and 10 we have discussed the economic and military policy instruments, the tangible means of policy implementation. Policymakers also have certain intangible instruments they can use. One of these is communication, and it is to this we now turn.

---

[64]Of course there can be disagreements about whether one actually has this capability. One of the major disagreements between supporters and opponents of the SALT II treaty in the U. S. Senate concerned precisely this point.

11
Intangible Implementation Instrument: Communication

Policymakers sometimes employ intangible instruments of policy implementation. One of the most important of these intangible instruments is communication. Almost all political activity involves communication of some sort.[1] Some communications are aimed at the policymakers of other parties. These, called "signals," will be studied later. Others are directed toward the populace of various countries and are termed "propaganda."

PROPAGANDA

The twentieth century communication revolution has had a significant impact on the conduct of international relations. Because of the information explosion and rapid technological progress it is feasible for policymakers to seek to influence the attitudes and behavior of foreign populations. The term given to these activities is propaganda, the deliberate attempt to alter the attitudes and behavior of foreign groups with the hope that the reaction of these targets will be that desired by the propagandist.[2]

Policymakers of nearly all states seek to influence the attitudes and behavior of parts or all of certain foreign populations. Leaders of LDCs frequently try to make a case for greater economic aid from industrialized states by appealing to portions of the public in those countries. For years a component of

---

[1] Richard N. Fagen, *Politics and Communication*, Little, Brown, Boston, 1966, p. 17.
[2] Terrence H. Qualter, *Propaganda and Psychological Warfare*, Random House, New York, 1962, p. 27.

Soviet policy was the repeated attempt to persuade the publics of a number of West European states that the territorial status quo in Europe was to their benefit. Moscow also worked to persuade policy influencers in LDCs that the Soviet Union, not the United States, provided the best model for LDC economic growth. In early 1979, following the establishment of diplomatic relations between the United States and the People's Republic of China, the PRC's vice-premier diligently sought to convince the American public that Peking's intentions toward Taiwan were peaceful. At the height of the Cold War both the United States and the Soviet Union sought to influence the attitude and behavior of people in uncommitted countries in such a fashion that those populations would pressure their leaders to join the "right" bloc. The Nazi propaganda ministry under Joseph Goebbels was very effective in employing propaganda techniques in the 1930s. Officials from Israel and the Arab states have worked strenuously to obtain the support of the American public for their respective parties' policies. With special emphasis on the United Nations, leaders of black African nations have quite successfully influenced the publics of some states against South Africa. Nonstate actors, too, frequently have extensive propaganda programs. For example, MNCs make major efforts to induce (actual and potential) host country publics to view the MNC's activities in a fashion that will allow the firm to optimize its economic position, and NLOs like the Palestine Liberation Organization employ a variety of propaganda techniques attempting to drum up support for the cause of "liberation."

Although deliberate efforts to influence the attitudes and behaviors of all or parts of the populace of foreign states are widespread, most policymakers deny that they engage in "propaganda." In some instances this is a deliberate deception, and sometimes it is (in part at least) a logical reflection of a different view of what constitutes reality. Frequently, however, it is the product of what is a rather commonly held, overly narrow view of what is or is not propaganda. To many people "propaganda" is simply another word for the lies of one's enemies. In the 1950s, to Communists many of the statements of Western capitalist leaders were "propaganda," and vice-versa. That is, they were lies told by a bitter adversary dedicated to one's destruction. Israeli and Palestinian Arab statements concerning who has "peaceful" and who has "aggressive" intentions demonstrate the same point. But such a conception of propaganda is both inaccurate and oversimplified. It is inaccurate because it posits that propaganda consists exclusively of deliberate lies, and that is not so. In the same vein, it is oversimplified; propaganda includes various mixtures, degrees, and types of both truth and falsity.[3]

---

[3]We are speaking in terms of conscious actions by the policymaker. Different people have different perceptions of "the truth," information may be inaccurate, and many other factors can prevent a "truthful" presentation. Such problems are not our concern here, although they are very important. Our analysis is concerned with the degree of *deliberate* truthfulness.

In the above discussion of the widespread use of propaganda we provided examples of a number of the objectives that policymakers employing propaganda have sought. A point of some moment is that the middle range objectives one is hoping to achieve or protect (via accomplishing the immediate objective of influencing foreign populations) are as varied as the objectives of all policy. Sometimes the goals are general, such as seeking to create a general climate of receptivity to a particular party's policy by projecting an image of trustworthiness or reliability. The British Broadcasting Corporation (BBC) has long had a history of accuracy in its presentations, thus establishing a base of credibility. Often, as indicated in the earlier examples, the goals are more specific. Employed as a means of implementing the orientation of indirect opposition, for example, propaganda may be designed to decrease societal cohesiveness by exploiting and increasing ethnic and racial hatreds. Many times parties use propaganda in an attempt to increase relative capability via the manipulation of their adversary's internal capability components. In this scenario decreasing popular support may be the middle-range goal. Perhaps one can capitalize on an already smoldering discontent and help fan it into a flaming rebellion; maybe it is possible to convince key nongovernmental policy influencers that their government is inept, thus creating a situation conducive to covert actions or even a coup; perhaps transnational attractions can be portrayed in a manner such that the masses' loyalty will be diverted from their current regime. The list could go on, but to no particular advantage. The number of possible middle-range objectives for propaganda is legion.

Techniques and Tools

It is obvious that a policymaker utilizing propaganda rarely is attempting to present an unbiased argument based on clearly established wholly unambiguous facts. This is important. It is absolutely essential to remember that the policymaker is hoping *to persuade, to favorably influence* the perceptions, images, attitudes, and behaviors of all or parts of the population of certain target parties. He or she is not presenting an objective, balanced, carefully reasoned analysis, and independent thinking is not desired.

In employing propaganda the policymaker can use a (combination of a) wide range of techniques. For analytical purposes, however, they can be usefully divided into two categories. *First, the policymaker can utilize the selective inclusion and arrangement of information.* Most times a propagandist does not include all the relevant information in the presentation. Instead, facts (and "evidence") are carefully selected; those (and that) which make the desired point are included, the remainder omitted. In a similar vein, often the included information is not arranged in the most logical, enlightening fashion. Instead, and regardless of these considerations, the material is carefully arranged in such a way as to create the maximum favorable impact on the target. Frequently, therefore, the entire picture is not presented, nor is everything put in perspective. Exaggeration, misrepresentation, and bias abound. This is not to say that logic is totally distorted or that no truthful information is presented. That would be inaccurate. Indeed, history indicates that in most instances the message will fail without at least a degree of evidence and organization, and without some basis in fact. But that's just the point: it is a "degree" of evidence and organization and "some" basis in fact. These are provided *only selectively* and only in a fashion such that a maximum impact is created.

A second major category of propaganda techniques is the "emotion-producing overs:" emotion-producing overgeneralization, and emotion-producing oversimplification. Propagandists constantly overgeneralize to the end of eliciting the maximum favorable emotional response; they don't want the target to dispassionately analyze the evidence and the complexities. It may be said, for example, that *"all* peace-loving people *know"* that such and such a government is "imperialistic," or that *all* Communists are *"aggressive,"* or that *all* capitalists *are* "monopolistic warmongers." Maybe "the people" do not have power in a particular state (are the individuals running the government "nonpeople?") Frequently, propagandists also drastically simplify what in reality are complex issues. The Nazis claimed "the Jews" were responsible for Germany's problems. Policymakers of LDCs may charge that neocolonialists are behind their state's economic difficulties (before independence it was "the colonialists"). Perhaps policymakers of a black African state will allege that progress in Africa is prevented solely by the "racists," while some of their opponents say it is "the Communists" who are the root of the problem. In instances such as these policymakers hope to produce the maximum favorable emotional response. To achieve this objective they ignore much evidence and a large part of the real world's complexity, and both overgeneralize and oversimplify. They hope their targets will do the same.

There are a number of tools available to convey their party's message. *Radio broadcasts* are one. In the 1970s, for example, the Soviet Union broadcast nearly 2000 hours per week in 88 foreign languages.[4] Washington's Voice of America broadcast more than 800 hours weekly in more than 30 different languages, and Radio Cairo has long been an important "information" source in the Middle East. All the major states (and, because it is relatively inexpensive, many of the LDCs) have extensive radio broadcasting programs. Propaganda also can be conveyed via *printed materials.* These include foreign language books, newspapers, scientific journals, literary classics, pamphlets, government documents and news releases, and so on. Related to the general use of printed materials is the effort to use such materials (and other tools) to *influence the target country's mass media.* Information in the form of "appro-

---

[4]Holsti, Third Edition, p. 239

priate" feature items, news releases, inside stories, leaks, exclusive interviews, photographs, or whatever, is provided free or at low cost to the target. Today, *films and photographs* also can be provided. The United States International Communications Agency, for example, supplies films to domestic television stations in many foreign states.

In recent years propagandists have made extensive use of another kind of propaganda tool, (various types of) *face-to-face relations*.[5] The U. S. State Department's Bureau of Educational and Cultural Affairs has played a major role in facilitating international cultural exchange programs between Washington and a large number of states. The Soviet Union repeatedly sends scientific, athletic, technical, expert, and artistic groups abroad, and invites equivalent foreign groups to visit the U. S. S. R. Many countries seek to induce foreigners to study in their country in hopes of influencing their perceptions and attitudes. States work hard to impress their counterparts at international gatherings, the degree of nationalistic competition at the Olympics being an excellent case in point. On occasion, major international exhibitions of particular types occur and states sponsor exhibits designed to project the optimum image. Because they (seemingly) are "nonpolitical" in character and are (purportedly) designed to enhance "understanding," and because most countries now engage in such activities and the participating groups want the trend to continue, it is likely that face-to-face relations will increase in the 1980s. It is essential though that one remember that such activities are engaged in, at least in part, for propaganda purposes. To lose sight of this would be a serious error.

Targeting

In developing a propaganda program one of the policymaker's first tasks is to determine precisely *who should be the target* of his or her communication. It is usually not feasible to consider an entire population as one's target.[6] Seldom are the masses as a whole susceptible to foreign influence (and most people usually are not very interested in international affairs anyway). But in all political systems there are certain "policy influencers" that have at least some impact on policymaking, that make demands on the leadership and expect a certain amount of satisfaction as the price for their support.[7] These same influencers become the target of a wide range of requests, promises, threats, and demands from policymakers. The propagandist must determine who the key

---

[5]The student should remember the definition of "propaganda" when evaluating this statement.

[6]The failure to recognize this fact was a distinct defect in American propaganda in the early years of the Cold War.

[7]For a more detailed discussion of policy influencers see Chapter 15.

policy influencers are in the particular target system and what their relationships are with the leadership, investigate their characteristics so as to discover the degree to which the various ones are or are not susceptible to propaganda, and focus his or her efforts accordingly.[8]

A second task is to *ascertain the types and depth of the images, perceptions, and attitudes held by the target(s)*. This is essential because some kinds of images and attitudes are quite susceptible to external manipulation but others are not. Experience is useful in this regard and allows the deduction of *some rules of thumb. First, propaganda that is supportive of the target's existing images and perceptions and reinforces existing attitudes tends to be more effective than that which urges change.*[9] Deeply ingrained attitudes and beliefs are resistant to external efforts to alter them. People who strongly believe in the American liberal ideology are unlikely to be persuaded by Soviet propagandists to reject that ideology in favor of communism, for example. A very important corollary of this proposition is that propaganda that reinforces (or activates latent) favorable perceptions and attitudes is more effective than that which seeks to alter deep hostility. In 1978 Egyptian President Sadat found that his efforts to moderate the hostility of West Bank Palestinians toward Israel were much less effective than were the statements of PLO and Syrian policymakers reinforcing that hostility. In contrast, Sadat's campaign to convince certain key American policy influencers of the sincerity of his desire for peace, policy influencers already somewhat favorably disposed because of the Egyptian leader's words and actions since the 1973 war (especially his 1977 trip to Jerusalem), was quite successful. People frequently tend to have a number of preconceptions about important matters and to possess relatively closed images. Often this leads to resistance to change, the selective incorporation and rejection of information on the basis of those preconceptions and images, and an interpretation of words and actions that reinforces existing favorable and unfavorable attitudes.

As a result of the facts discussed above, we can deduce *a second rule of thumb: propaganda is most effective with respect to one's allies, somewhat less with the populace of parties that are nonaligned, and least with respect to the public(s) of one's adversaries*. The historical record makes it quite clear that, as a generalization, this rule has considerable validity. But policymakers know that there are certain contingencies to which the generalization does not apply, situations in which even target policy influencers of adversarial (and/or nonaligned) parties may be effectively propagandized. First, it may be that at-

---

[8]For a useful discussion of this problem see W. Phillips Davison, *International Political Communication*, Praeger, New York, 1965.

[9]This statement, as the other "rules of thumb," assumes no change in other attitude-influencing factors.

titudes re a particular matter are weakly held, or that perceptions and images are vague and ill defined. In such instances there may be some susceptibility to external persuasion. Second, it may be that the object of the attitude is new, and perceptions, attitudes, and positions have not yet been formed and/or solidified. Third, in some situations there are a number of attitudes and views, and they may tend to counterbalance each other. When this condition obtains, the propagandist may be in a position to skillfully tip the balance.

Necessary Characteristics

When utilizing propaganda the policymaker recognizes that people form opinions, make judgments, and undertake actions on the basis of their mental images, perceptions, and attitudes, regardless of whether such square with objective reality. Earlier we discussed some of the general techniques that are used to affect those perceptions, images, and attitudes. Within the context of the general techniques, are there certain specific characteristics that communications must have if the propagandist is to have a reasonable chance of success? Are there certain particular attributes that are necessary if propaganda messages are to have at least a moderate chance of influencing the target policy influencer(s)? The answer, apparently, is yes. Although one can never guarantee success, it seems that the following characteristics are necessary, and without them ineffectiveness is probable.[10]

1. *The message must be short and simple.* Most elements of the general public, and of key policy influencers, are not interested in, nor do they comprehend, detailed sophisticated explanations or proposals. Indeed, as a rule they will be "turned off" by such messages. To be effective, propaganda must be direct, concise, and elementary.

2. *The communication must play on the target's emotions.* Calm, rational appeals seldom have much impact. In most cases simple slogans such as "ban the bomb" and "power to the people," or the use of emotion-laden terms such as "imperialist warmonger" or "racist," tend to affect images and attitudes much more than carefully reasoned arguments.

3. *The communication must be of some direct interest to the recipient.* If it does not deal with a problem that is of immediate personal concern then (usually) at best it will be ignored, and it may even be considered to be an attempt at deception or subversion (i.e., as "propaganda"). Because of this, communications related to improving a person's living standards or eliminat-

---

[10]Another way of putting this is that the specific attributes are necessary though not always sufficient. Useful here is Norman J. Padelford and George A. Lincoln, *The Dynamics of International Relations*, Third Edition, Macmillan, New York, 1976, pp. 354–356.

ing local injustices usually are more effectual than those dealing with great issues of war and peace (unless, of course, the recipients' own lives are involved in a war and peace situation).

4. *The message must be credible, believable.* If what is said is ludicrous, or at least it appears so to the target, once again the best one could hope is that the reaction will be neutral, and many times such propaganda is counterproductive. In early 1957 purported American concern for a supposed threat of overt armed aggression in the Middle East by states controlled by international communism was considered by many Arabs to be an obvious "red herring." There was no history of Communist aggression in the area. Furthermore, Egypt had just been attacked by Britain, France, and Israel and defended (diplomatically) by the Soviets.[11] Washington's professed anxieties just could not be believed.

5. *To be credible, the message must be visible.* There must be something tangible that makes this message "real" in the eyes of the target. After the Soviets launched Sputnik in 1957 their professions of technological capability seemed more real than they ever had before. U. S. claims that it desired to live in peace with the People's Republic of China carried greater weight after the establishment of diplomatic relations with Peking in January 1979 (and the breaking off of such relations with Taiwan) than they had before that occurred.

6. *The message must sympathetically identify with the local experiences of the targets.* American attempts to promote a capitalist economic system in many of the less developed countries, where a history of private exploitation by large landowners often exists, hardly identifies with local experience in a favorable way.

Having analyzed the particular situation, selected the target(s), determined which attitudes, perceptions, and images may be susceptible, chosen the most appropriate tool(s) and technique(s), and put together a message with the necessary characteristics, the policymaker is ready to employ the propaganda instrument. *There is another principle one needs to remember, however. Unless the message is repeated* and *repeated* and *repeated, it likely will prove ineffectual.* As any good advertiser knows, people are not much affected by a message they have seen or heard only once. The policymaker thus must utilize the principle of repetition almost endlessly.

Effectiveness

Even if the policymaker does all the right things there is no guarantee that propaganda will be effective. Indeed, it is almost impossible to know when success has been achieved. Even in small controlled groups it is difficult to

---

[11] See a discussion of the Suez crisis in Chapter 13, pp. 364–367.

measure the impact of messages on images, perceptions, attitudes, and behaviors, to discover if, when, why, to what extent, and in what manner changes have been induced. For obvious reasons, the problem is enormously compounded and magnified in the international political sphere. But even though definitive evidence of effectiveness seldom can be obtained, most policymakers feel it advisable to continue to use propaganda, for two reasons: (1) in *some* situations, on *some* occasions, in *some* degree, it probably has a constructive impact, and (2) *everyone else* is utilizing it and "we" just can't allow others to proclaim the message of "their" party with no one to proclaim the message of "ours."

Before closing, a final comment is in order. It has been perceptively stated that "we might liken the process of propaganda . . . to that of 'retouching' a photograph: Within limits, individuals engaged in both activities can do much to improve the image with which they are concerned, but the results are also fundamentally determined by the nature of the original picture."[12] In other words, a favorable image can be maintained only if policy actions have a favorable impact.

Mass communication can alter the degree and intensity of reaction, and might be very influential for a short time, but eventually the acts of the state will be more important than the pictures of those acts portrayed by the propagandist. Observer and policymaker alike must remember this point. All state actions influence attitudes to some extent and they all have propaganda connotations. As Lerche and Said pointed out, "effective propaganda may increase the policy impact of diplomatic, economic, or even military moves, but it can rarely accomplish a specific end by itself."[13]

SIGNALING

A second kind of international communication is signaling, the transmission of messages and cues from the policymakers of one country to their counterparts in another. In any communication relationship there are at least four parts: the message, the sender, the recipient, and the medium. As we have emphasized repeatedly, in analyzing international politics it is necessary to be situation-specific. The fact that all parties and policymakers are unique, that they have different objectives, ideologies, histories, orientations, capabilities, governmental systems, etc. cannot be overstressed. All the relevant particular factors must be studied and placed in their proper perspective with respect to the question at hand. What does this have to do with signaling? A great deal. It means that, regardless of the structure and content of the communications be-

---

[12]Cecil V. Crabb, Jr., *American Foreign Policy in the Nuclear Age*, Third Edition, Harper, New York, 1972, p. 400.
[13]Lerche and Said, Second Edition, p. 89.

tween policymakers, there are bound to be differences in perception and understanding because of the differences in situations and in the characteristics of the particular sender and receiver. The following discussion does not directly deal with these matters because they are covered in depth elsewhere in the book, but it is essential for the student to remember that in any real-life analysis of signaling such an examination is imperative.

As was mentioned at the beginning of this chapter, almost all political activity involves communication in some way. Sometimes, of course, what occurs is strictly communicative in nature such as when a policymaker of country X sends a private letter to a policymaker of country Y. Frequently, however, activities other than those obviously communicative in nature are undertaken, but they too "communicate" and are considered "signals." When are the policymaker's "noncommunication" activities "signals?" To some extent the answer is "always," but that is of little help. Although any classification is somewhat artificial (and in practice not always easy to make), as a rule one classifies an activity as "signaling" *when the importance of the activity lies primarily in the implications of its message and not in the activity per se; it is "signaling" when the activity is just the vehicle or medium for conveying that which is more important, certain meanings or cues.*

Signaling occurs with much more frequency in international politics than nonpolicymakers realize (and often with much more subtlety). Our discussion of this widespread phenomenon is divided into two sections: signaling via actions and signaling via language.

Signaling Via Actions

Many times policymakers signal their counterparts via actions. The American precautionary military alert to the perceived threat of unilateral Soviet intervention in the 1973 Middle East war, for example, clearly signalled Washington's determination not to allow any Soviet intervention to go unchallenged. Israeli raids on suspected guerilla bases in southern Lebanon in mid-November 1974 immediately prior to the appearance of the Palestinian guerrilla leader, Yasir Arafat, at the United Nations signalled Tel Aviv's determination not to allow its future to be determined by U. N. resolutions. The maneuvers of the American Sixth Fleet in the Eastern Mediterranean at the time of the 1970 Jordanian Civil War signified Washington's unwillingness to allow the situation in Jordan to deteriorate too far.[14]

Subtle Signaling. Much of the time, however, signaling occurs more subtlely. If negotiations should be sought in a particular case the diplomatic rank of the

---

[14]This was particularly important because of the 1958 landing of Marines in Lebanon discussed in Chapter 14.

negotiators and the location desired may be signals of the importance the parties attach to the talks. In authoritarian political systems the physical proximity of individuals to the chief policymaker on formal public occasions often is a reflection of the various individuals' relative influence. Unusual though unspectacular occurrences can be signals also. In early February 1974, following President Nixon's and Secretary Kissinger's talks with Soviet Foreign Minister Andrei Gromyko, Washington and Moscow issued a positively worded joint communique. A communique following the visit of a Soviet foreign minister is highly unusual, and its issuance in this instance was a clear indication of the importance the parties attached to maintaining a positive bilateral relationship, of their commitment to détente.

One of the more interesting instances of signaling occurred in August 1977. Following President Nixon's visit to Peking in 1972 and the 1973 Shanghai communique, the People's Republic of China had expected the United States to quickly take concrete steps toward the normalization of relations. Among other things, this required, in Peking's eyes, America's suspension of relations and abrogation of its defense treaty with Taiwan, and a total U. S. military withdrawal from that island. PRC leaders felt little progress had been made in these matters in the succeeding years, and with the administration with which it had begun the normalization process having been replaced by President Carter and his aides, Peking was unsure what to expect. Thus, when Secretary of State Cyrus Vance arrived in China for four days of talks, the Chinese subtly signaled that they were not pleased with the lack of progress toward normalization, they were noncommittal toward the new administration, and Mr. Vance had not yet earned sufficient respect (as Dr. Kissinger had done) to be treated with great dignity.[15] They did this in a number of unobtrusive yet unmistakable ways. Mr. Vance was met at the airport by a Chinese official who was not a member of the Politburo (a distinct change from the procedure that had been followed with Dr. Kissinger). Also, the evening's formal dinner was held in a room smaller than the one that had been used for Kissinger, there was no orchestra (like the one that had serenaded President Nixon with "Home on the Range"), and the guests at the head table were not senior political officials. Finally, only a few hours before Vance's arrival the Chinese press agency, Hsinhua, publicly restated the PRC's conditions for normalization. Through this combination of actions, the PRC signaled its attitudes very clearly.

Sometimes signals may be unintentional, and occasionally the absence of expected activities also "communicates." During the 1968 Czechoslovakian crisis there was no official statement, either on behalf of the Soviet Govern-

---

[15]The following is based on a *New York Times* special by Fox Butterfield, August 23, 1977, pp. 1, 6.

ment or the CPSU, about the invasion. Also there was a lack of the usual signatures of the Soviet leadership (Brezhnev, Kosygin, and Podgorny) on all official documents in the days immediately following the assault. These facts were an unintentional but clear signal that there was great confusion and disagreement within the Politburo.[16]

Of course, the absence of expected or usual activities sometimes is carefully planned, a consciously chosen signal from one party to another. The government of India signaled the United States in exactly this manner in early 1977. For several years leading Indian policymakers had vociferously condemned the existence of the American naval base on the island of Diego Garcia and the presence of U. S. nuclear vessels in the Indian Ocean. In January and February a U. S. nuclear task force with the aircraft carrier *Enterprise* and the guided-missile cruisers *Long Beach* and *Truxtun* was on routine maneuvers in these waters. The *Enterprise* in particular could have caused controversy, having been a part of the American task force that had been ordered into the Bay of Bengal in America's pro-Pakistan "tilt" in the 1971 war over Bangladesh. But instead of condemning the American naval presence, Indian policymakers kept a very low profile, making as few comments as possible. By refusing to respond in the usual fashion, New Delhi was conveying to the new Carter administration its desire to decrease the proportion of conflict in India's relations with Washington.

Shrewd Timing. Many times policymakers seek to add emphasis to their signals by a shrewd use of *timing*. In other words, not only can *what* is done be important in signaling, but *when*. In Chapter One we described in some detail President Carter's human rights campaign and the intensity of the Soviet reaction thereto. It was no accident in that connection that Moscow commenced the mid-July 1978 trials of Anatoly Shcharansky (for treason) and Aleksandr Ginsberg (for subversion) just two days before Secretary of State Vance was to begin Geneva talks with Soviet Foreign Minister Gromyko on a SALT II treaty.[17] The Kremlin chose to act at this particular time in order to emphasize its view that what went on inside Russia was none of Washington's business; if the United States wanted to make progress on limiting strategic weapons (which Moscow knew it did) it would have to stop violating the U. S. S. R.'s right of internal control.

The Israelis have often made use of timing in their signaling. One of the points of contention between Israel and the United States in the 1970s was the

---

[16]Windsor, p. 67. See Chapter 10, pp. 271, 273 for further comments on the crisis.

[17]Any more than it was coincidental that, knowing the United States planned to emphasize the human rights issue at the October 1977 Belgrade meetings re the implementation of the Helsinki Agreements, the Supreme Soviet of the U. S. S. R. adopted the country's new constitution (a document filled with numerous provisions relating to human rights) just as the Belgrade meetings were getting underway.

legitimacy of Israeli settlements in the territories taken from the Arabs in the 1967 war. Washington never agreed with the Israeli practice, and by 1976 American policymakers were labeling the settlements "illegal" and an "obstacle" to peace. Although not all Israelis viewed the issue identically and there were certain differences with respect to different settlements in the different territories, the settlements on the occupied West Bank were seen by nearly all Israelis as legitimate and permanent. Furthermore, they believed more could be built in what, after all, was (in Israel's view) the Promised Land.

With this as background, let's examine the issue of timing with examples from both 1977 and 1978. In July 1977 Israel's new Prime Minister, Menachem Begin, flew to Washington for his first meeting with President Carter. Prior to Mr. Begin's arrival the President had undertaken a number of steps to alleviate what seemed to be growing American-Israeli tension, and the meetings between the two leaders appeared to go quite well. *Just one day after the talks ended* Mr. Begin announced he was legalizing three previously unauthorized settlements on the West Bank. Coming right on the heels of this first meeting with Mr. Carter, Mr. Begin's action made the point very clear: no matter what the status of American-Israeli relations, whether Washington liked it or not Israel would continue to settle the West Bank as she saw fit. Jerusalem never departed from this position, and throughout the remainder of the year and most of 1978 there was friction with Washington on the issue. In mid-December of 1978 the Carter Administration was making a concerted effort to bring about the signing of an Israeli-Egyptian peace treaty by December 17, the goal established in the Camp David Peace Frameworks signed the preceding September. Secretary of State Vance was dispatched by the president to Cairo and Jerusalem to try to secure a final agreement. *On the eve of Vance's mission* Israel pointedly announced it felt free to build new settlements after December 17—an announcement specifically calculated to put Washington in its place. Such a statement would have irritated the Americans no matter when it was made, but by choosing to issue it at this particular time the Israelis significantly emphasized their determination to make independent decisions about settlements on the West Bank. Their signal was unmistakable.

The Meaning of Signals? The meaning of signals is not always as evident as this, however. The fact that "every act of international behavior involves communication in either an implicit or explicit sense" does not mean that such communication will be clear and unambiguous.[18] Indeed, acts may be interpreted in many different ways and there is no guarantee that the receiver will "get the message" in precisely the manner and to the extent that the sender desired.[19]

---

[18]The quote is from Warren R. Phillips, "International Communications," in Michael Haas, ed., *International Systems: A Behavioral Approach*, Chandler, New York, 1974, p. 178.

[19]Once again the problem of perception rears its ugly head. In addition to the relevance of many earlier examples, much of the analysis in Chapter 13 is pertinent here.

Here one must deal not only with the structure and content of communications but also with the elusive quality of intentions. What does the sender of a message "really" mean? Did the Soviet construction and testing of four new intercontinental ballistic missiles in 1974 mean that they were simply trying to gain a better bargaining position for the SALT II Talks, that they were only trying to upgrade their deterrent force, that they were trying to develop a first-strike capability, or what? In the 1967–1978 period the U. S. S. R. increased the number of divisions deployed in Eastern Europe from 26 to 31, increased divisional size, and introduced significant qualitative improvements. What was the Kremlin signaling in this regard? When in late 1978 and early 1979 China engaged in a considerable troop buildup along its border with Vietnam it was signaling its displeasure with the Vietnamese invasion of Kampuchea (Cambodia) and the SRV's ties with Russia, but what could one deduce about a possible invasion? The PRC was more prepared to launch an attack than it had been prior to such activities, but whether in fact an invasion would or would not occur was not determinable solely on the basis of this signal. If the implications of troop and logistical buildups and redeployments were always evident, the Czechs in 1968 and the Israelis in 1973 would have acted far differently than they did.

If the policymaker wishes to have the signal clearly understood it is essential that pains be taken to prevent the "message" from being misinterpreted. One needs to empathize with the receiver, visualize the situation in terms of that party's particular characteristics, perceptions, and policies, and as much as possible construct the signal in such a fashion that the target cannot help but interpret it in the desired manner. Sometimes it is necessary for the policymaker to act with this type of care to prevent a *third party* from interpreting a particular act to be an unfavorable signal when it was not so intended. A good example of such an effort occurred at the end of November 1974 when President Ford went to Russia for a summit meeting with Soviet Communist Party Secretary, Leonid Brezhnev. The conference was held in Vladivostok. The choice of this location could have been misinterpreted by the Chinese as signaling an American "tilt" toward Moscow in the Sino-Soviet dispute, since that city was a part of the territory taken from the Chinese by the Tsar in the mid-1800s. As discussed earlier this land is considered by Peking to be inescapably Chinese. In order to reassure the People's Republic of China that the site did not signify an American "tilt," Secretary of State Kissinger continued on to Peking after the Vladivostok meetings concluded.

Signaling Via Language

The second (and more apparent) means of signaling involves the use of language. Policymakers use language in communicating with their counterparts in a vast variety of ways, ranging from casual conversations to private letters to *aide memoires*. Three aspects of these communications are especially salient in signaling: the importance of particular words or phrases, the use of code words, and what is not said.

Particular Words or Phrases. *In diplomatic communication (usually) great care is taken to choose precisely the right word(s) or phrase(s).* Frequently, nonpolicymakers fail to understand this, fail to appreciate the fact that the policymaker usually labors diligently to select a particular word or phrase that conveys the desired specific meaning. If the nonpolicymaker is to really understand how policymakers, in fact, usually operate, it is essential that this be recognized. If this does not occur comprehension will be severely hindered. For example, if one skims through diplomatic communications in a general manner just to get an overall sense of what is being said, it is quite possible that he or she will fail to grasp the real essence of the "message."

On April 7, 1965, in his famous Johns Hopkins speech, President Johnson said that the United States was prepared to discuss the Vietnam conflict with all governments concerned.[20] While this may have seemed to indicate a willingness to talk with all interested *parties*, it did not. The key word here was "governments" and since the Vietcong was not a "government" it was not included. This phraseology was specifically designed to exclude the possibility of talking to them.

The same kind of problem has been reflected in the Middle East conflict. For several years after the passage of Resolution 242 by the United Nations Security Council on November 22, 1967, various Arab policymakers said they would be willing to make provisions for the security of all "states" in the area. Some people might have assumed that such comments promised a measure of security for Israel, but they did not. Many Arabs did not consider Israel to be a "state." Today when Israel talks of negotiating with "states" or "governments" it is excluding the possibility of negotiations with the Palestine Liberation Organization since the PLO is neither.

In the early 1960s the United States and the Soviet Union commenced negotiations on the subject of an agreement to prevent the proliferation of nuclear weapons. While both parties believed it was in their interests to prevent a broadranging proliferation, the United States, partly as a response to pressure from certain of its NATO allies and partly because some of its policymakers thought a degree of nuclear sharing might preclude independent force developments and enhance NATO unity, for a short time advocated what was called a multilateral nuclear force (MLF). In its effort to reach an agreement to halt general proliferation but not preclude the development of MLF, Washington

[20]See U. S. Department of State, *Bulletin*, April 26, 1965, pp. 606–610.

offered a proposal that would prohibit the existing nuclear states from disseminating nuclear weapons into the "national control" of states that were nonnuclear.[21] The words "national control" were chosen specifically because they would not prevent the creation of the MLF. The Soviets, who were adamantly opposed to any form of German control over nuclear weapons (which, in multilateral form, MLF would have allowed) immediately and strongly objected to this language; they were only too aware of the significance of these two words.

Early in 1968 radio Hanoi broadcast a statement concerning the effect that a complete unconditional bombing halt would have with regard to negotiations. This statement changed only one word from previous formulations but it was a critical change. Whereas previously most DRV statements had said that a bombing halt *could* bring negotiations, now it was said that it *would* bring negotiations.

Sometimes words or phrases that appear to be totally innocuous actually, at least in certain policymakers' eyes, have considerable significance. Following the signing of the Camp David Peace Frameworks in the fall of 1978, Egyptian and Israeli negotiators, aided by American mediation, sought to conclude a peace treaty. A major concern of Israeli policymakers was "linkage," the degree of connection between the proposed Israeli-Egyptian treaty on one hand, and the autonomy of the West Bank and Gaza Strip (as agreed to at Camp David) and subsequent peace treaties with the other Arab states, on the other. Jerusalem's position was that all agreements should stand on their own, that except in a very general nonobligatory sense there should be no linkage among them. During negotiations in Washington the United States offered a draft treaty that included the words "on this basis" in a clause in the preamble.[22] At first glance it does not seem that these three little words could cause problems, but they did. The Israeli cabinet objected to their inclusion on the grounds that such language could be interpreted to mean that subsequent peace treaties would be concluded "on the basis" of the present treaty, and since the agreement under negotiation provided for total Israeli withdrawal from the occupied territories, if that were true and such a linkage existed Israel would here be pledging to (eventually) completely withdraw from *all* the captured lands. Therefore, the three little words were rejected.[23]

Of course, while the particular terminology must be examined carefully, it must be analyzed in context. On October 1, 1977 Washington and Moscow issued a joint communique containing mutually acceptable principles for settling the Arab-Israeli dispute.[24] One of the agreed-on phrases provided that

---

[21]Barton and Weiler, p. 296.

[22]As reported in *The Jerusalem Post, International Edition*, November 21, 1978, p. 6.

[23]Interestingly, Israel's *negotiators* did not believe these words established such a linkage and had given their tentative agreement, only to be overruled by the cabinet.

[24]For the full text see U. S. Department of State, *Bulletin*, November 7, 1977, pp. 639–640.

any settlement should ensure the "legitimate rights of the Palestinian people." Previously, the United States had usually avoided employing the phrase "legitimate rights," because many thought that such terminology at least implied an endorsement of the concept of an independent Palestinian state, a concept Washington had opposed. Certainly this turnabout meant something, but did it signify a major policy change or, given the other provisions of the document and the circumstances of its issuance, was it simply an indicator of a minor alteration? Given the fact that Washington did not specifically endorse an independent Palestinian state, maintained its position of not insisting on a total Israeli withdrawal, supported the Israeli desire for the establishment of normal peaceful relations as a condition of peace, and did not even mention the PLO, it was apparent that the United States was not signaling a radical change. Indeed, it was promulgating what it believed to be a balanced, moderate set of principles, and the new phraseology was just a way of emphasizing, within that framework, Washington's belief in the importance of the Palestinian question. Unless particular words or phrases are read in context, one can easily misinterpret their real meaning.

Before terminating this discussion two important interpretive comments are in order. First, although what we have said above about policymakers carefully choosing and studying particular words and phrases holds true in most instances, it does not always; there are exceptions. To put it bluntly, policymakers make mistakes. On March 12, 1947 the Truman Doctrine was proclaimed. In sweeping language President Truman called on the United States "to help free people to maintain their free institutions and their national integrity against aggressive movements that seek to impose upon them totalitarian regimes." Such imprecise, broad generalizations as "free people," "aggressive movements," and "totalitarian regimes" were susceptible to widely varying interpretations, and if incautiously used could lead to an almost reflexive involvement in crises irrespective of situational specifics. And, of course, this is exactly what happened. Though obviously Mr. Truman could not have foreseen it, his pronouncement would eventually provide one of the major bases for America's involvement in the Vietnam war.[25]

Other problems that occur when imprecise language is used are that the recipients may be misled, misinterpreting the signal, or they may be able to turn the language to their own advantage. When the Eisenhower administration took power in 1953 it condemned the "blunders" of its predecessor and the failures of "containment." The United States ought to "rollback" the Soviets, it was said. Some people in Russia's East European satellites assumed Washington was making more than a verbal declaration, and expected some type of concrete assistance in case of rebellion. As many Hungarians found

---

[25]Much of the discussion of abstract generalization in Chapter 13 is relevant here.

out in 1956, they were wrong; the "signal" had been misleading. In 1959, after Nikita Khrushchev's visit to the United States, President Eisenhower used the word "abnormal" to describe the Allied position in Berlin.[26] This was the same word that Khrushchev always used, and it did not accurately reflect the United States' real view. If the situation was "abnormal," then presumably it should be made "normal." Eisenhower's slip of the tongue strengthened the Soviets' position and made Washington's task in justifying its presence in Berlin more difficult.

The second interpretive comment is this: while in most instances great care is exercised in choosing the precise words or phrases one wishes to employ, and in most cases those words or phrases are designed to convey particular messages, there are occasions when great pains are taken in choosing a particular word or phrase that is not, in itself, precise. In other words, at certain times and in certain circumstances policymakers deliberately choose words or phrases that themselves are vague or ambiguous. There are contingencies in which one would not want to transmit a clear signal. Indeed, when employing the orientations of limited support or cooperation, indirect opposition, or participatory or minimal nonalignment, recipient uncertainty can sometimes be an advantage; in such instances ambiguity and the lack of precision might be useful. Whether recipient uncertainty is actually advantageous was discussed in Chapter 5 and need not be repeated here.[27] The key point at this juncture is that there are certain times when policymakers can rationally choose words or phrases that do not clearly signal, that generalities are not always mistakes. Nevertheless, *in most situations* employing generalities is quite unproductive, and therefore it usually is not an advisable procedure. Consequently, it usually is not done. As a rule, within a given message there are a few key words or phrases that have been very carefully selected to signal specific meanings, and both sending and receiving policymakers know this.

Code Words. Policymakers when signaling sometimes utilize "code words," words that stand for or suggest something different from, and/or more than, they would appear to. The number of variations on this theme is enormous and we cannot possibly list them all here. For analytical purposes, however, they can usefully be divided into two categories: (1) words and phrases used by both situational and nonsituational parties that have come to have a generally accepted but specific meaning and (2) words and phrases used primarily by situational parties that have a specific operational meaning understandable in, and primarily relevant to, the particular situation.

There are certain words or phrases that occur with some frequency in international politics, words and phrases whose meaning is evident to both situa-

---

[26]This account is based on Spanier, *American Foreign Policy Since World War II*, Seventh Edition, pp. 144–145.

[27]See Chapter 5, pp. 119–124.

tional and nonsituational policymakers but not necessarily to observers. For example, many times following the meetings of Communist leaders communiques are issued and policymakers make public statements characterizing the talks' progress or the lack thereof. A word that sometimes is used in this regard is "frank"; it is said that the parties had "frank" discussions. To the untrained eye it might appear that these policymakers were saying only that their talks had been open, that the participants had been candid and honest with each other. While in part correct, such a conclusion also would be partly erroneous. "Frank" in this context does mean openness, candor, and honesty, but it also signifies a high level of disagreement and conflict; if Communist talks were "frank" there was a considerable amount of disharmony, and little progress was made re the subjects under discussion.

Another example involves a phrase used in arms control agreements. The SALT agreements, the Non-Proliferation Treaty, and the Threshold Test Ban Treaty provide that compliance with the various agreements' provisions will be monitored by "national technical means of verification." Although outsiders may not realize what the phrase denotes, policymakers know that "national technical means of verification" refers to the employment of intelligence capabilities located outside the monitored state in a means consistent with international law. More specifically, one is referring to reconnaissance satellites with high resolution photographic capabilities plus a vast array of electronic surveillance devices.[28]

There are code words of a second type, words that are not widely employed, either in terms of the number of parties using them or the number of situations to which they are pertinent, but words that nevertheless are utilized with frequency by certain parties with respect to particular situations. Here the words or phrases become a kind of policymakers' shorthand that is intelligible primarily with respect to a particular subject. Prior to the Sino-Soviet dispute becoming public, for example, Chinese policymakers condemned "Yugoslav revisionism" and Soviet leaders condemned "Albanian Stalinism" and "dogmatism." These were "code words" (or epithets) referring to the Russians and Chinese respectively and the situational parties knew it. In Chapter 5 we discussed the PRC's utilization of the orientations of limited support (for Kampuchea) and limited cooperation (with Japan) to the end of (among other things) countering a perceived Soviet expansionist threat.[29] To describe what they feel is a major Soviet effort to dominate Asia the Chinese consistently use the word "hegemony." When PRC policymakers speak of "hegemony" their meaning is abundantly clear.

If a policymaker is not cognizant of the particular meaning(s) of code words in specific situations, and/or if the importance of those meanings is un-

---

[28]Also see Chapter 10, p. 298.
[29]See Chapter 5, pp. 120–121, 123.

derrated, it's possible both that he or she will not truly understand the positions of the parties utilizing the words and/or that a greater degree of enmity will be produced than is necessary. The first point is obvious on its face and requires no further elaboration. With respect to producing unnecessary enmity, President Carter's misuse of language in early 1977 is a case in point. In early March, in a ceremony welcoming Israeli Prime Minister Yitzhak Rabin to Washington, Mr. Carter wholly unexpectedly endorsed Jerusalem's right to "defensible borders." U. N. Resolution 242 had provided for withdrawal from occupied territories and the right to live in peace within secure and recognized boundaries, and U. S. policy had been formulated to achieve these ends; nowhere had the term "defensible borders" been used. Policymakers in the Middle East knew that "defensible borders" had long been Israeli code words signifying the right to retain some of the occupied territories. Naturally, Mr. Rabin was greatly pleased, the Arabs angered by the president's language. Needless to say the parties were shocked when just two days later Mr. Carter said his statement did not signify a change in America's position, that the question of "defensible" as opposed to "secure" borders was just a matter of "semantics." This angered the Israelis, and it left Arabs and Israelis alike doubtful of the president's grasp of Middle Eastern realities; as they well knew, such differences are much more than matters of semantics.

What Is Not Said. A critical but often underrated task of the policymaker is determining the significance of *what was not said*. One must be very careful in generalizing about the meanings of a particular message and not automatically infer that certain things were meant even though they were not said. Sometimes one discovers that what is *not* said is the most critical "message" involved in a particular communication. For example, U. N. Security Council Resolution 242 provides that Israel shall withdraw from territories occupied in the recent conflict (referring to the 1967 Arab-Israeli War). It does *not* provide that Israel shall withdraw from *all* such territories or from *the* territories. This omission was deliberate. The Resolution's framers did not intend that the Resolution should automatically mean a total Israeli withdrawal, and the omission of either "all" or "the" was very significant.

In 1976, in his speech to the 25th Party Congress of the Soviet Communist Party, Party Secretary Leonid Brezhnev said that in its relations with the Socialist countries the CPSU followed the rule of dealing in a spirit of true equality.[30] If problems arose, they would be resolved in a spirit of friendship, unity, and cooperation. That, in fact, *was* how the Soviets shaped their relations with the "fraternal socialist states—Bulgaria, Hungary, Vietnam, the German

[30]See Compass Publications, Reprints from the Soviet Press, *L. I. Brezhnev: Report of the CPSU Central Committee and the Party's Immediate Objectives in Domestic and Foreign Policy: 25th Congress of the CPSU, February 24, 1976*, White Plains, New York, 1976.

Democratic Republic, the Korean People's Democratic Republic, Cuba, Mongolia, Poland, Rumania, Czechoslovakia and Yugoslavia.'' Notice the omission of China (and Albania) from Brezhnev's list of "fraternal socialist states"! This was a clear signal that relations between Moscow and Peking had in no way improved.

In 1971 and early 1972 there were three Egyptian-Soviet meetings concerning the continuation and/or increase of Soviet military assistance to Cairo. Each time the Egyptians sought to receive offensive weapons, aircraft that was equivalent in firepower to the Phantom jets that Washington was supplying to Israel. Each time they were turned down. The communiques that followed the meetings, while reiterating general Soviet support for whatever means were necessary to eliminate the "consequences of aggression," never mentioned the provision of offensive weaponry designed to achieve that objective. This omission was significant.

From July 31 to August 3, 1958 Soviet Premier Khrushchev was in Peking on a secret visit. The Lebanon crisis was just ending, and the Russians' obvious disinclination to become involved (plus the Kremlin's suggestion of a Big Four summit plus India but without China) had irritated Chinese policymakers greatly. In the week preceding the visit Peking had significantly stepped up its propaganda concerning the "liberation" of Taiwan, a fundamental objective of Chinese policy. Upon Khrushchev's return home a communique was issued. It made no mention of this objective. This omission was of immense significance for it made it quite clear that the Soviets had no intention of involving themselves in any activity in the Taiwan Strait that might lead to a confrontation with the United States.[31] Both Peking and Washington got the point.

With the development of the Cold War the problem of Germany became the focus of American-Soviet tension.[32] Unable to make any progress toward signing a peace treaty, East and West moved to consolidate and strengthen their positions in the respective occupation zones. Although the basic issues here were political they surfaced in the guise of economic problems. The Russians were printing occupation marks in unlimited quantities, creating severe difficulties. In reaction to this the Western zones were merged as a necessary preparatory step to reforming the currency situation, and in March 1948 plans were announced for a new federal government (for the merged Western zones). Shortly thereafter the Soviets instigated a few rather minimal restrictions on travel to Berlin.[33] Gradually additional limitations were imposed. In June the Western powers introduced the Deutschemark in West Germany. Two days later the Soviets responded with a new currency for their zone and

[31] Also see Chapter 6, p. 149 and footnote 31.
[32] Also see Chapter 13, pp. 362–364.
[33] Berlin was located more than 100 miles inside the Soviet zone.

for *all* of Berlin. On June 24 the West reacted by introducing their mark into West Berlin; on that same day the Soviets instituted a total blockade. As is well known, the United States soon responded to the blockade with an enormous airlift, and in June 1949 the blockade was lifted. The Soviet effort to drive the West from Berlin had failed.

Negotiations concerning the lifting of the blockade had commenced soon after its imposition.[34] Almost from the beginning the Soviets said the crisis had been caused by the West's introduction of a new currency; as a result, Moscow said, the West no longer had a juridical right to occupy (any part of) Berlin. Throughout the remainder of the year the talks were unproductive. Then, on January 30, 1949, in an interview with an American reporter, Stalin unexpectedly avoided any reference to the currency problem. American policymakers quickly noticed this omission—what was *not* said—and Washington's U. N. ambassador asked his Soviet counterpart if the omission had any particular significance. After consulting with his government the Soviet diplomat replied that it was "not accidental." Soon thereafter the pace of negotiations quickened, and in a short time an agreement was achieved.

The foregoing examples encompass a broad spectrum of situations. Different time periods are covered, illustrations being drawn from the 1940s, 1950s, 1960s, and 1970s; in some instances the omissions were agreed on multilaterally, in some bilaterally, and sometimes the signal was unilateral; they occurred in speeches, interviews, communiques, and U. N. resolutions. We purposely selected a wide range of examples in order to emphasize the *pervasiveness* of this type of signal; it is a type of (non) communication utilized by policymakers of all sorts in all kinds of times and circumstances.

When one is studying a policymaker's communication, then, it is not enough just to carefully examine the particular words and phrases used, analyze the message in context, and determine the meaning of the various code words it contains. It is imperative that one go further, that the communication be analyzed with respect to what was not said and the operational implications of those omissions.

It is essential that the communicators be cognizant of the importance of omissions. In the examples above they were, but sometimes such is not the case. If a policymaker does not draft and deliver the communication with sufficient regard for what is not said, detrimental effects may result. On January 12, 1950 Secretary of State Dean Acheson defined the U. S. defense perimeter in the Pacific as running from the Aleutian Islands to Japan, through the Ryukyus (Okinawa) to the Philippines. In this area, it was said, Washington

---

[34]The following is based on Frederick H. Hartmann, *Germany Between East and West: The Reunification Problem*, Prentice-Hall, Englewood Cliffs, N. J., 1965, Chapter 3.

had immediate responsibilities and would act, but beyond this the United States had no obligation (although it might help); South Korea thus was excluded from the American defense perimeter by omission. Some Communist leaders interpreted this omission to mean that the United States *would not* defend South Korea against military invasion.[35] In this case Secretary Acheson, by not saying South Korea would be defended, unwittingly emitted a signal that was perceived by some as almost an invitation to attack.[36]

Communications are an important part of the policymaker's arsenal. As we have seen, both propaganda and signaling are utilized extensively, and many times with considerable effectiveness. Before closing, one more point needs to be addressed. At various times in our discussion, for the purpose of analytical clarity we made a distinction between language and actions. In the world of international politics, however, much of the time such a distinction is artificial, and even when it is not it is not always of great value. Both as receivers and senders policymakers deal with a composite of communications, a composite that contains a mixture of actions and language. Thus, for policymaker and analyst alike it usually is productive to consider language and actions together, as one entire communications system.

The instrument of communications is only one of the two major intangible instruments of policy implementation. We now focus our attention on the second, negotiation.

[35]Also see Chapter 5, p. 125, and footnote 25.

[36]An interesting question in light of the subsequent attack is whether the statement was misinterpreted or this *was* Washington's position at the time, its later response representing a change in policy.

12

Intangible Implementation Instrument: Negotiation

The last of the major instruments of policy implementation is negotiation. *When policymakers speak of negotiation they (usually) are referring to various kinds of formal and/or informal meetings, conferences, consultations, and dialogues in which ideas and information are exchanged for the presumed purpose of reconciling differences and achieving an agreement that will essentially "solve" a problem.* We also will define negotiations in this manner.[1]

There is a rather pervasive and quite natural tendency for *non*policymakers to assume that the purported objective of negotiations—resolving differences and concluding a problem-solving agreement—is in fact the foremost objective of policymakers in all negotiations. Such a view is erroneous, however, oversimplifying and distorting what is a much more complex reality. While it is obvious that in many instances policymakers do undertake negotiations in the hope that it *will* be possible to achieve an agreement to solve a problem, *there are a number of contingencies in which they may opt to negotiate even if this does not appear to be the least bit likely.*[2] In some situations a policymaker may choose to enter the negotiating process to achieve one or more of a variety of nonagreement objectives. In these situations the negotiating process is de-

---

[1] Because attempts to influence and bargain are so prevalent in international politics, in the broadest sense "negotiations" occur almost constantly. We will use the term in the narrower policymaker's fashion, the other kinds of activities having already been analyzed in Chapters 9–11.

[2] See p. 332, for the four conditions essential to a problem-solving agreement.

signed primarily to yield benefits unrelated to any agreement, and in fact no agreement of any sort is expected.[3] And another variation sometimes occurs: that is, the policymaker seeks to achieve an agreement but the agreement is not expected to really "solve" the problem.

It is important that observers recognize that policymakers have variable motives and objectives in negotiations, and that one not assume that they necessarily are negotiating toward the end of achieving a problem-solving agreement. If this is not done various aspects of negotiations will remain forever incomprehensible. One must not assume anything with respect to policymakers' objectives in negotiations, but instead analyze each particular case in order to discover what those objectives actually are.

NONAGREEMENT OBJECTIVES

A policymaker may enter the negotiating process for many reasons unrelated to reaching an agreement.[4] Sometimes for example, he or she may just be *stalling*. In mid-1956 the United States withdrew an offer to help Egypt's President Nasser finance the High Aswan Dam and did so in a calculatedly offensive manner.[5] Responding to this diplomatic slap Nasser nationalized the Suez Canal Company and took over this strategic Canal's operation. Britain and France, the Company's major stockholders and states at odds with Nasser over many other issues, immediately began considering the use of force to remove him from control.

Secretary of State Dulles urged negotiation. In this regard he developed two different plans for the "nonpolitical" operation of the Canal. His efforts led to the convening of two international conferences, and each of these yielded proposals for a form of international control. If either had been implemented, of course, Nasser would have had to give back what he had won. Most observers doubted that he would do so, and they were right. Apparently Dulles did not think he would either, as former diplomat Robert Murphy has succinctly pointed out.[6]

If Dulles did not think Nasser would agree, what *was* he trying to do? To a great extent he was just stalling in the hope that something would "turn up" and the problem would be solved. Problems sometimes do just seem to slowly

---

[3]Not that in some cases the policymaker might not "like" one, of course, but his or her perception is that it just is not feasible.

[4]This section owes much to the work of Fred Charles Iklé, *How Nations Negotiate*, Praeger, New York, 1967, Chapter 4.

[5]Washington was very anti-Nasser because of his recent arms deals with the Russians. See Chapter 13 for a more detailed analysis of this crisis.

[6]Robert Murphy, *Diplomat Among Warriors*, Doubleday, Garden City, New York, 1964, p. 386.

die a natural death. This attempt to buy time also had the objective of keeping British and French eyes on the possibility of a peaceful settlement so that they would not resort to force. Dulles did not enter these negotiations with much hope that they would solve the problem; he was just stalling.

Another reason one may engage in negotiations was illustrated by British and French actions in the same crisis. As they saw things they were getting nowhere. Washington was using delaying tactics as it erratically shifted course between incompatible objectives, and Nasser was still in control of the Canal and seemingly on his way to an immense political victory.[7] Seeing no peaceful way of removing him London and Paris began to plan a military attack. But they wanted to appear reasonable. They therefore decided it would be useful to take the case to the United Nations before launching the assault.

They introduced a resolution which, for all practical purposes, just endorsed the proposals for international control that had been developed at the previous international conferences. There was no possibility such a resolution would be acceptable to Egypt (nor to the Soviet Union), and the sponsors knew it. The real purpose of entering these negotiations was to be on the record as having exhausted every means of peaceful redress so that when the attack was undertaken they could say they had no choice but to engage in a military operation. As this example shows *sometimes policymakers embark on negotiations recognizing no agreement can be reached, doing so only in an attempt to provide themselves with an excuse for undertaking other types of activities when the negotiations fail.*

There have been many other examples of this phenomenon, of course, of making proposals one knows full well will be unacceptable to the recipient in order to be able to say "we tried, we did everything we could to reach a settlement" before undertaking preplanned further action. A variation on this theme also has occurred frequently: a party claims it wants to "negotiate" but presents demands it knows cannot be accepted so that it can then accuse the other side of being unwilling to "negotiate." Following the assassination of Austrian Crown Prince Franz Ferdinand by Serbian nationalists in late June 1914 Austria-Hungary undertook to initiate "negotiations" with Serbia, but (as it well knew) its demands were so harsh that to have accepted them would have effectually destroyed Serbian sovereignty. When the demands were (as anticipated) rejected, Austria-Hungary "had no choice" but to attack. Because policymakers in fact do sometimes "negotiate" or evidence a "willingness" to do so to the end of providing themselves with an excuse or pretext for further action, it is essential that one not assume that simply because a party is involved in "negotiations," or indicates its "willingness" to become so involved, it is not planning aggressive action.

[7]For further analysis of the incompatible objectives see Chapter 13, pp. 362–367.

American and Russian policymakers entered negotiations at the 1954 Berlin Conference for still other nonagreement reasons. No real negotiations had occurred on the German problem since before the Berlin blockade of 1948–1949, and there was nothing to indicate that any would be successful now. The West's position of forming a unified government via free elections, and allowing it to ally with anyone it desired, was clearly unacceptable to Moscow (since both sides agreed that a free Germany would be anti-Russian). The Soviet plan advocated the creation of a provisional All-German coalition government formed on the basis of parity between Communists and non-Communists (despite the latter's vast numerical majority). This "government" would then supervise "democratic elections," but the resulting creature would not be able to ally against any of the World War II victors. This proposal was not acceptable to Washington.

Why then did the Soviets and Americans want the Conference? Each knew the other would not accept its proposals. First, each party was seeking to have a *particular impact on third parties.* In 1953 there had been serious riots in East Berlin that the Soviets had forcefully suppressed. This suppression had hurt the Russian image and the Soviets were seeking to show their Communist allies that Moscow "really" was interested in solving the German problem. Also, the Soviets were seeking to signal French leaders that perhaps the only way to prevent a resurgence of the hated Germans was through a deal with the Kremlin.

It was this latter problem, French antagonism and discouragement, that prompted Washington. At the same time that she was being humiliated by impending defeat in Indochina Paris was also being asked to consider the rearmament of her traditional enemy, Germany. The United States felt that NATO's strength had to be increased and this was feasible only with German participation. Since German armies had defeated the French three times in the last 100 years, Paris was understandably apprehensive. Thus American policymakers tried to use the Berlin Conference to reassure Paris that Washington *did* want to solve the German problem but only in a way that would prevent any possibility of German militarism developing independently. Therefore constant consultations occurred in the negotiating process and unified positions, strategy, and tactics resulted. It was made clear that a reunified German state would be acceptable only if it was carefully controlled by the Western states, including France.

In addition to having an impact on third parties each policymaker in this case was trying to appear to be the one who was the most "reasonable." And this is another nonagreement objective. Because negotiations are considered by many people to be inherently "good," *policymakers may negotiate simply to reap the possible psychological and prestige advantages that result from being considered the "good guy."* In the Berlin Conference each side wanted to appear to be the most dedicated to a "just" solution to the German problem and demonstrate that its proposals were the more ethical and practical.

Policymakers often seek such propaganda objectives. As an attempt to give the illusion or appearance of seeking an agreement and to reap the benefits therefrom, policymakers may engage in "posturing," assuming a public posture that conveys an attitude of reasonableness regardless of one's real positions. Both American and Chinese negotiators employed this device extensively in their various talks in the 1953–1967 period.[8]

Finally, a policymaker may enter into negotiations for the purpose of *gaining information*. Perhaps one is trying to assess more accurately military strength or determine the degree to which a particular policy is supported by all alliance members. Maybe one is seeking a more precise understanding of the views of a given policymaker and feels that a face-to-face meeting would be most helpful. Maybe one is seeking to more clearly define the issues or to understand different national perceptions of a given problem. Perhaps through the information obtained the policymaker can assess more accurately the degree to which the other party's policies are essentially the product of bureaucratic infighting, or maybe one can achieve a more precise comprehension of the functions performed by ideology. Frequently policymakers are able to obtain a highly useful understanding of the personality characteristics and physical and mental health of their counterparts via the negotiation process. And, of course, policymakers often approach arms control talks with a major objective being the gaining of information, both in terms of hard data and with respect to factors such as the other party's perception of threat and its view of the military capability relationship.[9] And the list could go on and on.

It is evident that there are a number of nonagreement objectives policymakers sometimes seek via the negotiation process. The failure to recognize this fact, or at least to give it sufficient consideration, sometimes leads to enormous efforts to get conferences convened and negotiations going almost without regard to what the outcome of such gatherings might be. The idea seems to be that if "we" can just get talks underway all differences will eventually be reconciled and all problems solved. After all, negotiations are inherently "good," aren't they? Obviously, as the discussion in this section has pointed out, such a view is always oversimplified, and it sometimes is patently incor-

---

[8]See Kenneth T. Young, *Negotiating with the Chinese Communists: The United States Experience, 1953–1967*, McGraw-Hill, New York, 1968, Chapter 13.

[9]More often than not this is only one of several objectives that are pursued simultaneously in arms control negotiations, one of which may well be the achievement of an agreement. The key point for our analysis though is that a policymaker may rationally decide to enter arms control negotiations even if no agreement seems likely in order to achieve this particular *non*agreement objective.

rect. And as Pearl Harbor made clear, just because a party is talking doesn't mean it isn't planning to fight.

NONSOLUTION AGREEMENTS

There is a second major difficulty with the idea that negotiations are always good and lead to a reconciliation of differences. Sometimes parties negotiate to reach an agreement that they do not expect will "solve" the problem, a pact that they do not believe can bring to an end or even severely diminish (at least for the foreseeable future) the difficulties that lie at the root of their conflict.[10] Here too, as in certain situations in which no agreement is likely, policymakers sometimes feel it useful to negotiate.

What might one's reason be for negotiating a nonsolution agreement? One objective could be *to gain time while preparing for further activity.* In this case the policymaker recognizes that the particular agreement does not solve the problem; its purpose is to provide a breathing space during which preparations can be made for later action. Throughout the Vietnam war policymakers of the Democratic Republic of Vietnam made it clear that they considered Vietnam to be one country that was only temporarily divided into two zones; at some point in the future it would be reunified. Hanoi knew the United States would not be a party to an agreement that explicitly provided for reunification under DRV control. Therefore, after its negotiators had extracted all the concessions they could, Hanoi signed the 1973 Paris Peace Agreement. By its terms American forces would withdraw and the people of South Vietnam would be able to exercise their right of national self-determination. The agreement did not reunify Vietnam under the DRV, of course, but it did "ratify" the elimination of the major obstacle thereto, the United States. A little more than two years later Hanoi's military forcibly reunified Vietnam.

Another example of buying time occurred with the Nazi-Soviet Nonaggression Pact of 1939. Following the remilitarization of the Rhineland in 1936 and the annexation of Austria in 1938, Hitler turned his efforts toward Czechoslovakia. Any movement in that direction had to be perceived by Soviet policymakers as a threat to the Fatherland. When the Czechs were scuttled at Munich and in early 1939 the remainder of the country was absorbed by the Nazis, Stalin intensified his existing efforts for an alliance with the British. Because of his ideological preconceptions and the series of Western capitulations to Hitler, however, he was deeply suspicious of their ultimate intentions and also be-

---

[10]This is different from a situation in which policymakers sign an agreement they believe will solve a problem only to later discover that it doesn't. Here the policymaker knows full well the agreement won't result in a solution but seeks an agreement anyway.

gan to negotiate with the Germans. As talks with the West deadlocked the Soviets began to turn more and more toward Hitler, and on August 23, 1939 the
Nonaggression Pact was signed. One week later Germany attacked Poland.

Stalin did not believe that this agreement eliminated the Nazi threat. He
constantly assumed that Hitler would eventually move against Russia.[11] But
the agreement gave the Soviets time to prepare to make the conditions under
which the battle would occur much more favorable.[12] Additional forces could
be trained and equipped, and the home front readied for the struggle. Because
the Pact contained a provision allowing the Russians to occupy eastern Poland
after the Germans defeated the Polish army, the Soviet defense line was moved
that much further west. Besides, Hitler's attack would test British and French
promises to defend Poland.

The signing of agreements for the purpose of obtaining a temporary res-
pite during which to prepare for further activity is not limited to the twentieth
century, of course. An earlier example occurred in the aftermath of the first
Opium War, the Anglo-Chinese War of 1839–1842. Prior to 1839 European
attempts to establish diplomatic and economic relations with China (the Manchu Empire) were thwarted. The Chinese treated Europeans as barbarians,
smug in their belief in the centrality of the Middle Kingdom and the superiority
of Chinese civilization. Although the war arose out of many causes too numerous to detail here, a major one was China's attempts to forbid authorized
British opium trade while corrupt officials made great personal profits from illegal smuggling.

The fighting ended in 1842 with the rupture of China's communication
lines from south to north and with the British threatening Nanking. The Treaty of Nanking signed in 1842 temporarily ended hostilities, but the policymakers on each side recognized that the issues involved were not really resolved. Each felt that it could have won a more favorable agreement, and each
fully expected that at some point hostilities would begin again (and indeed the
second opium war began in 1856, resulting in a second Chinese defeat and the
continuance of a process of concessions to the West).

---

[11]An interesting footnote here is that Hitler was very fearful that the Soviets would attack
Germany. Shortly after the conclusion of the Pact he warned his generals that Moscow would adhere to the Pact "only as long as Russia considers it to be to her benefit." Shirer, p. 657. And it
has been suggested that Stalin "seems to have contemplated opening hostilities himself in 1942, if
the Nazis did not start sooner." Wesson, p. 158.

[12]Despite this the Soviets were incredibly unprepared. There were no orders or plans, no mobilization, and Stalin was nearly in a state of nervous collapse. Apparently the Russians did not
feel that Hitler would launch an attack without at least presenting some prior demands, or that he
would move before crushing the British. Since neither of these conditions were present Stalin felt
no urgency and believed there was plenty of time to make the necessary arrangements. Also see
Chapter 13, pp. 371–373.

Sometimes a policymaker will sign an agreement in order to *deceive*. A good example of this occurred in Indochina shortly after World War II. For over half a century prior to World War II Indochina had been a French colony.[13] A series of nationalist groups had sought national independence, the most effective being the Indochinese Communist Party headed by Ho Chi Minh. Following the Nazi invasion of France, French authority in Indochina collapsed. Shortly thereafter the Japanese served a series of ultimata on the French and for all practical purposes took control.[14]

As the war progressed the Communists expanded their base of support and became the primary nationalist organization, changing their name to the Vietnamese Independence League or Vietminh. As the war drew to a close confusion reigned supreme. At the Potsdam Conference in July 1945 the Allies agreed that when the war ended British forces should occupy the southern half of Vietnam and Chiang Kai-shek's Chinese Nationalists the north.

The Vietminh had assumed they would receive Allied support after the war ended but this was not to be. France was determined to reassert control, and maintaining good relations with her was deemed by the other Allies more important than recognizing the role of the Vietminh.

When the war ended the appropriate occupation forces entered Vietnam, and Ho Chi Minh began guerilla operations. At the same time the French moved in, hoping to replace the occupation troops and reassert their authority. In late 1945 and early 1946 a series of military skirmishes occurred between the French and the Vietminh. Negotiations began and an agreement was signed on March 6, 1946.

The agreement provided that Ho's Democratic Republic of Vietnam would become a free state with its own government, parliament, army, and treasury, and that it would be a part of the Indochinese Federation and French Union. The French also agreed that there should be a referendum in Cochinchina (the southern portion of Vietnam) to determine whether or not its inhabitants wished to be united with the remainder of the country. Ho agreed to allow the French to introduce 15,000 troops into the north to relieve the departing Chinese, but with the understanding that each year thereafter 3000 troops would be withdrawn until all were gone.

Ho thought he was signing an agreement that would bring him nearly complete independence, but the French had no intention of allowing this to occur. Almost immediately they set up a puppet government in Cochinchina in open violation of the terms of the agreement, and quickly made it clear they intended to keep considerable administrative control over the remainder of the

---

[13]The colony of Indochina included the states we know today as Vietnam, Kampuchea, and Laos. This discussion is concerned primarily with Vietnam.

[14]The French did retain some local administrative control, however.

country. French policymakers had sought to deceive Ho, and they did.[15] Shortly thereafter war broke out anew, and this time it would last for many years.

Another purpose of reaching an agreement that one recognizes is not a final solution is to use it as a *stepping-stone toward a final settlement*. In this case it is usually hoped that some momentum toward resolution will develop, and it is believed that something is better than nothing.

A useful example of this would be the passage of United Nations Security Council Resolution 242 of November 22, 1967 following the 1967 Arab-Israeli War.[16] In the atmosphere of intense bitterness that followed the decisive Israeli victory, and with a number of interrelated issues each of which was dependent to some extent on the others but each of which in and of itself was immensely difficult to solve, it simply was not possible to reach a final definitive agreement in the months after the conflict. Most of the parties recognized this fact and a wide variety of draft resolutions were introduced and debated.[17]

Some type of compromise had to be reached if there was to be any agreement. The phraseology had to be sufficiently general to be acceptable to all parties. If this could be accomplished each party could interpret the various provisions as it saw fit. Differences had to be glossed over in an effort to reach some type of general statement on which all parties could agree and that could be used as a basis for a final settlement. This indeed, is precisely what occurred.

The Renunciation-of-Force Treaty signed by the Federal Republic of Germany and the Soviet Union in August 1970 provides another example of policymakers negotiating a stepping-stone nonsolution agreement.[18] The Bonn-Moscow treaty pledged the signatories to seek a "normalization" of the situation in Europe, refrain from the threat or use of force in their mutual relations, recognize the inviolability of existing frontiers, and disavow all territorial claims. With the Treaty's ratification by the Bundestag in May 1972 Soviet-West German tension decreased and the prospects for enhancing bilateral (and multilateral East-West) cooperation were considerably improved. But although the contours of the issue were changed somewhat, the root problem was (and is)

---

[15]Much has been written on this topic. I would suggest that the introductory student consult appropriate portions of the following works. Joseph Buttinger, *Vietnam: A Political History*, New York, Praeger, 1968; Bernard Fall, *The Vietminh Regime,* Ithaca, Cornell University Press, 1956; Ellen J. Hammer, *The Struggle for Indochina, 1940–1955*, Stanford, California, Stanford University Press, 1966; and Donald Lancaster, *The Emancipation of French Indochina*, London and New York, Oxford University Press, 1961.

[16]For more on Resolution 242 see Chapter 11, p. 318.

[17]See Arthur Lall, *The U. N. and the Middle East Crisis of 1967*, New York, Columbia University Press, 1968.

[18]For more on the context and the role of this agreement therein see Chapter 14, pp. 394–395.

still there: Germany was still a divided country, there still were more than half a million potentially adversarial and heavily armed troops deployed on either side of the dividing line, there was no peace treaty ending World War II, and "Germany's" borders were not definitively or juridically delineated.[19] Furthermore, West German policymakers, having altered their orientation but not their fundamental objective of the restoration of territorial integrity (reunification), made it clear that this treaty would not be binding on a reunified state. Both Moscow and Bonn realized that the root problem had not been solved. But policymakers on both sides had felt it useful to negotiate an agreement that might be a stepping-stone to that end.

In our earlier discussion of Resolution 242 we mentioned that policymakers in that instance were required to devise phraseology of a level of generality sufficient to allow differences to be glossed over and various interpretations to occur; this is highly characteristic of nonsolution agreements. Another frequent characteristic of such agreements is that many issues, usually the most difficult ones, are ignored. "By definition" they can not be resolved in a mutually satisfactory way; if they could, the parties would achieve a problem-solving agreement. The SALT I interim agreement limiting certain aspects of offensive strategic weapons was clearly a stepping-stone agreement. Russian and American policymakers visualized a continuing process of negotiations with this being but the first step, directly referring to the point in both the preamble and Article VII.[20] In SALT I only quantitative limits on missile launchers were established. The more difficult qualitative problems, and certain types of offensive weapons systems with respect to which agreement was impossible, were just not covered. American, Egyptian, and Israeli policymakers followed a similar course in negotiating the Camp David "Framework for Peace in the Middle East" agreement they signed September 17, 1978. It was wholly evident that the parties could not "solve" the West Bank-Gaza-Palestinian problem. Thus the Framework they established, a framework they hoped would be a stepping-stone toward an eventual resolution of the problem, simply did not deal with the core questions of sovereignty, the final status of the area, territorial boundaries, and Jerusalem. Had the policymakers tried to do so no agreement would have been possible.

It is essential that it be realized that policymakers may negotiate nonsolution agreements, that they may sign agreements in order to gain time while preparing for further activity, or to deceive, or as but a stepping-stone toward an eventual solution. The mere signing of an agreement proves nothing other than that an agreement has been signed. If this is not realized and one jumps to the

---

[19]For more on the background of the "German problem" see Chapter 13, pp. 362–364.
[20]For more on the SALT I agreement and the companion ABM Treaty, see Chapter 10, pp. 295–296.

conclusion that signatories always believe that agreements are designed and expected to solve problems, a highly erroneous assessment can result. As always, it is imperative that one be situation-and party-specific, investigating each case individually to see if in fact a problem-solving agreement is what is being sought in the particular situation.

NEGOTIATING FOR A PROBLEM-SOLVING AGREEMENT

Despite everything said previously, it is still true that many times policymakers enter the negotiating process with the objective of achieving an agreement that will solve a problem.[21] Reaching such an accord, of course, is not easy, and one entering the negotiating process can never be sure of success.

Before analyzing in detail the process of negotiating to achieve problem-solving agreements, two very important preliminary points should be made. First, in order for such an agreement to be concluded the following *four conditions* must be present:

1. The parties must truly desire such an agreement.[22]
2. The substantive interests involved and the objectives that the parties seek must be reconcilable.
3. Both the process and the outcome of the negotiations must be such that none of the parties' prestige is unduly harmed.
4. The negotiators must have sufficient skill in the use of bargaining tactics to achieve their objectives.[23]

Second, there are situations in which negotiations would be futile because some of the essential conditions are not present. It is useless to negotiate if the parties do not really want an agreement or simply have irreconcilable positions. An example of this situation occurred during the Chinese Civil War following World War II.[24] The United States was anxious to bring about a negotiated settlement of the conflict and sent General George Marshall to China to act as a mediator; and on February 25, 1946 an agreement was actually signed. It provided a basis for the reorganization of the military, the integration of forces, and the creation of procedures to bring about a common government.

---

[21]Our discussion will concern only voluntary negotiations, negotiations freely entered into by the respective parties; dictated agreements, such as the imposition of the Versailles Treaty on Germany after World War I, are not "negotiations" in this sense.

[22]Of course, this "desire" may be a result of threats or coercion by one's adversary, and not be solely the result of one's own wishes.

[23]Much literature today focuses on this last factor. Obviously it is important as the discussion below indicates. But it must be remembered that if the first three conditions are not present no amount of bargaining skill will induce an agreement.

[24]See Chapter 10, pp. 279–280 and corresponding footnotes for further comments on the Chinese Civil War.

Almost immediately, however, both sides violated both the terms and spirit of the agreement, and each accused the other of doing so first. As Mr. Acheson later pointed out, the United States had been too optimistic. Neither side wanted an agreement and neither was willing to make any reasonable concessions.[25]

The only type of agreement that could have lasted in this case would have been one that involved someone's surrender.[26] And this points out another situation in which it is futile (and often harmful) to try to achieve an agreement: one cannot solve the problem of aggression against oneself by negotiating with an aggressor bent on conquest.[27] Such an aggressor will make no meaningful compromise. Any concession he or she makes will be temporary and will be utilized to prepare the way for further action.[28]

NEGOTIATING: PRELIMINARIES

Once the policymaker has determined that he or she is in a situation in which there is a reasonable possibility that negotiations might prove fruitful, he or she must deal with certain preliminary factors.[29] The first issue is simply *who should be involved in the negotiations*? This question is deceptively difficult and involves two major considerations. First, most conflicts are multilateral rather than bilateral; that is, they involve several parties rather than just two. As a result the conflict can be definitively settled only when many viewpoints and objectives are reconciled. This does not automatically mean that all of the parties should be simultaneously involved in the negotiating process, however. Generally speaking, the more parties involved the more disagreement because there are more issues, more different perspectives, and more opportunity for tactics that are designed to serve purposes other than reaching an agreement. In consequence, very frequently large multilateral gatherings produce a rather vague consensus on broad guidelines and principles with little in the way of

[25]Acheson, Chapters 16 and 23. The most useful introductions to American-Chinese relations in this period are Tang Tsou, *America's Failure in China 1941-1950*, University of Chicago Press, Chicago, 1963, and U. S., Department of State, *United States Relations with China with Special Reference to the Period 1944-1949*, Washington, D. C., 1949.

[26]The Communists and Nationalists were each using the agreement for purposes of deception and stalling.

[27]This does not mean one should never enter the negotiating process with such a party, however. First, one may seek nonagreement objectives or nonsolution agreements. Second, there may be *other* issues on which meaningful agreements can be reached.

[28]The tragic concessions made to Hitler and his reiteration that each demand was the last Germany would make in Europe stand as vivid reminders of this fact.

[29]Many of these preliminary considerations are as important for the negotiation of nonsolution agreements as they are for negotiations designed to achieve agreements that will solve problems. Consequently, we will provide examples of both in the following paragraphs.

specific problem solving and commitments to action, and often they yield no agreement at all. Because of this policymakers often prefer to negotiate only a small part of the issue with a smaller number of parties and hope to build momentum toward a more comprehensive settlement.[30] Of course, the disadvantage with the smaller group is that not enough viewpoints are considered and one cannot resolve the problem until all the parties have their objectives sufficiently reconciled. The policymaker does not always know in advance which approach would be better; he or she can only try to make an intelligent judgment based on the facts of the particular situation.

The second consideration is that participation and the conditions thereof are often intimately related to prestige. This is particularly true when one of the parties either has no formal diplomatic status or at least is not recognized by some of the other participants. In the Middle East today one of the major questions concerning negotiations concerns what role the Palestine Liberation Organization should play. The same kind of question arose in the 1950s when the United States and her European allies were negotiating with the Soviets over Germany. Since the Western powers did not recognize the German Democratic Republic it was always a question as to whether or not policymakers from that party should be invited. In the early stages of negotiations concerning Vietnam the issue of Viet Cong representation was similarly critical.

Often the bargaining over such procedural matters is as intense as the bargaining that later occurs on substance. However, if the parties are really desirous of moving on to substantive negotiations ways can be found to handle the prestige element. At the 1959 Geneva Foreign Ministers Meeting, for example, West Germany and East Germany participated in the form of advisor groups and each was given a position at a small table on the circumference of the larger table at which the delegations of the major powers sat. In the Paris negotiations on Vietnam a round table was used with a line down the middle and each party could interpret it as he saw fit, namely, that there were two sides and thus only two delegations, or that there were four separate delegations.

Although the question of who should be involved and in what capacity sometimes appears foolish and petty to the general public, it is not; indeed, the issue reflects factors of basic importance such as bargaining strength and prestige. And in situations in which one of the potential participants is seeking to attain a certain degree of legitimacy, often legitimacy as a cocontender for the right to rule the particular land in question, if they participate on an equal footing there might be some degree of tacit inference that in reality they had al-

---

[30]This was the rationale for the 1974–1975 American approach of a step by step settlement of the Middle East conflict: the negotiation of small disengagement agreements first in the hope that these will, if they are observed, create conditions of trust that will then lead to, or create momentum toward, a final settlement.

ready achieved their objective of cocontender legitimacy. After all, when participating in negotiations to achieve a problem-solving agreement one is clearly implying that (in principle at least) it is willing to reach an agreement with the other parties with which it is negotiating.

In all but the most elementary and routine bilateral consultations *determining the location of the talks* is another preliminary matter of importance. This is important because of the prestige and bargaining strength factors it reflects. If negotiations occur on the home ground of one of the parties, or on the ground of one of its major allies, that party automatically appears to have gained the upper hand. The fact that in their early efforts to begin the process of normalizing Chinese-American relations United States' policymakers always went to China, and the Chinese did not come to Washington, made it quite evident which party would be making the most concessions in this matter. Because the venue is important, in negotiations that involve significant differences on major issues policymakers usually opt to defuse the location problem. In some instances this is accomplished via the selection of a neutral site such as Geneva. Or, the parties may choose to alternate between a site favoring one party and a location favoring another. In the SALT I talks the sessions were alternated between Helsinki and Vienna, and within each city between the respective parties' embassies.

Yet another preliminary matter of some significance is *the diplomatic rank of the negotiators*. The decision on this point reflects the importance the particular parties attach to the negotiations (or at least to the particular stage in the process). Generally speaking, the more the significance attached, the higher the rank. The fact that there was very little involvement by senior American officials during most of the negotiations in the Conference on Security and Cooperation in Europe (CSCE) clearly signaled that in Washington's eyes this was a relatively low priority affair. The rank also may reflect the "distance" one is from an agreement. On very technical matters it may be necessary to begin at a relatively low diplomatic level because so many technical factors are involved. As one approaches agreement on technical issues and the political issues become more paramount, however, the level of diplomatic rank will increase (assuming the parties at this point want to reach an agreement).

Another preliminary duty is determining the talks' substantive agenda. Formulating the agenda is a matter of considerable moment, for what will eventually be concluded will be, at least in part, determined by what is discussed in what form. Obviously, if certain matters cannot be talked about they will not be included in any agreement. Conversely, if the agenda is very broad a wide range of subjects may be considered. In February 1947 Britain, unable to resolve conflicting Arab and Zionist objectives within its Palestine Mandate, announced it would soon turn the problem over to the United Nations. In April a special session of the General Assembly was called to prepare for the consideration of the Palestinian question at the regular session in the fall. Arab leaders wanted the issue to be investigated in a fairly narrow manner and fought to have the agenda include consideration only of the termination of the mandate and a declaration of Palestine's independence. Their efforts were defeated by a British-American-led coalition, however. A United Nations Special Committee on Palestine (UNSCOP) was created and authorized to go to Palestine, gather and analyze any and all data it deemed useful, and make as many and whatever recommendations it felt useful. As we know, the later UNSCOP majority report provided the basis for the partition plan adopted by the General Assembly in November.[31]

Finally, during the preliminary phase the parties must agree on the procedures that will be followed in the substantive talks. These vary immensely, of course, depending on the circumstances, issues, urgency, and parties. Generalizations are of little value in this regard, but a few examples might prove instructive.

The SALT I talks (generally) were highly structured and formal. Meeting in seven sessions (or rounds) over a two-and-one-half-year period, the venue (as we noted earlier) was alternated from session to session between Helsinki and Vienna, and within each city (for the separate meetings) between the parties' respective embassies. Procedurally, during the formal ambassadorial-level talks only the ambassadors were permitted to make statements, each reading from a carefully prepared document with an original language copy being handed to the other side. No spontaneous discussion was allowed, no questions were raised re the statement, and no public record was kept. After the meetings ended the respective delegations would consult with their respective capitals, and whatever questions policymakers at home felt should be asked were raised at an appropriate juncture during a subsequent meeting. Those questions were not answered spontaneously either, the answers being provided at yet a later meeting. It was wholly evident that Washington and Moscow wanted their negotiating teams to proceed with the utmost care and circumspection, to avoid any spontaneous actions or comments that might unduly compromise a particular position.

The 35-state CSCE negotiations of the early and mid-1970s were somewhat less rigidly structured in the individual meetings, and more give and take was permitted. The major procedural questions in CSCE involved the degree to which there would be bloc-to-bloc (NATO-Warsaw Pact) talks, whether decisions would be made by vote or consensus, and the degree to which the work would be subdivided into committees. The way these issues were resolved made quite a difference. First, it was decided that there would be no bloc-to-bloc negotiations. This emphasized the degree to which members of the various alliances were independent of the superpowers, and allowed states such as

---

[31]For more on the events of this period see Chapter 8, pp. 233–235.

Rumania to play a more active role than might otherwise have been the case. Second, the parties opted to have all decisions be by consensus rather than formal votes. This tended to lengthen the sessions and enhance the influence of the smaller states. Third, a variety of working committees were created, leading to greater emphasis on consideration of details and less on general principles than would have been the case if all the work had been done in plenary sessions.

Although procedures are decided on during this preliminary phase, this does not mean they cannot be altered if the parties are mutually so inclined later. The September 1978 Camp David Summit began with President Carter and his aides meeting separately and somewhat informally with the Israeli and Egyptian delegations, discussing all pertinent issues first with one side then the other. When it became apparent that little progress was being made the parties chose to split the negotiations into a more manageable arrangement, the president continuing to follow the existing procedure (perhaps becoming even more personally involved and informal) but concentrating on issues of the Sinai, and separate minister-level talks being undertaken on the various facets of the difficult West Bank-Gaza-Palestine issue(s).

In some instances the basic procedures are not changed but a variety of additional arrangements are made to supplement them and overcome their deficiencies. As we explained above, the formal ambassadorial-level SALT I negotiations were rigidly structured and formal. Because as organized such meetings made the consideration of nuances and fine points very difficult, working-level delegations met to that end a couple of times each week. Second, because the ambassadorial-level meetings were clearly unsuited to the detailed examination of complex technical issues, separate technical sessions occurred almost daily. Third, at several points the negotiations seemed to bog down and the delegations appeared unable to reach a suitable compromise. What frequently happened in these instances was that Special Assistant Kissinger and various senior Soviet officials secretly undertook what were known as "back channel" exchanges, private negotiations aimed at reconciling the differences and agreeing on the mutual concessions necessary to achieve a satisfactory agreement.[32] Several times these back channel exchanges proved successful.

It is obvious that a great variety of procedural arrangements can be devised, and that the issue is important. Indeed, *all* of these preliminary issues— determining who should be involved, the location of the talks, the diplomatic rank of the negotiators, the substantive agenda, and the procedures to be followed—are matters of some importance and as such will themselves be subjects of hard bargaining. *But, and crucially, if the parties truly desire to negoti-*

---

[32]In some instances these exchanges were so secret and private that the respective ambassadorial-level delegations were unaware of their existence and didn't learn about them until they had ended. Dr. Kissinger has described these back channel activities in some detail at various places in *The White House Years.*

ate a problem-solving agreement and perceive that such really is possible, they will find a way to agree on the preliminaries; if policymakers believe there really is a reason to negotiate, in other words, they will find a way to do so.

THE NEGOTIATING PROCESS: BASIC FEATURES

Once having agreed on the preliminaries the parties are ready to commence substantive negotiations. It is essential that the policymakers involved (and observers too) continually remember that negotiation is a means to an end, not an end in itself. Presumably the parties have gone through the various steps in policy formulation, established certain objectives, and determined that negotiating a problem-solving agreement is the most cost effective way of achieving or protecting those particular goals. In any problem-solving negotiation each side will have to make concessions in order for any agreement to be concluded. Because obtaining a judiciously balanced compromise in a prestige-protecting (or prestige-enhancing) manner is essential to fulfill the four conditions necessary for an agreement, the effective policymaker seeks to strike a balance between what he or she will demand and what he or she is prepared to give. During the course of negotiations the policymaker will, via the utilization of a number of tactics (singularly and in combination), attempt to persuade his or her counterparts to make certain beneficial decisions in return for certain trade-offs that he or she is willing to make. If one is to be successful in this effort it will be essential to effectively empathize, to see things from one's counterpart's perspective, to understand that person's perception of the situation, determine what decisions that person could and might make, and then (and only then) act accordingly. In each case the policymaker will be trying to persuade his or her opposite numbers that the cluster of consequences resulting from the decisions the policymaker would like them to make would be more beneficial (*to them*) than the consequences resulting from other decisions or no decision at all.

The negotiating process usually begins with each policymaker stating his or her party's maximum positions. It is not expected that others will agree at this juncture. In its opening proposals in the SALT I negotiations, for example, the Soviet Union proposed that Forward Based Systems (FBS)—short-range American fighter-bombers deployed in Europe and on aircraft carriers in the North Atlantic, the Mediterranean, and the Northwestern Pacific—be included in the concept of the strategic balance. But the Kremlin knew Washington would not accept this since American policymakers viewed such weapons systems as tactical counters to Soviet ground forces and the approximately 600 Soviet IRBMs and MRBMs targeted on America's NATO allies (which were not to be included). But making this proposal allowed Moscow later to "compromise" by dropping its demands. As Hartmann has put it: "The negotiator, therefore, must begin with demands that are nicely calculated in their excessiveness to match what is considered excessive in the position of his opponent while making it clear that concessions may be expected.''[33]

After the presentation of opening statements the process continues as the parties study the various proposals and respond either by restating previous positions, attacking the other side's proposal, asking questions, making promises or threats, bluffing, or making new offers, proposals, or counterproposals. Throughout the negotiations policymakers (nearly) always intensively and extensively analyze the different positons, seeking to determine exactly what the other parties' objectives are, the costs and benefits of various alternatives, the firmness and intensity with which different views and positions are held, substantive and procedural areas with respect to which concessions might be made, the minimum that the other parties feel would be acceptable, the shadings and nuances underlying particular provisions, subtle signals that may be being sent, etc. The exact nature of the concession-inducing, -trading, and -compromising process, however, is enormously variable, and each set of negotiations has its own unique characteristics. Therefore, as policymakers well know, beyond what has been said above few generalizations are useful because there is no "typical" pattern.

In their quest for an agreement policymakers employ a number of tactics. Before discussing these directly, though, it would be useful for us to say a brief word about negotiating "styles." Different policymakers have different negotiating styles. Most Western European diplomats, for example, and Americans as well, have tended to assume that one should begin with a presentation of his most rational argument, couch it in very reasonable terms, and try to demonstrate why it is the most "ethical" solution possible. What "should" develop then is some degree of mutual accommodation and the result should be a compromise solution. Most such policymakers recognize that at least some element of *quid pro quo* also will be essential, that some compromises will have to be made and concessions given, but many of them really don't "like" this and concentrate their efforts on demonstrating why their argument is inherently superior. To a considerable extent such negotiators emphasize what they believe to be the *intrinsic merits of their position*, and efforts to devise trade-offs that will produce a mutually acceptable compromise are sometimes minimal.

Negotiators from authoritarian revolutionary states such as the Soviet Union, Nazi Germany, and the People's Republic of China, have frequently operated in a somewhat different fashion. In large part this seems to have been due to their view of the role played by negotiations in international politics. Policymakers from authoritarian revolutionary states have typically conceived of negotiation in the context of an overall dynamic of conflict, and have thought of it primarily in terms of a weapon to advance their cause. Because of

---

[33]See Hartmann, *The Relations of Nations*, Fifth Edition, p. 102.

this, much of the time they have assumed that no agreement could, in any fundamental sense, be truly problem "solving;" this being so, negotiations have often been undertaken for nonagreement reasons or to achieve nonsolution agreements. Furthermore, it has often been the case that when policymakers of such actors actually have sought an agreement to "solve" a problem, they have wanted only one that would do so in a way that was one-sidedly beneficial. In consequence, such negotiators often have used highly intemperate language, sometimes have sought to simply outlast or wear down an opponent in sort of a contest of stamina (often through the seemingly endless reiteration of irrelevant points), have been exceedingly inflexible, and have tirelessly repeated propagandistic and/or ideological generalizations. Such tactics have not been the most conducive to achieving mutually satisfactory compromises, of course, but usually that has not been the objective; the goal is victory, to overcome the adversary.

These and other differences in negotiating styles have been and are important, and policymakers and observers alike should be cognizant of the different characteristics. But while one should not erroneously assume identical styles, the differences and the resultant impact should not be overstressed either. While they have emphasized ethical factors and the perceived intrinsic merits of their position, American negotiators in fact have (if somewhat reluctantly) been able to compromise in a number of instances in the quest for problem-solving agreements. And in recent years the Soviets and Chinese have made slight changes in their negotiating styles on those occasions when they have determined it to be essential that an agreement with the West be obtained. Although they have not wholly dispensed with intemperate language, ideological bombast, and tactics of attrition, in several cases Russian and Chinese negotiators have "toned down" their language and offered the concessions essential to reaching agreement.[34] Thus, while styles differ, and some add to the difficulty of achieving a useful agreement, if the four essential conditions for negotiating a problem-solving agreement are present stylistic obstacles can be overcome.

NEGOTIATING TACTICS: MERIT ARGUMENTS

In negotiations policymakers employ a wide range of tactics.[35] Negotiators who are seeking to achieve a problem-solving agreement generally believe that

---

[34]Whether such changes reflect an altered view of the role and purpose of negotiations, however, remains an open question.

[35]Although henceforth our discussion is directed primarily toward negotiating problem-solving agreements, many (if not most) of the same tactics are employed in seeking to achieve nonsolution agreements, and sometimes they are used even in negotiating for nonagreement objectives. To reflect this complex reality we will present *examples* from all three categories. Nevertheless, our text *discussion* will emphasize the tactic's utility in achieving problem-solving agreements.

their party's position is the "best," that in terms of *intrinsic merit* their proposals and objectives are superior to those of everyone else. In the earlier discussion of negotiating styles we noted that utilizing merit arguments has been characteristic of American and some West European negotiators. In numerous contexts such individuals have repeated and repeated their "superior" arguments in attempts to demonstrate the merits of their positions to their counterparts.[36] But such activities are not the province of any single party or grouping. Though some policymakers may have more faith in the efficacy of merit arguments than others, and utilize them more frequently, *all* negotiators employ such tactics to some extent. And why not? They believe that their arguments, on the merits, *are* superior.[37]

To many nonpolicymakers it would seem only logical that such merit arguments would prove to be tactically effective. *In actuality, however, most generally they are not.* In the first place, as we noted previously each party entering negotiations considers its own argument superior, and from its own unique perspective it quite likely is. Second, given the nature of the international political environment most policymakers assume that each party is primarily "looking out for number one," is seeking objectives primarily designed to benefit itself, and merit arguments are simply tools to that end. Therefore, policymakers seldom believe their counterparts are really trying to discover what actually is or is not the most meritorious position. Finally, because of the system's decentralized anarchy it is imperative that one not rely just on the "merits" of someone else's position, because a mistake in this regard could endanger fundamental objectives; ultimately, no one can be relied on except oneself.

Perhaps an example would be helpful here. After World War II there was considerable international concern about the actual and potential dangers posed by nuclear weapons, and a number of proposals were made *re* their control. In June 1946 the United States presented the Baruch Plan to the U. N. Atomic Energy Commission. This proposal envisaged a treaty that would create an international authority that eventually would control all aspects of nuclear energy production and use, thus (presumably) eliminating any possibility of individual states producing and employing nuclear weapons. This organization would be permitted free inspection on the territories of all U. N. members to the end of verifying compliance with the treaty's provisions, and sanctions for noncompliance could be imposed by a majority vote of the Security Coun-

---

[36]Carried to its extreme this approach makes compromise almost impossible, and when one's counterparts are not convinced and do not give in it leads to charges that they really aren't interested in "negotiating."

[37]Many times, when each party's argument is viewed solely in terms of that particular party's unique perspective and circumstances, each party's merit arguement does seem unchallengeable. See Chapter 8, pp. 232–235.

cil. The United States, which possessed a nuclear monopoly at this time, would agree to turn over atomic information to the organization in stages as the control and inspection system was set up. Once it was operational, Washington would destroy its nuclear bombs.

The Soviets responded with a proposal for two agreements. One (the *first* one) would be a treaty prohibiting the production and employment of atomic weapons, and would require the destruction of atomic stockpiles within three months from the agreement's entry into force. Then, within six months of the first agreement, the parties should sign a second agreement establishing penalties for noncompliance, the sanctions eventually to be administered by the Security Council but with all decisions subject to permanent member veto.

Each party believed its argument, based on the merits, was clearly superior to that of the other (and from its perspective, it was). The Americans saw their position as highly ethical and unselfish; they were willing to ultimately simply give up the enormous capability advantage they possessed by unilaterally relinquishing nuclear weapons, weapons no one else in the world even had. All they wanted was to first establish procedures for verification and control so they could make sure that no one (especially the Russians) would be able to cheat and subsequently take advantage of American generosity. As they saw it, that was only reasonable. Clearly, they thought, if people "really" want to solve the nuclear weapons problem they will recognize the merits of the American position and commence negotiations. But the Soviets believed the merits of *their* position to be superior. In their eyes the first thing the American proposal provided for was the establishment of procedures for legalizing and then undertaking a massive breach in Soviet security; inevitably the proposed international authority would be dominated by the West, and it would not be subject to a Soviet veto. Furthermore, once the system was in place and Washington was ferreting out Soviet defense secrets, what was there to prevent the United States from simply reneging on its pledges and not destroying its atomic weapons? No, obviously the only argument with any validity was theirs. Let the United States agree to stop producing atomic weapons and destroy the ones it had if it truly wanted to solve the problem, let it agree to establish a relationship of nuclear equality and then do so. And the Security Council-administered control and sanctions system would have to be one where the Americans and Soviets were equal, where each party could use the veto.[38]

This example is typical; each side sincerely believed that its merit arguments were superior, and neither side could significantly alter the other's merit views. Because this in fact is the norm, unless other tactics are used, and unless the four essential conditions can be met (which was not possible in this case),

---

[38]At this time, given the preponderance of pro-Western states on the Security Council, the United States could almost always count on achieving a voting majority.

no problem-solving agreement will be concluded. Despite this, it would be erroneous to say merit arguments are wholly without value. They are one means by which each party attempts to communicate. They are a vehicle for expressing the intensity with which one holds a particular point of view and the degree of firmness that is involved. Arguments can also help clarify positions and provide an informational base for further negotiations. But as position-modifying tactics they are relatively unproductive.

NEGOTIATING TACTICS: PROMISES

A second negotiating tactic is the promise, a pledge that under certain conditions one will undertake or refrain from undertaking certain actions. In a negotiating context one (almost) never makes a promise without the expectation of receiving something in exchange, in the absence of an anticipated *quid pro quo*.[39] A promise is in some senses similar to a bribe. Party B pledges that (perhaps only under certain conditions) it will or will not do thus and so, the consequences of which will be beneficial to party C, if in return C will or will not do certain things as desired by B (again, perhaps only under certain conditions). The types of promises vary enormously, ranging from a pledge to perform relatively routine diplomatic services to assurances of the provision of certain kinds and quantities of foreign aid to obligations for total direct military support in combat.

Promises are not always made openly and explicitly. As noted in Chapter 6, for example, sometimes off-limits zones are created tacitly.[40] In effect what happens in these cases is that mutually agreeable tacit promises are exchanged. Sometimes even in direct negotiations a policymaker will choose to offer tacit promises. There are certain advantages to this procedure. For one thing, if the promise is not accepted no one's prestige is severely harmed because the promise's existence was not public knowledge. Also, a tacit promise by its very nature is somewhat vague and thus, everything else being equal, it commits the promising party less than an explicit promise would. But this is also a weakness; a tacit promise is not clear, and it does not establish specific rights and obligations relationships. In some situations that could be advantageous, but seldom is it a desirable attribute when one is seeking to conclude a problem-solving agreement. Therefore, though tacit promises may sometimes prove useful in certain stages of the bargaining process, policymakers almost always will want them made explicit before the signing of a binding agreement. Even

---

[39]There are times when this appears to be the case, however, such as when the expected response is much more vague than the promise, when it is a pledge of action to occur at a later date, or if it involves actions dependent on certain future contingencies and those contingencies never eventuate.

[40]See Chapter 6, p. 136.

if the terms of the promise itself are vague, policymakers still want that promise expressed explicitly if they are to sign a problem-solving agreement in which it is to play a significant part. They want to know what the agreement they are signing does and does not entail.

In order for a promise to have any effect it must fulfill two elementary conditions. *First, it must be credible*; the target state must believe you. As mentioned in the analysis of deterrence, credibility involves the perception of the target state with respect to a party's capacity to do what it said it would do, and one's willingness to do it.[41] Does one have the capability to fulfill one's promise, does the target know it, and is there some reason for believing that the promise will, in fact, be kept? In this latter regard a policymaker's reputation for performance will be particularly important. If a policymaker has a reputation of not carrying out promises, his or her current promise probably will lack credibility.

The second condition is the establishment of the perception in each party that the cost-benefit ratio of what it will be receiving in the exchange will be at least as favorable as the one it will be giving; the promising policymaker (promisor) must convince his or her counterpart (the promisee) that the net value offered is worth at least as much as the net value requested. The promisor must promise to do or not do something that the promisee considers important enough in a cost-benefit sense to do or not do what the promisor has requested. Sometimes the perception of an equivalent cost-benefit exchange ratio can be achieved via the process of the making of identical promises. In order to aid in the verification of compliance with the provisions of the SALT agreements each party made identical pledges not to interfere with the national technical means of verification employed by the other party and not to impede verification by deliberate concealment measures. But the key elements in most situations do not lend themselves to such treatment.[42] More often the scenario therefore is something like this: policymakers of party I need and try to convince the policymakers of party II that the cluster of consequences resulting from promises A-F that party I will make will be at least as beneficial to party II as the consequences of promises H-M that party II will make will be to party I. In this much more typical kind of situation it is not an identity of pledges that is the key but rather the perceived cost-benefit equivalence (or the lack thereof) of different mixes of disparate promises. Obviously, establishing such a perception in these situations is no easy task.

[41]See Chapter 10, pp. 283–284.

[42]Identical promises frequently do not produce equivalent impacts because of differences in circumstances and situational conditions, and the differences in objectives, capabilities, perceptual uniqueness, etc., of the parties. For example, identical promises not to produce more nuclear weapons certainly would have a different impact on the Soviet Union and China, and identical promises not to employ guerilla tactics would impact Israel and the PLO quite differently.

NEGOTIATING TACTICS: THREATS

In addition to presenting merit arguments and offering promises, policy-makers in negotiating contexts also may employ more coercive tactics and make threats.[43] In a sense threats, because of their coercive and potentially punitive nature, are the opposite of the promise of reward(s). The policymaker informs the target of the threat, whether it be by words or actions (or a combination of both), that unless the target does or does not do Y as desired it will be necessary to do or not do Z, and this will be harmful to the target.

Whether a threat will be effective depends to a great extent on its *credibility*. Once again it is necessary to view things from the point of view of the policymaker being threatened. He or she must believe that the threatener has the capability to carry out the threat and the willingness to do so.[44] What makes a threat credible? First, as discussed earlier, capability. Presumably some equivalence between the level of the threat and the objective to be obtained is also important.[45] If the threat is of a magnitude wholly disproportionate to the value of the objective the target probably will think its a bluff and not alter policy in the desired fashion.

Another important factor is the degree of commitment. Commitment may be established by public statements that involve the prestige and position of the policymaker's state (and perhaps his or her personal position or that of his or her regime as well). Also, one's reputation is a factor that has an impact on the credibility and the appearance of commitment. The United States partial mobilization and movement of the Sixth Fleet to the eastern end of the Mediterranean Sea at the time of the 1970 Jordanian Civil War was seen by many as a harbinger of possible intervention considering the fact that American Marines had landed in Lebanon in 1958. Specific actions also may add to or detract from the level of commitment. The stationing of American military forces in West Berlin where they would inevitably become involved in any European conflict gives some credence to the idea that the United States would

---

[43]Many writers make a distinction between warnings and threats. Usually the idea is that a warning means that if one's opposite number does not comply with his wishes then certain consequences will naturally occur. On the other hand, a threat is conceived to be a situation in which, if the opposite number does not do what is desired, the threatening party will make a special effort to harm him. See Iklé, pp. 62–63, and Thomas C. Schelling, *Strategy of Conflict*, Oxford University Press, London and New York, 1960, pp. 123ff.

[44]Weakness does not always detract from credibility as long as some capability is present. If a policymaker has little to lose because of weak political support or seems to have no other real choice but to carry out a threat that is made, he might be willing to take much greater risks than would be "reasonable" given his capability situation. William D. Coplin, *Introduction to International Politics: A Theoretical Overview*, Second Edition, Rand McNally, Chicago, 1974, p. 307.

[45]Kenneth E. Boulding, *Conflict and Defense: A General Theory*, Harper, New York, 1962, p. 255.

never allow Soviet forces to occupy Europe. The terms of the threat also are indicative of the level of commitment and thus affect the threat's credibility. Generally speaking, the more specific and direct the threat and the more likely that conditions will eventuate that will require its execution (such as the expiration of a time limit that probably cannot and will not be met), the greater the level of commitment; if a policymaker makes a direct precise threat and perceives that there is a high probability that the threat will have to be carried out, a major commitment has been made (and thus the threat's credibility is considerable).

Despite these particular means of establishing commitment, *the only real way of guaranteeing credibility is to leave as little room as possible for judgment or discretion in carrying out the threat.*[46] If a party puts itself in a position of having no choice but to carry out its threat, either in the sense that it will automatically follow or that there are no reasonable alternatives, then it has established a commitment and its threats will have maximum credibility (assuming one is able to communicate these facts to the target state and its policymakers' perceptions of them are accurate).

To this point the discussion has proceeded as if establishing maximum credibility was necessarily a good thing. But this is not always so. One may not always desire maximum commitment for the reason that, by definition, the greater the commitment the less the flexibility. In other words, as one proceeds to tie one's own hands in order to establish maximum credibility one loses a certain amount of flexibility, flexibility that may be necessary in order to negotiate effectively. This cuts down the possibility of changing and reformulating positions or perhaps retreating in case the target of the threat simply says "go ahead." In that case the threat may not induce an agreement but may in fact create a situation that prevents any possibility of an agreement and forces the policymaker to either carry out the threat or surrender.

This raises the entire question of *whether or not making a threat is a useful bargaining tactic.* Obviously, in some cases it is. The threatened policymaker believes that the threatener has the capacity and intention to carry out the threat, and that if the threat is carried out the consequences will be much worse than making the desired decision.[47] But there are other cases in which a threat may not be so valuable to the threatening state. As mentioned above,

---

[46]Schelling, p. 40.

[47]Often a threat that is designed to alter the target's negotiating position is made outside of the confines of the formal negotiations. With the negotiations to terminate the Korean War deadlocked in the early summer of 1953, via a series of public and private communications external to the negotiating sessions Secretary of State Dulles threatened to blockade and bomb China (possibly with nuclear weapons) if an armistice could not be obtained; in July the armistice was signed. Certainly this threat was not the *only* reason (Stalin's death in March being another) that Chinese negotiators modified some of their positions, but just as certainly it was *one* of them.

the establishment of maximum credibility ties the policymaker's hands. This means that he or she has relinquished the initiative and the outcome now depends solely on the other party's choice.

A second difficulty with employing threats is that presumably one's opposite number anticipated some costs when he began his actions, and possibly he may have anticipated this threat. If one acts as it was expected he or she would such action will hardly get an opponent to change his or her behavior. Furthermore, as indicated above in the discussion of the economic and military instruments of policy, people adapt quite rapidly and resent pressure being applied to them. Rather than submit to a threat they may believe that the costs of enduring an executed threat are preferable to the costs of giving in. Also, they may already have gone so far in the particular line of action that they feel that they have no choice but to continue.

Another set of reasons that mitigate against the use of threat involve the costs of actually carrying it out. Suppose, for example, A has threatened to withdraw economic assistance from B unless a certain political course of action is followed. Suppose B says, go ahead, either because he does not believe A will do it or because he simply reacts negatively. Is it to A's benefit to actually do it? In some ways, yes, because if he does not it will look as if he was bluffing and his reputation will suffer. On the other hand, if he does he will lose the opportunity of gaining influence that giving economic assistance would have provided. Sometimes one gets into a situation where he ends up doing something he would prefer not to do for no reason other than that he said he would, and this may not be beneficial.

Finally, perhaps the idea of executing the threat is that one will teach one's adversaries a lesson. But this may or may not be the case. They may find alternatives, for example, if we cut off economic assistance. It could be that rather than *them* learning *their* lesson the adversaries may have concluded that the policymaker has learned his as he suffers from the execution of the threat. They may believe that he will learn that such actions are not effective and he will not repeat them again.[48]

NEGOTIATING TACTICS: BLUFFS

Another tactic policymakers sometimes employ while negotiating is the bluff, claiming that unless the target modifies its position in the desired manner one can and will do something that in fact one can not or will not do. This is a very dangerous tactic and one that must be handled with care. The policymaker must always try to anticipate what his or her action will be if the bluff is called. Whether or not a bluff will be effective will, of course, depend on the percep-

---

[48]See Roger Fisher, *International Conflict for Beginners*, Harper, New York, 1969, Chapter 3.

tions of the parties involved, the degree to which the proposed action seems to be feasible, and the reputation of the policymaker. In 1936 Adolph Hitler ordered his troops to remilitarize the Rhineland, that area of Germany between the Rhine River and the border of France. This action was a direct violation of the Treaty of Versailles. Hitler was actually bluffing. His generals had orders to retreat if fired on. He was successful, however, because of the desire of the British to accommodate him to prevent the outbreak of a new war, the impression that the Western powers mistakenly had of German military readiness at the time, and the fact that the territory being remilitarized was "after all" German. In this case the successful execution of a bluff added greatly to Hitler's reputation and thus the credibility of future threats.

An opposite result occurred as a result of Soviet Premier Khrushchev's bluffs in the second Berlin crisis.[49] In late 1958 Khrushchev stated that the time had arrived for the Western powers to renounce their "occupation regime" in Berlin. Because of Western violations, he said, the Soviet Government no longer considered itself bound by the Four Power Agreements on occupation. At an appropriate time the Soviet Union would transfer its functions to the German Democratic Republic. The solution to the problem should be to convert West Berlin into an independent political unit, a free city, and the Western Powers would have up to a half a year to make such changes. If this did not occur then the Soviet Government would automatically transfer its powers over Berlin to East Germany and would terminate its contacts with the Western governments. Thereafter if the Western governments wanted to go to West Berlin they would have to deal with the East Germans. Furthermore, the Soviets would consider any Western "aggression" against East Germany as if the Soviet Union herself had been attacked.

But Khrushchev was bluffing. In the aftermath of the launching of Sputnik and the disarray in NATO following the Suez crisis, he had seized the initiative in the hope of solving the Berlin problem, probing for weaknesses on the part of Russia's perceived adversaries. Khrushchev did not really anticipate that the need would arise to actually confront the West and unilaterally turn the Soviets' functions over to the East Germans and sign a separate peace treaty purportedly terminating all Western rights, because he believed that the mere threat to do so would produce meaningful concessions. He was wrong. When the United States and its Allies simply confronted Moscow and refused Khrushchev's demands the Soviet leader backed down. He had been bluffing, and when his bluff was called his threat proved to be an empty one.[50]

---

[49]For a succinct, perceptive analysis see Frederick H. Hartmann, *Germany Between East and West: The Reunification Problem*, Prentice-Hall, Englewood Cliffs, N. J., 1965, Chapter 6.

[50]One consequence was a reduction in the credibility of some of his later threats.

Once in a while, if conditions are right, an unsuccessful bluff can later be turned to one's advantage. On numerous occasions in the last half of 1971 Egypt's President Sadat stridently proclaimed that 1971 would be the "year of decision"; one way or another, he said, the dispute with Israel would be settled. Nothing of the sort occurred, of course, with the result that Sadat's credibility was severely damaged; the Egyptian leader had been bluffing, and when his bluff had been called and he could not act he looked foolish. This, along with his expulsion of Soviet advisers in 1972, the Arabs' obvious military weakness in comparison to Israel, and the history of Israeli successes in the three previous wars, helped produce a perception in Israel to the effect that it would be totally irrational for Sadat to attack; therefore, he would not. In consequence, in 1973 he was able to make a number of moves that under other circumstances might have been regarded as clear signals of impending attack, and the Israelis thought he was bluffing.[51] Of course, they were wrong, and in October Egypt launched a limited war.[52]

It is obvious that bluffing is risky. When considering whether or not a bluff would be worthwhile the policymaker must very carefully analyze the peculiarities of the specific situational context and the specific individuals who will be the target; generalities at this point are wholly useless. In particular, it is essential that one empathize, that one role play and "be" the target for a while to try to assess the probable reaction. Finally, because bluffs are not always successful the prudent policymaker will have prepared a fall-back position, will be prepared to recover quickly if the bluff is called and undertake damage-minimizing actions.

NEGOTIATING TACTICS: CLOSING PLOYS

The discussion to this point has analyzed the major tactics that negotiators employ in seeking problem-solving agreements: merit arguments, promises, threats, and bluffs. For reasons of analytical clarity we have examined them separately in order that the reader can fully and accurately understand the usages, costs, and benefits of each. But while this is useful for study purposes, it is a somewhat inaccurate reflection of the real world. *In actual negotiations policymakers employ various mixes of these tactics simultaneously, and it is the net impact of the particular mix that is crucial. More than that, the mix is frequently changed.* As negotiators begin to reduce their demands and retreat from their maximum positions in the effort to persuade their counterparts to yield meaningful concessions, as they engage in the exchanges and the give and

[51] See Chapter 15, footnote 56 for some useful citations.
[52] See Chapter 10, pp. 277–278.

take that is essential if a mutually acceptable compromise is to be achieved, there is a constant reassessing of one's positions and tactics. Often this leads to both substantive and tactical reformulation. In other words, the mix (for all parties) tends to be dynamic, not static. Clearly, this has to be the case, at least to some extent, if a compromise is to be reached.

In many instances, despite the parties' diligent efforts a situation develops in which it appears that no more can be done and no agreement will be concluded. And, as we know, sometimes this appearance proves to be the reality and negotiations are broken off. But if the parties are not very far apart substantively and they really want an agreement there are certain ploys that sometimes can be effectively used to "close the deal." The list of such devices is long, and only a few illustrations can be mentioned here. If achieving the agreement is of considerable importance, if the other party has already made a number of concessions and there is no reasonable likelihood that more will be forthcoming, and if one's prestige will not be unduly harmed and domestic pressures will allow, the policymaker may choose to *offer a last minute "this is it" unilateral concession*. If one is proceeding optimally one will do this only after determining that no agreement is possible unless this action is taken, and that an agreement embodying this concession will yield a cost-benefit ratio superior to that produced by a situation that produces no agreement.

Sometimes certain procedural ploys can be beneficial. *The imposition of deadlines* occasionally has been productive. The knowledge that the summit meetings to sign both the SALT I and SALT II agreements were scheduled to occur on a specific date spurred negotiators to hammer out the final details in both cases. Perhaps even more to the point, in their September 1978 negotiations for Middle East Peace Frameworks Messrs. Carter, Begin, and Sadat agreed that if by a certain time they hadn't achieved an agreement they would pack up and go home with nothing.

Flexibility of procedure and form often become critical toward the end. For one reason or another (frequently domestic pressures or prestige factors), in some cases the policymakers are very close to success but there is a problem of form or procedure that threatens to prevent the agreement's consummation. When this is the situation policymakers can usually find a way to sufficiently minimize or disguise the problem so that an agreement can be reached. In the American-mediated negotiations for the 1974 Egyptian-Israeli Disengagement agreement President Sadat said he could not openly admit to limitations on Egyptian forces on sovereign Egyptian land. But without some such limitations the Israelis would not agree to any type of withdrawal. Sadat knew this, and did not oppose the concept, saying only that he could not publicly admit to it. The solution? The restrictions were spelled out in identical confidential letters from President Nixon to Sadat and Israeli Prime Minister Golda Meir, said letters then signed by each recipient.

Another example of the ploy of innovative form occurred in the American-Chinese talks during President Nixon's visit to Peking in February 1972. Both parties wanted to be able to issue a positive closing communique, but there were many problems on which their views differed considerably and no reconciliation was possible. How to achieve an agreement solving this problem? After futilely attempting to achieve common positions they hit on a solution: both sides agreed to write separate sections of the communique, one expressing the American view of a particular problem, the other the Chinese.[53]

There are still more possible closing ploys: raising a last-minute demand then dropping it so that the other party can enhance prestige and rebut domestic critics with a "victory"; appealing to precedents that previously had not been involved; reformulating the sticking points, in effect restructuring the issues procedurally even though the substance remains essentially the same; eliminating or establishing linkages to extrasituational matters in a beneficial manner; agreeing to negotiate the still-unresolved issues later in exchange for a signature on what already has been agreed on; and the list goes on. If the parties really want an agreement, are at a stage where most objectives have been reconciled and most substantive differences compromised, and no one's prestige has been unduly harmed, usually they will have the skill to develop the particular ploys that are necessary to "close the deal."

CONCLUDING COMMENTS

As we have seen, the instrument of negotiation is multifaceted and complex; it is used in many different ways for a variety of purposes. A few comments are essential in conclusion to put the analysis in perspective, to place it in a more realistic (although more complicated) context. First, a simple and perhaps obvious point: as is true with respect to all the other implementation instruments as well, sometimes negotiation proves effective, other times it does not. In the decentralized anarchy of international politics one is never guaranteed success, even if the correct instrument is chosen and it is utilized correctly.

Second, as we discussed earlier policymakers may rationally undertake negotiations to the end of achieving certain nonagreement objectives or nonsolution agreements, as well as for the more commonly assumed goal of negotiating an agreement that will solve a problem. Understanding that such a range of possible reasons exists is enormously important, and in each specific situation it is incumbent on policymakers to ascertain what their counterparts are after. But in the real world this task is more complicated than the analysis to this point has implied, because in most instances the various parties are seeking

---

[53]Stoessinger, *Henry Kissinger: The Anguish of Power*, p. 129.

to obtain and/or protect a multiplicity of objectives at the same time; therefore, in most situations one just cannot say that party A wants to achieve solely and only objective X. When entering negotiations policymakers usually have a number of goals they would like to accomplish, some of which are more important, some of which will be sought with greater intensity, and some of which are more likely to be achieved, than others. That this is the case, and it is, does not alter the necessity of recognizing the various possibilities. Parties have priorities in objectives and differences in expectations, and it is important to carefully investigate to determine the priorities and expectations in each case; ascertaining whether party C is primarily interested in achieving certain nonagreement objectives with some nonsolution agreement possibilities only secondarily in mind, or whether he is really after a problem-solving agreement but if compelled to will settle for certain types of nonsolution agreements, clearly is a task of great significance in laying out one's strategy. The point here is that because policymakers are usually seeking a multiplicity of objectives this important job is much more complicated than the earlier analysis may have implied.

Third, in Chapters 9–12 we analyzed the economic, military, communication, and negotiation instruments of policy implementation separately, examining the components and usages, the advantages and disadvantages, of each. This is a highly useful technique analytically, allowing an in-depth analysis and presentation. Nevertheless, it can have one drawback: by implication it may tend to give an oversimplified picture in that it may give the impression that policymakers in real-life situations simply choose which of the several instruments to use and then actually use only that one. While on any single day this may be what happens, on that day also certain instruments already are in operation because relations have existed prior to that time, and in the future more choices will have to be made. Therefore, with respect to each situation over time a combination of instruments will be utilized. The effective policymaker, therefore, has to be concerned with choosing the most productive *mix* of instruments. One must analyze the strengths and weaknesses of the many potential mixes and combine the components that are mutually compatible, reinforcing, and effect-multiplying into the most favorable cost-benefit package possible.

Finally, policymakers do not have the luxury of dealing with problems in isolation. The choices they make re instruments of implementation will in part be influenced by inputs from extrasituational parties and other existing and potential situations, and their choices and actions will also be somewhat affected by the anticipated effect their utilization will have on such extrasituational parties and other situations. A related point is that at any given time policymakers are involved in a number of situations and the choices and actions re one situation will partially influence and be influenced by those others. As a result, the real-world policymaker's task in choosing implementation instruments, and then in employing them, is complicated even more.

The first four parts of this book have provided an analysis of the international political environment within which policymakers operate, a discussion of the steps in policy formulation, an examination of the foundation of capability, and an analysis of the instruments of policy implementation. One point has been evident throughout: policymakers have an extremely difficult job. But things are even more complicated than Parts 1–4 have indicated. In the first place, all policymakers operate within a vortex of domestic influences. International and domestic politics are not wholly separate, as if they occurred in isolated, vacuum-sealed compartments with neither affecting the other. Consequently, policymakers are subject to varying degrees and types of domestic constraints and limitations, and often are not free to choose and act in whatever manner they deem would be most appropriate. In addition, there are a number of policymaking problems that occur with amazing regularity, both intellectual mistakes and difficulties seemingly "inherent" in the "system." These, too, limit effectiveness and are obstacles to formulating and implementing the optimum policy. These various domestic and regularly occurring policymaking limitations and difficulties provide the subject matter for Part 5, to which we now turn.

Part 5

MISTAKES, PROBLEMS, AND CONSTRAINTS

In Parts 1–4 we have analyzed the international political environment within which the policymaker works, the steps in the formulation of policy, the foundations of international influence, and the major instruments of policy implementation. Presumably by now the student is fully aware of the fact that the policymaker's task is awesomely complex. But it is even more difficult than we have so far indicated. There are a number of problems, constraints, and obstacles to optimum policymaking that to this point we have covered only peripherally, if at all. These must be examined in some depth, however, if we are to have a comprehensive realistic analysis. Such policymaking difficulties fall into three basic categories. First, there are a number of intellectual errors that policymakers make with considerable regularity, mistakes that presumably are not inevitable but that nevertheless occur over and over again; these are discussed in Chapter 13. Second, there are a number of pragmatic problems policymakers confront, problems that occur with such frequency that it's almost as if they were "inherent" in international politics; these are analyzed in Chapter 14. Finally, all policymakers are in some degree constrained by a web of domestic pressures; domestic influences provide the subject matter of Chapter 15.

13
Common Intellectual Errors

There are, in international politics, certain kinds of intellectual errors that occur with amazing frequency, certain types of mistakes that policymakers seem to make over and over again. They are: formulating policy on the basis of overly general and abstract concepts, seeking to achieve incompatible objectives, following inconsistent policies, acting on the basis of incomplete and distorted preconceptions, and failing to empathize, to put oneself in the other person's shoes. These intellectual errors presumably are not inevitable, and therefore they "ought" somehow to be avoidable. Despite this, they continue to occur with considerable regularity and to present major obstacles to the formulation and efficient implementation of an optimum policy.

ABSTRACT GENERALIZATION

The first obstacle a policymaker needs to avoid is the formulation of objectives in terms that are too abstract and/or generalized. It is emotionally satisfying, of course, to employ broad concepts and the type of sloganeering that prevails in democratic political campaigns. In the United States it has been popular since World War II to speak in terms of defending "democracy," protecting the "Free World," opposing "communism," supporting "peace," opposing "aggression," opposing "colonialism," and so on.

Unfortunately, this deceptively simple approach has many defects. *In the first place, the concepts are of such a generalized nature that they hide as much as they reveal*. When speaking of defending democracy, for example, how does one define "democracy?" There are any number of definitions but people would be hard put to reach one that was universally acceptable. Even if this could be done, it is highly unlikely that one could find a nation-state in the real world to which it would apply. Even if this should occur, could a policymaker develop a meaningful definition that would apply to all of those states he or she wished to defend? It is doubtful. And beyond this, could policymakers of different governments agree on a precise definition of "democracy" and also agree which countries deserve that appellation? Probably not. The point is that such abstract generalization provides the policymaker with no specifically applicable basis for handling the concrete problems with which he or she must deal daily. The policymaker's world is one of practical specifics, not abstract generalities.

A second basic difficulty with this approach is that it drastically oversimplifies reality, categorizing and compartmentalizing factors of great complexity and obliterating significant distinctions. Formulas become a substitute for thought, and the hard thinking necessary to make discriminating judgments is avoided. This often leads to an extremely rigid situation in which the status quo is seen as permanent. For example, for years after World War II American policymakers perceived all Communists to be basically alike, as interchangeable parts of an expansionist monolithic bloc directed by Moscow. Washington accepted the world's division into two hostile camps as unalterable fact, and sought to develop policies to contain "the other side."[1] Because this was assumed to be a permanent situation, seldom was any thought given to devising policy options that might aid and encourage Communist bloc fragmentation. A policymaker must have the capacity to discern the differences and nuances in and between situations, and the ability to refine his or her policies accordingly. This is nearly impossible if abstract generalizations provide the policy foundation.

A third defect with overabstraction concerns the tendency to include within such concepts a sense of moral imperative.[2] If a policymaker considers the problem before him or her to be primarily an ethical issue it inevitably becomes emotion laden. The practical problem is transformed into a question of "Good" and "Evil," and naturally each party tends to feel that it has

---

[1] In this connection the student would be well-advised to read the famous article proclaiming "Containment" (actually written by George Kennan, Director of the Policy Planning Staff of the State Department, under the initial "X"), "Sources of Soviet Conduct," *Foreign Affairs*, July 1947, pp. 566–582. For an excellent discussion of the question of whether the United States had any real alternative to containment in the immediate post-war world, see Charles Gati, ed., *Caging the Bear: Containment and the Cold War*, Bobbs-Merrill, New York, 1974, Part Two.

[2] For more on the role of ethics see Chapter 2, pp. 33–40. Also pertinent is the discussion of the American Liberal Ideology, Chapter 2, pp. 47–50.

"Right" on its side.[3] When this occurs negotiation and compromise are nearly impossible. How does one negotiate concerning an absolute moral principle? If a policymaker compromises in this situation it is considered a "sellout," or "appeasement." The practical impact of this fact is that a great element of rigidity is introduced into the situation, making resolution of a conflict via mutual agreement extremely difficult.

Example: Anticommunism

The practical results of a policy based on generalized abstraction can be demonstrated by briefly considering some of the implications of one of the major bases for American policy for nearly two decades after World War II, "anticommunism." When American policymakers analyzed the events of the immediate post-war period they perceived a major Communist threat. Developments such as the establishment of Soviet domination in Eastern Europe and the Balkans, the deepening division of Germany and the Berlin Blockade, the coup in Czechoslovakia, the "fall" of China to the Red Chinese (assumed to be controlled by Moscow), the North Korean attack on South Korea (assumed to have been ordered by the Russians), these and many other factors all seemed to point to this conclusion.[4] The situation seemed clear enough: these events were part of an attempt by a monolithic Communist bloc to conquer the world.[5] Gone were the unity and hopes of World War II. In their place were disillusionment, anger, and conflict. Thus it was "obvious" that anticommunism had to be one of the foundations of policy.

This belief had considerable practical impact. It led policymakers to assume that American relations with Russia were totally conflictual.[6] Because of

---

[3]It can be argued that this is not *always* bad. If one believes that there are standards of Right and Wrong, then clearly he or she can say that there have been "good" and "bad" nations, policymakers, actions, and so on. It could further be stated that there are limits to compromise and certain principles *must* be defended if there is to be any civilized order in the world. Thus, perhaps "rigidity" and conflict may be "good" in certain circumstances.

[4]This is not to say that such perceptions were inevitable, however. As is now known, and a more discriminating analysis then might have ascertained, both the Chinese and North Koreans possessed considerable independence of Moscow. Also, the Soviet tactics in Europe could have been viewed as defensive in nature, a means to protect their vulnerable Western approaches. The point is, however, that the American perception was understandable.

[5]It should be pointed out that, to many Americans, this was not only an instance of yet another power-hungry state attempting to conquer its neighbors but also an attack on the very way of life of Westerners by a centrally directed, monolithic, atheistic ideology committed to world revolution.

[6]Particularly useful for this discussion are Hartmann, *The New Age of American Foreign Policy*, Chapters 10–12; Spanier, *American Foreign Policy Since World War II*, Seventh Edition, Chapters 2–6; and Ulam, *The Rivals: America and Russia Since World War II*.

this little effort was expended to determine whether or not there might be common interests (such as the creation of a unified, neutralized Germany). Every issue was a matter of the triumph of Right; there could be no compromises, no agreements with the Devil.

Another effect, since the Soviets were Evil and were presumed to control all Communists, was that American relations with other Communist states also "had to be" adversarial.[7] Thus there was little consideration given to the possibility that various Communist states might have different objectives and that these differences might yield opportunities to exert American influence (let alone the possibility that a degree of cooperation might develop). Instead there was undifferentiating hostility, and this put pressure on all communists to sublimate any potential differences in favor of the common interest of opposing the United States.

The tendency of American policymakers in the first two decades or so after World War II to formulate policy on the basis of abstract generalizations had another significant effect: *it created a kind of reflexive tendency to become involved in conflicts without really investigating to see either if involvement was warranted, or if it was whether less confrontational orientations could be productively employed.* As explained above, Washington saw the world as divided into two totally separate and wholly hostile camps, the "Free World" and the Communists, and the Communist camp was perceived as "inherently" aggressive. Furthermore, history had "proved" that if aggression was not halted at once the states surrounding the aggressee would fall like a row of dominoes.[8] Therefore, active opposition to the Communists was essential to preserve freedom. In 1947 President Truman added to this series of general concepts when in requesting Congress to provide emergency economic and military aid for Greece and Turkey he proclaimed what later became known as the Truman Doctrine. Mr. Truman stated that the "peoples of a number of countries have recently had totalitarian regimes forced upon them against their will." The United States should help free people "maintain their free institutions and their national integrity against aggressive movements that seek to im-

---

[7]An interesting exception occurred, however, with respect to Yugoslavia. The one Balkan state in the Communist bloc not "liberated" by the Red Army, she refused to accept Soviet dictation. In 1948 Yugoslavia broke with Moscow (without renouncing communism) and American policymakers responded with economic and military assistance. In this case Washington *was* able to discern the advantages of helping an anti-Russian Communist state. One should note the significant situational difference here between Communist states under tight Soviet control and Yugoslavia, which was outside Moscow's sphere. Whereas American policymakers made some distinctions in the Yugoslavian case, they assumed that all states within the Soviet bloc were unreachable (and it was assumed that all other Communists *were within this bloc*).

[8]For more on the domino theory see Chapter 4, pp. 103–105.

pose upon them totalitarian regimes." Who were these "free people?" All non-Communists, of course. And what is the "aggressive movement" that seeks to impose on them "totalitarian regimes?" International communism directed from Moscow.

The consequences of policies based on such abstract generalizations were never thought out in detail because there was no perceived need to do so; everything was "obvious." Thus, as we noted earlier, formulas became a substitute for thought, nuances and situational differences were ignored, and rigid, reflexive actions became commonplace. From one administration to another the United States chose to become involved in a myriad of conflicts to the end of containing the Communists (who, Washington assumed, were the cause of the problem), to defend the Free World and its people against aggression. Unable to carefully analyze each situation in terms of its own unique circumstances (indeed, oblivious of the need to do so), the United States laid down commitments and principles that eventually led to an "inevitable" involvement in the Vietnam war.[9] When broad, all-encompassing generalizations are used one is not equipped to make discriminating judgments, and if the generalizations are of such a nature as to require involvement and commitment (and one does not ignore his or her own generalizations) such will occur willy-nilly, regardless of situational peculiarities and whether other types of orientations would be more productive.

It is evident that the degree to which these particular abstract generalizations provide the operational rationale for American policy has somewhat diminished; anticommunism in its various manifestations is still important, but it no longer is quite as pervasive and overarching as it once was. Most policymakers are opposed to communism in principle and believe that many conflicts exist, but they tend to be rather pragmatic in their analysis of the concrete problems of the day. They have witnessed the fragmentation of the Communist bloc and the bitter Sino-Soviet dispute, and realize that monolithic communism does not exist (and never did). They have seen that it is possible for common interests to exist between potential adversaries; the wide range of agreements coming from the May 1972 Summit Meetings provided ample evidence of this.[10] Generally speaking one can say that most policymakers have

---

[9]This analysis owes a considerable debt to the ideas of Frederick Hartmann. See both *The New Age of American Foreign Policy*, pp. 126ff, and *The Relations of Nations*, Fifth Edition, pp. 427–430.

[10]The Soviet-American meetings of May 22–29, 1972 yielded a broad range of bilateral agreements in various technical and scientific spheres, a series of economic agreements designed to invigorate trade and reform the entire pattern of US-Soviet economic relationships, two agreements partially limiting strategic weapons, and agreement on twelve basic principles of conduct for future actions.

learned that all states have a variety of objectives, and although some of these are in conflict, some are common or complementary.[11]

INCOMPATIBLE OBJECTIVES AND INCONSISTENT POLICIES

The problems of overabstraction and overgeneralization are often tied in with two other common errors, namely, formulating objectives that are incompatible with each other and following inconsistent policies. Unfortunately, it is often the case that to the extent one objective is achievable another is not. The crippling effect that the simultaneous pursuance of incompatible objectives can have on policy is magnified when the objectives are formulated on a generalized, abstract basis. Inconsistency in policy itself is often the result of trying to achieve incompatible objectives.

Before examining a case in which all of these elements were present, it should be pointed out that there have been numerous instances in which policymakers have sought to achieve or protect very concrete objectives that were incompatible. In these kinds of situations even if policy is consistent it cannot be more than partially successful because the very accomplishment of certain goals creates conditions that prevent the accomplishment of others. Policymakers (usually) are not stupid, and it usually is not evident during the formulation process that the eventual incompatibility will exist. Instead, what generally happens is that judgments concerning the projected impact of the achievement of certain objectives are faulty, policymakers anticipating either that certain consequences will eventuate which do not, or expecting that certain developments will not occur that eventually do.

Example: The Adenauer Case

A good example of trying to achieve incompatible concrete objectives was provided by West Germany's first chancellor, Dr. Konrad Adenauer. When World War II ended Germany lay in utter devastation. She was temporarily divided into four military occupation zones, the United States, Britain and France sharing what later became West Germany, the Soviet Union occupying what became East Germany. In addition, vast territories historically German came under direct Polish and/or Russian administration, and have remained outside the "Fatherland" to this day.

In 1949 an all-West German government was created and Dr. Adenauer was elected chancellor. A strong nationalist, he believed that reunification was an objective of fundamental importance. He also recognized the absolute necessity of rebuilding his country politically and economically however, and felt

[11]See also Chapter 2, pp. 62–64.

that this had to occur first. He knew outside assistance was necessary and shared American perceptions of the Soviet threat; thus complete support of the United States seemed the logical orientation to adopt, so he did. Much economic assistance was received, particularly through the Marshall Plan, and the economy boomed.[12] With American blessings a limited rearmament was undertaken and West Germany joined NATO in 1955.

Dr. Adenauer also believed, however, that the alliance with the West could help achieve the fundamental objective of the restoration of territorial integrity, that is, German reunification. His idea was that when Russian policymakers saw what became known as a "position of strength," the combined power of the United States and Western Europe, they could be induced to make concessions that would allow progress toward reunification. In his view the West had the capability to build a position of strength which the Soviets simply could not match. Once such a situation developed, because of their relative inferiority (plus what Adenauer believed would also develop, namely, domestic economic problems and/or increased friction with China) the Soviets would be responsive to the intelligent exercise of power and be willing to evacuate their exposed position in East Germany. Thus, as Adenauer saw things, alignment with the West would help bring about a reunified Germany.[13]

But Adenauer was in error. Given Soviet perceptions and policies, that which the German leader believed necessary to achieve recovery and protection would, if accomplished, lead to conditions precluding reunification. Look at the situation from Moscow's perspective. The Soviets, above all, would have preferred a united Germany in their bloc. This however, was most unlikely. Failing such a situation their objective most certainly would be to hold East Germany and keep West Germany unarmed. A powerful, rearmed Western-oriented Germany, given the history of twentieth-century German-Russian relations, could be perceived as nothing but a threat in the Kremlin. Adenauer's belief that a Western alignment would induce Russian concessions ignored the Soviet fear of possible German desires for revenge. The simple geographical fact that now there would be German troops facing Russian troops on German territory, and that no free German regime was willing to acquiesce in the permanent occupation and subjugation of fellow Germans and their lands, inevitably heightened tension. Furthermore, Moscow believed that its military strength was sufficient to deter any military attack; control of this area would provide geographical defense-in-depth against any assault. Thus once the Federal Republic was rearmed and aligned with the West, the Soviets decided to dig in permanently. Adenauer's objectives of recovery and protection via an

---

[12]From the vast devastation of World War II West Germany has risen to become one of the four or five most economically powerful nations in the world. See Tables 7 to 10, Chapter 7.

[13]See Hartmann, *Germany Between East and West: The Reunification Problem*, p. 159.

alignment with the West were simply incompatible with reunification. *The closer he came to achieving the one, the less chance he had of achieving the other.*

Example: The 1956 Suez Crisis

Now let's turn to a case in which abstract overgeneralization, inconsistent policies, and incompatible objectives were all apparent: the 1956 Suez Crisis. Before analyzing the crisis *per se* some background information would be helpful. With the exception of Soviet pressure on Turkey and Iran at the end of World War II, until the mid-1950s the Middle East had been an area characterized by disputes that were largely extraneous to the Cold War. In 1955, however, Turkey, Iraq, and Great Britain signed military agreements that eventually culminated in the Baghdad Pact, thus "filling" the West's alliance gap between NATO and SEATO.[14] This development, plus a massive Israeli raid against the Egyptian-controlled Gaza Strip on February 28, impelled Egypt's President Nasser to intensify his existing quest for military assistance. Unable to obtain the types and quantities of arms he wanted from the West on terms he considered to be acceptable, he turned to Communist sources. On September 27, 1955 he announced the signing of an arms agreement with Czechoslovakia, irreparably shattering the Western arms monopoly and allowing the Russians to leapfrog the Baghdad Pact into the heart of the Arab world. In one bold stroke Nasser did more to break Arab dependence on the West than had any Arab leader in history.[15]

The United States, which had been on reasonably good terms with Nasser since the Free Officers overthrow of King Farouk in 1952, sought to counter further Soviet penetration and in December of 1955 announced it would help Egypt finance the construction of a High Dam at Aswan, a project of immense political, economic, and psychological importance.[16] Great Britain and the World Bank also made offers to participate in the financing, but their offers were contingent upon Washington's.

Negotiations about the precise conditions of the American loan dragged on through early 1956. True to his orientation of participatory nonalignment, Nasser continued to deal with any and all who would help him irrespective of

---

[14]Iran and Pakistan also became members, and the United States a very interested observer and unofficial participant.

[15]An American diplomat said, "If Nasser ran for President in Lebanon, Syria or Jordan today, he would be elected unanimously." Quoted in Wilton Wynn, *Nasser of Egypt: The Search for Dignity*, Arlington Books, Cambridge, 1959, p. 120.

[16]In its announcement, the U. S. Department of State used the phrase "inestimable importance." See U. S., Department of State, *American Foreign Policy, 1950–1955: Basic Documents*, Vol. II, p. 2230.

their problems with each other. In May he granted diplomatic recognition to Communist China, at that time the bogeyman of the United States, and made it quite clear that he was dickering for more aid from the Russians, including assistance in financing the High Dam. The American Secretary of State, John Foster Dulles, deeply resented the fact that Nasser was negotiating with Moscow, feeling that this playing of East against West really amounted to no more than simple blackmail. On July 17, 1956 Nasser publicly announced that Egypt would accept the American offer, but on July 19 Mr. Dulles brusquely withdrew it.[17] On the next day the British and the World Bank followed suit.

Secretary Dulles was correct in his assumption that the Soviets would not immediately move in to pick up the tab (although they did a couple of years later), but he made a gross miscalculation in not anticipating a strong reaction from Nasser. On July 26, 1956 Nasser nationalized the Universal Suez Maritime Canal Company, and the Suez crisis proper began.

Washington immediately received a cable from British Prime Minister Eden stating that Britain would not allow Nasser to succeed and would use force to "bring Nasser to his senses" if necessary.[18] Now America's generalized abstract objectives made it extremely difficult, because some indicated one line of policy and some another. Policymakers naturally wanted to support those countries who supported or furthered the achievement of the underlying policy principles, and oppose those who opposed or hindered the achievement of said principles. The United States was anti-Communist, pro democracy, and pro West (i.e., Free World), but also prointernational law, antimilitary aggression, and anticolonial. Britain was clearly anti-Communist, democratic, and a bastion of the Free World, but she was an ex-colonial power considering violating international law via military aggression. To the extent that Washington tried to support one set of principles, it inevitably could not support the other. As long as a final decision could be avoided this inherent inconsistency might not cause trouble. But suppose a full-scale showdown should occur; what standards could policymakers use to determine which abstractions were most worthy of support, and what would this mean in terms of specific policies?

With no coherent guidelines to follow Washington erratically sought a middle course, hoping to dissuade the British from any type of aggressive action, trying to develop a plan for international control of the canal, and yet making it clear that it did not agree with Nasser's action.[19]

---

[17]An interesting discussion may be found in Herman Finer, *Dulles Over Suez: The Theory and Practice of His Diplomacy*, Quadrangle Books, Chicago, 1964, pp. 47–48.

[18]For complete text see Anthony Eden, *Memoirs: Full Circle*, Houghton Mifflin, Boston, 1960, pp. 476–477.

[19]In fact, the American Ambassador to Egypt, Henry Byroade, "was instructed . . . to make clear to Nasser some possible consequences of his act of force." Finer, p. 89.

An international conference was called. Nasser said he would not attend since the conclusion was foreordained and no real negotiations would occur.[20] The result of the conference was a plan for international control of the canal by a nonpolitical board. This was immediately rejected by Nasser, who considered it to be collective colonialism. A mission to convince him to consider otherwise ended in failure.[21]

Dulles developed another plan for international control, the Suez Canal Users Association. This was designed to create an international organization of primary countries using the canal which would "insulate" the canal from the politics of "any one country" (i. e., Egypt). Mr. Eden had been leery of this approach, but gave in to the importuning of Dulles and officially announced it on September 12, 1956. The very next day Dulles said the United States did not plan to shoot its way through, thus cutting the rug out from under him.[22] Naturally Egypt did not accept SCUA, and said its implementation would mean war.

The United States, caught in the web of its contradictory generalizations, continued to flounder erratically as the scene shifted to the United Nations Security Council. Although a set of six principles were agreed upon, they were so ambiguous that each party could "interpret" them to its own satisfaction.[23] The British and French had made up their mind that force would be necessary, and began to implement a plan for a collusive action with the Israelis. On October 29 the Israelis struck, and on October 31 the British and French joined in.

American policymakers were now in a very difficult situation, because the showdown had come. The prodemocracy, anti-Communist, antineutral, and pro "Free World" principles indicated that they should at least adopt a policy of neutrality, and certainly should not oppose the attack. But they were also prointernational law, antiaggression, and anticolonial. Obviously these abstractions dictated opposition to the attack.

A decision had to be made, however, and Washington opted for the prointernational law principles and the like, pressing the case with evangelical fervor.[24] It led the fight for adoption of a cease-fire and withdrawal resolution by

[20]See Egypt, Ministry for Foreign Affairs, *White Paper on the Nationalization of the Suez Maritime Canal Company*, August 12, 1956.

[21]Given his political gains from the nationalization, and the obvious losses that such a plan would entail, it is hard to see how anyone could have expected him to do anything different. See John C. Campbell, *Defense of the Middle East: Problems of American Policy*, Second Edition, Praeger, New York, 1960, p. 101.

[22]Eden was extremely bitter. See Eden, pp. 539–540.

[23]For text, see U. N. Security Council, *Official Records, Supplement for October, November and December, 1956*, Document S/3671, pp. 19–20.

[24]See Noble Frankland, ed., *Documents on International Affairs, 1956*, Royal Institute of International Affairs, London, 1959, p. 269; U. N. General Assembly, *Official Records*, First Emergency Special Session, Plenary Meetings, pp. 10–12; Beal, p. 288; Murphy, p. 381.

the General Assembly, and this was followed by the creation of the United Nations Emergency Force. Under intense pressure from Washington and amid threats of rocket warfare by the Soviets to "crush the aggressors," the British agreed to a cease-fire on November 6.[25] The French and Israelis reluctantly concurred and the worst was over.

Seldom is total success possible in international politics, and when dealing with a situation as multifaceted as the Suez crisis policymakers always are compelled to choose from a variety of options the consequences of which inevitably would be mixed. Because of the situational complexity any policy the United States adopted at Suez would have involved some element of risk and produced less than perfect results. Nevertheless, had American policymakers formulated policy in accordance with the procedures outlined in Part 2, made prudent choices at each point, and then chosen the most appropriate combination of implementation instruments and used them wisely, they would have maximized the chances of achieving or protecting certain limited objectives at minimal cost. At the same time they would have avoided activities that were detrimental to middle-range political and prestige goals. Instead, they managed to accomplish very little, not really convincing Arab nationalists that there was a genuine desire to establish a relationship of limited cooperation, and bitterly antagonizing their closest NATO allies and Israel. At Suez the generalized principles were incompatible, there were no criteria on the basis of which one could make a rational selection, and the resulting inconsistency achieved a high degree of alienation on all fronts. Policymakers simply had no sense of direction, operating much like ships without rudders.

PRECONCEPTIONS

One of the most dangerous pitfalls a policymaker must avoid is distortion due to preconception. To put it somewhat differently, he or she must be very careful to avoid prejudgments based on preconceived ideas about the sources of information one would believe, its interpretation, about the intention and objectives of various parties, their capabilities, even about the identification of who is involved and what the issues may be.

Examples of misperception due to preconceived ideas are legion. John Stoessinger, in his excellent book, *Nations in Darkness: China, Russia, and America*, gives us a detailed analysis of several flagrant examples. One of the most interesting examples concerns the American view of Red China and Peking's view of Washington during the Korean War.[26] Given the self-image

---

[25]Many, including top United States officials, were surprised at the British action. See Murphy, p. 391.

[26]John G. Stoessinger, *Nations in Darkness: China, Russia, and America*, Chapter 4.

each nation had, that is, the American view that it was the defender of the Free World, the nation destined to protect the world against the scourge of communism, and the Chinese view that Peking was the proper and natural leader of all Asia and a leading Communist power, and given the fact that each side viewed the very existence of the other system as a threat to itself, it was inevitable that each would misperceive the objectives of the other. This, indeed, was precisely what occurred.

The Chinese, assuming that the United States was inherently hostile and aggressively imperialistic toward all Communist states, assumed that the objectives of the United States included not only the protection of the hated Nationalist regime on Formosa (Taiwan) and the rehabilitation and rearming of China's archenemy Japan, but also preparation for an invasion of China. Thus all assurances to the contrary were dismissed out of hand. The United States, assuming the People's Republic of China to be part of a monolithic Soviet directed Communist bloc whose basic objective was the eventual domination of the world, assumed that the attack on South Korea by the North Koreans, and the later entrance into the war by "volunteers" from the People's Republic of China, were simply a part of this overall program. Therefore, Washington believed that Peking's professions of concern about American intentions were misunderstandings at best, and more likely were fabrications. As Stoessinger points out, these misperceptions influenced the policy alternatives chosen for implementation.

Preconception may lead to either a refusal to consider certain information that does not conform to one's preconceived mental images, or to an "interpretation" that distorts the information to make it fit. To the extent that the mental image one possesses is "closed," unable to adjust to new or conflicting information, one will have a distorted view of reality as conditions change. In the months preceding the outbreak of World War I the French General Staff adopted Plan 17, the strategic plan they expected to follow in case of war.[27] It envisaged the following scenario: if hostilities occurred they would be initiated by Germany. The Germans would attack frontally, avoiding any right-wing enveloping movements that would massively violate Belgian neutrality. In such circumstances France would respond by seizing the initiative, offensively attacking the onrushing German armies in the most flexible manner possible, finding and then hitting their weakest points.

Because of this preconception concerning what the Germans would and would not do, the French saw no need to develop a defensive strategy; why plan for defense when one is going to seize the offense? Consequently, nearly two-thirds of the Franco-Belgian frontier was left undefended. Over a period

---

[27]Useful and succinct is Barbara Tuchman, *The Guns of August*, Dell, New York, 1962, pp. 59–62, on which the following is based.

of years French intelligence had passed many signals to the General Staff indicating that a right-wing envelopment was exactly what Germany *would* do. Indeed, an officer of the German General Staff several years earlier had betrayed his country and specifically said this was what was planned; furthermore, corroborating documentation was provided. And the patterns of the Germans' use and training of reserve forces provided further substantiation. But the General Staff dismissed such evidence, rejecting all information that did not fit the preconception. Only later, when the Germans stormed through Belgium, would they admit their mistake.

Example: 1958 Lebanon Crisis, Early Stages

Let's examine another case in a little more depth: the early stages of the 1958 Lebanese crisis. First, a little background. Following the Suez crisis relations between the United States and Egypt ranged from cool to antagonistic. In February 1958 Egypt and Syria merged into the United Arab Republic (UAR). As indicated many times, the United States had been hostile to President Nasser of Egypt because of the belief that he was willingly or unwittingly a tool of the Communists. Washington's conception of the significance of Nasser's dedicated pan-Arabism was that he intended to be the leader of a unified Arab world, and he was actively pursuing this goal with a policy that was designed to create instability and perhaps even rebellion throughout the area. Therefore, American policymakers assumed that much if not all of the unrest in the Middle East was due to the active instigation of Nasser in the furtherance of his own particular objectives. Naturally, this being the preconception, it was assumed that the formation of the United Arab Republic was part and parcel of his plan.

In point of fact, the Syrians had taken the initiative in the formation of the UAR and Nasser had been very cool to the idea. Early in the negotiations he laid down a number of highly restrictive conditions for his assent, conditions of such a demanding nature that it seemed very unlikely the Syrians would accept. Somewhat surprisingly they did, however, and soon thereafter the merger was consummated.[28] Because of its relatively closed image, Washington peremptorily dismissed the possibility that Nasser was the pursued and not the pursuer, that the Syrians had taken the initiative and come to him.

Shortly after the UAR was formed disturbances erupted in Lebanon, a country which was approximately half Muslim and half Christian and split by loyalties to the West and to its Arab brothers. Throughout late 1957 and early 1958 there had been a series of civil disturbances that often found the factions divided along religious lines. When President Chamoun, a Christian, became

[28]See Chapter 5, pp. 125–126.

the only Arab leader to formally accept the Eisenhower Doctrine, for example, he was generally supported by the Christians but opposed by the Muslims.[29] It also was clear that the mid-1957 elections had been rigged, resulting in a sweeping victory for the Christian government.

The announcement of the formation of the UAR had considerable impact, and pan-Arabist feeling was evident in the Muslim community. Chamoun added fuel to the fire by giving indications that he was going to have the country's Covenant (Constitution) amended to allow him to succeed himself. The assassination of an antigovernment newspaper editor provided the spark that brought about a full-fledged crisis, and soon armed rebellion was in full swing.

The Western reaction, given its preconception of Nasser, was swift, horrified, and one-sided. It was automatically assumed that Nasser and the Communists were causing the problem. On May 13, 1958 Lebanon's foreign minister, Charles Malik, specifically accused the UAR of instigating the rebellion. Nasser charged that the Lebanese rulers had to create this impression so they could ask for Western assistance to maintain their internal political position. The United States contributed to the unrest on May 20 by emphasizing that there was a provision of the Eisenhower Doctrine which provided that the independence of the Middle Eastern countries was *vital* to the peace and national interests of the United States. Another basic clause provided for U. S. military assistance against overt armed attack by a nation controlled by international communism if the authorities requested this assistance, a "request" that could be easily arranged. This American reaction, resulting from its preconception of Nasser, reciprocally increased Nasser's suspicions that it was a pretext for a possible invasion.

Lebanon then took the issue to the U. N. Security Council charging that the UAR was intervening in Lebanon's internal affairs. The United States echoed this charge. The fact is that there was no substantial *hard* evidence at this point to support this conclusion. On the contrary, many sources indicated that this was *not* the case but American policymakers assumed that Nasser "must" be behind the problem and convinced themselves that *their* sources were the more trustworthy.[30]

The Swedish representative, Gunnar Jarring, developed the concept which the Security Council adopted. A United Nations Observer Group (UNOGIL) was created to go to Lebanon and report on the charges of infiltra-

---

[29]For more on the Eisenhower Doctrine see pp. 374–376.

[30]One is reminded of events in the fall of 1950 in the Korean War. As U. N. forces under the command of General Douglas MacArthur penetrated far into North Korea and approached the Chinese border, the Communist Chinese and many neutral nations (especially India) warned that Peking would not tolerate the approach of U. N. forces to the frontier. MacArthur, however, said his sources indicated otherwise and kept on. Shortly thereafter Chinese "volunteers" entered the war.

tion of personnel and equipment. The United States was pleased with this since it assumed that the report would validate Washington's position. What actually happened, however, was that UNOGIL determined that the affair was primarily an internal dispute. The report minimized outside support for the rebellion, stating that the vast majority of those involved in the fighting were Lebanese. A second UNOGIL report had basically the same import. American information was incorrect.

Changing one's image is difficult. It is difficult to admit one has been wrong, and the problem is compounded by the fact that policymakers often have an investment in being right once they are on the public record. In such a case contrary information may not be wanted because it is a threat. To President Eisenhower's credit, however, he began to accept the fact that this was primarily a domestic power struggle; he began to recognize that his preconceptions had prevented him from accurately assessing the situation.[31]

Example: Stalin and the German Attack

But sometimes a person's preconceptions are so strong that even when confronted with overwhelming contrary evidence he won't budge. In such cases, instead of analyzing the specifics in order to figure out what is happening one simply dismisses or "interprets" all information contrary to the preconception in a manner that supports the preexisting view. Joseph Stalin's refusal to alter his belief that the Nazis would not attack the U. S. S. R. in the summer of 1941 provides a truly incredible example of this phenomenon.

As we have mentioned on several earlier occasions, in September 1939 the U. S. S. R. and Nazi Germany signed a Nonaggression Pact.[32] Stalin, suspicious of the capitalist West and persuaded by Hitler that cooperation would allow both Germany and Russia to achieve certain territorial objectives, concluded this agreement even though he had no illusions about the Nazi's ultimate objectives. Stalin knew the agreement would not solve the German problem, but it would allow the Soviets time to prepare so that when the attack eventually came conditions would be as favorable as possible.

In late 1940 and early 1941 Stalin rigidly clung to the belief that no attack was imminent. Prior to such an operation, he believed, the Germans would make a number of demands and create certain pretexts, as they had done elsewhere. Moreover, Germany was too shrewd to again make the mistake of becoming involved in a two-front war. Therefore, Hitler would not move against Russia until the British had been defeated (or maybe not at all, if the capitalists exhausted themselves against each other). Because of these views Stalin felt no

[31]See Ralph K. White, *Nobody Wanted War: Misperception in Vietnam and Other Wars*, Doubleday, New York, 1968 for a fascinating example of what he called Washington's "selective inattention" to events that failed to fit its "black-and-white" picture in the Vietnam conflict.

[32]See especially Chapter 6, pp. 143–146, and Chapter 12, pp. 327–328.

urgency. Plans to bring the army up to levels sufficient to meet the Germans were undertaken, but they were not expected to be completed before early 1942, and the timetable for completing the shiftover of Soviet industry to war production (adopted June 6, 1941) was not scheduled for completion until the end of 1942. Individuals who presented information contrary to Stalin's preconceptions were ignored or reprimanded, and in some cases even were dismissed as *provocateurs*. And in order not to provoke the Germans into commencing hostilities Stalin bent over backwards to be accomodating, in early 1941 increasing Soviet deliveries of the supply shipments already agreed on, closing the diplomatic missions of countries occupied by the Germans, etc. On June 22, 1941 Germany initiated Operation Barbarossa, the attack on the Soviet Union.

It is a generally accepted fact that the U. S. S. R. was probably the most well-informed, highly warned nation in history. Yet Stalin was taken completely by surprise. Some of this can be explained by ideological factors, by his distrust of all capitalists. On several different occasions the British warned Stalin of the impending attack, in early and mid-June even providing information on the identity, characteristics, quantity, and location of the German forces to be used in the attack; the British even went so far as to make predictions of the date.[33] The United States, too, warned the Russians more than once. But Stalin believed the capitalists wanted to draw the Soviets into a war with Germany, and he rejected their warnings out of hand.

What is less understandable is the fact that Stalin ignored the seemingly "obvious" implications of numerous factual developments and an encyclopedic mass of warnings from his own foreign policy, military, and intelligence organizations. We cannot do more than present a representative sampling, but it will suffice to make the point.[34]

1. The NKGB, the Soviet intelligence agency, in June 1940 reported the Germans were developing data on rail capabilities to move troops from west to east; on March 25, 1941 it compiled a special report disclosing the Nazis had moved 120 divisions toward the Soviet border; on April 10 it reported that Hitler had told Prince Paul of Yugoslavia Germany would take action against Russia by the end of June; on June 6 it estimated that Germany had concentrated four million men on the Soviet frontier; and on June 11 it reported the German Embassy in Moscow was preparing to evacuate.

---

[33]Particularly significant was a June 10 meeting between British Under-Secretary Sir Alexander Cadogan and the Soviet Ambassador to Britain, Ivan Maisky. See Barton Whaley, *Codeword Barbarossa*, MIT Press, Cambridge, Mass., 1973, pp. 107–108.

[34]There are several sources of value in this regard. For the reader's convenience we have chosen illustrations all of which can be found in one work: Harrison E. Salisbury, *The 900 Days: The Siege of Leningrad*, Avon, New York, 1970, Chs. 6–7.

2. Soviet defense and military officials also forwarded significant information. In February 1941 the naval commissariat reported German military specialists were arriving in Bulgaria. By March the daily bulletins of the General Staff carried items about the almost daily German reconnaissance flights over the Baltic; in April the Soviet military attaché in France specifically warned that Germany planned to attack in late May, later advising the attack had been delayed a month because of bad weather; and about June 1 the naval attaché in Berlin advised Admiral Kuznetsov in Moscow that the Germans would attack about June 20-22!

3. Political-diplomatic officials told the same story. In February the Embassy in Berlin reported more and more items in the German press accusing the Soviets of military preparations; the same kinds of stories had preceded the attacks on Poland and Czechoslovakia. German overflights of Soviet territory increased, and on April 22 the Foreign Commissariat protested, claiming there were 80 overflights from March 28 to April 18 alone. In May the Embassy in Berlin reported that the Germans were almost ready and an attack on Russia should be expected at any moment.

4. Finally, the Soviets had a master spy, Richard Sorge, a German Communist. As early as November 1940 he reported German plans for an eastern offensive; on March 5, 1941 he sent Moscow a microfilm of a telegram from Ribbentrop to the German Ambassador in Tokyo which gave the date of the attack as mid-June; and in mid-June he sent Moscow a telegram specifically stating that nine armies of ten divisions would attack on June 22.

It's incredible isn't it? Stalin still was caught by surprise.

Preconceptions are obstacles to effective policymaking much more often than many people realize, indeed, more than seems to "make sense." Our examples covered a wide spectrum of situations and time periods, involved French, American, Chinese, and Soviet policymakers, represented different political systems and ideologies, etc., all to the end of illustrating how widespread this phenomenon is. In each of the cases individuals in important policymaking positions did not carefully investigate the situation in question to discover the answers, because (they believed) they already "knew" them. Sources and types of information were believed or not believed, other parties' objectives, policy orientations and implementation patterns were ascertained, and policy choices were made accordingly, on the basis of preconceptions.

It is important to realize how pervasive this phenomenon is, and how much of an obstacle to effective policymaking it constitutes. Policymakers, in fact, act on the basis of what they believe, irrespective of the sources of their beliefs or the degree to which said beliefs correspond to "reality." When analyzing a given situation, therefore, it is incumbent on the investigator not to assume that rationality will govern but instead investigate to find out. If strongly held preconceptions indeed are prevalent, whether they are accurate or not they will by highly significant in actually determining policymaker choices.

FAILURE TO EMPATHIZE

Another problem develops if the policymaker sees things only in terms of his or her own perspective, if he or she does not empathize and put himself or herself in the other person's shoes. It is absolutely necessary when attempting to "understand" a problem that one try and see it from the point of view of each of the parties.[35] One must analyze the situation as *they* would in light of *their* perceptions. This requires the development of what has been called "tough-minded empathy;" one must see things from the other person's perspective but also have the strength to independently evaluate that point of view.[36]

This seems to be an obvious point, but how often in practice do people really empathize? When in 1979 American policymakers were trying to determine whether or not to continue work toward testing and deploying a new, invulnerable MIRVed mobile missile system so as to strengthen U. S. deterrent capability, did they strive to see how threatening this would *have* to be to the Soviets? When in the mid- and late 1970s the Kremlin provided aid to the MPLA in Angola, the government of Ethiopia, and the new regime in Afghanistan, did Soviet policymakers really try to see how this would *inevitably* be perceived in Washington? When Vietnam signed a Friendship Treaty with Moscow in late 1978 and then invaded China's ally Kampuchea (Cambodia), did its policymakers put themselves in Peking's shoes to anticipate what the PRC's reaction would be? Did President Carter empathize with the Russians in early 1977, criticizing them for alleged human rights violations then sending Secretary of State Vance to the Soviets with strategic arms control proposals that were wholly unacceptable in the first place? Did the new Communist government of Russia empathize with Germany during their 1917–1918 negotiations for a separate peace treaty when the Bolsheviks refused to conceal their determination to bring about the German government's overthrow as soon as possible?

Example: The Eisenhower Doctrine

The failure to empathize can lead to extremely harmful policies. Let's take an example, the Eisenhower Doctrine of 1957. The Suez crisis had effectively destroyed British and French influence in the Middle East. Viewing the world

---

[35]Such "understanding" implies nothing in the way of agreement or disagreement.

[36]Ralph K. White, *Nobody Wanted War: Misperception in Vietnam and Other Wars*, Doubleday, New York, 1968, pp. 32–33.

through the Cold War prism of containing the Communist bloc, American policymakers were distressed. The Middle East was an important region in this struggle and now the ramparts of the West had been breached. This left a power vacuum, at least in terms of non-Middle Eastern states. It was believed that it was inevitable that someone would fill this vacuum; if the West did not do it the Communists would. Washington's response was the Eisenhower Doctrine.

The wheels were officially set in motion on January 5, 1957 in a Presidential message to Congress. Stating that it was essential that the United States manifest through the joint action of Congress and the President its determination to assist nations desiring that assistance, the President requested authorization to provide military assistance, including the use of American armed forces, to secure and protect the territorial integrity and political independence of nations requesting such aid. What would be the purpose of this aid? To protect the asking nation "against overt armed aggression from any nation controlled by International Communism."[37]

American policymakers felt that the situation was critical and wanted Moscow to know that they would fight if necessary. Secretary of State Dulles indicated that unless the President's proposal was passed immediately the chances of war would be greater than they had been at the time of the Berlin airlift; any major delay in Congressional action would mean that the area would "be in a short time dominated by international communism."[38] With this as the context Congress quickly passed the President's proposal and the Eisenhower Doctrine was born.

Now, just suppose you were an Arab. It is true that there had just been an overt armed attack against an Arab country, but by whom? Certainly not a nation controlled by international communism. The attack had been by Great Britain, France, and Israel, and the Soviet Union had been one of the strongest political defenders of Egypt and, along with the United States, had led the United Nations effort to condemn the aggressors. From the Arab point of view, nothing could have been more remote from their experience, not only in the Suez crisis but throughout their history, than the possibility of an overt armed attack by a nation controlled by international communism.[39]

[37]U. S. Department of State, *U. S. Policy in the Middle East, September 1956–June 1957: Documents*, p. 20.

[38]U. S., House of Representatives, Committee on Foreign Affairs, *Hearings on H. J. Res. 117, A Joint Resolution to Authorize the President to Undertake Economic and Military Cooperation with Nations in the General Area of the Middle East in Order to Assist in the Strengthening and Defense of Their Independence*, 85th Cong., 1st Sess., 1957, p. 34.

[39]Mohammed Heikal, one of Nasser's most influential and trusted advisers, put it this way: "It has seen imaginary Russian plans of aggression even before they take shape but has completely failed to see the sinister plans of Britain, France and Israel, which are not based on conjecture but have actually taken the shape of bloodshed, devastation and arson." *New York Times*, January 10, 1957, p. 7.

The Arabs thus felt that the Eisenhower Doctrine "had" to be an attempt by the United States to fill the void left by the departure of the British and French via the use of American armed forces. After all it is not too difficult to arrange a call for military assistance. And since no nation in the Middle East could conceivably be considered controlled by international communism, outside perhaps of Syria if one were to stretch rationality all out of proportion, it also looked like a direct thrust at those Arab nations who were neutral or somewhat left of neutral, and a possible warning that American military forces might be used against them. It looked like a naked exercise of power.[40]

Example: European Leaders and World War I

The American response to the perceived consequences of Suez can be aptly characterized as monumentally inappropriate; the failure to empathize led to policies that did much to eliminate whatever the potential for better relations that had been created by the opposition to the invasion. If the policymakers of more than one of the situational parties are unable to empathize the difficulties are compounded. This seems to have been the case among European leaders in the last days before World War I.[41]

In the wake of the formation and consolidation of the Triple Entente (with the Anglo-French Entente of 1904 and the Anglo-Russian Entente of 1907) Europe went through a series of crises in which the states of the Triple Entente were arrayed against the Triple Alliance of Austria-Hungary, Germany, and Italy. Major hostilities were only narrowly averted several times as policymakers confronted each other in a wide range of potentially war-producing situations. Although none of the parties was seeking war, each recognized it might occur and prepared accordingly. No one could be sure that policymakers would continue to be able to prevent a major conflict. It was in this volatile setting that on June 28, 1914 a Serbian nationalist assassinated the heir apparent to the throne of the Austro-Hungarian Empire, the Archduke Franz Ferdinand.

In the aftermath of the assassination, as the Austrians considered what their response should be, Germany's ruler, Kaiser Wilhelm II, assured Austria of Germany's full support no matter what the action undertaken. Thus encouraged, desirous both of territorial gain and maintaining imperial prestige, on July 23 Austria-Hungary presented the Serbian government with an ultimatum, an ultimatum with demands so harsh that to have accepted them would

---

[40]The only Arab state to formally accept the Eisenhower Doctrine was Lebanon. However, Jordan, although never formally accepting it, did not hesitate to invoke its protection in the 1957 crisis. See Chapter 10, pp. 269–270, for further discussion.

[41]Stoessinger, *Why Nations Go To War*, Second Edition, Chapter 1, is useful and succinct.

have virtually destroyed Serbian sovereignty. When the expected occurred and the ultimatum was rejected Austria-Hungary made ready for war. On July 28 war was officially declared and the next day hostilities commenced.

Meanwhile, on July 25 Russia, as always concerned about Austrian efforts in the Balkans, decided it would go to war if Serbia was attacked. Consequently, once Austrian-Serbian hostilities commenced Russia ordered a general mobilization. Kaiser Wilhelm, who until now had believed the hostilities could be localized, suddenly awakened to the danger and sought to mediate. The Russian Tsar (Nicholas II, Wilhelm's cousin) at first responded to Wilhelm's initiative by canceling the general order and replacing it with one for only partial mobilization. The next day (July 30), however, at least in part because of the practical difficulties involved in mobilizing on that basis, the Tsar was persuaded by his advisers to change his mind again, and once more general mobilization was ordered. On the same day Nicholas wired Wilhelm to the effect that this action was undertaken only because of Austria-Hungary's activities; indeed, it had been decided upon five days earlier. But the Kaiser, seeing the Russian mobilization, did not believe him. Wilhelm had concluded that the Russians had been deceiving Germany to gain time for their preparations, and he responded with a 12-hour ultimatum demanding the Russians demobilize. When the ultimatum's deadline expired on August 1 with no reply Germany mobilized and declared war on Russia.

These European leaders surely were in a difficult situation. The tension level was very high, a number of crises already had occurred in which war had been only narrowly averted, the underlying problems had not been resolved, the rigid confrontational two-alliance configuration had done much to eliminate policymaking flexibility, etc. In a setting as volatile and restrictive as this if one is to formulate and conduct the optimum policy thoroughgoing empathy is a necessity. Yet empathy is precisely what was lacking. The Austrians, making no effort to "put themselves in the Russians' shoes," did not see that their ultimatum to Serbia and the subsequent mobilization and attack could not help but be perceived by the Russians as a considerable prestige challenge and potential territorial threat. Given that perception Russia would believe itself faced with either acquiescing in humiliation and possibly some territorial loss, or adopting an orientation of confrontation; in such a contingency it most assuredly would choose confrontation. Yet the Austrians never even considered this. Tsarist Russia was equally unable to empathize. Nicholas did not see that the combination of the order to mobilize against Germany's ally and the statement that the mobilization decision had actually been made well before Wilhelm's mediation effort could not but be viewed by the Kaiser as proof that all Russia's protestations about avoiding hostilities were a trick, that in fact Russia had fully intended to become involved all along. And surely Wilhelm was devoid of empathy. The assurance of faithful support he had given Austria-

Hungary was interpreted by the Austrians as a blank check, and it encouraged them to destroy Serbia. Had Wilhelm put himself in their shoes he would have seen it could hardly have been otherwise. And when Russia mobilized Wilhelm failed to see that, in the Russians' view, such action was primarily "defensive," a response to a perceived security threat. Instead, the Kaiser (perhaps also in part because of his anti-Slavic prejudices) attributed to the Russians a desire to (along with Britain and France) wholly destroy Germany.

If a policymaker is to truly grasp the essence of the policies of his or her counterparts it is absolutely essential that he or she tough mindedly empathize and "be" those counterparts for a while. All situations are different, and (as we pointed out in depth in Chapter 8) each party is unique.[42] When party X is dealing with party Y and planning certain things, it doesn't make much difference how X would respond to these things because X is not the target; Y is. The policymakers of X must role play and imagine what would be most appropriate for Y to do or not do, based on Y's political system, capability, ideology, history, etc. This does not mean that after doing this they will then agree with Y. On the contrary, such an exercise may produce the sure knowledge that Y and X cannot possibly agree, or even that Y might well be planning to provoke a confrontation or launch military operations. Empathy is not a synonym for cooperation. What it does mean is that one cannot really understand the policies of a given party without empathizing whatever those policies may be, and thus one cannot formulate and implement the optimum policy in response thereto.

We have seen in this chapter that there are a number of intellectual errors that occur with considerable frequency, errors which presumably are not inevitable yet continue to happen. Policymakers often formulate policy on the basis of highly general, abstract concepts, seek to achieve incompatible objectives and follow inconsistent policies, act on the basis of incomplete and distorted preconceptions, and fail to empathize, to put themselves in the other person's shoes. These mistakes continually are obstacles to the formulation and implementation of a productive, cost-effective policy. There is another category of problems that pose additional difficulties, practical problems over which the policymaker has less control and which seem in some sense to be almost "inherent" in international politics. To these we now turn.

[42]See Chapter 8, pp. 231–235

14

"Inherent" Practical Difficulties

In the effort to formulate and implement a policy that produces maximum results at minimum cost the policymaker often is confronted by a number of rather pragmatic problems not of his or her own making, difficulties that occur with such frequency that it's almost as if they were an "inherent" part of the international political scene. When dealing with such obstacles the policymaker needs to be flexible, adjust to their existence to the extent they are unavoidable and uncontrollable, avoid or control them as much as possible, and minimize the degree to which their existence produces negative consequences.

UNANTICIPATED EVENTS AND SNOWBALLING

A major problem for policymakers is that no one can possibly be aware of everything that is going on, have perfect information with respect to the situation at hand, or always be able to accurately anticipate the course and tenor of future developments. Things are made even worse because of the fact that no party has absolute power and much happens that is beyond its control. Many times developments occur that one could not reasonably be expected to predict, and about which little could be done anyway.

Beginning in the mid 1960s the United States commenced to advocate arms control negotiations to the end of limiting strategic weapons. After a number of exchanges with Moscow, in May 1968 the Soviets announced their willingness to undertake such talks, and in July President Johnson stated that negotiations would begin in the "nearest future." A summit meeting between Johnson and Chairman Alexei Kosygin was scheduled for the end of August, and on August 19 Soviet Ambassador Anatoly Dobryin informed Washington that the Soviets would be willing to begin negotiations at that time.[1] But on August 20 the Russians and some of their Warsaw Pact allies invaded Czechoslovakia to crush the Prague spring. In consequence, plans for the summit were immediately canceled. The unanticipated invasion, an event over which Washington had no control, destroyed the plans to commence strategic arms control talks.

Hitler was confronted by two similarly unanticipated and uncontrollable events during his early 1941 preparations to attack the Soviet Union.[2] First, in October 1940 Italy had invaded Greece in a surprise attack. To Hitler's disgust by early 1941 Mussolini's forces unexpectedly were in disarray. When the Italian leader pleaded for help Hitler complied, and by April 1941 Nazi tanks rolled into Athens. Twelve divisions were tied down, however, divisions that previously had been scheduled for Russia. Second, in March 1941 a coup suddenly occurred in Yugoslavia overthrowing the pro-Nazi government of Prince Paul. The new regime plainly intended to follow a more independent course than its predecessor had. In response, German forces invaded. This action necessitated a postponement of the take off date of Barbarossa from May 15 to June 22. Six months later, when German forces were mired in the snows of the U. S. S. R., perhaps only a few weeks short of victory, the consequences of these unanticipated events and the decisions made in response thereto seemed enormous.

Example: The 1967 Arab-Israeli War

Another problem for policymakers is that at times events seem to "just happen" and to develop a momentum of their own.[3] Difficulties are compounded by the fact that the process is often cumulative and a kind of "snowballing" effect develops. In such circumstances the parties feel that their feasible options have been so severely restricted that they have no real choice except to do certain things, that they are being swept along by events they can't control. When snowballing is mixed with unanticipated events policymakers feel they can do little more than react. Let's take an in-depth look at a case in which

[1]Barton and Weiler, p. 177.
[2]See Stoessinger, *Why Nations Go To War*, Second Edition, pp. 43–44.
[3]One noted ex-diplomat calls this "the most potent of all factors—the chain of circumstances." See Harold Nicolson, *The Congress of Vienna*, Harcourt Brace, New York, 1946, pp. 19–20.

these elements were present: the events preceding and leading to the Arab-Is-raeli war of June 1967.

From the time of the Suez Crisis until the mid-1960s the Arab-Israeli con-flict had been relatively dormant. The majority of Middle Eastern political ac-tivity had revolved around a variety of inter-Arab disputes and attempts by the United States and the Soviet Union to consolidate their positions with their re-spective client states.

Egypt's President Nasser had become too involved in inter-Arab prob-lems to consider challenging the Israelis, and had also recognized the fact that his military machine was simply no match for theirs.[4] He said many times that he did not want another round with the Israelis unless and until the Arabs were unified and they had drastically increased their military capabilities. The Is-raelis, relatively content with the existing territorial situation and recognizing their military superiority over the Arabs, also had adopted a policy based largely on the status quo.

It is difficult to know precisely when the dispute began to heat up again but it appears as if it may have begun with a coup in Syria in February of 1966. The new Syrian leaders, a leftist faction of the Ba'ath party, called for the lib-eration of Palestine via military means and began to take operational steps to bring this about. They began to assume more and more control over the Pales-tinian guerila organization El-Fatah and to encourage its raids via Jordanian territory into Israel.[5] The Israelis knew full well that these raids were originat-ing in Syria, but they also held Jordan partially culpable for allowing the gue-rillas to use Jordanian territory. These developments obviously were outside of the control of the United States. Most of the raids occurred without Washing-ton's prior knowledge, and they were certainly contrary to the American in-terest of maintaining stability without conflict.

Following two particularly serious incidents in the late fall of 1966, the Is-raelis launched a major retaliatory attack against the Jordanian village of Samu; the stated purpose was to destroy a guerila base. This unanticipated Is-raeli response was a key factor in the development of the crisis. It demon-strated Jordan's vulnerability, putting extreme pressure on King Hussein to be "ready" next time. It did not soothe Israeli public opinion because the citizen-

---

[4]In addition, by the end of 1963 he had committed 40,000 Egyptian troops to the cause of rev-olution in the Yemen Civil War, the number growing to perhaps 70,000 by the mid-1960s. Most of these troops were still there (and remained there) when the new Arab-Israeli crisis developed. See Malcom H. Kerr, *The Arab Cold War: Gamal 'Abd al-Nasir and His Rivals, 1958–1970*, Third Edition, Oxford University Press, London, 1971, pp. 96–97, 106–114. Also useful is John S. Ba-deau, *The American Approach to the Arab World*, Harper, New York, 1968, Chapter 7.

[5]See Walter Laqueur, *The Road to War: The Origin and Aftermath of the Arab-Israeli Con-flict 1967–8*, Penguin Books, Middlesex, England, 1969, pp. 67–72. This was also published as *The Road to Jerusalem.*

ry knew that the guerillas were based in Syria. It led Hussein to castigate Nasser for Egypt's involvement in the Yemen Civil War where it was killing Arabs instead of Israelis. It encouraged the Syrians to continue their incitement since they had gotten away unscathed. And it contributed to Egyptian and Syrian boldness since it occurred shortly after their signature of a mutual defense pact and made them feel that the pact had had a deterrent effect on the Israelis (since the attack had not been directed at Syria).

Throughout early 1967 terrorist activity increased. In April a small scale incident escalated into an exchange of fire between Syrian and Israeli tanks, and this in turn led to an aerial clash in which six Syrian MIGS were downed by Israeli Mirages. Although in retrospect one can see that momentum was building toward another Arab-Israeli clash, this was not at all clear to the participants or to interested observers. As late as May 1 Nasser accused Hussein and King Feisal of Saudi Arabia of being in league with the United States and Israel against Egypt, clearly demonstrating his unawareness of the impending war with Israel.

As things continued to deteriorate the Israelis began to take a harder and harder line. On May 11 Prime Minister Eshkol spoke of "drastic measures" if things got worse. Two days later he once more said that Israel knew full well that the terrorists were primarily based in Syria, and indicated that Tel Aviv would choose the appropriate time and place to retaliate. American policymakers to this point had been concerned but they did not really feel that the dispute would explode into armed conflict. Then on May 13 the Egyptians received messages from the Syrians and from the Soviet Union to the effect that the Israelis were massing troops on the Syrian border and that an attack was very likely.

Events seemed to be snowballing. Nasser ordered a partial mobilization and, with great fanfare, sent a small force into the Sinai.[6] Stung to the quick by the many Arab comments concerning his unwillingness to help his Arab brothers and his "hiding behind the skirts" of the United Nations Emergency Forces (which had been established along his borders with Israel after the 1956 Suez War), angered by the constant accusations concerning his willingness to kill Arabs in Yemen but not Israelis, Nasser apparently felt that he had no choice but to at least make some type of move in this regard.

By now it seemed evident that the Israelis were planning to take *some* type of action against Syria if the raids did not cease, but it was not clear precisely what kind of operation was envisaged. It appears as if (with the advantage of hindsight) one can see that Israel did not at this point have troops mobilized for a massive attack. However, Egypt felt that it must never again be unpre-

---

[6]For a very interesting analysis of both the contents of the messages and the reasons for Nasser's reactions, see Nadav Safran, *From War to War: The Arab-Israeli Confrontation, 1948–1967*, Pegasus, New York, 1969, pp. 272–285.

pared as it was in the 1956 Suez War, and also felt that it had no choice, given the nature of inter-Arab politics, but to be ready.[7]

What happened next is another example of unanticipated events. The Egyptian field commander, moving his troops to the Sinai border, asked the commander-in-chief of the United Nations Emergency Forces to withdraw his men. As Nadav Safran has accurately stated, "there is absolutely no doubt that the Egyptian Government wanted the U. N. troops to be removed only from the Egyptian border with Israel."[8] Thus, only the UNEF forces along the Sinai front were to be involved, not those at Sharm al-Sheikh or in the Gaza Strip. The field commander immediately informed Secretary General U Thant, who in turn immediately contacted the Egyptian Representative. The secretary in essence said that only *he* could make such a decision, and that a temporary or partial withdrawal was unacceptable. He went on to say that the UAR (Egypt) had the right to request a *general* withdrawal of *all* UNEF forces because the UNEF was there only with Egypt's consent. If it so requested then he would order a withdrawal of all troops, not only from the Sinai *but also from Gaza and Sharm al-Sheikh*.[9]

But this was not what the request had been. This certainly was an unanticipated development and a tragically significant one. Sharm al-Sheikh, commanding the Straits of Tiran at the entrance to the Gulf of Aqaba, the passage through which the Israelis must go to reach their only southern port, Elath, was of immense strategic importance. This was the last location from which the Israelis had withdrawn in 1957 following the Suez attack, and they had withdrawn then only on the condition, as they understood it, that there would be guaranteed freedom of navigation. They had time and again stated their position, that if the Straits were ever closed it would mean war. If the UNEF forces were withdrawn from this point, the psychological pressure on Nasser to reoccupy it would be immense. Confronted with this choice of alternatives from U Thant, however, Nasser felt that it was necessary, once again to a great extent for reasons of inter-Arab politics, to take up the challenge. He requested that all UNEF troops be removed, and Egyptian forces then moved in to Sharm al-Sheikh. On May 22 Nasser announced the reinstitution of the blockade of the Straits.

---

[7]Prior to the Israeli attack in 1956 Nasser had thought that Israel was preparing to attack Jordan, and his forces had been unprepared for the Sinai assault.

[8]Safran, p. 285.

[9]It is not very clear why U Thant posed the alternatives in this all-or-nothing fashion, especially since the Egyptian request had been so limited. The most commonly accepted explanation is that he thought Nasser would back down when confronted with this choice, although Thant himself explained it on legal grounds. See "*Special Report of the Secretary-General of the United Nations, U Thant, to the General Assembly, May 18, 1967, on the United Nations Emergency Force*," Document A/6669, May 18, 1967.

In retrospect it seems that from this point on the die was cast; it was only a question of time before some type of war occurred. Even at the time most parties believed that there would be some kind of military response. What amazed people, however, was the fact that Israel did not strike immediately. Prime Minister Eshkol, in fact, delivered a very moderate speech calling for a mutual withdrawal of UAR and Israeli troops to prevent conflagration, and suggested negotiations. All this did was to contribute to Nasser's prestige among the Arabs, and his speeches became more bellicose.

By this time both American and Soviet policymakers recognized the extreme danger and both sought to prevent the outbreak of violence; they soon discovered how powerless they really were, however, how "uncontrollable" events had become.[10] Both parties talked to the Israelis and the Egyptians urging negotiations, almost pleading that there be no resort to violence. Yet the situation continued to deteriorate. On May 26 Hussein signed a defense treaty with Egypt, contributing to Israeli fears of military encirclement. Nasser stated that the situation was no longer a question of the Gulf of Aqaba but was now the rights of the people of Palestine; if a battle were launched it would be total, and its result would be destruction of Israel. Apparently the Soviet Union had convinced Nasser that it would at least neutralize the United States if war should occur, and this contributed to his confidence.

Israeli policymakers had become quite confused because they "knew" of their military superiority, or at least they thought they knew, and also "knew" of Nasser's previous moderation on the issue of another war. When Nasser became more and more bellicose, given the fact that he had been so moderate and given the fact he had said he would not reach a point of conflict unless the Arabs were united and superior, it made the Israelis think twice. After considerable reassessment, however, and some domestic political infighting, Moshe Dayan was appointed Minister of Defense (June 2, 1967). And, of course, on June 5, 1967 Israeli aircraft took off and the Six Day War began.

With the advantages of hindsight it is possible to identify several key events that contributed to, and were a part of, the snowballing process that culminated in war: the Syrian coup and the ensuing raids by El-Fatah; the unexpected Israeli retaliation on Samu; the reciprocal escalation of early 1967; the Soviet and Syrian intelligence received by Nasser and Nasser's resultant movement of forces; U Thant's totally unanticipated response to Nasser's request for troop removals; and the imposition of the blockade.

This case provides a prime example of the impact that unanticipated events can have, as well as demonstrating the development of a kind of "snow-

---

[10]The illusion of omnipotence dies hard. An excellent discussion of the general topic may be found in Dennis W. Brogan, "The Illusion of Omnipotence," *Harper's*, December 1952, pp. 21–28.

balling" effect. Of course, there were key points at which decisions *could* have been made differently and they might have stopped this "chain-of-circumstances," but the simple fact is that they were not, and it is plain that many of the participants felt themselves to be "swept along by the current of events."[11] Nasser did not seek war but the pressures of inter-Arab politics and specific events made him feel as if he had no choice but to take certain actions (mobilization, seizure of Sharm al-Sheikh, blockade, etc.). Israeli policymakers did not seek war but certain actions (the removal of UNEF forces and the blockade) made them feel as if they had no choice. And so the list goes on. As the American diplomat, Charles Yost, remarked, though "no government plotted or intended to start a war in the Middle East in the spring of 1967," war did occur.[12]

What "lessons" can one learn from this episode? How does it help to know that not all events can be anticipated, that many things occur that seem to be beyond one's control, and that events can develop a snowballing "uncontrollability" of their own? First, it helps the policymaker keep things in their proper perspective; sometimes things will not work out no matter how hard one tries. Second, it makes one emphasize flexibility and adaptability in his approach. A policymaker must be able to adjust to changing conditions, to unanticipated developments. Third, it illustrates the need for preparing for a variety of contingencies so that one has a range of options from which to choose. Hopefully one of them will be appropriate (or at least close). Fourth, it makes one cognizant of the dangers that may develop if things do get out of control and points up the necessity of making a concerted effort to prevent this from happening.[13] And fifth, it underlines the importance of obtaining accurate information, correctly interpreting it, and anticipating as accurately as possible; one should not be caught unaware any more than is absolutely unavoidable.

INFLUENCE OF THE PAST

Another major practical difficulty policymakers often encounter is the fact that the feasible alternatives are limited by the past and one usually has only a narrow range of options from which to choose. This unpleasant truth seldom receives sufficient emphasis with the result that observers tend to exaggerate the number of *realistic* choices a policymaker actually has.

[11]Badeau, p. 168.
[12]Yost's analysis of the entire sequence of events leading to the war supports this author's thesis. See Charles W. Yost, "The Arab-Israeli War: How it Began," *Foreign Affairs*, January 1968, pp. 304–320.
[13]See the discussion of the Cuban Missile Crisis, pp. 402–405.

There are several facets to this concept. *First, a nation's historical experience influences the content of its policymakers' perceptions of various features of the international environment such as ethics, law, and ideology.* The fact that the United States is the only major state in the world "whose historical experience occurred so predominantly in the rather unusual—even peculiar—century between 1815–1914," for example, is a matter of immense significance.[14] This was an era of peace and Americans came to assume that peace was the normal state of affairs, that the policies they followed in that era "must" be correct, and that things would just get better and better.[15]

A second point is that one's perception of the past significantly influences the content of objectives, and his choice of policy implementation instruments as well. Certain options will be eliminated from consideration and certain objectives just taken as "givens."[16] Soviet attempts to develop defense in depth along her western frontiers by assuring that Central European regimes are "friendly," for example, must be assumed as a constant because of the number of times she has been attacked through that area. Israeli policymakers could not even consider the option of reducing their military forces unilaterally, given what has happened to the Jews throughout the centuries, the fact that it was only through force of arms that the state was created and three additional wars have since occurred, and the fact that Israel still is confronted by a combination of states and NLOs that (the Israelis believe) have not accepted her creation as irreversible. The fact that modern Germany was first united by force of arms led to a belief in the efficacy of the military instrument and to an intimate association in the German mind between national unity and military strength. The American view that the United States failure to take an active role in stopping the Nazis in the 1930s was a major contributory cause to the onset of World War II led to a pendulum swing toward commitment and involvement in all situations. And the list goes on.

Third, once a particular policy has existed for a while a degree of inertia seems to set in. Operations become routinized and the underlying assumptions are not questioned. The fundamental assumptions underlying the American policy of anti-Communist containment went for nearly two decades without being challenged. No one bothered to investigate to see if certain negative consequences were being produced and/or if certain tension-reducing and/or security-enhancing opportunities were being missed.[17] It was all "obvious," wasn't it? There was no Soviet attack, so the policy "must" be correct.

---

[14]Hartmann, *The New Age of American Foreign Policy*, p. 27.

[15]See Chapter 2, pp. 47–50, for further discussion. Hartmann's analysis, *ibid*, Chapters 1–3, provides an excellent examination of this subject.

[16]See Chapter 3, pp. 83–84.

[17]See Chapter 13, pp. 358–362, for further discussion.

Fourth, once a policy is undertaken those policymakers responsible for its formulation and implementation have a vested interest in its success.[18] Therefore, they would prefer to have the existing policy succeed rather than undertake other options, and will make every effort to see that it does. In the Vietnam war President Johnson reached a point where he had so committed himself to not being "the first American president to lose a war" that all "nonwinning" options were foreclosed. The record of past commitment and the prestige invested therein can sometimes produce a situation in which policymakers feel no other alternatives can be considered.

There are three more ways in which the past limits policymakers' choices. One is that the execution of any policy inevitably brings about commitment of some of the state's resources for its success. These may be economic, military, and psychological, as well as political in the broadest sense. It is not easy to suddenly rearrange the allocation of resources. Also, once a policy is undertaken the state inevitably has invested some of its prestige. It is not only the individual policymakers who may lose by failure, but also the nation itself.[19] Finally, it is often assumed that there is some value in having a degree of certainty and stability in foreign policy; sudden changes would tend to produce just the reverse.

These influences from the past often combine to produce what has been termed a policy of incrementalism.[20] Roger Hilsman puts it this way:

> Rather than through grand decisions on grand alternatives, policy changes seem to come through a series of slight modifications of existing policy, with the new policy emerging slowly and haltingly by small and usually tentative steps, a process of trial and error in which policy zigs and zags, reverses itself, and then moves forward in a series of incremental steps.[21]

A critically important point to remember is that the policymaker must deal with *the situation as it is today, not as it might have been.* For him or her, for example, if in charge of American policy toward Vietnam, the general wisdom of past policy in terms of his or her value judgements is less important than a knowledge of what that policy *actually has been* and the recognition that *he or she cannot change what has occurred.* The policymaker must act on the basis of what *has* happened, whether it was wise or not; he or she does not start with a blank sheet of paper.

[18]See Chapter 15 for a discussion of bureaucratic politics in this connection.

[19]See pp. 402–405, for a discussion of the Cuban Missile Crisis. Both Khrushchev and the U. S. S. R. suffered as a result of the outcome.

[20]For more on incrementalism see Charles E. Lindblom, "The Science of Muddling Through," *Public Administration Review*, Spring 1959, pp. 79–88.

[21]Roger Hilsman, *The Politics of Policy Making in Defense and Foreign Affairs*, Harper, New York, 1971, p. 5.

This is a fundamental difference between the position of the policymaker and the position of all those who are not forced to take the responsibility of making the decision. The latter have the luxury of discussing the wisdom or lack thereof of particular previous decisions and can totally reject the past. The policymaker is forced in the very nature of things to accept the fact that certain decisions were made and he must now proceed from there.

Let's take a specific practical example. It is not a feasible option for an American policymaker today to consider whether or not it is wise for the United States to commit itself to the existence of the country of Israel. Even though there is no formal treaty commitment to such existence it is absolutely clear that the United States would fight to prevent Israel's destruction.[22] This has been determined to be an objective of fundamental importance. Thus it really is an exercise in irrelevance for a policymaker to speculate concerning the wisdom of such a decision and whether this decision *should* be made, because in fact it is already a generally accepted axiom of policy. This being so it is one of the bases from which the policymaker must act, regardless of his personal evaluation. One result, of course, is that an option has been eliminated because of what has gone on in the past.

Flexibility and Change

Although very often observers fail to give sufficient weight to the constraints of the past, it also is possible to give them too much; the point also can be overstressed. One should not conclude that because the past is an important influence there is no room for change, that policymakers in all cases are inexorably restricted to certain courses of action no matter what. As we have repeatedly emphasized, there are a number of factors impinging on and helping to produce policymakers' choices. History is one of these, but only one. To ignore the past would be foolish, but it also would be fallacious to ascribe to it a wholly determinative influence.

Because of this, in most situations policymakers, though constrained in certain ways and having to accept certain historical facts as givens, have a degree of flexibility. The fact that the United States is committed to the preservation of Israel's existence does not mean American policymakers must humbly acquiesce in all the policy decisions made in Jerusalem, nor does it necessarily mean there is no room for the employment of various orientations and combinations of policy instruments in most situations. In fact, it does not *necessarily*

---

[22]The precautionary alert of American armed forces to the perceived threat of unilateral Soviet intervention in Arab-Israeli War No. 4, October 25, 1973 provided eloquent testimony to this commitment. The issue of whether the response itself was appropriate and solely the result of the perceived threat is a different question.

even mean (although it may) that the United States is committed to ensure the survival of the state of Israel within any particular geographical boundaries. All it really says is that the United States will do everything in its power to make sure that the state of Israel, within some as yet undefined boundaries, will not be eliminated from the face of the earth.[23]

Because history is neither wholly nor rigidly determinative policymakers generally have the opportunity to explore the possibilities for change, and if they conclude it would be productive to do so they can undertake the appropriate actions. The extent to which policy alterations will be inhibited by influences of the past will vary, of course, depending on the situation, but in all but the most unusual of circumstances at least incremental changes can be undertaken. Over a period of time the cumulative effect of a number of these incremental changes may be considerable.

Example: The United States and the PRC

An example of the degree to which flexibility may ensue despite past policy is provided by the change in American policy toward the People's Republic of China with the advent of the Nixon administration. The new leadership could not, of course, eliminate what had gone on before. Previous policy had been based mainly on the concepts of military containment and diplomatic isolation; the Chinese were an enemy and had to be dealt with accordingly.[24]

Actually, feelings of suspicion and distrust had dominated policymakers on *both* sides.[25] Each viewed the other as the incarnation and epitome of Evil, and each policymaker automatically interpreted the actions of his counterparts in the most unfavorable way. For over two decades relations remained rigidly adversarial and neither side seemed particularly interested in changing.

President Nixon and Dr. Kissinger, however, felt change was necessary. The People's Republic of China was potentially very powerful, and would just have to be dealt with if there was to be any hope of real peace in the world. Of course, changes would take some time. Mutual perceptions would have to be altered, public opinion conditioned, and some feeling of American-Chinese trust would have to be developed. But the effort had to be made.

[23]One can, of course, question the extent of *any* commitment and postulate extreme circumstances in which a state may not fulfill its obligations. States have even "acquiesced" in their *own* partition as the Czechs did at Munich in 1938, and in their complete elimination as Poland did (in three stages) in 1772, 1793, and 1795. Basically, however, it means that if the United States will fight to protect the independence of anyone besides Uncle Sam, it will fight to protect Israel.

[24]One should keep in mind the pertinent points in several topics discussed earlier including the discussion of ideology, the role of abstract principles and anti-communism, the assumptions of containment, American views on who was involved in Vietnam, and so on. Also useful in this regard is Stoessinger, *Nations in Darkness: China, Russia, and America*, Third Edition, Chapters 3–6.

[25]See Chapter 13, pp. 367–368

The process began in late 1969 when American officials told the Chinese that they were ready to resume Ambassadorial discussions at Warsaw. The Chinese responded and a meeting was held in early 1970.[26] President Nixon also undertook a series of unilateral actions. Trade and travel restrictions were eased on July 21, 1969, and some items were taken off the embargo list in December. Controls on oil companies were lifted in August 1970, and restrictions on the visits of PRC citizens to the United States were relaxed by April 1971. Coupled with these actions were speeches of American officials that now called China by its correct name, the People's Republic, instead of Red China or something much less flattering. Washington also worked through a series of third parties to let Peking know it really meant what it said: it wanted better relations.

In early 1971 the Chinese responded, the invitation to the American table tennis team to come to China being one of the manifestations of change. In July and again in October of 1971 Dr. Kissinger visited Peking and had extensive discussions with Premier Chou En Lai, one of the major purposes being to pave the way for President Nixon's visit. From February 21 to February 28, 1972 an American president for the first time was welcomed to the People's Republic of China.

This was clearly a watershed in international politics, even though the immediate objectives for the talks were simply a sharing of perspectives rather than concrete agreements (which clearly would not have been possible yet). A statement of principles (generalized and abstract admittedly, but nevertheless constructive in their import) was agreed upon. And it was agreed that various bilateral personnel exchanges should be increased, there should be more trade, and continuing efforts should be made through cultural and diplomatic channels to normalize relationships. Through the remainder of the year trade did in fact increase as did these personnel exchanges, and there were additional movements toward normalization. Today the process continues with full diplomatic relations having been established in 1979.

The fact that such an innovative approach could develop underlines a critical point: despite the fact that one's options are limited by the past, there still may be sufficient latitude for an immediate incremental change, and over a lengthy period this incremental change may culminate in a substantially different policy.[27]

---

[26]In 1955 the United States and the People's Republic of China had begun talks at the ambassadorial level, first in Geneva and then in Warsaw. Since neither government officially "recognized" the other, these were, for all practical purposes, their only direct contacts. From 1955 to 1969 134 talks were held. In February 1969 the Chinese canceled the 135th session and no direct communication occurred again until late in the year.

[27]It should also be pointed out that sudden crises may force (or allow) one to substantially change policy. The Japanese attack on Pearl Harbor "allowed" a major change in American policy.

The question of the degree to which one's options are limited by the past is also related to the question of generalized abstractions as a basis for policy. If one states his objectives in specific terms he is much more able to be flexible because it is much easier to change a concrete alternative than one based on an abstract principle. After all, the People's Republic of China is still a Communist system but when one concerns himself or herself with the possibility of specific mutual objectives and carefully defines what those objectives might be, there is some possibility of a significant alteration of policy.

To sum up, it is very important that one realize that, to a considerable extent, policymakers are limited by, and act on the basis of, the accumulated record of the past.[28] Whatever has happened *has happened*, irrespective of personal judgments as to whether or not it "should" have. Because of the past what can be done in the future has already been partly determined, and policies have to be formulated and implemented in light of this fact. As a result, certain choices that might ideally seem possible in actuality are not, and barring sudden crises it is unlikely that more than incremental policy alterations can and will occur; the kinds of radically different, all-encompassing problem solutions that observers so often advocate usually are but fantasies to policymakers. Given the pervasive impact of history, clearly it is imperative that the unique record of each and all of the parties be studied with great care in order to determine as accurately as possible the influence which the past will have in each specific case. But one must also remember, as the example of the change in United States' policy toward the PRC demonstrated, that within certain constraints there is an opportunity for considerable flexibility of action if one acts via a process of cumulative incremental change.

INTERRELATED EVENTS

Another fact of international politics is that, like it or not, events are interrelated. Policymakers, therefore, cannot deal with situations in isolation, as if they were in no way linked to extrasituational developments or were not themselves in part a product of preceding events. Indeed, in many instances one's situational perceptions and actions are directly and intimately related to extrasituational occurrences, sometimes even to the extent of being largely determined by them. And frequently it simply is not possible to begin work on a certain matter until a number of interrelated demands and preconditions have been met.

Extrasituational Impacts

In almost (if not) all cases situational developments and external factors are interrelated. Policymakers seeking to formulate and implement the optimum

---

[28]Party uniqueness and perceptual differences are enormously important in this regard. See Chapter 8, pp. 233–235 for a useful example.

situational policy thus find their task is enormously more complex, and frequently they have much less control over the number and types of influencing factors, than they would like.

Example: U. S. Marines in Lebanon. Aspects of the 1958 Lebanon crisis exemplify the impact of extrasituational developments. As we pointed out in Chapter 13, by early June 1958 the United States had begun to change its view of the origins of, and stakes involved in, the crisis.[29] President Eisenhower and Secretary of State Dulles had started to realize that their preconceptions had prevented them from accurately assessing the situation; they had begun to understand that the problems in Lebanon were primarily internal, not the result of external instigation by Gamal Nasser and the Communists. As a result of this changed perception they had shelved their thoughts of possible armed intervention, preferring instead to adopt the orientation option of limited support for the government of President Chamoun. Suddenly, on July 14 a coup occurred in nearby Iraq. The pro-Western government of King Feisal and Nuri Said was deposed by a leftist military regime headed by General Kasim and his followers, men who had previously made known their sympathies to Egypt's President Nasser. When this occurred Washington "reinterpreted its reinterpretation." With the most pro-Western government in the area overthrown by "pro-Nasser" elements, it was felt that the existing framework of American Middle Eastern policy was in danger of being completely destroyed, and because of the interrelationship of events in the Middle East and the preconceived generalization that President Nasser was out to subvert the entire Arab world in his quest for Pan-Arab leadership, the United States responded to a call from the President of Lebanon for military assistance. Thus American Marines landed in Lebanon.

Clearly the dispatch of these Marines was not primarily due to events in Lebanon but rather was the result of developments in Iraq and the perceived interrelationship of these factors. The point here is that all calculations of policy with respect to Lebanon, if viewed only in that narrow perspective, would not have (and indeed previously had not) required the deployment of American Marines. It was only the perceived relationship of events in one country to those in another that brought about this decision.

Example: Perceptions of Ho Chi Minh. Another pertinent example was provided by the changes in the way American policymakers perceived Ho Chi Minh in the first decade after World War II.[30] As pointed out earlier, in the first few months after the war the situation in Indochina was chaotic, British troops, Chinese nationalist forces, the French, various Vietnamese organizations, and the Vietminh competing and collaborating in a maze of confusing interac-

---

[29]See Chapter 13, pp. 369–371.
[30]Useful is Stoessinger, *Nations in Darkness*, Third Edition, Chapter 5.

tions.[31] In late 1945 and early 1946 as the Chinese and British withdrew military skirmishes occurred between the French and the Vietminh. Negotiations were undertaken and an agreement was signed in March 1946, but by year's end full-scale hostilities were underway.

During this period and up until 1949 the United States was not really very concerned about Indochina; its priorities lay elsewhere. To the extent that it did pay attention Washington evidenced a certain disapproval of France's activities, viewing Paris as a colonial power seeking to reestablish control over nationalist groups seeking independence. Though somewhat skeptical of the true nature of Ho Chi Minh's "nationalism" given the facts that he had been one of the founders of the French Communist Party, had founded the Indochinese Communist Party, had been a delegate to the Comintern, and had spent most of the 1930s in Russia, during these years such elements tended to be seen as secondary in significance to his fight to lead his people to independence from France.

But as the Cold War developed American perceptions began to change. By the summer of 1949 the postwar crises over Greece, Turkey, and Iran, the establishment and consolidation of Soviet control over the East and Central European satellites, the February 1948 coup in Czechoslovakia, and the Berlin Blockade all had occurred, and in consequence the abstract generalizations of containment and anticommunism had become the basis of U. S. policy. As a result of these developments *outside* Indochina Washington's view of what "really" was going on *inside* Indochina was changing. When China "fell" to the Communists in October 1949 this process was accelerated, and when the Korean war commenced in June 1950 the perceptual alteration was complete. Now Ho Chi Minh was perceived as a bona fide Communist, and his "nationalist" tendencies were dismissed as secondary; Ho was part and parcel of the efforts of monolithic communism to subjugate the "Free World." Naturally, therefore, he had to be opposed. Soon Washington began providing foreign aid to France for use in Indochina, and by 1954 the United States was paying well over half the cost of the war. Here, as in the marines in Lebanon example, situational and extrasituational events were intimately interrelated and policy-makers altered their situational assessment because of the impact of external factors.

Conditions Precedent

Situations do not just "spring out of thin air"; circumstances and conditions at any particular time are in part a product of what has occurred previously. Frequently the interrelationship between present and past is such that certain

[31] Also see Chapter 12, pp. 329–330.

developments *had* to occur before the present parameters could be established; in many instances policymakers had to act and interact in a manner that allowed certain conditions precedent to a particular situation to be developed and certain demands to be fulfilled. In this sense possible successes re situation X are possible only because of the interrelated events of S, T, U, V, and W that already have occurred.

Example: Events Leading to CSCE. An example of the interrelationship between a particular situation and the events preceding it, of the creation of the precedent conditions essential to the development of the desired situation, was provided by the events leading to the Conference on Security and Cooperation in Europe (CSCE). For most of the 1950s and 1960s the Soviet Union had sought to convene an all-embracing European Security Conference. The United States and its NATO allies had balked, fearing that such a gathering would probably yield no substantive agreement and would simply provide a forum for Communist propaganda. Washington's position had been that it was wiser to negotiate on specific issues. Once some measure of success could be shown, then, with the hope that more progress might be forthcoming, a general conference might have some value.

Due, in considerable measure, to the efforts of West German Chancellor Willy Brandt and his predecessor Kurt Kiesinger, conditions were eventually created that allowed this to come to pass. Breaking with the Adenauer "position of strength" approach the West German leaders sought a relaxation of tensions with the Eastern European countries and the Soviet Union. The first steps involved the establishment of diplomatic relations with Rumania and Yugoslavia. By late 1969 Brandt began speaking of two German states within one German nation, and suggested various areas of potential cooperation. Clearly his words were directed to Moscow. In March and in May of 1970 he broke precedent by meeting with Willi Stoph, the East German Chairman of the Council of Ministers. In August of 1970 West Germany signed a treaty with the Soviets "normalizing" relations with Moscow and recognizing the "inviolability" of existing frontiers, and in December a similar treaty was signed with Poland.[32]

[32]The eastern borders of post-World War II Germany have never been definitively delimited. Approximately 40 percent of present Polish territory was obtained as a result of World War II. Much of this land was historically German, and until these treaties were signed and ratified no West German regime had given any credence whatever to Poland's western frontier. The Polish-West German Treaty binds the Federal Republic and the Polish Government on this issue but does not substitute for the definitive delimitation a peace treaty would provide. That is the responsibility of the Four Powers who defeated Germany in World War II. The present treaty would not be binding on a reunified German state either. Useful on this point is the statement of West Germany's Foreign Minister, Walter Scheel, reprinted in *The Treaty between the Federal Republic of Germany and the People's Republic of Poland*, Bonn, Press and Information Office of the (West German) Federal Government, 1971, pp. 41–53. It should also be pointed out that the Final Act of

The various West German initiatives were concrete signs of progress and this contributed to much greater flexibility in European relations. This led to some optimism that other issues in conflict might receive the benefit of this momentum. But the treaties, although signed, were not ratified immediately. West German policymakers made it clear that Bonn would not act so unless the Four Powers could achieve an agreement on freer access to Berlin, and freer movement and communication between the sectors.[33] The clear relationship between these events, however, gave impetus to Four Power negotiations, and a Quadripartite Agreement was signed in September of 1971. Once this occurred many West Germans felt that the normalization treaties could be ratified without injuring German interests, and on May 17, 1972 this was accomplished by a very narrow margin.

While these Germany-focused agreements had been in the process of negotiation, the United States had been engaged in an extensive and intensive series of bilateral negotiations with the Soviet Union. As mentioned above, the Moscow Summit meetings of May 1972 yielded a wide range of United States-Soviet Union agreements including two limiting strategic armaments. The willingness to sign these agreements had been greatly influenced by the fact of the reduction in tensions due to the German treaties and the Quadripartite Agreement over Berlin. The momentum continued when on November 6, 1972 the two Germanies initialed the Basic Treaty, an agreement designed to somewhat improve intra-German cooperation. By its terms the Federal Republic formally "takes note" of East Germany as a sovereign state but not as a foreign country.

All of these agreements were interrelated, and their conclusion met the American demand that concrete progress had to be demonstrated before a European Security Conference could be held. Now that this condition had been fulfilled the first preparatory meetings could be held, and they were in November 1972. Stage I of the Conference on Security and Cooperation in Europe took place in Helsinki in early July 1973, and the Stage II meetings (the working level negotiations) began at Geneva in September.

DIFFERENTIAL EFFECTS

Another very practical problem with which policymakers must deal is the fact that all policies produce differential effects. This really means two things.

---

the Conference on Security and Cooperation in Europe (the 1975 Helsinki Agreements), whose signatories declared that they regarded the frontiers of all the states in Europe as inviolable, was only a political statement of intent; it was neither a treaty nor a legally binding agreement.

[33]Berlin was located deep inside the Soviet occupation zone at the end of the Second World War, and there were no written provisions for Western access thereto. It soon became a focal point in the Cold War.

First, all policies yield both costs and benefits. There is no such thing as a policy without disadvantages; nothing is perfect. When the Soviets signed the ABM Treaty with the United States in 1972 both parties agreed that the agreement added a degree of stability to their strategic relationship. The limitations imposed, however, foreclosed the very real possibility that Moscow could have developed an ABM capability sufficient to provide effective defense against French or Chinese missiles. In January 1977 Canada, seeking to do its part to prevent the possible proliferation of nuclear weapons, embargoed all uranium ore shipments to the states in Euratom (and Japan) until better safeguard arrangements could be worked out.[34] This positive result was offset by the fact that the embargo, along with uncertainty about future Australian production, prompted West Germany, Japan, and France to sign contracts for uranium supply with South Africa.[35] The increasing importance of South Africa as a major source of uranium ore is a matter of concern to many.

An important factor in this regard, as in most, is that different parties view and interpret the same facts differently. Although disagreeing on numerous facets of the issue, Americans generally viewed the exodus from Vietnam, given the pros and cons of the various alternatives, in a positive light. Leonid Brezhnev also evaluated it "positively," but for an entirely different reason. In Brezhnev's view, because of the "victory" of the Vietnamese people:

> Imperialism's strongest post-World War II bid to destroy a socialist state by armed force and crush a national liberation revolution ended in failure. . . . The Soviet people take great pride in having rendered considerable aid to Vietnam in its struggle against the imperialist invaders. . . . It was a glorious victory, and will be inscribed forever in the annals of the peoples' struggle for freedom and socialism.[36]

Example: Effects of Lebanon Landings

The "ever-present" 1958 Lebanon crisis provides a useful example. As discussed above, because of its perception of the interrelationships involved in the Middle East the United States landed Marines in Lebanon. When deciding to so use the military policy instrument American policymakers believed they could achieve a number of positive results. The landing would prevent the subversion of the Middle East by President Nasser, maintain a certain element of

---

[34]It was from Canada that India had obtained the nuclear reactor from which the plutonium was produced that was used in the May 1974 explosion. As a consequence the Canadians had undertaken a major effort to control the transfer of nuclear facilities, materials, and expertise.

[35]The International Institute for Strategic Studies, *Strategic Survey, 1977*, London, 1978, pp. 110–111.

[36]Brezhnev, *25th Congress Report*, pp. 11–12.

stability in the area, and therefore prevent a further degree of penetration by the Soviet Union. It was designed to show Nasser that there were limits to what the United States would tolerate, and it was felt that it demonstrated to the Russians that the United States would act whenever and wherever it considered its fundamental objectives threatened. Finally, it was also believed that it would show the Arabs that the Soviets would *not* come to their aid in each and every case. These were the perceived benefits of the decision.

There were many costs, however. First, the decision gave the illusion of validity to the charges made by Nasser and the Soviets earlier in the year to the effect that the crisis was all a pretext for the intervention of Western military forces. Second, the landing of troops inevitably gave rise to suspicions about ultimate Western intentions in the area. As soon as the British and French were gone (because of Suez) another Western Power intervened militarily. The landings also did much to reunite the Arab world behind Nasser, certainly a development Washington did not desire. It also angered the Arabs because it demonstrated Washington's doubts over the Arabs' ability to solve their own problems. And finally, this was the first time the *United States* had landed its forces on Arab soil and it raised the specter of specifically *American* colonialism. Perhaps the charges against the Eisenhower Doctrine were correct. Obviously there were many disadvantages as well as advantages to this particular move.

Example: Strategic Doctrine For Europe

The fact that all options have both advantages and disadvantages also has plagued efforts to devise strategic military doctrine for Europe. For most of the 1950s the United States Strategic Air Command provided the major deterrent for all of the "Free World" via a strategy known as "massive retaliation." In essence this concept postulated that the Communist bloc would be deterred from all acts of aggression by the knowledge that, if aggression occurred, there might be a devastating nuclear response on military targets and urban centers within the Soviet Union itself. The perceived advantages of this approach were its apparent simplicity and certainty. But there was an offsetting disadvantage, namely, what if the threat's credibility was questionable? Suppose, in other words, one's adversary just did not believe him. If he acted on that basis and one had no other options he would be forced either to acquiesce in aggression or initiate a nuclear war, neither of which were pleasant alternatives.

By the latter 1950s the logic of this dilemma had permeated official thinking. This had been reinforced by two basic situational changes. First, the Soviets had developed considerable operational nuclear capacity of their own, eliminating the possibility that a nuclear war would be a one-way street.[37] Second, there had in fact been a wide variety of ambiguous, low level military conflict situations, which obviously the threat of massive retaliation had not deterred and to which its use seemed totally inappropriate.

One way to mitigate the dilemma was to give NATO forces a wider range of possible options so that a differentiated series of flexible, graduated responses would be available.[38] The West would not be forced to risk national survival or capitulate on every issue. Thus, by a kind of cost-benefit analysis, each act of aggression would be met with a response of appropriate severity; the punishment would fit the crime.

Unfortunately this concept too has some offsetting disadvantages. The idea of minimum threat with maximum credibility assumes a high degree of rationality on both sides, certainly a dubious assumption for a warfare situation. It assumes acceptance by all parties of a limited warfare "game" and the concept of a limited nuclear war in Europe strains credulity. It assumes the capacity to determine what punishment is appropriate to the crime. To put all of this a different way, graduated deterrence and flexible response demand a cool rational analysis by all parties, the avoidance of emotion, precise calculation, and a conscious refusal to escalate no matter what the circumstance or provocation. Ideally this is possible. Whether in the midst of actual hostilities such could take place is certainly an open question.[39]

The second basic meaning of the term differential effects is that each decision has an impact on more than one party, and each affects each party differently. The impact of the Israeli attack on Samu (see above) provided us with an excellent illustration.[40] This can also be seen in the continuing saga of the Lebanese crisis. The advantages and disadvantages of the American decision to deploy Marine units as related to United States relations with Egypt and the Russians were discussed above.

But this decision also had an impact on American relations with Great Britain, France, and Israel. Washington's action was compared with its refusal to assist, or even be neutral toward, these countries in the Suez crisis. Clearly

---

[37]This development led the French to conclude that there were circumstances in which the United States might not be willing to use its nuclear forces to defend Europe. Therefore, the French decided to develop an independent nuclear force.

[38]Another proposed remedy was a nuclear sharing program, some procedure by which NATO members would participate in the decisional and operational aspects of strategic warfare. Suggested by many in the early 1960s, this concept never was satisfactorily implemented. For an excellent, very brief discussion see Cecil V. Crabb, Jr., *American Foreign Policy in the Nuclear Age*, Third Edition, Harper, New York, 1973, pp. 257–258.

[39]Many of the comments made in the discussion of limited war in Chapter 10 are also pertinent here.

[40]See pp. 381–382.

the differential impact of Suez had been immense: the weakening of United States ties with its major allies and closest friend, the deterioration in NATO cohesion, the elimination of British and French influence in the Arab world and the corresponding decline in the capacity of the British-supported states of Iraq and Jordan to combat "Nasserism," the increase in Soviet influence, and the increase in Nasser's political prestige despite a military debacle. Despite all of this, Washington had led the opposition. Yet in Lebanon it had responded unilaterally with the deployment of Marines. A major but often overlooked effect of this decision was its reinforcement of a growing European belief that the United States was only willing to use force unilaterally to protect narrowly defined American objectives, and that therefore the NATO nations had better begin to look out for themselves a little more.

All policies affect more than one party and affect each one differently whether policymakers (or observers) want them to or not; such is inherent in the process. Consequently, it behooves policymakers when formulating policies to take this into account and to try to develop policies that maximize the net benefit-cost ratio. Sometimes they do this. For example, during the Vietnam peace talks Dr. Kissinger's activities were, to a considerable extent, designed as much (if not more) for their impact on the Soviet Union, China, and America's allies as they were for the DRV.[41] Of course, the recognition of the principle of differential effects by policymakers in no way ensures that they will select an effective policy. In the crisis following Italy's attack on Ethiopia in the mid-1930s, for example, British policymakers were fully aware that whatever they did or did not do it would affect not only Ethiopia and Italy but also the perceptions and policies of Germany and France (and perhaps others). This knowledge did not prevent London's adoption of policies that managed to anger the French, assist the Germans, worry the Russians, and encourage the Italians.

Before closing this section one more comment is in order. Because of the increasing power of the People's Republic of China and the development of the Sino-Soviet dispute, it has become common to speak in terms of a diplomatic triangle involving the United States, Russia, and China. In a sense, this triangle involves a series of bilateral relationships, United States-Russia, United States-China, and Sino-Soviet, varying in the degree of common, complementary, and opposed objectives. As the United States has directed its policies toward a "normalization" and "betterment" of relations with each of the other two, and as the Sino-Soviet breach has deepened and intensified, a highly flexible and uncertain situation has developed. The United States has received the benefit of a split among its adversaries, and China and Russia have each gained a new enemy. But the triangle is more than just a series of bi-

---

[41]Also see Chapter 3, p. 87.

lateral relationships, because each party is continuously and to some extent simultaneously interacting with the other *two*; the "triangle" is more than just the sum of its bilateral parts. Each party has two potential opponents, and each is constantly faced with the possibility of collusion by its potential adversaries against itself. A primary objective of each party is to prevent such collusion. At the same time, there tends to be a primary adversary for each party, either generally or on a given issue, and this inevitably brings about pressure for collusion.

In this situation every decision has a differential impact. Each party must watch the other two very closely. Each movement toward a Soviet-American détente must also be evaluated in terms of its effect on Peking. Every time Washington and Moscow work closely together it inevitably increases Chinese fears of collusion. And, as Washington has proceeded to normalize relations with Peking, it has made cooperative relations with Russia more difficult. The diminishment of Peking's perception of an imminent United States threat, especially with Washington's 1978 acquiescence to the PRC's conditions for the establishment of diplomatic relations, has allowed Chinese policymakers to pay more attention to the Soviets, a fact not unnoticed in Moscow.[42] Obviously as policymakers in this case exercise external means of increasing capability, they must proceed with extreme care and caution, constantly guarding against actions that would drive the other two parties in the triangle together.[43]

As a policymaker analyzes each situation then, he or she must consider the potential differential effects of each choice. The policymaker must recognize that all alternatives have both advantages and disadvantages, and choose the one with the best ratio. But he or she must do this within the confines of the second facet of differential effects, namely, the fact that every choice has an impact on several parties and the effect is different for each. Thus the alternative the policymaker is seeking is the one that yields the best *net* cost-benefit ratio when calculated in terms of the anticipated impact on *all* the parties affected.

INSUFFICIENT TIME

The final difficulty policymakers often encounter is insufficient time. Frequently, there is not time to carefully go through the various steps in policy formulation, assess the relative merits of different combinations of implemen-

---

[42]Peking demanded that Washington shift its formal recognition from Taipei, withdraw all military forces from Taiwan, and terminate the 1954 mutual security pact. It did (although technically, on the last point, it did not abrogate but gave notice it would allow the treaty to lapse).

[43]For more on the effective utilization of such external means see Chapter 6, pp. 147–150 and p. 143.

tation instruments, etc.; things just happen too fast. The world does not always wait until one has completed the analysis, and decisions must be made. Sometimes one simply has no choice but to act, whether ready or not.

Example: The Korean War

Developments at the beginning of the Korean War illustrate this point well. First, a little background.[44] When World War II ended the allies occupied Korea to take over from the defeated Japanese (who had annexed Korea, and renamed it Chosen, in 1910). United States forces took over south of the 38th parallel, the Russians to the north. Unfortunately, final plans for the future of Korea had never been made, the sudden termination of hostilities catching the allies unprepared. With the occupation forces in place American-Soviet negotiations produced an agreement for a Joint Commission to set up a provisional Korean government with a view to eventually reestablishing Korea as an independent unified state. The Joint Commission also was to work out an agreement for a four-power trusteeship for Korea for five years until such independence could be achieved. Quickly the Joint Commission's activities reflected the growing Cold War, however, and little progress was made. In reaction the United States laid the matter before the United Nations where the General Assembly voted Washington's proposal to establish a Temporary Commission to oversee free all-Korean elections. In a short time elections were held in the American occupied zone. On August 15, 1948 the Republic of Korea was officially proclaimed, and on December 12 it was recognized by the General Assembly as South Korea's lawful government. But the Soviets refused the Commission access to North Korea, so free elections were never held there. Instead, the Soviet-style Democratic Republic of Korea was established. Shrewdly the Russians, who had extensively trained and equipped North Korea's army, now began to call for the withdrawal of all foreign troops. By the end of June 1949 the last American troops had departed, leaving behind only some 500 members of a military advisory group. No progress at all was made toward establishing a unified independent Korea (which both south and north wanted), and border incidents occurred regularly.

On Sunday June 25, 1950 at 4:00 A.M. Korean time (3:00 P.M. Saturday, June 24, Washington time) the North Koreans attacked.[45] A U. N. commission on the scene quickly verified that it was an unprovoked full-scale invasion. A

---

[44]Useful is Carl Berger, *The Korea Knot: A Military-Political History*, Revised Edition, University of Pennsylvania Press, Philadelphia, 1968, Chapters 1–7.

[45]Excellent on the first few days of the war is Glenn D. Paige, *The Korean Decision, June 24–30, 1950*, Free Press, New York, 1968.

few hours later the news reached Washington. Immediately a meeting of the U. N. Security Council was called, and it adopted a U. S.-sponsored resolution calling for a cease-fire and a withdrawal of North Korean forces.[46] But on the ground the North Koreans were advancing rapidly, and from Japan General MacArthur reported that all evidence indicated South Korea's army was collapsing. Convinced that the Soviets were behind the attack President Truman authorized MacArthur to use his air and sea forces to stem the onslaught. This was far too little, however, and the situation continued to deteriorate. On June 29 MacArthur flew to Korea to get a firsthand look. He was dismayed by what he saw; it was a rout. MacArthur therefore cabled Washington to the effect that unless American ground combat troops were committed, and fast, South Korea would be lost. MacArthur requested authority to immediately move an American combat team to Korea. The president consented to this request, and also authorized the Air Force and Navy to blockade and attack the North. Simultaneously, the wheels were put in motion to bring in additional ground forces.

As we noted in Chapter 5, on January 12, 1950 Secretary of State Acheson had defined the U. S. defense perimeter in the Pacific in such a way that it seemed to exclude Korea. A few months later war had broken out. Policymakers would like to have been in a situation that permitted them sufficient time to dispassionately analyze their alternatives and then, on the basis of this analysis, decide whether to stick with the earlier decision or opt to stop the assault. But they did not have that luxury; the pace of military events demanded immediate decisions. By the time one carefully went through all the "proper" steps the North Koreans would have conquered the whole peninsula and the ballgame would have been over.

Policymakers are only too aware of the difficulties caused by insufficient time. Sometimes, as in the example above, they are in situations in which much of what occurs is beyond their capacity even to significantly influence, let alone to control. But frequently though they cannot control each and every development they are in a position to have a major impact on the pace and flow of events and thus to make a strong effort to provide sufficient time for rational thought and decision.

Example: The Cuban Missile Crisis

President Kennedy's actions in the 1962 Cuban Missile Crisis provide an excellent example of an effort to manage and control events in order that the parties have as much time as possible to analyze the significance of information

---

[46]The Soviets were absent, having earlier walked out in protest of the United Nations' refusal to seat Red China.

and consider the likely consequences of various alternatives.[47] In the summer and early fall of 1962 American policymakers received considerable soft evidence indicating the Soviets might be installing intermediate and medium range ballistic missiles in Cuba. Because the Kremlin had never before placed such weapons outside Russia, because the possibility of discovery was high, and because the risks such action would produce were enormous, United States officials were skeptical of the incoming soft evidence. Since there was always a chance they were wrong though, via a wide range of public statements and private messages Washington made its position abundantly clear: such action would not be tolerated. Any number of times Moscow stated there was no reason for concern; the Soviet Union had no need to deploy missiles outside its frontiers. In light of all these facts policymakers considered it highly unlikely that missiles actually were being emplaced. Therefore, when the National Security Council's Executive Committee met on the morning of October 16 and was confronted with unmistakable evidence that, in fact, that was exactly what was happening, "the dominant feeling was one of shocked incredulity."[48]

Once it was clear that Soviet missiles *were* being put into Cuba, President Kennedy, after assessing the options with his Executive Committee, selected an approach with as low a level of violence as possible so that the Russians would have the time to consider the real impact of each step by the United States, and the consequences that would flow from each projected response.[49] Even then Kennedy sought to avoid a confrontation. On October 18 he met with Soviet Foreign Minister Gromyko, a conference arranged prior to his knowledge of the Russian action. Gromyko, unaware of Kennedy's knowledge, assured the President again that there were no offensive weapons being delivered. For Kennedy this was the last straw. The president announced the American quarantine on all offensive military equipment under shipment to Cuba in the evening of Monday, October 22, 1962.[50] In the same speech he evidenced his ultimate resolve when he stated that any nuclear missile launched from Cuba against any nation in the Western Hemisphere would be considered as an at-

---

[47]"Information" is used here in the broadest sense, referring to all messages, signals, and cues of a transnational nature, including the impact of actions.

[48]Robert F. Kennedy, *Thirteen Days: A Memoir of the Cuban Missile Crisis*, Norton, New York, 1969, p. 8. Upon being informed of the presence of the Soviet missiles in Cuba the president assembled an ad hoc group of his most trusted advisers. Even though it existed outside the formal National Security Council apparatus this ad hoc group became known as the Executive Committee of the National Security Council (Ex Comm). Also see Chapter 15, pp. 438, 441.

[49]One of the questions that the Executive Committee had to consider, of course, was "why" did the Soviets put the missiles into Cuba. In a brilliant study Graham Allison indicates that one's answer is highly dependent on his analytical model. See Graham T. Allison, *Essence of Decision: Explaining the Cuban Missile Crisis*, Little, Brown, Boston, 1971.

[50]In actuality, of course, this was a naval blockade. The term "quarantine" was used because a blockade could be considered an act of war under International Law.

tack by the Soviet Union on the United States, and would require a full retaliatory response directly on the Soviet Union.

The determination to pace and manage events so as to give the Soviets
time to think out the consequences of each move illustrated Kennedy's fear of
the situation getting out of control, and the possibility that an incorrect assessment of the information being received might lead to that. He worried that the
Soviets might feel pushed into a corner and have a spasm reaction. Although
the quarantine was announced on Monday, he waited until Tuesday, until
after he had received approval of the Organization of American States, to issue the actual proclamation, and it was not to become effective for another 24
hours. He ordered the Navy not to intercept a Soviet ship until absolutely necessary, and did so publicly so that the Soviets would be fully aware of what
was going to happen. The first ship intercepted obviously carried no arms, and
it was hailed but not boarded. The first boarding occurred the next day, and
the ship was not a Soviet ship but rather a Lebanese freighter under Russian
charter.

Meanwhile the administration had been taking steps to demonstrate that
this was not a bluff. Troops and ships were deployed, B-52s with nuclear
weapons were put on airborne alert, and the Polaris fleet was moved into operational range. Diplomatically, Washington asked for and received unanimous
support from the Organization of American States for the quarantine, a rare
occurrence indeed, and in the United Nations Ambassador Adlai Stevenson
had pressed the United States case with unusual vigor and decisiveness.

The President clearly hoped that Moscow would "get the message." On
October 26 he received a private communication from Soviet Premier Khrushchev suggesting a removal of the missiles under international supervision in
exchange for an American no-invasion pledge.[51] On the following morning,
however, the Russians publicly presented a much more uncompromising position, suggesting a removal of the missiles in exchange for removal of U. S. missiles from Turkey.

Kennedy's crisis management had been designed to allow the Soviets time
to think, but it also had involved the concept of gradual escalation. Now the
time had come to give the screw another turn. He ignored the uncompromising
Soviet proposal of October 27 and responded favorably to Friday evening's
private message. He then sent his brother Robert, the attorney-general, to
meet Soviet Ambassador Dobrynin. Robert emphasized the Soviet deception,

---

[51]Also, on this same day, John Scali, diplomatic correspondent of the American Broadcasting
Co., received a similar message from Alexander Fomin, purportedly a counselor at the Soviet Embassy but actually a KGB colonel. Scali communicated this to the State Department. See Elie Abel,
The Missile Crisis, Bantam, New York, 1966, pp. 155–164. The Russians had claimed that there
were only defensive weapons being given to Cuba to protect them against an American attack. Because the Central Intelligence Agency had helped to plan and execute the ill-fated Bay of Pigs assault in April 1961 a plausible case could be made.

made it clear that "if they did not remove those bases, we would remove them," and stated that Washington had to have a commitment to this effect by Sunday morning.[52] The next morning such a commitment was received. Moscow had "gotten the message."[53]

The pace at which the Soviet missiles were arriving and becoming operational had placed President Kennedy under considerable time pressure. Moscow had "kindly" assured the president that it would not raise the Berlin issue again until after the November 6 congressional elections, but it had indicated that it *would* do so then. At that juncture, American intelligence estimated, Russia's nuclear capability would be 50 percent greater than before the missiles were emplaced; obviously the Soviets would be in a much better bargaining position than they had ever been previously. Mr. Kennedy, therefore, wanted the crisis terminated quickly, before such a scenario could develop. He could not, of course, specifically control the Kremlin's actions; all he could do was bend every effort possible to prevent things from snowballing, to avoid being swept along by the chain of circumstances, and hope that Mr. Khrushchev would reciprocate. Fortunately, with the spectre of nuclear war looming on the horizon, the Soviet leader did.

As the Korean example shows, there are situations in which policymakers have to act rapidly and simply do not have sufficient time to analyze all the relevant information, logically consider each alternative, and so forth. In these cases hopefully contingency plans have been developed that can be applied, the foreign-policy machinery functions efficiently, and the parties exert every effort to keep things as logically controlled as possible. But as President Kennedy's actions in the missile crisis demonstrate, there are times even under conditions of severe stress and time pressure when a policymaker can do much to manage and pace the tempo of developments. Such activities can maximize the efficiency with which time is utilized and some of the debilitating effects that insufficient time often creates can be lessened (or even eliminated).

In this and the preceding chapter we have analyzed a number of rather common policymaking problems. Some are essentially intellectual errors, mental mistakes that presumably are not inevitable but nonetheless occur with remarkable regularity; others are pragmatic problems not of the policymaker's own making but with which he or she nevertheless must deal, problems that occur with such frequency that its almost as if they were "inherent" in the international political world. As if these obstacles to the formulation and implementation of the optimum policy were not enough, policymakers also must operate within a vortex of domestic influences. These provide the subject matter for Chapter 15.

[52]Kennedy, p. 86.
[53]See Allison, pp. 62–66.

15

Domestic Influences

Up to this point our analysis has proceeded as if the policymaker were able to act without regard to domestic pressures and considerations, as if international relations and domestic politics could be separated into vacuum-sealed compartments and neither would affect the other.[1] Unfortunately things are not this simple; nearly all decisions are taken within a vortex of internal pressures and policymakers often do not have the freedom to just go ahead and make whatever decisions they feel would be best.

In most situations the "official" policymaker is only one of the participants in the policymaking process. A variety of other parties also are involved, each attempting to influence the course of action.[2] As a result the policymaking process usually is much more complicated than even the admitted complexities of international politics would dictate. A staggering quantity and variety of mutual interactions occur yielding a very hazy web of complex, reciprocal relationships.

Because in all political systems the leadership needs some degree of domestic support, policymakers often attempt to build a coalition that will provide a consensual base for themselves and their policies. The major groups and individuals who are needed and who are in a position to provide the requisite

[1] For years international relations was studied with little regard for domestic pressures and this is still the approach in many courses and textbooks today.

[2] As Hilsman pointed out when analyzing the Cuban Missile Crisis there was "an appalling array of rival interests and competing factions." Hilsman, *To Move A Nation*, p. 196.

support thus become the target of a wide range of requests, promises, threats, and demands. At the same time that policymakers are wooing these elements they are returning the favor. Each "policy influencer" makes certain demands and expects a certain amount of satisfaction as the price for its support.[3] If a particular policymaker is unwilling or unable to provide this satisfaction the policy influencer may not give him or her the support he or she seeks.

Of course, there may be specific situations in which the policymaker does not have to respond positively. Perhaps the party in question is very weak, or maybe offsetting pressures are more powerful. Maybe he can convince it that the demands cannot be filled or another course of action is better. In some systems there are such tight restrictions on group and individual activity that they may have no choice but to support him much of the time, or maybe there is no alternative. Perhaps the party is willing to give in this time in the hope of making a gain on another issue or to pave the way for more influence in the future. Despite all these qualifications, however, the policymaker eventually will find that there is a certain core or minimum level of demands that one must meet if one hopes to succeed. If the policymaker does not do so he or she will at some point become ineffective (and perhaps even be removed from power).

An enormously important caveat must be introduced at this juncture to preface the analysis to follow. As we have pointed out many times, all international parties are unique, each possessing a distinctive blend of characteristics that to some extent sets it apart from every other. With respect to the topic at hand this means that the domestic influences on policymakers are different in varying degrees in every case. Consequently, our discussion can only be highly focused and selective, emphasizing certain elements (those deemed by the author to be the most significant) while barely touching others; this is inevitable. Furthermore, the analysis can only present hypotheses and generalizations that can be productively utilized as guidelines in the requisite separate examinations that must be undertaken in each specific case, because commonly accepted all-embracing conclusions do not exist. Accomplishing these limited objectives is a not unimportant task. Nevertheless, it is important for policymaker and observer alike to be cognizant of these analytical limitations and to again recognize the essentiality of being situation—and party—specific.

POLICY INFLUENCER: PUBLIC OPINION

What are the major types of policy influencers? The first is *public opinion*. In many states policymakers profess that they are significantly influenced by the

---

[3]See William D. Coplin, *Introduction to International Politics: A Theoretical Overview*, Second Edition, Rand McNally, Chicago, 1974, Chapter 3, from which the term "policy influencer" is taken.

public. Is this really the case or is it just a pretense? If public opinion does have an impact, what is it?

Before beginning this analysis directly it is necessary to make the distinction between the general public, what has been termed the "attentive" public, and opinion elites.[4] When one speaks of the "general public" he or she is referring to all of the people within a society. The term "attentive public" refers to a much smaller group and is defined as that body of informed citizenry that constitutes the primary nongovernmental audience for foreign policy discussions. The "opinion elites" are the articulate policy-influencing *core* of the population that gives some kind of structure to policymaking discussions and provides the effective means of access to those in charge.

In analyzing the influence of public opinion a very important consideration is the nature of the political system. Although a wide variety of classification schemes are possible, for the purposes of this analysis the basic distinction between authoritarian and democratic systems is sufficient. In every situation one who is seeking to ascertain the impact of public opinion should seek to determine the location of the system in question on the continuum from authoritarian to democratic.

What are the fundamental differences? Basically, authoritarian systems are characterized by the vast and stringent control of society by the government, very little competition, low levels of popular participation, either a single political party or none at all, usually a very powerful and influential internal police force, intensive and extensive controls of the activities of individuals by the policymakers, and control of the structures of society by a relatively small number of people. In a system that is more democratic the government does not control everything, competition and popular participation are fairly extensive, political parties are allowed to operate with relative freedom, police forces are limited by laws, individual rights are protected and there are relatively few restrictions on individual activities, power tends to be somewhat diffused, and the governors themselves operate under certain limitations.

Authoritarian Systems

In authoritarian political systems, such as exist in the Soviet Union and the People's Republic of China, public opinion plays almost no role in policy determination. Usually, in fact, the general public is just a tool in the hands of the policymakers. Because the government controls the media of communication the people hear and see primarily what the government wants them to; seldom do they make any serious demands. To the extent that the general public is involved at all in policy its participation is largely reactive or responsive.

[4]See Gabriel Almond, *The American People and Foreign Policy*, Praeger, New York, 1960.

And in many cases, of course, it is simply unaware of the policies undertaken (a phenomenon not unknown in democratic countries).

The attentive public in these systems is either nonexistent or terribly small and uninfluential. If there *is* a real foreign policy audience, it acts only as a sounding board on relatively unimportant issues. On major issues decisions are made by the policymakers; the public, including the attentive public, is expected to do as it is told. Similarly, in authoritarian systems nongovernmental opinion elites are of little significance (except, as is seen below, as they may be leaders of important interest groups). In many cases there may not even *be* any opinion elites because there just is not any policy-influencing core of the population.

This does not mean that the public *never* exercises any influence, however. Because all states today are much more permeable than was the case a few years ago, and because knowledge of other countries continually increases (even if policymakers seek to prevent it), the various publics in authoritarian states are becoming somewhat more aware of international realities. Because people's awareness is increasing, consistent or massive reverses in foreign policy may lead to real pressure on policymakers as general disenchantment or antagonism develops. Also, on a few occasions there may be certain deeply held specific opinions that operate at least vaguely as constraints. The Syrian general public's antipathy to Israel certainly places limitations on the policymaker's freedom of choice, for example. Despite these considerations, however, as a generalization one can still say that usually public opinion has very little effect on the policymaker in an authoritarian country.

Democratic Systems

In more democratic systems public opinion *sometimes* is more significant. In what ways can it have an impact? First, usually the general public has some notion about what policies, methods, and objectives it will tolerate. Although these notions are usually vague and amorphous they do exist; at some point they will *provide a set of boundaries* which a policymaker will transgress only at considerable risk.[5] For example, although in the years after World War II the American public usually supported its President in national security-related affairs, it eventually became disenchanted with American policy in Vietnam. After it became clear that the war was not being "won," there were certain limits established beyond which governmental action would not be tolerated (e.g., a permanent reescalation of the conflict). In a similar vein, the general public in the United States simply would not allow its government to follow a policy that would permit the destruction of Israel. The high level of pacifism

[5]Obviously some of this "risk" is the risk of electoral reverses.

demonstrated by Japanese public opinion in the first years after the termination of the post-World War II occupation limited that government's discretion with respect to the development of military strength.

The general public can also be influential in *positively marking out at least the general direction that policy should take.*[6] This delineation too is usually imprecise and vague, but that does not detract from the reality of its existence. Once again referring to the Vietnam situation, general public sentiment in the United States placed considerable pressure on the government to change its policy from one of confrontation and commitment to one of conciliation and withdrawal. British public opinion was strongly noninterventionist and antiwar in most of the 1930s, and this had much to do with Chamberlain's efforts to try to avoid conflict by conciliating Hitler.[7] The Japanese general public has acted as a strong stimulus to government policymakers in recent years toward the end of obtaining greater policy independence from the United States yet retaining the security of the American-Japanese alliance.[8]

There are other examples of influencing the general direction of policy. The reaction of the American public to the "loss" of China and the stalemate that developed in the Korean War were important factors in the major electoral reverses the Democratic Party suffered in the 1950 midterm elections. This setback indicated that those who had advocated a more vigorous anti-Communist policy would be more influential in future policymaking. The resulting "hardening" of American policy toward the People's Republic of China was at least partially due to this manifestation of public displeasure. And in both 1956 and 1967 Israeli public opinion put pressure on the government to adopt very bellicose policies.[9]

The general public plays another role to the extent that it *provides support for governmental policies.* Support is most pronounced when there is a strong national consensus which policymakers both clearly perceive and agree with. In the June 1967 war Israeli forces captured the Old City of East Jerusalem ("Arab" Jerusalem to the Arabs) from Jordan.[10] The deep spiritual, historic, political, cultural, and emotional ties of the Jews to Jerusalem, are well known.[11] Because of the government's military successes policymakers and

[6]The word "general" needs to be emphasized. Seldom is public opinion sufficiently coherent, informed, and precise to delineate specific policy directions.

[7]See Lord William Strang, *Britain in World Affairs: The Fluctuation in Power and Influence from Henry VIII to Elizabeth II*, Frederick A. Praeger, New York, 1961, pp. 319–324.

[8]Akio Watanabe, "Japanese Public Opinion" in Robert A. Scalapino, ed., *The Foreign Policy of Modern Japan*, University of California Press, Berkeley, 1977, p. 145.

[9]Samuel J. Roberts, *Survival or Hegemony? The Foundations of Israeli Foreign Policy*, Johns Hopkins Press, Baltimore, 1973.

[10]Jordan had achieved control of East Jerusalem as a result of the 1948–1949 war. Israel had obtained control of West Jerusalem, the New City, in the same conflict.

[11]Jerusalem is also a Holy City to both Christians and Moslems, and they also have deep ties to it.

nonpolicymakers alike saw the opportunity to end the Holy City's division, to achieve reunification. There was almost no division of public opinion on the desirability of undertaking such action. On June 18, 1967 the government of Israel decided to annex East Jerusalem and surrounding areas, and the move was almost wholly supported by the populace.[12]

The degree of public support is important in crisis situations, and often at such times it is pronounced.[13] In noncrisis times people become involved in the joys and frustrations of daily living and neither strongly support nor oppose particular policies, but in time of crisis the general public often rallies behind its leaders. Witness the immense support for their government by the people of England during the Battle of Britain, and the high morale and support of the government of the United States by its people during World War II.

But, there are times when the general public does *not* give its government support in a crisis. Although one cannot be certain, it seems that the level of support is related to the attributes of the crisis' perceived importance and its duration. For example, in short crises of high importance the American public seems to rally behind its president. The positive reactions to President Nixon's mining of Haiphong Harbor in 1972, President Johnson's massive increase of the bombing of North Vietnam in 1965, President Kennedy's actions in the Cuban Missile Crisis, and President Truman's decisions at the beginning of the Korean War, are just a few examples.

But if a crisis is long lasting and if the objective is perceived to be out of proportion to the time, effort, and resources expended, public support seems to decrease. World War II was a long crisis but there the obvious importance of the struggle plus the fact that positive results were forthcoming led the American public to continue to give strong support. When stalemates developed in the Korean and Vietnam conflicts and they dragged on and on the public eventually began to turn away; it just was not worth it. *Policymakers thus must remember that there is at least a danger that unless a crisis is resolved swiftly, or at least considerable progress can be shown toward its resolution, the public may withdraw its support.* Obviously this fact places pressure on policymakers to at least give the appearance of success, and this in turn often leads them to attempt to deceive the public, a point mentioned earlier.[14]

In each of the cases discussed above the attentive public and the opinion elites successively summarized and articulated the feelings of the mass society. In these situations what seems to exist is a two-step, two-way process.[15] Atti-

[12]This is carefully analyzed in Michael Brecher, *Decisions in Israel's Foreign Policy*, Yale University Press, New Haven, 1975, Chapter 2.

[13]See John Spanier and Eric M. Uslaner, *How American Foreign Policy is Made*, Second Edition, Praeger, New York, 1978, pp. 91–102. Also see Barry B. Hughes, *The Domestic Context of American Foreign Policy*, W. H. Freeman, San Francisco, 1978, Chapter 2.

[14]See Chapter 8, p. 215.

[15]See Elihu Katz and Paul Lazarsfeld, *Personal Influence*, Free Press, New York, 1955.

tudes flow from the general public to the community and opinion leaders and then to the policymakers, and vice versa. Information is filtered, interpreted, and transmitted in both directions with key elites, including the mass media, acting as the conduit and mediator between policymakers and the public at large.

Despite the fact that public opinion *can* have considerable impact in relatively democratic systems, *as a general rule it is not very important.*[16] Most of the time people are primarily concerned with domestic matters and are ill informed about foreign policy issues.[17] To put it very bluntly, most people don't know much about foreign policy matters and don't care (unless they feel it affects them directly). Re U. S. policy and the Berlin blockade, for example, "the fluidity that characterized American public opinion, largely a result of apathy and lack of expertise, gave Truman a carte blanche in dealing with the Russians."[18] In addition, inconsistency of views, contradictory ideas, and lack of coherence and direction abound. Actually, *instead of influencing the policymaker the general public usually looks to him or her for guidance.* In most cases the public is more of a *follower* than an *influencer.* Although there are the kinds of exceptions discussed earlier, usually the policymaker has pretty much of a free hand.

This public dependence on the policymaker (rather than vice versa) often leads him or her to attempt to manipulate the public mood instead of being guided by it. In democratic as well as authoritarian systems public opinion is often "used as an active and manipulable resource."[19]

POLICY INFLUENCER: POLITICAL PARTY

The second major type of policy influencer is the *political party.* As used here the concept of political party includes all party members, those who have ob-

---

[16]This fact is not, of course, restricted to the United States. In his study of the politics of the British military Kenneth Waltz states that a former British Minister in the Foreign Office felt that there was *no* occasion on which he or his superiors had been significantly affected on important decisions by public opinion. See Kenneth Waltz, "The Politics of the British Military," in Roy C. Macridis, ed., *Modern European Governments: Cases in Comparative Policy Making*, Prentice-Hall, Englewood Cliffs, N.J., 1968, p. 40.

[17]See James N. Rosenau, "Foreign Policy as an Issue Area," in James N. Rosenau, ed., *Domestic Sources of Foreign Policy*, Free Press, New York, 1967, pp. 24-36; also see Almond, p. 54.

[18]Morton Berkowitz, P. G. Bock, and Vincent J. Fuccillo, *The Politics of American Foreign Policy: The Social Context of Decisions*, Prentice-Hall, Englewood Cliffs, N.J., 1977, p. 51.

[19]Milton J. Rosenberg, "American Public Opinion on Cold-War Issues" in Herbert C. Kelman, ed., *International Behavior*, Holt Rinehart, New York, 1965, p. 279. Although the phrase is Rosenberg's, he was not specifically referring to democratic systems. One should also add that public opinion is sometimes manipulated as a means of increasing international capability; it is not always manipulated for domestic reasons.

tained official political office as well as those who have not.[20] To what extent are policymakers influenced by political parties?

Authoritarian Systems

Once again the distinction between authoritarian and democratic systems is relevant. In authoritarian systems there is usually just one political party, and it supplies all (or nearly all) policymaking personnel. One may wonder whether the idea of a policy influencer is even appropriate in such cases since the key policymakers are also party members. It *is* relevant, however, because most of these parties have a number of factions within them (each with its own power base, interests, and commitments) and each *faction* acts as an influencer.

A useful example of party influence in an authoritarian system is provided by the Communist Party in the Soviet Union (CPSU). The CPSU is the only political party in Russia and it controls the entire policymaking process. All general policy guidelines and specific blueprints are formulated within various party organs (with the Politburo usually being dominant), and implementation is similarly concentrated. Although two parallel hierarchies exist, the party and the governmental, only the former is really significant. All key government figures are party members and it is to the party that they owe first allegiance. For this reason the major governmental organs have little independent importance. The legislative body, the Supreme Soviet, acts primarily as a sounding board and rubber stamp for party leadership. The executive, the Council of Ministers, supposedly has wide authority, but it too is run by party elites; its chairman (premier) is always one of the two or three most powerful party leaders. Similarly, although various administrative personnel may have some role in policy execution, they also must operate within the guidelines and under the watchful eye of the party faithful. Thus Soviet foreign policy is CPSU policy.

Although the CPSU's control is complete, it is not always unified. Indeed, there has been *much* intraparty factionalism as various individuals and groups have competed for control of the party apparatus. Following Khrushchev's denunciation of Stalin at the Twentieth Party Congress in 1956, for example, those who were threatened such as Molotov, Malenkov, and Kaganovich allied themselves with men who sought greater power in their own right, like Bulganin, and battled Khrushchev for control.[21] And from the time of the beginning

---

[20]Obviously there is some overlapping of categories here since some individuals are both party members and policymakers. Nevertheless the distinction is analytically valid for most situations.

[21]In the struggle for control in the 1956–1957 period the Central Committee actually "overruled" the Politburo (at that time called the Presidium), a majority of which had voted to oust Khrushchev. This was a highly unusual occurrence, however, since major decisions are usually made by the Politburo. For an analysis of this interesting period see Robert Conquest, *Power and Policy in the USSR*, Macmillan, London, 1959.

of the Second Berlin Crisis of the late 1950s until Khrushchev's fall in 1964 there were serious factional differences within the Politburo.[22] Despite the continuing internal struggles, however, there was little public awareness of the various disputes until later (if then), and party officials continually sought to maintain the facade of unity; although there actually was a good deal of conflict it occurred behind closed doors and was denied or minimized in public.

Obviously, in authoritarian states such as the Soviet Union the political party is very influential. In some authoritarian systems, however, it means much less. In Egypt, for example, for years there was only one political party, the Arab Socialist Union, and all key policymakers belonged just as they did in the Soviet Union. But in contrast to the Russian situation the ASU had little importance. Egypt's single party functioned primarily as an arm of the leadership instead of as a determiner of policy, and usually was little more than a facade behind which decisions were made (and power struggles occurred). What went on in the ASU, therefore, had little immediate influence on Egyptian policymakers.

Thus when one is seeking to ascertain the influence of political parties in authoritarian systems he or she once again is faced with the necessity of becoming specific. There are few generalizations of any value. It is clear that conditions in these systems allow room for a great deal of party influence and that sometimes such a degree of influence exists. In some cases it does not, however, and whether or not it actually does in a given situation can be determined only by means of considerable specific analysis.

Democratic Systems

With respect to more democratic systems it is also difficult to generalize. This can be usefully illustrated through some comments about the influence of parties in Japan, West Germany, and the United States.

In post-World War II Japanese politics, the impact of political parties on the foreign policy process has been considerable. In fact, it has been said that "the most important domestic determinant of Japanese foreign policy is the intra-party decision making process of the Liberal-Democrats. All other components of the political system . . . reach the major foreign policy decisions primarily through access to this process."[23]

The Liberal-Democrats were a parliamentary party without a strong popular base. Party leadership was recruited from various distinct factions, each

---

[22]See Tatu, Parts 1-4.

[23]Hellman, p. 50. In addition to Hellman's work, very useful is I. M. Destler, Hideo Sato, Priscilla Clapp, and Haruhiro Fukui, *Managing an Alliance: The Politics of U.S.-Japanese Relations*, Brookings, Washington, D. C., 1976, Chapter 2.

faction having its own independent sources of finance, promoting its own candidates, and regularly caucusing on matters of strategy and policy. These factions existed primarily for the purpose of gaining and using power, and no policymaker could remain in a position of authority without responding to their demands. Reciprocal self-interest was the glue holding them together.

Within the Liberal-Democratic Party there was a continuing process of bargaining, the result being that policy usually was a compromise based on the accommodation of factional demands. This often led to a stifling of initiative and support of the status quo. This was reinforced because of the traditional Japanese notion that decision making should be based on a consensus and not be simply the result of a majority vote.

Due to the fact that though the factions of the Liberal-Democrats often achieved consensus such consensus usually was vigorously opposed by opposition parties, policymakers frequently sought to minimize public discussion of foreign policy and defense issues. When this tactic was not successful the opposition occasionally was able to take advantage of the belief in consensus and influence both political debate and the substance of policy. Generally, however, policy was the product of the Liberal-Democrats' intraparty factional struggles.

It is important to point out that this policymaking process has been significant not just in the sense of providing the context for decisions, although it has done that, but also in producing specific policy choices. For example, the 1956 decision to normalize diplomatic relations with the Soviet Union was preceded by two years of factional maneuvering and bargaining; domestic political victory was the prize and the intraparty power struggle was the prime element in determining the outcome.[24]

In the Japanese case policymakers definitely were influenced by the political party, particularly the faction(s) from which they drew their support. In the West German system parties have often had less of a policy-determining influence but they still have been important. Let's briefly examine one aspect of the role of the party system during the reign of Chancellor Konrad Adenauer. The leader of the Christian Democrats, Adenauer was the dominant force in West German politics for well over the first decade of his government's existence. As noted in Chapter 13, he sought West German recovery via an alliance with the West. Adenauer was seeking to develop a European political order that would tie the direction and structure of German society to the cultural and political forces of Western Europe.[25] He assumed that once these purposes were accomplished German reunification would follow.

[24]Hellman, p. 52.

[25]Wolfram Hanrieder, *The Stable Crisis: Two Decades of German Foreign Policy*, Harper, New York, 1970, p. 131.

The opposition, mainly the Social Democrats, had foreign policy priorities that were almost exactly the opposite. While they agreed that both recovery and unification were desirable, they believed that Adenauer's commitment to the West would eliminate any possibilities of German unity. They therefore advocated reunification as the first step with recovery and alliance with the West following to whatever extent possible.

The opposition was not very successful because Adenauer's policy recognized the political essentiality of attaching first priority to German recovery. With the country so war devastated it simply was not feasible to focus on any other objective in the early years of government, and if alliance with the West was necessary to achieve this goal then that is what the majority of the people would support. Of course, as discussed in Chapter 13, the Social Democrats were correct in their contention that this recovery and Western orientation would prevent unification. The problem for them, however, was that their policy was not domestically realistic.

The political parties in this case did not determine or even significantly influence the policymakers with respect to their choice of policies; Adenauer's positions were not the result of party pressure, from either the Christian Democrats or the opposition. But the party system was important in a less direct way. Because the Social Democrats provided a viable coherent opposition with a program of reasonable alternatives the policymakers in power were compelled to defend their positions publicly, make clear what their priorities were, and be answerable in case their policies failed. To this extent the party system fulfilled a valuable function for a democratic system in that it helped make the policymaker answerable to the public. The specific content of the policies, their anticipated results, and their actual consequences all were kept in the public eye through the process of debate over the various strategic alternatives.

The United States provides us with yet a third variation. The American party system is characterized by moderation, decentralization, and pragmatism.[26] In a sense there are no truly national parties but rather congeries of local and state parties that combine once every four years in an attempt to elect a president. Party discipline is very weak. Individual members often have their own organizations and independent bases of power. Party leaders possess little formal authority and almost no sanctions; whatever influence they have is a result of nonparty powers. In terms of influence there really is no hierarchy. A system of decisionmaking *layers* exists with as much power running from the local to the national level as vice versa.

---

[26]There are any number of useful analyses of this topic. I would recommend that the introductory student begin with a traditional text such as Robert K. Carr, Marver H. Bernstein, Walter F. Murphy and Michael N. Danielson, *Essentials of American Democracy*, Eighth Edition, Dryden Press, Hinsdale, Illinois, 1977, Chapter 7.

Due to these facts a large variety of political views are expressed within and between the parties. Intraparty conflicts abound and interparty coalitions form and reform. Because party discipline is so weak there seldom is a "party line" (although this is not always the case); even when there is it cannot be enforced. Although Congress is organized on a party basis most of its conflicts with the president are not primarily *party* struggles.[27]

The net result of all this is that American policymakers are seldom influenced significantly by the political parties per se. Because they owe little of their success or failure to party officials they seldom pay much attention to them in the normal processes of policy formulation and implementation.[28]

In each of the three examples of democratic systems described above the political party policy influencer had a different impact. In the Japanese case it was quite influential in policy determination; in the West German situation it did not directly influence policy choices but was indirectly important as an agent to keep the policymaker "on his toes" and publicly accountable; in the American case parties had almost no significance.

What conclusions can be drawn from this? Perhaps the only sure one is that no generalizations are possible (as was true with respect to authoritarian systems). The mere fact that a system is democratic gives one little clue as to how important a policy influencer the political parties in that system will be. In some they are very significant, in some moderately so, and in some they hardly matter. When attempting to ascertain their influence one must proceed on a case by case basis, carefully analyzing the specific facts before him and reaching his conclusions only on the basis of those facts.

POLICY INFLUENCER: INTEREST GROUPS

Interest groups are another major category of policy influencer. An interest group is (1) an association of individuals; (2) external to major policymaking positions; (3) who are "tied" together by a more or less common set of interests and (4) one of whose objectives is to influence the policymaker with regard to specific policies that would advance these particular interests.[29] These associations are often economic in nature, but this is not a requisite and various professional, ethnic, social, and occupational groups exist.

---

[27]Sometimes the features of governmental structure have a significant impact on the policymaking process, as noted in Chapter 8, pp. 212–217. Today the U. S. Congress is attempting to enlarge its role vis-à-vis the president, for example. As stated in the text, however, this is not primarily a *political party* issue.

[28]For a thoughtful, concise analysis see Gene E. Rainey, *Patterns of American Foreign Policy*, Allyn & Bacon, Boston, 1975, Chapter 8.

[29]Bureaucratic factors that could be considered here will be analyzed in succeeding sections.

Authoritarian Systems

The distinction made earlier between relatively democratic and authoritarian systems is important here. Fewer independent groups are allowed to exist in most authoritarian states than in their democratic counterparts. For this reason one can say that generally interest groups tend to be less important. But although fundamentally correct, this "obvious" conclusion is to some extent misleading. Even though formal independent associations are fewer, a myriad of informal "groupings" exist and people with common interests *do* work together to achieve common objectives. As defined in this manner interest groups or groupings exist in authoritarian as well as in democratic systems.

In the Soviet Union, for example, there are several factions competing for control of the party and governmental machinery.[30] Although Soviet ideology officially allows no room for competing interest groups (which could only be "hostile classes"), these groups do exist. Economic managers, technocrats, the cultural intelligentsia, the scientific community, the police, and the ever-present armed forces compete for supremacy along with the party and governmental bureaucrats. Instead of a process of competition and accommodation such as occurs in many democratic systems, however, the objective in this case sometimes is the attainment of dominance and the elimination of rivals. Because of this the composition of the various party and governmental organs often tends to reflect the mosaic of power relationships in existence at a given time.

In an authoritarian system the policymaking apparatus is centrally controlled and directed, and thus in many ways it is relatively impervious to pressure. Nevertheless, policymakers are sometimes forced to depend on outside sources for certain kinds of specialized information, a certain degree of expertise, and some cooperation in the implementation of decisions. Because often there are groups (or "groupings") that possess these special characteristics, they may have an opportunity to exercise some influence. Generally speaking, the degree of influence will be proportional to the policymaker's *dependence* for information and advice on such outside sources, his *need* for their expertise in handling various matters, and the *extent* to which their cooperation is necessary for the effective implementation of his decisions. Leaders of the military in the U. S. S. R., for example, because of the armed forces' near monopoly of information and expertise on technical military issues (and the secrecy pervading the Soviet system) frequently are in a position to have a significant impact on Politburo members as they consider either overall strategy or specific mat-

---

[30]See especially Vernon V. Aspaturian, *Process and Power in Soviet Foreign Policy*, Little, Brown, Boston, 1971, Chapters 15–16. Also see Philip D. Stewart, "Soviet Interest Groups and the Policy Process," *World Politics*, October, 1969, pp. 29–50.

ters of doctrine, force posture, arms control, etc. In authoritarian as well as democratic systems policymakers sometimes have certain needs that can best be met by special interests. It is evident that there are differences from system to system, just as there are between different parties with similar systems, but to a considerable extent they are differences in degree, not kind.

There is another aspect of interest group activity to be considered with respect to authoritarian systems—the fact that various groups often struggle to advance their special interests by taking control of the policymaking apparatus. In this situation the objective is not to influence certain specific policies but rather to attain decisive influence within the policymaking organs themselves.

The policymaker in an authoritarian system thus may find himself or herself subject to two kinds of interest group stimuli. The first is the traditional demands-supports relationship based on reciprocal need and advantage. When the need factor is minimal he will be little influenced *if* the group is not too powerful. But the second impinging factor concerns the matter of competition for control of the policymaking apparatus, and in these situations one must always be aware of the power dynamics of group politics.

Democratic Systems

With respect to more democratic systems it is useful to distinguish between those in which policymaking is relatively centralized and those in which it is not. Great Britain provides us with an example of considerable centralization. With its parliamentary system and fusion of powers, policy is made primarily by the governing political party rather than via any kind of interparty bargaining and compromise. The parties organize and operate the governmental system on a straight, party-line basis. They are highly disciplined and centralized, with sanctions and authority flowing from top to bottom through a well-defined hierarchy. Members seldom depart from the leadership's positions, and when they do they may be risking their political careers. In this kind of a situation there is precious little room for interest group influence external to the party structure. A wide variety of groups *do* seek to influence policymakers at both the executive and parliamentary level, *but they do so primarily by working through and in connection with the parties themselves.*

Because the parties have different although somewhat overlapping bases of support, some groups are much more influential with one party than another. But even with respect to important supportive groups the key point remains: seldom can a group compel a policymaker to depart from the accepted party line. A group's influence exists primarily within the confines of the party structure and is limited to attempting to persuade the party leadership that what is good for the particular group is good for party and country.

In some democratic systems decision making is much more diffused. Because of the system of separate institutions with an intermingling, checking, and balancing of functions and powers, decentralized political parties, federalism, and a variety of other structural features, American policymaking is extremely fragmented.[31] Decisions are made in a wide variety of places and circumstances by a number of different individuals, groups, and coalitions. This means that there are a multitude of points at which one may gain access to the policymaking process. Interest groups investigate these, constantly seeking access to the "key" policymaker. Because these groups sometimes have significant financial resources, occasionally can be important in an electoral contest, sometimes can provide valuable information and assistance, and sometimes are in a position to apply coercive pressure, policymakers on certain issues may be very sensitive to group viewpoints. Various Zionist organizations, for example, have played a significant role in influencing American policy toward Israel.[32] Similarly, for years the notorious China lobby was influential in preventing reconsideration of American policy toward the People's Republic of China.[33]

These examples are the exception rather than the rule, however. Generally interest groups are not very influential with respect to foreign policy issues. In the passage of the Foreign Assistance Act of 1967, for example, their impact was "marginal."[34] Even those groups that sometimes, in fact, are influential and whose public reputation for influence is considerable frequently have little impact. William Quandt discovered this in his study of American policy in the June 1967 Arab-Israeli war, stating:

> Noteworthy by their unimportance during the crisis were the allegedly powerful pro-Israeli interest groups and the oil lobby.[35]

Why are interest groups usually not significantly influential in the formulation and execution of U. S. foreign policy? What are the reasons that,

[31]This analysis owes an intellectual debt to the classic and ever valuable work of David Truman, *The Governmental Process*, Knopf, New York, 1951.

[32]Jewish groups are among the most active and the most successful. See Bernard C. Cohen, *The Public's Impact on Foreign Policy*, Little, Brown, Boston, 1973, pp. 104–105. Also see Earl Huff, "A Study of a Successful Interest Group: The American Zionist Movement," *Western Political Quarterly*, March, 1972, pp. 109–124.

[33]See A. T. Steele, *The American People and China*, McGraw-Hill, New York, 1966. Also useful is Ross Y. Koen, *The China Lobby in American Politics*, Macmillan, New York, 1960.

[34]Berkowitz et. al., p. 217.

[35]Quandt, *Decade of Decisions*, p. 70. The student should remember we are speaking here of influence on the policymaker. Just because an individual makes a decision that benefits a particular group, that does not necessarily mean he or she has been *influenced by* that group. Only if one's policy is different from what it otherwise might have been has influence been exercised.

contrary to what many times is the public perception, policymakers generally do not have their decisions impacted in a major way by so-called special interests? There are several. In the first place, most major groups such as the AFL-CIO and Chamber of Commerce are large organizations composed of many members who are also members of other groups. Because of this overlapping membership individuals have competing loyalties and most of the time the group's leaders cannot possibly influence their membership sufficiently to have them act as a cohesive body.

A second point is that usually there are a myriad of groups lined up on opposite sides of various issues. For example, with respect to foreign trade bills there are certain groups that tend to be protectionists and others that tend to be oriented toward freer trade. Many times this competition has an offsetting effect as the groups neutralize each other.[36] This allows the policymaker to pick and choose. Similarly countervailing, off-setting coalitions occur with respect to arms control agreements, military spending proposals, economic aid bills, and most other specific issues.

Another point is that most interest groups are concerned with only a few problems and are not really operational a good share of the time. Thus policymakers are simply relatively free of interest group pressures on many issues. Also, there are so many competing elements within the policymaking process that even if interest groups should happen to be united and cohesive on some issue they might well be offset or relegated to subsidiary importance by other factors. Furthermore, whereas interest groups are often important in domestic politics because of their capacity to provide critical information, on foreign policy questions they simply do not have such information to provide.[37] Finally, on some issues perceived to have a significant relationship to national security, interest groups sublimate their special needs to the national good; in certain cases politics "stops at the water's edge."

The net result of all of this is that in most situations policymakers' decisions are not significantly shaped by interest group pressures. Although this is a fact, and an important one, it is essential not to overstate the case; there can be exceptions. Such are particularly likely in circumstances in which the focus is on certain kinds of economic-political issues that are perceived to have a major domestic economic-political impact. Energy problems often fall in this category. These *are* the exception rather than the rule, but they do exist. Consequently, as is typically the case, it is necessary to be situation specific. Although the generalization of little impact is valid for enough instances to have some value, enough exceptions exist to make it imperative that policymakers analyze each case on its own merits.

[36]Raymond A. Bauer, Ithiel de Sola Pool, and Lewis Anthony Dexter, *American Business and Public Policy*, Second Edition, Aldine-Atherton, Chicago, 1972.
[37]Spanier and Uslaner, Second Edition, pp. 83–84.

Before concluding this analysis it is necessary to deal with what has been called the military-industrial complex, that conglomeration of industries, bureaucratic agencies, congressmen, interest groups, communities, and states that are concerned with and purportedly influential in the development of defense policy. With the annual American defense budget now over the $130 billion mark it is easy to understand why various organizations seek to influence the policymaking process in their favor. More and more groups are becoming involved, not only because of the size of the pie but also as a result of two other factors: (1) the distinction between foreign and domestic policy is becoming increasingly obscure (and meaningless?), and (2) more and more sectors of the economy are being geared specifically to defense and defense-related activities. In recent years completely new industries have developed that depend almost totally on military expenditures, for example, and basic research and development have been closely tied to military requirements. Decisions such as whether or not to develop a new weapons system or whether to maintain, expand, or close a particular military installation can have an immense impact.

Policymakers expect to be the targets of activity in defense-related areas, and they are. Sometimes the pressures are immense and occasionally a policymaker's decision is definitely influenced. *This is the exception rather than the rule, however, despite misconceptions to the contrary.* The basic reason is that the "complex" is both less coherent and less powerful than is sometimes supposed. There are several reasons for this. In the first place, specific industrial representatives, interest groups, contractors, and whatever usually align with the specific armed service they feel will do them the most good. Different ones choose different services and the services often are in competition. This contributes to an intensification of natural interservice rivalries with the result that presidents and their advisers are able to play one against the other, to pick and choose. Second, more times than is recognized the military is simply overruled by the civilians in control. President Carter's decision not to produce the B-1 bomber was just such a case. Third, very often there is intense infighting among the various elements; instead of a unified complex controlling policymakers there is vigorous factional competition and conflict within "the complex." In such situations rather than being compelled to do something the policymaker is able to choose from the maelstrom of contending forces. Fourth, the elements of the complex are but some of the domestic organizations and actors competing for the policymakers' attention, and there is nothing that automatically guarantees their superiority over any of the others. And finally, as we have consistently pointed out, policymakers are subject to a whole host of influences. The elements of the military-industrial complex are one, but only one, of this vast array.

None of this is to gainsay the fact that the military-industrial complex has a role in American policymaking. It has sometimes been important before and will occasionally be so in the future. But the matter should be kept in perspective: this "complex" certainly is not dominant, much of the time it is not unified, and usually policymakers are not significantly influenced by it.

Our analysis of the significance of the three types of policy influencers (public opinion, political parties, and interest groups) has led to the general conclusion that most of the time they really are not very influential in democratic systems. With the notable exception of the importance of political parties in certain authoritarian states, in most authoritarian systems they are similarly insignificant. Very seldom are these policy influencers able to compel the policymaker to do what he does not want to do, and most of the time they cannot even influence him significantly. But does this mean that policymakers are usually free from meaningful domestic pressures? The answer is "no," and the reason is that they often are greatly influenced by bureaucratic politics, the subject of the remainder of this chapter.

BUREAUCRATIC POLITICS

Former President Harry Truman was quoted as saying, "I make American foreign policy."[38] At another time, however, he said, "I sit here all day trying to persuade people to do things they ought to have enough sense to do without my persuading them," and he said of incoming President Eisenhower's problems, "He'll sit here and he'll say do this, do that, and nothing will happen."[39] These quotations point up the discrepancy between what the chief policymaker occasionally feels able to do and what he or she is so often prevented from doing because of bureaucratic difficulties.

All chief policymakers operate within some sort of bureaucratic context. Because of the fact of party uniqueness, each state's policymaking machinery is different in some respects from that of every other, that is, the size, complexity, structure, and specific features of each party's bureaucracy are in some manner and to some extent unique. It is evident, for example, that a major power with global involvements such as the Soviet Union will have a much larger and more varied policymaking apparatus than would a small state with essentially regional concerns such as Costa Rica. Although the existence of manifold organizational differences is a fact, it also is well established that the general trend in nearly all countries is toward the development of a fairly extensive policymaking apparatus. To the extent that such a condition actually obtains there will be a number of similarities among states, even though at the

[38]Louis E. Koenig, *The Chief Executive*, Third Edition, Harcourt Brace, New York, 1975, p. 213.

[39]Richard Neustadt, *Presidential Power: The Politics of Leadership*, Wiley, New York, 1960, pp. 9–10.

same time there also will be many peculiarities. The analysis that follows focuses primarily on the similarities, on those features that appear to be common in some measure to all bureaucracies. In the analysis of each specific situation one would have to investigate to discover the degree to which these features actually existed, and to the extent that they did not it would be necessary to make the requisite adjustments accordingly.

What is a bureaucracy? Although there are a wide variety of definitions, for the purposes of this analysis it is useful to define it as a large, formal organization that possesses the following characteristics: first, a hierarchical pattern of authority and communication with specific superior-subordinate relationships; second, a specialization of both role and function; third, a complex division of labor; and fourth, internal operations conducted via set procedures that emphasize formal rules and regulations. An example of such an organization would be the U. S. Department of State.

The presumed purpose of a foreign policy bureaucracy is to aid the chief policymaker(s) in formulating and implementing the optimum policy. It is designed to reflect the need for specialization and expertise in the conduct of foreign affairs, and to provide for the gathering, interpreting, and transmitting of accurate information as swiftly as possible to the correct people. It is also supposed to ensure a certain degree of stability and regularity in the policymaking process. It is supposed to provide records of what has been done so that one has a basis on which to make intelligent judgments concerning the future. It (hopefully) can partially remedy the problem of the leader's having "too much to do and not enough time to do it" by handling routine matters and freeing the chief policymaker for higher priority tasks. Often the bureaucracy is expected to generate innovative yet sound ideas and recommendations in the policy formulation stage, to provide the managerial tools to ensure cost-effective implementation, and to have the capability to monitor and effectively evaluate performance. Finally, in many states the bureaucracy is also charged with the crucial task of policy coordination.

The foreign policy bureaucracies of today's world fulfill these functions and achieve these objectives to varying degrees, sometimes performing well, other times not. Often such organizations exhibit certain characteristics and produce certain kinds of outputs that adversely impact policymakers, however. In other words, on some occasions instead of being a positive influence the bureaucracy's impact is detrimental. One cannot know in advance of the particular case. Therefore, one cannot productively generalize with any certainty on this point. The outcome is always mixed, and each party and situation must be studied separately.

As we mentioned earlier, our analysis will focus primarily on those features that to some extent are common to all bureaucracies. Within this framework we will study these organizations from four related and somewhat overlapping perspectives. First, we will view the bureaucratic political process in terms of the standard operating procedures that exist within most large organizations. Second, we will examine the significance of bureaucratic fragmentation and the competition between organizations. Third, we will analyze the role of small groups in policymaking. And fourth, we will comment on the bureaucratic process as a whole, emphasizing in particular the relationship of the chief policymaker to his or her bureaucracy.

BUREAUCRATIC POLITICS: STANDARD OPERATING PROCEDURES

The first point to remember is that in states with medium or large policymaking organizations the vast majority of foreign policy decisions are made in accordance with standardized procedures set up well in advance of the particular situation. Such procedures are designed to anticipate a wide variety of contingencies, and responses are preprogrammed according to specific routines. Policymaking often becomes a matter of selecting the appropriate routine and implementing it according to prescribed rules and regulations. The vast majority of these activities involve low- and middle-echelon "bureaucrats" who act within the framework of the procedures and general policies established by their superiors.

The *Fait Accompli* Problem

Because of the immense volume of issues confronting any state these routinized procedures are necessary. *But the consequence for the chief policymaker is that the vast majority of the "decisions" that are made, although presumably being within the prescribed policy and procedural framework, occur without his or her specific knowledge.*[40] This means that he or she is removed from the day to day operation of most policy and often wakes up to a *fait accompli.*[41]

Sometimes these low- and middle-level decisions have immense significance. For example, in the Eisenhower administration specific decisions con-

---

[40]For reasons of textual clarity we always use the term "chief policymaker" in the singular and proceed as if that person's identity were quite clear. It is apparent that this is an oversimplification. As we pointed out in Chapter 8, a major task in analyzing governmental effectiveness is to discover who the key individuals are. It is evident that regimes vary enormously, that much of the time several people are involved in the decision-making process, and that the locus of decision may vary with time and circumstance. But the point here is that irrespective of these concerns, no matter the identity and number of "chief policymaker(s)," whoever it is he, she (they) will find him, her (them)self(ves) to some extent enmeshed in the bureaucratic web.

[41]A useful study in this regard is Vincent Davis, "The Development of a Capability to Deliver Nuclear Weapons by Carrier-Based Aircraft" in Morton H. Halperin and Arnold Kanter, eds., *Readings in American Foreign Policy: A Bureaucratic Perspective*, Little, Brown, Boston, 1973, pp. 216–275.

cerning U-2 overflights (spy flights) were taken as a matter of course by the Central Intelligence Agency in accordance with guidelines set down by the president. In the early summer of 1960 such an aircraft was shot down over the Soviet Union shortly before a scheduled summit conference. This led to a series of events that culminated in the Russians torpedoing of that conference, and the spy-plane incident provided the rationale. The decisions had been taken on a routine basis without any direct guidance from above and apparently without sufficient awareness of what embarrassment a failure could cause.[42]

Another example occurred in the Truman administration. In the fall of 1947 the United States had played a major role in securing the U. N. General Assembly's passage of the resolution to partition Palestine. By early 1948 as violence increased and it was evident that partition could not be achieved peacefully, because of their view that the Soviets would exploit any conflict situation American policymakers reexamined their support of partition. As a result of their study a number of departments urged a policy alteration. Representatives of the Zionists' Jewish Agency picked up these vibrations and sought a meeting with the president to head off any change. Following the bureaucracy's advice Mr. Truman altered course and gave preliminary approval for a speech by Washington's U. N. Ambassador, Warren Austin, to the effect that the partition plan should be set aside and a temporary trusteeship installed; the ambassador was given the document on March 16 with instructions to deliver the speech as soon as the time was appropriate. On March 18 Mr. Truman met with the Jewish Agency's representative, Dr. Chaim Weizmann, and as a result of this meeting decided to continue to work for partition, to go back to the original policy and reverse the alteration. But Ambassador Austin hadn't even known this meeting was going to occur, let alone that the president would reverse his position, so his people had gone ahead and scheduled the speech; since they had already gotten preliminary approval from the president they did not think they needed to ask for clearance again, and since their instructions were to deliver the speech when the time was appropriate they didn't inform him of the timing. On March 19, the day after Truman promised Weizmann the United States would continue to support partition, Ambassador Austin told the United Nations that the partition plan should be abandoned and a U. N. trusteeship should be created. The president did not find out until he read the story in the newspaper the next morning.

American leaders sometimes have had *fait accompli* difficulties with the CIA's covert activities.[43] From 1949 to 1952, for example, the Director of Central Intelligence (DCI) had the capacity to approve CIA projects strictly on his

---

[42]See David Wise and Thomas B. Ross, *The U-2 Affair*, Random House, New York, 1962.

[43]A useful summary is U. S. Senate, Select Committee to Study Governmental Operations with respect to Intelligence Activities, *Final Report, Book I, Foreign and Military Intelligence*, 94th Cong., 2nd Sess., 1976, pp. 48–61.

own authority (though he usually consulted with an NSC panel prior to undertaking action); from 1953 to early 1955 the DCI had to coordinate project approvals with certain NSC subcommittees only. In both cases although certain covert activities were brought to the president's attention this was not required, and it took place only at the DCI's initiative. As a result of two NSC directives in 1955 "designated representatives" of the president and the secretaries of state and defense were brought into the process, and from this point on most covert action programs were approved by what became known as the "Special Group." But not *all* projects were submitted to the Special Group for clearance, so the president's "designated representatives" were not always informed, and even when they were they did not always communicate effectively with the president. A restructuring occurred in 1970 with the creation of the so-called 40 Committee. The 40 Committee consisted of the president's assistant for national security affairs, the deputy secretary of defense, the under secretary of state for political affairs, the chairman of the Joint Chiefs of Staff, and the DCI. The DCI was responsible for obtaining prior approval for all sensitive covert projects from the 40 Committee. However, although "sensitive" covert programs required 40 Committee approval, low-risk, low-cost operations did not, and some of what the DCI did not feel to be sensitive and thus did not refer to the 40 Committee in actuality was pretty important. Furthermore, some of what the 40 Committee perceived to be routine and/or relatively unimportant actions were not referred to the president, and these too were subsequently undertaken without his knowledge. It is quite clear that with these kinds of organizational arrangements (or the lack thereof), on numerous occasions the president of the United States had little to do with day to day operations and found himself confronted with a *fait accompli*.

Naturally, the above does not describe what occurs in all cases; decisions are not always made at lower levels, nor are they always the result of the application of preprogrammed routines. States differ considerably in this regard. In some, Britain being a prime example, it is standard operating procedure to have as many matters as possible handled through the application of routines, and to make decisions at as low a level as is feasible.[44] In others, especially in many of the LDCs, top policymakers prefer to keep the influence of low- and mid-echelon bureaucrats to the minimum, to have them participate in policymaking only to the extent that it cannot be prevented. Although there thus can be no hard and fast rules in this matter, it still is accurate to say that generally, in most bureaucracies most of the time, the following is true: the more unanticipated the problem the less routinely it can be handled, and the more complex and important the issue the more likely decisions will be made at higher and higher levels within the bureaucracy.

---

[44]William Wallace, *The Foreign Policy Process in Britain*, London, Royal Institute of International Affairs, 1975, p. 69.

There is yet another factor to be considered in this regard, however. The very judgments concerning whether or not a problem is highly important and complicated are often made by the person with whom the problem first comes in contact, namely, a low- or mid-level bureaucrat. If this person perceives the problem to be relatively simple or believes that it can be handled within a pre-arranged framework he or she may make a decision that has far-reaching operational consequences (when he or she should refer it to a higher level). Indeed, one of the most significant and difficult responsibilities of low- and mid-level officials is the determination of which matters they may dispose of themselves and which need to go to a higher authority.[45]

The Stifling of Innovation and Initiative

A major difficulty that often arises in a bureaucratic setting is the *stifling of initiative and innovation*. Decisions tend to be made that are considered safe, that conform to existing procedures, and that will not require significant judgment concerning whether or not departures from established rules are required. Because procedures are set up on the basis of the results of *past* policy, decisions based on such experience involve very few radical departures. To the extent that these factors operate the policymaker may never even get the chance to consider new ideas.

There are several other factors that tend to inhibit innovation within a bureaucratic setting. First, the individual whose views or actions differ widely from organizational policy tends to adjust his or her views or be rejected.[46] If he or she cannot be convinced to change his or her views, his or her ideas will have very little influence. Second, there is a rather natural tendency on the part of subordinates to advocate policies that they perceive to be in accord with the views of their superiors. It is usually safe to propose alternatives that one knows will not "rock the boat" and that will reinforce his or her superior's power and policies. As Hedrick Smith has pointed out, in the U. S. S. R. a bureaucrat with too much initiative and knowledge can get into trouble. The prudent course is to anticipate the wishes of one's superiors and act accordingly.[47] To the extent that the superior-subordinate relationship prevents the consideration of new ideas, either because of formal sanctions or informal coercion, innovation is repressed.

[45]Useful is R. Barry Farrell, *The Making of Canadian Foreign Policy*, Prentice-Hall of Canada, Scarborough, Canada, 1969, pp. 45–46.

[46]Joseph De Rivera, *The Psychological Dimension in Foreign Policy*, Charles E. Merrill, Columbus, Ohio, 1968, pp. 209–211.

[47]Hedrick Smith, *The Russians*, Quadrangle/New York Times Book Co., New York, 1976, p. 294. In the Vietnam war many American bureaucrats followed such a course, prudently telling their superiors what they wanted to hear. See Leslie H. Gelb, with Richard K. Betts, *The Irony of Vietnam: The System Worked*, Brookings, Washington, D. C., 1979, Chapter 11.

A third reason that new policies tend to be eliminated is the mere fact that many decisions must ascend several horizontal layers within the organization. As proposals traverse their hazardous way up the administrative hierarchy the more extreme ideas tend to be weeded out at each level. By the time a proposal reaches the top it very often can be described as the least common denominator, the least innovative and most compromised point of view.

And there is another reason. A bureaucracy contains a wide variety of specialists with differing perspectives, sources of information, and points of view. Because many people take part in a given policymaking situation, in order for a common policy to be developed compromise is necessary. And compromise itself usually involves a rejection of extremes or radical departures from established policy. This too contributes to a lack of innovation.

Parochialism

This discussion of the pressure toward caution and conformity has raised several other important points. As mentioned above, within a bureaucracy there is immense task specialization. While this is necessary because of the detailed expertise required to formulate an effective policy, it also poses certain problems. For example, the *further one is down the hierarchy, the narrower his or her perspective becomes.*[48]

All people quite naturally tend to view a problem in terms of their particular position. Within the U. S. State Department, for example, it is quite natural for the country director of Egypt to view the Arab-Israeli conflict with particular emphasis on the role of the Egyptians and the impact of various policies on Cairo. However, there are other considerations which people at higher levels with broader responsibility will need to take into account. The assistant secretary for the Near East would have to consider the possible impact and importance of all the various factors within that geographical region (many of which will have been presented to him or her by the various country directors). Even the assistant secretary's perspective is not sufficiently broad, however, because there are a wide variety of ramifications for international organization, economic development and, of course, for the interrelationships from one geographical region to another. The secretary of state will need to coordinate all of the specialized inputs, and the process continues this way right up to the top.[49]

---

[48]I. M. Destler, *Presidents, Bureaucrats and Foreign Policy: The Politics of Organizational Reform*, Princeton University Press, Princeton, New Jersey, 1974, p. 57.

[49]Another problem sometimes crops up in this regard. Because of their differences in perspective and objectives lower level bureaucrats may refuse to comply with established policy or procedure. In some cases they may even go beyond this and sabotage the leadership's positions, trying to impose their own solutions to problems.

The problem of parochialism requires that compromises be effected but this must be done in such a way that the specialists do not react too negatively and in such a fashion that high level coordination of various recommendations can occur. This is often easier said than done, and the many compromises tend to inhibit major policy changes. But the only way to avoid this is to not consider certain points of view and simply make whatever decisions one feels appropriate. This would both fail to take advantage of all relevant information and expertise and lead to a low level of morale and intraorganizational efficiency. So there is no perfect answer to this one.

Inertia

The many factors that contribute to the stifling of initiative, the parochialism and compromise, and the problem of "layering," lead to another troublesome problem: *often it takes forever and a day to get anything done.* So many clearances are required, there are so many "bases to be touched," that the policymaker sometimes just cannot seem to get started. President Kennedy was continually frustrated by what he felt was a kind of "built-in inertia."[50] Leaders in other states, of course, face similar difficulties. The Soviet bureaucracy, for example, has long been noted for its rigidity and inertia.[51] This type of problem frequently impels policymakers to bypass the foreign policy bureaucracy in those circumstances when quick decisions are imperative, as in most crises.

Information and Communication Deficiencies

For a party to formulate and implement the policy that produces the best attainable net benefit-cost ratio it is important that large quantities of high quality information be obtained, that it be interpreted correctly, it be sent to the appropriate parties in a timely manner, and that they act on it. Standard operating procedures can be highly significant in this regard. We have already mentioned one frequent difficulty: whether or not information is communicated will in part depend on a subordinate's perception of the rewards or costs that will result from the communication. If one insists on communicating information his or her superior feels is unimportant or contradictory to the superior's interests there may be excessive costs, and if a subordinate envisages such a result it's likely no communication will occur.

To some extent, of course, information *must* be selected, evaluated, and filtered from one level to another. There are too many decisions for all of them

---

[50]Theodore Sorensen, *Kennedy*, Harper, New York, 1965, p. 287.

[51]A recent study indicated that in many instances Soviet organizations tend to be even less innovative than the bureaucracies of most Western nations. Arthur J. Alexander, *Decision-Making in Soviet Weapons Procurement*, IISS, London, Adelphi Papers Nos. 147 and 148, 1978.

to be made at the top level, and there is simply too much information for any one party to digest. Therefore, synthesis and summarization must occur, and judgments made as to what should and should not be communicated. Because of this, systematic procedures and routing systems are established to help "rationalize" the process and ensure that the right people get the right information, and criteria are set up to enable those who are responsible for the routing to know what data goes to whom.

Despite such organizational efforts personal judgments still play a major role. No matter how effective the system is in general there still will be many situations in which much individual discretion will be exercised; the "rules" cannot cover all contingencies. In March and April 1970 top U. S. policymakers were evaluating the pros and cons of a limited military incursion into Cambodia to the end of destroying the sanctuaries and bases being used by DRV forces.[52] In April analysts in the Office of National Estimates prepared a long memorandum that included a discussion of possible future developments in Cambodia. Although the analysts were not aware that an assault was being planned, they nevertheless briefly addressed the question and gave a rather gloomy prognosis of its likely impact. Thirteen days before the planned incursion CIA Director Richard Helms received the memorandum. Top U. S. policymakers had been planning on the basis of a February National Intelligence Estimate plus current reporting from various departments and agencies. Although he had this new memorandum in hand, Helms unaccountably decided *not* to send it to the White House; acting within the prescribed framework Helms exercised his personal judgment and withheld the memo.

Much of the time lower- and middle-level bureaucrats play key roles in the information-communication process. They are the ones through whom most information is funneled and the ones who usually make the judgments concerning the kind, frequency, direction, and content of communication. Because of this role it is they who often "really" make policy and the individuals at the top, reputedly the chief policymakers, are sometimes relatively powerless.[53]

It was noted in Chapter 13 how information can be distorted by preconception or perceptual bias. But even that which is communicated without such handicaps may receive insufficient consideration or be lost in the mass of data that threatens to inundate all bureaucracies. Because of this problem there seems to be an increasing tendency on the part of top level policymakers to consider only a small fraction of that which is directed to their attention and to

---

[52]This example is taken from U. S. Senate, Select Committee to Study Governmental Operations with respect to Intelligence Activities, *Foreign and Military Intelligence, Book I, Final Report*, 94th Cong., 2nd Sess., 1976, pp. 79–82.

[53]See John C. Ries, *The Management of Defense*, Johns Hopkins Press, Baltimore, 1964, pp. 49–50.

place more emphasis on the source of the information than on the informational content.

Sometimes the bureaucrats do their job well but either can't get the right people to pay much attention, or the chief policymaker(s) just think the information and/or recommendations are wrong; in these situations the problem is not in the bureaucracy but at higher levels. For example, in May 1960 a poll indicated that the Cuban majority was heavily supportive of the Castro regime. Obviously in such a situation any attempt at an invasion in the hope of a mass revolution would be very unwise. The poll was distributed widely both inside and outside of government but apparently no one paid much attention since the Bay of Pigs episode occurred early the next year.[54] Before the October 1973 war in the Middle East most American intelligence officials did not believe hostilities would occur; some did, however, but they could not get either Mr. Nixon or Dr. Kissinger to pay much attention.[55] In the fall of 1964 the Johnson administration was assessing the possibility of escalating the war in Vietnam via a systematic, calculated bombing of the north. The intelligence community had a pessimistic view of the effect the bombing would have on Hanoi's leaders, believing it would not be productive. It so informed the president but its views were ignored.[56]

Of course, sometimes this is not what occurs; in some instances inaccurate information is provided. On April 24, 1965 a military revolt occurred in the Dominican Republic. The Dominican president resigned, his place taken by a man with close ties to former President Juan Bosch. Military skirmishes occurred as anti-Bosch elements in the armed forces organized. U. S. intelligence community and diplomatic reports (especially those of the ambassador) indicated that if the rebels were victorious there was a strong chance that a Communist government would be the result. This fit in well with President Johnson's preconceived generalization of anticommunism, so he ordered in the Marines to prevent such an outcome. Though a Communist regime did not materialize it was hardly because of Johnson's action since the Communists had had little to do with the revolt in the first place.

In some instances it is not a question of the quantity or accuracy of the data, or of getting it to the right people; indeed, with the extensive and sophisticated intelligence gathering systems that exist today there often is a veritable flood of information. Much of the time the problem is one interpretation;

[54]Hadley Cantril, *The Human Dimension: Experiences in Policy Research*, Rutgers University Press, Brunswick, N. J., 1967, Chapter 1.

[55]See Ray S. Cline, "Policy Without Intelligence," *Foreign Policy*, Winter 1974–1975, pp. 121–135.

[56]See *The Pentagon Papers*, pp. 330–332. In 1964 the CIA also argued against the validity of the domino theory. As a result "President Johnson never again asked for the CIA's opinion." Gelb, with Betts, p. 230.

what does it all mean? As Roberta Wohlstetter has so effectively demonstrated, the Pearl Harbor disaster simply would not have occurred if intelligence had been interpreted correctly.[57] Perhaps even more to the point (since
there were some bureaucratic "foul-ups" in the Pearl Harbor case) is the example of the failure of Israeli policymakers to interpret intelligence information correctly prior to the 1973 October war. In this instance the procedures
worked well, produced the data, and routed it to the right people. Policymakers just misinterpreted its meaning.[58]

To this point our analysis has described and given examples of a number
of things that can happen in the information-communication process. One
more comment must be made, a comment of considerable significance: *frequently* (and this occurred in most of the preceding examples) *the policymaker
receives conflicting data and recommendations.* The summer and early fall of
1963 found the internal situation of South Vietnam chaotic. In an attempt to
get as much accurate information as possible to use as a basis for a decision as
to whether or not to continue to support the regime of Ngo Dinh Diem (whose
continued repression of the domestic opposition was eroding its base of support), Washington dispatched the Krulak-Mendenhall mission to the scene.[59]
Upon the mission's return General Krulak told President Kennedy that the war
was going well and would be won if current policies were followed, regardless
of defects in the regime. Joseph Mendenhall, a State Department diplomat,
concluded the situation was dismal and likely would not get better unless major changes were made. The president, somewhat chagrined, asked: "You two
did visit the same country, didn't you?"[60]

BUREAUCRATIC POLITICS: FRAGMENTATION AND COMPETITION

Another series of problems that the policymaker must face arises largely because of the fact that the bureaucratic policymaking machinery is terribly fragmented. Although there is a difference in degree depending on the system, circumstances, issues, and personalities involved, it is almost always true that
several organizations or factions participate in the policymaking process.
Whereas previously this analysis has been concerned with problems that arise

---

[57]Roberta Wohlstetter, *Pearl Harbor: Warning and Decision*, Stanford University Press,
Stanford, Cal., 1962.

[58]See Chaim Herzog, *The War of Atonement: October 1973*, Little, Brown, Boston, 1975,
Chapters 1–4, and Michael I. Handel, "The Yom Kippur War and the Inevitability of Surprise,"
International Studies Quarterly, September 1977, pp. 461–502. Also see Chapter 10, pp. 277–278,
and Chapter 12, p. 349.

[59]Interestingly described in Hilsman, *To Move A Nation*, Chapter 32.

[60]Quoted in ibid., p. 502.

within a given bureaucratic organization, now our attention is directed to the fact that there are several such organizations and/or factions interacting.

The United States represents perhaps the extreme in bureaucratic policy-making fragmentation.[61] The president, of course, is the chief policymaker. In his Executive Office the members of his White House Staff and the Office of Management and Budget often play important roles, and in recent administrations the assistant for national security affairs has been extremely influential. In addition, the National Security Council, created in 1947 and consisting of the president, vice-president, secretaries of state and defense, and having as statutory advisors the director of the CIA and the chairman of the Joint Chiefs of Staff, also may play a major role.

The Department of State, of course, is also a primary participant. Headed by the secretary of state, the senior member of the president's cabinet, it tends to be at the center of routine policymaking activities. It is organized on both a geographical and functional basis in recognition of the fact that both kinds of expertise are needed for effective decisionmaking.[62] As noted earlier, this leads to certain problems of coordination, specialization, parochialism, compromise and so forth.

There are many other agencies. The Department of Defense obviously is concerned with matters of military and defense posture, the development of strategic concepts, the allocation of resources, preparation for the most likely military contingencies, and the management of alliance military policies. Headed by a civilian, the secretary of defense, it incorporates within it the branches of the armed services and the Joint Chiefs of Staff. There are several intelligence agencies (of which the CIA is the most important), and they have a significant impact on a variety of security-related matters. The Arms Control and Disarmament Agency plays an important role in the sphere of arms limitations. On some kinds of problems an agency whose functions are primarily domestic may have a meaningful input. For example, when dealing with issues of world hunger the Department of Agriculture is deeply involved. The Treasury and Commerce Departments are major participants in decisions concerning international finance and trade. If oil imports are the issue the Energy Department will play a major role. Of course, the list could be extended even further.

---

[61]This analysis focuses on the American system. Obviously the policymaker (and the student) would need to adjust his or her views to whatever level of fragmentation was characteristic of the particular system under study. To illustrate, one would need to recognize that if a state is relatively small, has an authoritarian political system, has only a small bureaucracy, has comparatively few external relationships, and deals with only a restricted range of issues, it likely will experience bureaucratic fragmentation and the effects thereof much less than will the United States.

[62]Such a breakdown is typical. The headquarters staff of the Soviet Ministry of Foreign Affairs, for example, consists of several functional divisions and "about sixteen geographic divisions or desks." Morton Schwartz, *The Foreign Policy of the USSR: Domestic Factors*, Dickenson, Encino and Belmont, Cal., 1975, pp. 174–175.

Lack of Policy Coordination

Fragmentation such as this can have harmful effects. One of these may be the lack of policy coordination. The right hand may not know what the left is doing with the result that each faction may develop its own particular approach to a problem. At best this leads to duplication and waste, to an overlapping of jurisdictions with several agencies attempting to do the same thing. But sometimes things are not even this "good." If the right hand does not know what the left is doing, perhaps the job simply will not get done. Each organization assumes that the particular task is someone else's responsibility, so no one undertakes it. Sometimes one unit will act in such a way (unintentionally) to undercut the effectiveness of another. For example, in March 1978 President Carter gave a major speech on defense policy. The speech, written by an aide to National Security Adviser Zbigniew Brzezinski and reflecting the latter's rather "hardline" approach, was designed to dispel any Soviet doubts about Washington's "firmness" and signal Moscow that a continued Russian military buildup might jeopardize U. S.-Soviet cooperation. Shortly before the address was given, however, a high-ranking State Department official telephoned the Soviet Embassy in Washington and urged that the complete text of the speech be transmitted to Moscow so Russian leaders could read the *conciliatory portions*.[63] Obviously, this diminished the speech's impact on the Soviets. It has been hypothesized that this is what happened in the Cuban missile crisis when the Russians took great care to deceive the United States with respect to the clandestine shipment of missiles but their installation proceeded with almost no efforts at camouflage. Traditionally, Soviet arms shipments were the province of Soviet military intelligence whose work emphasized secrecy and deception; missiles were usually installed by the Strategic Rocket Forces who seldom were concerned with such things.[64]

The supposed "solution" for these problems is to establish clear lines of authority and give the appropriate officials "authority" commensurate with their "responsibility." Hopefully by now the student is aware of the substantive complexity of international politics and realizes how difficult this "answer" is to put into practice. Problems are just too large, interrelated, and complex for such a simple solution to work.[65] As Destler has put it:

> More generally, who in the broader government should have "authority" on the issue of possible U. S. troop withdrawals from Europe? The Secretary of State and his European Affairs Bureau? His Politico-Military Affairs Bureau? The Sec-

[63]*New York Times*, April 17, 1978, p. 3.
[64]See Allison, pp. 109–111.
[65]Of course, this does not mean that one should not try to come as close to this goal as possible.

retary of Defense? The Secretary of the Treasury, given his role as protector of the balance of payments? The Director of the Arms Control and Disarmament Agency, given the relation of troop withdrawals to the military balance? For each of them, "responsibility" on this issue far outruns the "authority" to deal with it.[66]

Organizational Competition

A second major difficulty develops because *organizations tend to develop interests of their own.*[67] Just as is true with respect to states and their leaders, organizational leaders seek to develop the capabilities necessary to protect their interests. Generally this involves acquiring and preserving a certain structural, personnel, and financial base, and some degree of policymaking autonomy; in some ways it is as if they were seeking bureaucratic "territory" and the right to exert primary influence over its future.[68]

There is another factor that exacerbates this problem. Bureaucrats are human beings who have career concerns and seek personal advancement. Since an individual works within an organization, how that organization fares will affect his or her personal welfare. If it gains influence, becomes widely respected, is assigned new and better programs, and receives economic, political, and psychological rewards, then its members will usually benefit. If not, or if the reverse is true, the members will tend to suffer.

Within each organization there are certain patterns of communication and authority and certain rules and regulations that define the expectations of those in various positions. Career advancement is often dependent on serving the organization's interests and it obviously is much safer to promote what seems to be best for the organization than to "cross" the organization in favor of policies that might benefit others.

It is important to note, however, that much of the time these acts are not perceived as "selfish" by their perpetrators.[69] Generally speaking, the representatives of a given organization, while advocating policies that benefit that organization, honestly believe that these policies are also the "best policy" for

[66]Destler, p. 24.

[67]It has been persuasively argued that certain organizations in the Soviet Union have a stake in maintaining an atmosphere of tension. Because of this they automatically oppose a policy of detente with the West because any real relaxation would cause their role to be reduced. For a perceptive yet concise analysis see Schwartz, pp. 182–188.

[68]This concept is developed in Anthony Downs, *Inside Bureaucracy*, Little, Brown, Boston, 1967.

[69]Of course, in many situations motives are mixed. See ibid., p. 88 and the classification scheme of Robert Presthus, *The Organizational Society*, Knopf, New York, 1962. In fact, in some cases one may even support policies whose impact is at least partially counter to increased organizational influence. See Hilsman, *To Move A Nation*, p. 112.

the resolution of the problem. For example, whereas the Joint Chiefs of Staff generally advocate a high level of spending for the military services, which presumably would have the result of increasing the power and prestige of the armed services, they also genuinely believe that this is essential for the security of the United States. Similarly, when representatives of the Agency for International Development advocate more foreign aid, a result of which would be a greater role for their organization, they also believe this is what is best for the country. It should not automatically be assumed that what is occurring is a cynical manipulation in the interest of organizational influence *at the expense* of the interests of the state; one needs to understand that various policies are often advocated in the belief that the interests of the organization are coincident with the interests of the country.

The product of acting in terms of organizational interests is bureaucratic competition.[70] The parochialism generated by the specialization required to solve complex problems is combined with the desire to accomplish organizational objectives, and the result is a process of competitive bargaining. When this occurs the "policy" that emerges is less the result of rational choice than simply the product of bureaucratic interaction. This outcome may provide an effective policy but there is no guarantee that this will occur. It may yield a stalemate, a compromise, an ineffective policy, or no policy at all.

Before leaving this topic one final point should be made. As mentioned many times, it is flesh and blood human beings with all of their qualities and frailties who make decisions. Therefore *interpersonal conflict also can be a very important element in a policymaking situation*. This is true in any context, of course, but it is likely to be exacerbated in this setting because of the fact that the particular individuals represent different interest constituencies when they are members of different organizations; this may aggravate whatever existing tendencies there may have been toward personal conflict.

In the discussions concerning the appropriate policies to be undertaken with regard to the Korean War, for example, there were genuine differences of opinion, to some extent based on organizational interests, between the Department of Defense and the Department of State. But these differences were made much worse by the personal conflicts that existed. It was quite clear that the president had a closer relationship with the secretary of state than he did with the secretary of defense, and in addition to "the tension created by various interdepartmental conflicts, the two Secretaries obviously disliked and distrusted each other personally. Reportedly the Secretary of Defense undercut the Secretary of State whenever he could."[71]

---

[70]Allison, Chapters 3–4, is excellent on this topic. Also very useful is Matthew Holden, Jr., " 'Imperialism' in Bureaucracy," *American Political Science Review*, December 1966, pp. 943–951.

[71]de Rivera, p. 215.

BUREAUCRATIC POLITICS: SMALL GROUPS

There is another phenomenon apparent in much of the policymaking process—that a significant part of the daily activity occurs within the framework of various small groups.

Types of Groups

There are any number of variations in such groups, of course, each unit to some extent being unique, but for analytical purposes they can be divided into three basic types. *First, there is the informal group with no permanent structural base.* Usually the membership of this kind of group transverses organizational lines, and it is held together by a wide range of personal and professional ties. Sometimes, if there is sufficient need and the unit demonstrates a capacity to act, meetings may be held over an extended period of time and the group may take on some degree of permanence. If the group is composed of high level leaders and increased trust develops, a kind of policymaking "inner circle" may result.[72] When Lyndon Johnson was president there was a small group known as the "Tuesday Lunch Bunch," which constituted an inner circle.[73] Made up of Secretaries Rusk (state) and McNamara (defense), the special assistant, director of the CIA, chairman of the Joint Chiefs of Staff, and Johnson, this group provided the "real" policymaking forum for years.

A second kind of small group is that which is created specifically to deal with a particular problem or crisis (and the assumption is that it will disappear when its job is finished). These groups may be variable in membership and meet intermittently. In the Korean War, for example, there were six critical meetings during the first week of the crisis, four involving groups of from 12 to 14 members, two with 6.[74] Sometimes groups are created that meet more or less continuously for the duration of the problem. In the Cuban missile crisis President Kennedy appointed a small group known as "ExComm," a group of about 15 trusted advisers whose advice he considered significant, and this group was important throughout the dispute. As was the case in the other examples, a small group made critical decisions outside of the formal policymaking machinery.[75]

The third type of small group is one whose existence is institutionalized, a small transdepartmental entity that is created to perform certain functions and whose existence is presumed to be permanent.[76] Upon taking office, President

---

[72]See Hilsman, *The Politics of Policymaking in Defense and Foreign Affairs*, pp. 118–120.

[73]See Hartmann, *The New Age of American Foreign Policy*, p. 80.

[74]See Paige, *The Korean Decision*, for a discussion of these meetings.

[75]It was recognized that in this setting the members represented the president, not various organizational interests. Sorensen, *Kennedy*, p. 679.

[76]"Permanent" in the sense that it has no foreseeable or specific termination date. In a bureaucratic setting no organization can be said to be permanent in an infinite sense.

Nixon undertook to restructure the policymaking apparatus in a manner that would elevate the National Security Council to a preeminent position. But the Council could not handle the quantity of detailed work policymaking involved, nor could it carefully investigate all the relevant options. To achieve these ends a series of small, permanent, interagency subcommittees were established. These units bypassed the usual departmental chains of command, reporting to one or another of the units chaired by the ubiquitous Dr. Kissinger.[77]

Perceived Advantages

As policymakers have been increasingly frustrated by the difficulties engendered by standard operating procedures and bureaucratic fragmentation and competition they more and more have utilized the small group. Such entities are perceived to have a number of positive features.

1. Other things being equal, there will be relatively little conflict because presumably there will be comparatively few viewpoints to reconcile.
2. These "extracurricular" organizations have no organizational interest to protect and are free to deal directly with the substantive issues.
3. Usually the group's members can subordinate the interests of the organizations from which they come to the purposes of the informal group and thus organizational parochialism can be avoided.
4. The members are not prevented from a free and frank interchange by organizational rules and procedures; there are no artificial barriers to open communication.
5. Action often can be taken swiftly and decisively.
6. Innovation and experimentation are not stifled by various bureaucratic devices.
7. Secrecy is much more probable than in larger organizations.

Negative Attributes

But small groups do not provide a panacea for policymaking ills; indeed, they frequently exhibit a number of negative attributes. Quite clearly, for example, the purported advantage of secrecy also can produce highly negative consequences. Another problem is that orientations that are not immediately action oriented, such as avoidance or minimal nonalignment, seldom receive sufficient consideration. When an item is referred to a small group it is highly unlikely that that group will recommend zero or minimal action.

---

[77]Kissinger also was a member of some of these subcommittees.

There are other problems. Members of small groups tend to rely on their own memories and perceptions rather than on organizational data (stored, interpreted, and coded information that exists within the policymaking bureaucracy). Often personal recollections are seriously incomplete and/or distorted. Members of the Soviet Politburo bitterly recall that the Western allies did not open a second front in Europe until June 1944, failing to take into account that they could not effectively do so before then. And, of course, personal perceptions can be extremely inaccurate, as British Prime Minister Eden's likening of Nasser to Hitler in the 1956 Suez crisis demonstrates.

Another difficulty arises because the particular group members may not be experts in the specific matters under consideration. The inordinate complexity of international politics requires that a variety of specialists be heard on most issues of significance; although a small group could make an effort in this regard, in practice it often fails to do so. For example, President Johnson's "Tuesday Lunch Bunch" contained no Asian specialists, no one with much knowledge about Vietnam, (indeed, few with much knowledge about international politics at all?). Although the individuals were briefed by various specialists in different organizational settings, when it came time for decision the specialists were dispensed with.

Another difficulty with small groups is that many times the unorthodox personality either is rejected quickly or is required to subordinate his viewpoint. Unusual ideas are very noticeable when only a few people are involved, and there is much pressure to conform. In a large bureaucracy one has a degree of anonymity and usually is secure as long as standard operating procedures are followed. This is not the case in small groups, where procedures are established *ad hoc* and individuals are highly visible. As a consequence sometimes those with unpopular and/or unorthodox views may seek to avoid the humiliation (or even reprisal) that presenting their ideas might cause, and remain silent; to the extent that this occurs the group will be dominated by a relatively few individuals and the potential contributions of those who are stifled will never be made.

Personal relationships are of paramount importance in small groups. Depending on what they are, of course, they can be either useful or harmful, but because they are so significant there is always the possibility that a consensus will be achieved because of actual or potential personal pressure. Indeed, in some situations one individual may be (or become) dominant and the others "just go through the motions." In July 1969 the Washington Special Actions Group (WSAG) was established to oversee crisis management. As the India-Pakistan-Bangladesh crisis quickened in late November and December 1971 WSAG met more than 20 times to determine American policy.[78] President Nixon and Dr. Kissinger believed that India's objective was to defeat and possibly

---

[78]For more on the crisis see Chapter 6, pp. 134–135.

conquer Pakistan, that India and the Soviet Union were working hand in glove, and that if India were successful the subcontinent would be controlled by an India-Russia tandem. Because of these beliefs they wanted the United States to "tilt" toward Pakistan. The WSAG meetings were wholly dominated by Kissinger amid an atmosphere of unspoken tension. Those who disagreed felt intimidated and remained silent. Occasionally Dr. Kissinger would ask whether anyone wanted to disagree, but those who might have did not.[79] Clearly this kind of *modus operandi* does not allow for (let alone stimulate) the search for alternatives and a careful weighing of the benefits and costs of each potential option.

The characteristics and methods of conduct of small group meetings are important. The relationship(s) of leader(s) and followers, the degree to which the meetings are effectively and efficiently run with regard to the objectives at hand, the extent to which there is a concerted effort to examine alternatives and receive thoughtful input from all members prior to decision, even the details of the procedures themselves can have a critical impact. One must remember that the absence of the regularized procedures that exist in an organized bureaucracy means that the procedures for a small group are set by the group itself, and they may either inhibit or facilitate efficient policymaking. President Kennedy was well aware of this problem, so in order to keep the "Ex-Comm" discussions from being inhibited or biased during the Cuban missile crisis, to negate the possibility that individuals would not speak up or would seek to curry favor if he were present, he often did not attend. Quite a contrast to the way things were done in the WSAG and the "Tuesday Lunch Bunch."

BUREAUCRATIC POLITICS: THE POLICYMAKING PROCESS

To this point the analysis of bureaucratic politics has examined the impact of bureaucratic procedures, analyzed the results of bureaucratic fragmentation and interorganizational competition, and discussed the role of small groups. It remains for us to look at the policymaking process as a whole, make some comments as to its overall characteristics, and discuss the relationship of the chief policymaker to the bureaucratic organization.

Decisional Flow

Perhaps the first point one should note is that *it is misleading to think in terms of a single "decision." In reality policymaking is the product of many bits of*

---

[79]Some studies have even indicated that those who might have dissented refrained from doing so because they believed that if they did they would be summarily fired. See Dan Haendel, *The Process of Priority Formulation: U.S. Foreign Policy in the Indo-Pakistani War of 1971*, Westview Press, Boulder, Colorado, 1977, especially pp. 162-169. See Kissinger, *The White House Years*, Chapter 21, for a different view.

decisions emerging and interacting continuously over time. Ideas and information flow into the process from a variety of official and unofficial sources, actions are taken by people at various levels in different organizations, and information is transmitted and communicated laterally and hierarchically to other people in positions of authority. Each "piece of the action" is the result of many different factors and in turn shapes and influences the succeeding ones. Rather than single discrete decisions there is really a stream or flow of decisional fragments. Because of this process the policymaker often has his or her "decision" already largely determined by actions taken as a result of bureaucratic bargaining, fragmentation, or operating procedure. Whatever one speaks of as a person's "decision" in such a case is actually a part of the entire chain rather than a self-contained individual choice.

Just Another Participant?

Because of this fact the chief policymaker is frequently just another participant in the process. Of course the chief policymaker possesses certain attributes and advantages that others do not have, but in many cases he or she is not in a position of "command" even with respect to his or her own policymaking organization. Instead, the "boss" finds that his or her "power" is essentially a power of persuasion, a capability that is exercised primarily via a bargaining process. As Neustadt has effectively demonstrated, this is true even of the President of the United States. He, too, often finds that his power is primarily just a power to persuade, and that "the power to persuade is the power to bargain."[80]

While the chief policymaker is frequently just another participant in the policymaking process, clearly this is *not always* the case. In some situations the chief policymaker is "first among equals," and sometimes he or she is wholly preeminent. A number of factors impact in this regard, and they must be assessed in combination. While hard fast rules are not possible, the following generalizations provide useful starting points for the specific situational analysis necessary in each case:

1. The type of political system and the nature and unity of the regime have an impact. Other things being equal, chief policymakers in authoritarian systems are less susceptible to bureaucratic influences than are their more democratic counterparts, and policymakers of unified regimes can be more assertive than those in regimes characterized by fragmentation, competition, and conflict.
2. The nature of the issue makes a difference. Generally speaking, the more a situation is perceived to be a crisis that endangers fundamen-

[80]Neustadt, Chapter 3.

tal objectives the more chief policymakers are likely to be preeminent and the less the role played by bureaucratic politics; conversely, the more routine the problem the greater the impact of the bureaucracy and the more the chief policymaker will be just another participant.

3. Differences among individual policymakers are important variables. The more action oriented and assertive the individual the more likely he or she will not be "just another participant" in the process.

4. The time available and the degree to which the leader is interested in the problem also are salient. If the chief policymaker is busy elsewhere he or she may not have enough time to participate in more than a marginal manner (unless the situation involves a crisis, in which case he or she will "make time"), and if the issue is one in which an individual has relatively little interest he or she may be content to leave its resolution to the wheels of the bureaucratic machine.

The degree to which the chief policymaker is just another participant then is variable, depending on a number of things. It is important to note that we are talking in terms of degrees, of various points on a continuum; it is not an all-or-nothing question.

Pervasiveness of Bargaining

A third characteristic of the bureaucratic policymaking process is *the pervasiveness of bargaining*. Instead of participating in a rational planning and implementing process as one might assume, all participants in the policymaking process negotiate in order to attain maximum influence. This occurs within organizations, between organizations, and between the chief policymaker and all of the other organizational and individual participants. Thus the entire process in many ways consists of a gigantic contest in which the stakes are influence and the outcome is what is sometimes called the policymaking "decision."

This activity occurs in all political systems although it is much more obvious and open, and is extended to a wider variety of participants, in more democratic structures. Nevertheless, for reasons mentioned earlier (the information required, insufficient time, the necessity of expertise, specialization of function, and so forth) in all situations there is some degree of bargaining and bargaining occurs to some extent in all political systems (even though in some cases it may be tacit rather than explicit). Indeed, as Paul Cocks has put it:

> Even in highly authoritarian regimes, like under Stalin and Hitler, elements of bargaining exist at certain stages down the bureaucratic hierarchy. They are an in-

trinsic part of the decision process and impose limits on the function and power of the top political leadership.[81]

Time Pressure

Another factor that is evident in the bureaucratic process is that the individuals enmeshed there frequently operate under immense time pressure. The perception of some nonpolicymakers to the effect that bureaucrats put in a rather leisurely eight hours five days a week seldom is accurate, and often it is very far from the truth. And unfortunately the problem is getting worse. One reason is the greatly increased number of nations in the world as compared with 20 years ago and the resulting increase in the number of interactions. Also, there seem to be more problems to deal with and in many ways they seem to possess greater urgency. Policymakers are also under time pressure because as the bureaucracy grows larger there are simply more and more different interests to be taken into account.

To a much greater degree than is sometimes realized individuals in the foreign, defense, and intelligence communities have their priorities determined by external demands, being compelled to deal with matters as they arise and are brought to their attention. Because there so often is too much to do and not enough time to do it bureaucrats seldom can give any single topic careful detailed study. Consequently, to the extent possible they frequently employ standard operating procedures in as efficacious a manner as they can, and quickly move on to the next problem; if the preprogrammed routines are incorrect so be it. And rarely is there adequate time for reflection on the past and/or the development of a coherent plan for the future. This is not the way they would like to proceed, of course, but in the real world it is often the way they must; much of the time they don't have much choice.

People in policymaking positions for international parties, whether they be relatively low echelon bureaucrats or individuals holding top level positions, have no more hours in the day than do you and I. And, again just as you and I, when they are compelled to deal with a number of important issues almost simultaneously the product is sure to be mixed. Some problems will be handled well but others will not, some will receive attention corresponding to their intrinsic importance but others will receive too much or too little, etc. Such a situation is hardly conducive to produce the optimum policy, but it is the rule in most foreign policy organizations today.

---

[81]Paul Cocks, "The Policy Process and Bureaucratic Politics" in Paul Cocks, Robert V. Daniels, and Nancy Whittier Heer, eds., *The Dynamics of Soviet Politics*, Harvard University Press, Cambridge, 1976, p. 175.

Search for Consensus

Another characteristic attribute of bureaucratic policymaking is what has been called the *"strain toward agreement."*[82] All of the participants are involved in an effort to build a consensus, to "push" for an accommodation or compromise that all participants eventually can support. Sometimes this leads to a tendency to "oversell" particular policies.[83] In the effort to build a consensus the various participants naturally try to present their case in the most favorable light. As a result they often exaggerate the merits of their particular position. This process of overselling may continue once a decision is reached and policymakers oversell the policy both to the public and to other states. This sometimes leads to self-deception on the part of the very policymakers who made the decisions.

Another danger in this process is that since, as noted earlier, policy may just be the outcome of bargaining, the capacity to achieve consensus may become the test of whether or not a particular policy "should" be adopted. Furthermore, once a consensus is reached people may automatically assume that it is the *appropriate* policy, when in fact it may well not be. The achieved consensus may actually have little or no relationship to the optimum policy; it may be simply a reflection of the power and skill of the participants.[84]

Naturally there are times that despite everyone's efforts no consensus can be reached. Often the product in such instances is a *"minimal decision,"* the avoidance of deciding any more than absolutely necessary. For example, because of interorganizational disputes American officials could not reach a consensus on the development of a hydrogen bomb in 1950. As a result President Truman made only a very limited commitment, ordering only continued research and the development of a few prototypes. It seems that, for him, the major "issue" was minimizing conflict and building consensus within the bureaucracy, and the minimal decision was the method he deemed appropriate.[85] In 1967 President Johnson followed a similar course of action in his decision on the development of an antiballistic missile system (ABM).[86] Here too differ-

[82]Warner R. Schilling, "The Politics of National Defense: Fiscal 1950," in Warner R. Schilling, Paul Hammond and Glenn Snyder, eds., *Strategy, Politics and Defense Budgets*, Columbia University Press, New York, 1962, p. 23.

[83]See Theodore Lowi, "Making Democracy Safe for the World: National Politics and Foreign Policy" in James N. Rosenau, ed., *Domestic Sources of Foreign Policy*, Free Press, New York, 1967, pp. 295–332.

[84]See Roger Hilsman, "The Foreign Policy Consensus: An Interim Research Report," *Journal of Conflict Resolution*, December 1959, pp. 361–382.

[85]See Warner R. Schilling, "The H-Bomb Decision: How to Decide Without Actually Choosing," *Political Science Quarterly*, March 1961, pp. 24–46.

[86]See Morton H. Halperin, "The Decision to Deploy the ABM: Bureaucratic and Domestic Politics in the Johnson Administration," *World Politics*, October 1972, pp. 62ff. Also see Spanier and Uslaner, pp. 115–126.

ent organizational actors viewed the stakes differently, bargaining was pervasive, and consensus appeared unachievable. In a fashion reminiscent of Mr. Truman, Johnson opted to decide as little as possible, hoping to avoid antagonizing any of the conflicting elements. Consequently, he neither rejected nor supported ABM deployment. Instead, the president asked Congress to fund the acquisition of certain ABM components, and allowed Secretary of Defense Robert McNamara to state that the administration believed in the concept of a small, anti-Chinese system. But concerning deployment, the "decision" was to postpone any decision.

As a result of the effort to achieve consensus and the myriad of factors discussed in the preceding sections, certain other characteristics abound (some of which are simply a magnification of problems that exist within and between organizations). Because so many different views must be accommodated, radically different proposals tend to be eliminated and innovative ideas stifled. Because so many actors participate the process is time-consuming and prone to excessive delay, and much conflict is generated. Policies once established acquire an immense momentum, inertia sets in, and change is extremely difficult. Finally, frequently people become so enmeshed in their daily routines, in handling the never ending cascade of immediate demands, that long-range planning and projects receive little attention. With all the international parties that exist and the incredible maze of interactions that occur, there just doesn't seem to be time to plan beyond the moment.

Personal Objectives

There is one more subject to be discussed, one that sometimes receives insufficient emphasis. To this point, with minor exceptions, the analysis has proceeded as if each of the individuals within the bureaucracy was primarily concerned with developing the optimum foreign policy. Unfortunately this characterization is both oversimplified and inaccurate.[87] Bureaucrats are human beings who have careers and seek personal advancement. Naturally they hope to advance up the hierarchy of influence and/or to maximize their influence at any given level.

Because of this their perceptions and goals may be substantially determined by bureaucratic factors, and their attention may be directed away from international problems to intrabureaucratic concerns.[88] Since they want to succeed, they bargain, manipulate, and attempt to persuade in an effort to

---

[87]Allison, p. 146, says "The gap between academic literature and the experience of participants in government is nowhere wider than at this point. For those who participate in government the terms of daily employment cannot be ignored.

[88]Halperin and Kanter, p. 3.

achieve their *personal* objectives. Because this is so it obviously is inaccurate to view them as homogeneous unselfish lumps; they are particular human beings with particular interests and perspectives who desire to advance their own careers, and the policymaker *must* evaluate them accordingly.

The logical implication of these facts is that *the process of interaction within an organization is eminently political.* There are a wide range of actions based on interpersonal rivalry, the various processes are characterized by bargaining in both formal and informal settings, and personal gain is often as much a determinant of the decisions made (or not made) as concern for the "best" policy.

Although these statements are true, it should also be pointed out that people often believe that what is best for them and a maximization of their own power *is* the "best" policy, and that their actions are not all cynical manipulations. Furthermore, it is obvious that a great many people *do* legitimately concern themselves with developing the "best" policy at any particular time, and personal influence and prestige are not all that count. Also, as should be evident by now, the substantive problems are so terribly complex that differences among policymakers are inevitable even when they are seeking the optimum decision. Nevertheless, the fact remains that it would be unwise of the policymaker to assume that the maximization of personal power and prestige is not a significant part of the bureaucratic process.

IN LIEU OF CONCLUSION

There really is no appropriate conclusion for a text such as this. We have provided an in-depth analysis of international politics via the policymaker focus, examining in detail the international political environment, the steps in policy formulation, the foundation of capability, the instruments of policy implementation, and policymaking limitations, problems, and constraints. To now present a thorough summation would be both repetitious and an insult to the reader's intelligence. I do have a few personal observations that might be of some value, however, and I would like to share them with you in lieu of a conclusion.

First, throughout the research for this book, both that conducted via the printed word and through my interviews with policymakers, I could not help but (continually) be struck by the extraordinary difficulty of the policymaker's task. In the decentralized anarchy of the international political environment there are few generally accepted "rules of the game" except trying to achieve or protect one's fundamental objectives. Beyond that even the most basic concepts are controversial; often there is disagreement about content, and even when there is not it seldom is evident how particular concepts should be applied to specific situations. In consequence, few generalizations have much utility to the policymaker and an immense amount of situation-specific analysis is necessary in every case. Not only are there few generally accepted rules of the game, even if there were the difficulties would be enormous because the international political arena is an incredibly complex, fluid, dynamic mosaic of interrelated interactions; sometimes it is a wonder that anyone (ever) knows what is happening. With a multiplicity of actors seeking a variety of objectives via varying combinations of implementation instruments, with each action producing differential effects, and with extrasituational inputs and impacts being ever present, situations are incredibly complicated and problem solutions terribly difficult. In many cases it is evident that genuine grounds for conflict exist, that there are basic substantive differences of considerable proportions. And because all parties are unique and policymakers operate from different perspectives phenomena are perceived differently, and these perceptual differences and distortions magnify the substantive differences; yet from each party's perspective they are both understandable and legitimate. The individual policymakers who must grapple with these issues, the real people who formulate and implement policy, operate from within different systems and cultures, possess any number of idiosyncratic personality features, etc.; this exacerbates matters even more. About the only certainties one can be sure of are that the job is extremely difficult and change is certain.

This brings me to a second point: given the difficulty of the policymaker's job it is imperative that policymakers and observers alike have only modest expectations. When one carefully studies and reflects on the uncertainties, complexities, disparities and limitations that exist, and recalls the essentially decentralized anarchical nature of the international environment, it is evident that the vast majority of the time the most that can reasonably be hoped for is a moderate degree of effectiveness; policymakers usually can produce counterpart policy changes, increase the degree to which objectives are achieved, and decrease the costs of so doing, to only a limited extent. All policies produce mixed results, and even optimum policies will have certain negative consequences. It is important to understand this fact; otherwise understandable but unwarranted frustration, disenchantment, and cynicism take over, just making matters worse. Often the fault really lies in the observer's unrealistic expectations, not in the policy. No policymaker can always formulate and implement the optimum policy, of course, but even if he or she could it often would not "succeed" to the extent and in the manner that observers would like (and mistakenly assume is possible).

Third, it is my hope that this book has made the reader highly cognizant of and interested in both the basic features and specific nature of many of the most important facets of contemporary international politics. There is a world out there with real problems that affect all of us, and real flesh-and-blood human beings make judgments about how to deal with them; perhaps the reader may even become one of these people. In any event, I hope that the student now has some understanding of the types of options that are and are not feasible, of the choices realistically available to policymakers as they confront the concrete complexities of real world situations.

Finally, it has been my intent to provide the student with an enduring, flexible analytical approach that allows a pragmatic means of understanding the real world of international politics. Certainly complexities, uncertainties, and problems do exist, but the utilization of the policymaker focus enables one to obtain a significant degree of comprehension. Additionally, by concentrating on the investigation of various options in terms of their cost effectiveness in producing desirable outcomes, this approach has provided some tentative prescriptive guidelines as to how one ought to try to proceed in certain contingencies in light of the advantage-disadvantage ratios of the various alternatives. It is my fervent prayer that the comprehension obtained and the guidelines developed will be used to bring about a better quality of life for all humankind.

SELECTED BIBLIOGRAPHY

PART 1

Barnet, Richard, and Ronald E. Muller, *Global Reach: The Power of the Multinational Corporations*, Simon & Schuster, New York, 1974.

Black, Cyril, and Richard Falk, eds., *The Future of the International Legal Order*, Vol. I, Princeton University Press, Princeton, N. J., 1969.

Brzezinski, Zbigniew, *Ideology and Power in Soviet Politics*, Praeger, New York, 1962.

Carr, Edward H., *The Twenty Years' Crisis, 1919–1939*, Macmillan, London, 1939.

Claude, Inis L., Jr., *Swords into Plowshares: The Problems and Progress of International Organization*, Fourth Edition, Random House, New York, 1971.

Cook, Thomas I., and Malcom Moos, *Power Thru Purpose: The Realism of Idealism as a Basis for Foreign Policy*, Johns Hopkins Press, Baltimore, 1954.

Coplin, William D., *The Functions of International Law*, Rand McNally, Chicago, 1966.

Coulombis, Theodore A., and James H. Wolfe, *Introduction to International Relations: Power and Justice*, Prentice-Hall, Englewood Cliffs, N. J., 1978.

Duchacek, Ivo D., *Nations & Men: An Introduction to International Politics*, Third Edition, Dryden Press, Hinsdale, Ill., 1975.

Feld, Werner J., *International Relations: A Transnational Approach*, Alfred, Sherman Oaks, Cal., 1979.

Goodman, Elliot R., *The Fate of the Atlantic Community*, Praeger, New York, 1975.

Haas, Ernst B., *The Uniting of Europe*, Stanford University Press, Stanford, Cal., 1958.

Hartmann, Frederick H., *The Relations of Nations*, Fifth Edition, Macmillan, New York, 1978.

Herz, John, *International Politics in the Atomic Age*, Columbia University Press, New York, 1959.

Hoffman, Stanley, *Contemporary Theory in International Relations*, Prentice-Hall, Englewood Cliffs, N. J., 1960.

Holsti, K. J., *International Politics: A Framework for Analysis*, Third Edition, Prentice-Hall, Englewood Cliffs, N. J., 1977.

Kennan, George, *On Dealing with the Communist World*, Harper & Row, New York, 1964.

Keohane, Robert O., and Joseph S. Nye, "Transgovernmental Relations and International Organizations," *World Politics*, October 1974, pp. 39–62.

Levi, Werner, "International Law in a Multicultural World," *International Studies Quarterly*, December 1974, pp. 417–449.

Lindberg, Leon N., and Stuart A. Scheingold, *Europe's Would-Be Polity: Patterns of Change in the European Community*, Prentice-Hall, Englewood Cliffs, N. J., 1970.

Mansbach, Richard W., Yale H. Ferguson, and Donald E. Lampert, *The Web of World Politics: Nonstate Actors in the Global System*, Prentice-Hall, Englewood Cliffs, N. J., 1976.

Meyer, Alfred G., *Communism*, Third Edition, Random House, New York, 1967.

Morgenthau, Hans J., *Politics Among Nations*, Fifth Edition, Alfred A. Knopf, New York, 1973.

Morgenthau, Hans J., *Scientific Man vs. Power Politics*, University of Chicago Press, Chicago, 1946.

Nicholas, H. G., *The United Nations as a Political Institution*, Fifth Edition, Oxford University Press, New York, 1975.

Osgood, Robert E., and Robert Tucker, *Force, Order, and Justice*, Johns Hopkins University Press, Baltimore, 1967.

Paxton, John, *The Developing Common Market: The Structure of the EEC in Theory and in Practice, 1957–1976*, Third Edition, Westview Press, Boulder, Colo., 1976.

Plano, Jack C., and Robert E. Riggs, *Forging World Order: The Politics of International Organization*, Macmillan, New York, 1967.

Puchala, Donald James, *International Politics Today*, Dodd Mead, New York, 1971.

Quandt, William B., Fuad Jabber, and Ann Mosely Lesch, *The Politics of Palestinian Nationalism*, University of California Press, Berkeley, 1972.

Reprints from the Soviet Press, *L. I. Brezhnev: Report of the CPSU Central Committee and the Party's Immediate Objectives in Domestic and Foreign Policy, XXVth*

Congress of the CPSU, 24 February 1976, Compass Publications, White Plains, N. Y., 1976.

Rosen, Steven J., and Walter S. Jones, *The Logic of International Relations*, Second Edition, Winthrop, Cambridge, Mass., 1977.

Rubinstein, Alvin Z., ed., *The Foreign Policy of the Soviet Union*, Third Edition, Random House, New York, 1972.

Said, Abdul A., and Luiz R. Simmons, eds., *The New Sovereigns: Multinational Corporations as World Powers*, Prentice-Hall, Englewood Cliffs, N. J., 1975.

Scheinman, Lawrence and David Wilkinson, eds., *International Law and Political Crisis: An Analytical Casebook*, Little, Brown, Boston, 1968.

Spanier, John, *Games Nations Play: Analyzing International Politics*, Third Edition, Praeger, New York, 1978.

Spero, Joan Edelman, *The Politics of International Economic Relations*, St. Martin's Press, New York, 1977.

Stoessinger, John G., *The Might of Nations: World Politics in Our Time*, Fourth Edition, Random House, New York, 1973.

Tannenbaum, Frank, *The American Tradition in Foreign Policy*, University of Oklahoma Press, Norman, Oklahoma, 1955.

Vernon, Raymond, *Sovereignty at Bay: The Multinational Spread of U. S. Enterprises*, Basic Books, New York, 1971.

PART 2

Beer, Francis A., *Integration and Disintegration in NATO*, Ohio State University Press, Columbus, Ohio, 1969.

Brzezinski, Zbigniew, *The Soviet Bloc: Unity and Conflict*, Revised Edition, Praeger, New York, 1961.

Churchill, Winston S., *The Second World War. Vol. I: The Gathering Storm*, Houghton Mifflin, Boston, 1948.

Claude, Inis L., Jr., *Power and International Relations*, Random House, New York, 1962.

Coplin, William D., Patrick J. McGowan, and Michael K. O'Leary, *American Foreign Policy: An Introduction to Analysis and Evaluation*, Duxbury Press, North Scituate, Mass., 1974.

Crabb, Cecil V., Jr., *The Elephants and the Grass: A Study of Nonalignment*, Praeger, New York, 1965.

Crankshaw, Edward, *The New Cold War: Moscow v. Peking*, Penguin Books, Baltimore, 1963.

Fedder, Edwin H., *NATO: The Dynamics of Alliance in the Postwar World*, Dodd Mead, New York, 1973.

Freedman, Robert O., *Soviet Policy Toward the Middle East Since 1970*, Praeger, New York, 1975.

Friedman, Julian R., Christopher Bladen, and Steven Rosen, eds., *Alliance in International Politics*, Allyn Bacon, Boston, 1970.

Griffith, William E., *The Sino-Soviet Rift*, MIT Press, Cambridge, Mass., 1964.

Gulick, Edward Vose, *Europe's Classical Balance of Power*, Cornell University Press, Ithaca, N. Y., 1955.

Halberstam, David, *The Best and the Brightest*, Random House, New York, 1969.

Hartmann, Frederick H., *The New Age of American Foreign Policy*, Macmillan, New York, 1970.

Holsti, K. J., "National Role Conceptions in the Study of Foreign Policy," *International Studies Quarterly*, September, 1970, pp. 233–309.

Jordan, Robert S., ed., *Europe and the Superpowers: Perceptions of European International Politics*, Allyn Bacon, Boston, 1971.

Kahin, George McTurnan, and John W. Lewis, *The United States in Vietnam: An Analysis in Depth of America's Involvement in Vietnam*, a Delta Book, New York, 1967.

Kennedy, Robert F., *Thirteen Days: A Memoir of the Cuban Missile Crisis*, W. W. Norton, New York, 1971.

Laqueur, Walter, *The Struggle for the Mediterranean: The Soviet Union and the Middle East, 1958–68*, Macmillan, New York, 1969.

Legg, Keith R., and James R. Morrison, *Politics and the International System: An Introduction*, Harper & Row, New York, 1971.

Lentner, Howard H., *Foreign Policy Analysis: A Comparative and Conceptual Approach*, Charles E. Merrill, Columbus, Ohio, 1974.

Lerche, Charles O., Jr., and Abdul A. Said, *Concepts of International Politics*, Second Edition, Prentice-Hall, Englewood Cliffs, N. J., 1970.

Lovell, John P., *Foreign Policy in Perspective: Strategy, Adaptation, Decision Making*, Holt, Rinehart and Winston, New York, 1970.

Martin, Lawrence W., ed., *Neutralism and Nonalignment*, Praeger, New York, 1962.

Neustadt, Richard E., *Alliance Politics*, Columbia University Press, New York, 1970.

New York Times, *The Pentagon Papers*, Bantam, New York, 1971.

Organski, A. F. K., *World Politics*, Second Edition, Alfred A. Knopf, New York, 1968.

Paul, David W., "Soviet Foreign Policy and the Invasion of Czechoslovakia: A Theory and a Case Study," *International Studies Quarterly*, June 1971, pp. 159–202.

Pfaltzgraff, Robert L., Jr., *The Atlantic Community*, Van Nostrand Reinhold, New York, 1969.

Sayegh, Fayez A., ed., *The Dynamics of Neutralism in the Arab World: A Symposium*, Chandler, San Francisco, 1964.

Wilkinson, David O., *Comparative Foreign Relations: Framework and Methods*, Dickenson, Belmont, Cal., 1969.

Wolfers, Arnold, " 'National Security' as an Ambiguous Symbol," *The Political Science Quarterly*, December 1952, pp. 481–502.

Young, Oran R., *The Intermediaries: Third Parties in International Crises*, Princeton University Press, Princeton, N. J., 1967.

Zagoria, Donald S., *The Sino-Soviet Conflict, 1956–1961*, Princeton University Press, Princeton, N. J., 1962.

PART 3

Adie, W. A. C., *Oil, Politics, and Seapower: The Indian Ocean Vortex*, Crane, Russak & Company, National Strategy Information Center, New York, 1975.

Allon, Yigal, "Israel: The Case for Defensible Borders," *Foreign Affairs*, October 1976, pp. 38–53.

Bhagwati, Jagdish, ed., *Economics and World Order*, Macmillan, New York, 1972.

Black, Cyril E., *The Dynamics of Modernization*, Harper & Row, New York, 1966.

Cline, Ray S., *World Power Assessment 1977: A Calculus of Strategic Drift*, Westview Press, Boulder, Colo., 1977.

Ehrlich, A. H., and P. R. Ehrlich, *Population, Resources, Environment: Issues in Human Ecology*, W. H. Freeman, San Francisco, 1970.

Finley, David J., and Thomas Hovet, Jr., *7304: International Relations on the Planet Earth*, Harper & Row, New York, 1975.

German, F. Clifford, "A Tentative Evaluation of World Power," *Journal of Conflict Resolution*, March 1960, pp. 138–144.

Gray, Colin S., *The Geopolitics of the Nuclear Era: Heartlands, Rimlands, and the Technological Revolution*, Crane, Russak & Company, National Strategy Information Center, New York, 1977.

Greenstein, Fred I., *Personality and Politics*, Markham, Chicago, 1969.

Hopkins, Raymond F., and Richard W. Mansbach, *Structure and Process in International Politics*, Harper & Row, New York, 1973.

International Institute for Strategic Studies, *The Military Balance, 1978–1979*, London, 1978.

Jackson, W. A. Douglas, and Marwyn S. Samuels, eds., *Politics and Geographic Relationships: Toward A New Focus*, Prentice-Hall, Englewood Cliffs, N. J., 1971.

Knorr, Klaus, *Military Power and Potential*, D. C. Heath, Lexington, Mass., 1970.

Pierre, Andrew J., "America Down, Russia Up: The Changing Political Role of Military Power," *Foreign Policy*, Fall 1971, pp. 163–187.

Potholm, Christian P., *The Theory and Practice of African Politics*, Prentice-Hall, Englewood Cliffs, N. J., 1979.

Rostow, W. W., *The Stages of Economic Growth*, Cambridge University Press, New York, 1960.

Sawyer, Jack W., "Dimensions of Nations: Size, Wealth, and Politics," *American Journal of Sociology*, September 1967, pp. 145–172.

Scott, Andrew M., *The Revolution in Statecraft: Informal Penetration*, Random House, New York, 1965.

Sprout, Harold, and Margaret Sprout, *Toward A Politics of Planet Earth*, Van Nostrand, New York, 1971.

Sterling, Richard W., *Macropolitics: International Relations in a Global Society*, Alfred A. Knopf, New York, 1974.

Stockholm International Peace Research Institute, *World Armaments and Disarmament: SIPRI Yearbook, 1979*, Stockholm, 1979.

Stoessinger, John, *Henry Kissinger: The Anguish of Power*, Norton, New York, 1976.

Stookey, Robert W., and James A. Bill, *Politics and Petroleum: The Middle East and the United States*, King's Court Communications, Brunswick, Ohio, 1975.

Szyliowicz, Joseph S. and Bard E. O'Neill, eds., *The Energy Crisis and U. S. Foreign Policy*, Praeger, New York, 1975.

Tachau, Frank, ed., *The Developing Nations: What Path to Modernization?*, Dodd Mead, New York, 1974.

Tatu, Michael, *Power in the Kremlin: From Khrushchev to Kosygin*, Viking, New York, 1968.

United Nations, *UN Statistical Yearbook, 1977*, New York, 1978.

U. S. Congress, Joint Economic Committee, *Allocation of Resources in the Soviet Union and China—1977: Hearings Before the Subcommittee on Priorities and Economy in Government of the Joint Economic Committee*, 95th Cong., 1st Sess., June 23 and 30, and July 6, 1977, Part 3.

U. S. Congress, Office of Technology Assessment, *The Effects of Nuclear War*, May 1979.

U. S. Department of Defense, *Department of Defense Annual Report Fiscal Year 1980, Harold Brown, Secretary of Defense*, January 25, 1979.

U. S. Department of Energy, *Monthly Energy Review*, various.

U. S. Department of State, *Special Report: The Planetary Product "Back to Normalcy" in 1976–77*, June 1978.

U. S. Department of State, *The Trade Debate*, Revised, May 1979.

U. S. Department of State, *World Population: The Silent Explosion*, 1978.

Waterlow, Charlotte, *Superpowers and Victims: The Outlook for the World Community*, Prentice-Hall, Englewood Cliffs, N. J., 1974.

Wicker, Tom, *JFK and LBJ: The Influence of Personality Upon Politics*, William Morrow, New York, 1968.

World Bank, *1978 World Bank Atlas: Population, Per Capita Product, and Growth Rates*, Washington, D. C., 1978.

PART 4

Art, Robert J., and Kenneth N. Waltz eds., *The Use of Force: International Politics and Foreign Policy*, Little Brown, Boston, 1971.

Baldwin, Robert E., *Nontariff Distortions of International Trade*, Brookings, Washington, D. C., 1970.

Barghoorn, Frederick C., *Soviet Foreign Propaganda*, Princeton University Press, Princeton, N. J., 1964.

Barton, John H., and Lawrence D. Weiler, *International Arms Control: Issues and Agreements*, Stanford University Press, Stanford, Cal., 1976.

Blechman, Barry M., and Stephen S. Kaplan, *Force Without War: U. S. Armed Forces as a Political Instrument*, Brookings, Washington, D. C., 1978.

Bottome, Edgar M., *The Balance of Terror: A Guide to the Arms Race*, Beacon, Boston, 1971.

Brodie, Bernard, *Strategy in the Missile Age*, Princeton University Press, Princeton, N. J., 1959.

Brodie, Bernard, *War and Politics*, Macmillan, New York, 1973.

Davison, W. Phillips, *International Political Communication*, Praeger, New York, 1965.

Fagen, Richard N., *Politics and Communication*, Little, Brown, Boston, 1966.

Fisher, Roger, *International Conflict for Beginners*, Harper & Row, New York, 1969.

Frank, Thomas M., and Edward Weisband, *Word Politics: Verbal Strategy Among the Superpowers*, Oxford University Press, New York, 1972.

Galtung, Johan, "The Effects of Economic Sanctions, with Examples from the Case of Rhodesia," *World Politics*, April 1967, pp. 378–416.

George, Alexander, David K. Hall, and William R. Simons, *The Limits of Coercive Diplomacy: Laos, Cuba, Vietnam*, Little Brown, Boston, 1971.

Giap, Vo Nguyen, *Banner of People's War: The Party's Military Line*, Praeger, New York, 1970.

Halperin, Morton H., *Defense Strategies for the Seventies*, Little Brown, Boston, 1971.

Hartmann, Frederick H., *The Game of Strategy*, unpublished manuscript.

Hoffman, Arthur P., *International Communication and the New Diplomacy*, Indiana University Press, Bloomington, Ind., 1968.

Huntington, Samuel P., "Foreign Aid, for What and for Whom," *Foreign Policy*, Spring, 1971, pp. 114–134.

Iklé, Fred Charles, *How Nations Negotiate*, Praeger, New York, 1967.

Johnson, Chalmers A., "Civilian Loyalties and Guerilla Conflict," *World Politics*, July, 1962, pp. 646–661.

Joy, C. Turner, *How Communists Negotiate*, Macmillan, New York, 1955.

Kahn, Herman, *On Thermonuclear War*, Second Edition, Free Press, New York, 1969.

Kaufman, John, *Conference Diplomacy: An Introductory Analysis*, Oceana Publications, New York, 1968.

Kaufmann, William W., *The McNamara Strategy*, Harper & Row, New York, 1964.

Kindleberger, Charles P., *Power and Money: The Economics of International Politics and the Politics of International Economics*, Basic Books, New York, 1970.

Kissinger, Henry, *Nuclear Weapons and Foreign Policy*, Harper & Row, New York, 1957.

Kissinger, Henry, *The White House Years*, Little, Brown, Boston, 1979.

Knorr, Klaus, *On the Uses of Military Power in the Nuclear Age*, Princeton University Press, Princeton, New Jersey, 1966.

Knorr, Klaus, *The Power of Nations: The Political Economy of International Relations*, Basic Books, New York, 1975.

Lall, Arthur, *How Communist China Negotiates*, Columbia University Press, New York, 1968.

Lall, Arthur, *The U. N. and the Middle East Crisis of 1967*, Columbia University Press, New York, 1968.

Mao Tse-tung, *On Guerilla Warfare*, Praeger, New York, 1961.

Montgomery, John, *Foreign Aid in International Politics*, Prentice-Hall, Englewood Cliffs, New Jersey, 1967.

Morgenthau, Hans, J., "A Political Theory of Foreign Aid," *American Political Science Review*, June 1962, pp. 301–309.

Mosely, Phillip E., *The Kremlin and World Politics: Studies in Soviet Policy and Action*, Vintage Books, New York, 1960.

Nelson, Joan M., *Aid, Influence and Foreign Policy*, Macmillan, New York, 1968.

Newhouse, John, *Cold Dawn: The Story of SALT*, Holt, Rinehart and Winston, New York, 1973.

Nicolson, Sir Harold George, *Diplomacy*, Third Edition, Oxford University Press, New York, 1964.

Orbis, Fall, 1974, pp. 655–790.

Osgood, Robert, *Limited War: The Challenge to American Strategy*, University of Chicago Press, Chicago, 1957.

Padelford, Norman J., and George A. Lincoln, *The Dynamics of International Politics*, Third Edition, Macmillan, New York, 1976.

Phillips, Warren R., "International Communications" in Michael Haas, ed., *International Systems: A Behavioral Approach*, Chandler, New York, 1974, pp. 177–201.

Pranger, Robert J., and Roger P. Labrie, eds., *Nuclear Strategy and National Security: Points of View*, American Enterprise Institute for Public Policy Research, Washington, D. C., 1977.

Progress in Arms Control? Readings from Scientific American with Introductions by Bruce M. Russet and Bruce G. Blair, W. H. Freeman, San Francisco, 1979.

Qualter, Terence H., *Propaganda and Psychological Warfare*, Random House, New York, 1962.

Quester, George H., *Nuclear Diplomacy: The First Twenty-five Years*, Dunellen, New York, 1970.

Raser, John R., "International Deterrence," in Michael Haas, ed., *International Systems: A Behavioral Approach*, Chandler, New York, 1974, pp. 301–324.

Rosi, Eugene J., ed., *American Defense and Detente: Readings in National Security Policy*, Dodd Mead, New York, 1973.

Schelling, Thomas C., *Arms and Influence*, Yale University Press, New Haven, Conn., 1966.

Schelling, Thomas C., *Strategy of Conflict*, Oxford University Press, London and New York, 1960.

Sheehan, Edward R. F., *The Arabs, Israelis, and Kissinger: A Secret History of American Diplomacy in the Middle East*, Reader's Digest Press, New York, 1976.

Snyder, Glenn H., *Deterrence and Defense*, Princeton University Press, Princeton, N. J., 1961.

Spanier, John W., and Joseph L. Nogee, *The Politics of Disarmament: A Study in Soviet-American Gamesmanship*, Praeger, New York, 1962.

Stern, Ellen, ed., *The Limits of Military Intervention*, SAGE, Beverly Hills, Cal., 1977.

Strange, Susan, "The Politics of International Currencies," *World Politics*, January 1971, pp. 215–232.

Strausz-Hupé, Robert, and Stefan T. Possony, "Economics and Statecraft," in Robert L. Pfaltzgraff, Jr., ed., *Politics and the International System*, Second Edition, J. B. Lippincott, Philadelphia, 1972, pp. 308–318.

Thayer, Charles W., *Diplomat*, Harper & Row, New York, 1959.

Thayer, Charles W., *Guerilla*, New American Library, New York, 1963.

Trager, Frank N., "Wars of National Liberation: Implications for U. S. Policy and Planning," *Orbis*, Spring 1974, pp. 50–105.

U. S., Central Intelligence Agency, National Foreign Assessment Center, *Communist Aid to Less Developed Countries of the Free World, 1977*, November 1978.

Windsor, Philip, and Adam Roberts, *Czechoslovakia: Reform, Repression and Resistance*, Columbia University Press, New York, 1969.

Young, Kenneth T., *Negotiating with the Chinese Communists: The United States Experience, 1953–1967*, McGraw-Hill, New York, 1968.

PART 5

Alexander, Arthur J., *Decision-Making in Soviet Weapons Procurement*, International Institute for Strategic Studies, London, Adelphi Papers Nos. 147 and 148, 1978.

Allison, Graham T., *Essence of Decision: Explaining the Cuban Missile Crisis*, Little, Brown, Boston, 1971.

Almond, Gabriel, *The American People and Foreign Policy*, Praeger, New York, 1960.

Aspaturian, Vernon V., *Process and Power in Soviet Foreign Policy*, Little, Brown, Boston, 1971.

Bauer, Raymond A., Ithiel de Sola Pool, and Lewis Anthony Dexter, *American Business and Public Policy*, Second Edition, Aldine-Atherton, Chicago, 1972.

Berkowitz, Morton, P. G. Bock, and Vincent J. Fuccillo, *The Politics of American Foreign Policy: The Social Context of Decisions*, Prentice-Hall, Englewood Cliffs, N. J., 1977.

Brecher, Michael, *Decisions in Israel's Foreign Policy*, Yale University Press, New Haven, Conn., 1975.

Brogan, Dennis W., "The Illusion of Omnipotence," *Harper's,* December 1952, pp. 21–28.

Campbell, John C., *Defense of the Middle East: Problems of American Policy*, Second Edition, Praeger, New York, 1960.

Cline, Ray S., "Policy Without Intelligence," *Foreign Policy*, Winter 1974–75, pp. 121–135.

Cohen, Bernard C., *The Public's Impact on Foreign Policy*, Little, Brown, Boston, 1973.

Coplin, William D., *Introduction to International Politics: A Theoretical Overview*, Second Edition, Rand McNally, Chicago, 1974.

De Rivera, Joseph, *The Psychological Dimension in Foreign Policy*, Charles E. Merrill, Columbus, Ohio, 1968.

Destler, I. M., *Presidents, Bureaucrats and Foreign Policy: The Politics of Organizational Reform*, Princeton University Press, Princeton, N. J., 1974.

Destler, I. M., Hideo Sato, Priscilla Clapp, and Haruhiro Fukui, *Managing an Alliance: The Politics of U. S.-Japanese Relations*, Brookings, Washington, D. C., 1976.

Elowitz, Larry, and John W. Spanier, "Korea and Vietnam: Limited War and the American Political System," *Orbis*, Summer 1974, pp. 510–534.

Esterline, John H., and Robert B. Black, *Inside Foreign Policy: The Department of State Political System and Its Subsystems*, Mayfield, Palo Alto, Cal., 1975.

Feld, Werner, "National Economic Interest Groups and Policy Formation in the EEC," *Political Science Quarterly*, September 1966, pp. 392–411.

Finer, Herman, *Dulles over Suez: The Theory and Practice of his Diplomacy*, Quadrangle Books, Chicago, 1964.

Gelb, Leslie H., with Richard K. Betts, *The Irony of Vietnam: The System Worked*, Brookings, Washington, D. C., 1979.

Haendel, Dan, *The Process of Priority Formulation: U. S. Foreign Policy in the Indo-Pakistani War of 1971*, Westview Press, Boulder, Colo., 1977.

Halperin, Morton H., *Bureaucratic Politics and Foreign Policy*, Brookings, Washington, 1974.

Halperin, Morton H., and Arnold Kanter, eds., *Readings in American Foreign Policy: A Bureaucratic Perspective*, Little, Brown, Boston, 1973.

Hammer, Ellen, *The Struggle for Indochina, 1940–1955*, Stanford University Press, Stanford, Cal., 1966.

Hanrieder, Wolfram, *The Stable Crisis: Two Decades of German Foreign Policy*, Harper & Row, New York, 1970.

Hartmann, Frederick H., *Germany Between East and West: The Reunification Problem*, Prentice-Hall, Englewood Cliffs, N. J., 1965.

Hilsman, Roger, *The Politics of Policy Making in Defense and Foreign Affairs*, Harper & Row, New York, 1971.

Hilsman, Roger, *To Move A Nation: The Politics of Foreign Policy in the Administration of John F. Kennedy*, A Delta Book, New York, 1967.

Holsti, Ole R., "The Belief System and National Images: A Case Study," *Journal of Conflict Resolution*, September 1962, pp. 244–252.

Hoopes, Townsend, *The Limits of Intervention: An Inside Account of How the Johnson Policy of Escalation in Vietnam Was Reversed*, Revised Edition, David McKay, New York, 1973.

Huff, Earl, "A Study of a Successful Interest Group: The American Zionist Movement," *Western Political Quarterly*, March 1972, pp. 109–124.

Jervis, Robert, *The Logic of Images in International Relations,* Princeton University Press, Princeton, N. J., 1971.

Kennan, George, *American Diplomacy, 1900–1950*, University of Chicago Press, Chicago, 1951.

Koen, Ross Y., *The China Lobby in American Politics*, Macmillan, New York, 1960.

Lindblom, Charles E., "The Science of Muddling Through," *Public Administration Review*, Spring 1959, pp. 79–88.

Love, Kenneth, *Suez: The Twice-Fought War*, McGraw-Hill, New York, 1969.

Macridis, Roy C., ed., *Modern European Government: Cases in Comparative Policy Making*, Prentice-Hall, Englewood Cliffs, N. J., 1968.

Morgenthau, Hans J., *In Defense of the National Interest*, Alfred A. Knopf, New York, 1951.

Neustadt, Richard, *Presidential Power: The Politics of Leadership*, Wiley, New York, 1960.

Pachter, Henry M., *Collision Course: The Cuban Missile Crisis and Coexistence*, Praeger, New York, 1963.

Paige, Glenn D., *The Korean Decision, June 24–30, 1950*, The Free Press, New York, 1968.

Quandt, William B., *Decade of Decisions: American Policy Toward the Arab-Israeli Conflict, 1967–1976*, University of California Press, Berkeley, Cal., 1977.

Qubain, Fahim I., *Crisis in Lebanon*, Middle East Institute, Washington, 1961.

Rosenau, James N., ed., *Domestic Sources of Foreign Policy*, Free Press, New York, 1967.

Rourke, Francis E., *Bureaucracy and Foreign Policy*, Johns Hopkins Press, Baltimore, 1972.

Safran, Nadav, *From War to War: The Arab-Israeli Confrontation, 1948–1967*, Pegasus, New York, 1969.

Salisbury, Harrison E., *The 900 Days: The Siege of Leningrad*, Avon, New York, 1970.

Schilling, Warner R., Paul Hammond, and Glen Snyder, eds., *Strategy, Politics and Defense Budgets*, Columbia University Press, New York, 1962.

Schwartz, Morton, *The Foreign Policy of the USSR: Domestic Factors*, Dickenson, Encino and Belmont, Cal., 1975.

Simon, Herbert A., *Administrative Behavior*, Macmillan, New York, 1959.

Simon, Richard C., H. W. Bruck, and Burton Sapin, eds., *Foreign Policy Decision-Making*, Free Press, New York, 1962.

Spanier, John, and Eric M. Uslaner, *How American Foreign Policy is Made*, Second Edition, Praeger, New York, 1978.

Stewart, Philip D., "Soviet Interest Groups and the Policy Process," *World Politics*, October 1969, pp. 29–50.

Stoessinger, John G., *Nations in Darkness: China, Russia, and America*, Third Edition, Random House, New York, 1978.

Stoessinger, John G., *Why Nations Go to War*, Second Edition, St. Martin's Press, New York, 1978.

Truman, Harry S., *Memoirs, Volume II, Years of Trial and Hope*, Doubleday, New York, 1956.

Tuchman, Barbara, *The Guns of August*, Dell, New York, 1962.

Waltz, Kenneth M., *Foreign Policy and Democratic Politics*, Little, Brown, Boston, 1967.

White, Ralph K., *Nobody Wanted War: Misperception in Vietnam and Other Wars*, Doubleday, New York, 1968.

Wohlstetter, Roberta, *Pearl Harbor: Warning and Decision*, Stanford University Press, Stanford, Cal., 1962.

X, "Sources of Soviet Conduct," *Foreign Affairs*, July 1947, pp. 566–582.

Yost, Charles W., "The Arab-Israeli War: How it Began," *Foreign Affairs,* January 1968, pp. 304–320.

Index